SAP® Business Information Warehouse Reporting

About the Author

Peter Jones is a Principal/Platinum Business Applications Consultant with SAP Professional Services Consulting specializing in Controlling, Enterprise Controlling, Auditing, Business Intelligence, Strategic Enterprise Management (Corporate Performance Management – CPM), Enterprise Information Architecture, and Enterprise Data Warehouses. He has over nine years of consulting and educational experience in a variety of strategic and leadership roles, focused on Costing, Profitability Analysis, Strategic Enterprise Management, Corporate Governance, Data Warehousing, Business Intelligence, and Business Analytics. Peter's diverse professional background includes not only consulting experience but participation in the academic areas of Finance, Controlling, Data Warehousing, Enterprise Management, and Corporate Governance. He is serving as an SAP Principal/Platinum Business Consultant for areas including CO/FI/BW/SEM and Auditing. He has been involved with numerous implementations for BI, in the 3.x and 7.0 versions, from the Blueprint phase through to the Go-Live Process. His responsibilities include being an SME (Subject Material Expert) in all of the areas listed above, active presenter at conferences including ASUG, BI conferences and Shappire, and editor/writer for FICO Expert and BI Expert. Along with consulting he has been involved with the academic world in developing and presenting numerous topics for the University Alliance which included topics in the areas of BI, Auditing, and SEM. He has an MBA from Drexel University in Finance and is SAP certified in the areas of FI, CO, BW, and SEM.

About the Technical Editor

Charles Soper has worked in the industry at Eastman Kodak Company in Rochester, New York in a variety of Finance and Accounting Roles. He has an undergraduate degree in Economics and an MBA in Finance from the University of Rochester. He is a Senior Applications Instructor with SAP Educational Services specializing in the areas of Controlling, Finance, Business Intelligence, and Strategic Enterprise Management. He has over eight years of experience in the Educational Group at SAP and is involved with the development of training material for areas such as Business Planning and Business Intelligence. He has taught in areas including Finance, Controlling, Business Intelligence, and Strategic Enterprise Management (CPM). He is SAP certified in the areas of BW and SEM.

SAP® Business Information Warehouse Reporting: Building Better BI with SAP® BI 7.0

Peter Jones

New York   Chicago   San Francisco
Lisbon   London   Madrid   Mexico City
Milan   New Delhi   San Juan
Seoul   Singapore   Sydney   Toronto

The McGraw·Hill Companies

Cataloging-in-Publication Data is on file with the Library of Congress

McGraw-Hill books are available at special quantity discounts to use as premiums and sales promotions, or for use in corporate training programs. To contact a representative, please visit the Contact Us pages at www.mhprofessional.com.

SAP® Business Information Warehouse Reporting: Building Better BI with SAP® BI 7.0

1234567890   DOC DOC   0198

ISBN   978-0-07-149616-2
MHID   0-07-149616-5

Sponsoring Editor
Wendy Rinaldi

Editorial Supervisor
Patty Mon

Project Management
Vasundhara Sawhney,
International Typesetting
and Composition

Acquisitions Coordinator
Mandy Canales

Technical Editor
Tim Soper

Copy Editor
Bart Reed

Proofreader
International Typesetting
and Composition

Indexer
Broccoli Information
Management

Production Supervisor
George Anderson

Composition
International Typesetting
and Composition

Illustration
International Typesetting
and Composition

Art Director, Cover
Jeff Weeks

Cover Designer
Pattie Lee

Contents at a Glance

Contents

Acknowledgments

This endeavor has been an exciting and interesting process. Having worked with smaller documents, such as journal articles and presentations, I was not sure what to expect with the task of writing a technical book on SAP reporting functionality in Business Intelligence. It is the difference between running a 5-mile race versus a marathon. The amount of effort is not linear but geometric in nature, and the process of organizing, cataloging, and managing all the information and documents is incredible. With all the changes and upgrades that occur with any software system, this process was a challenge. I thought that my background in technical writing and having worked on course material for SAP Education would give me a good idea of what kind of effort would be needed to write a reference book. I found that there is a world of difference between writing the type of book one would use during instructor-led training for a week-long class and the process of writing this book—which is meant to be read and used as a reference rather than as a guide for instructor lead classes. Much more planning is involved in creating examples and explaining processes versus coming up with material that will flow correctly in a class environment. I found that writing a book is much more than just sitting down and starting to write. Having to focus on each chapter and understanding how I, as a reader, would look at this book was a real eye-opener. I believe weaving examples into each chapter makes sense, and I hope this approach makes sense to anyone who is willing to work through this book.

Because this version of BI is growing by leaps and bounds each time a support package comes out, which is about every 2 months, functionality may/will change. Therefore, I had to put a stake in the ground and go from there in terms of functionality and configuration. The timeline to get this book finished was very important—if it took longer, the book would have to go through its first revision before it was completed. Even as I write this, SAP version 7.1 BI is ready to be released and shortly thereafter will be generally available for purchase. Therefore, my timeline had to be more aggressive than I realized. Of course, all these issues are coming from a new writer's point of view—and probably a naïve view of writing. I know I said many times, "How hard can it be to write a book?" Well, I found out quickly.

But along with all the time spent researching different functionalities of the reporting tools and web-based components came additional knowledge and insight concerning the uses of each of these different components, which I hope will serve me and the readers well in the future. I have always said that if you really want to learn something, teach it. Now I can add to that: If you really want to learn something, teach it and write a book.

I would like to thank the people at McGraw-Hill, especially Wendy and Mandy, for offering me this opportunity. Without their help I would have been lost and floundering numerous times, and the amount of time needed to complete this task would have doubled.

They supported me every step of the way and were patient to a fault during the times when I felt like an idiot having to figure out the process of writing. I would also like to thank Tim for his support and for suffering through the pain he must have felt going through each one of these chapters, reviewing the information and offering additional ideas for how I could better explain some functionality or configuration.

Finally, to my wife, Lisa, for helping me along the way and giving me the time, opportunity, and support to work on and finish this project. Without your help and all of the time and sacrifice on your part, this project would never have been completed. To add to that, a sincere thanks to our dear friend Pam, for helping to keep Lisa company during the entire process of writing this book. Without her help, I'm not sure whether Lisa and I could have made it through this whole process without going crazy.

Introduction

This book is constructed in a series of chapters, ranging from the high-level overview of what SAP NetWeaver 7.0 (NW2004S) is all about and what InfoProviders are, to the detailed processes of query construction and implementation. I will probably say this many times during the course of this book, but I am not looking to make this a "technical" reference book but rather something that can aid developers, power users, business users, and casual users of SAP Business Warehouse (BW) in organizing and developing their reports and reporting strategy. Don't get me wrong: This book is definitely focused on being your reference book for all the functionality within the reporting strategy and, as we call it today, the Enterprise Reporting Process. However, it is a reference book for *all* users. The initial chapters discuss the functionality and process of building queries, workbooks, and other components of BW. The latter chapters will focus on providing information and examples so that during the final process of configuration, you are able to see what each step looks like and can better navigate within your systems.

There are a number of other areas in the BW system I could include in the book, such as authorizations in BW (new authorization concepts in BW 7.0) and performance tuning (we will cover this topic at a high level, but not anywhere near the level needed to give you a complete picture) in BW for queries (reports), but doing so would make the book too big. What's more, many of these activities are for groups other than the ones this book addresses. It has been mentioned many times that trying to use the BW reporting tools is a bit difficult and seems to be geared more toward the technical/basis person rather than the business analysts. I believe that after you start reading this book, you will see that you have many options when configuring your queries and that many of the activities are definitely not rocket science. With a little work, you can be creating ad-hoc queries in a matter of hours. Of course, depending on the other activities (authorizations, roles, security), access to different areas and processes may be limited. We will get into this in more detail as we work our way through the material.

We begin by discussing the different segments of NetWeaver 7.0 (2004S) and how they are integrated together to structure a single platform for your SAP systems. It is important for everyone who is working in the SAP environment to be aware of, at a high level, how the system and platform work so that the data results make sense. One of the other comments you might hear is that the backend activities are not easily understood or clearly explained, so it's hard to know whether the data is correct and consistent. This book will give you a 50,000-foot overview of the basic BW process, just so some of your questions can be answered without having to work though additional documentation and explanation.

Once we work our way through the initial discussion, we will then get into the details of the query toolkit offered to you by SAP BW version 7.0. There are many options, and we will break these down into reasonable portions so you can digest each one before getting another helping of information. We'll start out by discussing the basic objects that store data for reporting purposes. Understanding these objects and their structures, to an extent, will make the construction of the queries easier and make the available query information more consistent. We will not get into a deep technical discussion of these objects, but you will learn what the difference is between an InfoCube and an InfoSet, as well as what each object can do and in what situations you might use it.

Next, we'll review the functionality of one of the more popular frontends of BW—the BEx Analyzer. We will discuss the navigation options and review the functionality available to the business user directly from the query/report once it is executed. Now, this is not to say that the BEx Analyzer is the frontend of choice, nor is it to say that SAP feels the BEx Analyzer is the preferred frontend (as a matter of fact, based on best business practices, SAP has been leaning toward the Web as the preferred frontend). However, because so many companies are used to the Microsoft Excel look and feel, the BEx Analyzer is comfortable to many of their users. We then follow this up with a discussion of the BEx Query Designer. We will work through, in detail, the use of the BEx Query Designer for both the BEx Analyzer (BEx) and the Web Application Designer (WAD). The BEx Query Designer offers numerous options, and we will go through as many as possible. However, for some of the functions that are not used as much, you will need to experiment in the BW system itself, but with the basics explained in this book you should be able to navigate your way through many examples and functionality. There's also a chapter on additional options and functionality in the queries, such as the Unit of Measure conversion, the use of Variants, time-dependency and other WAD objects.

The next set of chapters focus on a new set of tools for the BW 7.0 system—the Report Designer. The Report Designer helps in developing formatted reporting for those business users who need to print out their reports. The Report Designer allows you to format your reports with all the bells and whistles a third-party frontend user interface (UI) would offer, including sorting, rearranging, reformatting, and designing your reports. We will go into the details of this tool so that you are aware of all the options.

The Information Broadcaster (IB) is the topic of the next series of chapters. The IB has taken on all the tasks that once were the responsibility of another area of the BW system—the Report Agent. This means that the Information Broadcaster is the main tool for disbursing information and queries to all the business users and analysts. The IB can distribute your information via e-mail, fax, alerts, print media, and other avenues. Depending on how you configure the IB, you will be able to proactively push query information to the necessary users so that they can be updated on their metrics immediately or at specific times during the day.

Next we will cover Standard Business Content (SBC) in the BW reporting component and the use of this functionality in the reporting strategy. We will discuss in detail the advantages of the SBC and how to use it. This includes only the SBC involved in the query portion of SAP BW and not the SBC involved in the configuration of the other backend activities. We wrap up this section with a discussion of advanced BEx functionality and what additional information and options are available to you for enhancing the final version of your queries.

The previous chapters focused on providing a basic foundation in the functionality and implementation of the BW reporting tools, which will be a great start to using the BW Reporting Toolkit. We next turn to the Web and the toolkit available for us for generating web-based queries. As you know, more and more information is coming to us via the Web, and this is no different with the BW reporting strategy. The BW offers two options for using the Web. The first option we will discuss is the BEx Web Analyzer. This is a mirror-image web option of the BEx Analyzer. Once we discuss the additional functionality of this component, we turn to the second option—the Web Application Designer. The Web Application Designer (WAD) is the main tool we use to construct web-based query templates to publish our queries to the Web and assign them to an Enterprise Portal. As mentioned, the amount of information and configuration options available in the BW reporting component is considerable. Therefore, in the web configuration area we will focus on the basics of both the BEx Web Analyzer and the Web Application Designer and leave the detailed, advanced configuration for another book on web functionality. After working our way through the functionality on the Web, we can look at the other options and functionality linked to and included in BW.

There are many different additional add-on components to the reporting aspect of BW that we will cover, making sure you understand the uses of these different frontends. Therefore, the next set of chapters highlights the Enterprise Portal, Visual Composer, and the Integrated Planning functionality. These sets of activities you can use in conjunction with the SAP BW reporting tools; each one has additional enhancements that it offers. Enterprise Portal offers you a method of organizing numerous reports and also provides user friendly web access to your reports. Visual Composer offers the flexibility of all the query configuration functionality at the end user's fingertips. Integrated Planning provides the reporting functions to improve your planning process (building what-if scenarios into your queries). We will get into some detail in each of these areas, but we won't dig as deeply because each of these tools is worthy of a reference book of its own.

There are many differences between the 3.x version of BW and the 0.7 version. In each chapter, I will comment on the new features and functionalities of the various areas of the BW 7.0 version. As you already know, nothing is for certain except change—and this version is no different. The support package (SP) and support pack stack (SPS) are being updated on a regular basis, and as you work your way through this book, there may be some differences between what you see in your system and what is displaying in the book's screenshots. There are two likely reasons for this:

- The authorizations you have are not as extensive as those used in the examples.
- The level of the SP or SPS you have is not the same as what this book is based on.

Another component that should be reviewed is the OSS notes applied in your system. Make sure your OSS notes and SP levels are as up to date as possible. Realizing certain situations will not allow you to update your system on an ongoing process, you can schedule these events at a convenient time and not impose them on your current business users.

A final note about the contents of this book: If we were to try to cover *all* the different scenarios, circumstances, and situations in this book, we would never get the book published. There are so many different options and functionalities in this area of BW that as many as we cover, there are as many still around left to try—and that's the key with the BW reporting options: You should try as much of the functionality as your schedule and deadlines allow you. You'll find yourself in numerous situations where something very specific needs to be developed for your business users. Although it's probably 99.9% possible to fulfill their needs, the amount of time available to you to work through the issue using the appropriate tools is likely at a premium. Review your business requirements and from there understand what functionality the system can offer. You will, more than likely, have a successful reporting strategy.

SAP Business Intelligence Overview

Before we delve into the details of the functionality of NetWeaver 2004S (7.0) BI reporting, we need to review some of the architecture and concepts of the SAP systems that support these analysis tools. This chapter explores the overall architecture and structure of the SAP NetWeaver System and then goes into further detail concerning the BI architecture and options. In this way, you will be able to position the details of BI 7.0 report functionality within the larger picture of the new NetWeaver platform. We will start with an analysis of the different areas and elements of NetWeaver, of which BI is a part, so as to understand the integration between all the different components. Then we'll take a more detailed view of the data-flow process within the BI system to understand what more there is in support of the reporting functionality.

One of the challenges of current business processes is that they are made up of multiple, different systems, all trying to talk to each other in various languages, different platforms, and different landscapes. Companies want to reduce their costs, find new ways of increasing turnover and profitability, and be able to flexibly adjust to all types of changes. In this context, the question of how to adjust or integrate existing applications and flexibly implement new applications plays a central role. Existing investments should be used optimally, and at the same time new business processes have to be supported quicker and in a more intelligent way. These days, realistic system landscapes often consist of many systems. This situation may have grown out of a specific corporate strategy of going with best of breed, or perhaps with numerous mergers and acquisitions, the system landscape has just grown out of control. The business processes that are to be mapped in these complex system landscapes contain process steps that run over multiple, different systems. For all system transitions, sending systems are connected to receiving systems by means of interfaces (point-to-point connections). Different interfaces are often implemented using the technology that is considered to be ideal for the respective interface. Due to this, administrators not only have to take care of complex system environments, but must also know many different system technologies.

In Figure 1-1, every interface is represented by a connected line. This illustrates the complexity of an integration solution.

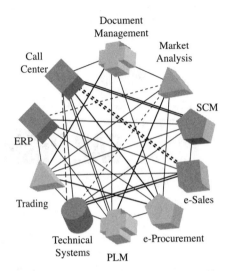

FIGURE 1-1
Challenges of the
current IT
landscapes

Copyright by SAP AG

Challenges of the Current IT Landscapes

After a merger, the existing company will have a very heterogeneous IT infrastructure. To map processes, not only SAP systems and functionality are used but also software components from other providers as well as business applications that have been developed internally. The business processes are then extended over the multiple system landscapes. The ability to map these business processes as effectively as possible is a complex and time-consuming activity for the parent corporation. Even the basic processes of Order-to-Cash and Pay-to-Procure are difficult to analyze due to the inconsistency of the mapping process. In addition to the actual implementation of this scenario, the company is faced with the overall cost of maintenance, the integration of different types and formats of master data, the need for uniform reporting across the processes and across the companies, and the task of making sure all parties are getting the information they need to complete their tasks.

Studies on how long it takes to change existing business processes or introduce new processes still show that it takes quite a bit of time, ranging from months to years, depending on the process. The people surveyed attribute about a third of this to the inflexibility of IT, another third attributed to concerns around the corporate culture and the final third is attributed to the concerns with change. With SAP NetWeaver, the process of implementing and adjusting complex business scenarios is much quicker, easier, and more flexible. For example, SAP NetWeaver reduces the complexity of system landscapes by

- Being a single platform for integrated information and systems.
- Providing functions that make time-consuming, expensive integration projects unnecessary.
- Ensuring compatibility with .NET and WebSphere objects.
- Making it possible to increase the flexibility of business processes with the new Enterprise Services Architecture concept.

Figure 1-2
Integrated system
infrastructure

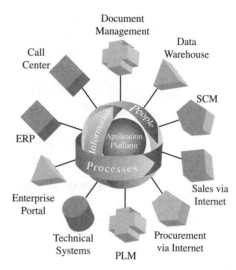

Copyright by SAP AG

In Figure 1-2, you can see that rather than having to integrate with each different system separately and then attempt to consolidate these activities, you are integrating with a single point of communication and then consolidating these activities and processes through a single platform. It is possible to work with the SAP NetWeaver system in terms of a number of modules that can also be implemented separately. The most important thing, though, is that the whole is more than the sum of the individual components. SAP NetWeaver enables you to flexibly develop business processes on tailored components without having to give up existing investments.

SAP NetWeaver: Overview of Components

SAP NetWeaver is the technical foundation on which almost all mySAP solutions are currently based. SAP NetWeaver is the functionally enhanced successor of the SAP application platform mySAP Technology, and it serves as the basis for the Enterprise Services Architecture in order to meet requests for flexibility and integration among systems, interfaces, users, and processes. It connects information, business processes, and people across systems and organizational boundaries. It is the central tool for reducing the total cost of ownership (TCO) of complex system infrastructures.

As you can see in Figure 1-3, the SAP NetWeaver platform has four integration levels. It provides the core functions for the technical infrastructure of business solutions. These integration levels are People Integration, Information Integration, and Process Integration, and Application Platform. SAP NetWeaver also supports cross-application software, so-called composite applications or xApps (xApps connect heterogeneous systems in continuous cross-function processes so that the underlying applications can be more or less ignored). In addition, different software interfaces ensure full interoperability of applications that are running on Microsoft .NET and IBM WebSphere.

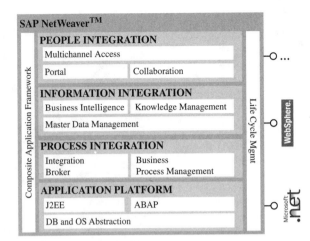

FIGURE 1-3
An overview of the
SAP NetWeaver
components

Copyright by SAP AG

People Integration: The Use of an Enterprise Portal

An enterprise portal is the gateway to the end user. Based on the end-user view, this section illustrates how a user-friendly interface makes it possible to access relevant data from very different systems. In addition, it illustrates the meaning of role-based user and content management and shows that using business packages can significantly reduce the amount of resources required for implementing a portal.

An enterprise portal offers a central point of access to information, applications, and services in your enterprise. All SAP and non-SAP systems, data warehouses, desktop documents, as well as web content and web services are brought together on one uniform interface. By using single sign-on, users benefit from the convenient authentication and communication between IT systems. Knowledge management in the portal turns unstructured data into important information for the enterprise and the regional business users, collaboration facilitates the communication among people across enterprise borders, and personalization adapts the structure to the requirements of individual users.

Figure 1-4 shows an overview of the architecture of the SAP Enterprise Portal. Basically speaking, a well-defined Enterprise Portal can offer the business users the right information and the right functions at the right time from any location and in the right format. To do this, SAP Enterprise Portal provides an infrastructure you can use to retrieve and edit data from information sources in your company as well as from the Internet by means of iViews. SAP provides iView templates to help facilitate the implementation of the portal, but you can also create customer-specific iViews. The SAP Enterprise Portal also provides powerful search functions with which you can selectively and intuitively retrieve files and documents from different sources of information, such as local database applications, websites, or pools of enterprise documents. Collaboration functions allow you to use common resources and content. The individual tools and services include virtual project rooms and tools for real-time interaction, regardless of geographical distance. You can use discussion forums to exchange data and information with colleagues whose workplace is not in the same area or even in the same time zone. The core functions of SAP Enterprise Portal are written in Java; therefore, you need a J2EE runtime environment, which is provided by the SAP Web

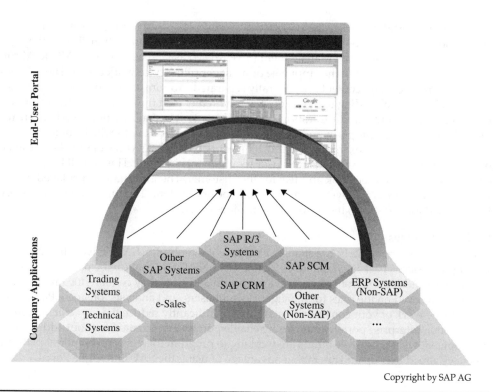

FIGURE 1-4   SAP Enterprise Portal

Application Java Server. SAP Enterprise Portal uses an open architecture. The standards it supports include SOAP (Simple Object Access Protocol), UDDI (Universal Description Discovery and Integration), and XML (Extensible Markup Language). The portal has powerful security functions, including extensive support of directory services, digital certificates, and the SSL protocol. It is also highly scalable and designed to be used by any number of business users, from small groups to large departments. It also supports mobile devices.

Roles in the SAP Enterprise Portal

Roles determine which navigation paths, specified using the file structures, can be used to access which content, specified using the integrated iViews and pages. Roles can be assigned to individual users or groups of users.

NOTE *The term* content *covers all types of content available to a user in their role-based portal view. A Content object can be an iView (a program that determines data from different sources of the enterprise or Internet, displays it in the SAP Enterprise Portal, and, if applicable, makes it available for processing), a page (a layout of one or more iViews), or a workset (a collection of tasks, services, and information that can be used to create roles). Worksets consist of iViews and pages, arranged in a folder structure that determines the navigation paths.*

Either the portal is used as the users' central workplace, with access to different applications, or it serves as the user interface within a specific application. This is the situation in SAP Master Data Management (SAP MDM) as well as in xApp SAP xRPM for multiproject management of the employee or manager self-service work center. The roles for administering users and content are generally separated. Administrators of users and roles define both objects according to the enterprise requirements in the system and then assign roles to users. Content administrators define which content is available in the system, ensure that it is administered properly, and decide which roles can work with which content.

Figure 1-5 shows an example of the SAP Enterprise Portal. As you can see, the portal is divided into sections with the business user requirements in mind. This can all be customized for the correct look and feel for the customer. The information displayed can be from multiple sources and systems or from one specific system. The functionality of the SAP Enterprise Portal adapts to the needs of the business user.

Business Packages

In addition to approximately 100 standard business content roles, SAP delivers Business Packages. Business Packages contain predefined portal content that can be used to call up transactions and reports from all sorts of systems. In addition, they contain documents and information based on the roles for managers, casual users, and analysts. Business Packages facilitate the work of your content managers and significantly reduce the implementation time of your enterprise portal because they enable portals to be created without additional development work. So, while others are working to program their enterprise portal platform, you have already set up and are taking advantage of using the SAP Enterprise Portal.

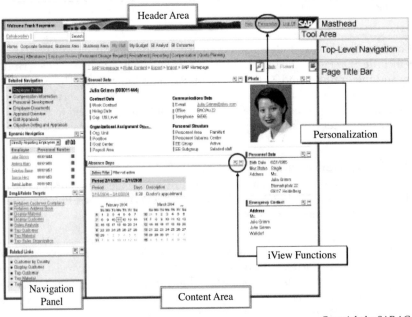

Copyright by SAP AG

FIGURE 1-5 Look and feel of SAP Enterprise Portal

FIGURE 1-6
Target groups
of Business
Packages

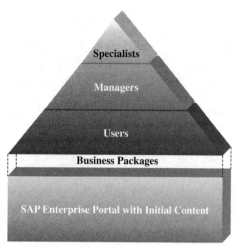

In Figure 1-6, you can see the specific target groups identified based on Business Packages. Business Packages are classified according to target groups that consist of end users, specialists, and managers. Business Packages for end users contain the tasks that a portal user may carry out in the portal, regardless of their other roles in the enterprise. The tasks help beginners familiarize themselves with the portal as quickly as possible and thus increase the acceptance of the enterprise portal. The content includes functions such as e-mail, task lists, calendar administration, travel expense settlement, administration of benefits, employee self service, e-learning activities, and additional search functionality for the employee directory. Business Packages for managers or decision makers can use the content for efficient analysis and for gaining decision-relevant information. They offer extensive tools for planning and administering the portal and its budget. Line managers, team managers, and project managers can reduce the time they have to spend on administrative tasks and focus on strategic tasks. The most widespread Business Packages for managers include the Manager Self-Service (MSS). The final Business Packages are for specialists, which are aimed at the experts from different departments in the enterprise, such as Sales, Human Resources, Marketing, Finance, and Production. They provide appropriate analysis tools, which enable users to act quickly based on the right information. These packages can also provide operational tools, such as campaign management for marketing employees. You can purchase Business Packages from the iView Studio, a central marketplace for portal content. As a registered user, you will find the individual packages at www.sdn.sap.com. You can display and review them, and then download the content required.

SAP Mobile Infrastructure

SAP Mobile Infrastructure (SAP MI) is a technology solution of SAP NetWeaver, which is the basis for the SAP solutions for Mobile Business. This is usually an enhancement to an existing SAP application, as shown in Figure 1-7.

For example, an enhancement for SAP Human Resources can be used to enter travel data and working times on the go. In the same way, service employees can be directly informed of new orders via a mobile device, and they can confirm data directly with the

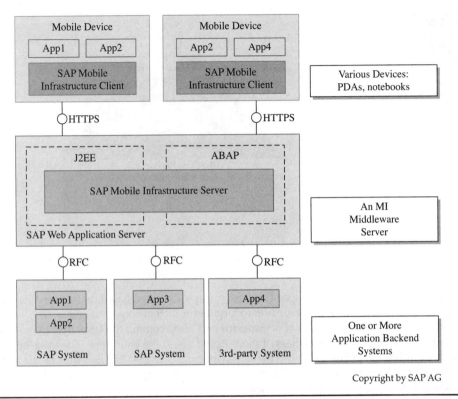

FIGURE 1-7   Architecture of the SAP Mobile Infrastructure

customers instead of writing down data on sheets of paper and entering it into the backend system later on. Mobile business increases flexibility as well as makes it easier to provide information to field sales representatives. A sales employee can dynamically access customer and order data without having to download and save it from the back end before visiting a customer. This also leads to getting rid of piles of paper, where data has to be reentered into the IT systems afterward. This speeds up processes, reduces the amount of work required for field sales representatives, and is less error-prone because the data is entered when it is created. SAP MI can also be used to mobilize non-SAP-based applications. SAP MI can be locally installed on a mobile device and is equipped with a web server, database layer, and dedicated business logic. Therefore, remotely working employees never have to wait for a network connection to complete time-critical business transactions but can instead work offline. To synchronize the data on a mobile device with the back end, SAP MI provides tools for synchronization and data replication. SAP MI is equipped with a Java Virtual Machine and provides an open programming model with which developers can create mobile applications. This open-system architecture facilitates platform independence of mobile devices and networks as well as supports mobile devices such as personal digital assistants (PDAs), laptops, and smart phones.

Information Integration

Each solution supplied by SAP offers reporting options via the data of the respective application. Usually, the application provides a large number of standard reports for this purpose, but user-defined reporting is also possible. Customers can use the query interface to program their own reports in the ABAP workbench and then read the data of the production system as needed. This type of reporting can also be used with SAP NetWeaver. At this time, more than 8,000 customers are successfully using the software solution SAP Business Intelligence (system component SAP BW), either in parallel to the ABAP workbench process or exclusively. One reason for this is the increasing requirements for integrated solutions for the enterprise-wide analysis of data. In times of globalization and market expansion, it is important to have access to the relevant information from one's own enterprise at any time and to be able to analyze it flexibly, including in aggregated form and without placing a performance strain on the transactional system. In heterogeneous system infrastructures, the extraction and preparation of consolidated transaction and master data from SAP systems and source systems by other suppliers are particularly challenging. Apart from integrated data procurement, options for detailed data analysis and the multimedia display of the analysis results are required to meet the increasing quality requirements for enterprise information.

We will be looking at this in more detail (at the 30,000-foot level rather than the 50,000-foot level) in the next section of this chapter. Therefore, this discussion introduces the information for the following section. However, it's obvious that you need to understand the transaction-oriented OLTP and the integration with the analysis-oriented OLAP environment (online analytical processing). As Figure 1-8 shows, the uses of each type of data are specific to the level of granularity.

In the current business environment, huge amounts of information are created from the data for business processes that is not easily used for practical analysis. Therefore, the data is cleansed and, due to its different origins, technically and semantically formatted (homogenized). The result can be used to generate knowledge that's helpful to the enterprise management to define its enterprise strategy and the business processes it derives. Figure 1-8 illustrates this process. In many cases, you are receiving information from multiple sources; therefore, the homogenization process will not only cleanse the data in terms of master data inconsistencies but also for the differences between the sources.

Figure 1-9 shows an overview of the architecture of the SAP BW system. The architecture for the SAP BW system has three levels. The lowest level shows the source systems. SAP provides extraction mechanisms for production data from SAP systems. For non-SAP systems, there are the BW BAPI interfaces, the interfaces for accessing relational database systems and multidimensional applications, and finally an interface for processing XML files. There are multiple ways to upload data into the BW system, including the use of flat files.

The second level is where the metadata and application data (master and transaction data) are managed in the Business Information Warehouse server. When a report (query) is executed, the OLAP processor reads the data. The third level shows the different reporting tools: BEx Analyzer, embedded in Microsoft Excel, and BEx Web Analyzer, embedded in BEx Web. You can use the Web Analyzer to execute queries in the browser. There are numerous approaches to viewing the data, and we will get into each one in a later chapter. You can access the information via your cell phone or any other portal interface. The structuring and

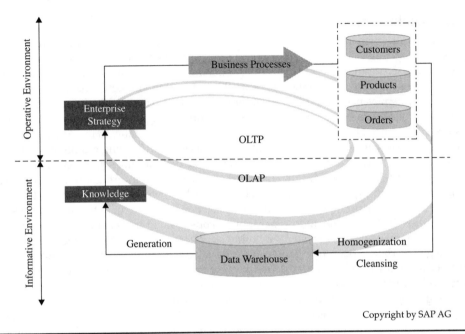

Copyright by SAP AG

FIGURE 1-8   Distinguish between Operational and Informational Environment

visualization of all information is ensured by the use of BW database structures and the requirements and expectations on reporting. This data can be from both SAP and non-SAP sources and is extracted and uploaded into the SAP BW system.

One of the fastest approaches to implementing SAP BW is the use of Standard Business Content (SBC), which is composed of preconfigured models based on best business practices from all the different industries that have implemented the SAP systems. All of this content can be used by any of the industries and can be adapted to individual enterprise requirements. As shown in Figure 1-10, the structures available in the SBC of SAP BW consist of roles, workbooks, queries, InfoCubes, InfoObjects, InfoSources, Update Rules, Transformation Rules, and many other objects. We will be looking specifically at the SBC for the reporting process in Chapter 14 of this book.

The Standard Business Content (SBC) is shipped as an add-on to the SAP BW system. The documentation provides detailed information on the Business Content of the individual applications. The distinct advantage of the Business Content is that it is based on a data model process and you can activate all required and related objects at the same time. Therefore, you can set up and demo the functionality of BW quickly and easily.

Knowledge Management

Knowledge Management (KM) enables users to access all sorts of internal and external content via intelligent search functions. The functionality of the KM system allows users to publish documents, browse, classify, or manage content. The publication cycle of documents can be controlled by means of online communication or workflow functions found in KM. Access to information is controlled by means of authorization profiles. The two major areas are Content Management, which supports the life cycle of documents from creation to

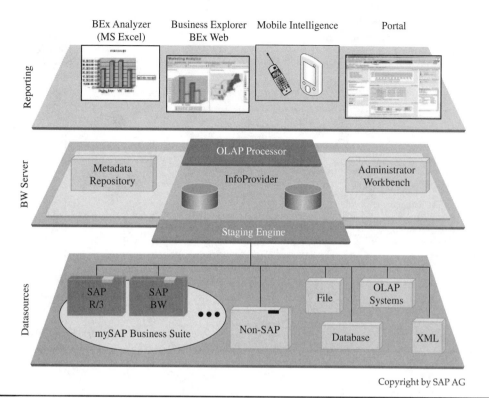

FIGURE 1-9   The Three-Level Architecture of the SAP BW

archiving, and Search & Classification, which allows full-text searching across all types of documents and enables their automatic classification.

Master Data Management

The last area is the integration of master data via Master Data Management (MDM). When an enterprise stores master data in different locations and systems at the same time, this can lead to redundancies and variances, which might significantly disrupt business processes. SAP MDM enables you to create master data that is uniform across the enterprise and to distribute it to different dependent systems. SAP MDM uses the technological basis of the SAP Exchange Infrastructure (SAP XI) to distribute the data. Not only does it distribute the data, but for new master data, it checks whether identical master data objects are already available and generates comprehensive information duplicates, which can in turn be transferred into the SAP BW or used in analyses. This reduces data management costs and significantly simplifies the correction of data errors.

Figure 1-11 shows that MDM is able to help by

- Offering to generate content that is consolidated.
- Working to harmonize the master data.
- Having an identified location for the Central Master Data Management.

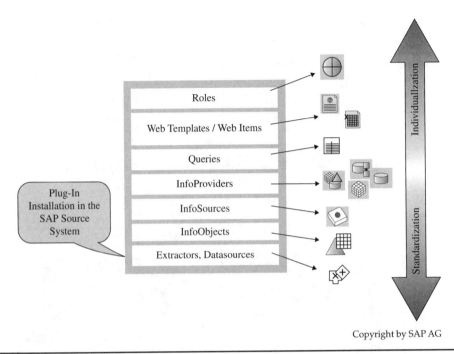

FIGURE 1-10   SAP BW: Standard Business Content

Process Integration

At the Process Integration level, the system offers the ability to implement cross-system business processes, with the help of the SAP Exchange Infrastructure (SAP XI). Within the overall architecture of SAP NetWeaver, SAP XI takes care of the process integration. It enables the connection of SAP and non-SAP systems from different suppliers in different versions on different platforms—whether it is Java, ABAP, or any other source system. SAP XI is based on an open architecture, mainly used for open standards (specifically for XML and Java) and offers services that are essential in a heterogeneous and complex system infrastructure, such as a runtime infrastructure for exchanging messages, configuration options for controlling business processes and the flow of messages, as well as options for transforming message content between sender and receiver. Basically, the SAP Exchange Infrastructure includes

- **System Landscape Directory**   This is where the system landscapes are mapped.
- **Integration Repository**   This repository stores all the required interfaces entered in the design phase. These are used for mapping the master data and checking the format of the data to be exchanged.
- **Configuration phase**   During this phase, the mappings completed in the Integrated Repository are assigned to each other based on the system infrastructure and business processes in question. Once this is complete, the application content is transferred from the sender to the receiver via messages in a freely definable XML structure.

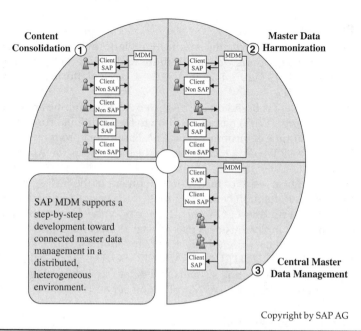

Copyright by SAP AG

FIGURE 1-11   Integrated Master Data Management with SAP MDM

In Figure 1-12, the sending system makes the data available in the document format, IDocs, and sends it to the adapter via a protocol. The adapter transforms the document to SAP XI format and sends it to the Integration Server using HTTP(S). During configuration, you specify which adapter the receiver is to use to receive the message. The Integration Server sends the message to the corresponding adapter, which converts the message to the receiver's protocol and sends the message to the receiver.

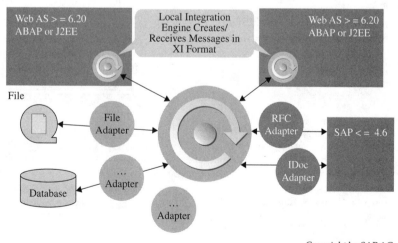

Copyright by SAP AG

FIGURE 1-12   Connecting different systems to SAP XI

Application Platform

With the SAP Web Application Server, the Application Platform has the J2EE and ABAP runtime environments and supports web applications and web services in an open development environment. As Figure 1-13 shows, these basic platform structures support all areas of NetWeaver 2004S.

Nearly every SAP system is based on the SAP Web AS as a runtime environment. The SAP Web Application Server (WAS) has, in addition to the traditional runtime environment for ABAP programs, a runtime environment for J2EE-based Java programs, called the SAP Web AS Java. Thus, the SAP Web AS, together with the database, is the Application Platform of SAP NetWeaver.

SAP Web AS is the logical result of further development of the SAP Application Server technology with particular attention being paid to the web-based application. This platform offers a reliable and tested runtime environment that has evolved over more than 10 years, a framework for executing complex business processes that meet the highest security standards, and a reliable and user-friendly development environment. It supports open technical standards such as HTTP, HTTPS, SOAP, SSL, SSO, Unicode, XML, WML, and others, and supports various operating systems and database systems. Figure 1-14 offers a view of each of the options within the Web Application Server (WAS).

SAP Business Warehouse Administration

Before we move into the details of the reporting process and the objects that support the creation and execution of queries, I would like to go over the process in SAP BW that supports data processing and the management of data loading. Much of what we will be

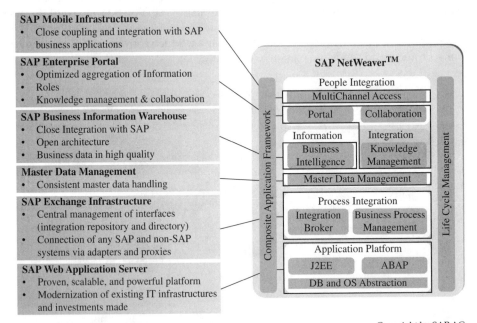

Copyright by SAP AG

FIGURE 1-13 Components of SAP NetWeaver

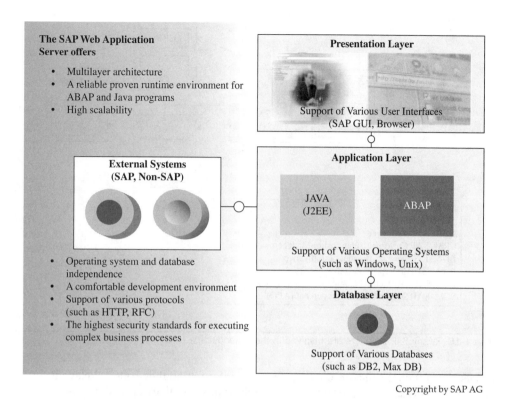

The SAP Web Application
Server offers

- Multilayer architecture
- A reliable proven runtime environment for ABAP and Java programs
- High scalability

**External Systems
(SAP, Non-SAP)**

- Operating system and database independence
- A comfortable development environment
- Support of various protocols (such as HTTP, RFC)
- The highest security standards for executing complex business processes

Presentation Layer

Support of Various User Interfaces
(SAP GUI, Browser)

Application Layer

JAVA
(J2EE)

ABAP

Support of Various Operating Systems
(such as Windows, Unix)

Database Layer

Support of Various Databases
(such as DB2, Max DB)

Copyright by SAP AG

FIGURE 1-14   SAP Web Application Server (SAP Web AS)

looking at in the next chapters is dependent on the setup and processing that you do during the configuration and implementation of BW data uploading. Therefore, I believe it is worthwhile that we look at this activity and understand that it can provide you data for reporting in the best possible format and structure. In the end, it's all about reporting the data and having the information in exactly the correct format for your business users— whether this is the CEO, CFO, or a line manager. Therefore, we need to look at some of the options we have in the way of processing the data initially in order to have the data in the right place at the right time and in the best possible format. This portion of BI, Business Warehouse, is the data warehousing solution and supports many of the other products and functionalities of the SAP systems. If you were to look at the architecture of the various applications supported by the BW area, you would see that it is the foundation of many activities and is the main platform for the reporting of information and storage of data. As you can see in Figure 1-15, NetWeaver supports many of the applications shown here, and within NW2004S, Business Warehouse is the central storage location for data.

In this case, the information from SCM (Supply Chain Management) is used in the Customer Relationship Management (CRM) process, which is processed through the ECC environment and then moved through the Business Intelligence system to be displayed in the Enterprise Portal (EP). All this data moves through Business Warehouse.

As a core component of SAP NW2004S, BI provides data warehousing functionality, a Business Intelligence platform, and a suite of Business Intelligence tools that enable

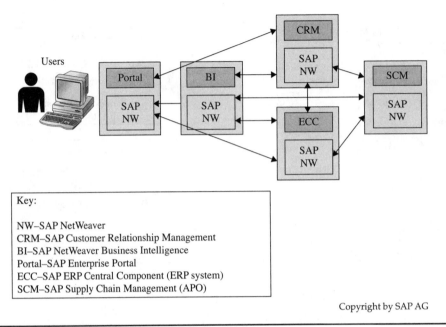

Key:

NW–SAP NetWeaver
CRM–SAP Customer Relationship Management
BI–SAP NetWeaver Business Intelligence
Portal–SAP Enterprise Portal
ECC–SAP ERP Central Component (ERP system)
SCM–SAP Supply Chain Management (APO)

FIGURE 1-15   Many SAP products are involved in the BI landscape

businesses to attain the maximum value from the information they collect. Relevant business information from productive SAP applications and all external datasources can be integrated, transformed, and consolidated in BI. BI provides flexible reporting and analysis tools to support you in evaluating and interpreting data and distributing that information to others in your company, even across the globe. With this capability, businesses are able to make informed decisions and determine target-oriented activities on the basis of this analysis. Figure 1-16 defines what SAP believes are the key components of a BI system. We will focus the majority of our time on the BI suite and touch on portions of the BI platform where they pertain to reporting and analysis. The actual Data Warehouse area of BI is discussed at a high level in the next section.

Data Warehouse Layer

The Data Warehouse layer is responsible for the cleansing, loading, storage, and management of the data needed for enterprise reporting and analysis. To help facilitate the implementation of this data layer, SAP delivers Standard Business Content. This is a preconfigured set of objects that have been developed based on best business practices and should be used to bridge the gap in functionality between your current system setup and what the SAP data warehouse can offer. With this BI content, SAP provides all the structures, objects, queries, and transfer processes that cover a large portion of what a typical project requires. Here are the Data Warehouse requirements that were taken into account in the development of this layer:

- A data warehousing system must have optimized data structures for reporting and analysis.
- The data warehouse needs to be a separate system so that it supports all types of data, both SAP and non-SAP.

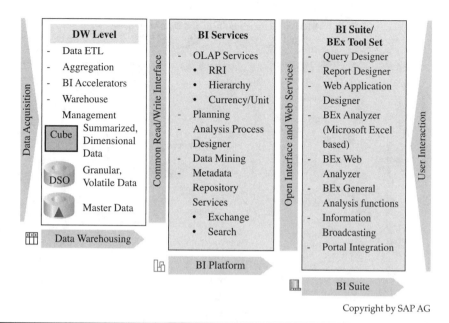

Copyright by SAP AG

FIGURE 1-16   Key components and features of BI

- The data warehouse needs to be an automated system to process data.
- The data warehouse must have preconfigured objects based on specific industries and businesses.

Figure 1-17 identifies the different items in the BI Platform and Data Warehouse level. As you can see the Data Warehouse architecture is structured in three layers: sourcing the data, storing the data, and reporting on the data.

This discussion focuses on the bottom two layers—the data warehouse and data acquisition process. *Data acquisition* refers to the source system that provides the BI system with data. BI can integrate with many source systems of data, including an SAP business suite, SAP XI, non-SAP systems (including flat files), other data providers (other BW systems), databases (DB Connect), and complex sources (universal data integration, or UDI).

Data Acquisition

SAP business suites include any SAP-related source of data, such as SAP CRM, SAP SCM, SAP SEM, and others. In this area, SAP offers predefined extraction structures and programs that help with sourcing the data and uploading it into the BW system. Figure 1-18 shows numerous source systems and the connection to BW. In this process, the datasource is used as the structure to extract the desired transactional data from the source systems tables into the BW tables (specifically InfoCubes and DataStore objects). You can also send data from SAP and non-SAP sources to BI using SAP Exchange Infrastructure (SAP XI). Once in BI, the data is queued and is available for further integration and consolidation. Data transfer using SAP XI is based on the Simple Object Access Protocol (SOAP). SAP has an open system standard and enables all external systems to be integrated. At the center of the infrastructure

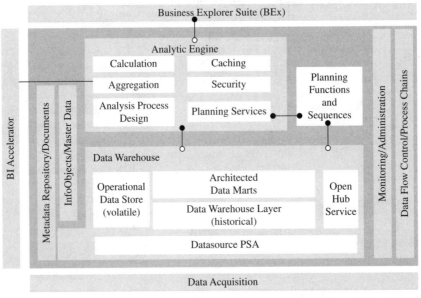

Copyright by SAP AG

FIGURE 1-17 Architecture of the BI platform services and warehouse components

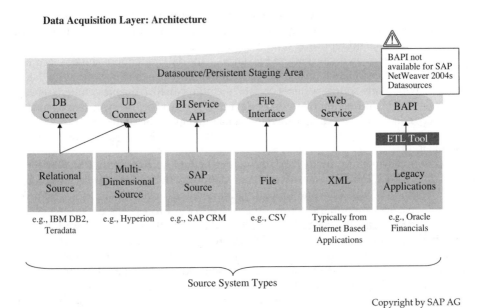

Copyright by SAP AG

FIGURE 1-18 Data acquisition

is XML-based communication using HTTP. The application-specific contents are transferred in messages in user-defined XML from the sender to the receiver using the Integration Server (part of SAP XI). Another datasource would be non-SAP systems; the BI architecture offers the ability to integrate with any external source of data. One of the methods within BI to facilitate this process is the Open Hub Service. This functionality offers the ability to link external file systems to BI, then upload the data directly into another database file or flat file (Excel document) from the InfoCube. You can also access information from one BW and upload it to another BW (specifically to a Data Target in that BW system) system or share information within a BW system with other data targets in that same system (InfoCube-to-InfoCube exchange of data—DataMarting) so that you can stage the granularity of the data in the BI system in storage layers. Another method of uploading data into the BI data warehouse is via the use of DB Connect, which offers direct connections to an Oracle Database system. For example, the DB Connect functionality offers a direct connection to a legacy Oracle DB and the ability to create a series of structures that directly link the BI objects to the Oracle DB and offer direct uploads of data. For more complex uploads, you can use the UDI (Universal Data Integration), which offers an integration process similar to the use of a third-party system, to integrate BW with another source of data such as Hyperion.

ETL is the process of extracting, transforming, and loading data. It describes the process of moving data from one source system to another. The source system types describe the extraction activity (see Figure 1-18). In the data extraction process, the transformation process can take place. This can be any sort of manipulation of the raw data—cleansing of the data, aggregation of the data, and other activities to make the data ready and usable in the BI system. As of 7.0 BI, this process is enabled with a new drag-and-drop visual transformation tool for configuration purposes. There are numerous topics in this area, such as the management of delta uploads, full uploads of data, real-time sourcing of data (new for 7.0 BI), currency conversion, and more. These are critical topics that are too involved to get into during this overview, but they are important to understand and manage. Transformation of the data can involve the summary of the data, enhancing the data (adding more characteristics to a record—for example, if customer is A100, then customer group is R45), developing calculations that occur during the upload (for example, based on sales volume, a salesperson receives a bonus; if the sales volume is $1,000,000, the salesperson receives a bonus of $10,000, and that calculated bonus is included in the record), or any number of different realignments of the data. This is important to understand so that as you query the information, you understand what has happened to the data between the source system tables and the InfoCube you are querying against for strategic information.

Data Transformation

The InfoPackage (IP) and the Data Transfer Process (DTP) are the objects used to execute the transfer of data through the transformation process. As you can see in Figure 1-19, these two items can be used to manage the data loads by filtering the data uploaded (for example, only upload the data from North America) or to manage a check for data consistency, among other responsibilities. The PSA (Persistent Staging Area) is the physical storage level that holds a set of data that is exactly what the source system has, and it can therefore be used for a number of tasks, such as a consistency checks against the data in the source system table to validate the accuracy of the uploaded data.

Figure 1-20 shows the configuration screen from the SAP BI Transformation Rule. The basic process is to map the fields from the source system to the fields in the target system.

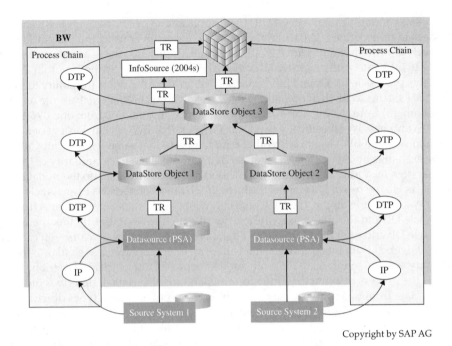

FIGURE 1-19   Basic transformation in SAP BI 7.0

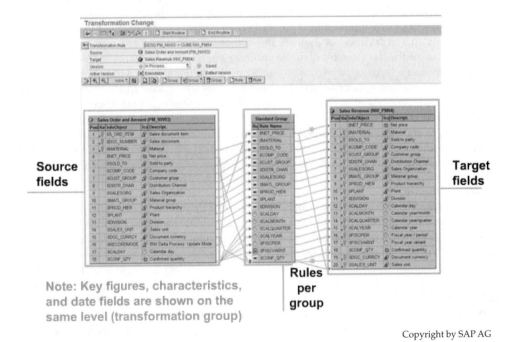

Note: Key figures, characteristics, and date fields are shown on the same level (transformation group)

FIGURE 1-20   Transformation Rule in SAP BI

These source and target fields can be combinations of a number of different systems, including other BI systems. The portion in the middle of the screen is called the Standard Group, and it can be used in a situation where common rules are used for a number of different source and target combinations. Thus, you can set up a reusable set of rules. You will usually see the two groups linked directly to each other without the Standard Group option. To review the details of each of the rules, right-click the connecting line/link and choose Rule Details to analyze any changes or manipulations being used to upload the data.

In Figure 1-21, you can see the different options that can be used to work with the data during the upload. These are all standard business content elements that are available without any configuration to be used. This is one of the areas where the configuration of system processes can be applied. The Rule Types go from the basic direct assignment between fields to the use of ABAP routines to create complex calculations before the data reaches the InfoCube for reporting. In addition to this, the currency can be converted during the upload, the key figures can be aggregated or adjusted to hold the maximum or minimum of a range (for example, the maximum stock price during a 24-hour session), and you have the ability to assign routines and formulas to the structures to adjust or validate the data as it is uploaded.

The next layer is the Physical Storage layer for the data. I cover this information in more detail in the next chapter and will therefore only expand on this here at a high level. Numerous data storage objects can be used for this task, but specific to this process you use an InfoProvider that is a Data Target. There are Data Targets and Non-Data Targets, and we discuss the differences in more detail in the next chapter. The Data Targets that can store data and are generally used here include the DataStore objects (commonly referred to as the Operational Data layer), InfoCubes (generally the Reporting layer), and InfoObjects (used to store the master data from the source systems). The queries are then created using these objects as their sources of data. We will discuss all these items in detail in Chapter 2.

Transformation Rule
- **Rule Type**
  - Constant
  - Direct Assignment
  - Reading master data
    - Only available for InfoObject-based sources (not PSA)
  - Routine
  - Formula editor
  - Time Conversion/Distribution
- **Currency / Unit conversion**
  - Not available if the source of the transformation is a DataSource
- **Aggregation**
  - Summation (+) / Minimum (<) / Maximum (>)
  - Symbol for aggregation shown on the graphical UI
  - Overwrite (for DataStore objects)
- **Source fields**
  - Usually one source field (plus unit/currency)
  - For routines/formulas, several source fields are possible
- **Target fields**
  - Usually one target field (plus unit/currency)
  - For return table, several fields are possible

Copyright by SAP AG

FIGURE 1-21   Functionality in the Transformation Rule

Summary

The SAP NetWeaver 2004S platform is the overall system architecture that supports the SAP applications. Within the NetWeaver platform you have a number of different groupings of activities, and one of them in the information level is BI. BI offers a toolkit of options for uploading and accessing data from numerous sources as well as for storing that information for reporting purposes. More specifically, the Business Warehouse is the data warehouse that facilitates the storing and reporting of all the integrated data. It is the only area in the platform that has the breadth of reporting options to give you the ability to format and structure the queries required by your business users.

Storing the Data—
SAP/Business Warehouse
InfoProviders

Before we start working our way through the details of the navigation and building of an SAP BI query, you first need to understand the tables and objects used to store the data for use in a query. In the previous chapter we talked very briefly about these "InfoProviders". Here, we'll get into more detail about the uses, the construction, and the functionality of each one. A number of different InfoProviders are supplied by BI, and it's very important that we use the correct one for the purpose of running the specific queries effectively and efficiently. We will discuss each InfoProvider in terms of the group it belongs to. Therefore, this discussion will not follow the format of listing the most used to the least used InfoProvider, but rather will be in terms of whether the InfoProvider is a Data Target or Non–Data Target.

NOTE *You will see many new terms as we go through this chapter.*

Simply put, Data Targets are those InfoProviders that hold data in tables for the purposes of reporting/querying. Non–Data Targets are InfoProviders that are views—they don't hold data but are used as a conduit for the purposes of reporting/querying. This is a very basic definition of each of these items, and we will expand on these definitions as we work our way through the chapter. You will see that quite a bit of analysis and data modeling takes place before you can decide which InfoProvider is right for your purposes.

Introduction to SAP BI InfoProviders

When you're deciding which InfoProvider to use, it is important to understand several concepts within BI, as well as which one of the concepts your corporation is using in the process of implementing or maintaining BI. For example, if the agreed-upon architecture is an Enterprise Data Warehouse (EDW), you will have a series of layers in which your data will be stored. Depending on the types of reports you are required to generate, you will look to different layers for the data in the specific format and granularity required by your business users. This initial architecture is identified and formatted during the initial stages of the implementation and is something that will need to be ironed out so that all the other concepts of BI will work in that environment. Figure 2-1 shows an example of a standard view of a BW(Business Warehouse) architecture and the positioning of the InfoProviders in that architecture. Notice that an InfoProvider is used as the final location for all the transactional data. Before starting the process of creating queries, you should review your corporate architecture to identify the types of data, where they are stored (that is, what tables are used), and what attributes (such as time dependency of the data, level of granularity, and so on) are being stored in the specific tables. After this chapter, we will address the "tables" in BI by the appropriate naming convention. Up until now, I've tried to control the number of additional terms used to describe BI-specific objects so that we can work into these concepts in a consistent manner.

InfoProviders, as mentioned, are initially grouped as Data Targets and Non–Data Targets. We then break them down into specific types within these groups. Figure 2-2 shows the breakdown of these objects based on the flow of data to the queries. Notice the symbols associated with the different objects. For instance, the symbol associated with an InfoCube looks like a cube. Whether you are in the configuration administration workbench of BI or the Query Designer, you will be seeing these symbols.

Table 2-1 shows the further breakdown of each different type of InfoProvider and the detailed naming convention of each object.

We will discuss each of these objects in this chapter. I approach this process from two different angles. Initially we will discuss each object based on the configuration view. Then we will move to the view of these objects from the front end or query point of view. Therefore, during our discussion you will be presented with two illustrations, each covering

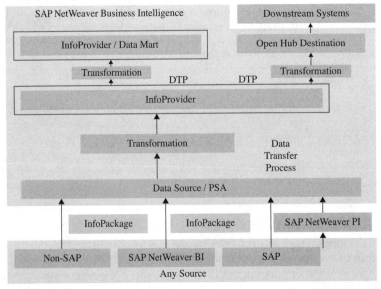

Copyright by SAP AG

FIGURE 2-1   Overview of InfoProviders' positions in the data process flow

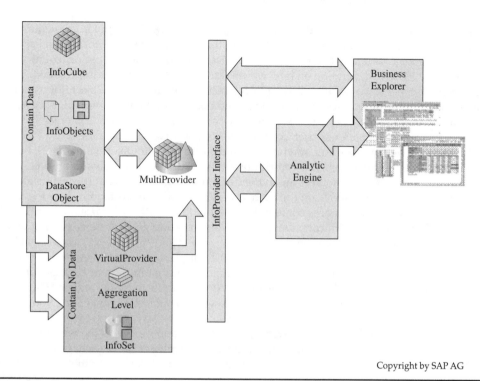

FIGURE 2-2   Overview of InfoProviders and queries

a different view of an object. The discussion around the configuration view is limited due to the nature of this book. Therefore, areas of interest in the configuration such as the details behind the structures of the tables, the relational database architecture of these objects, and other important topics for configuration will not be discussed at length. It would be easy to turn this discussion into a technical commentary, but that is for another time.

We first need to discuss the object that is the foundation of much of the architecture in BI—the Characteristic InfoObject. The InfoObject is the smallest unit in BI. From the viewpoint of configuration, the InfoObject is a series of tables that holds master data, texts, and hierarchies. If you think of the process of creating something such as a customer list, the

Data Targets	Non–Data Targets
InfoCubes—Standard and Real Time	MultiProviders
InfoObjects—Characteristic	InfoSets
DataStores—Standard, Direct Update, and Write-Optimized	Virtual InfoCubes—Data Transfer Process, BAPI, and function module
	Aggregate Levels—Integrated Planning Objects (specific to BW-IP)
	InfoSet Queries

TABLE 2-1   Types of Data Targets and Non–Data Targets

question would be, What information about the customers I have and am I interested in saving and storing so that I can retrieve it later? In this case, a customer information list might include the customer's name, address, contact, telephone number, region, country, and many other attributes, depending on how we want to recall this customer information. This list of informational items can be called an InfoObject. Therefore, an InfoObject (for example, Customer) has a series of tables that holds the customer master data (the individual customer information). Each of these objects is also an InfoObject (Customer Name, Customer Address, Customer Phone, Customer Contact, and Region), as shown in Table 2-2.

In this case, we are interested in reporting on the primary InfoObject (Customer), but we are also interested in reporting on the attributes of the customer. This helps us answer questions such as, Which customers are in the Central region? Notice that the technical name of each object starts with zero (0), such as 0CUSTOMER. This is to introduce the idea that most of the standard business content delivered with SAP BI starts with a zero (0). Therefore, if you see any technical naming convention beginning with a zero, you know that the object was delivered with the system.

InfoObjects are divided into characteristics (for example, customers), key figures (for example, revenue), units (for example, currency, amount unit), time characteristics (for example, fiscal year), and technical characteristics (for example, request number). Figure 2-3 shows some different InfoObjects you might be using in the process of analyzing your business information.

It is very important that you understand the InfoObject and its uses in the reporting process. We will be using both the characteristics and the attributes of these characteristics while building queries. All InfoProviders are constructed using InfoObjects; therefore, getting the InfoObject architecture correct allows you to construct your InfoProviders accurately and deliver the required data and information in the appropriate format consistently.

Characteristics are sorting keys, such as company code, product, customer group, fiscal year, period, and region. They specify classification options for the dataset and are therefore reference objects for the key figures. In the InfoCube, for example, characteristics are stored in dimensions. These dimensions are linked by dimension IDs to the key figures in the fact table. The characteristics determine the granularity (the degree of detail) at which the key figures are kept in the InfoCube. In general, an InfoProvider contains only information on a subset of the characteristic values from the master data table based on the transactional data that is being loaded. The full set of master data is stored in the InfoObject tables, which

0CUSTOMER Primary InfoObject	0CUSTNAME Attribute/Text of Customer	0ADDR_NUMBR Attribute of Customer	0PHONE Attribute of Customer	0CONTACT Attribute of Customer	0REGION Attribute of Customer
Customer Number	Customer Name	Customer Address	Customer Phone Number	Customer Contact	Region
1000123	Smiths	123 Anywhere Dr.	123-234-4567	Jim	Central
1000234	Anderson	234 Everywhere Ave.	444-567-7890	Albert	South

TABLE 2-2   Attributes of the Characteristic InfoObject Customer

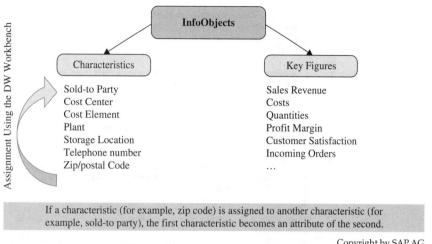

FIGURE 2-3   InfoObjects: characteristics and key figures

include the permitted values for a characteristic. These are known as the *characteristic values*. See the "InfoCube" section, later in this chapter, for additional information.

Key figures provide the values that are reported on in a query. Key figures can be quantity, amount, or number of items. They form the data part of an InfoProvider. *Units* are also required so that the values for the key figures have meaning. Key figures of type Amount are always assigned a Currency key, and key figures of type Quantity also receive a unit of measure. There are a number of other types of key figures, and we will cover them during our discussion of the uses of key figures in a query. *Time characteristics* are characteristics such as date, fiscal year, calendar month, and so on. These types of characteristics are standard delivered (therefore Standard Business Content that is delivered with BI), and even though you can create a characteristic that looks like time, the system doesn't allow you to create a time characteristic. Time characteristics are only delivered with the system. *Technical characteristics* have only one organizational meaning within BI. An example of this is the request number in the InfoCube, which collects IDs when loading data. It helps you to find groups of data that were loaded together (for example, uploading on a daily basis will generate a unique request ID). Figure 2-4 illustrates the different InfoObject types and their symbols.

If characteristics have attributes, texts, or hierarchies at their disposal, they are referred to as *master data–bearing characteristics*. Master data is data that remains unchanged over a long period of time. Master data contains information that is always needed in the same way. References to this master data can be made in all InfoProviders that hold the specific InfoObject. You also have the option of creating characteristics with references. A reference characteristic provides the attributes, master data, texts, hierarchies, data type, length, number and type of compounded characteristics, lowercase letters, and conversion routines for other new characteristics. The hierarchy is another addition to a characteristic that we will discuss during the query-creation process. The characteristic that holds the hierarchy is the basic characteristic for the hierarchy. Like attributes, hierarchies provide a structure for the values of a characteristic. For example, using the customer as a characteristic, you could have a hierarchy made up of Region, Customer Group, and Customer. Therefore, Customer

> **Key Figure InfoObjects** provide the values to be evaluated. Examples of key figure InfoObjects:
>
> - Quantity (0QUANTITY)
> - Amount (0AMOUNT)
>
> **Characteristics InfoObjects** are business reference objects that are used to analyze key figures. Examples of characteristics InfoObjects:
>
> - Cost center (0COSTCENTER)
> - Material (0MATERIAL)
>
> **Time Characteristics InfoObjects** form the time reference frame for many data analyses and evaluations. They are delivered with BI content. Examples of time characteristics InfoObjects:
>
> - Calendar day (0CALDAY) – Time characteristic with the largest granularity
> - Calendar year (0CALYEAR) or fiscal year (0FISCYEAR) – Time characteristic with the smallest granularity
>
> **Units InfoObjects** can be specified along with the key figures. They enable key figure values to be paired with their corresponding units in evaluations. Examples of units InfoObjects:
>
> - Currency unit (0CURRENCY) – Holds the currency of the trasacttion ($, EUR, and so on)
> - Value unit (0UNIT) – Holds the unit of measure (Gallon, Inch, cm, PC)

would be the base characteristic for this hierarchy. If you use this hierarchy in the query, you could define the information more clearly in terms of the location of a specific customer.

The properties of a key figure are additional information about the key figures that will help us with the development of the query format and information. A key figure is assigned additional properties that influence the way data is loaded and how the query is displayed. This includes the assignment of a currency or unit of measure, setting aggregation and exception aggregation, and specifying the number of decimal places in the query. We will run into these properties again directly in the Query Designer while creating queries.

NOTE *We will use the Query Designer to create a query definition. This definition can be used in the Web Application Designer, BEx Analyzer, Report Designer, or the Workbooks.*

Now that you have a better understanding of the InfoObject basics, we can discuss the definition(s) of an InfoProvider. InfoProviders are different meta-objects in the data basis that can be seen within a query definition as uniform data providers. They are a combination of characteristics and key figures based on the structure of their data and can be analyzed in a uniform way. The type of data staging and the degree of detail or proximity to the source system in the data flow diagram of a specific company differs from InfoProvider to InfoProvider. However, in the BEx Query Designer, they are seen as uniform objects. Depending on the type of InfoProvider, you will see the InfoObjects that comprise these InfoProviders, organized and mapped differently for the defined requirements and responsibilities of that InfoProvider. We will discuss the unique architecture as we work our way through the details of each object. As you will see, not only do InfoObjects comprise an InfoProvider, but an InfoObject can also be an InfoProvider. This makes sense if we remember that an InfoProvider is an object in the BI system against which a query/report is generated. Therefore, we can use this fact, and the fact that an InfoObject is an InfoProvider, to assume that we can create/run a query against the master data of an InfoObject.

Data Targets

As mentioned, Data Targets are InfoProviders that hold data. They are used as the final uploading component for the transactional data and offer the ability to generate queries against the data for analysis. The architecture for uploading data from the datasource to the InfoProvider is a discussion for another time, but it is important to understand some of the options you have during this uploading process that will affect your queries, both from a display point of view and a performance point of view.

One of the initial questions that needs to be answered for the purposes of both uploading and querying involves the granularity of the data being loaded. As you will see, the granularity of the data will direct you to use a specific InfoProvider—either the InfoCube or the DataStore Object (DSO). For example, we need to determine whether we are uploading the data at the material item level or at the material group level? In this case very different levels of granularity can be seen—number of materials equaling 400,000 versus material groups equaling 5,000. In this situation we would be able to report to different areas of the corporation—at the middle management level reports at the material level versus at the 'C' level reports at the material group level.

Another question to be answered involves the time element. It is important to collect the data at the correct time level, whether it is months, days, years, quarters, or some other time group. This can have a significant effect on the performance of the data because if you are collecting the data at the monthly level, everything you upload has a level of at least 12 months (versus collecting data by day, for example, which would mean you are collecting the data and multiplying it by 365). As you can see, this would result in a significant difference in data being stored and possibly performance of the query.

Another question during the process of setting up the architecture of the uploads involves the uploading process for currency and unit of measure (UOM). In the 7.0 BI version, we can upload the transactional currency or UOM and then have the query execute the currency or unit of measure conversion on the fly, or we can execute the conversion of the UOM or currency during the upload. Your decision depends on the use of the data in the querying process and the performance effort for the query. If you are looking to store the currency in the "local" version and want to be able to query at either the local level (transactional level) or global level (view based on the corporate level), you would be uploading the currency of the original transaction and setting up the currency translation process in the query. If the only type of reporting you are developing is at the global level (global currency view), the option of executing the conversion during the upload would be more consistent with the data the query is reporting. Therefore, the query performance would not be affected by the requirement to execute the currency conversion at query runtime. A similar questioning process would be used in decisions concerning the unit of measure and whether the upload would generate a consistent unit of measure (based UOM, such as "pieces" or "each" or "bottles") or you would use the approach of generating a consistent UOM during the querying process.

Another question during the decision of what to upload and in what format is the idea of whether or not to precalculate the data. Precalculation of data refers taking the basic information and, during the upload, summarizing or manipulating it in some way that we have a "grouped" view of the information. Therefore, rather than uploading all the elements of net profit, based on specific general ledger accounts we can upload the data and, during the upload, calculate the net profit. We can then store this number as one amount rather than as the basic elements, and then during the querying process we can complete the calculation. Depending on the use of each of these elements, we can answer this question. If the identified component will always be used as a precalculated number and, more importantly, the underlying calculations will not change (as in the calculation of net profit), then we can look at precalculations to help with the querying process. If we find that the calculation may change over time (as in the approach we use for the planning process or the manufacturing process for a specific material) or that we need to use underlying basic key figures for some other activity, then we should upload the data as the basic key figures and let the query do the calculation. One of the more prevalent concerns surrounding the uploading of data is the need for consistency in the uploaded data. By that I mean, will the data be uploaded so we can combine the information together in a query, and will this make sense as well as be accurate and consistent? Take, for example, the uploading process for a specific material. The material is sold throughout the world, and in each country you can buy the same product, but under different names and SKUs. For example, suppose the same widget is sold in both North America and Europe. In North America the characteristic value is 1234, but in Europe the value is 4567. We need to be sure that either during the upload or during querying these two material values are grouped together so that we can get the total picture rather than just one region's information.

This means that the same material will be identified with different numbers and possibly different naming conventions. Now, in an ideal world we would use the functionality of MDM (Master Data Management) to do all the consistency checks to make sure that the master data is consistent and can be consolidated to generate a true view of the total amount of inventory of that specific material. In the real world, we may not be implementing MDM, so BI would have to take care of this for us. Therefore, we would need to look to the consolidated InfoObjects that are used for this purpose. These InfoObjects allow us to group/consolidate the data to query and get the appropriate information. These consolidated InfoObjects are part of Standard Business Content (SBC) and are discussed at length in Chapter 14.

These are just of a few of the questions you'll need to consider—many more questions are involved in the uploading process and the integration of the uploaded data and the query performance and format. This topic will come back numerous times during our discussions of query properties and the functionality of queries. Now that you understand the basics of a Data Target, InfoProvider, and InfoObject, we can review the specific types of Data Targets.

InfoCubes

An InfoCube is the central object in BI for the storage of data. It is the most used object for storing data and generating queries due to the relational structure of the tables. (Based on the architecture of your BI system, you may decide to generate all queries from a MultiProvider object, but that would be a decision specific to each company.) The structure of the InfoCube was set up specifically to be able to execute and run query processes as quickly as possible. Therefore, it's about 99.9% sure you will be using InfoCubes during your BI implementation. InfoCubes can answer numerous questions for you concerning reporting. For example, depending on the characteristics and key figures you have grouped together in your InfoCube, you can ask questions such as

- How much product am I selling in a specific region during a specific period of time?
- What is the total P&L and balance sheet information for a company code during a specific year?
- How much has a customer purchased of a group of materials and how does that amount for the current period differ from the previous period?

Therefore, any of the basic requests for information you use to run your business, the InfoCube can answer. Just remember, the InfoCube can answer any question about events that have happened, not events that have *not* happened. For example, suppose you are interested in knowing the product orders that have run during the month that have *not* had any variance between standard costs and actual costs. The InfoCube doesn't hold information about any event that has not happened—and the production orders that don't have a variance have not happened. You will learn later that another InfoProvider is used for this situation.

An InfoCube describes (from an analysis point of view) a self-contained dataset (for example, for a business-orientated area). You analyze this dataset in a BEx query. Here's another way to describe an SAP BI InfoCube: It is a set of relational tables arranged according to the extended star schema. InfoCubes are filled with data from one or more datasources or other InfoProviders. As you can see from Figure 2-5, the Fact table is the central table of the InfoCube and stores the combinations of dimension IDs and key figures that make up the transactional data.

NOTE *An extended star schema is an enhancement of the classic star schema. In the extended star schema, the InfoCube itself doesn't hold any master data of the characteristics. The master data information is stored in separate tables in the InfoObjects, called* master data tables. *Thus, the master data tables "extend" the star schema—hence the name "extended star schema." Figure 2-5 shows a diagram of an extended star schema.*

The dimension IDs hold groups of characteristics. In the case of the Cost Center dimension table, you can see that Cost Center, Controlling Area, and Person Responsible are all held in one dimension. Review the other dimensions—Cost Element and Time—to see what characteristics are being held in those. You can see that the grouping of characteristics within

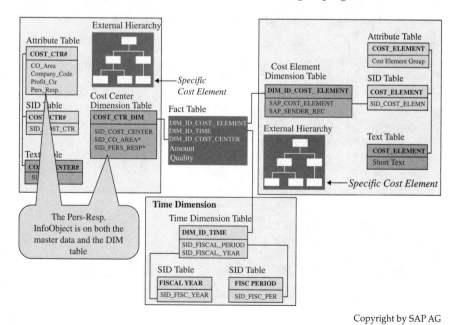

Copyright by SAP AG

FIGURE 2-5   BI InfoCube: extended star schema

a dimension is important for the performance of the query because having the appropriate characteristics grouped together allows the query to reduce the amount of data processing needed as well as to organize the data for the queries. But that's a data modeling concern, and even though the data model of the InfoCube is of great importance, it is more of a configuration discussion and therefore beyond the scope of this book. Data modeling for data warehousing has been well documented in other books such as *The Data Warehouse Toolkit* by Ralph Kimball. A number of key data modeling concepts are of importance and specific to SAP BI InfoCubes, but again this is a configuration issue and therefore not directly discussed in this book.

Standard InfoCubes   The preceding is an overview of InfoCubes, but really this discussion is consistent with the structure of Standard InfoCubes. In Figure 2-6, you can see a view of the configuration of an SBC Standard InfoCube, 0FIGL_C01. Object Information and Settings are closed in order to view the additional information for Key Figures and Characteristics. The three dimensions—Data Package, Time, and Unit—are always delivered with an InfoCube. The other dimensions are in this case delivered by SAP, but you can create additional dimensions (a total of 13 dimensions) that group characteristics. In this figure, one dimension—Organizational Units—groups together the characteristics Company Code and Business due to the consistency of the information that is delivered by the combination of these two characteristics. Notice the icon for the dimensions—the grouped green triangles. You will see these shortly in the querying process. Characteristics that logically

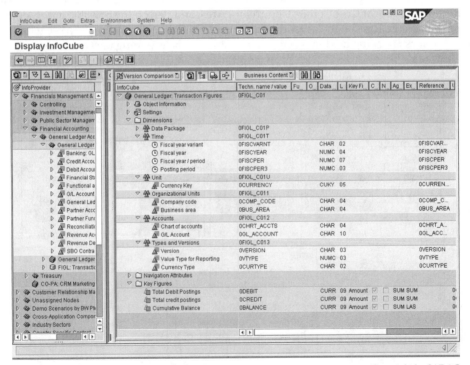

Copyright by SAP AG

FIGURE 2-6   Data model display for a Standard InfoCube

belong together are grouped in a dimension. By adhering to this design criterion, dimensions are to a large extent independent of each other, and dimension tables remain small with regard to data volume. This is beneficial in terms of performance.

In Figure 2-7, you can see the Standard InfoCube in the Query Designer as it is viewed by the Power User in the process of creating the query definition. As you can see, the Dimension icon groups the different characteristics for use. In this case, the Material dimension holds just one characteristic, Material, whereas the Sales Area Data dimension has three characteristics—Distribution Channel, Division, and Sales Organization—grouped together. Again, one of the factors in defining the Dimension structure (characteristics that are grouped together) and the data modeling process would be the reporting process of the Business User. Also notice the folder identified as Key Figures; this is where all the key figures that are listed and available to use in a query definition. We will be discussing and defining all the different areas in the Query Designer in Chapter 4 and therefore will not dwell on the actual structure here.

Real-Time InfoCubes   Real-Time InfoCubes differ from Standard InfoCubes in their ability to support parallel write accesses. Standard InfoCubes are technically optimized for read accesses to the detriment of write accesses, whereas Real-Time InfoCubes are technically optimized for writing access. The Real-Time InfoCubes are used in connection with the entry of planning data. They are used in the BI-IP (Integrated Planning) and BW-BPS (Business Planning and Simulation) components of BI. We will discuss the functionality of BI-IP in Chapter 18 due to the integration with BI and the querying process, but we will

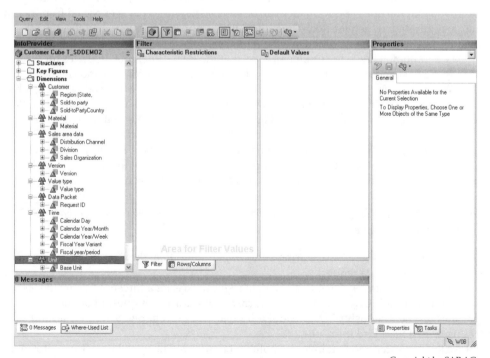

Copyright by SAP AG

Figure 2-7   InfoCube display in the Query Designer

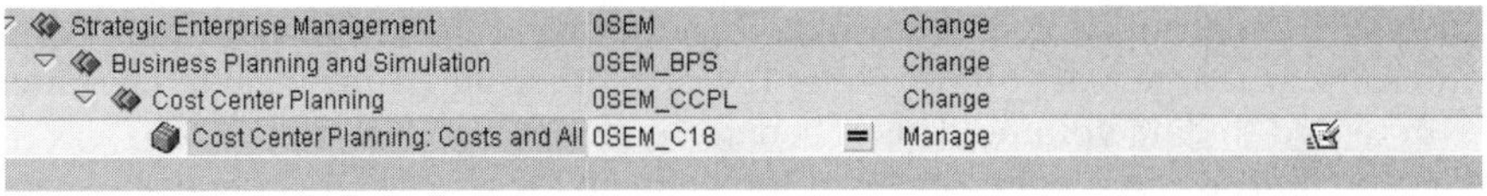

⟡ Strategic Enterprise Management	0SEM		Change	
▽ ⟡ Business Planning and Simulation	0SEM_BPS		Change	
▽ ⟡ Cost Center Planning	0SEM_CCPL		Change	
🗄 Cost Center Planning: Costs and All	0SEM_C18	▬	Manage	⬚

FIGURE 2-8   Real-Time InfoCube identifier icon

defer the discussion of BW-BPS because the configuration of BW-BPS is unique from BI and queries. Whereas Standard InfoCubes are filled using the uploading process in BI, as explained in Chapter 1, the Real-Time InfoCubes can be filled with data using two different methods: You can enter data directly into the queries by posting manually or by executing planning functions for manipulating the data, or you can opt to convert a Real-Time InfoCube back to a format that allows for the uploading of data the same as a Standard InfoCube. Depending on the use of the Real-Time InfoCube, you can either post planning data or upload data, but not both at the same time. Figure 2-8 shows the icon that indicates whether the InfoCube is a Real-Time InfoCube. This icon—paper with a pencil—allows you to create an aggregation level for that Real-Time InfoCube to use in integrated planning.

There are approximately 14 technical differences between the Standard InfoCube and the Real-Time InfoCube and how they hold data and are used for data analysis. A basic rule of thumb is that if you are going to create queries using a Real-Time InfoCube, the performance will be effected by the architecture of a Real-Time InfoCube. Therefore, depending on the specific reporting requirements, it may be good to discuss the possibility of uploading the data from a Real-Time InfoCube to a Standard InfoCube and then report on the Standard InfoCube so that the query performance can be consistent with what is expected from BI. The actual configuration screen for Real-Time InfoCubes is not any different than the one for Standard InfoCubes. The one difference that you need to be aware of involves the creation of the query definition. Due to the unique process that the Real-Time InfoCube uses for collecting the data and the request ID (one of the standard dimension IDs and characteristic groups in the InfoCube), the last request ID in the InfoCube is yellow instead of green, which is the status a normal InfoCube request ID would have if an upload of data via the data flow process were executed. As you can see in Figure 2-9, the request ID is yellow instead of green. Therefore, the flag for reporting purposes that is required against the request ID group is not available against the last request ID of a Real-Time InfoCube. Therefore, you have to use the SBC variable "Most Current Data" (technical name, 0S_RQMRC) or another SBC variables that is now available in 7.0 BI as part of the query definition.

NOTE *In the BI 7.0 version, this functionality is also available using the transaction code RSRT to display the query results.*

This is shown in Figure 2-10. During entry of planning data, the data is written to a Real-Time InfoCube data request.

As soon as the number of records in a data request exceeds a threshold value (50,000 records), the request is closed and a rollup is carried out for this request in defined aggregates (asynchronously). You can still roll up and define aggregates, collapse, and so on, as usual in a Standard InfoCube.

If we look at a scenario that involves both Standard InfoCubes and Real-Time InfoCubes, we can understand the responsibilities of each InfoCube. In one instance, actual data (read-only access) and planned data (read-only and write access) have to be held in different

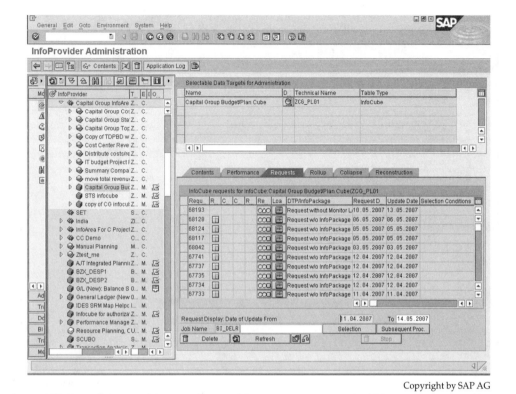

Copyright by SAP AG

FIGURE 2-9   Real-Time InfoCube request ID

InfoCubes. Therefore, we use a Standard InfoCube for actual data and a Real-Time InfoCube for planned data. Data integration is achieved using a MultiProvider that contains both of the InfoCubes. Access to the two different InfoCubes for planning purposes is controlled by the aggregation level that is created with the MultiProvider as the basis. Access to the specific InfoCube is controlled by the use of the unique characteristic 0INFOPROV (contains a list of the InfoProviders used), which is created upon the activation of a MultiProvider.

DataStore Objects

A DataStore object serves as a storage location for consolidated and cleansed transaction data on a document (operational) data level, or it can be used for the storage of master data for analysis. A DataStore object contains key fields (for example, document number/item) and data fields that contain both character fields (for example, order status, customer) as well as key figures. Another task that the DataStore object can be used for is the update of the current data in another object. This uses the delta updating functionality and can update data into an InfoCubes and/or other DataStore objects or master data tables (attributes or texts) in the same system or across different systems. Unlike multidimensional data storage using InfoCubes, the data in DataStore objects is stored in transparent, flat database tables. The system does not create fact tables or dimension tables for the DataStore object. The cumulative update of key figures is supported for DataStore objects, just as it is with InfoCubes, but with DataStore objects it is also possible to overwrite data fields. This is

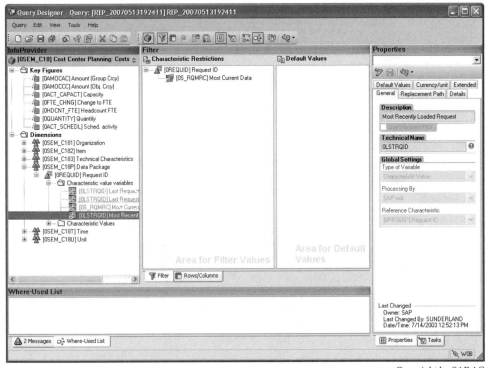

FIGURE 2-10   Query Designer view of a Real-Time InfoCube definition

particularly important with document-related structures. If documents (for example, sales orders transactions) are changed in the source system, these changes include both numeric fields, such as the order quantity, and nonnumeric fields, such as the ship-to party, status, and delivery date, can be updated into the DataStore object and the change statuses can be tracked by the "change log" in the DataStore object. To reproduce these changes in the DataStore objects in the BI system, you have to overwrite the relevant fields in the DataStore objects and set them to the current value. Furthermore, you can use an overwrite of the existing change log to render a source delta enabled. This means that the delta that is further updated to the InfoCubes, for example, is calculated from a delta process. This is a very basic outline of the back-end functionality of the DataStore object.

As for the use and functionality in relationship to reporting, the DataStore object plays a very important role. Because it is structured to be able to store and manage line item detail and operational data, we can use it to do report-to-report interfacing for ease of access to detailed data.

NOTE   *Report-to-report interfacing (RRI) is the process of using one query to filter information for another query. You access one query from the executed query and identify a characteristic value that you drill down against for more detailed data. For example, suppose you are looking to review the details of a division. You execute a report that shows information for the division at a summary level; you then execute a query jump (RRI) to another query with the detailed data around the division.*

This approach eliminates the need to do an RRI back to the source system data and then effectively push additional query effort back onto the source systems tables. We can also use the DataStore object to execute and store precalculated information or enhance the transactional data as it is moved through the table structures in the DataStore object. Due to the flat table structures, if you query against the DataStore objects, you will see that query performance suffers a bit.

The different types of DataStore object are Standard, For Direct Update, and Write-Optimized. In Table 2-3, you can see the differences in the structures, data supply, and BEx querying of the three DataStore objects.

Figure 2-11 shows the architecture of a Standard DataStore object with the combination of three tables, as described in Table 2-3. An InfoCube fact table only contains key figures, in contrast to a DataStore object, whose data part can also contain characteristics. The characteristics of an InfoCube are stored in its dimensions. The "dimensions" of a DataStore object are the key fields and the data fields. The key fields are the combinations of characteristics that make up the critical key fields that identify whether a transaction that is being uploaded is either a *new* record or a *changed* record. The data fields are the combinations of characteristics and key figures being tracked in the DataStore object. Figure 2-12 shows the format of the DataStore object's key and data fields. Within the structure of the DataStore object, you can also create secondary indexes for use during the query process to increase the performance of the DataStore object during reporting.

Standard DataStore Objects   The Standard DataStore object is filled with data during the extraction and load process in the BI system. As shown, the Standard DataStore object has three tables: The Active Table, the Activation Queue, and the Change Log. Each has a responsibility in the upload and query process. The Activation Queue is used for the processing of the initial data that comes in the DataStore object. This offers the ability to run serialization against the transactional data. As Figure 2-11 shows, the Activation Queue receives the data and passes it along to the Active Table and the Change Log for final storage. The Active Table is used for supplying the queries with information at a summary level.

Type	Structure	Data Supply	SID Generation	Are BEx Queries Possible?
Standard	Consists of three tables: activation queue, table of active data, and change log	From data transfer process	Yes	Yes
For Direct Update	Consists of the table of active data only	From APIs	No	Yes
Write-optimized	Consists of the table of active data only	From data transfer process	No	Yes

TABLE 2-3   DataStore Object Types and Attributes

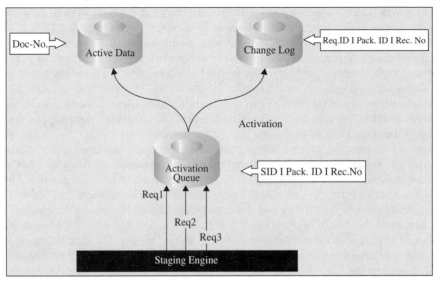

FIGURE 2-11 Architecture of the Standard DataStore object—three tables

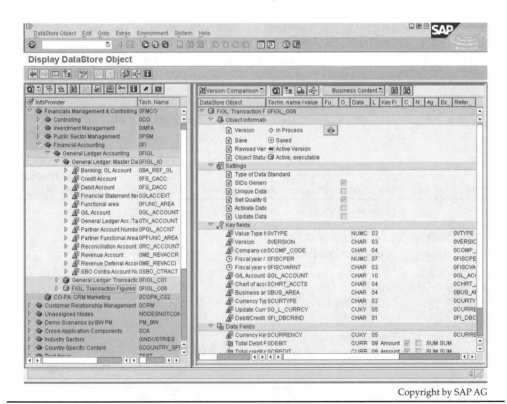

FIGURE 2-12 DataStore object's data model display—key fields and data fields

Finally, the Change Log is used for the uploading of the changed records to another Data Target such as an InfoCube. This is the most popular and most used structure for the DataStore objects. The tables of active data are built according to the DataStore object definition. This means that key fields and data fields are specified when the DataStore object is defined. The data arrives in the Change Log from the Activation Queue and is written to the table for active data upon activation. During activation, the requests are sorted according to their logical keys. This ensures that the data is updated to the table for active data in the correct request sequence. In terms of the uses of the Standard DataStore object for querying and reporting on the data it follows the same concept as discussed above in terms of the detailed level of data that is stored for reporting purposes and the use of this level of data for querying.

Direct Update DataStore Objects   The DataStore object for direct update differs from the Standard DataStore object in terms of how the data is processed. In a standard DataStore object, data is stored in different versions (active, delta, modified), whereas a DataStore object for direct update contains data in a single version. Therefore, data is stored in precisely the same form in which it was written to the DataStore object for direct update by the application. In the BI system, you can use a DataStore object for direct update as a Data Target for an analysis process such as for use with the Analysis Process Designer for data mining. In Figure 2-13, you can see the structure of the Direct Update DataStore and the use of APIs to execute the uploading of data. The DataStore object for direct update is also required by diverse applications, such as SAP Strategic Enterprise Management (SEM), for example, as well as other external applications. In SEM, the Direct Update DataStore object is used for capturing the detailed data for the consolidation process via SEM-BCS. DataStore objects for direct update ensure that the data is available quickly. The data from this kind of DataStore object is accessed transactionally. The data is written to the DataStore object (possibly by several users at the same time) and reread as soon as possible. It is not a replacement for the standard DataStore object. It is an additional function that can be used in special application contexts. The DataStore object for direct update consists of a table for active data only. It retrieves its data from external systems via fill or delete APIs. One of the

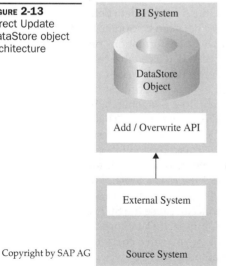

Figure 2-13
Direct Update
DataStore object
architecture

Copyright by SAP AG

advantages to the way it is structured is that it is easy to access data. Data is made available for analysis and reporting immediately after it is loaded. Figure 2-14 shows the format of the DataStore object displayed in the Query Designer. Notice that there are only two "dimensions": key fields and data fields. It is important that you remember to use at least one of the key fields during the creation of the query so that the transactional data can be queried and show consistent results.

Write-Optimized DataStore Objects   Write-Optimized DataStore objects are new to the 7.0 version of BI and are used for faster uploading to the BI environment. They are used to store large amounts of data, such as the master data of materials that a company has, or to upload a large amount of transactional data that has

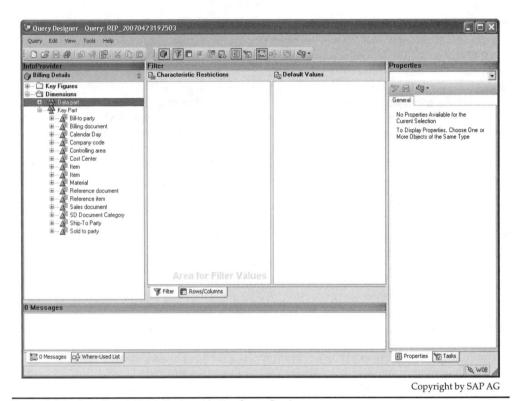

FIGURE 2-14   DataStore object displayed in the Query Designer

already been identified as consistent and cleansed. This type of DataStore object only consists of one table of active data. Data is loaded using the data transfer process. Data that is loaded into Write-Optimized DataStore objects is available immediately for further processing. You use a Write-Optimized DataStore object as a temporary storage area for large sets of data if you are executing complex transformations for this data before it is written to the Standard DataStore object. Subsequently, the data can be updated to further (smaller) InfoProviders. You only have to create the complex transformations once for all data—for example, when storing sets of mapped InfoObjects used as a table to enhance the records as they are uploaded into standard DataStore objects. You use Write-Optimized DataStore objects as the EDW layer for saving data. Business rules are only applied when the data is updated to additional InfoProviders. The system does not generate SIDs for Write-Optimized DataStore objects, and you do not need to activate them. This means that you can save and further process data quickly. Reporting is possible on the basis of these DataStore objects. However, I recommend that you use them as a consolidation layer, and update the data to additional InfoProviders, Standard DataStore objects, or InfoCubes.

For performance reasons, SID values are not created for the characteristics that are loaded. The data is still available for BEx queries. However, in comparison to Standard DataStore objects, you can expect slightly worse performance because the SID values have to be created during reporting. If you want to use Write-Optimized DataStore objects in BEx queries, I recommend that they have a semantic key and that you run a check to ensure that the data is unique. In this case, the Write-Optimized DataStore object behaves like a

Standard DataStore object. If the DataStore object does not have these properties, unexpected results may be produced when the data is aggregated in the query.

InfoObjects

You can indicate an InfoObject of type Characteristic as an InfoProvider if it has attributes and/or texts. The data is then loaded into the master data tables using the transformation rules. You can only designate a characteristic as an InfoProvider if it contains texts or attributes. It is not possible to use transformation rules to load hierarchies. You also need to have the field for the connection to the InfoArea so that the InfoObject can be identified as an InfoProvider and therefore execute a query against this object. Figure 2-15 shows the field in the InfoObject Master Data/Texts tab that the InfoArea is assigned to allow the InfoObject to be classified as an InfoProvider. The characteristic is subsequently displayed in the InfoProvider tree in the Data Warehousing Workbench.

During InfoObject maintenance, you can select two-level navigation attributes (the navigation attributes for the characteristic and the navigation attributes for the InfoCube) for this characteristic in the Attribute tab page. These are then available like normal characteristics in the query definition. If you want to turn a characteristic into an InfoProvider, you have to assign an InfoArea to the characteristic. Figure 2-16 shows the view of the InfoObject InfoProvider from the Query Designer.

During the process of identifying this as an InfoProvider, you include a key figure (number of records) that is automatically added to the structure so that you can query off this object as well as another formatting process that is generated from the two "dimensions" for the InfoObject—a Key Field node and an Attribute node. In the process of querying against the InfoObject, you need to remember that Time objects are unavailable using the InfoObject InfoProvider. You will have to create an InfoSet to take advantage of this type of reporting

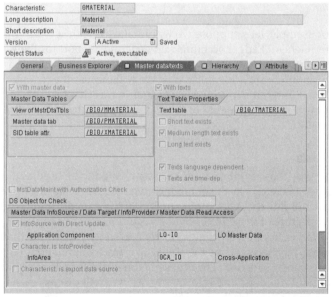

Copyright by SAP AG

FIGURE 2-15   InfoObject Master Data/Texts tab for the field entry for InfoArea

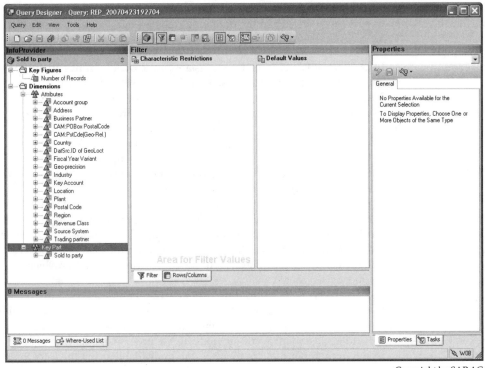

FIGURE 2-16   InfoObject used as an InfoProvider in Query Designer view

requirement. For example, let's suppose we would like to create a report that uses time to integrate with the General Ledger accounts and generate a report for the AR/AP aging process. We would not be able to do that type of reporting on a specific InfoObject, so we need to organize an InfoSet to accomplish this. We will discuss the required fields for an InfoObject that are of interest to business users later in this chapter.

As a summary of the functionality of the DataStore object and the InfoCube, refer to Table 2-4.

Non–Data Targets

Non–Data Targets are those InfoProviders that are created to be used as a *view* of the data from other sources. Therefore, as the naming convention suggests, these InfoProviders do not hold any data but rather create a union or join of the data during the query execution process. The architecture of these InfoProviders is unique for this purpose. As mentioned before, the Data Target InfoProviders are only able to show you events that have happened, but with Non–Data Targets you have the ability to create combinations so that additional reporting requests can be satisfied. The types of Non–Data Targets are MultiProviders, InfoSets, Virtual InfoProviders, and InfoSet Queries. We will discuss each of their advantages as we work through these InfoProviders.

Object/Property	DataStore Object	InfoCube
Method/purpose	Harmonization/consolidation and mass storage (as part of the warehouse data layer of an EDW architecture)	Aggregation/optimization of query performance
Data storage	Storage for transaction data and, less often, consolidated master data: permanent, one to ten years	Storage for transaction data: permanent, five to ten years
Source of data	Cleansed data (source system independent)	Cleansed data (source system independent)
Manipulation	Change/Add/Delete	Add
Architecture	Relational DB tables, normalized, records have business meaningful keys	BW extended star schema: denormalized
Reporting	High data granularity (flat reporting)	Low data granularity (multidimensional reporting)

TABLE 2-4 Comparison of DataStore Object and InfoCube Parameters

MultiProviders

A MultiProvider is a type of InfoProvider that combines data from a number of InfoProviders and makes it available for analysis purposes. The MultiProvider itself does not contain any data. Its data comes entirely from the InfoProviders on which it is based. These InfoProviders are connected to one another by a union operation. A MultiProvider can consist of different combinations of the following InfoProviders: InfoCube, DataStore object, InfoObject, InfoSet, Virtual Provider, and aggregation level. Figure 2-17 shows an example of the combinations possible. A union operation is used to combine the data from these objects in a MultiProvider. Here, the system constructs the union set of the datasets involved; all the values of these

FIGURE 2-17
MultiProvider
graphical model
view

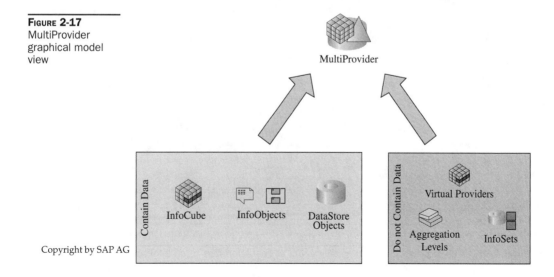

datasets are combined. As a comparison, InfoSets are created using joins. These joins only combine values that appear in both tables. In contrast to a union, joins form the intersection of the tables. In a MultiProvider, each characteristic in each of the InfoProviders involved must correspond to exactly one characteristic or navigation attribute (where available). If this is not clear, you have to specify the InfoObject to which you want to assign the characteristic in the MultiProvider. You do this when you define the MultiProvider. It is important that in the process of creating a MultiProvider you have at least one characteristic that is in both tables so that a successful set of combinations can be generated. For example, if you have DataStore objects—one with sales order data, one with billing data, and another with delivery data—and you are using these in a MultiProvider, it's very important that a characteristic that's an intersection of all DataStore objects be available (such as sales order number) so that the information generated will have a unique value that can be linked. As another example, suppose you have actual data in one InfoCube and planned data in another InfoCube, and you have to report on the data in combination/comparison. The answer is to build a MultiProvider to offer you information from two separate InfoCubes. The underlying concept here is that a query can only be created based on one InfoProvider, but with a MultiProvider you can create a query on many InfoCubes via the structure of the MultiProvider. Attempting to organize the information into a query without a characteristic that is the same in both InfoCubes would be difficult, if not impossible. In Figure 2-18, you can see that during the

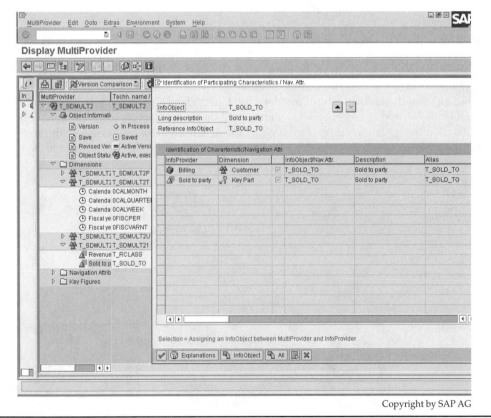

FIGURE 2-18   MultiProvider data model assignment of characteristics to an InfoProvider

creation of a MultiProvider we identify the connection by checking the link between the characteristics of the different InfoProviders. In this case, the characteristic T_SOLD_TO (Sold To Party) is assigned to the InfoCube Billing and also to the InfoObject Sold To Party. Therefore, this will be a combination of the master data from the InfoObject Sold To Party and the transactional data from the Billing InfoCube. Both the characteristics and the key figures are assigned to specific combinations or single InfoProviders. The key figure assignments are as (or even more) important than the characteristic assignment, because if you assign a key figure to two different InfoProviders, you need to make sure that in the Query Designer process you identify the specific source of data. Otherwise, you will get double the amount because of the combination of information.

MultiProviders only exist as a logical definition. The data continues to be stored in the InfoProviders on which the MultiProvider is based. A query based on a MultiProvider is divided internally into subqueries. There is a subquery for each InfoProvider included in the MultiProvider. These subqueries are usually processed in parallel. Technically there are no restrictions with regard to the number of InfoProviders that can be included in a MultiProvider. However, I recommend that you include no more than ten InfoProviders in a single MultiProvider, because splitting the MultiProvider queries and reconstructing the results for the individual InfoProviders takes a substantial amount of time and is generally counterproductive. Modeling MultiProviders with more than ten InfoProviders is also highly complex. In Figure 2-19, you can see the format of the MultiProvider in the Query Designer. Notice that in the list of characteristics (green triangles) a new characteristic is

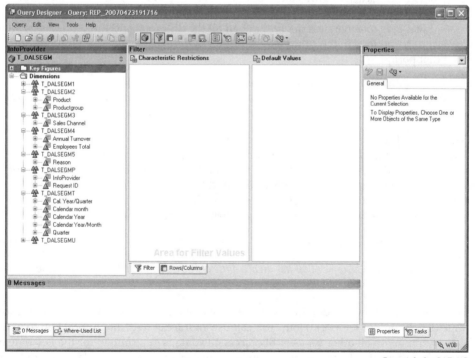

Copyright by SAP AG

Figure 2-19   MultiProvider in the Query Designer view

added that is specific to the MultiProvider (that is, the characteristic InfoProvider (0INFOPROV). This characteristic allows the power user creating a query from the MultiProvider to choose the specific InfoProvider to restrict the data being read. Therefore, if you have a MultiProvider that has a key figure being read from two different InfoProviders, you can limit this to only by combining the InfoProvider (0INFOPROV) characteristic with the key figure you are reading.

NOTE *This process is known as creating a restricted key figure, and we will discuss and create this object in Chapter 5.*

InfoSets

InfoSets are a specific kind of InfoProvider that describe datasources that are defined as *joins* of DataStore objects, InfoCubes, and InfoObjects (not other MultiProviders). BI InfoSets are objects that serve to collect and join any of the targets into a logical view that can be used for accessing the data to be read by a query. Because the InfoSet is a join of data, you can control the view of the information from an InfoSet. By this I mean that you can set up the InfoSet so that the query can answer questions, such as questions about an event that has not happened. For example, if you use a master data–bearing InfoObject during the creation of the InfoSet and identify this as the *outer join*, the master data will be a required value in the column and therefore show situations were there has been no activity. As a real-world example, I worked with a company that wanted to see what each of its different divisions sold during each month—and not only what they did sell, but also other products that they didn't sell. Therefore, setting up an InfoSet and using the master data as the *left outer join*, I was able to generate a query that had all the divisions and the products listed in the rows and the periods in the columns. All products were displayed, even if there were no sales for that period.

NOTE *A join condition determines the combination of individual object records that are included in the results set.*

The InfoSet is a semantic layer over the datasources and reads the data similar to a database view. Unlike the classic InfoSet, this InfoSet is a BI-specific view of the data. InfoSets allow you to analyze the data in several InfoProviders by using combinations of master data–bearing characteristics, InfoCubes, and DataStore objects. The system collects information from the tables of the relevant InfoProviders. When an InfoSet is made up of several characteristics, you can map transitive attributes and analyze this master data.

NOTE Transitive attributes *are attributes at the secondary level. Suppose, for example, you have an InfoObject called Customer that has an attribute of Region, and that attribute, Region, has an attribute of Country. You can set up a process so that you can report on Country via Customer.*

If one of the InfoObjects contained in the join is a time-dependent characteristic, the join is a time-dependent (or temporal) join. You can use an InfoSet with a temporal join to map periods of time. With all other types of BI objects, the data is determined for the key date of the query, but with a temporal join in an InfoSet, you can specify a particular point in time at which you want the data to be evaluated. The key date of the query is not taken into consideration in the InfoSet.

A join can contain objects of the same object type, or objects of different object types. You can include individual objects in a join as many times as you want. Join conditions connect the objects in a join to one another (equal-join condition). A join condition determines the combination of individual object records that are included in the results set. In Figure 2-20, you can see that the configuration screen for the InfoSet is very different from those for either the InfoCube, MultiProvider, or DataStore object. It is more of a display of a transformation rule that offers you the drag-and-drop process of linking up characteristics. The boxes that are checked on the far left side of each column are for those characteristics and key figures that are to be used in the structure of the InfoSet. The links that connect the series of tables are used as integration points for the InfoSet. To the far right in each column you can see boxes to check. These are for the configuration of the temporal joins that can be used to identify the correct information for a key date of the InfoSet.

In the BEx Query Designer, each InfoProvider in the join of type DataStore or characteristic-bearing master data displays two separate dimensions (key and attribute). With InfoCubes, the dimensions of the InfoCube are mapped. These dimensions contain the fields and attributes for the selected InfoSet. If the InfoProvider is an InfoObject of type Characteristic, all the characteristics listed in attribute definition and all the display attributes are assigned to the characteristics (and the compound characteristics, if applicable) in the Key dimension. If the InfoProvider is a DataStore object or an InfoCube, *no* field objects with the "exclusive attribute" property are listed in the directory tree of the InfoProvider. If the join is a temporal join, there is also a separate Valid Time Interval dimension in the BEx Query Designer.

Copyright by SAP AG

FIGURE 2-20   InfoSet data model display

InfoSets offer you the *most recent* reporting for characteristics that bear master data; in reporting and analysis, the newest records are displayed, even if they are not activated yet. In Figure 2-21, you can see the InfoSet as formatted in the Query Designer.

The results set of a join is made up of fields from all the tables involved. One row of this results set contains a valid combination of rows from each of the tables involved. The join condition and the filter for the query that you specify determine which combinations are valid.

You can set join conditions between fields from the key part of the tables and between fields from the data part of the tables. For two InfoObjects, for example, you can define an equal-join condition between two attributes. The filter for the query determines which values are allowed for individual columns of the results set, or the combinations of values that are allowed for various different columns. This further restricts the results set that is produced by the join condition. Depending on how join conditions have been designed, every record from table1 and table2 can be included several times in a combination for a record in the results set. For example, if for a single record in table1 there are a total of three records in table2 for which the conditions F1(T1) = F2(T2) apply, there are potentially three records in the results set in which the record from table1 is included. If table1 contains a key figure, depending on the filter condition in place, this key figure can appear one to three times or not at all in the results set. The data for the query is determined from the results set. Another standard key figure that is included in every InfoSet is the Number of Records key figure. This key figure tells you how many records in the results set for the join feed into a record in the query.

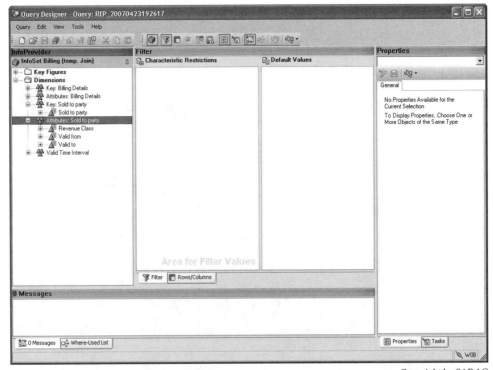

Copyright by SAP AG

FIGURE 2-21   InfoSet in the Query Designer view

In the following examples, it is assumed that master data exists for all the characteristics in the data part of DS_ORDER (otherwise, you would have to work with a left outer join):

- An InfoSet contains a join from DataStore object DS_ORDER and characteristic PLANT. You have defined the join condition PLANT(DS_ORDER) = PLANT(PLANT). In this example, for each record in DS_ORDER, there is exactly one record in PLANT. The AMOUNT key figure cannot be included more than once in the results set.

- An InfoSet contains a join from DataStore object DS_ORDER and characteristic BPARTNER. You have defined the join condition PLANT(DS_ORDER) = PLANT(BPARTNER). A number of records from BPARTNER may have the same value for PLANT. This means that more than one record from BPARTNER may be determined for a single record in DS_ORDER. As a result, there is more than one record in the results set of the join and the AMOUNT key figure appears several times. You can avoid this by activating local aggregation.

- An InfoSet contains a join from DataStore object DS_ORDER and time-dependent characteristic PERSON. You have defined the join condition PERSON(DS_ORDER) = PERSON(PERSON). Although physically a person is unique and can exist only once, the fact that the PERSON characteristic is time-dependent means that several records can exist for a single person. Using time-dependent characteristics results in a situation like that described in the previous example.

Virtual InfoCubes

As with MultiProviders and InfoSets, Virtual InfoCubes are InfoProviders with transaction data that is not stored in the objects themselves, but is read directly for analysis and reporting purposes. The relevant data can be from the BI system or from other SAP or non-SAP systems. Virtual Providers only allow read access to data. The different Virtual Providers are based on the data transfer process, on a BAPI (Business Application Program Interface), or on the function module. Each has a specific responsibility and use in the view of data and may be used in the process of a specific application involved with BI.

Based on Data Transfer Process   Data Transfer Process (DTP) Virtual Providers are those whose transaction data is read directly from an SAP system using a DataSource or an InfoProvider for analysis and reporting purposes. The DTP Virtual InfoCube allows you to define the queries based on direct access to transaction or master data in other source systems. This Virtual Provider is used if you require up-to-date information from an SAP source system, but it is suggested that you only access a small set of data and that you only use this process for a specific set of users. This Virtual Provider is not meant to be used for accessing large amounts of data, or having large numbers of users accessing data via this approach. There are specific situations where the use of this type of Virtual Provider is important—for example, if you are looking to validate information that was uploaded into the BI system and you use this Virtual Provider to access the same table you used for the upload. You could create a query against this Virtual Provider to review the information directly from the source system and then compare it to the uploaded data (more than likely you would compare the data from the Virtual Provider query with the data in the PSA (Persistent Staging Area) since this is the initial table that is used for an uploading/staging area and the data in the PSA has not be altered by any programs in BI). This type of Virtual Provider is defined based on a datasource or an InfoProvider and copies its characteristics and key figures.

NOTE *In addition to this option, in 7.0 BI is a new feature that allows you to configure your datasource as a "reconciliation datasource," which offers you a functionality similar to what's discussed in the previous paragraph.*

One unique item about the structure of a DTP Virtual Provider is that once the Virtual InfoCube is created from the datasource, you will have a Virtual InfoCube with one dimension. This can be changed, but it makes sense that if you are copying from a source system that is one dimensional, the outcome should be one dimensional. As you can see in Figure 2-22, the three different Virtual Providers are listed on the Create screen and the DTP Virtual Provider is linked directly to an infosource/datasource or can be linked to an InfoProvider. Unlike with other Virtual Providers, you do not need to program interfaces in the source system. To select data in the source system, you use the same extractors that you use to replicate data into the BI system. When you execute a query, every navigation step sends a request to the extractors in the assigned source systems. The selection of characteristics, including the selection criteria for these characteristics, is transformed according to the transformation rules for the fields of the transfer structure. They are passed to the extractor in this form. The delivered data records pass through the transfer rules in the BI system and are filtered again in the query. Because hierarchies are not read directly by the source system, they need to be available in the BI system before you execute a query. You can access attributes and texts directly.

With more complex transformations, such as routines and formulas, the selections cannot be transferred. It takes longer to read the data in the source system because the amount of data is not restricted. To prevent this, you can create an inversion routine for every transfer routine. Inversion is not possible with formulas, which is why I recommend that you use routines instead of formulas. In Figure 2-23, you can see the final view of the DTP Virtual Provider in the BI configuration.

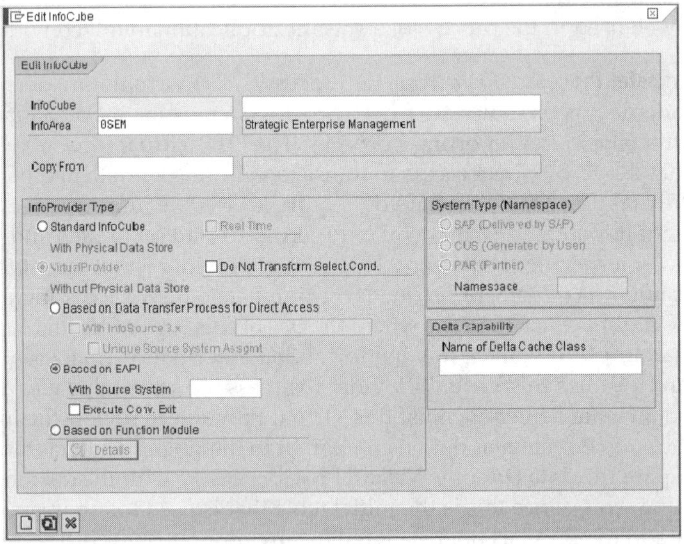

Copyright by SAP AG

FIGURE 2-22   Create screen for the Virtual Providers

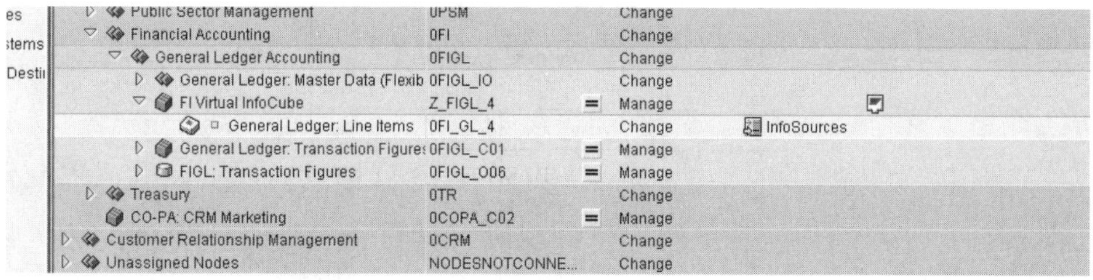

▷ ⬧ Public Sector Management	UPSM		Change	
▽ ⬧ Financial Accounting	0FI		Change	
▽ ⬧ General Ledger Accounting	0FIGL		Change	
▷ ⬧ General Ledger: Master Data (Flexib	0FIGL_IO		Change	
▽ ⬧ FI Virtual InfoCube	Z_FIGL_4	=	Manage	⬚
⬦ ▫ General Ledger: Line Items	0FI_GL_4		Change	⬚ InfoSources
▷ ⬧ General Ledger: Transaction Figure	0FIGL_C01	=	Manage	
▷ ⬧ FIGL: Transaction Figures	0FIGL_O06	=	Manage	
▷ ⬧ Treasury	0TR		Change	
⬧ CO-PA: CRM Marketing	0COPA_C02	=	Manage	
▷ ⬧ Customer Relationship Management	0CRM		Change	
▷ ⬧ Unassigned Nodes	NODESNOTCONNE...		Change	

FIGURE 2-23   DTP Virtual Provider view from the Administration Workbench

Based on BAPI   This Virtual Provider is different from the DTP Virtual Provider because the transaction data is read for analysis and reporting from an external system using a BAPI (Business Application Program Interface) and not specifically from an SAP source. The BAPI-based option allows reporting using data from non-SAP systems. The external system transfers the requested data to the OLAP processor via the BAPI. This could be used by a company that wants to provide an access solution to its data for its SAP customers. When you start a query with a Virtual Provider, you trigger a data request with characteristic selections. The source structure is dynamic and is determined by the selections. For this type of Virtual Provider, a non-SAP system transfers the requested data to the OLAP processor using the BAPI. This Virtual Provider allows you to connect non-SAP systems that are not relational in nature. Because the transaction data is not managed by the SAP system, you must code an application or utilize one that was coded in support of this interface. The uses of this Virtual Provider include carrying out analyses on data in external systems without having to physically store transaction data in the BI system. You can, for example, use a Virtual Provider to include an external system from a market data provider. Because the transaction data is not managed in the BI system, you have very little administrative effort on the BI side and can save memory space. Figure 2-24 gives an example of the architecture for a Virtual Provider with BAPI functionality.

When you use a Virtual Provider to analyze data, the data manager calls the Virtual Provider BAPI instead of an InfoProvider filled with data, and it transfers the parameters for the selections, characteristics, and key figures. The external system transfers the requested data to the OLAP processor.

Based on Function Module   The list of Virtual Providers ranges from the basic Virtual Provider to the complex Virtual Provider using a function module to gather the appropriate information from the source system to use for query display. The Virtual Provider with a user-defined function module reads the data in the Virtual Provider for analysis and reporting purposes. You have a number of options for defining the properties of the datasource more precisely. According to these properties, the data manager provides various function module interfaces for converting the parameters and data. These interfaces have to be implemented outside the BI system. You use this Virtual Provider if you want to display data from non-BI datasources in BI without having to copy the dataset into the BI structures. The data can be local or remote. You can also use your own calculations to change the data before it is passed to the OLAP processor. This Virtual Provider is used primarily in the SAP Strategic Enterprise Management (SEM) application for SEM-BCS reporting purposes. In comparison to other Virtual Providers, this one is more generic. It offers more flexibility, but also requires a higher implementation effort.

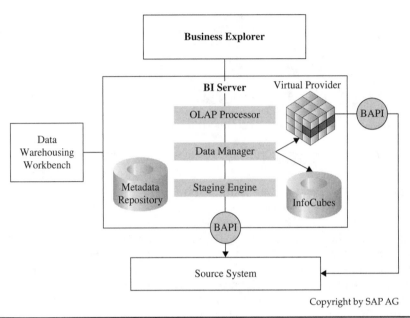

Copyright by SAP AG

FIGURE 2-24   Architecture for the use of a BAPI Virtual Provider

You specify the type of the Virtual Provider when you create it. If you choose Based on Function Module as the type for your Virtual Provider, an extra Detail pushbutton appears on the interface. This pushbutton opens an additional dialog box, in which you define the services. You enter the function module that you want to use as the datasource for the Virtual Provider. There are different default variants for the interface of this function module (these will not be discussed in this book due to the configuration process) and there are numerous options to support the function module selection conditions. These manage and control the processing of the data and whether the BI system or the external system will be in control. Figure 2-25 shows the final view of the Virtual Provider being configured.

InfoObjects as Virtual Providers   This Virtual Provider can be used in a situation where you don't want to upload master data but rather can satisfy the requirements by reading the master data directly from the datasource. However, that direct access to data has a negative impact on query performance. As with other Virtual Providers, you have to decide whether direct access to data is actually useful in the specific case in which you want to use it. You can access data in the source system directly for this characteristic. Furthermore, you can create additional DTPs for the characteristic. If you create additional DTPs for the

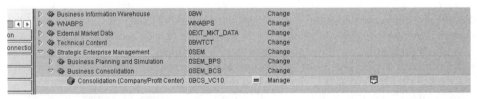

Copyright by SAP AG

FIGURE 2-25   Virtual Provider with services being configured

characteristic, you can deactivate direct access to a particular source system again, depending on the source system from which you want to read data. In the context menu of the attributes or texts for your characteristic, choose Activate Direct Access.

InfoSet Query

The final Non–Data Target has been around for quite sometime and is supported in the 7.0 BI version. However, its use is not suggested due to the enhancements in the InfoSet and MultiProvider for combining all the different InfoProviders, the requirements of assigning the results to a role, and the fact that you are not using the standard query front end for the execution of the report, even though the name (InfoSet Query) seems to reflect the fact that you would be using this front end. A classic InfoSet provides a view of a dataset that you report on. The classic InfoSet determines which tables, or fields within a table, an InfoSet query references. The InfoSet query can be used to carry out tabular (flat) reporting on these InfoSets. As of Release BW 3.0, these InfoSets are called *classic InfoSets*.

As you can see from Figure 2-26, the creation of an InfoSet Query can be accomplished by assigning it directly to a DataStore object. For technical reasons, all additional definitions of the classic InfoSet (additional tables, fields, text fields, limits, and coding for the various points in time) are not transferred into the new InfoSet. Comparable definition options are not available in the new InfoSets. In Figure 2-27, you can see the second step in the configuration of an InfoSet Query, where you choose the specific tables to be used. You *cannot* transform InfoSet Queries. The InfoSet Query is designed for reporting using flat data structures (that is, InfoObjects, DataStore objects, and DataStore object joins). The following functions are supported for the InfoSet Query: joins from several master data tables and DataStore objects, the report-to-report interface (RRI), and authorization checks. The authorization check in the InfoSet Query is simpler than the authorization check in the

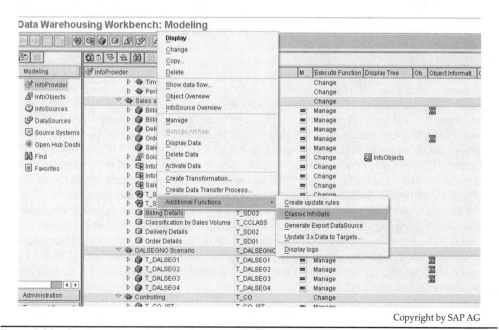

Copyright by SAP AG

FIGURE 2-26   Creation of an InfoSet Query via a DataStore object

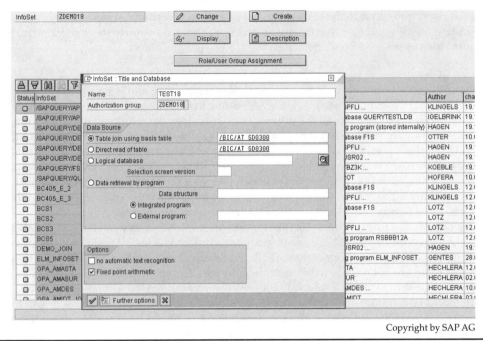

FIGURE 2-27 Step 2 in the creation of the InfoSet Query—the selection of the tables for the datasource

BEx query. The report is displayed either in the SAP List Viewer or on the Web. I recommend you *not* use the InfoSet Query for reporting using InfoCubes. The InfoSet Query does *not* support the following functions: navigation, hierarchies, delivery of BI content, currency translation, variables, exception reporting, and interactive graphics on the Web.

Aggregation Levels

Aggregation levels are used as InfoProviders for planning: with an aggregation level, you model levels whose data can be changed manually using input-ready queries or automatically using planning functions. An aggregation level is set using a set of characteristics and key figures from the underlying InfoProvider. The key figures included in the aggregation level are aggregated using the characteristics that are not included in the aggregation level. In the simplest case, an aggregation level is located on a Real-Time-enabled InfoCube. In Figure 2-28, you can see the results of creating the aggregation level from the InfoCube. Aggregation levels can also be created on MultiProviders. You can create multiple aggregation levels for an InfoProvider using the Planning Modeler or the Planning Wizard for this process.

In the Modeling functional area of the Data Warehousing Workbench, the system also displays the aggregation levels and the underlying InfoProviders in the InfoProvider overview. When you double-click the aggregation level, you can branch to the Planning Modeler and edit the selected aggregation level. Figure 2-29 shows the web-based view of the Planning Modeler and the creation of the aggregation level based on the Real-Time InfoCube. In the Planning Modeler or Planning Wizard, we have selected (and if necessary edited) an InfoProvider to act as the basis of the aggregation level. This InfoProvider includes at least one Real-Time-enabled InfoCube. A simple aggregation level consists of a Real-Time-enabled InfoCube. A complex aggregation level consists of a MultiProvider that includes at least one

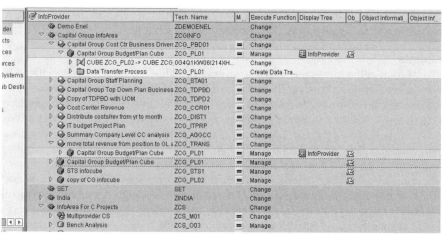

FIGURE 2-28   Aggregation level assigned to the InfoCube being configured

Real-Time-enabled InfoCube, but no simple aggregation level. With a complex aggregation level, note how data records from the InfoProviders included in the MultiProviders are embedded in the MultiProviders (and thus also the aggregation levels) and how the system writes changes to data records of the aggregation level back to the InfoProviders included in

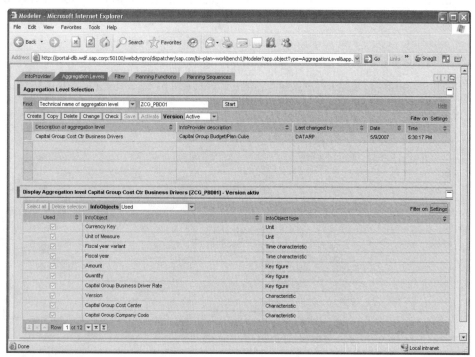

FIGURE 2-29   Aggregation level in the Planning Modeler

the MultiProviders. Additional information on aggregation levels and the uses and processes in the integrated planning process will be discussed in Chapter 18.

InfoObjects

We'll now look at the InfoObject and the definition within the InfoObject specific to the query definition. As mentioned during the discuss of the InfoObject as an InfoProvider, the components that are specific to the InfoObject being an InfoProvider are different from those used to define what format the data/values will have and display in the queries. We will discuss each field that appears in the tabs on the InfoObject that impacts the query design and format. On each of the tabs within the InfoObject are specific indicators that impact the query—some more than others. Therefore, we will start from the initial screen and work our way back.

Figure 2-30 shows the General tab. On this screen, the field "Characteristic is document attrib," is of interest. All objects within BI are available to assign documents to during the configuration process; if defined, they can assign documents during the query process. This indicator allows you to assign documents not to just the characteristic or characteristic value, but to a combination of characteristics and key figures. Therefore, if you are required to assign a document to a specific cell in a query (for example, you are required to explain the reason why revenue for a specific region and product is only increasing by 10%, so you need to assign a document to a specific cell in the query), you can use this indicator for all that functionality. Just remember that if you are interested in doing this, you must have this indicator turned on for all characteristics involved in the query. Otherwise, this functionality will not be available.

Figure 2-31 shows the Business Explorer tab. This tab has the most indicators involved in the query process, as discussed in the following list:

- **Display**   For characteristics with texts. In this field you select whether you want to display text in the Business Explorer and, if yes, which text. You can choose from the following display options: No Display, Key, Text, Key and Text, or Text and Key. This setting can be overwritten in queries. This will be your default setting for the display in the query.

FIGURE 2-30
General tab of the
InfoObject

Copyright by SAP AG

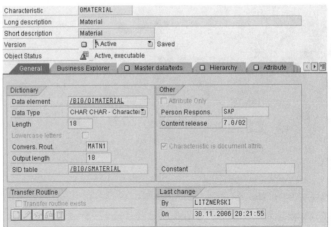

- **Text Type**   For characteristics and texts. In this field you set whether you want to display short, medium, or long text in the Business Explorer. You, of course, also need to upload that specific text type for this to work.

- **BEx description**   In this field, you determine the description that appears for this characteristic in the Business Explorer. You choose between the long and short descriptions of the characteristic. This setting can be overwritten in queries.

- **Selection**   The selection describes if and how the characteristic values are to be restricted in queries. If you choose the Unique for Every Cell option, the characteristic must be restricted to one value in each column and in each structure of all the queries. You cannot use this characteristic in aggregates. Typical examples of this kind of characteristic are Plan/Actual ID and Value Type. This is normally set to No Selection Restriction.

- **Filter Selection in Query Definition**   This field describes how the selection of filter values or the restriction of characteristics is determined when you *define* a query. Therefore, within the Query Designer, when you restrict characteristics, the values from the master data table are usually displayed. For characteristics that do not have master data tables, the values from the SID table are displayed instead. In many cases, it is more useful to only display those values that are also contained in an InfoProvider. Therefore, you can also choose the setting Only Values in InfoProvider, and this will restrict the total number of values you see during the query definition.

- **Filter Selection in Query Execution**   This field tells you how the selection of filter values is determined when a query is *executed*. When queries are executed, the selection of filter values is usually determined by the data selected by the query. This means that only the values for which data has been selected in the current navigation status are displayed. In many cases, however, it can be useful to include additional values. Therefore, you can also choose the Only Values in InfoProvider setting and the Values in Master Data Table setting. If you make this selection, however, you may get the message "No data found" when you select your filter values.

Figure 2-31
Business Explorer
tab of the
InfoObject

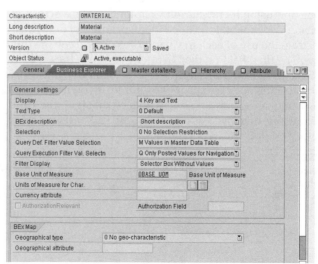

These settings for input help can also be overwritten in the query:

- **Filter Display**   This indicator is new to the BI 7.0 functionality. This allows you to define the format of the Filter Display in the Query Designer. As you can see in Figure 2-32, you have the ability to select the use of radio buttons, drop-down boxes, and so on, to enhance the look of your query. This can also be changed in the query or BEx Analyzer.

- **Base Unit of Measure**   You specify a unit InfoObject of type Unit of Measure. The unit InfoObject must be an attribute of the characteristic. This unit InfoObject is used when quantities are converted for the master data–bearing characteristic in the Business Explorer.

- **Units of Measure for Char.**   This is part of the new 7.0 BI functionality for use in the conversion of UOM during the uploading process. We will discuss this in Chapter 13.

- **Currency attribute**   You select a unit InfoObject of type Currency that you have created as an attribute for the characteristic. This way, you can define variable target currencies in the currency translation types. The system determines the target currency using the master data when you perform currency translation in the Business Explorer or loads dynamically from a predefined table for the currency translation.

- **Authorization Relevant**   You choose whether a particular characteristic is included in the authorization check when you are working with the query. Mark a characteristic as "authorization relevant" if you want to create authorizations that restrict the selection conditions for this characteristic to single characteristic values. You can only mark the characteristic as "not authorization relevant" if it is no longer being used as a field for the authorization object.

Figure 2-33 shows the Hierarchy tab. Hierarchies are used quite frequently in the process of displaying the data in a query. This allows the end user to see the integration of many layers of one characteristic or the layers of many characteristics all in one list. Therefore, if you are looking to view the integration between the characteristics Region, Division, and Customer, you can create a hierarchy to display the combinations in a query. We will be discussing and using hierarchies in Chapter 6. On this screen, you can enable the hierarchy to be version dependent, time dependent, or interval dependent. All are important, and as I demonstrate the use of each in Chapter 6, you will see the differences they offer in terms of display. The final field on the Hierarchy screen is the option to reverse the plus and minus signs for nodes. If this indicator is turned on, it allows the end user to change the signs for a specific node of data. For example, if you have uploaded the financial data as posted in a source system (revenue with a credit sign), then you can reverse the sign and have the revenue displayed as a plus (+) sign rather than a minus (−) sign.

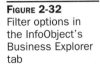

Figure 2-32
Filter options in the InfoObject's Business Explorer tab

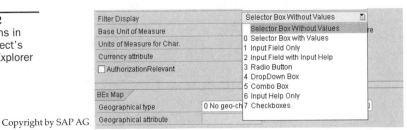

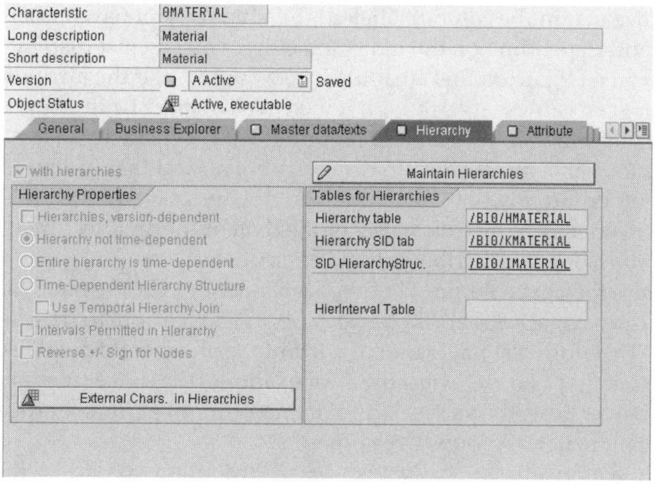

FIGURE 2-33
Hierarchy tab in
the InfoObject

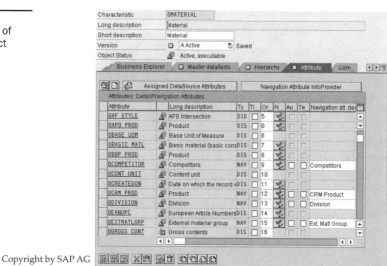

Copyright by SAP AG

If you want to create a hierarchy, or upload an existing hierarchy from a source system, you have to set the With Hierarchy indicator. The system generates a hierarchy table with hierarchical relationships for the characteristic. We will discuss additional options with the structures of hierarchies in Chapter 6.

In Figure 2-34, the Attribute tab shows the attributes available for this particular InfoObject to display. Remember from our previous discussion that we have attributes that are assigned to the InfoObject that offer additional explanation of the root InfoObject but realize that these attributes are also InfoObjects themselves. As you can see in Figure 2-34, the attributes for Material are Product, Competitor, Product, Division, and so on (there are a total of 78 attributes for Material listed on this tab). You can use all or some of these attributes for your analysis.

FIGURE 2-34
Attribute tab of
the InfoObject

Copyright by SAP AG

Notice that in the column labeled "TY (Type)," you have either DIS or NAV. This is very important. Depending on the indicator, either you can just display this attribute in the query or you can navigate on this attribute in the query. So, if the attribute is set as a navigational attribute, you can use it as though it were a characteristic in your query and then slice and dice this information the same as though it were a characteristic. Now, there are specific reasons to enable an attribute to be navigational, and that discussion could use up an entire book. Suffice it to say that, depending on a series of requirements, including the need for time dependency or historic views of the data or the architecture of the InfoCube, you may need to turn on these attributes to be navigational.

Notice the next column, TI (Time Dependency), for the navigational attributes. This allows the navigational attributes to support a From and To date against the characteristic values. Therefore, the navigational attributes can generate displays of the characteristic values that may change over time—for example, the movement of a person from position to position over time, the status of a customer order over time, or the movement of a material to different material groups over time.

The column labeled "N (Navigational Attributes On/Off)" is the indicator for switching an attribute. This process should not be taken lightly because with the switch from display to navigational come additional concerns with uploading and tables created. In Chapter 6, we will discuss navigational attributes in detail, but for now you need a better understanding of what they do and what the ramifications are for their use.

Two additional options on this screen are located above the list of attributes: Assigned DataSource Attributes and Navigation Attribute InfoProvider. Each has different responsibilities but are similar concepts. For the assigned datasource attributes, we are referring to the attributes to be used by the InfoObject for navigational attributes and properties. On the other hand, the navigation attribute InfoProvider is used for the InfoObject when it is being used as an InfoProvider. Therefore, each manages the properties of the attributes, but in different situations—one if the InfoObject is really being used as an InfoObject, and the other if the InfoObject is being used as an InfoProvider.

Finally, the column labeled "AU (Authorization Relevant)" and its ramifications were explained earlier in this section.

Summary

As you can see, we could very well develop a complete book on just this information and all of the steps in creation of an InfoProvider. There's much more information to review around when to use each and detailed discussion on the creation and configuration and finally the expected results for each InfoProvider. A full and detailed discussion of these items is beyond the scope of this book. However, this basic overview of the different InfoProviders should give you enough information to understand the process behind identifying the required objects for your implementation. As we go through the rest of the book, I will display the query creation process and results and, in most cases, will be using InfoCubes as a basis of display for these activities. I will identify some of the differences between the queries created using each of the different InfoProviders. If there are no differences, we will concentrate on the results rather than the provider of the data.

Navigating Through the
BEx Analyzer

In this chapter, we will discuss the functionality of the BEx Analyzer from the point of view of the executed query. I find that showing some of the final functionality helps get your thoughts and concepts around the BI front-end functionality while working toward specific aspects of the query process, such as how it can be presented, what approach you want to use for distribution of the query information, and how much you are looking to have the business user work with versus what the power user might be responsible for in the query-design process. After this chapter, we will begin working through the details of the query design process, starting with the functionality of the BEx Analyzer. Then we'll move into the web functionality of the BI front end. We will only cover the BEx Analyzer portion of the front end in this chapter and therefore work exclusively with the functionality you will see in the BEx Analyzer. We will work with the Web Query and Web Application Designer functionality in Chapters 15 and 16.

In the process of walking through the different aspects of the BEx Analyzer front-end functionality, you will see certain activities show up in multiple places, which means you can control certain activities either at the query execution level or at the query configuration level. We will discuss all functionality, but don't get confused as you work through this chapter and the ones that follow: I am just making sure you are aware of all the different points where you can effect the display or outcome of a query view. Many areas we will not be able to cover directly in this book will have an effect on the query process, such as authorizations, the new 7.0 BI analysis authorization process, and the many ways of impacting query performance tuning. These topics alone could fill another book with information. Therefore, as we go along, you will see that we mix up the different types of data we are using for demonstration purposes and therefore will not be concerned with SOX (Sarbanes-Oxley) compliance or other areas of compliance. We will also look to use a basic naming convention as we work our way through the process of saving the queries or workbooks, but we have not yet identified a specific naming or numbering convention and therefore may stray from the SAP best business practices of the identifier X, Y, Z options. In all, we will have our hands full just trying to identify, reference, and demonstrate all the functionality for just the BEx Analyzer, the Web Application Designer, and other integrated tools for reporting purposes.

Introduction to the BEx Analyzer

Let's start by defining the BEx Analyzer. The BEx Analyzer (Business Explorer Analyzer) is one of the front ends to the SAP BI system. It provides flexible reporting and analytical tools for the analysis of reports, consistent information to develop dashboard reporting, and it supports much of the decision-making activities within a business. The Business Explorer Analyzer offers querying, reporting, and analysis functions, and with version 7.0 of the BI system, it is fully integrated into the planning process. With the structure of the NetWeaver 2004S architecture, two versions of the BEx Analyzer are offered, as well as other tools such as the Query Designer, Web Application Designer, and Broadcaster. We will be concentrating on and using all the 7.0 BI functionality and not really getting involved with the 3.x functionality because that information has been around for quite a while. In Figure 3-1, you can see that from the Start | All Programs | Business Explorer menu, you have two options—you can either use the 7.0 version of the BEx Tools or the 3.x version of the BEx Tools. BI 7.0 supports both versions. Therefore, if your version of Windows does not support the 7.0 functionality, you can use the 3.x version of the tool set.

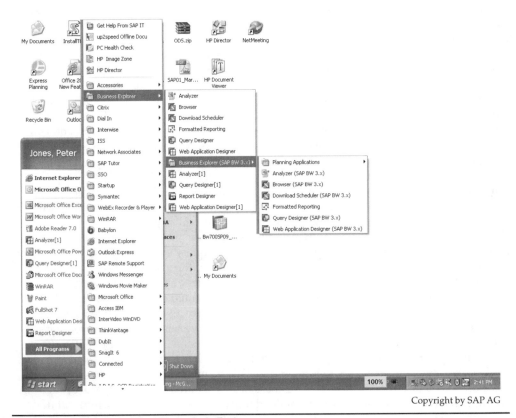

Copyright by SAP AG

FIGURE 3-1 Initial view of the BEx Analysis Tools

In the following illustration, you see all of the different tools we will be discussing in detail in this book.

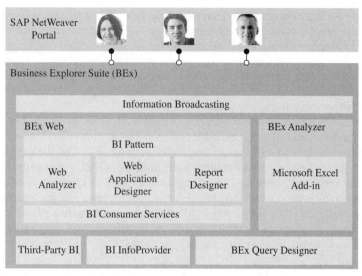

As we discussed previously, the initial location of data used for querying is in the InfoProviders. You analyze the dataset of the BI system by defining queries for InfoProviders in the Query Designer. By selecting and combining InfoObjects (characteristics and key figures) or reusable structures in a query, you determine the way in which you navigate through and evaluate the data in the selected InfoProvider. Analyzing data on the basis of a relational database (OLAP reporting) makes it possible to analyze several dimensions at the same time (for example, time, customer, and product).

You have the option of implementing any number of variance analyses (for example, plan-actual comparison or customer-region-division by period comparison). The data, displayed in the form of a table, serves as the starting point for a detailed analysis for answering a variety of questions. A large number of options, such as sorting, filtering, ascending and descending characteristics, and local calculations, allow for flexible navigation through data at runtime. You can also display data in graphics (for example, bar charts or pie charts). In addition, you can evaluate geographical data (for example, characteristics such as customer, sales region, and country) on a map. You can also use Exception Reporting to determine deviation and critical objects, another option would be to broadcast messages on deviating values by e-mail, or distribute these results to the universal worklist in the portal. You can perform a detailed analysis of BI information both on the Web and in Microsoft Excel. This is why I suggest that while you are identifying the different reports and queries you will be using, you should start to understand the functionality available to you and see where it can help simplify some of your design issues. As we go through each of the possible options for query navigation, you will see many different ways to adjust the display of data. We can't possibly display and demo all the options, so we will simply discuss them all and display only the results of some of the more interesting ones.

Other options available include the Web Application Designer, which allows you to use the generic OLAP navigation in web applications, as well as Business Intelligence Cockpits for simple or highly individual scenarios. You can use standard XML to implement highly individual scenarios with user-defined interface elements. Web application design comprises a broad spectrum of interactive web-based business intelligence scenarios that you can adjust to meet your requirements using standard web technologies. The Web Application Designer is the desktop application used to create web applications and to generate HTML pages that contain BI-specific content (such as tables, charts, or maps). Web applications are based on web templates you create and edit in the Web Application Designer. You can save the web templates and access them from a web browser or the portal.

The BEx Web Analyzer provides you with a stand-alone, convenient web application for data analysis that you can call using a URL or as an iView in the portal. You can also distribute and save the results of your ad-hoc analysis as needed. The Report Designer is an easy-to-use design tool you can use to create formatted reports that are optimized for presentation and printing. Extensive formatting and layout functions are available in the Report Designer, which you can use to create standard formatted reports for any internal or external business stakeholder. The connected PDF generation function allows you to print web applications and reports in various formats. BI Patterns are web applications tailored to the requirements of particular user groups and are used for the unification of the display of BI content. You can design the interface for your queries by inserting design items such as drop-down boxes, radio button groups, and pushbuttons into your Excel workbook. In this way, a workbook becomes a complete query application. Information Broadcasting allows you to make objects with Business Intelligence content available to a wide spectrum of users, according to your requirements. With the Broadcaster, you can precalculate web templates, queries, query views, reports, and workbooks, and publish them in the portal, distribute them by e-mail, or print them. In addition to precalculated documents that contain historical data, you can generate online links to queries and web applications.

The Business Explorer portal role illustrates the various options available to you when working with content from BI in the portal. Finally, in this overview of a reporting strategy, you can integrate business BI content seamlessly into the portal. Integration is carried out using the Broadcaster, KM content, SAP Role Upload, or the Portal Content Studio. The objects you create and their display types in the portal depend on the type of integration. The portal enables you to access applications from other systems and sources, such as the Internet or an intranet. Using one entry point, you can reach both structured and unstructured information. In addition to content from Knowledge Management, business data for data analysis is available to you from the Internet/intranet.

Access to the BEx Analyzer

You can access the BEx Analyzer via the Start button on your computer. (As mentioned earlier, you can access either version of the BEx Analyzer tools.) Once you access the 7.0 BI BEx Analyzer, choose Open | Open Query on the BEx Analyzer toolbar. You are now required to log on to the appropriate server. Figure 3-2 shows the initial logon screen you will be presented with for access to the BI server.

After accessing the server by logging on with your username/password combination, you will be presented with the Open dialog box. The following illustration shows a view of this dialog box. As you can see, a series of buttons appear down the left side and allow access to different lists of (in this case) queries. We will discuss each option and its

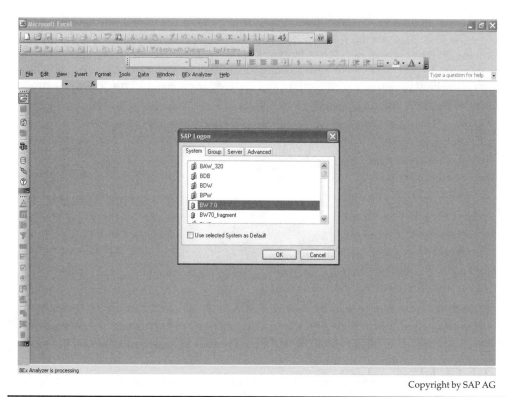

Copyright by SAP AG

FIGURE 3-2 Access to the server via the BEx Analyzer

responsibilities. Generally speaking, the dialog box will default to the History folder, but we will discuss this option last because it requires some configuration behind the scenes to work properly.

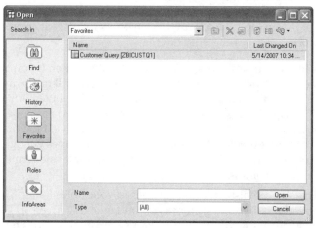

Copyright by SAP AG

First in the list we have the Find folder. The Find folder is not necessarily new, but we do have some additional options for performing a Find operation on queries of interest. In the following illustration, you can see the Find functionality. There are numerous approaches to using the Find option. They help with locating all the queries that may be of use to you. In the past, the Find option was a bit limiting and therefore a bit less user friendly in the process of searching for the queries of interest.

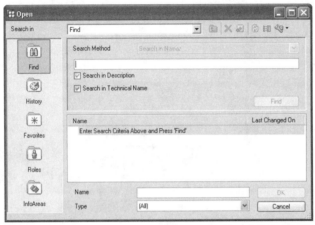

Copyright by SAP AG

To the right of the Find function you will see a series of icons. These icons look like they are grayed out, but some are actually active. Table 3-1 describes the function of each icon.

You can search by description and/or technical name using the appropriate check box in the dialog box. You can also search in the lower portion of the dialog box. Simply fill in the search term in the Name field and filter the search by using the Type option (either All, InfoProvider, Query, or Query View) and then choose OK to start the search. As a word of caution, if the search is too wide ranging, it may go on for quite a while. Therefore, you should narrow down the search to be as detailed as possible.

Below the Find option you have four different folders that offer the ability to view and store the definition of the queries that are used. Each offers a different approach but all are very useful in the process of accessing your queries.

- **Favorites folder**   You save a query to your Favorites folder. If you do this, the query will be located only in your Favorites folder and will not be available to anyone else. Depending on the approach you use to distribute your queries, this is a reasonable decision. Unless the query you have developed has gone through the process of review and approval, you will probably not save it to your Role folder for others to access and execute. Thus, the Favorites folder gives you additional time to analyze your query and confirm that it is, in fact, accurate and strategically positioned for the business users.

- **Roles folder**   You can also save your queries to your Roles folder. The reason for doing so depends on the strategy for saving and allowing access to your queries. For example, if you are going to have one role for saving your queries for a short time, so that you can do an initial analysis of the validation of the query for consistency,

Icon Object	Description of Functionality
One Level Up	This icon allows you to navigate through the different levels of the objects faster and easier. Use this icon to move up levels.
Delete	This icon allows you to delete an object in specific cases. It allows you to delete from your Favorites and History folders, but not from the InfoAreas or Roles (unless you allow this via authorizations).
Add to Favorites	This icon allows you to add a specific query or other objects to your Favorites folder. A pop-up box appears when you use this icon, and you can decide where to add the object.
Refresh	This icon allows you to refresh the view of your queries. Thus, any changes made in another session will appear here after the Refresh operation.
Display Properties	This icon allows you to view the details of an object. The properties include Type, Description, Technical Name (if the object is a query or workbook, you will see Name of the InfoProvider), Created By, Last Changed By, Last Changed At, and Released for OLE DB for OLAP Indicator.
Display Object Name As	You can switch the display of the information from Description, to [Technical Name] Description, to Description [Technical Name], to [Technical Name].

TABLE 3-1   Options in the Open Dialog Box

performance, and other concerns, then move the query to a standard role for all users who have access to that role to use. Another reason someone can save to the Role folder is that this person is a Power User and is authorized to save to the Role folder queries they have created and confirmed based on requirements documented by the business users. This allows direct access to the queries that have been identified for analysis. Therefore, from a query access point of view, the Role folder could be a list of all available queries for the user based on their responsibilities.

- **InfoAreas folder**   The InfoAreas folder is the access point for all the queries available to you for review and execution based on the InfoProvider to which they are attached. Therefore, if you are searching for a specific query and you know the InfoProvider to which it is attached, this is another avenue for you to research and/or execute the query. In many cases, the InfoAreas folder may not be available to business users to see either in the configuration or display process, because they will probably not be doing any configuration against the InfoProviders. On the other hand, the folder will be available for power users because they will probably be handling most of the configuration via the InfoProviders.

- **History folder**   The History folder offers the most direct and easy access to queries, InfoProviders, and workbooks you have been reviewing or using in the recent past. This list of objects is collected based on your activities in the Open dialog box over a period of time. To be able to use this functionality, you must do some initial setup. You need to activate the option for the BEx History to collect the information on the

queries and other objects you have used. To do this, you have to access the
Implementation Guide (IMG) in BI – *transaction code* – SPRO. Use this transaction
code in the command field of your BI system, and you will be able to access the
Reference IMG button (once you access the IMG). Figure 3-3 shows the structure
path to use to activate the History folder. Use the following path:

SAP Customized Implementation Guide | SAP NetWeaver | Business Intelligence |
Settings for Reporting and Analysis | General Settings for Reporting and Analysis |
Activate Personalization in BEx

This directs you to the screen you see in Figure 3-4. In this screen, you will see three
options, but we will only talk about the first—Activate BEx History. As you can see, this box
is *not* checked. Note that when the box is *not* checked, the functionality is *active*. If the box *is*
checked, the functionality is *inactive*. Because this approach is backward in logic, you need
to be aware of it.

Once you decide whether you will activate this option, you need to direct your attention
to a bit of standard business content that will need to be activated. This is the DataStore
object, which collects the information surrounding activity within the BEx Open dialog box.
The technical name is 0PERS_BOD—Personalization Data for the BEx Open Dialog, and
this DataStore object collects and stores all objects, including queries, workbooks, and
InfoProviders you have worked with and reviewed in the past. It allows you direct access

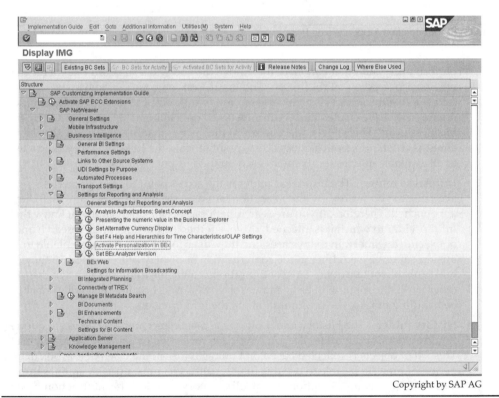

Copyright by SAP AG

FIGURE 3-3   Path in the IMG to activate the History folder in the Open dialog box

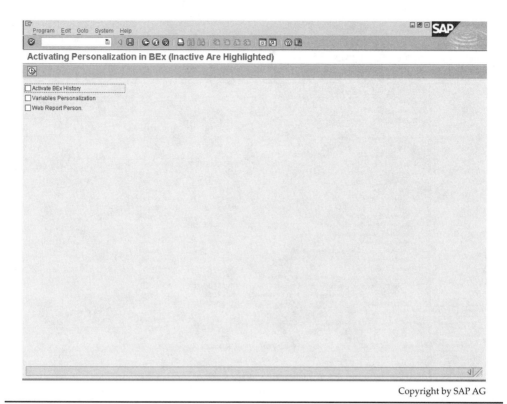

FIGURE 3-4   Activation of BEx History

to the objects you have worked on in the past. Figure 3-5 shows the activated DataStore in our BI system. You can see that we have been working with one query, if you access the Open Dialog Box and either default to the History folder or access it by clicking on the History Folder button, the Customer query is the only query that is listed. In the following illustration, you can see that the details of two elements (one query and one workbook) have been stored in the DataStore object, and we are able to navigate to the table contents and see one entry based on User—BWUSER01. This information is automatically updated in this DataStore object every time the user accesses the Open dialog box and executes any functionality against any objects.

Data Browser: Table /BI0/APERS_BOD00 Select Entries   2

Table: /BI0/APERS_BOD00
Displayed Fields: 8 of   8 Fixed Columns: 6 List Width 0250

User	Object Version	BW System	Actions with Query	Object Metadata	Object Type Metadata	Record Mode	UTC Tim
BWUSER01	A	FB4CLNT800	1	D0WK3IWI5UUIQ617D32MSE3SN	ELEM		2007051
BWUSER01	A	FB4CLNT800	1	EXP_O60WZ1DL5RKYON6X23ZBF5179	VW3X		2007051

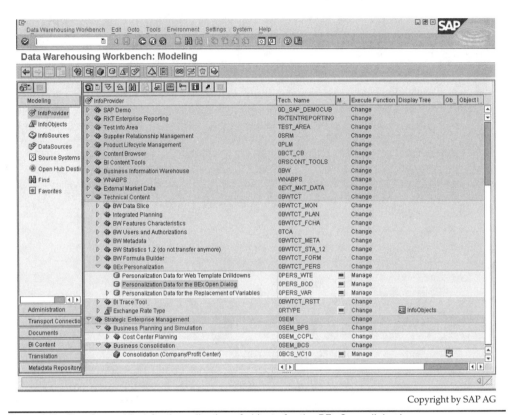

FIGURE 3-5 DataStore object for the collection of objects for the BEx Open dialog box

Now that we have reviewed the options of the Open dialog box, we can review the options on the Analysis Mode toolbar. As the following illustration shows, the BEx Analyzer toolbar (Analysis Mode) has several icons assigned. We will discuss the functionality of each:

- **Open**   You can open workbooks or queries in BEx Analyzer. The Open tool has two submenus, and two Open items appear on the BEx Analyzer menu.

  To open a query, choose Open | Query from the Analysis toolbar, or select BEx Analyzer | Open Query from the menu bar. When you open a query, it is embedded into the workbook you have currently defined as the default. The query is automatically executed and the current state of the result is returned from the server. Typically, a power user will open a query and work in design mode to customize it, and then save the query to a workbook that the business user can use for analysis.

  To open a workbook, choose Open | Workbook from the Analysis toolbar, or select BEx Analyzer | Open Workbook from the menu bar. A workbook delivers the interface for your query. This is the typical interface a business user would use to access queries.

  In addition to the Open function for queries and workbooks, you can also access Local History from the Open function's submenu. The number of workbooks or queries displayed in Local History is determined by the Maximum Number of Objects in Local History setting in the Global Settings dialog box.

- **Save**   You can save workbooks or views in BEx Analyzer, either under existing names or with new names. The Save tool has three submenus, and three Save items appear on the BEx Analyzer menu.

  To save a workbook, choose Save | Save Workbook As from the Analysis toolbar, or select BEx Analyzer | Save Workbook As from the menu bar. After you have opened a workbook or embedded a query into a new workbook, you can navigate the query and generate different views of the data. If you want an end user to be able to save the state of the query after analyzing and navigating it, uncheck Reference the View in each data provider. Otherwise, the workbook will open with the original state of the query or query view. In this way, the power user who creates and configures the workbook determines the extent to which the end user can interact with and navigate the query.

  To save a workbook with a new name, choose Save | Save Workbook As from the Analysis toolbar, or select BEx Analyzer | Save Workbook As from the menu bar.

  To save the current navigation state (view) of the data provider assigned to the design item in the currently active cell, choose Save | Save View.

  In any case, after the Save operation, you will be required to enter a text name for the workbook.

NOTE   *To save a workbook to your local file system, choose File | Save or choose File | Save As from the menu bar in Microsoft Excel.*

- **Refresh/Pause Automatic Refresh**   You control the refresh status (to enable or disable the request of current valid data from the server) with the Refresh function, which is a toggle function.

  To enable refreshing, requesting the current valid data from the server, choose Refresh from the Analysis toolbar, or select BEx Analyzer | Refresh from the menu bar.

  If you have already activated the Refresh function and you wish to pause automatic refreshing of current valid data, choose Pause Automatic Refresh from the Analysis toolbar, or select BEx Analyzer | Pause Automatic Refresh from the menu bar. This allows you to navigate the query without having to wait for it to update with the current data. The Pause Automatic Refresh state is recommended for performance reasons—for example, if you intend to make several changes to the query properties and several navigational steps in succession without displaying the corresponding data immediately. After opening a query or a workbook, you should ensure that the Refresh function is active in order to be able to continue navigating with the current state of the data. A query can only be refreshed if a connection exists between BEx Analyzer and the BI system. When a query is refreshed, the data, format, rows, and column widths of the analysis grid (in which the results display) automatically adjust to the updated query data. You can adjust this display using the properties for the analysis grid.

NOTE   *When you activate a Refresh operation, variables are not automatically processed by default (in other words, you don't get the chance to change variable values). You can change this behavior so that you are always prompted to enter new variable values when you activate Refresh by selecting Process Variables on Refresh in the properties for the workbook.*

- **Change Variable Values**   You can change the variable values associated with the queries in your workbooks. When you initially refresh your workbook, all queries embedded in it are processed. Use this function to change values for all variables associated with queries in your workbook. All variables saved in any of the queries must at that time be replaced by concrete values, which are then saved in a session on the server. Changing the value of a variable involves recreating this state and might be time-consuming. Therefore, variables are not automatically processed when you navigate a query, and you can specifically evoke this function to change them.

  Choose Change Variable Values from the Analysis toolbar, or select BEx Analyzer | Change Variable Values from the menu bar. When the Select Values for Variables dialog box appears, select a value to assign to the variable.

- **Tools**   You can launch other tools from within BEx Analyzer via the Tools function and its submenu.

  To launch BEx Query Designer and create a new query, choose Tools | Query Designer from the Analysis toolbar, or select BEx Analyzer | Tools | Query Designer from the menu bar.

  To precalculate and distribute workbooks with the BEx Broadcaster, choose Tools | Broadcaster from the Analysis toolbar, or select BEx Analyzer | Tools | Broadcaster from the menu bar.

  To launch the Planning Modeler and create objects for planning, choose Tools | Planning Modeler from the menu bar.

  To launch the BEx Report Designer and create formatted reports for the queries, choose Tools | BEx Report Designer from the menu bar.

  To launch the BEx Web Analyzer and create web objects for reporting, choose Tools | BEx Web Analyzer from the menu bar.

- **Global Settings**   You can configure global settings, which are defaults valid for the whole application rather than for individual workbooks. You can configure global settings in four different areas using this option—the trace file, behavior, statistics, and default workbook. Behavior is the first tab, and the options available under this tab are

  - **Maximum Number of Objects in Local History**   Use this drop-down box to configure the maximum number of objects that should display in your local history. Local History is a submenu that appears on the Open tool on the Analysis toolbar, and it lists the workbooks and queries you have opened, providing easy access to these workbooks and queries. The submenu will not display more than the number of queries or workbooks you configure with this setting. If you have not opened this many items, the submenu will only display as many as you have opened. To turn off the display of the Local History submenu, set this value to zero.

  - **Display System Name in Local History**   The Open function on the Analysis toolbar displays the workbooks or queries (shortcuts) you have opened earlier in the same session. If you want to open one again, you need not browse to locate the workbook or query. However, if you want to open a workbook or query from a specific system, you do not know whether the available shortcut refers to the system you want. This feature allows the system to display system names alongside the workbook or query shortcuts. This allows you to check whether the workbook or query you want to access refers to the system that you want.

- **Log On with Attached SAP GUI**   When this function is checked, you will receive messages (such as transport messages) from the server. In some situations this is necessary—for example, if you save a workbook while you have the standard transport system activated. Typically, you will want to leave this function unchecked for performance reasons.

- **Launch Legacy Version from Easy Access Menu**   This feature determines which version of the BEx Analyzer should be launched from the RRMX transaction of the SAP BW system. If you select this option, the SAP BW 3.x release of the BEx Analyzer is launched when you use the RRMX transaction in the SAP BW system. If you do not select this option, the SAP BW 7.0 release of the BEx Analyzer is launched.

- **Launch Analyzer when Excel Starts**   If this option is selected, BEx Analyzer starts as soon you open Microsoft Excel. If this option is not selected, you must start BEx Analyzer manually.

- **Cancel Pop-up Delay**   Set this to the amount of time you are interested in viewing any pop-ups on your screen. Set this option to a longer time to review comments.

Select Default Workbook is the second tab, and its options are just a few:

- **Current Default Workbook**   To execute this option, you must be viewing a workbook and therefore be able to effect that workbook. Thus, you can set the current workbook as Current Default Workbook or you can select the Use Default option for the workbook that has been system assigned to you as the default. Finally, there's the option Use SAP Standard Workbook as the Default Workbook. One of the uses of this function is to identify a default workbook for all your queries and thus control the format, style, and functionality of the queries so that they're all saved with the same look and feel.

Trace is the third tab on this dialog box, and the options on this tab allow you to manage some of the processing of queries. The trace file is a text file that contains a log of BEx Analyzer's activities. It is stored in your system's temporary folder. You can view and set several trace file properties. The Trace File Name field displays the path to and name of the trace file (e.g.,BWUSER01Trace.txt). Select the Record Trace check box to record trace information to this file. You can delete the contents of the trace file by switching Record Trace off and back on again. Save the contents of your trace file before you turn off Record Trace. Choose the Display Trace button to display the file using your system's default text editor. The trace display is not constantly updated, meaning you must repeat the Display Trace command whenever you want to see the most recent entries.

Statistics is the final tab. It allows you to record statistical data (for example, the time taken to execute a query). You can use this data to analyze performance issues, or to get technical support if needed. Select the Collect Statistic Information check box to enable this setting. The system then records the statistical information. When you choose the Display Statistic Information button, the system displays the statistical information in a separate workbook.

Choose Global Settings from the Analysis toolbar, or select BEx Analyzer | Global Settings from the menu to access this setting.

- **Context Menu for Selected Cell (menu only from the BEx Analyzer drop-down)**   You can access the context menu—to perform OLAP functionality, access item properties, or delete items—via the menu bar if you don't have access to a secondary mouse click. The context menu provides access to OLAP functionality (if available for the selected cell) in analysis mode, and allows you to delete an item and access its properties in design mode. If you cannot access the context menu with the right mouse button (secondary mouse button), you can access it with the following menu function: BEx Analyzer | Context Menu for Selected Cell.

- **Design Toolbar (menu only from the BEx Analyzer drop-down)**   The same functions that appear on the Design toolbar are available via the BEx Analyzer menu bar. This offers another option to access the icons and functionality for the Design toolbar that show up as a separate toolbar on the screen. We will be going through all these functions in Chapter 8 and therefore will not expand on them at this time.

  From the menu bar, choose BEx Analyzer | Design Toolbar, and then select the submenu item that corresponds to the tool you want.

- **Connect/System Information**   You can connect to a system, display system information, and disconnect from the system with the Connect function (available on each of the tab displays), which is a toggle function.

  Here's the information displayed in this pop-up:

  - **User**   Client Number, User Name, Language, and Application Server
  - **System**   System Name, System ID, Host, SAP Release
  - **Database**   Database, DB Host, Database System
  - **Hardware**   Machine, Operating System, IP Address, Time Zone, Datastamp
  - **RFC**   Protocol, Character Type, Integer Type, Floating Type

    To connect to a system, choose Connect from the Analysis toolbar, or select BEx Analyzer | Connect from the menu bar.

If you are already connected and wish to view system information (which also allows you to disconnect from a system), choose System Information from the Analysis toolbar, or select BEx Analyzer | System Information from the menu bar.

- **About (menu only from the BEx Analyzer drop-down)**   You can display BEx Analyzer's splash screen. From the menu bar, choose BEx Analyzer | About.

- **Application Help**   You can launch the SAP Library documentation for BEx Analyzer. This allows you to access SAP help for use with the functionality of the BEx Analyzer. From the menu bar, choose BEx Analyzer | Help.

Navigation Options

When you navigate a query in analysis mode, you interactively work with the query to generate different views of its data. This allows you to perform OLAP analysis, which helps you to evaluate query results from different points of view. After you open a query or insert a query into a workbook, the distribution of dimensions (including characteristics and key figures or structures) into the rows and columns from the query definition is displayed in the first view of the analysis grid. With the help of navigation functions such as drilling, filtering, and hierarchy expansion, you can change the query and thereby generate additional views of the InfoProvider data. Most of the design items provide navigation functions. The two key design items in which you can navigate in analysis mode are the Analysis Grid and the Navigation pane. You can navigate using the context menu, drag and drop, or icons. The initial screen you see once you access the query might look similar to Figure 3-6. Of course, depending on the key figures and characteristics you use in the initial screen of the query, you will have more or less information showing. However, we can start with this view and move deeper into the functionality as we go. Again, after we have completed the adjustments, made changes to the styles, and performed other formatting on this query, it will only resemble the original query based on the data.

Toolbar Functionality

On the initial screen of the query, three standard buttons appear: Chart, Filter, and Information. The addition of Sold-To Party as the initial column was done to have some sort of identifiable object in the initial set of rows.

The Information button offers you additional information for the parameters of the query. The information available is customizable, but initially you will see the list of information shown in Table 3-2. Most of the items in this table are self-explanatory, but items such as Last Refreshed need some further explanation.

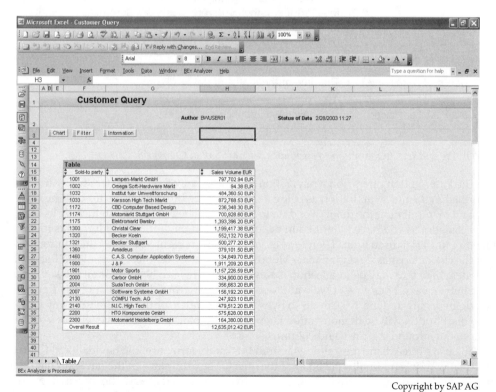

Copyright by SAP AG

FIGURE 3-6 Initial view of a query in the BEx Analyzer

Information Button Item	Description and Relevance
Author	The person who created the query.
Current User	The person who is currently running the query.
Last Changed By	If the query was changed by a specific person, you can find out here. Therefore, you need to have a historical trace of the changes to a query.
InfoProvider	The InfoProvider supporting the query information.
Query Technical Name	The technical name of the query.
Query Description	A description of the query.
Last Refreshed	When the query data was last refreshed. This is the point at which you display the text elements, because refreshing the query is necessary for displaying the text elements.
Key Date	The key date is the date for which time-dependent master data is selected that will be used to sort the transactional data.
Changed At	The last time and date this query's format was changed. (That is, adjustments to the format, key figures, and characteristics.)
Status of Data	The point in time when data for the latest request that can be used for reporting was posted to the InfoProvider. For MultiProviders, the current requests are determined from the individual basic cubes, and from these the basic cube with the oldest data validity date is called.
Relevance of Data (Date)	The date of the status of data.
Relevance of Data (Time)	The time of the status of data.

TABLE 3-2   Toolbar Functionality of the Information Option

NOTE *We will review the option to customize this text box in Chapter 8.*

The Filter button offers you a navigation box for all the other characteristics you identified in the query definition as being available to the business users for drilling down into and manipulating the display of data in the query. The Filter box can include as many characteristics as you have identified in the query definition, but we will limit this to only a few for our initial discussion. Therefore, as you can see in Figure 3-7, the Filter button gives you the characteristics Calendar Year/Month, Division, Key Figures, and Sold-to Party. The only item here that may be in question is Key Figures. This is a header for all the key figures used in the query. Therefore, if we want to swap the axes from characteristic/key figure to key figure/characteristic, we can do so by using this header for the grouping of key figures. The Chart button will be demonstrated later in this chapter. Therefore, we will look at the information around the rows and columns.

There are three distinct groupings within this query structure: the navigational filter, the information box, and finally the body of the query. The groupings of the navigational filter and the body of the query are the most interactive in a normal query. The information box

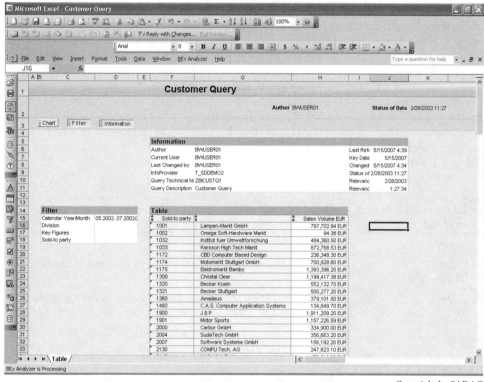

Copyright by SAP AG

FIGURE 3-7   The display of a query with the Filter and Information buttons executed

in the context menu has the options Back, Back to Start, and Query Properties, as detailed in Table 3-3.

NOTE *Context menus are accessed by right-clicking the mouse.*

Information Box Option	Description of Functionality
Back	Moves you back one step
Back to Start	Moves you back to the initial screen, based on the initial execution of the query
Query Properties	Query properties are the same for the rows, columns, navigational filter, and information box. Therefore, we will break down this functionality later in the chapter.

TABLE 3-3   Options in the Information Box of the BEx Analyzer

Navigational Filter Functionality

In the navigational filter are a number of functions available from the context menu. Some of these functions are similar to the ones you will find in the context menus of the body of the query. I will try not to duplicate some of this functionality because it has the same purpose whether you access it via the navigational filter or via the query itself.

In the navigational filter, you can use the functionality of double-clicking with the primary mouse button to either add (drill down) a characteristic to your query or remove it from the query. Thus, if the characteristic is already in the query and you double-click it, you will remove it from the query. You can also double-click an empty cell to select a filter value for a key figure or a free characteristic. The options in the navigational filter are listed in Table 3-4, along with their description and functionality.

Navigational Filter Options from the Context Menu	Description and Functionality
Back	Undoes the last navigational step.
Back to Start	Restores the query to the initial view of the data at the time of execution.
Select Filter Value	A dialog box is displayed that allows you to identify a single value, range of values, or other combination to show specific information.
Remove Filter Value	Removes the filter value and shows all values in the query.
Drill—Characteristic/Key Figure – Down or Across	Drills down on the characteristics or key figures of that specific item. If a filter was identified initially, the drilldown will only use the remaining values.
Sort Characteristic – Sort Ascending by Text; Sort Ascending by Key; Sort Descending by Text; Sort Descending by Key	Sorts the characteristic or key figure by either the key or text in either ascending or descending order.
Add Local Formula (Key Figures Only)	This function allows the business user to create a local formula directly in the executed query. A dialog box appears that has a limited list of functions that can be used for doing basic calculations with the key figures used in the query.
Properties (Characteristics Only)	This list of attributes is discussed in Table 3-5.
Query Properties (Both Key Figures and Characteristics)	This list of attributes is discussed in Table 3-5.
Drill Key Figure/Characteristic Across Sheets	This function allows the business user to drill across the query with the characteristics or key figures available in the query and create worksheets for each of the characteristics. The following illustration shows the results of this function used in the query against Division.

TABLE 3-4   Navigational Options Within the BEx Analyzer

NOTE *As an additional option, you can change the naming convention in the navigational filter by just typing in the change in the title of the characteristic. This can make the characteristics more recognizable to the business user. Remember, once you leave the query and come back, it will revert back to the original naming convention. To make sure this change is "saved," you will need to convert the query to a workbook. We will discuss this in Chapter 8.*

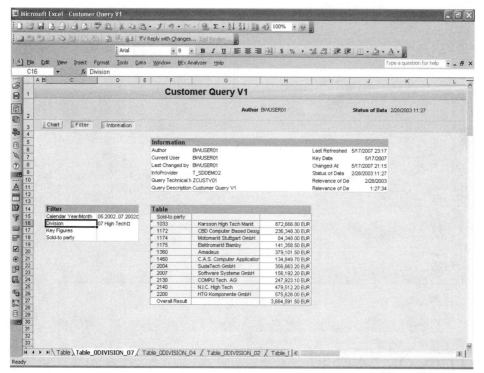

As you can see, this function creates additional worksheets for each of the divisions involved.

The following two illustrations show the context menus for the navigational filter for key figures and characteristics. These are examples of what you will see as you use the navigational filter functionality.

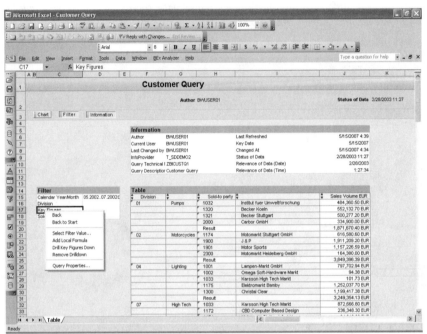

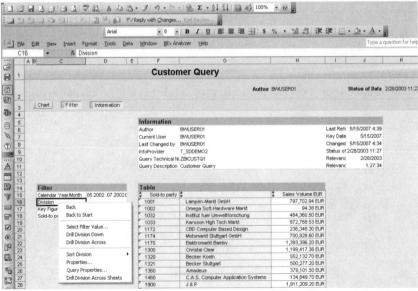

In these context menus, you can also access Properties and Query Properties to change the display and help create new views of your data. If you access the option Properties, you are accessing functionality that will affect the specific characteristic you are prompting. If you are accessing the functionality of Query Properties, you are looking to change the format and display of the entire query and/or workbook (again, remember that any changes made here will be reverted back to the original format once you leave the query, unless you save it as a workbook). We will break down both of these options now because the same functionality is used in the rows and columns of the analysis grid (body of the query).

Properties can be accessed via the context menu from the navigational panel (navigational filter) or from the analysis grid (body of the query). With your cursor on either the characteristic or the characteristic value, you can access this option. It has the same parameters from either of these areas. Listed in Table 3-5 are the fields, the options to fill those fields, and the results you would view in the query. The following illustration shows the initial screen for the Properties option. In addition to these parameters, you have an icon at the very bottom of the screen to turn on the technical names for the objects.

Copyright by SAP AG

Query Properties can be accessed via the context menu from the navigational panel (navigational filter) or from the analysis grid (body of the query). With your cursor on either the characteristic or the characteristic value, you can access this option. It has the same parameters from either of these areas. Listed in Table 3-6 are the fields, the options to fill those fields, and the results you would view in the query. The following illustration shows the initial screen for Query Properties. In addition to these parameters, you have an icon at the very bottom of the screen to turn on the technical names for the objects. This dialog box contains seven tabs: Navigation State, Data Formatting, Presentation Options, Display Options, Currency Conversion, Zero Suppression, Properties, and Conditions.

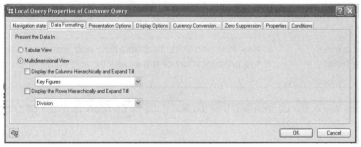

Copyright by SAP AG

Properties Field Name	Description and Functionality
General Tab	**General Information and Sorting Options**
Presentation	None, Key and Text, Key, Text and Key, and Text. This item adjusts the view of the values for this characteristic based on the option chosen. Thus, if Key and Text is chosen, the value will show Key, then Text, and so on.
Text Type	Default Text, Middle Text, Short Text, Long Text. Based on this option, the query will display the Text table information.
Sort According to	Key, Text, Selection (plus Hierarchy, if a hierarchy is being used). This functionality sorts the view by the Key, Text, or Selection option.
Characteristic Name	Characteristic or attribute of the characteristic on which you are basing your sort.
Sort Direction	Ascending or descending order for display in the query.
Suppress Result Rows	Never, Always, Conditional. Conditional is for when the item has only one line of data. If so, this will suppress the result row. For example, suppose you are querying by Division and Sold-To Party. If the number of Sold-To Party values is one, there will be no Results row created, and only the one line will appear. Never and Always are both self-explanatory.
Result Access	Default, Booked Values, Characteristic Relations, Master Data. This is a very important option. It allows you to show values that have no transactional data posted to them. If you use master data, this option accesses the master data table and shows all the values for master data, regardless of whether postings have occurred.
Attribute Tab (if the Characteristic Has Attributes)	**Available Attributes to Display**
Available Attributes	A total list of all attributes available for use as additional descriptions of the characteristic.
Selected Attributes	A list of attributes that have been chosen to display along with the characteristic. These attributes are for display purposes only. You can access either Properties or Do Not Display from the context menu of the attribute.
From the context menu from the characteristic – Text	Default, Short, Medium, and Long Text can be used.
From the context menu from the characteristic – Presentation	Key, Key and Text, Text and Key, and Text are used to adjust the presentation of the characteristic value in the query.

TABLE 3-5   Options Within the Context Menu of the Navigational Component of the BEx Analyzer

Tab of the Query Properties Dialog Box	Property Field Names	Description and Functionality
Navigation State	Columns, Rows, Free Characteristics	Use this tab to change the arrangement in the analysis grid of the characteristics and key figures on the rows and columns and the free characteristics for the query. The navigational state of the query is displayed in the form of three list boxes: • **Columns** Lists the dimensions currently appearing on the columns. • **Rows** Lists the dimensions currently appearing on the rows. • **Free Characteristics** Lists the free characteristics (those dimensions that do not currently appear in the results). This is equivalent to the Local Query View found in the 3.x version.
Data Formatting	Presenting the Data in: Tabular View	In this view, the InfoObjects are displayed only in the columns. The multidimensional result is flattened to display in a table. Note that this function is only available in Query Properties, and *not* in the Query Designer.
	MultiDimensional View: Display the Columns Hierarchically and Expand Till Display the Rows Hierarchically and Expand Till	Select the Display of the Columns Hierarchically and Expand Till check box to place characteristics that spill over several columns into *one* column in a hierarchy. Specify in the drop-down box the node to which you want to expand this hierarchy. Select the Display of the Rows Hierarchically and Expand Till check box to place characteristics that spill over several rows into *one* row in a hierarchy. Specify in the drop-down box the node to which you want to expand this hierarchy.
Presentation Options	Result Position for the Rows	Right (default), Left.
	Result Position for the Columns	Bottom (default), Top.
	Display of +/− Signs	X-, -X, (X), Default.
	Display of Zeros	Here are the options available: • **Display** Zeros are displayed with actual currencies. • **Do Not Display** Cells will be empty. • **Display No Units** Zeros will be displayed without currencies. • **Display As** Zeros will be displayed in a customized format.
	Show Zeros As	If you chose Display As, you will be offered the ability to display zeros in other formats.

TABLE 3-6   Query Properties in the BEx Analyzer

Tab of the Query Properties Dialog Box	Property Field Names	Description and Functionality
Display Options	Display Scaling Factor	Displays options for the scaling factor.
	Display Document Links on Data, MetaData, Master Data	Displays document links for data (InfoProvider), metadata (MetaData – InfoObjects and so on) and master data (Master Data Values).
	Suppress Repeated Key Values	Suppresses repeated key values in the query. You will only see one entry for all values of a specific characteristic value.
	Allow Input of Plan Values	If this option is available, the query is available for planning purposes and data entry.
Currency Conversion	Show Original Currency	Shows the currency for the transaction uploaded into the InfoProvider or displayed in the source system. This will deactivate all other currency options.
	Convert to Currency and Use Currency Translation	Convert to Currency identifies the currency required in the query. Use Currency Translation uses the appropriate currency translation key to calculate the currency values. You can see an example of this functionality in the following two illustrations.
	Consider Translation from Query Definition	Use this option to convert the currency first to the currency defined in the query, then to the currency as customized in these settings.
Zero Suppression	Zero Suppression	To suppress results rows or columns that contain zeroes, thus removing them from the display in the analysis grid, select from the following options: • **None** Rows or columns with zeros are displayed. • **Active** If characteristics are in the rows and columns, every row or column that has a result of zero is not displayed. • **Active (all values = 0)** Columns or rows containing zero values in all cells are not displayed.
	Apply To	Rows and Columns, Rows, Columns.
	Apply as Well to Members of Structure Key Figures	Applies the treatment of zeros to the key figures in structures.
Properties	Author, Last Changed By, Changed On	Displays the author, the person who last changed the query, and the date/time the change occurred.
Conditions	Conditions	If there are conditions, you can sort the conditions here for display purposes.

TABLE 3-6   Query Properties in the BEx Analyzer (*continued*)

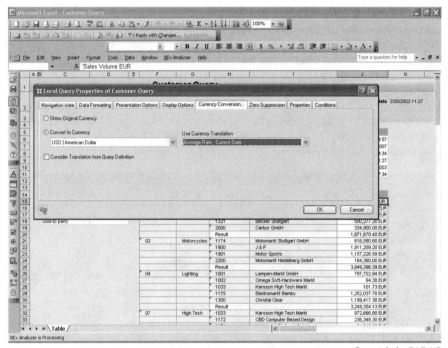

Copyright by SAP AG

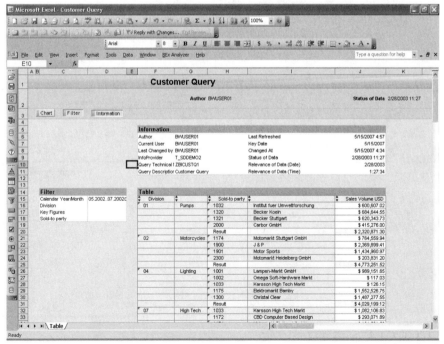

Copyright by SAP AG

Context Menu Functionality in the Columns

In the context menu of the columns you have a series of additional options offered to adjust the display of the query. In the following illustrations, you can see a basic list of activities in the context menu for both the header and the values. A number of options are redundant in the lists for rows and columns (characteristics and key figures), so to make the lists shorter, I will not repeat any duplicate options after this initial list. Instead, I'll simply highlight the differences between the two lists. The following Table 3-7 reviews all of the options available in the Context Menu of the Columns. In many cases a significant amount of functionality can be achieved by just using the components of this Context Menu in conjunction with the characteristics and key figures available in the query.

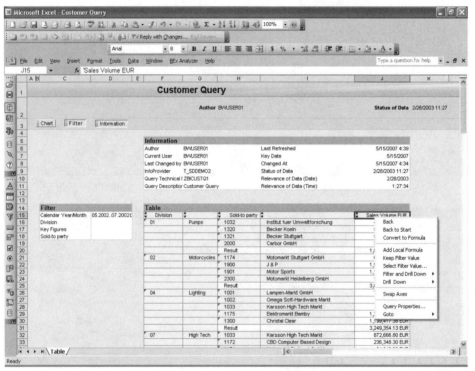

Copyright by SAP AG

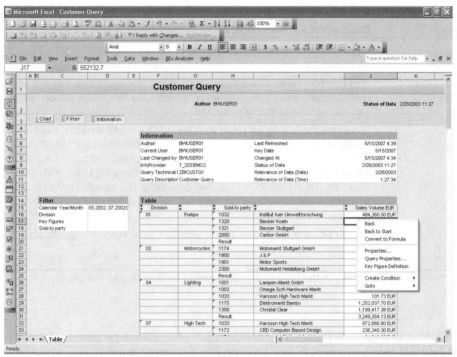

Context Menu Function in the Columns	Description and Functionality
Back	Goes back to the previous step.
Back to Start	Goes back to the start of the query.
Convert to Formula	If you have created a local formula based on the Key Figure heading (navigational panel), you can use this option to "convert to formula" the results or the single values in the Key Figure column. This can also be used for working with Excel based formulas.
Add Local Formula	This option allows you to create a local formula based on the key figures in your query. A dialog box appears for the creation of the formula.
Keep Filter Value	This option is used to keep the filter values of the key figures.
Select Filter Value	This option offers a dialog box to select specific key figure values.
Filter and Drill Down	Allows filtering and drill-down functionality based on any filter characteristics in the query.
Drill Down	Allows drill-down functionality in the query by the filtered values (characteristics in the query).
Swap Axes	Allows the switching of axes' values. Therefore, if the key figures are in the columns and the characteristics are in the rows, this function will switch their positions.

TABLE 3-7   Context Menu Functionality in the Body of the BEx Analyzer for Key Figures

Context Menu Function in the Columns	Description and Functionality
Properties	See table 3-5 with the definition of the Properties functionality.
Query Properties	See table 3-6 with the definition of the Query Properties functionality.
Key Figure Definition	This function generates a Web Query of the key figure summarized by the characteristic values associated to the specific level. This generates a web-based view of the information.
Create Condition	Based on the key figure value you use for this context menu, you can create a condition. The options to create the condition are Via Dialog, Set Threshold (you can identify a customized threshold for the value), Top 10 or 10%, Bottom 10 or 10%, Greater Than, Greater, Less, and/or Less Than. As you create these you can deactivate the specific conditions or activate the conditions, as needed, using the Toggle Condition State function.
Go To	Go To I Documents allows you to view the documents assigned to this value.

TABLE 3-7   Context Menu Functionality in the Body of the BEx Analyzer for Key Figures (*continued*)

In addition to these options, we have another dialog box for the properties of the key figures. In this dialog box, you will find additional options to alter the display of the key figures. Listed in Table 3-8 are the options in the Key Figure Properties box. Numerous options are available here. We will review only the basics and will go into more detail in Chapter 5 due to the overlap of functionality. There is also an option at the bottom of this dialog box to turn on the technical names of the information available (icon symbol of a wrench). In the following illustration, you can see a view of the Key Figure Properties box.

Copyright by SAP AG

Tabs of the Dialog Box	Property of the Key Figure	Description and Functionality
Number Format	Scaling Factor	This option allows you to display the results in a specific scaling factor (1, 10, 100, and so on).
	Decimal Places	This option allows you to display the results in a specific decimal view (0, 1, 2, 3, and so on).
	Highlighting	Select this option to display all values of the selected key figure in a different color.
(Calculation applied to displayed data only) Calculations	Calculate Results As	Here are the available options: • **Average of all values**. • **Average** Indicates not to take zeros into account. • **Count all values** Number of values in the list. • **Count all values not equal to zero** Number of values in the list not including zeros. • **First value** Initial value in the list. • **Last value** Last value in the list. • **Maximum**. • **Minimum**. • **Standard deviation** A calculation of the mean of all values, then a calculation of the average variance from that mean. • **Summation**. • **Summation of rounded values**. • **Suppress results** Results are not displayed. • **Undefined**.
	Calculate Single Values As	Here are the available options: • **Average of all values**. • **Average** Indicates not to take zeros into account. • **Count all values** Total of lines. • **Count all values not equal to zero**. • **Maximum**. • **Minimum**. • **Normalize** Shows the values as percentages of the total. • **Normalize result (exclusive filter)** This result shows up as a percentage exclusive of the filter. • **Normalize result (inclusive filter)** This result shows up as a percentage inclusive of the filter. • **Normalize subtotals** Shows subtotals as percentages. • **Ranked list** List of 1st, 2nd, 3rd, and so on (may have ties). • **Ranked List (Olympic)** List of 1st, 2nd, 3rd, and so on. Ties will be taken into account with the next value. Therefore, the ranking may look like this: 1st, 2nd, 2nd, 4th. • **Suppress results**. • **Undefined**.

TABLE 3-8   Context Menu Options for Key Figure Properties in the BEx Analyzer

Tabs of the Dialog Box	Property of the Key Figure	Description and Functionality
	Cumulated	A totaling of the results of each cell.
	Also Apply to Results	Use Default direction, calculate along the rows (from top to bottom), or calculate along the columns (from left to right).
Sorting	Leave Sorting, Descending, Ascending	Sort key figures by ascending, descending values or leave sorting alone.

TABLE 3-8 Context Menu Options for Key Figure Properties in the BEx Analyzer (*continued*)

Context Menu Functionality in the Rows

The last context menu we will review is the one associated with the rows—in this case, the characteristics Division and Sold-To Party. In Figure 3-8, you can see that we have to drill down on the division to see the query expand for additional detail. Quite a bit of redundancy exists between the context menus for the columns and rows, so Table 3-9 only details the additional areas of interest. Listed in the table are the last new options shown in the context menu for rows. The following illustrations provide examples of the two context menus.

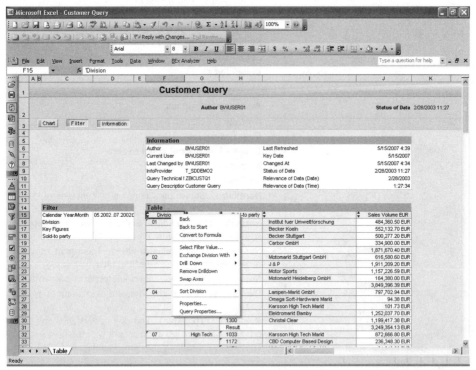

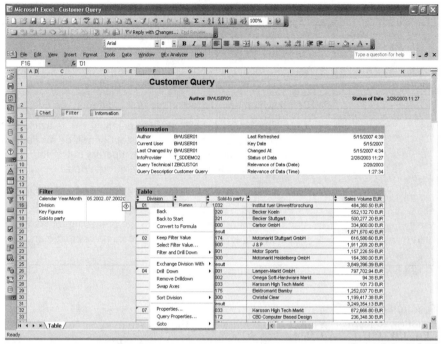

Copyright by SAP AG

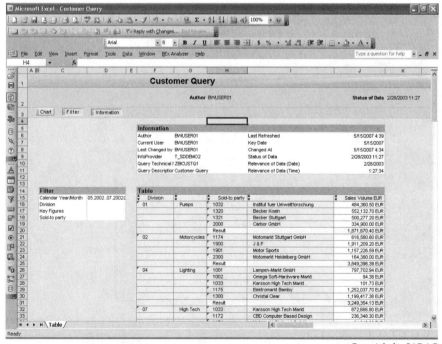

Copyright by SAP AG

FIGURE 3-8 Drilldown by Division in the Query Analysis Grid

Context Menu Function for Rows	Description and Functionality
Exchange (characteristic) With	Exchanges a characteristic with other characteristics or key figures available in the query.
Sort Characteristic	You can sort in ascending order by key or text, or sort in descending by order by key or text.
Drill Down	Drill down on any characteristic that is filtering the query.
Transfer Values	If the query is enabled to perform planning and is available to post values for the key figures, this option will be available. It allows you to transfer data into a temporary buffer for storage until you post to the InfoCube or delete the data.
Save Values	If the query is enabled to perform planning and is available for posting data, you can save the values to the InfoCube.
Other Functionality	All other functions are covered in the preceding tables for Properties, Query Properties, and column context menu options.

TABLE 3-9   Context Menu Functionality in the Rows of the BEx Analyzer

Chart Functionality

The last option will cover in terms of navigation via the BEx Analyzer is the ability to switch from a table to a chart in the analysis grid. As you can see in Figure 3-9, we can easily switch to a chart from a table, and the chart automatically uses the data in the table to build the

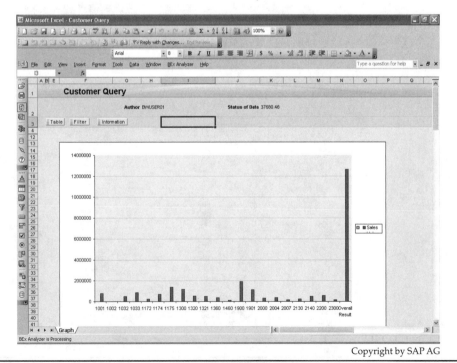

Copyright by SAP AG

FIGURE 3-9   Converting a table to a chart for the query display

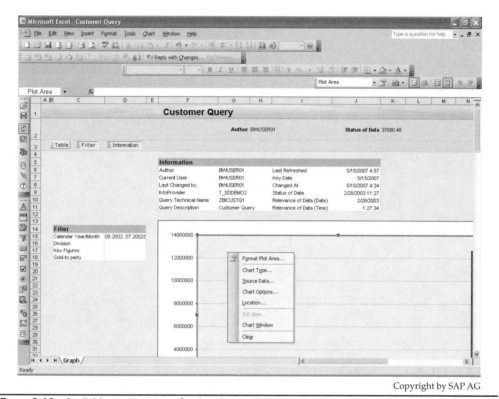

Figure 3-10   Available context menu for the chart options

chart axes. In this case, the chart has assigned Sold-To Parties to the X axis and Total Sales to the Y axis. This format can be customized, as you can see in Figure 3-10. You can alter the view of the chart based on the context menu options. These options are based on the standard Excel chart functionality—Format Plot Area, Chart Type, Source Data, Chart Options, Location of Chart, and so on. We will be looking at the capability and components of customizing a chart in Chapter 13 and therefore will withhold a detailed discussion of this process until then.

Summary

As you can see, the functionality even in the initial stages of query analysis is very powerful and detailed. Many of your reporting requirements can likely be accomplished by just using some of these initial functions. Some topics could have been expounded upon at length, but as we go through the process of creating, changing, presenting, and distributing the results of queries and workbooks, we will see much of this information in action. We haven't gotten to what the capabilities are of the workbook and the Design Toolbar of the BEx Analyzer. This chapter has offered us a view of the majority of the functionality of the BEx Analyzer and other tools during the process of using BI reports by the Business User Group. The following chapters will take us from a high-level review to an increasingly more detailed view of the processes for queries, both Excel based and web based.

Where It All Starts—
The Query Designer

In the BEx Query Designer, you will be building almost all the components you'll use in the process of creating a query, Web Query, Report Designer report, and anything that can be used in the Web Application Designer for a Web Template. These components include but are not limited to, restricting characteristics, restricted key figures, calculated key figures, exception reporting, conditions, defining formulas, variables, formatting, exception cells, attaching documents, and all the properties of the characteristics and key figures. We'll now get into the activities in the BEx Query Designer. Tons of options are available in this toolset—in fact, too many for you to remember everything the first time through, or even the second time through. Therefore, you might find the step-by-step procedures for specific activities a bit challenging, so you'll need to get some hands-on system time to gain some additional experience and confidence using these different options. For this reason, I have included as many screenshots as possible without burdening you with too many. Also, keep in mind that even though we will be working with specific screenshots, once the next support pack or upgrade comes out, these may change a little (or a lot). For example, a function that was used in the 3.x version—Tabular Display—was available in the 3.5 version directly on the toolbar for the BEx Query Designer, but currently it is only available in the BEx Analyzer components from the Workbook functions, not the Query Designer functions. It may, in a future support pack, come back to being available in the Query Designer.

Access the Query Designer

Some of the general concepts incorporated into the Query Designer include the ability to generate error-handling methods, correction help, messages, and warnings. This is something that was lacking in the previous versions, and in some cases you were left to find an error without any direction. These new capabilities have helped enormously in the process of building a query. The Tasks section of the screen helps anyone new at building queries to gain additional help and support. Another new function of the 7.0 BI system is its ability to automatically generate technical names for reusable objects such as variables, restricted key figures, structures, and queries. In some cases, you might want to edit multiple objects at the same time. This is now possible with the Edit function. For example, you now have the ability to edit multiple objects' text names simultaneously. Another new option is the ability to have reusable properties of a specific object. For example, you might want to have all the objects in a structure use a specific setting, such as default text. Therefore, you can give the highest object that setting and establish a reference to all subordinate objects to inherit that setting from the upper reference object.

Now that we have set the stage for the Query Designer, let's access it. You have several ways in which to access the BEx Query Designer:

- You can access it directly from Start | Programs | Business Explorer | Query Designer. (Keep in mind we are working with version 7.0, not 3.5.)

- From the BEx Analyzer accessing the BEx Query Designer, you can go to BEx Analyzer | Tools | Create New Query.

- From the BEx Report Designer, you can go to Tools | BEx Query Designer.

- From the Web Application Designer (WAD), you can use the Menu toolbar to go to Tools | BEx Query Designer

- Finally, from Crystal Reports, you can use Tools | BEx Query Designer.

We will concentrate on using the first option and access the BEx Query Designer toolkit from the Start menu. Starting the BEx Query Analyzer in this way, you have to access the server and log on. Once that task is complete, you will be presented with a view of the BEx Query Designer, shown in Figure 4-1. This view of will become very familiar to you as you work through this chapter. We will be using the BEx Query Designer for all the query definitions in this book. Therefore, it is very important that you get acquainted with the functionality of this screen. As you look at the BEx Query Designer, you can see that three partitions are available: InfoProvider, Filter, and Properties. Within these partitions you have additional options, and we will review all of them. You can also see that you have some toolbars available at the very top of the screen: Query, Standard, and View. These toolbar functions are involved in all of the activities of the BEx Query Designer. Some of the options include Copy, Save, and Create, as well as the ability to change the view of the Query Designer. We will discuss each option and define its functionality and responsibilities. Using the options under the View component of the Query toolbar, you can hide certain sections of this initial screen. You can change the view of the Query Designer via View | Predefined | Standard View or 3.x View.

NOTE *The terms "BEx Query Designer" and "Query Designer" are used interchangeably in this chapter.*

Once you access the BEx Query Designer, you need to find a query to work with or create a new query. In either case, you will be accessing the BEx Open dialog box, discussed in the previous chapter. If you access the Open dialog box based on the Create option, you will be able to use the Find, History, or InfoAreas folder to access the InfoProvider you are

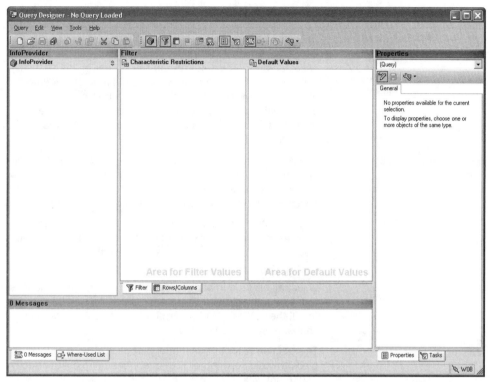

FIGURE 4-1   Initial view of the BEx Query Designer

using to create your query. If you use the Open option on the Standard toolbar, you will be presented with the options Find, History, Favorites, Roles, and InfoAreas to access the objects you want to work with to design your queries.

NOTE *The options you see could be influenced by your authorization access. Therefore, you may not see the InfoAreas button.*

Format of the Query Designer Screen

Figure 4-1 shows the different portions of the Query Designer screen, and you need to know what to expect to see in each of these areas so you can understand where you can define specific items and where you can set up different types of functionality. Table 4-1 lists the different areas that are defined.

If we switch the screen view from what's shown in Figure 4-1 to what's shown in Figure 4-2, you can see that the section labeled Filters is now named Rows/Columns, the section labeled Properties is now Tasks, and the section labeled Message is now

Query Designer Heading	Description and Functionality
InfoProvider – Directory Tree of the Selected InfoProvider	Once you have selected the specific InfoProvider you are interested in using for the building the query, all the objects associated with this InfoProvider will appear in this section. This includes both the objects included in the architecture of the InfoProvider and those structures that are or will be created in the Query Designer and connected to the InfoProvider, such as structures, restricted key figures (RKF), and calculated key figures (CKF).
Filter – Characteristic Restriction	In this section, you drag and drop characteristics that will be filtered and applied to the entire results set for the query. For example, you might want to filter all the queries based on a specific sales organization, company code, or division.
Filter – Default Values	In this section, you define the characteristic filter values used for the initial view of the results set for the query. The user may decide to modify these filters in the result.
Properties	This section is used to display the current settings for an object highlighted in another section. You can make changes to these settings here. There are multiple tabs in this section for all the settings, and we will investigate these based on characteristics and key figures.
Messages	This section is for informational purposes. This is a good place to indicate whether your query has been built correctly and, if not, where the error is located. You can also provide some additional information like what to do to fix the error.

TABLE 4-1   Definition of the Panes in the Query Designer

Where-Used List. This is where you can see any additional panes available for use in query definitions. These are explained in Table 4-2.

Toolbars of the Query Designer

In the initial view of the Query Designer, three toolbars offer us additional functionality. Each is appropriately named for the responsibilities it has. Thus, the Query toolbar has all the functions related to the query itself, the Standard toolbar has all the functions required for basic activities in the query, and the View toolbar is used to view the initial sections of the Query Designer as well as the dialog boxes for other functions, such as creating exceptions and conditions.

Standard Toolbar

The Standard toolbar doesn't really have any unusual functions, but they are all important for basic query activities. In the following illustration, you can see the different icons for the

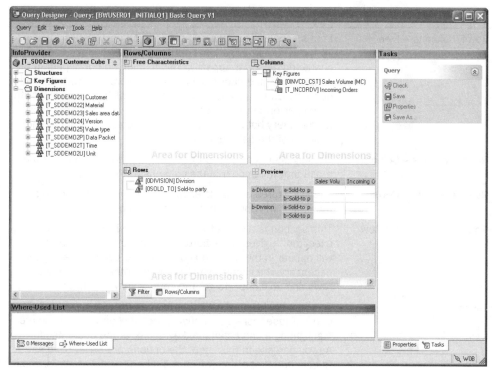

Copyright by SAP AG

FIGURE 4-2   Query Designer with rows/columns displayed

objects in the Standard toolbar. In Table 4-3 are the executables and the functionality and description.

Copyright by SAP AG

View Toolbar

The View toolbar is responsible for all the different dialog boxes for additional functionality in the Query Designer. It also manages the view of the different sections of the Query Designer. In the following illustration, you can see the different icons for the objects in the View toolbar. Table 4-4 lists the View toolbar items and their functionality and description. As mentioned previously, a number of items are available in different areas of the Query Designer but are used for similar functionality. Therefore, it is not necessary that you remember specifically where every function is, only that you know a certain function exists can find it when you need to use it.

Copyright by SAP AG

Query Designer Heading	Description and Functionality
Rows/Columns – Free Characteristics	In this section, you drag and drop the characteristics you would like to offer as navigational options to the business users. The characteristics that appear in this section do not appear in the initial view of the query result and therefore help with the initial query execution against the database, which in turn helps with query performance. These are not, in their current state, filters for the query but rather navigational options used during the analysis of the data in the query.
Rows/Columns – Columns	The key figures or characteristics you drag and drop here are those that will appear in the columns of the query.
Rows/Columns – Rows	The key figures or characteristics you drag and drop here are those that will appear in the rows of the query.
Rows/Columns – Preview	This section is a view of what the query will look like once executed. It gives you a better idea of the information that will appear in the rows and columns. You can then realign, if necessary, the choices you have in the other two sections—rows and columns—to get the correct view of your data.
Tasks	This is a basic list of activities you can execute against the query. These tasks will change depending on whether you are highlighting a characteristic, key figure, or the query itself. As you can see in this case, the options are Save, Save As, Check, and Properties (which will take you back to the previous screen options).
Where Used	In this section, you will find information related to the use of the current object in other areas of BI. To access this information, you need to use the context menu item Where Used from the specific object. This executes the search for all the other objects that use the currently highlighted object.

TABLE 4-2   Definition of the Panes in the Query Designer Screen

Query Toolbar

The Query toolbar is responsible for all functionality surrounding the activities of the query, including Save, Copy, Edit, View, and Application Help. Some of the functionality in the Query toolbar is redundant with respect to the Standard and View toolbars, so where appropriate I will refer to a prior discussion. Table 4-5 breaks down the functionality in terms of the heading and the context menu items associated with each heading.

Query   Edit   View   Tools   Help

Standard Toolbar Item	Description and Functionality
New Query	This function allows you to create a new query.
Open Query	This function allows you to open an existing query for changes and review.
Save Query	This function offers the ability to save the query.
Save All	This function offers the ability to save not only the query but also other objects and structures that are not specific to the query but are assigned to the InfoProvider, such as the RKFs and CKFs created for use by all queries assigned to this InfoProvider.
Execute	This function executes the query via the Web view, not the BEx Analyzer view. To see the BEx Analyzer view, you have to execute the BEx Analyzer and open the query.
Check Query	This option allows the user to execute a check on the query to validate the different functions and objects built.
Query Properties	This function switches the pane to the far right of the Query Designer Tool to the Query Properties view. We will be discussing all these tabs and options later in the chapter.
Cut	You can use this function to remove an object from a specific area in the query. It can then be placed in another portion of the query using the Paste function.
Copy	This function inserts an object into a particular section of the query in the Query Designer. Unlike the Cut function, this function only copies the object and doesn't affect its current position in the query.
Paste	This function is used to insert the copied or cut object in the query definition (be sure to mark the place you want the query object to be inserted).

TABLE 4-3   Components of the Standard Toolbar of the BEx Query Designer

Basic Navigation in the BEx Query Designer

You have accessed the Query Designer and decided to create a new query, so you have chosen the New Query icon and decided to use a specific InfoCube. Now, to start the process of creating a new query, you have to start to fill the areas of the Filter and Rows/Columns portions of the Query Designer with characteristics and key figures. We will be doing quite a bit of this, so let's start with a basic example. Then in the next few chapters we'll move into more complex functionality in terms of creating the query and adding functionality such as variables, RKFs, and CKFs to the query. We have chosen an InfoProvider—Customer Cube—for our

View Toolbar Item	Description and Functionality
InfoProvider	This function opens the InfoProvider section of the Query Designer.
Filter	This function opens the Filter section of the Query Designer.
Rows/Columns	This function opens the Rows/Columns view of the Query Designer.
Cells	This function is only available and highlighted for queries with two structures. You can define formulas and selection conditions for cells explicitly. In this way, you control the values of cells that appear at the intersections of structural components. This function enables you to access individual cells in queries or to assign special values to individual cells. You can use this function to create unique formulas for each cell. It is important to remember that using this function will impact the performance of the query, so be sure to use this function wisely.
Conditions	You use this function to define conditions for a query. For each characteristic, you can give limit conditions to the key figure values in order to determine, for example, all sales revenue above or below a specific amount. This function is used to identify groups of values—for example, the top 5% of all customers in sales revenue or the bottom 10% of all customers for total sales in this quarter.
Exceptions	You can use this function to create or define exception reporting in the query. Exceptions are variances from a specific norm that you define. For example, an exception is any sales revenue below a certain number for the quarter, or a certain number of returned sales items by a customer. Nine different levels are standard with exceptions to define.
Properties	This function displays the properties of the object being highlighted in the Query Designer. You can then change/adjust or display the parameters for each item.
Tasks	Using this function, you can display the activities available for a unique object in the Query Designer.
Messages	This function opens the Message pane. In the Message pane is a list of outstanding messages relating to the status of the query and the objects used or created. These messages are normally informative in nature. Use the Check Query function to display a list of messages in the Message pane
Where-Used List	Using this function, you can identify other objects where the query is being used.
Documents	This option adds an additional tab onto the Query Designer to display all documents assigned to the objects. It also displays the Application Help functionality.
Technical Names	This function allows you to display the technical name and text of the objects being used in the Query Designer. This allows you to hide/display the technical names.

TABLE 4-4   Components of the View Toolbar of the BEx Query Designer

Heading I Context Menu Item	Description and Functionality
Query I New	Described in Table 4-3.
Query I Open	Described in Table 4-3.
Query I Check	Described in Table 4-3.
Query I Save	Described in Table 4-3.
Query I Save As	This function allows you to save the existing query under another name. This is important in cases of testing a query. This way, you can make changes and adjustments to test the query without adjusting the original. You can also use this in terms of managing the key figure structures for referencing purposes. This is discussed in detail in Chapter 5.
Query I Delete	To delete the query, choose Delete. You can only delete the query if it is no longer being used (in any workbook, Web template, report, or broadcast setting).
Query I Properties	Details of the Query Properties are discussed later in this chapter. You'll see a series of tabs that include additional parameters you can use to alter the display of the query information.
Query I Execute	Described in Table 4-3.
Query I Publish I To Roles, BEx Broadcaster	You can publish queries that you have edited and saved in the Query Designer so that they are available to other users. You can choose to save in a role. The Save dialog box appears and you can select a role in which you want to publish the query. The system saves a link to the current query in the selected role. You can choose to save to a portal. The Publish dialog box appears, which enables you to publish the query in the Portal Content Directory (PCD) as an iView. The BEx Broadcaster is a web application for precalculating and distributing queries, query views, Web templates, reports, and workbooks. You can precalculate the query you edited in the Query Designer, or you can generate an online link. You can broadcast the generated document or link by e-mail, print it, or publish it in a portal.
Query I End and Discard Changes	Choose this function to leave the Query Designer. Your entries will not be saved.
Edit I Display/Change	You can use this function to change between the display and change modes in the properties of a query or query component.
Edit I Cut, Copy, Paste and Remove	Described in Table 4-3.

TABLE 4-5 Functionality of the Query Toolbar in the Query Designer

Heading I Context Menu Item	Description and Functionality
View I Predefined I Standard View and BW 3.x View	Using the View I Predefined I Standard View menu option, you can return to the standard view. If you prefer the view you are familiar with from the Query Designer in SAP BW 3.x, choose View I Predefined I View SAP BW 3.x.
View I Standard Toolbars I View and Standard	You can use this function to show and hide the View, and Standard toolbars.
View I Technical Names, Properties, Tasks, InfoProviders, Filter, Rows/Columns, Cells, Exceptions, Conditions, Messages, Where-Used List, Documents	Described in Table 4-4.
Tools I Save All	Described in Table 4-3.
Tools I Expand Node, Collapse Node	You can use this function to fully expand the hierarchy nodes you have selected, in one step. You can also use this function to fully collapse the hierarchy nodes you have selected, in one step.
Help I Application Help	When you choose Application Help, the SAP NetWeaver online documentation appears. The Query Design: BEx Query Designer section in the documentation for the Business Explorer is displayed automatically.
Help I About	Using this function, you see the version of the Query Designer with the number of the support package and the revision. You can use this information if you need to send problem messages.

TABLE 4-5   Functionality of the Query Toolbar in the Query Designer (*continued*)

initial query. In Figure 4-3, you can see that this InfoCube shows dimensions, key figures, and also something called a *structure*. (We will discuss this in Chapter 5.) Needless to say, this object is assigned to the InfoCube T_SDDEMO2. You can see that the Dimensions node is opened to show the different dimensions of the InfoCube. Under the Dimension folders, you will find the characteristics and navigational attributes we have turned on for use in reporting. You will be opening up the Dimension nodes to get to the characteristics and navigational attributes. These are the objects you will be dragging and dropping onto the different portions of the Query Designer (not the complete dimension, but what is stored in the dimension).

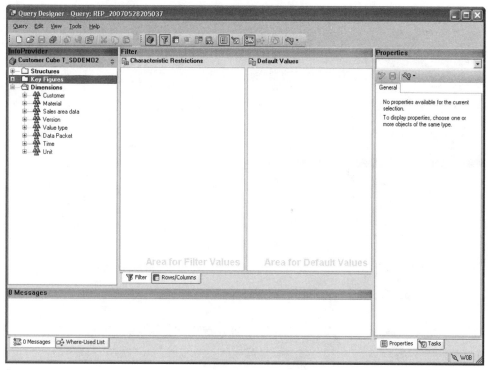

Copyright by SAP AG

FIGURE 4-3   Initial screen for the creation of a query

Initial Drag-and-Drop Functionality

Now that we have identified the InfoProvider and the dimensions, we are going to look at the dimension Sales Area Data. As you can see in Figure 4-4, three characteristics are listed: Sales Organization, Division, and Distribution Channel. Figure 4-4 shows the initial drag and drop of the characteristics into other areas of the Query Designer. In this case, we are moving the Sales Organization characteristic to the area Characteristic Restrictions. You do this by using your cursor and clicking a particular characteristic or key figure and then dragging it to the appropriate portion of the Query Designer. We'll continue to fill the different portions of the Query Designer with the characteristics and key figures we require for reporting. In Table 4-6, you see the positioning of the other objects. This is a common format where the key figures are placed in the columns and the characteristics are placed in the rows.

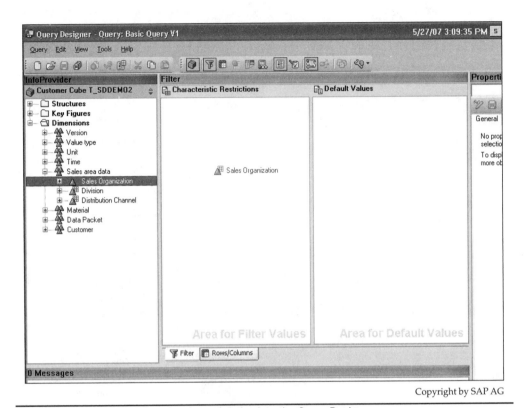

FIGURE 4-4 Dragging and dropping characteristics into the Query Designer

Position in the Query Designer	Characteristic or Key Figures Assigned; Technical Name/Description
Free Characteristics	0DIVISION/Division
Rows	0SOLD_TO/Sold To Party; 0SOLD_TO_0REGION/Region
Columns	0INVCD_CST/Sales Volume; T_INCORDV/Incoming Orders
Characteristic Restrictions	0SALESORG/Sales Organization; 0SOLD_TO_COUNTRY/Sold To Party Country
Default Values (These characteristics default to this position based on their position in Rows, Columns, and Free Characteristics.)	0DIVISION/Division; 0SOLD_TO/Sold To Party; 0SOLD_TO_0REGION/Region

TABLE 4-6 Drag-and-Drop Positions for Characteristics and Key Figures in the Query Designer

The following two illustrations show the end result of this process.

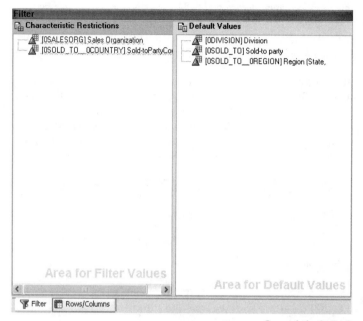

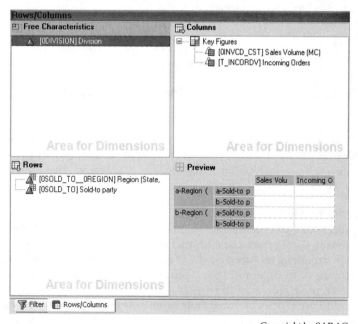

NOTE *Notice that the technical names of the characteristics are significantly different in terms of look. Some use a single technical name (for example, 0DIVISION) and others use two (for example, 0SOLD__TO_0REGION). This is due to the fact that one of the ways to identify a characteristic versus a navigational attribute is based on the technical name format. Those with one technical name are actually characteristics, and those with two technical names are navigational attributes.*

The end result of this query configuration initially is shown here, once you execute and display it on the Web or BEx Analyzer. Once it's executed, you can drill down and incorporate the characteristics in the left navigation block into the query or switch the current view (for example, remove Region and replace it with Division). At this point, if you have a system on which you can create a query, do so now and use some of the functionality we talked about in the previous chapters to test the results.

New Analysis | Open | Save As... | **Display as** Table ▼ | Information | Send | Print Version | Export to Excel | Comments | Filter Settings				Sales Volume (MC) ⇕	Incoming Orders ⇕
▼ Columns	Region (State, ⇕	Sold-to party ⇕			EUR
• Key Figures	AE/#	AE/Not assigned	2402	Jashanmal International Trading Co	1.265.530,00 EUR
▼ Rows				4.727.300,00
• Region (State,			Result	1.265.530,00 EUR	4.727.300,00
• Sold-to party	AU/#	AU/Not assigned	1990	Int. Computers. Inc.	$ 0,00	1.492,72
▼ Free characteristics			Result	$ 0,00	1.492,72
• Division	CA/AB	Alberta	4000	North Energy Ltd	0,00 CAD	10.936,73
			Result	0,00 CAD	10.936,73
	CU/#	CU/Not assigned	1908	Caribbean Computer Supply Corp	$ 0,00	2.985,45
			Result	$ 0,00	2.985,45
	DE/#	DE/Not assigned	1508	Deutsche Computer AG	$ 1.000,00	24.310,09
			100026	Reference Customer for Internet	0,00 EUR	0,00
			CUSTOMER00	Becker 00	1.329,98 EUR	7.000,00
			R110	SB Warenhaus R110	3.010.924,88 EUR	0,00
			R111	SB Warenhaus R111	1.116.852,00 EUR	0,00
			R112	SB Warenhaus R112	1.320.369,14 EUR	0,00
			T-S11A00	CompuMax GmbH	0,00 EUR	7.750,00
			T-S11A01	CompuMax GmbH	0,00 EUR	7.750,00
			T-S11B00	PC-World Stuttgart KG	0,00 EUR	5.000,00

I have saved our query definition. Notice that the characteristic restrictions have disappeared. This is due to the fact that we didn't restrict these characteristics before saving. You may have noticed a warning message in the Messages area stating that if we didn't restrict these objects, they would be ignored. Therefore, we need to restrict these objects before saving.

Restriction of Characteristics

The restriction process has different results depending on where you set up the restriction. Filters or restrictions in the Characteristic Restriction section are always applied to the query result, which cannot be modified by the user. These are often regarded as global or static filters. The filters or restrictions in the Default Values section are applied immediately once the query is executed. However, the user is able to navigate within these filters. The user cannot add additional filters to the default values; therefore, the filter establishes the maximum set of values allowed for the user to view. However, the user can reduce the number of values and apply an additional restriction to the filter and thus reduce the amount of information they can see.

The restriction process is very similar for all the characteristics, so let's take a look at the characteristic Sales Organization (0SALESORG) from the Characteristic Restriction section of the Query Designer. You can access the dialog box for the restriction using the context menu of the characteristic (right-click and select Restrict) or by double-clicking the object. The first of the following illustrations shows the context menu with Restrict highlighted. Once you execute this option, you will see a dialog box with options for finding the restricted values. The second illustration shows the dialog box for the initial restriction process. Now we'll start to investigate the options in this dialog box. In the third illustration, you can see an expanded section—the Show section. If you look at the information available, you can see that we have the ability to filter the restricted values by using History, Favorites, Single Values, Value Ranges, and Variables. The History, Favorites, Single Values, and Value Ranges selections are self-explanatory. Depending on which one you choose, you will get a screen showing that specific option. For example, with Value Ranges, you get an option to identify the To value and From value and whether these values are between, equal, less equal, greater equal, less than, or greater than. Just beside this option are two additional components: Display of the Values with Key and/or Text, and the Settings button. The option to display the values as a combination of key and text is similar to others of the same nature, but the Settings button offers some additional information. The fourth of the following illustrations shows the initial view of the dialog box invoked via the Settings button. Table 4-7 lists the options and offers descriptions and functionality of these parameters.

Copyright by SAP AG

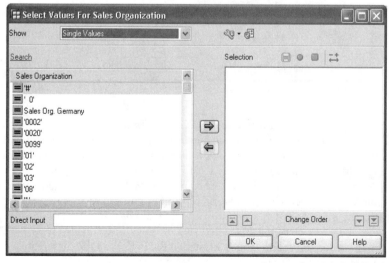

Copyright by SAP AG

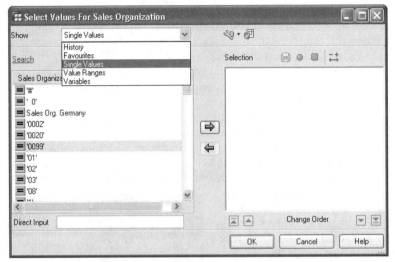

Copyright by SAP AG

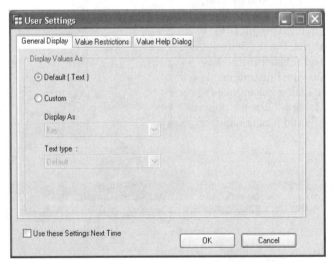

Copyright by SAP AG

Additional search functions allow you to search by attributes of the characteristic and combinations of these attributes. If you choose Search in the Input dialog box, you will see three search rows available for the characteristic and its attributes. Compounded characteristics and the text of the characteristic are considered attributes in this context. As long as the characteristic has text, you can search in the text or in the key. If there is text, you can enter text for the search into the input field. With keys and attributes, you can restrict the search to the required values using input help. Choose Input, and help appears in a new dialog box and provides you with the selection of the associated single values. You can also type in a direct input to find the characteristic value—this is located at the bottom of the dialog box.

Tab	Option	Description and Functionality
General Display	Default Value (Text)	This is the default view of the text identified in the characteristic or from the Query Designer settings.
	Custom – Display As; Text Type	This option allows you to adjust the view of the characteristic. If you choose a different display (for example, Text and Key), you will get the following options: Default, Long, Medium or Short Text.
	Use These Settings Next Time	This allows you to define the settings and reuse them rather than having to reset them each time.
Value Restriction	All Values	This allows you to display all the values for the search, which can take quite a bit of time if your master data is a long list (for example, Materials).
	Maximum Values Displayed	Allows you to customize the number of values displayed at one time.
	Read Mode Setting – Default	This reads the values based on the default setting in the system. Normally this reads the values used in the InfoProvider.
	Read Mode Setting – Custom	This allows you to read the master data tables or just the values already posted in the InfoProvider.
	Use These Settings Next Time	See previous description.
Value Help Dialog	Default (No Attributes)	With this option, no attributes are shown or used for the search.
	Custom	Select the desired attributes in the left selection window and click the arrow pointing to the right. The selected attributes now appear in the right window. This allows you see the attributes during the search for values of the characteristic.
	Use These Settings Next Time	See previous description.

TABLE 4-7   Options in the Settings Dialog Box

The last set of options you have to review are on the right side of the dialog box. These are directly above the box that holds the restricted values once you transfer them from the complete list to the restricted list. Beside the word Selection are four options: Save Selection, Include the Selection, Exclude the Selection, and Set Offset for Variables. These options are used after you have selected the values for the restriction. You can save the selection as well as include or exclude specific values. For example, suppose you have a list of characteristic values you use quite a bit, and rather than removing specific values, you exclude them for a particular list, thus saving yourself the time of removing them and then having to find them again. You can just include them the next time. You'll normally use the Set Offset for Variables option while setting up time intervals or rolling yearly values. For example, suppose you are interested in using the same variable for all 12 columns for a monthly analysis. You can employ the offset variable setting to use the same variable, but offset by -1 or +1, to identify the next month. Thus, if the variable is directed to the month of May, your offset of -1 will direct that column to collect data for the month of April, and +1 will be June. This is demonstrated in detail throughout the book. The first of the following illustrations shows the context menu options for the text/technical name display, and second illustration shows the

final view after you have selected the value to transfer. In this case, we have decided to restrict the query to read only values directly related to Sales Organization 1000 – Germany. To choose the value, you can highlight the value and use the selection arrows, or you can just double-click the value and it will automatically be transferred to the Restricted Values box.

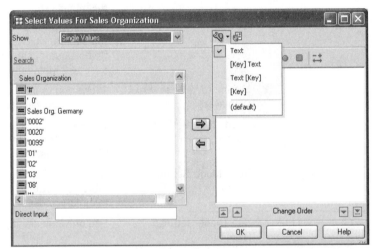

Copyright by SAP AG

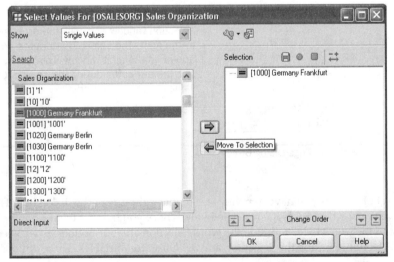

Copyright by SAP AG

Again, we will be adding quite a few options to this query before we are finished, so questions concerning variables, exceptions, and so on, will be answered shortly. Once you have finished this process, you can save the query. Enter a technical name and a description for the query. The technical name must uniquely identify the query; this means the name may appear only once across all InfoProviders of the BI system. The technical name can contain a maximum of 30 characters and must begin with a letter. Once you have saved the query, you can execute it in the BEx Analyzer and include it in a workbook. This allows you to add functionality from the workbook to the query and be able to save the format and executables. You can also display the query on the Web via the Execute function directly on the context menu of the Query toolbar. Go to Query | Execute to execute the query to the Web. (In this case, this would technically be classified as a Web Query.) You can also use the query as a data provider in the Web Application Designer (WAD). Once you have finished setting up a WAD query, you can execute it to a portal. In this case, this type of display would be known as a Web Template Query. You can also use this query as a data provider for the Report Designer.

Query Properties for the Query Designer

Because we are working through the basics of the Query Designer, this is a good place to discuss the Query Properties. Again, you will find some overlapping functionality, but

because we will be using this portion of the Query Designer quite frequently, we will discuss all of the functionality and uses.

You can get to the Query Properties by clicking the Query Properties icon at the top of the Query Designer, or you can use the context menu from the Query toolbar (select Query | Properties). Either way, the right side of the Query Designer shows the tabs of the Query Properties, as shown in the illustration at right. If you use these properties, and the ones you have from the BEx Analyzer (functionality in the context menu of the characteristics and key figures), you can probably satisfy a large number of your business requirements without even going to the other functions and calculations.

The Query Properties dialog box is divided into tabbed pages; each tabbed page provides different settings. The Table 4-8 describes each item and its functionality.

Tab	Component	Description and Functionality
General	Description	You can change or adjust the description of the query here. You can use a text variable in the description. This allows you to customize the text to reflect something in the query or allow manual text entry. You can also enter the query description when you save the query.
	Technical Name	The technical name of the query is displayed.
	InfoProvider	The technical name of the InfoProvider on which the query is based is displayed.
	Key Date	Every query has a key date. For time-dependent data, the key date determines the time for which the data is selected. The default value for the key date is the date on which the query is executed (that is, today's date). The Select Values for Date dialog box appears. Choose a date from the calendar and use the arrow button to add it to the selection window on the right. You can also select a variable key date. In the Select Values for Date dialog box, choose the Variables tabbed page. Choose a variable and use the arrow button to add it to the selection window on the right. Additional information on all variables can be found in Chapter 6.
	Last Changed Information	Displays details of the owner of the structure, the person who last changed the structure, and the date and time when the query was changed.
Variable Sequence	List of Variables	Any entry variables the query contains are listed here. You can use the two arrow buttons to determine the sequence in which the variables appear in the variables screen when the query is executed. This is purely for display of the variables, not for creating or changing them.

TABLE **4-8**   Components of the Query Properties in the Query Designer

Tab	Component	Description and Functionality
Display (The first illustrations at the end of this table shows the options on this tab.)	Display Options – Adjust Formatting After Refresh	This setting is useful in the BEx Analyzer and is therefore the default setting. The formatting for the query underlines the type of data contained in a cell and highlights the structure of the delivered results. The position and size of the cell area in the analysis grid changes when the query is refreshed. The Adjust Formatting After Refreshing function guarantees that the format is adjusted when the updated query data is refreshed. You can deactivate the function for adjusting the format, for example, if you want to display the data more quickly, or if you use a workbook with your own format template. This should be deactivated if you are formatting your workbook for specific column widths, sizing of the rows, or using other formatting options.
	Display Options – Hide Repeated Key Values	You can specify whether identical key figures are to be displayed more than once in the query. The Hide Repeated Key Values setting is active by default, such that only the first key value is displayed for each characteristic; additional, identical key values are suppressed. You may want to deactivate this function if you are using the data in the query for a flat file to be uploaded in another data warehouse. In this way, you will have all the cells filled in and available for uploading. This parameter must be set again to be functional on the Web.
	Display Options – Display Scaling Factors for Key Figures	Key figures can have scaling factors and units or currencies. Units or currencies are displayed for every key figure, but not the scaling factors. If you activate the Display Scaling Factors for Key Figures setting, an additional header row is added to the row or column header in the query. Information about the scaling factor and unit or currency appears in this additional header row, as long as it is consistent (for example, EUR 1,000). This setting is deactivated by default. This parameter must be set again to be functional on the Web.

TABLE 4-8   Components of the Query Properties in the Query Designer (*continued*)

Tab	Component	Description and Functionality
	Document Links – For InfoProviders, Master Data, Metadata	For metadata, master data, and InfoProvider data for a query, you can display links to documents that you have created for these objects. If documents exist for these objects, the icon appears next to them. You can choose this icon to navigate to where the document is displayed on the Web. These documents are available to be assigned to the InfoProvider, Master Data, and MetaData levels.
Rows/Columns (The second illustration at the end of the table shows the options on this tab.)	Result Position – Rows and Columns	Here you specify where the result (that is, total) is displayed. Rows: Above or Below. Columns: Left or Right. By default, the results are displayed at the bottom right. Note: As you adjust the view of the result position, you can view the display on this same tab.
	Suppress Zeros	You can use this setting to specify whether columns or rows containing zeros are to be displayed. The following options are available under Suppression: • **Do Not Suppress** The rows or columns with zeros are displayed. • **Active** If characteristics are in the rows and columns, any row or column with a result of zero is not displayed. If the rows or columns include, for example, the values 1, −1, 1, −1, the result is 0. If you select this setting, the whole row or column is hidden. • **Active (all values = 0)** If this is set, the columns or rows containing zero values in all cells are not displayed.
	Effect On	Defines whether suppression of zero values should be applied to rows and columns, only to rows, or only to columns.
Value Display (The third illustration after the table shows the options on this tab.)	Display of +/− Signs – Before, After, in Parentheses	Here you specify how the minus sign (−) is displayed. Either before the number or after the number, or the number is displayed in parentheses.

TABLE 4-8   Components of the Query Properties in the Query Designer (*continued*)

Tab	Component	Description and Functionality
	Zero Value Display – Display Zeros, Show Zeroes as	The following options are available for displaying zeros. • **Zero with Currency/Unit** Zeros are displayed with the currency or unit (for example, EUR 0.00). This is the default setting. • **Zero Without Currency/Unit** Zeros are displayed without a currency or unit entry. • **Zero as Space** Cells containing a zero value remain empty. • **Zero as Default Text** If you choose this setting, the Show Zeros As field is activated. You can now enter the required value (character, number, or letter), such as an asterisk (*). Cells that contain a zero value are filled with this value.
Planning	Start Up View	Here you can specify that the query is only started in display mode. At runtime, the user can switch on the input-ready field to use the query for manually entering plan data or executing planning functions. This guarantees that users can use the query in planning applications without locking each other out. For queries that are not input ready, this function is always active and cannot be changed. For input-ready queries, this function is not active by default, but can be switched on. Queries are input ready as soon as they contain a structural component that has one of the following properties: • Data can be changed by planning functions • Data can be changed by user input or planning functions
Extended	Enterprise ID	This is the technical number that the Excel sheet gives to the query. This is the location that the query holds in the Excel database.

TABLE 4-8 Components of the Query Properties in the Query Designer (*continued*)

Tab	Component	Description and Functionality
	Release for OLE DB for OLAP – Allow External Access to This Query • **OLE** Object Link Enabling • **DB** Database • **OLAP** Online Analytical Processing	External reporting tools that communicate using the OLE DB for OLAP interface use queries as data sources. If you want to release this query as a data source for external reporting tools, select Allow External Access to This Query. Queries that contain formulas with the operators %RT, %CT, %GT, SUMRT, SUMCT, SUMGT, and LEAF cannot be released for OLE DB for OLAP. These operators depend on the display of the list in the BEx Analyzer, and the formulas would return unexpected values when OLE DB for OLAP is used.

TABLE 4-8   Components of the Query Properties in the Query Designer (*continued*)

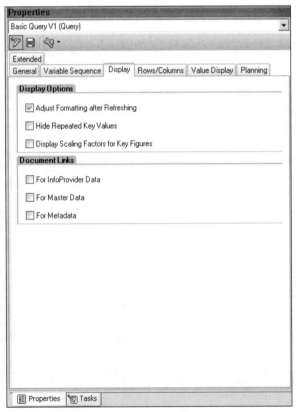

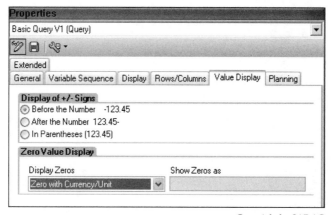

Copyright by SAP AG

Summary

We have now covered all the basic information surrounding the Query Designer and the functionality of the BEx Analyzer. You should try to gain access to a BI server to test out these options and get some hands-on experience to see what each of these parameters can do for you. We will be using and working with many of these functions in later chapters and referring to options for configuring certain calculations and settings. For example, if you use the properties of the key figures, you can set up a query that has the initial column with the raw data (for example, sales revenue by customer), then in the next column you can use that same key figure and the key figure ranking property to create a numbering system to identify the highest-priority customers. Then in another column you can use the same key figure but this time use the option "as %", which will give you the percentage of the total sales revenue by customer. This offers your business users tremendous value—rather than just viewing raw data, they can now look at an analysis of the data that offers strategic information. They can answer questions such as, what customer generates the largest percentage of my business? What is the overall ranking of my customers by sales revenue? These functions are just the initial set of options the BEx Query Designer and BEx Analyzer have to offer. In the next three chapters we will discuss numerous other components and tools.

Configuration in the BEx Query Designer— Working with the Numbers

W e are now getting into the details of the design and configuration portion of the SAP BI reporting tools. Because there is so much to explain and review, I've decided to divide the information and discussions across three chapters. This chapter focuses on the use of the key figures in our InfoProviders and what we can do with them to help enhance the information we get from our queries. Included in this discussion is the use and configuration of restricted key figures (RKFs) and calculated key figures (CKFs), working with other parameters in the key figures (such as the Constant Selection option), and finally the use of the key figure properties. Certain areas are introduced in this chapter and also included in Chapter 13—such as the configuration of the Unit of Measure option. You will notice the number of screen shots increasing in these chapters. I believe that these will be reasonable views of the options in the BEx Query Designer for quite a while and will probably not change much in terms of look and feel for a number of years.

Introduction to the Key Figures

Normally when you fill your InfoProviders (actually Data Targets) with data, you are uploading a series of records. You will need to decide on the granularity of the records being loaded, and that granularity will depend on a number of requirements—from the source system information to the level in BW you are loading. As mentioned, in many cases, you will want to store the data at a level that can satisfy all parties. That being said, the data will then have to be manipulated at the query level to get the required results. This is where the use of restricted key figures (RKFs) and calculated key figures (CKFs) comes to the rescue. They are very useful in these situations. You can create a detailed column or row to filter the information and then generate a detailed report. Remember that in the query itself you can define a filter, at the top level of the query, and have that filter apply to the entire query, however, what if you need to have that particular restriction apply to only one column or a series of columns? For example, suppose we would like to have a report that shows a different region's sales revenue for the year. We need to apply a filter to each of the columns to accomplish this view of the data. I would definitely not suggest that we upload the data with these specific combinations because using that information for other queries would be very difficult. We want to upload the data at a level that helps us develop the queries, but not at a level that hurts our flexibility at the query level and also hurts the uploading process.

NOTE *Too many precalculations going on during the data upload process will affect performance times of the data load.*

Another example of a report that lends itself to RKFs is one that needs each column to show a different year's sales revenue or costs by division, or where we want to see both Actuals and Planned Data. We would need to create a restricted key figure to include in each column a different year. Table 5-1 has an example of what the RKF might include.

As you can see, there are a number of applications for this option. Realize, however, that you need to plan out what your RKFs should be and not create excess characteristic restrictions in the process, because this would affect query performance.

Restricted Key Figures

Restricted key figures are key figures filtered by one or more characteristic selections. RKFs can include other RKFs, basic key figures, or CKFs, and can be available to be reused in other queries created against a particular InfoProvider. Therefore, RKFs can be at the InfoProvider level or the query level, depending on where you decide to create them. This is an important decision because you want to make sure the RKFs developed at the InfoProvider level are consistent and can be reused to apply the same restrictions to other queries and arrive at the appropriate results set for the business user. Think what would happen if you allowed business users to create InfoProvider-level RKFs and were reusing them in other queries, only to find out that the RKF definitions were incorrect. Therefore, not everyone is allowed to create these components at the InfoProvider level. Using these restrictions, you can focus the query result on certain values. Finally, these are calculations you are not interested in storing, filling up your InfoCube with too much data. You are comfortable with the calculation done on the fly in the query OLAP engine.

One other comment that applies to all components discussed here: Be sure to turn on the statistical SBC so you can manage the performance of the queries. In 7.0 BW, you can use the statistics in the SBC technical area to identify the total number of cells being calculated as the query is executed. This is important information because if the total

Rows (Lead Column)	Column 1	Column 2
Characteristic: Division	Key figure: Sales Revenue Characteristic: Year Characteristic: Actual Data (Version)	Key figure: Sales Revenue Characteristic: Year Characteristic: Planned Data (Version)

TABLE 5-1 Restrictions That Create an RKF in the Columns

number of cells being calculated in the OLAP process is in the thousands, you will need to be very careful as the data volume grows. You may be looking at a deterioration of the query performance, and the system can alert you of this. Figure 5-1 shows the location of the InfoProvider-level and query-level RKFs.

NOTE *The term "basic key figure" refers to the InfoObjects in the InfoProvider that will be storing either amounts, quantities, or numbers based on the uploading of data from the source system.*

Restricted Key Figures at the InfoProvider Level

To define an RKF at the InfoProvider level, from the Query Designer right-click the node Key Figures. If RKFs have already been created, you will find a node specifically for them. Then you can either right-click the key figure or the restricted key figure node. The first of the following illustrations shows the result of this action. Notice that you have a choice of New Restricted Key Figure or New Calculated Key Figure. We will discuss CKFs a bit later in this chapter. Once you click the option New Restricted Key Figure, the system creates another place in the list for a new restricted key figure. This is just a placeholder for the process of creating the RKF. The second illustration shows the next step. In the

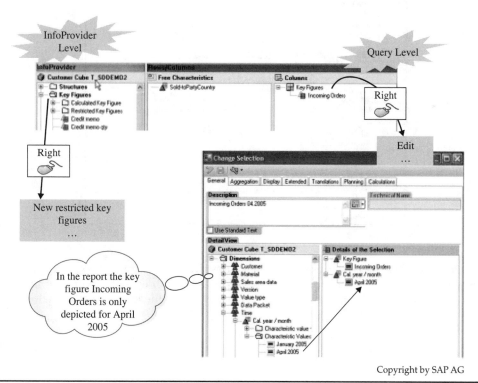

Copyright by SAP AG

FIGURE 5-1 Defining restricted key figures

context menu of this placeholder, you choose Edit to access the dialog box for the actual setup of the RKF.

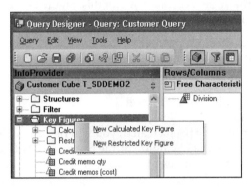

Copyright by SAP AG

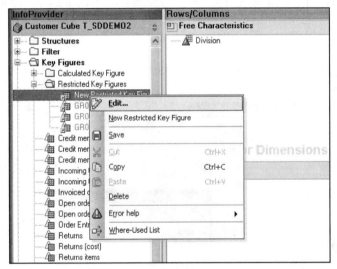

Copyright by SAP AG

Once you click the Edit option, the Change Restricted Key Figure dialog box appears, as shown here. You will see a list of tabs across the top, which we will cover later in the chapter. For now we'll concentrate on the list of objects on the left side of the dialog box.

In the General tab you will see a series of fields. Table 5-2 offers a detailed description of the functionality of each of these fields.

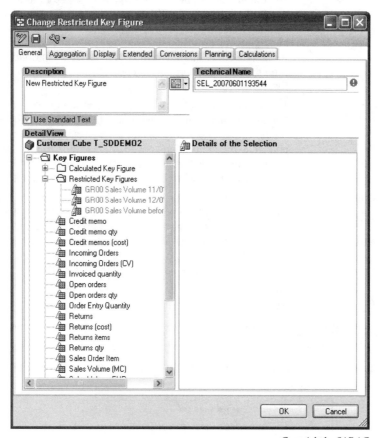

Copyright by SAP AG

In this example, we have dragged the key figure Sales Volume (EUR) to the selection side of the dialog box. We have also moved a time characteristic to the selection section—0CALMONTH, calendar year/month. Next, we will be accessing the context menu for the calendar year/month and looking to restrict this in a manner similar to what we did before, as shown in the first of the following illustrations. Finally, we will restrict this key figure to the information for Sales Volume before January of 2003. Thus, this RKF will be supplying the query all of the years of data in the InfoCube before January 2003 (not including January 2003). The second illustration shows the selection dialog box for this

Field	Description and Functionality
Description	The default description, which will be changed to reflect what the RKF will represent. This is initially New Restricted Key Figure. What you manually type into this field shows up as the column heading. Notice that you can use variables (via icon to the left of the field). We will cover variables in Chapter 6. Directly below is an option to use standard text—this would be the default text from the key figure.
Technical Name	This is the technical name/number that will identify the RKF. The system automatically generates this for you, but depending on the company's technical naming conventions, this should be changed. The generation convention is (RKF/CKF)_<date><time> (for example, RKF_20050818122045). As long as the generated technical name has not been saved, you can change it.
Detail View – InfoProvider Information	This list includes all the objects within the InfoProvider that are available for you to use in the process of creating an RKF. In this list will be all the characteristics, navigational attributes, key figures, other RKFs, CKFs, and possibly other objects created by the Cell Editor functionality (virtual key figures). You can use any combination of these objects to create your RKFs.
Detail View – Details of the Selection	This is the area where you drag and drop the objects you select to be included in your RKFs.

TABLE 5-2   Sections of the Change Restricted Key Figure Dialog Box

activity (we discussed these parameters in the previous chapter), and the third illustration shows the final result of the RKF.

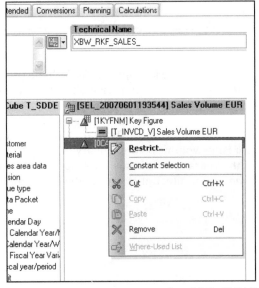

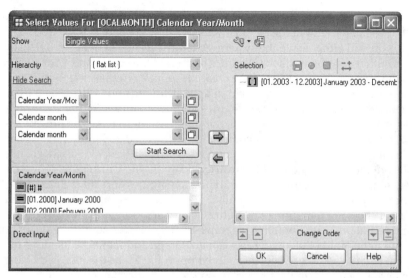

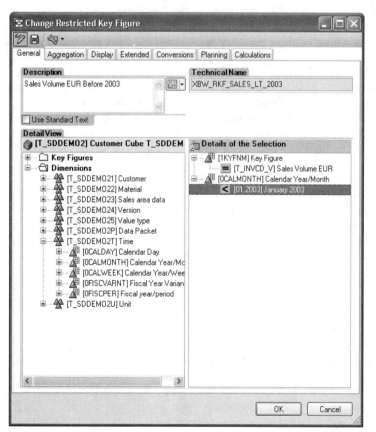

You can use other items within the RKF tabs to enhance the final result, and we will work with those items later in the chapter. We have now created an RKF. Once this has been done, you will either leave the system-generated technical name or delete the system number and fill in your own. Click OK at the bottom of the screen and your RKF will default to the area where you started the creation process. In this case, it will be placed in the InfoProvider section and be included in a list below the node Restricted Key Figures (or you create the node Restricted Key Figures and the slot itself in under the node).

If we need to edit an existing RKF, its not much different from the process just demonstrated. Remember that when you change a restricted key figure, these changes are effective in all queries that use it. To check on where the RKF is being used, choose Where-Used List from the context menu of the restricted key figure. During this process, I find it very useful to turn on the technical names of the key figures and characteristics because the text for many of the key figures is similar. Therefore, I rely on the technical names to be sure that I am choosing the correct key figures, especially if I am using a MultiProvider for the final presentation layer. If you have a number of InfoCubes supplying data to one MultiProvider, the number of key figures can get larger, and therefore the need to know exactly what key figures to use becomes more important. Make the required changes to the definition and, if required, to the properties on the associated tab page. Click OK. You have now defined a restricted key figure for reuse. You can use this restricted key figure in all queries based on the InfoProvider by moving the key figure into the rows or columns of the query using drag and drop. The restricted key figure is not an actual element in this query, but rather a placeholder referenced to the restricted key figure in the InfoProvider.

Restricted Key Figures at the Query Level

Now we can review the process at the query level, which is very similar to the process at the InfoProvider level. The big difference is that these RKFs are not connected to the InfoProvider and therefore are only available to one specific query. This can be a definite blessing because each company has a process to define whether an RKF is correctly configured. Therefore, use it in a query that is being developed and reviewed by the power users. During this review, the definition of the RKF is also reviewed and confirmed to be correct. Once this is complete, if needed, we can identify a query-level RKF as an InfoProvider-level RKF. To initiate this process, you need to have dragged and dropped a basic key figure into the column or rows sections. Alternatively, you can access the context menu of the heading of rows or columns and create a structure, and then drag and drop a basic key figure into that area. Then go to the Rows/Columns section of the Query Designer and access the context menu on the heading Key Figure. This was created once you moved the basic key figure over. The first of the following illustrations shows this activity. Once this is complete, you will see that a placeholder has been created below that structure. The label is a bit different from the InfoProvider-level RKF. In this case, the heading is Selection 1. Within the context menu, choose Edit (not New Selection, because that will just add another placeholder for you in the Key Figure node). The second illustration shows this activity.

We will use this RKF to provide our second column with information about the year 2003 only. Therefore, we will use the same basic key figure—Sales Volume EUR—and drag and drop over the calendar year/month and restrict it to the values within 2003. The first of the following illustrations provides a view of the results. The process of restricting at this level is the same as what we did with the InfoProvider-level RKF. We'll now add one more RKF to the picture, but rather than starting from scratch, we will copy over the RKF we just finished creating. The second illustration shows the start of this process. From the context menu of the new RKF, select Copy and then Paste as Child, as shown in the third illustration, which places the RKF at the level of the Key Figure node. This allows us to add one more restriction to this existing RKF.

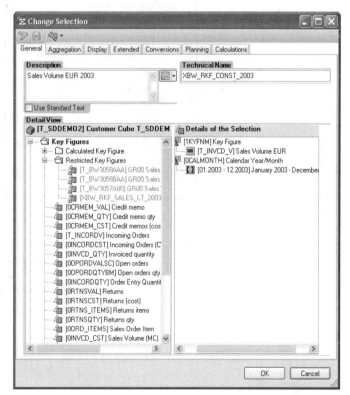

Copyright by SAP AG

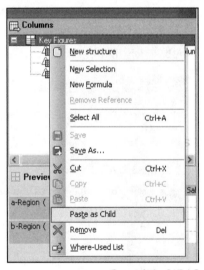

Copyright by SAP AG

Finally, we add the characteristic for Distribution Channel to this RKF. We are interested in the sales revenue for 2003 for the specific distribution channel Final Customer Sales. The following illustration shows the final view of this RKF. Click OK, and we now have three RKFs in our query. The entire process is complete. We can now look at the results of our RKFs in the executed query. The illustration on the next page shows the query results for this process. As you can see, we now have more detailed information for sales revenue and even more detail for sales revenue for a particular distribution channel.

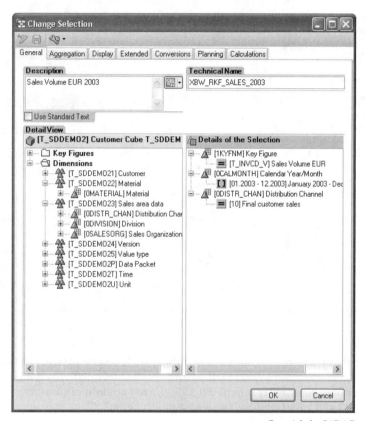

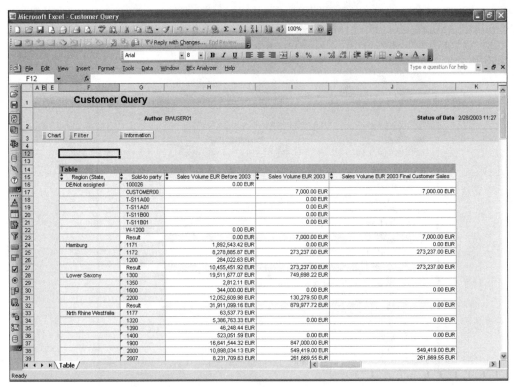

You'll notice that we have a customer that didn't purchase any products before 2003, but in 2003 that customer purchased 7,000 EUR's worth (CUSTOMER00). Even more important, another customer (customer 1171) purchased a significant amount of products through 2002 (a total of 1,892,543.42 EUR), but didn't purchase anything in 2003.

Constant Selection

Another important option is Constant Selection. It basically allows you to "freeze" the values within a column or RKF, no matter what the filtering process is during the drilldown into the query. This is helpful if you need to make sure a calculation is using the same value every time a process executes. You are able to freeze the denominator so you can have a consistent calculation. To go about this, let's use an RKF we developed in the last section— the RKF that has the sales revenue for the year 2003. The following illustration shows this RKF in our query.

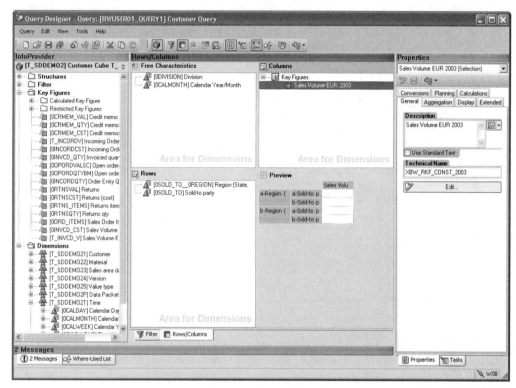

We will copy this RKF and then go back to the Change Restricted Key Figure dialog box and turn on Constant Selection against the calendar year/month, as shown in the following illustration. We need to change the column heading a bit so that we can identify the different RKFs because this minor change will not alter the look and feel of the RKF.

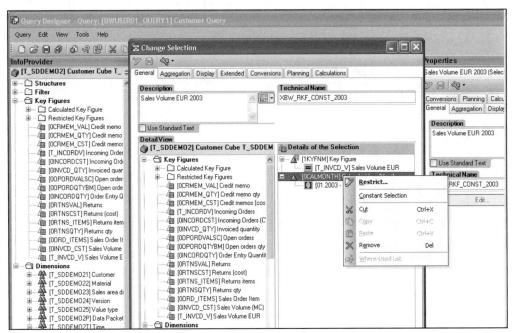

With that complete, we can now execute the query again and see the results of this adjustment. In the first of the following illustrations, you can't see any difference in the totals of the columns. We'll now filter the query a bit to see what happens. In the second illustration, you can see that we filtered against the calendar year/month and filtered to just the month of January 2003 (see the filter component beside Calendar Year/Month in the navigational selection). Now we can investigate what happened. Look at the column with the heading Sales Volume 2003. Constant Select has not changed it. It is holding the full value of the year 2003. On the other hand, the column with the heading Sales Volume EUR 2003 has been filtered to show just the data for the month of January 2003. This may not be something you show in the query, but it will come in handy in the background when you need to execute a calculation.

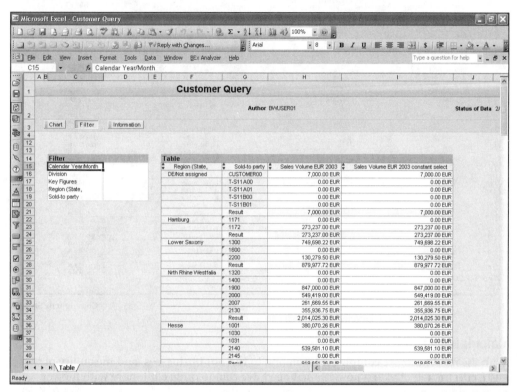

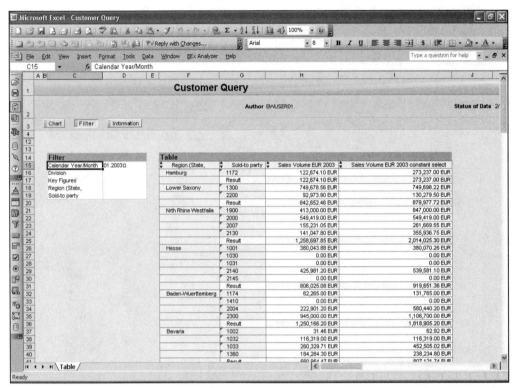

Calculated Key Figures

With the need for more complex information to run our businesses, and the ability of the system technology to keep up with that need, we can do quite a bit more with the key figures stored in our InfoProvider. This brings us the use of calculated key figures (CKFs). A CKF is a combination of key figures, RKFs, other precalculated key figures, and characteristics using a mathematical calculation to derive a formula definition. This formula definition can be saved at the InfoProvider level and reused by anyone creating queries against that InfoProvider. The use of these complicated calculations for information analysis is a basic requirement for any front end of a data warehouse. We won't even attempt to store every possible combination we need to satisfy all the business requirements for information directly in the InfoProvider. Therefore, we need to be able to flexibly use what we have and let the OLAP (online analytical processor) do the rest of the work for us.

To do this, we need to have access to mathematical, basic, percentage, and other functions to give us the ability to pull together different levels of data and calculate the required information. The BEx Query Designer provides many different calculation functions to offer as much standard functionality as possible. We will discuss some of the specific functions, but we can't cover all of them here. (That would take a book of its own.) However, what we will do is identify many of the frequently used functions and discuss their uses. Depending on what types of calculations you are working with, you will be using some of these functions more often then others and therefore will be comfortable with their functionality. You can manually type in some items in the Detail View of the Formula Editor, but you should use the operators as much as possible. You create the CKF in the General tab, much like you create an RKF. You have three different fields when creating the CKF, as identified in Table 5-3.

To follow this up, Table 5-4 provides a short definition of each of the more popular functions.

Sections of the General Tab	Description and Functionality
Detail View	This field is used to create the formula. You will either drag and drop the component of the formula to this area or double-click the component, which will make it appear in the next position in the formula. No period is needed at the end of the formula or line—this is not as close to ABAP programming code as is the formula calculates of Integrated Planning (IP) which does require the syntax specific to ABAP programming.
Available Operands	The available operands are similar to those in the RKF. These are all the objects you can use in the creation of your CKF, including (but not limited to) characteristics (in the format of an RKF), basic key figures, precalculated key figures, and other RKFs.
	You will notice another node that is for the use of variables in this area. You can include a variable in the formula and thus have the business user include a piece of information before the calculation is completed. For example, suppose one of your requirements for bonus calculations is to have the manager change the percentage bonus paid out. Thus, using a variable in the formula, you can allow, at execution time, the manager to change the bonus percentage from 10% to 5% and perform "what-if" calculations.
Operators	The operators are numerous. There are a series of nodes in this area—Basic, Percentage, Data, Mathematical, Trigonometric, and Boolean. In the Mathematical and Trigonometric nodes, you will find functions you might never use in the BI system. For example, when was the last time anyone asked for the arc cosine of Sales Revenue? Or the hyperbolic sine of Costs? In the Mathematical node, you will find Logarithms, Exponential Functions, and Square Roots. Therefore, I would say there's a slim chance of using something in the Mathematical node, but very little chance of using anything in the Trigonometric node. The most used are those found in the Basic, Percentage, Data, and Boolean functions.

TABLE 5-3   Sections in the General Tab of the Calculated Key Figure

Operators	Description and Functionality
Percentage Function – (%) Percentage Variance	Gives the percentage variance between Operand 1 and Operand 2. Plan Sales % Actual Sales provides the percentage difference between the plan sales and actual sales.
Percentage Function – (%A) Percentage Share	Generates the percentage share of Operand 1 and Operand 2. Fixed Costs %A Costs provides the proportion of the total cost of a product that is the fixed cost.
Percentage Function – (%CT) Percentage Share of Result	Generates the percentage share of the subset of the total amounts. %CT Sales Volume (the query will have division and customer data) provides the percentage at the Division/Customer level, not the Total/Customer level.
Percentage Function – (%GT) Percentage Share of Overall Result	Generates the percentage share of the overall results. If the query has a filter, this percentage ignores that filter. %GT Sales Volume (same scenario as the previous item) generates the percentage of Customer/Total, ignoring any filters in the query.
Percentage Function – (%RT) Percentage Share of Report Result	Generates the percentage share of the query results. Therefore, if the query has a filter, this percentage will pick it up. %RT Sales Volume (same scenario as before, but Division is restricted) generates the percentage of Customer/Total and uses the filtered value for Division.
Data Functions – COUNT	Delivers the value 1 if the expression named in <expression> is not 0. Otherwise, it delivers the value 0. COUNT<expression>
Data Functions – DATE	Delivers the values in a Date format. DATE<Expression> mmddyy
Data Functions – DELTA	Delivers the value 1 if the change is 0. Otherwise, it delivers the value 0. DELTA <Expression>
Data Functions – NDIV0	Delivers the value 0 if the division results in a DIV/0 expression. NDIV0<expression>
Data Functions – NODIM	Delivers the quantity without units. NODIM<Expression>

TABLE 5-4   Operators Available for the Formula Editor for Calculated Key Figures

Operators	Description and Functionality
Data Functions – NOERR	Delivers a 0 if the calculation is undefined. Otherwise, it will generate the actual result. NOERR\<Expression>
Data Functions – SUMCT (Column Total)	Similar to Constant Selection in nature. Delivers a constant result in all rows. SUMCT \<Operand>
Data Functions – SUMGT (Grand Total)	Delivers the overall results of the operand. SUMGT\<Operand>
Data Functions – SUMRT (Report Total)	Delivers the report results of the operand. SUMRT\<Operand>
Data Functions – TIME	Displays the results of the expression in TIME. TIME\<Expression> hhmmss
Boolean Operators	These are all the Boolean operators required to incorporate logical IF, THEN, and ELSE statements in your formulas. Refer to the example given in the following section.

TABLE 5-4   Operators Available for the Formula Editor for Calculated Key Figures (*continued*)

Calculated Key Figures at the InfoProvider Level

To define CKFs at the InfoProvider level, you can use all of the objects in the InfoProvider. However, realize that you do not have access to all the operators because some operators only make sense at the query level. Remember that after you create your CKF, you will need to drag and drop that CKF into the query for it to be used. The illustration at right shows the initial view of the CKF from the InfoProvider level.

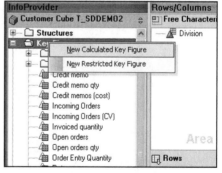

Copyright by SAP AG

As you can see, we are in the same area where we created the RKF. If CKFs are already available, you will see the node for the list of calculated key figures, and you can use this to obtain the context menu. Once you have done this, a placeholder is created in the list of CKFs. You will then use the context menu for this object and edit the CKF. The following illustration shows this step.

NOTE   *Creating a CKF at the InfoProvider level should require a power user who is very familiar with the requirements of the business. These CKFs will be available to all users to add to their queries.*

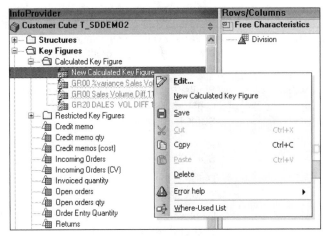

After selecting the Edit command, you will see the dialog box for creating the CKF, shown next. As you can see, the system suggests a technical name, as it did with the RKF. We've already discussed the options available here, so we will move forward with the configuration process.

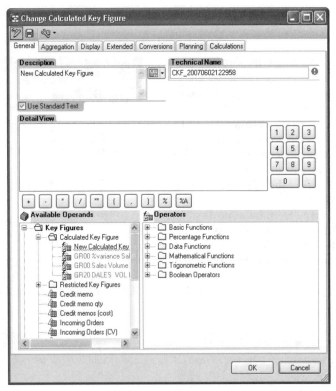

We will be using several of the RKFs we have created to demonstrate the different functionality in the CKFs. Therefore, in some cases, we will not create all the components of the example, but rather will use key figures that have already been developed. In this first case, we will be using two RKFs and combining them to create a CKF. We will take an RKF for the Sales Volume in February 01 and subtract the Sales Volume of January 01 to arrive at a variance by month. Assign a description and a technical name to this new CKF and select OK (at bottom of dialog box). The following illustration shows the final result of the configuration. You can either drag and drop the elements of this CKF into the Formula Editor or double-click the object and it will default to the Formula Editor.

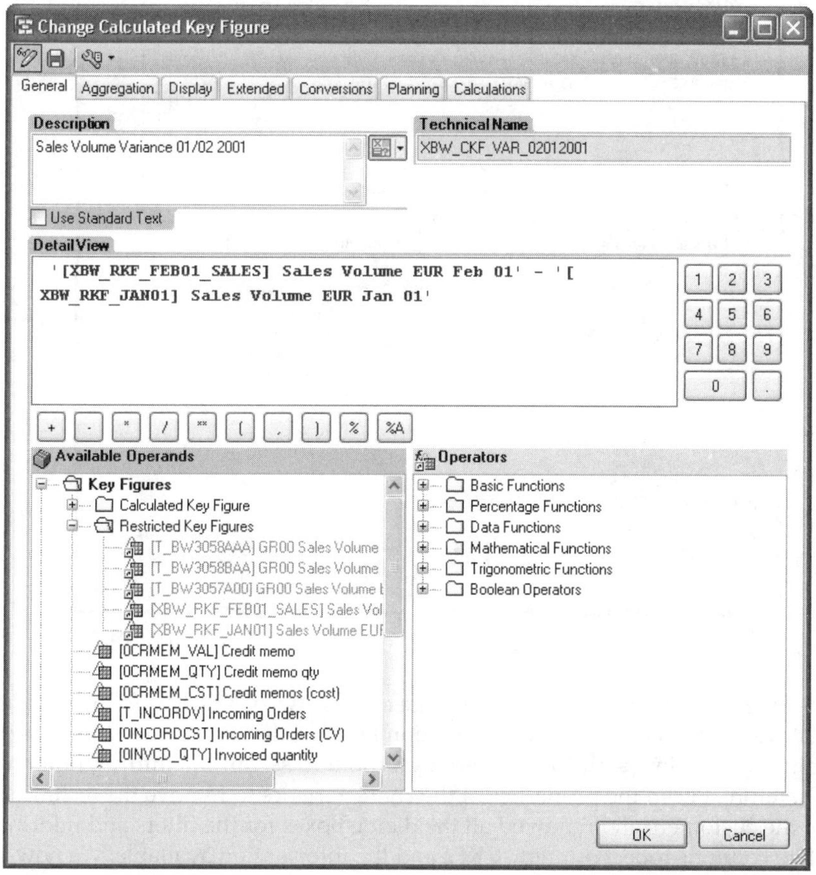

Before we see the results, let's create another CKF. This CKF will use one of the Percentage functions to help with the creation process. We are looking to create a CKF to show the % Variance of Sales Volume. To accomplish this, we use the same two RKFs as before, but we will use the % function instead of subtraction. Thus, double-click the required RKFs and under the Percentage node you will find (%) Percentage Variance. The following illustration shows the configuration in this case. I've turned on the Text and Key display to show the different display options. Include some text and a technical name, and the second CKF is complete.

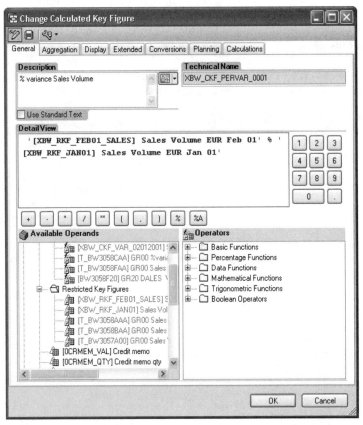

Copyright by SAP AG

Execute the query to see what the results are of these two CKFs. The following illustration shows that we now have even more information to make decisions in the business process. I have adjusted the view a bit to allow enough room to see all the information on one screen. Therefore, I used the properties of the characteristics to remove the technical name of each of the customers and removed all the dialog boxes for the filters and information. The last two columns reflect our new CKFs and the information available. We now know what customer sales were in January and February, we know the variance between the two months, and we also know the percentage variance from one month to another. As you can see, depending on the number of scenarios we develop, we can continue to create more CKFs.

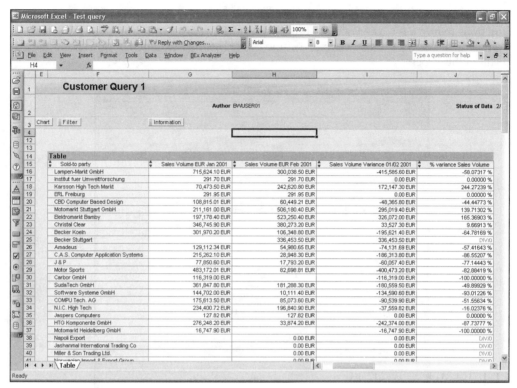

NOTE *DIV/0 can be changed. This is covered in the Chapter 14.*

Rather than continuing at the InfoProvider level, we will move to the query level and continue creating CKFs from that area of the BEx Query Designer.

Calculated Key Figures at the Query Level

Creating CKFs from the query level is very similar to the process for RKFs. The illustration at right shows the initial screen from the query side of the Query Designer. Here we will choose the option New Formula to create the CKF. This invokes the dialog box for the creation of the CKF, which is the same as it is on the InfoProvider side. Rather than going through the process of creating CKFs from scratch, we will use some of the functions available to help us to develop the final view of the CKFs faster and more efficiently.

We will use the Percentage functions first and then look at others. We want to see the percentage share of the result, so we can use %CT to do this.

In this case, drag and drop or double-click the %CT symbol in the list of Percentage functions to move it to the Formula Editor screen. Then drag and drop the RKF Sales Volume EUR Feb 2001 onto the screen behind %CT. The following illustration shows the result of this process.

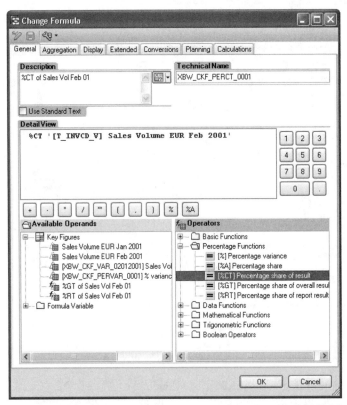

Copyright by SAP AG

Rather than reviewing each of the results of the CKFs, we will create a few more and then execute the query to see the results. We will now use %GT to create another CKF. Take %GT (Percentage Share of Overall Results) and drag it into the Formula Editor as well as

the same RKF as before and assign it to the Formula Editor after the %GT symbol. The
following illustration shows the results of this process.

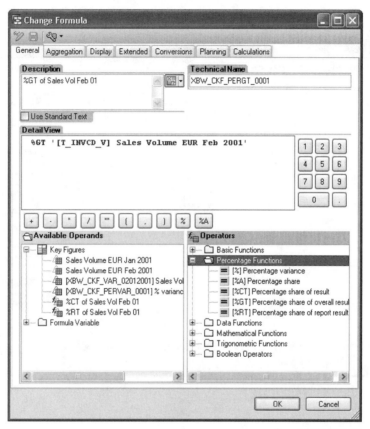

I've used the distinctive names %GT and %CT so we can identify them in the query. For
good measure, we will create the final CKF—%RT. We will create %RT in the same manner

as the other two. The following illustration shows the final configuration view of the three different CKF using the Percentage functions.

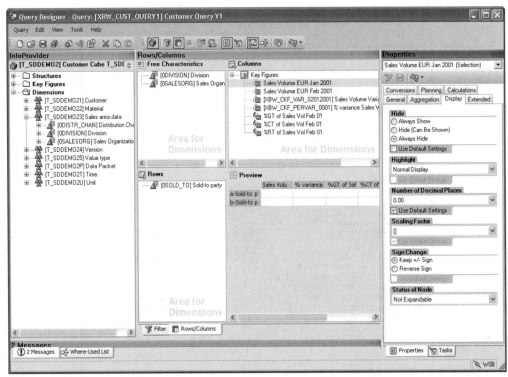

The following illustration shows the initial results from the query point of view.

Microsoft Excel - Customer Query V1

Customer Query V1

Author BWUSER01   Status of Data   2/28/2003 11:27

Filter   Information

Table

Sold-to party	Sales Volume Variance 01/02 2001	% variance Sales Volume	%GT of Sales Vol Feb 01	%CT of Sales Vol Feb 01	%RT of Sales Vol Feb 01
1001	415,585.60 EUR	-58.07317 %	8.19593 %	8.19593 %	8.19593 %
1032	0.00 EUR	0.00000 %	0.00797 %	0.00797 %	0.00797 %
1033	-172,147.30 EUR	244.27239 %	6.62750 %	6.62750 %	6.62750 %
1034	0.00 EUR	0.00000 %	0.00797 %	0.00797 %	0.00797 %
1172	48,365.80 EUR	-44.44773 %	1.65125 %	1.65125 %	1.65125 %
1174	-295,019.40 EUR	139.71302 %	13.82696 %	13.82696 %	13.82696 %
1175	-326,072.00 EUR	165.36903 %	14.29325 %	14.29325 %	14.29325 %
1300	-33,527.30 EUR	9.66913 %	10.38765 %	10.38765 %	10.38765 %
1320	195,621.40 EUR	-64.78169 %	2.90505 %	2.90505 %	2.90505 %
1321	-336,453.50 EUR	DIV/0	9.19066 %	9.19066 %	9.19066 %
1360	74,131.69 EUR	-57.41643 %	1.50187 %	1.50187 %	1.50187 %
1460	186,313.80 EUR	-86.55207 %	0.79076 %	0.79076 %	0.79076 %
1900	60,057.40 EUR	-77.14443 %	0.48604 %	0.48604 %	0.48604 %
1901	400,473.20 EUR	-82.88419 %	2.25902 %	2.25902 %	2.25902 %
2000	116,319.00 EUR	-100.00000 %			
2004	180,559.50 EUR	-49.89929 %	4.95212 %	4.95212 %	4.95212 %
2007	134,590.60 EUR	-93.01226 %	0.27621 %	0.27621 %	0.27621 %
2130	90,539.90 EUR	-51.55634 %	2.32389 %	2.32389 %	2.32389 %
2140	37,559.82 EUR	-16.02376 %	5.37696 %	5.37696 %	5.37696 %
2141	0.00 EUR	0.00000 %	0.00349 %	0.00349 %	0.00349 %
2200	242,374.00 EUR	-87.73777 %	0.92532 %	0.92532 %	0.92532 %
2300	16,747.90 EUR	-100.00000 %			
2401	0.00 EUR	DIV/0	0.00000 %	0.00000 %	0.00000 %
2402	0.00 EUR	DIV/0	0.00000 %	0.00000 %	0.00000 %
2502	0.00 EUR	DIV/0	0.00000 %	0.00000 %	0.00000 %
2503	0.00 EUR	DIV/0	0.00000 %	0.00000 %	0.00000 %

As you can see, there is very little difference in the three columns and the results of the calculations. Now, before you think that something is wrong, let's investigate a bit further and drill down on the query to identify the actual benefits and results. The following illustration shows a bit more with some help from the properties we can use from the BEx Analyzer. In this view of the BEx Analyzer query, we have reduced the view of the characteristics by using just the technical name in the query (versus the text and technical name in the query). We also hide the rest of the key figures, RKF, and CKF so that we can see the three CKFs clearly, all on one screen.

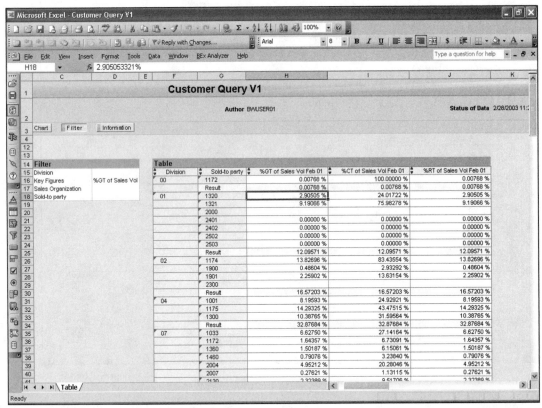

Copyright by SAP AG

In this scenario, we can see that there is a difference between %GT, %RT, and %CT. %CT is calculating the total per characteristic. Therefore, the percentages by division are 100% totals, and the others are still a percentage of the total in the query. If we focus on Division 2, this difference is clear. %CT is calculating by the subset of Division/Sold To Party. Therefore, Sold To Party 1174, 1900, and 1901 total 100%, whereas in %RT and %GT they total about 16% to 17%.

We will now see if there's any difference in these two final percentage calculations. The first of the following illustrations shows that we will be filtering by Sales Organization in this case. We will filter based on Sales Organization 1000 to see the outcome. The second illustration shows the outcome of the last filtering by Sales Organization 1000. Now we can easily review the differences. If we look at the information, we can see differences in the postings this time. The difference is that for %RT, we are expecting to the results based on them showing in the query, whereas %GT is the results based on the grand total. It doesn't take into account the filter (in this case, the Sales Organization). This illustrates the need to review the results of the different reporting functions included in the standard functions.

In this case, the final adjustment would be to correct the results total or hide the results row so that the totals are not misleading.

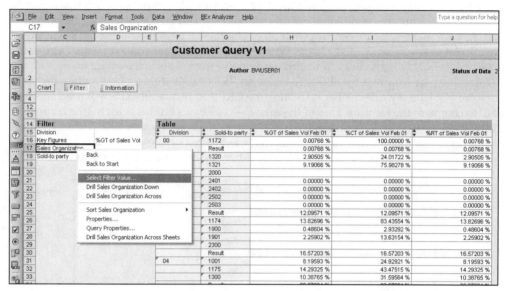

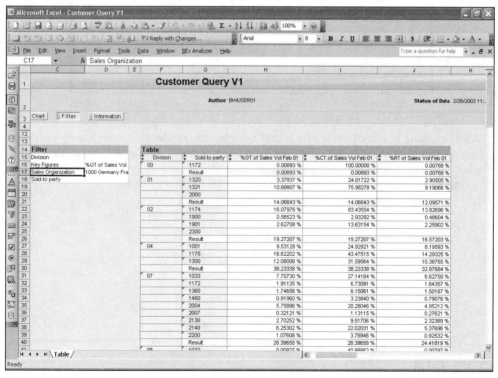

To edit an existing CKF, you would need to access it either from the InfoProvider level or the query level, depending on where it was created. Then you open the Formula Editor and make the necessary changes. Another important concern with editing is the fact that a specific CKF is used in a number of different queries, workbooks, and WADs. Therefore, before you edit the CKF, make sure you confirm what other objects will be effected. You can see where the calculated key figure is used, choose Where-Used List from the context menu. Once you have made your changes, click OK to close and review the results in the actual query.

Another new feature is the ability to create an RKF or CKF directly from within the CKF. For example, let's say a developer is creating the CKF and realizes that he will need another RKF to complete the formula. One of the many ways he can do this is to use the context menu at any section of the formula that has a "space" to create another RKF. The following illustration shows an example of a formula that was created on the query side of the Formula Editor. Here, the developer is in the process of either creating or changing the formula.

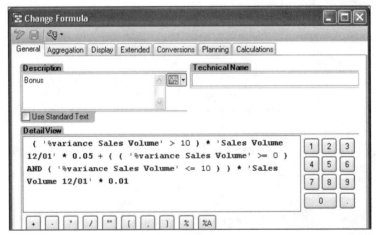

Copyright by SAP AG

Right-clicking in any of the spaces found between the operands causes another series of options to become available. All the options are normal ones, but the fact that a "new selection" or "new formula" can be created directly from this area is new functionality. The following illustration shows the context menu options for this process.

Copyright by SAP AG

Boolean Logic

Another very useful set of functions in the Formula Editor is the Boolean Logic functions. These functions allow you to make comparisons within the formulas and use conditional calculations. The most popular example of Boolean logic is the statement IF, THEN, ELSE. By using this type of function, you don't have to immediately look to ABAP programs or other methods to offer the ability to string these types of conditional formulas together in the Query Designer. The following operators are available:

- **Is less than** <
- **Is less than or equal to** <=
- **In not equal to** <>
- **Is equal to** =
- **Is greater than** >
- **Is greater than or equal to** >=
- **Logical AND** AND

  The result is 1 if both expressions do not equal 0. If this is not the case, the result is 0.

- **Return 1 for single values, 0 for aggregated values** LEAF

  The result for result rows is 0 (aggregated values). Otherwise, the result is 1 (for postable levels).

- **Logical NOT** NOT

  The result is 1 if the expression is 0. Otherwise, the result is 0.

- **Logical OR** OR

  The result is 1 if one or the other expression does not equal 0. If both equal 0, the result is 0.

- **Logical exclusive OR** XOR

  The result is 1 if one or the other expression—but not both—does not equal 0. If both do, the result is 0.

The following illustration shows an example of the use of Boolean logic in the Formula Editor. As you can see, this is a calculation, based on a condition, of bonus amounts based on the sales revenue increase from February. I have also added the NDIV0 data function so that any divisions by zero or negative numbers are calculated to be zero. Therefore, you can read this from left to right as follows:

IF (Percentage Variance in Sales Volume is GREATER THAN 5%) THEN (Total Sales Volume for Feb 2001 multiplied by 10%) AND (Percentage Variance in Sales Volume is GREATER THAN 0%) AND (Percentage Variance in Sales Volume is LESS THAN OR EQUAL TO 10%) THEN (Total Sales Volume for Feb 2001 multiplied by 5%)

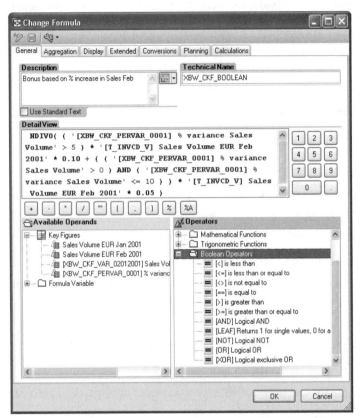

Copyright by SAP AG

As you might suspect, the IF is silent in the initial space of this logic, and the THEN is the multiplication sign (*). The following illustration shows the results of this calculation. Notice that the bonus is 10% of the sales volume for those variances that are over 10% (for example, Sold To Party 1033). For the percentages that are either negative or 0%, the bonus calculation is 0 and not a DIV/0 symbol thanks to the DIV/0 function.

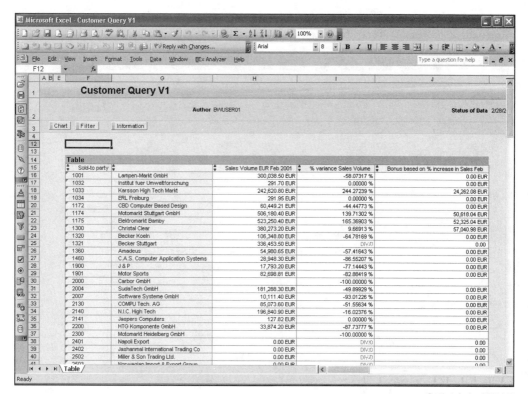

Properties of Key Figures

We have now looked at the use of RKFs, CKFs, and other options within the key figure process. We have another option available to us—to use the key figure properties. In this area many standard parameters replicate the use of RKFs and CKFs, and its normally better to use a system-generated calculation rather than having to create one. This can help to possibly optimize your queries and is also an easier approach to getting the strategic view of the data to the business user. Various components of a query have specific properties that reproduce important functions. These properties can have an effect on the presentation of the key figure, the function, or both.

Before we get into the analysis of all the different key figure properties, I would like to give you an idea of what types of reports can be created using just these properties. To do that, we need to take one of the basic queries we have been working with and identify one key figure that we can use. The following illustration shows a query using just the information for Sales Volume and Incoming Orders.

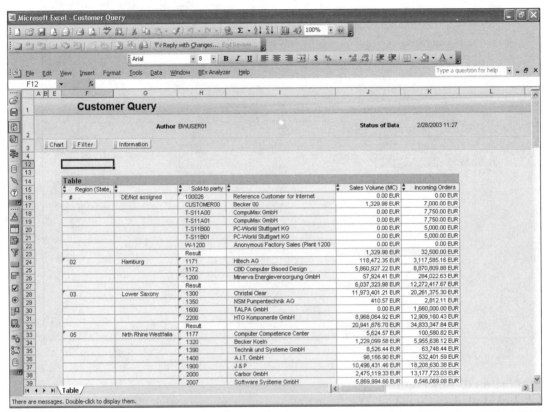

We will use this query and see what additional information we can supply to the business users for their analysis. In this case, we have used the basic key figure for Incoming Orders and changed the parameters in the Calculation tab to facilitate these functions rather than using the actual calculation functions in the Formula Editor. The following illustration shows the use of Incoming Orders with the following additional parameter:

- Calculate Results As – Standard Value
- Calculate Single Values As – Normalization of Overall Results

Note that the box for Also Apply to Results has been checked.

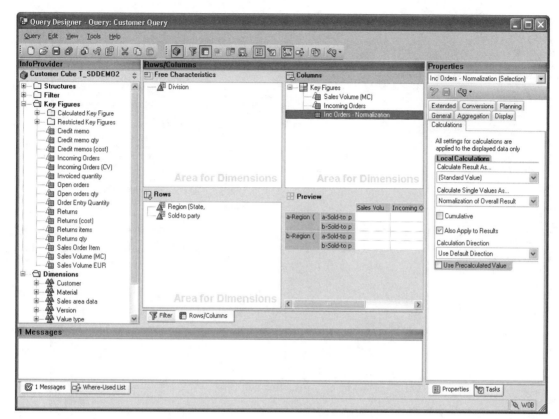

In the next illustration, we are using the same key figure (just copy the key figure three times into the column field) and adjusting the parameters in the Calculation tab (Calculate Single Values As – Ranked List). The box for Also Apply to Results has been checked.

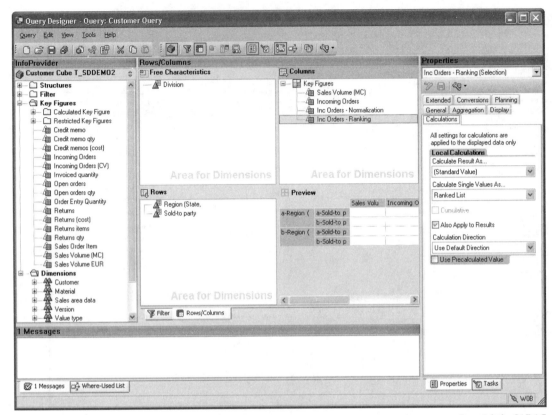

In the following illustration, we are using the same basic key figure, but this time we are changing the parameters in the Calculation tab to Calculate Single Values As – Normalization of Result. The box for Also Apply to Results has been checked.

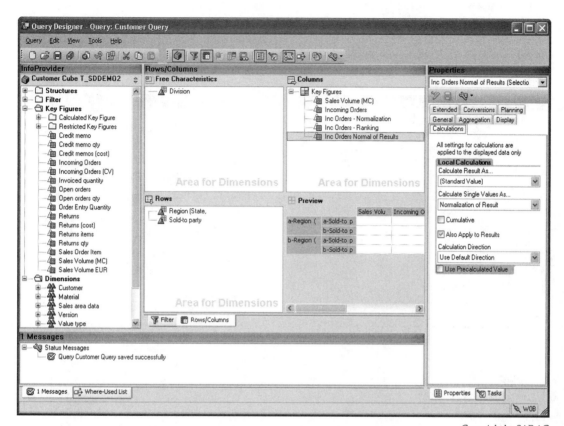

Once we have completed this configuration, we can review the results of our work. One thing to remember here: Much of what we did in the BEx Query Designer can also be accomplished directly in the BEx Analyzer once the query has been executed. The next illustration shows the results of the parameters in the Calculation tab. The third column identified as Normalization has taken the raw data and calculated the percentage of it based on the overall results (thus the naming convention for the parameter). This shows us not only the individual percentages but also the results have been calculated to show the percentage. The next column has taken the raw data for Incoming Orders and has calculated a ranking list based on the sold-to parties. This ranking has occurred based on the region/sold-to party combinations, but the subtotals have been ranked based on the total of the results. Finally, the next column – Inc Orders – Normal of Results – has generated the percentage using the individual line items with percentages that are calculated based on the region/sold-to party combinations, but the results rows calculated based on the total of the query. For example, if we take the initial eight (8) rows you can see that the percentages of the characteristic value combinations total to 100% for Region DE and its Sold-To Parties but if you review the RESULT line you can see that it has a total of 0.012% which reflects the total for the entire query result rather than the total for the percentages that are listed above. This information forms a very powerful initial view of the information around the customers and their purchasing habits within and outside of the regions. All this strategic information is available to the business user without the use of the CKF Formula Editor. Therefore, review the key figure properties before moving to the CKF process. You may find that some of your business requirements are met without creating any calculations.

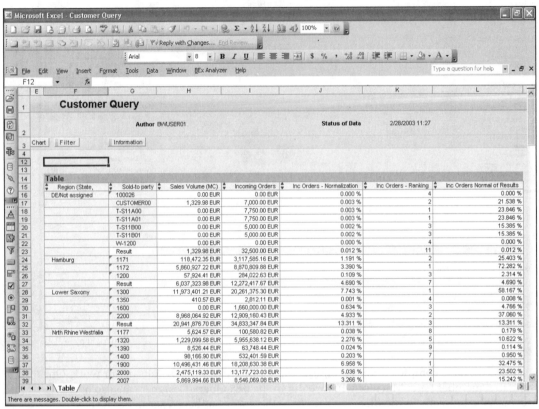

Now, let's look at all the functionality available in the key figure properties. To access these key properties, you can either use the tab "Properties" at the right side of the screen or use the context menu from the specific key figure to display the dialog box for the properties. I will use the context menu for the examples because the display is better and a bit easier to work through versus using the right side of the screen. The following illustration shows the two options. Generally the indicator normally set is Use Default Settings. If this is the option you choose, you will be using the information from the base InfoObject. Once you override the default setting, this check box will automatically be unchecked to show that the setting has been changed and is now nonstandard. It is possible to maintain properties of multiple characteristics simultaneously. Just highlight all the characteristics you want to include. The Properties pane will then display the properties. If there are any conflicts between the different characteristics, you will see the text "Multiple Values Selected" where the setting would normally appear. In this case, you will need to select the individual characteristics to see their respective settings. We will look at each of the tabs of the Key Figure Properties dialog box. Once we work our way through these, we can look at the query and, using just the key figure properties, see what we can come up with for data display. We have already discussed the General tab in the initial RKF section. Table 5-5 provides a breakdown of the functionality in the Key Figure Properties dialog box. I will be emphasizing some of the more complex functions available, such as the Exception Aggregation, Currency Translation, and the Formula Collision.

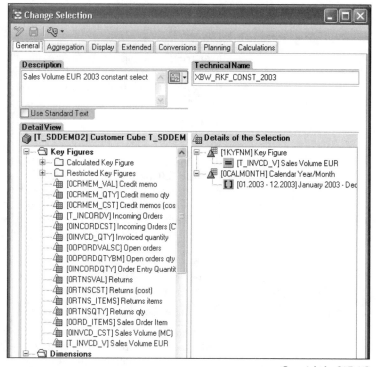

Copyright by SAP AG

> **NOTE** *Remember, it is possible to use the features in Excel to change the name of a characteristic directly in the query. Just click the field so that it is highlighted. You can then type in whatever description you want.*

Tab	Component	Description and Functionality
Aggregation	Exception Aggregation	A more detailed discussion of Exception Aggregation appears later in this chapter.
	Reference Characteristic	A more detailed discussion of Reference Characteristic appears later in this chapter.
Display (see the first illustration at the end of this table)	Hide	You can hide key figures that you only need for calculating formulas and do not want to display. If you hide the key figure, you can still select it in the navigational process and display the results.

TABLE 5-5   Functionality in the Key Figure Properties Tabs

Tab	Component	Description and Functionality
	Highlight	You can choose whether the key figure is to be highlighted in the report. This will allow the presentation tools to identify the key figures that need additional formatting so that the values are clearly shown in the results.
	Number of Decimal Places	You can define the number of decimal places here.
	Scaling Factor	You can set the scaling factor here. This is a nice option if the values in your key figure are large—for example, in the billions. Therefore, identify the scaling factor in the query and reduce the actual display to millions (six zeroes versus nine).
	Sign Change	You have the ability to remove the sign or reverse the sign here.
	Status of Node	Defaults to Not Expandable.
Extended	Enterprise ID	ID for the Enterprise location for the key figure. RKF and CKF have system-generated numbers, whereas the base key figures have a virtual ID. In this field, the unique ID (UID) that is used for unique identification is displayed. This field is only used for information purposes. For example, you can use the UID in URLs of the Web API to address this element. However, I recommend that you use technical names, because UIDs can change when an object is deleted and then created again.
	Constant Selection	You can set Constant Selection here.
Conversions	Currency Translation	In the query, you can set a currency conversion key and a target currency. You can also use a variable to allow the translation setting to be determined at runtime. We will discuss currency translation in more detail later in this chapter.
	Unit Conversion	In the Query Designer, you can set a unit of measure (UOM) conversion key and a target unit. You can also use variables to allow the translation setting to be determined at runtime. We will discuss UOM conversion in Chapter 13.
Planning (see the second illustration at the end of this table)	Change Data	You can define the use of planning in the query. Therefore, you have the ability to change the data directly in the query and post it back to the InfoProvider. This is used in the process of BI-IP more than in the reporting process. You have the ability to set manual input, calculations based on planning functions, or both.

TABLE 5-5   Functionality in the Key Figure Properties Tabs (*continued*)

Tab	Component	Description and Functionality
	Disaggregation	This option allows the use of a calculation to distribute or allocate the values down to more granular levels by use of this executable. This, along with Type of Distribution, identifies how the data is to be distributed.
	Type of Distribution	You can define how the data is to be distributed: • **Equally among the characteristic values** • **Analog distribution (on itself)** Distribution using the current key figure values in combination with a specific characteristic value • **Analog distribution (to following structure elements)** The distribution of the values based on a specific set of characteristic values in combination with the key figure amount
Calculations (applied to display data only—not posted or saved to the InfoCube)	Local Calculations	Similar functions are available directly in the BEx Analyzer (these options were discussed in Chapter 4). The settings can be used to formulate additional calculations specifically within the query once it is executed.
	Cumulative or Also Apply to Results	These two indicators, in conjunction with the calculation settings, define whether the amounts will be specific to the key figure or will be cumulative totals. The results can be applied to the individual lines of data, to the results rows, or both.
	Calculation Direction	Default calculation directions are not always what's expected. You can change the calculation direction as required • Use the default direction (from top to bottom and from left to right) • Calculate along the rows (from top to bottom) • Calculate along the columns (from left to right) Therefore, if the required calculation is to be derived from the row, use the Calculate Along the Rows option. If you're using a column calculation, use the Calculate Along the Columns option.

TABLE 5-5   Functionality in the Key Figure Properties Tabs (*continued*)

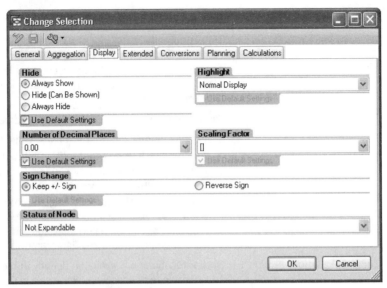

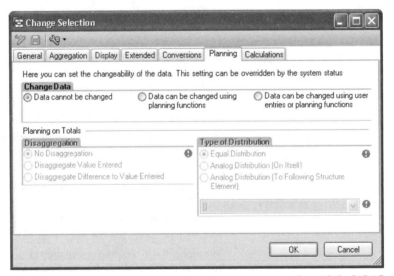

Aggregation

Aggregation is available in the Key Figure Properties dialog box and also in the properties from the BEx Analyzer. This function is only available for formulas and calculated key figures. You can also make settings for aggregation at calculation time (for the detail level of the calculated key figure or formula). By default, the aggregation of the data to the display level takes place first, followed by the calculation of the formula (= standard aggregation). The Exception Aggregation settings allow the formula to be calculated before aggregation, using a reference characteristic, and afterward to be aggregated with exception aggregation. You can select the following settings in the Calculate Result As field if the exception aggregation is Standard.

Use Standard Aggregation   You use this setting to define that aggregation will take place first, followed by the calculation of the formula (therefore, you do not use exception aggregation):

- Total
- Maximum
- Minimum
- Exception, If More Than One Record Occurs
- Exception, If More Than One Value Occurs
- Exception, If More Than One Value <> 0 Occurs
- Average of All Values
- Average of All Values <> 0
- Average for Calendar Days
- Average for Working Days
- Count All Values
- Count All Values <> 0
- First Value
- Last Value
- Standard Deviation
- Variance

NOTE   *You determine the ID of the factory calendar in Customizing. For more information, see the SAP Reference IMG under SAP Customizing Implementation Guide | SAP NetWeaver | Business Intelligence | Reporting-Relevant Settings | General Reporting Settings | Set F4 Help and Hierarchies for Time Characteristics/OLAP Settings.*

There are similar settings for the field Calculate Single Values As. These have been discussed in this and previous chapters. They are available for creating a CKF based on key figure properties only, and not with the aid of a formula. If you use exception aggregation against a CKF, which is a formula, you must select a characteristic from the Reference Characteristic field that the system can use to calculate the formula before aggregation. In the Reference Characteristic field, all characteristics available in the InfoProvider can be selected. This is used for display, and it stipulates that the formula of the calculated key figure is calculated after aggregation. If you use calculated key figures you defined in SAP BW 7.0, you can use this field to determine whether the calculation of the formula takes place before or after aggregation. An example of how you would use this would be that you could display the cumulative calculations for a percentage based on all the values for a particular characteristic. In the following illustration, we are using a calculated key figure (%Share Sold-To Parties) and an exception aggregation (Exception Aggregation – Count All Values) and including the reference characteristic Sold To Party, for further analysis of the Exception Aggregation. There are no additional parameters set for this key figure.

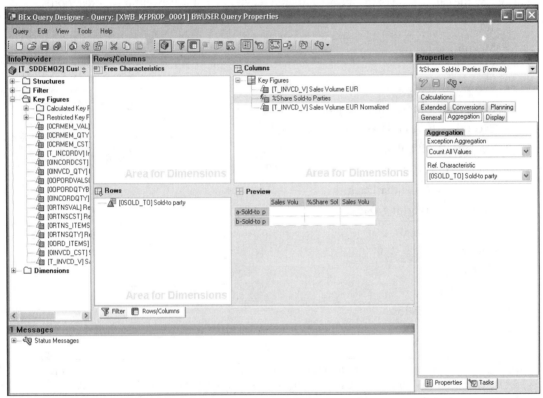

We can then go to the Key Figure Properties dialog box and, using the Calculations tab, set the display to be Count All Values for Exception Aggregation, as shown next.

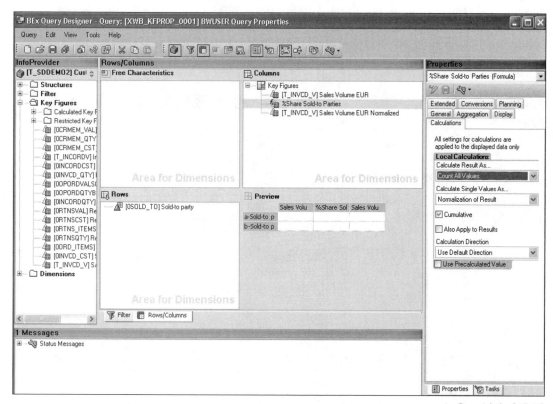

The results of this configuration are shown in the following illustration. Notice that the column %Share Sold-To Parties is a cumulative percentage total of each of the sold-to parties in the list. Therefore, this is a straightforward percentage based on the total number of sold-to parties (each sold-to party has the same percentage no matter what its total sales contribution) versus the next column, which calculates the percentage of sales volume against the total sales volume of all the sold-to parties. This can be helpful in other calculations where you would need to have a fixed percentage of the total number in a group.

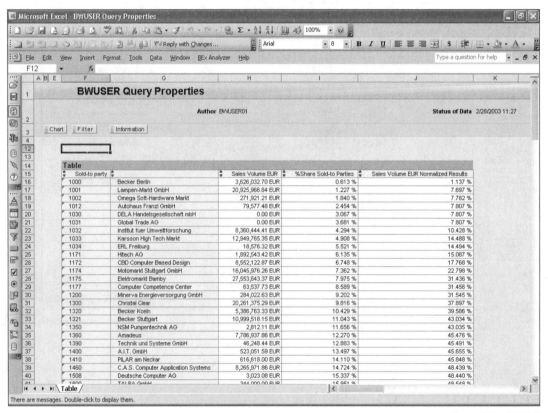

Another example of the use of aggregation is the ability to arrive at the correct results of a query total. As we have discussed, the system has two different types of calculated key figure aggregation: before aggregation and after aggregation. Depending on the formula, these two approaches can give widely different key figure results. The type of aggregation can be set individually on each calculated key figure; however, the system initially sets all key figures to "after aggregation" by default. Therefore, as shown in the following illustration, the Results total seems to be a bit off from what's expected. The Total Sales Volume CKF is showing the calculation from the row and therefore is executing the following calculation at the Results Level:

$$246.931 \times 39{,}516{,}289.24 = 9{,}736{,}458{,}022{,}132.84$$

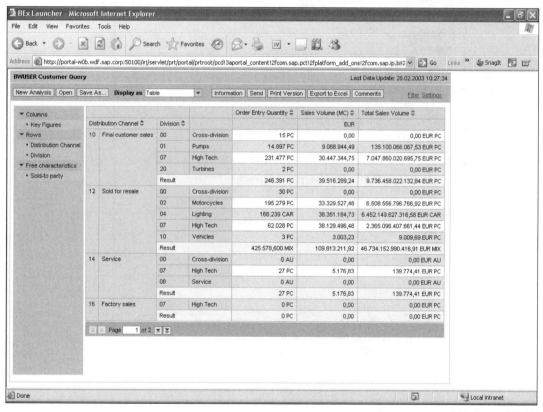

The question is, Is this the correct calculation? The answer to this question is *no*. Due to, in part, the sales volume in some cases being 0, the calculations across the row are incorrect. This is where the ability to change the aggregation to "before" is important. Reviewing the setup of the CKF shows that there is nothing unusual about this formula. The following illustration shows this configuration.

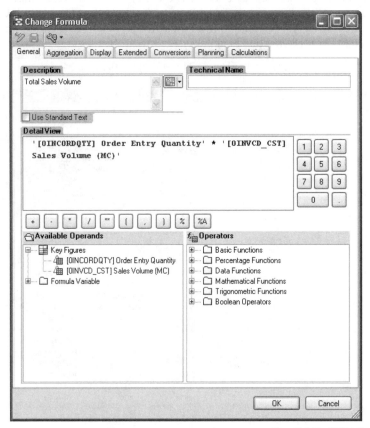

To correct this calculation, we rely on the use of exception aggregation, and the first of the following illustrations shows that we can adjust the calculation by using the Exception Aggregation Total with the Reference Characteristic Region (technical name 0Sold-To Region). The final result of this adjustment is shown in the second illustration. Notice that the Total Sales Volume calculation is done using the amounts in the columns, not the row calculations. This result is consistent with the actual calculations. Needless to say, check the results of your formulas with some real data before you decide that all the calculations are correct and accurate.

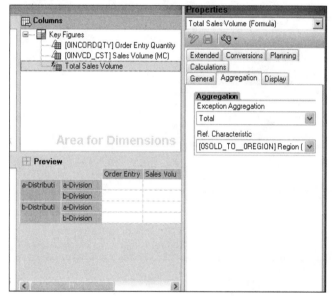

Copyright by SAP AG

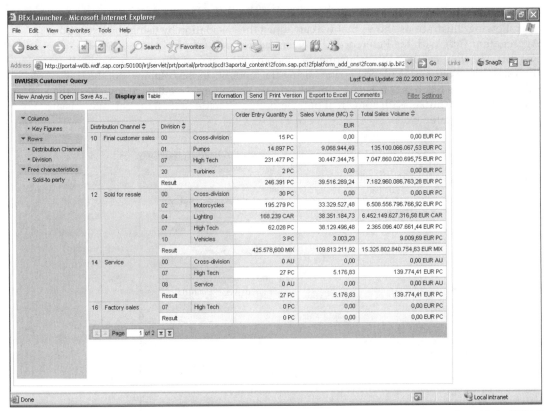

Currency Translation

Currency translation can take place either during the upload of the data into the InfoProvider or during the query process. You either assign the currency translation to the query in configuration or access the currency translation during the execution of the query. There is a significant amount of configuration in the Administration Workbench for currency translation to work correctly. You have to create translation keys for currency translation under SAP Menu | Modeling | Object Maintenance | Currency Translation Keys. This and other steps of back-end configuration are necessary to be able to identify the source and target currencies and have the appropriate translation by date and combination of currencies available for use. Normally you would upload the currency tables from another source system such as ECC or a flat file. Once that has occurred, you will need to review and update a few tables and settings—review the exchange rate types, define the translation ratios for currency translation, confirm that all currency exchange rates have been uploaded, then create your currency translation types. Once all of this is complete, you are ready to use the currency translation process in the queries.

You can set a target currency for a structural component in the Query Designer. Select a translation key in the Translation Key drop-down box. Depending on how the currency translation key has been created, you have the following options:

- **Select the Target Currency When Translating**   The target currency is not fixed in the translation key but can be determined when translating. Select the required translation key and enter the required currency in the Target Currency drop-down box. You can also select a currency from the drop-down box.

- **Fixed Target Currency**   The target currency is determined by the translation key. Select the required translation key with the fixed target currency. In the Target Currency drop-down box, the fixed target currency for this translation key appears.

- **InfoObject Determines Target Currency**   The target currency is determined in the translation key so that it is determined from an InfoObject. Select the required translation key with the target currency from the InfoObject. The text From InfoObject appears in the Target Currency field when you select this translation type.

- **Target Currency from Variable**   In the translation type, a variable is specified for 0CURRENCY. In the Target Currency field, the text From Variable appears during the selection of this translation type.

The following illustration shows the currency translation in the Query Designer. Here you can set up the translation so that once the query is displayed, the appropriate translation has already occurred.

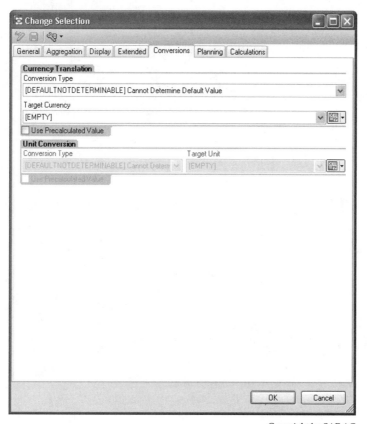

In the next illustration, you have the initial steps in the query itself to use the currency translation process. In the BEx Analyzer, you would have to access the Query Properties node from the context menu. From there, use the Currency Conversion tab to set up your translation.

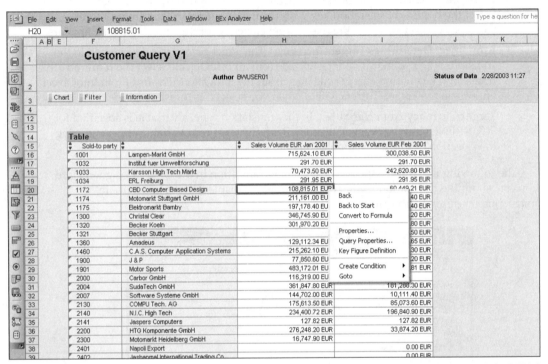

The next illustration shows the Currency Conversion tab in the Query Properties dialog box. In this case, we are translating everything into USD using the translation type Average Rate – Current Date.

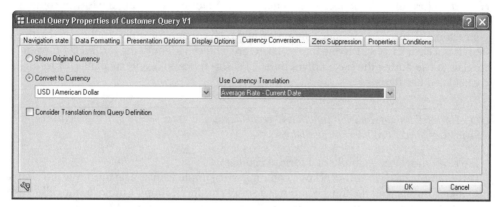

Finally, in the following illustration, you can see the results of the translation process. All the values are converted to the USD ($) values for Average Rate – Current Date, defined in the Administration Workbench.

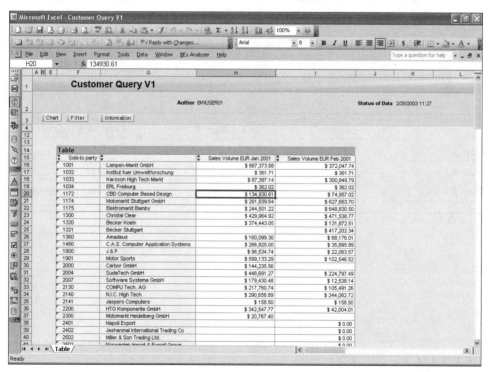

Formula Collisions

One of the results of all the functionality in the Query Designer is that we can have formulas in rows and/or columns. However, this causes an issue with the cells that are at the intersection of conflicting formulas. What does a particular cell do in terms of reading the row or column calculation. The Formula Collision function is only displayed in the Properties dialog box if two structures are used in the query definition and both contain formulas. In these cases, the system is not clear as to which one to use. Therefore, you can identify the formula you want these cells to use during the execution of the query. This function is only available for formulas and calculated key figures.

NOTE *For the Formula Collision function to be available, you must be using two structures. Structures are defined later in this chapter.*

Table 5-6 shows an example of a formula collision.

This example has two rows and two columns with simple values. The third row is a simple summation formula, and the third column is a simple multiplication formula. In the cell where the row and column formulas meet, it is not clear which calculation should be made.

If you calculate according to the column formula in this cell, the cell contains $(A + C) \times (B + D)$. If you calculate according to the rows formula in this cell, the cell contains $(A \times B) + (C \times D)$. Each produces a different result.

If a formula collision occurs, you can, as described in this example, determine which formula is used in the calculation. You can make the following settings in the Trigger Formula Collision field:

- **Nothing defined** If you do not make a definition, the formula that was last saved and defined takes priority in a formula collision.

- **Result of this formula** The result of this formula has priority in a collision.

	Column 1	Column 2	Column 1 × Column 2
Row 1	Value A	Value B	A × B
Row 2	Value C	Value D	C × D
Row 1 + Row 2	A + C	B + D	? Formula Collision?

TABLE 5-6   Formula Collision Example

- **Result of competing formula** The result of a competing formula has priority in a collision.

The following illustration shows the Extended tab in the Key Figure Properties dialog box. It offers the Formula Collision option. The setting Use Result of This Formula is used so that the system can correctly calculate the data.

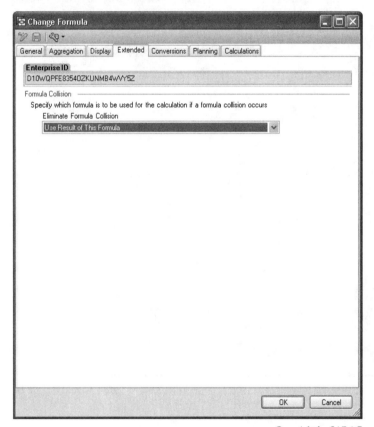

The first of the following two illustrations shows an example in the system of formula collisions. You can see that there are two structures (nodes holding all of the objects) and that we have defined formulas in both. The result of this is shown in the second illustration. In the query results, you can see that the third cell in the column Sales Volume % Share of Incoming Orders is using the formula from the column to calculate the results of the cell.

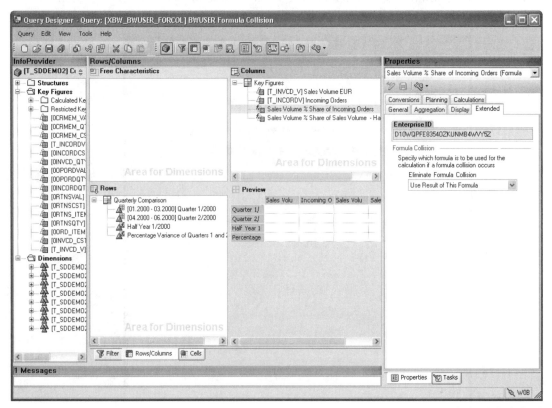

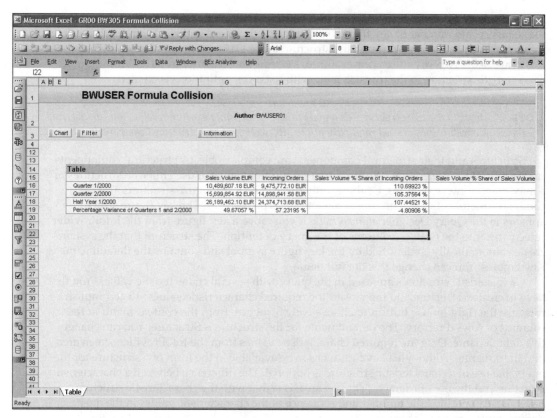

Structures

After you spend all this time going through and creating these great formulas, restrictions, key figure settings, and so on, you'll want to save this information so that others can take advantage of all your hard work. To do this, you create a structure.

A structure forms the basic framework of the axes in a table (rows or columns). It consists of structural components. We differentiate between key figure structures and characteristic structures. Structural components of key figure structures are always based on the key figure selections (basic key figures, restricted key figures, and calculated key figures). These are structures *with* key figures. Characteristic structural components cannot contain key figure selections (structures *without* key figures). The setup of the structure determines the sequence and number of key figures or characteristic values in the columns and rows of the query. You can navigate through the structure in the executed query and set filters for it. If you are using two structures (for example, a key figure structure in the columns and a characteristic structure in the rows), a table with fixed cell definitions is created.

NOTE *You have to use two structures as a prerequisite for defining exception cells. You can override the value of cell values created implicitly at the intersection of two structural components.*

Structures and their structural components are complex objects. Structural components can be formulas or selections. Within a query definition, you can use either no structures or a maximum of two structures. Of these, only one can be a key figure structure. You can combine structures freely with other characteristics on the axes. The key figure structure appears in the Query Designer *automatically* if you move a key figure from the InfoProvider screen area into the rows or columns of the query definition. The structure that the system creates automatically is identified by the key figure symbol and contains the default name Key Figures. You can change this default name.

Characteristic structures are used in the query with several characteristic values. You first have to create a structure and then insert the required characteristic values. To accomplish this, use the right mouse button to choose New Structure from the context menu in the columns or rows directory. The default name for the structure is Structure. You can change this default name. Drag the required characteristic values from the InfoProvider screen area into the structure. Although a key figure has to be available in the form of a structure for the query, the use of a characteristic structure is optional. The difference between a characteristic structure and the use of characteristics on an axis is that with the characteristic structure, you have already specified the number and sequence of the characteristic values in the query definition. If you use a characteristic on an axis, all posted characteristic values for the characteristic are displayed in the query. You can restrict the selection of specific characteristic values by setting a filter.

Another available option with structures is that you can copy them and reuse the components. The components of key figure structures often contain very complex objects that are made up of formulas or selections. If you want to reuse the definition of a structural component within a structure, you can copy the structural component, paste it into the structure, and continue to work with it. This enables you to create similarly structured structural components quickly and easily. From the context menu of the structural component, choose Copy. Then, from the context menu of the structure, choose Insert. You can also copy structural components using temporary storage locations (CTRL-C, CTRL-V). Once you have completed the configuration of the structures, you can then save them to the InfoProvider level for reuse in any query assigned to the particular InfoProvider. These structures are called *reusable structures*. The following illustration shows a query in the Query Designer with two structures, and the context menu from the node of the structure is being used to perform a Save As operation.

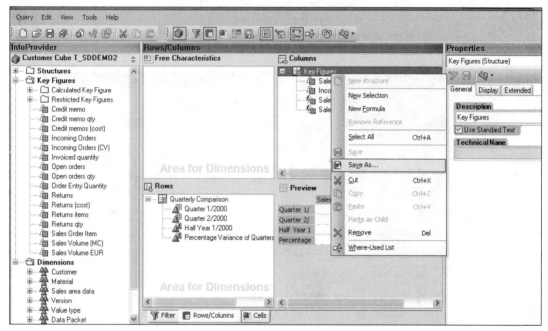

Copyright by SAP AG

You will then see a dialog box requesting that you assign a technical name and text, as shown in the first of the following two illustrations. After completing this task, click OK to save. The result is shown in the second illustration.

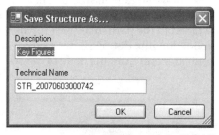

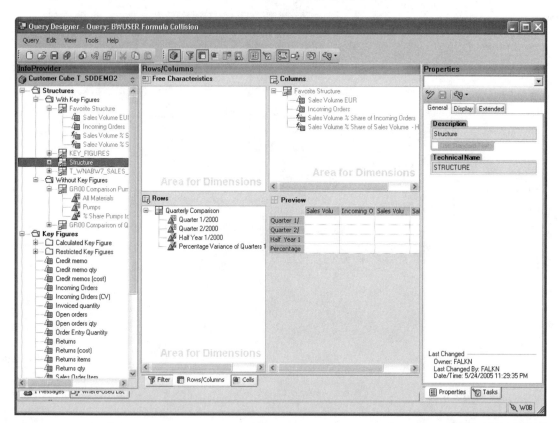

The structure named Favorite Structure is now stored at the InfoProvider level and is available for all other query builders. This is a very good option because many times you will have created a P&L statement or will have worked through business requirements and will use this specific combination of key figures and characteristics in the future. Notice the two nodes With Key Figures and Without Key Figures; these are the nodes referred to in the prior discussion. You can also make changes to the structures without affecting all the queries using the structure. If you need to change a portion of the structure for your specific query, drag and drop the structure into your query and then in the context menu at the Key Figure level select Remove Reference. This allows you to change the structure without changing the "global" definition. The next illustration shows the context menu for the Remove Reference option.

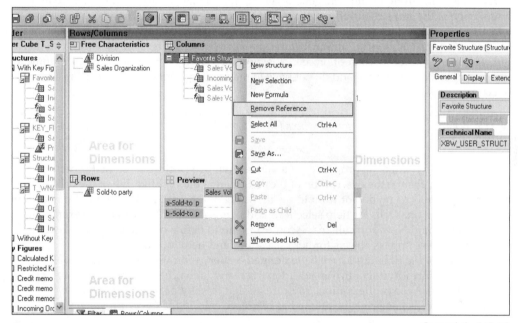

Copyright by SAP AG

NOTE *The Remove Reference function is currently not active. Therefore, to use the structures without changing the global definition, you will need to choose the structure and, rather than using the Remove Reference option, use the Save As function and then make the changes to your saved copy. This particular function will be active in a future support pack.*

Cell Editor

In certain situations where you need to define each specific cell of a query, you may need to use the Cell Editor. For example, suppose you are looking to create a query that has the divisions listed in a particular manner and you want to hold all the divisions in the list, even though there are months where certain divisions don't have any sales or data. This may be a reason for using the Cell Editor. The Cell Editor allows you to directly define specific cells in the query via the Query Designer. If you define selection criteria and formulas for structural components and there are two structural components of the query, generic cell definitions are created at the intersection of the structural components that determine the values to be presented in the cells. Cell-specific definitions allow you to define explicit formulas and selection conditions for cells as well as implicit cell definitions. This means you can override cell values. This function allows you to design much more detailed queries. In addition, you can define cells that have no direct relationship to the structural components (virtual key figures). These cells are not displayed and serve as containers for help selections or help formulas. The prerequisite for this is that the query must have two structures.

NOTE *A cell is an intersection of two structures in a query definition.*

A new cell reference is a cell you have defined that can be reused in a formula. If you want to reuse the value from the implicit, generic cell definition that is automatically created at the intersection of the two structural components of a query, select this cell in the Cell screen area and, using the secondary mouse button, choose New Cell Reference. A description taken from the two structural components automatically appears in the cell. The symbol shows you that a cell reference exists for this exception cell. Now you can reference this cell. You can continue to use the implicit cell definition and do not have to manually generate this value using a new selection.

NOTE *Before you delete a cell, you can check for the formulas in which the defined cell is used in the Where-Used List.*

You can also change the properties of a defined cell by selecting it. In the Properties screen, you can change the description of the cell, change the highlighting of the cell, and even hide the cell (if you do not want to see the value of the cell). In the Help Cells area, you can define additional cells for help selections and help formulas. You can use the functions New Selection and New Formula in the context menu to define help cells not displayed in the query to serve only as objects for help selections and help formulas.

In the following illustration, we have defined a query (you've seen this query before) with two structures. You'll notice an additional screen that has been created. The tab Cells is available to use in the configuration. You can see that this is a preview of the query. Currently two cells have been positioned as reference cells in the query preview. At the bottom of the screen you can see the option to create help cells. As mentioned, these cells store formulas for use in the query and do not automatically display in the query.

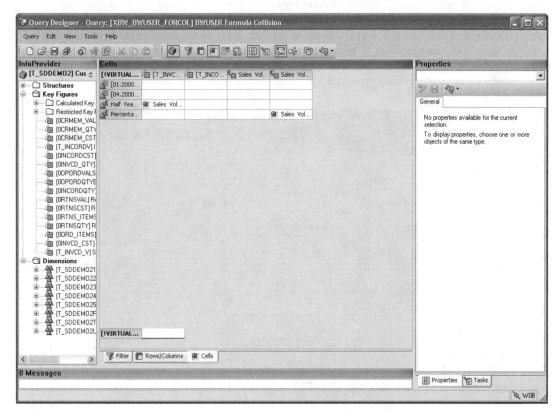

The next illustration shows the context menu from the reference cells. The options are New Cell Reference, New Selection (creates a new RKF), and New Formula (creates a new CKF). In the case of the New Selection or New Formula option, you would be changing the information that this particular cell displays. Therefore, you would be creating a specific calculation for this cell to use. If you are going to do this, make sure sufficient documentation is available for the business user to recognize this fact. If you use the New Cell Reference option, you are not changing the data that the particular cell is displaying but rather allowing more flexibility in creating other formulas.

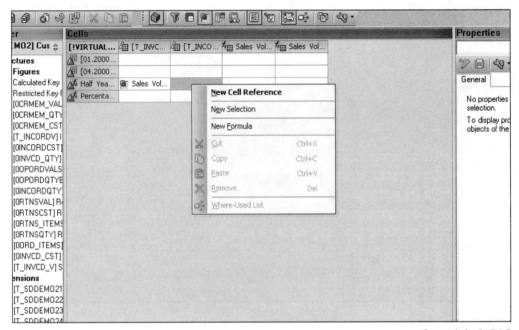

Copyright by SAP AG

The next illustration shows the use of the cell reference by creating two additional cell references and showing the functionality of the help cells. These help cells can store either RKFs or CKFs.

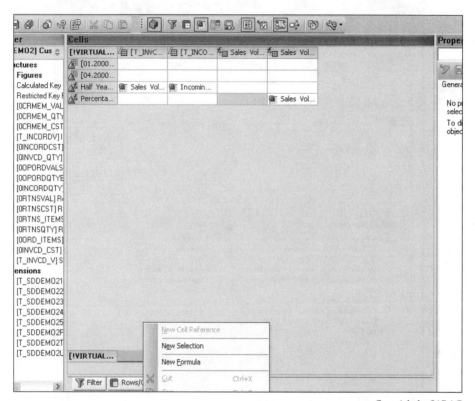

In the final illustration, we are in the Formula Editor and the cell references are available for us to use in creating additional calculated key figures. These can be identified by the node in which they are stored—Cells. This functionality might never be something you need, but if at any time an unusual request for a query design is requested, think Cell Editor.

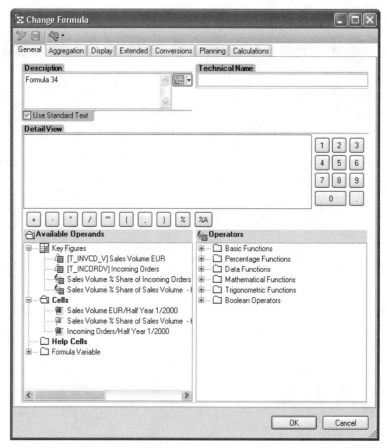

Summary

With the combination of all these different calculation functions included in the BEx Query Designer for building formulas—the Cell Editor, currency translation, exception aggregations, Percentage functions, Boolean Logic functions, Data functions, restricted key figures (both individually and included in the calculated key figures), plus the functionality directly used in the BEx Analyzer, you have a powerful tool set for creating effective queries. Having worked with BW for quite some time, I can say that the functionality and flexibility of this version of the Query Designer in the use of the key figures is excellent. Although many options were demonstrated in this chapter, still many others are available—and depending on your needs, they may come in handy. If you have access to a system, the best approach to working with all these options is to experiment with data that is consistent and familiar to you so that the outcome to all these different calculations will be easier to test and confirm.

Enhancing the Use of the Characteristics in the BEx Query Designer

We have now covered quite a bit of information and material. You have seen what we can do with the functionality of the key figures, directly in the BEx Query Analyzer. We've worked with the BEx Query Designer and have touched on some of the system configuration options in addition to these for queries. Unlike in the previous chapter, where we were almost completely in the BEx Query Designer, in this chapter we will step into the Business Administration Workbench and review the characteristic InfoObjects and their attributes, and then we'll look at the use of hierarchies in BW. We will review these in different portions of the chapter. In between these two topics, we will cover other activities you can do with characteristics, such as creating variables. We will also look at setting up and executing exceptions and conditions, and finish our discussion on personalization. We talked a little bit about the use of characteristics and their attributes in the process of creating queries and I held off going through the details of the attributes in the initial chapters so that we could get up and running on the functionality of queries before we discuss the use of characteristic attributes. The attributes we'll discuss are those that start within the configuration of the characteristic—the use of navigational attributes. I once heard someone define a navigational attribute as an attribute you turn on if you've made a mistake in the architecture of the InfoCube and need to have another object available for reporting, just like the characteristic. That definition is as far from the truth as you can get. There are specific reasons for turning on navigational attributes in the InfoObject, then continuing the process and turning them on in the InfoProvider configuration. So, based on that you know, this is a two-step process: First, identify the navigational attributes in the InfoObject configuration that you would like to use in the reporting process and turn them on at that time. Second, turn them on in the InfoProvider at the time of configuration. These are the mechanics of using navigational attributes, but the reasons for doing so are a bit more involved. We will talk briefly about one reason to turn on these attributes, but a full discussion would be more appropriate when we cover the architecture of the back-end objects.

If we look at the functionality of the navigational attribute, we can identify some of the benefits of these components and thus understand the need to turn them on. A navigational attribute can be used in the same manner as a characteristic in the query. As mentioned in an earlier chapter, the navigational attribute can be identified in the Query Designer if you turn on the technical names of the objects in the InfoCube. You can see that the navigational attributes are those that have a double-characteristic naming convention. You can see this in the following illustration. Notice that in this dimension there are three objects—0SOLD_TO, 0SOLD_TO__0REGION, and 0SOLD_TO__0COUNTRY—that you see from the BEx Query Designer. Therefore, the root characteristic is first in the list, and the navigational attribute is the second technical name in the list (for example, 0CUSTOMER__0CUSTOMER_GROUP). In many cases, if you are interested in tracking and reporting on a specific object that changes over time, you would activate the navigational attribute process. In other situations, we were using a specific method of reporting on a characteristic, and to get a true picture of the total inventory, we have to use an attribute so that we can group together the information. Therefore, we use a navigational attribute to accomplish this process, basically consolidating the information.

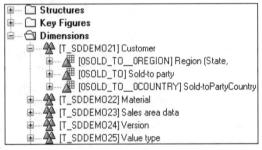

Copyright by SAP AG

NOTE *In this example, a specific material is identified with two different technical names for different parts of the world. Therefore, we need to report on these materials at the global level. We use a navigational attribute to "link" these two different numbers under one global numbering system and thus are able to report by that "link" attribute.*

This is just one situation where a navigational attribute is useful. Another more common use is to report on a grouping type characteristic, such as material group, customer group, or profit center group. These characteristics are attributes of the root characteristic, and we can use this integration between different InfoObjects to help us report. Therefore, reporting on the material group rather than the material can offer different views of the data.

Characteristics and Navigational Attributes

To start this process, we can look at a characteristic that is used quite a bit and definitely has navigational attributes as a part of the standard business content. The following illustration shows the initial step of getting to the attribute list of the InfoObject SOLD_TO. Notice that 0SOLD_TO is a reference InfoObject to 0CUSTOMER. Therefore you, in fact, use the tables of 0CUSTOMER for this InfoObject.

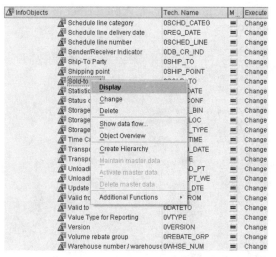

Copyright by SAP AG

In the next illustration, you can see the list of attributes and the indicator box checked for specific attributes, such as 0COUNTRY being a navigational attribute. Type (NAV) is turned on as Navigational, and you can see that the check box for time dependency has also been turned on for this object.

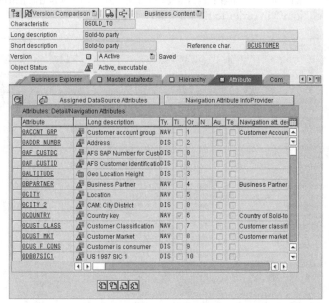

Copyright by SAP AG

Once the list of navigational attributes is identified, we can move to the next step. Go to the InfoProvider (in this case an InfoCube) and turn on the use of the navigational attributes. The following illustration shows the view of the dimension that stores the characteristics for Customer. Notice that there is only one characteristic—0SOLD_TO—in the Customer dimension viewed from this InfoCube approach. A bit further in this discussion you will see the final step in this setup process.

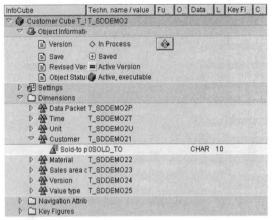

Let's look at the navigational attributes that have been turned on in the InfoCube. In the first illustration, there are no navigational attributes turned on, but in the second you can see that 0SOLD_TO_0COUNTRY has its box checked. From a technical viewpoint from the query side, during the data selection for the query, the data manager connects the InfoProvider and the master data table ("join") in order to fill the query.

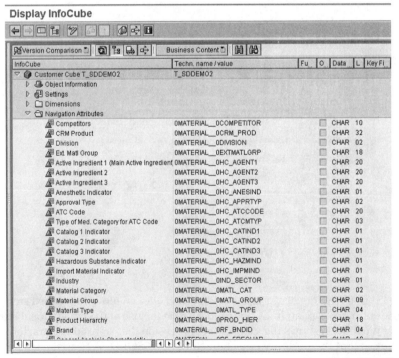

Display InfoCube

InfoCube	Techn. name / value	Fu	O	Data	L	Key Fi
Predefined Source	0MATERIAL__0RT_PRRULE		☐	CHAR	01	
Season	0MATERIAL__0RT_SEASON		☐	CHAR	04	
Season Year	0MATERIAL__0RT_SEAYR		☐	CHAR	04	
Size	0MATERIAL__0RT_SIZE		☐	CHAR	18	
Source of Supply	0MATERIAL__0RT_SUPS		☐	CHAR	01	
Industry Standard Description	0MATERIAL__0STD_DESCR		☐	CHAR	18	
Type of Certificate Requirement	0MATERIAL__0UCCERTIFTY		☐	CHAR	02	
Construction Class	0MATERIAL__0UCCONSTCLA		☐	CHAR	08	
Function Class	0MATERIAL__0UCFUNCCLAS		☐	CHAR	08	
Vendor	0MATERIAL__0VENDOR		☐	CHAR	10	
Customer Account Group	0SOLD_TO__0ACCNT_GRP		☐	CHAR	04	
Business Partner Number for Sold-to Par	0SOLD_TO__0BPARTNER		☐	CHAR	10	
0SOLD_TO__0CITY	0SOLD_TO__0CITY		☐	CHAR	35	
Country of Sold-to Party	0SOLD_TO__0COUNTRY		☑	CHAR	03	
Customer classification	0SOLD_TO__0CUST_CLASS		☐	CHAR	02	
Customer market	0SOLD_TO__0CUST_MKT		☐	CHAR	04	
D&B D-U-N-S Number	0SOLD_TO__0DBDUNS_NUM		☐	NUMC	09	
0SOLD_TO__0DBEMPTOT	0SOLD_TO__0DBEMPTOT		☐	NUMC	07	
Industry of the sold-to party	0SOLD_TO__0INDUSTRY		☐	CHAR	04	
Key Account	0SOLD_TO__0KEYACCOUNT		☐	CHAR	01	
Nielsen ID	0SOLD_TO__0NIELSEN_ID		☐	CHAR	02	
Branch category	0SOLD_TO__0OUTL_TYPE		☐	CHAR	04	
Postal Code	0SOLD_TO__0POSTAL_CD		☐	CHAR	10	
Region (state, county)	0SOLD_TO__0REGION		☑	CHAR	03	
0SOLD_TO__0SALESEMPLY	0SOLD_TO__0SALESEMPLY		☐	NUMC	08	
Pre-defined call frequency	0SOLD_TO__0VISIT_RYT		☐	CHAR	04	

Copyright by SAP AG

A bit of a caution concerning the use of navigational attributes: Extensive use of navigation attributes leads to a large number of tables in the connection ("join") during the selection and can impede the performance of the deletion and creation of navigation attributes (construction of attribute SID tables). This can also affect changes in the time-dependency of navigation attributes (construction of attribute SID tables) for time dependency the loading of master data (adjustment of attribute SID tables), and the calling up of input help for a navigation attribute and the execution of queries. Therefore, only change those attributes into navigation attributes that you really need for reporting. Technically speaking, it is sometimes appropriate to manually create additional indexes for master data tables, to improve system performance for queries with navigation attributes. As a typical scenario, suppose you encounter performance problems during the selection of characteristic values—for example, in BEx queries containing navigation attributes, where the corresponding master data table is large (more than 20,000 entries). In such a case, there is usually a restriction placed on the navigation attributes. We talked about the use of transitive attributes from the navigational attributes in a previous chapter, so I will just comment that this is another option in the use of attributes that you might investigate, depending on the system architecture you have developed.

NOTE *If a characteristic was included in an InfoCube as a navigation attribute, it can be used for navigation in queries. This characteristic can itself have further navigation attributes, called* transitive attributes. *These attributes are not automatically available for navigation in the query. As described in Chapter 2, they must be switched on.*

Characteristic Properties

In this section, we will be looking at the characteristic properties from the point of view of the BEx Query Designer rather than the BEx Analyzer. Because quite a few of the different options are similar, we will only go into additional detail for the ones specific to the BEx Query Designer.

In the Characteristic Properties dialog box for a specific characteristic, you can set a range of functions. These settings affect all the key figures for this characteristic in a query drilldown. Even though these can all be set at their default settings here, they are still available to be changed in the executed state of the query. The following illustration shows the initial view of the different tabs available for this topic. In the General tab, the name of the characteristic appears automatically. You can overwrite this text. The new text is different from the text provided in InfoObject maintenance and is used in the query display. The check box Use Standard Text offers you the ability to indicate that the default value is always used. In this case, the standard text is the text from the characteristic determined in InfoObject maintenance. The technical name of the characteristic is also displayed in this tab.

Copyright by SAP AG

The Display tab offers a number of options. In the Value Display section you have Display As. Here you can determine whether and in which format you want to present the individual values of the characteristic. Here are your options:

- **No Display**   The characteristic display is hidden. This function is useful, for example, with the currency/unit characteristic because the currencies are also shown in the key figures.
- **Key and Text**   The characteristic values are displayed by their technical key and text.
- **Text**   The characteristic values are displayed by their text.
- **Key**   The characteristic values are displayed by their technical key.
- **Text and Key**   The characteristic values are displayed by their text and technical key.

If you set a display type that contains text, you can choose which text type you want to set under Text View. The following options are available:

- **Standard**   The shortest available text for the characteristic values is used as the text.
- **Short text**   The short text for the characteristic values is used as the text.
- **Long text**   The long text for the characteristic values is used as the text.
- **Medium text**   The medium text for the characteristic values is used as the text.

In the Sorting section of the Display tab, you can set the sorting within the characteristic according to the key or text in ascending or descending order. If a characteristic has attributes, you can sort the characteristic by attribute. The attribute involved does not have to be selected for the display. Under Sort Characteristic you can choose the characteristic or the required attribute. Under Sort By, choose Key or Text. Choose Ascending or Descending under Sort Direction.

NOTE *Let's say you want to sort your articles according to specific criteria. To do this you create an attribute for the Article characteristic that contains these criteria. Then you are able to sort the articles by this attribute.*

The values are sorted as they are defined in the query definition by default. If you have not specified a filter value in the query definition, the system sorts the values according to the key.

In the Characteristic Setting dialog box, you can specify that the default value is always used. In this case, the default value is the setting from the characteristic determined in InfoObject maintenance. In the Results Rows section, you can choose whether the results row is Always Displayed, Always Suppressed, or Displayed with More Than One Single Value. Display with More Than One Single Value means that the result rows are displayed when there are at least two single values and any results row is suppressed that aggregates only one value.

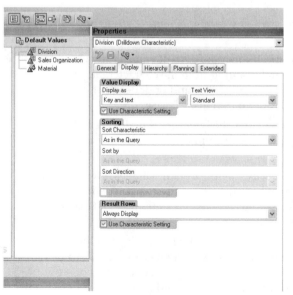

In such a case, the value and the result are identical, and the results row repeats the same value. We will see an example of the use for this later in this chapter. Decisions made in the Results Rows section are more debatable than you might think. The illustration at left shows a view of these options.

The next tab, Hierarchy, is for hierarchical display. To show this in change mode, we will use 0material to view the options. You can present the characteristic as a hierarchy. If you choose to select a hierarchy, it is flagged automatically as an active presentation hierarchy. If you deactivate the Activate Hierarchy Display check box, the characteristic is not displayed in the query as a hierarchy but as a basic list. If you restrict the characteristic to a hierarchy node, the node hierarchy is adopted automatically as the presentation hierarchy. You can deactivate the presentation hierarchy here if necessary. The following illustration shows a view of these different functionalities.

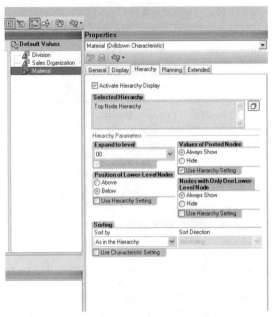

In the Hierarchy Parameters section, each hierarchy has certain properties you specify in the hierarchy definition. You can override the following hierarchy properties for the current hierarchy:

- **Expand to Level**   Choose up to which hierarchy level the hierarchy is to be displayed when it is expanded.

- **Use Hierarchy Setting**   Here you can specify that the default value is always used. In this case, the default value is the hierarchy setting from the characteristic determined in InfoObject maintenance. This option is found under each of the options for display and has a very similar definition in each case.

- **Position of Lower-level Nodes**   Select whether the lower-level nodes are to be positioned above or below. For example, choose the option Above if you want to see the overall result at the bottom.

- **Use Hierarchy Setting**   Here you can specify that the default value is always used. In this case, the default value is the hierarchy setting from the characteristic determined in InfoObject maintenance. As you can see, this option is available for each item in the tab, and its use is very similar in each case.

- **Values of Posted Nodes**   Select whether you want to always display or hide the values of posted nodes. In hierarchies, nodes always display the aggregated values of the subordinate nodes and leaves. If a node has a posted value, you cannot see this. To display this posted value, an additional leaf is inserted that has the same name as the node. This leaf displays the value posted to the node.

NOTE   *In the following illustration, you see that for Cost Center A1, an additional leaf has been added and the value of Cost Center A1 itself (10) is displayed. This additional leaf does not exist in the hierarchy. You can display or hide this leaf (with the value of the posted node). We will run into this situation again during our discussion of the configuration of hierarchies, but this offers you the application functionality.*

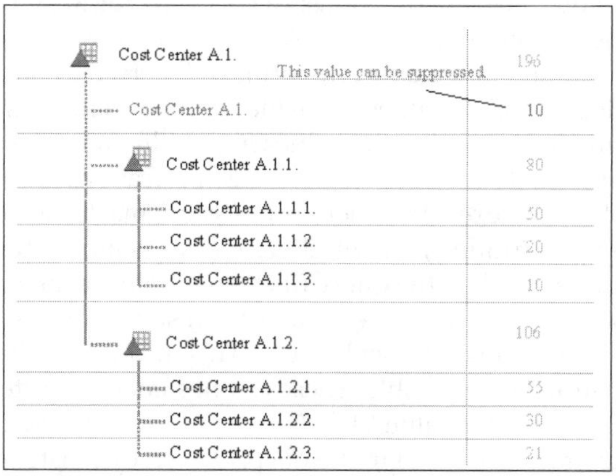

Copyright by SAP AG

- **Use Hierarchy Setting**   Here you can specify that the default value is always used. In this case, the default value is the hierarchy setting from the characteristic determined in InfoObject maintenance.

- **Nodes with Only One Lower-level Node**   Select whether you want to always display or hide the values of posted nodes. Hiding nodes with only one lower-level node helps you to reach the more detailed information quickly. In Figure 6-1, Cost Center A and Cost Center A.1 contain the same information because Cost Center A has only one lower-level node in the hierarchy. If you are interested in the detailed data for the individual cost centers, you can hide the uppermost node with only one lower-level node because this does not contain any additional information.

FIGURE 6-1
Lower-level node
structure

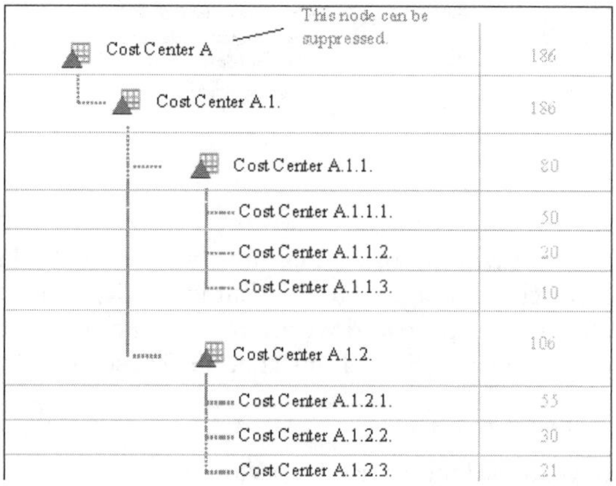

Copyright by SAP AG

- **Sort Settings** You can set the sorting within the hierarchy according to the key or text in ascending or descending order. If you do not make any entries, the values are sorted as determined in the hierarchy. Depending on the option you choose here, the other field for Sort Direction will offer you the ability to sort in ascending or descending order.

In the Extended tab, you can set two options: Access Type for Result Values and Query Execution for Filter Values Selection. In terms of Access Type for Result Values, you are affecting the result set identified in the query. In terms of Query Execution for Filter Values Selection, you are affecting the set of values available for the business user to choose from for navigation. This setting indicates that the values in the filter area are always unique at runtime. This setting is especially required in planning applications. You can also determine which data the value help in the executed query is based on: master data, fact table, or dimension table. Generally, at runtime, the selection of filter values in the value help is determined from the data selected by the query (fact table). This means that only the values for which data has been selected in the current navigation status are displayed. In many cases, it can make sense to include additional values. This means that the settings Master Data and Dimension Table are also possible. These settings enable shorter access time. However, after the selection of filter values, the "No data found" message may occur. This would occur if we wanted to see the data in the query driven by master data rather than transactional data. This is a key enhancement in the 7.0 version of BI to help with unique reporting requirements. The following illustration shows these components.

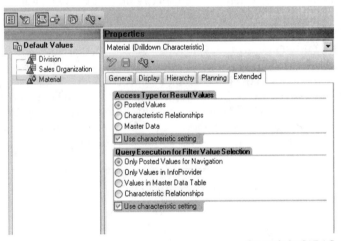

Copyright by SAP AG

The final tab we will discuss is Planning, shown next. The setting here is only available if a display hierarchy is assigned to the characteristic, which means that an actual hierarchy is to be used for this purpose and we are not using a presentation hierarchy. We will discuss this in detail in the next section of this chapter. These options for this setting are

- No Budgeting
- Bottom-Up Budgeting (Roll Up Value)

- Top-Down Budgeting (Posting to Higher-level Nodes)
- Top-Down Budgeting (Posting to Root Node)

These options are new to the BI environment and are available after SP11. They identify the methodology for how the values are rolled up and/or managed. Therefore, if you choose any of the options for budgeting, the hierarchy will roll up the budget and post to a higher-level node or the root node, or will just roll up the values. With budgeting, we are managing the values that are posted, and error messages are generated if the amount entered exceeds the total value at the upper nodes.

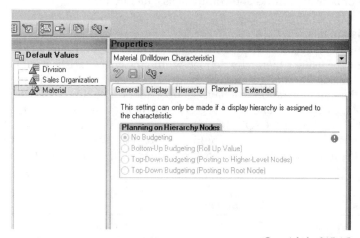

Hierarchies

Hierarchies are useful for managing the positioning of the characteristic values and thus the display of the key figure values. Hierarchies are a set display of characteristic values in the manner in which the business user is required to view them. You can increase the clarity of your reports by arranging characteristics and key figures in a hierarchical format. Therefore, you can develop a hierarchy to satisfy an alternative view of the data that is of interest to the business user. Display hierarchies are created in Administration Workbench and are assigned/attached to an InfoObject. A number of steps are involved in creating a hierarchy and identifying what type of hierarchy you are interested in using. You can have a hierarchy against characteristics, key figures, or both, in one query. You can also have multiple hierarchies used in either the rows or columns, and you can combine hierarchies with individual characteristics in a query. The hierarchies for key figures are a bit more flexible and are created in the BEx Query Designer. The hierarchies for characteristics can be created in the BEx Query Designer or against the InfoObject itself in the Administration Workbench of BI. We will discuss both options, and I offer suggestions for their uses. To assign terminology to these hierarchies, we have a *display hierarchy* (created against the InfoObject in the Administration Workbench) and a *presentation hierarchy* (created in the BEx Query Designer).

SAP NetWeaver Business Intelligence offers different options for modeling hierarchical structures. We will be focusing on the characteristic hierarchy. Table 6-1 gives you an overview.

The appropriate type of modeling depends on each individual case. The modeling types differ, for example, with regard to the following factors: how data is stored in the source system, performance, authorization checks, the use of aggregates, and whether parameters can be set for the query.

In addition, you can organize the elements of a structure hierarchically in the query definition. Display hierarchies for characteristics are not required for these functions. You can display one or both axes (rows and columns) as a hierarchy.

Presentation Hierarchies

Our initial discussion will cover creating hierarchies within the BEx Query Designer. This means we will not be using a hierarchy defined within the characteristic itself but rather one defined directly during the configuration of the query. We start with a basic query design, as shown in the following illustration. We have set up a query with three characteristics in the rows: 0DIVISION, 0SOLD_TO, and 0SOLD_TO__0REGION. You now know that the last characteristic, 0SOLD_TO__0REGION, is really a navigational attribute. It looks like a characteristic, works like a characteristic, but is not a part of the InfoCube structure but rather a part of the InfoObject structure. We have turned on the functionality for it being

Hierarchy Type	Description
Characteristic hierarchy—Hierarchy Definition for Characterisitics	Characteristic values in a tree structure. Characteristic hierarchies are stored in their own data tables. Like master data, they can be used in all InfoProviders. Example: A hierarchy of cost centers assembled in cost center groups.
In the dimensions of an InfoCube—Determining Hierarchical Structures in an InfoCube Modeling	In a time dimension, the definitions of InfoObjects OCALDAY, OCALMONTH, and OCALYEAR form a hierarchy. Example: 04.09.2003 | 04.2003 | 2003
In the attributes of a characteristic—Specification of Hierarchical Structures in an InfoCube Maintenance	The definitions of InfoObjects OMATERIAL, OMATL_GROUP, OMATL_TYPE, and OIND_SECTOR form a hierarchy. To use attributes in the query as hierarchy levels, you have to define them as navigation attributes.

TABLE 6-1   Hierarchy Types in BI

a navigational attribute. That being said, we can now define this as a presentation hierarchy by changing the setting in the properties of the Query Designer.

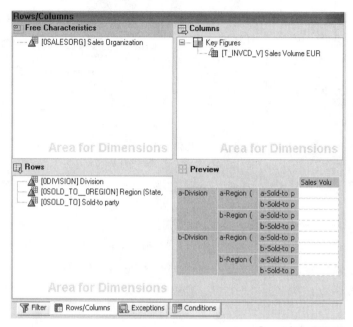

The first of the following illustrations displays the settings. To begin, you will need to highlight the "ROW" line. Once you have done this, review the settings presented in the Properties area on the pane to the right. You will see the Active option under the General tab in the Display as Hierarchy field. You will also see the setting to define the level as initially expanded. As you can see, we have made "activate" the hierarchy and have defined that the hierarchy open initially to the Sold-To Party level, which is the third level. Also, notice that the key figures have been positioned to make a hierarchy view of this information. Therefore, once you open your query, you will see the highest level of the key figures—Sales Volume—and have the ability to open up the rest to see the underlying key figures. Once you have defined this, save the query and execute the BEx Analyzer to see the results. The second illustration shows the results of these settings. Some important differences between

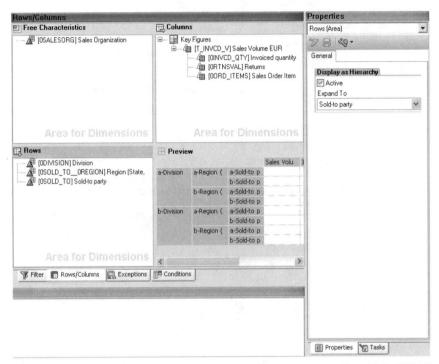

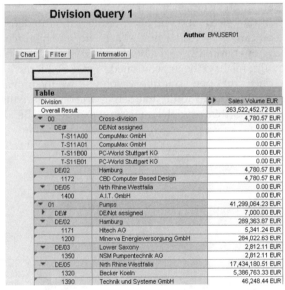

these three characteristics listed in the query and being executed as a presentation hierarchy could help in the display to the business user. First, setting these characteristics up as a presentation hierarchy will display all three objects in *one* column versus having the three setup to be presented in *three* columns. Hierarchies, no matter the number of nodes, will always display in one row versus whatever number of characteristics you would have in the normal characteristic display. Second, using a presentation hierarchy, you can see that nodes are created by the system and therefore you can close and open the hierarchy to the desired level versus having them show as three characteristics. In this case, you will see all three levels and not have control over the display. Third, a presentation hierarchy is driven by the transactional data versus the master data. This is probably the most important concept of the three. You will see the hierarchy structured based on the transactional data and what was posted, not based on a "fixed" structure that is defined in the Administration Workbench of BW. Also, notice that the key figures have been closed up to a higher level. This was defined in the BEx Query Designer during configuration. In the following illustration, you can see that we have opened up the key figures to show the lower level ones. This is the first option you have with hierarchies, but again this will not offer you a "fixed" view of the information. What it will offer you is the ability to use this type of hierarchy to track information over time as a sold-to party moves from division to division. This is good for other types of information such as tracking a person as they move from department to department over time. Your query might have as columns months of the year, and you are tracking personnel costs over time. You can see the movement of cost and employees between departments by the month. With a "fixed" hierarchy, this type of report would not be possible.

Division Query 1

| | Author BWUSER01 | | Status of Data | 2/28/2003 11:27 |

Chart | Filter | Information

Table

Division		Sales Volume EUR	Invoiced quantity	Returns	Sales Order Item
Overall Result		263,522,452.72 EUR	653,302.520 MIX	347,600.00 EUR	6,760
00	Cross-division	4,780.57 EUR	17 AU	0.00 EUR	8
DE/#	DE/Not assigned	0.00 EUR	0 PC	0.00 EUR	6
T-S11A00	CompuMax GmbH	0.00 EUR	0 PC	0.00 EUR	2
T-S11A01	CompuMax GmbH	0.00 EUR	0 PC	0.00 EUR	2
T-S11B00	PC-World Stuttgart KG	0.00 EUR	0 PC	0.00 EUR	1
T-S11B01	PC-World Stuttgart KG	0.00 EUR	0 PC	0.00 EUR	1
DE/02	Hamburg	4,780.57 EUR	17 AU	0.00 EUR	1
1172	CBD Computer Based Design	4,780.57 EUR	17 AU	0.00 EUR	1
DE/05	Nrth Rhine Westfalia	0.00 EUR	0 PC	0.00 EUR	1
1400	A.I.T. GmbH	0.00 EUR	0 PC	0.00 EUR	1
01	Pumps	41,299,064.23 EUR	13,627 PC	0.00 EUR	332

Display Hierarchies

In the next type of hierarchies, we have a bit more work to do versus the presentation hierarchies. These hierarchies are the display hierarchies. They come in a number of different formats and can be uploaded from another source system, such as an ECC/R3 system, and in many cases the initial hierarchies are uploaded from the specific module that uses them in the source system. Some of the standard hierarchies we have heard of are Cost Center hierarchies, Product hierarchies, Profit Center hierarchies, and so on. Each of these hierarchies definitely has a different look and feel. For example, the Cost Center hierarchies

from the ECC systems have only *one* characteristic in them with a Text node as the Cost
Center Group, whereas the Product hierarchies from the ECC systems has a series of *three*
characteristics in them—Material Group, Material Type, and Material. Therefore, these
types of hierarchies have one Text node at the top, but all the other nodes are actual values
you can post data against. Finally, there can be hierarchies that have only one characteristic
involved but also have only one Text node, and all other nodes are characteristic values.
Therefore, you have the same values nested under other values of the same characteristic.
The following illustration is a good example of a mix of these hierarchies. As you can see,
there are several levels of nonpostable nodes (EMEA, DE, and DE North) but under DE
South you have a series of values that are postable and are nested (4714 has 4714A and
4714B nested under it). Because this is a mixture of two types of hierarchies, you need to
look at the levels. Because we have at least three levels that are nonpostable, this hierarchy
is identified as a Text hierarchy. The other hierarchies are thought of as *external* hierarchies.
BW uses and incorporates these hierarchies into the queries in the same manner. The
difference is how the data is rolled up based on the nonpostable and postable nodes. You
will see that BW has an answer for this. With certain attributes that are used and defined in
the hierarchies, we can sort out the rollups and summaries.

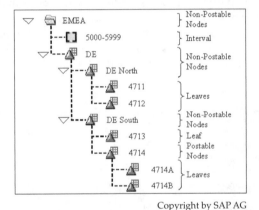

Copyright by SAP AG

NOTE *You may also see the Text hierarchy grouped under this heading in some situations.*

Now that you have a basic idea of the different types of hierarchies, we can take a look
at the configuration that goes into them. As mentioned, we can upload these hierarchies
from other systems, we can upload them from flat files, or we can create them and maintain
them in the BW system. The preference would be that they are maintained in other systems
and uploaded to BW, starting with a full upload and continuing with a Delta uploading
process. These hierarchies are saved in their own specific tables and are similar to master
data in nature. You can modify them in BW and can have several hierarchies (no limit)
assigned to one characteristic. Therefore, you can have hierarchies by version (12/31/2006
versus current) or you can have time-dependent hierarchies (hierarchies that change over
time, either as the corporation changes or as different events occur, such as a new product
being sold, customers changing regions, and so on). You determine whether a characteristic
can have a hierarchy in InfoObject maintenance. This is also where you would define the
hierarchy as well as the attributes of that hierarchy. The following illustration shows the

initial screen for hierarchies. As you can see, a number of parameters can be set against the hierarchies. Table 6-2 details these setting and their functionality.

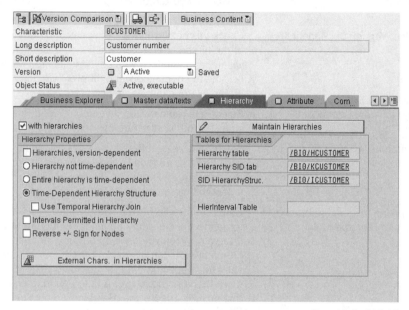

Another parameter, shown in the following illustration, is the executable for "External Chars. in Hierarchies." This component is specifically for adding additional characteristics to the configuration that you might be using to create the hierarchies. In our case, we will add the InfoObject 0REGION to the external characteristics so that we can build a hierarchy with region and customer values included.

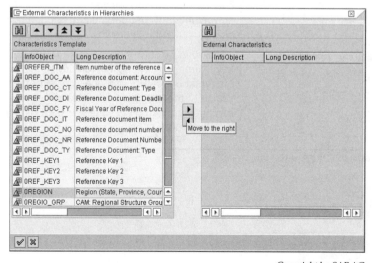

Setting in the Hierarchy Tab	Description and Functionality
With Hierarchies	Select this button to set up the hierarchy tables in the InfoObject.
Hierarchies, Version-Dependent	Check this box if you want to maintain different versions of the hierarchies. When you define each hierarchy, you will need to supply a version identifier. You will then be able to choose between different versions of the hierarchy (for example, financial versions).
Hierarchy Not Time-Dependent	Select this radio button if you don't need to store the changes to the structure over time.
Entire Hierarchy Is Time-Dependent	Select this radio button if you want to define hierarchy structures in relation to time intervals. When you develop a query that uses the hierarchy, you can also select the hierarchy valid for a specific date.
Time-dependent Hierarchy Structure I Use Temporal Hierarchy Join	Select this radio button if you want to be able to define the individual nodes in relation to time intervals. When you develop a query that uses the hierarchy, you can also select the hierarchy nodes valid for a specific date. If members appear in more than one node over a time period, a check in this box will ensure you are able to report on these movements in the same result. For example, if you have an interval of master data and posted data, such as employee absentee occurrences and employee managers, then using this indicator will allow the reporting of this information in the correct node of the hierarchy based on a key date.
Intervals Permitted in Hierarchy	If you need to set up intervals within the hierarchy, you should report by grouping rather than individually. Any new member of that particular range will automatically be included in the hierarchy.
Reverse +/– Sign for Nodes	Check this box if it makes sense to present the key figures with the sign reversed. This is purely a presentation feature and does not alter the actual values of the key figure. For example, if you upload revenues as a credit (–) and you want to display them as + instead.

TABLE 6-2   Hierarchy Settings in the InfoObject

The next illustration shows the InfoObject in the correct position to be used for building hierarchies. The requirement is, if you need to use a specific characteristic in the hierarchy, it must be included in the External Characteristics list. Therefore, move the characteristics to the right side of this screen. Now that this is complete and you have changed the characteristic, you need to save and activate the characteristic. Hierarchies have to (and can only) be created for hierarchy basic characteristics. All characteristics that reference a hierarchy basic characteristic automatically inherit the corresponding hierarchies. A hierarchy basic characteristic can have as many hierarchies as required. Therefore, we will be using 0CUSTOMER to build our hierarchies against. However, because the InfoObject 0SOLD_TO PARTY is a reference to 0CUSTOMER, we will see the built hierarchies included in this characteristic also.

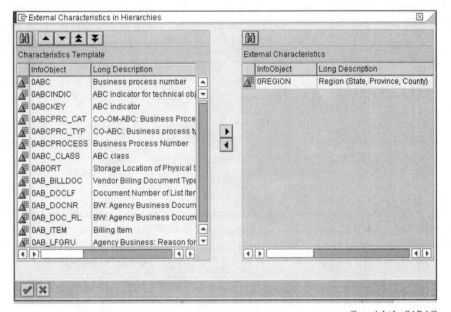

Copyright by SAP AG

The next illustration shows both locations where you can maintain and edit hierarchies directly in the BW system. You can use the context menu of the specific characteristic and select **Create Hierarchy**, or you can use the option **Maintain Hierarchies** directly in the

InfoObject. We will start to build our hierarchy from the Create Hierarchy option (however, either way you arrive at the same screen).

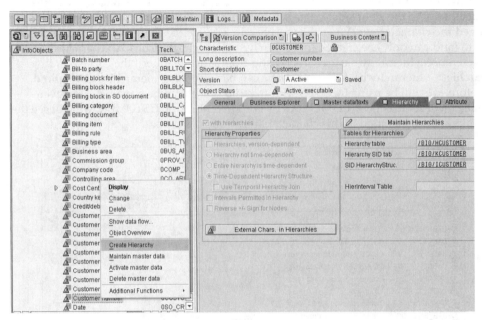

Once you have accessed this option, you are presented with a screen titled "Initial Screen Hierarchy Maintenance." Use the Create button (the icon that looks like a sheet of paper) to start the build. The following illustration shows this initial screen. The necessary entries for the hierarchy name and descriptions have been filled in manually.

The first of the following illustrations shows the next step, which is to start the creation process. Notice that the hierarchy we will be building is time-dependent because we have to include the From and To dates in the configuration of the hierarchy. We are continuing to build the hierarchy by adding Text nodes to the list—Group A and Group B. The second illustration shows this step.

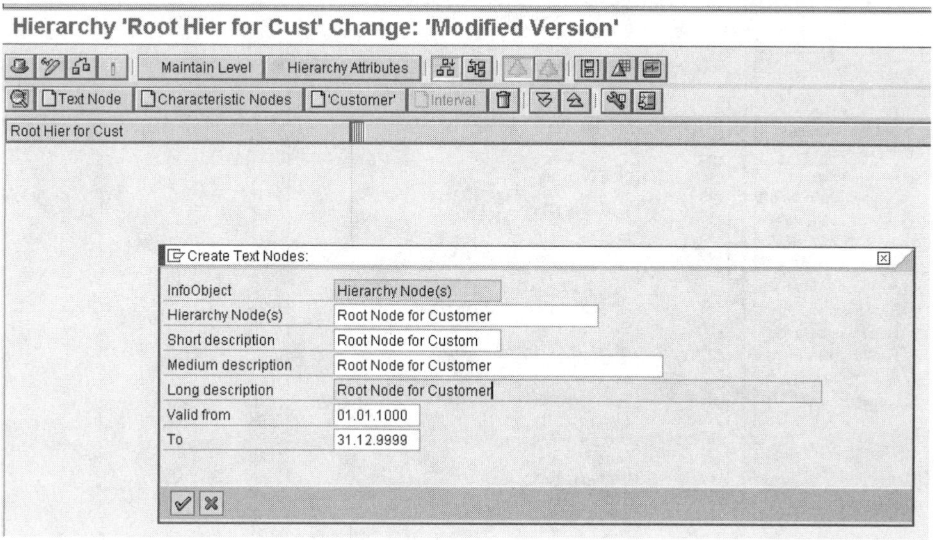

Hierarchy 'Root Hier for Cust' Change: 'Modified Version'

| Maintain Level | Hierarchy Attributes |

Text Node | Characteristic Nodes | 'Customer' | Interval

Root Hier for Cust

Create Text Nodes:

InfoObject	Hierarchy Node(s)
Hierarchy Node(s)	Root Node for Customer
Short description	Root Node for Custom
Medium description	Root Node for Customer
Long description	Root Node for Customer
Valid from	01.01.1000
To	31.12.9999

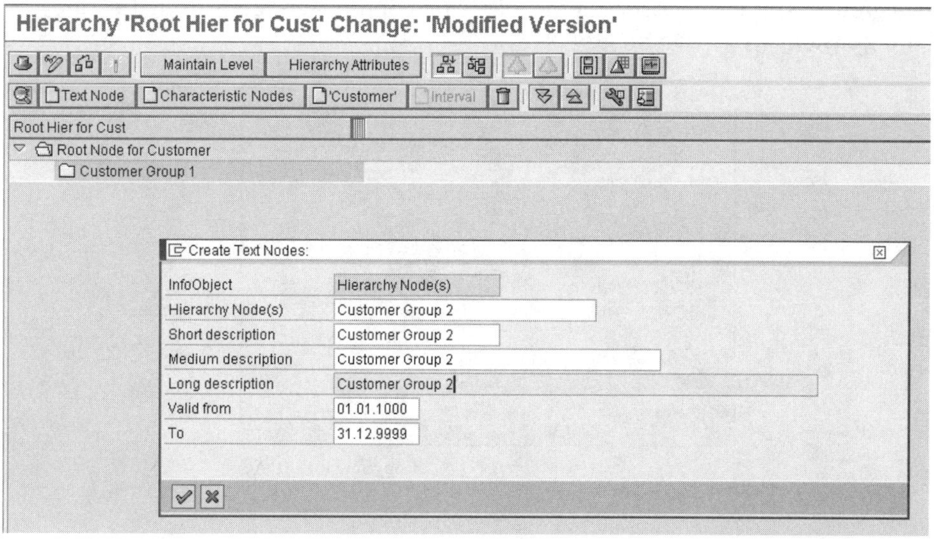

Hierarchy 'Root Hier for Cust' Change: 'Modified Version'

| Maintain Level | Hierarchy Attributes |

Text Node | Characteristic Nodes | 'Customer' | Interval

Root Hier for Cust

▽ Root Node for Customer

Customer Group 1

Create Text Nodes:

InfoObject	Hierarchy Node(s)
Hierarchy Node(s)	Customer Group 2
Short description	Customer Group 2
Medium description	Customer Group 2
Long description	Customer Group 2
Valid from	01.01.1000
To	31.12.9999

The next step is to fill in the lower-level characteristic values for each of the Text nodes. The next illustration shows the build in this process. To create the Text node, use the Text Node Create button (an icon of a blank sheet of paper). To add characteristic values to this hierarchy, use the button for "Customer" to display a list of values, as you see here.

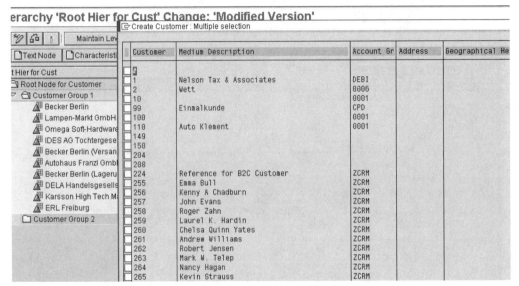

During this process, we find that we are trying to include the same characteristic value in both groups. This is the reason for the following pop-up. This alerts us that we are including customer 1000 in both groups.

As you can see, you have choices. Table 6-3 details the functionality for each option. You will use whatever option works for your situation, but its important to understand the display that will be available to the business user. The following illustration shows the outcome of this linking process.

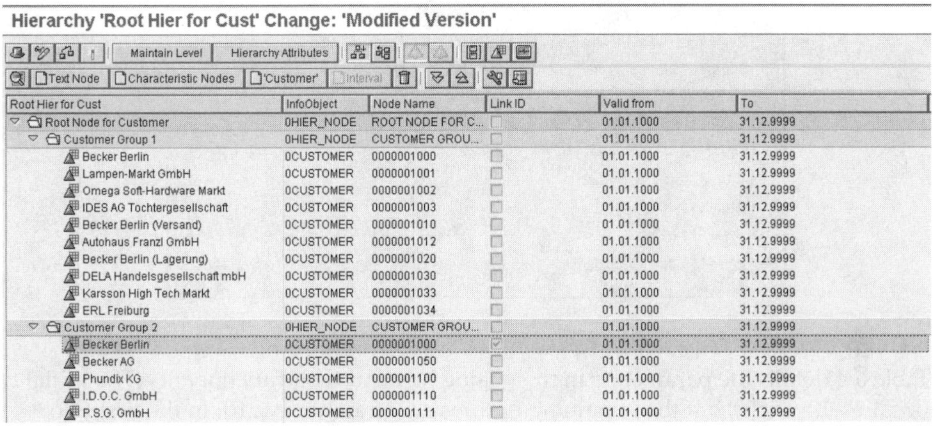

Hierarchy 'Root Hier for Cust' Change: 'Modified Version'						
Maintain Level	Hierarchy Attributes					
Text Node	Characteristic Nodes	'Customer'	Interval			
Root Hier for Cust	InfoObject	Node Name	Link ID	Valid from	To	
Root Node for Customer	0HIER_NODE	ROOT NODE FOR C...		01.01.1000	31.12.9999	
▽ Customer Group 1	0HIER_NODE	CUSTOMER GROU...		01.01.1000	31.12.9999	
Becker Berlin	0CUSTOMER	0000001000		01.01.1000	31.12.9999	
Lampen-Markt GmbH	0CUSTOMER	0000001001		01.01.1000	31.12.9999	
Omega Soft-Hardware Markt	0CUSTOMER	0000001002		01.01.1000	31.12.9999	
IDES AG Tochtergesellschaft	0CUSTOMER	0000001003		01.01.1000	31.12.9999	
Becker Berlin (Versand)	0CUSTOMER	0000001010		01.01.1000	31.12.9999	
Autohaus Franzl GmbH	0CUSTOMER	0000001012		01.01.1000	31.12.9999	
Becker Berlin (Lagerung)	0CUSTOMER	0000001020		01.01.1000	31.12.9999	
DELA Handelsgesellschaft mbH	0CUSTOMER	0000001030		01.01.1000	31.12.9999	
Karsson High Tech Markt	0CUSTOMER	0000001033		01.01.1000	31.12.9999	
ERL Freiburg	0CUSTOMER	0000001034		01.01.1000	31.12.9999	
▽ Customer Group 2	0HIER_NODE	CUSTOMER GROU...		01.01.1000	31.12.9999	
Becker Berlin	0CUSTOMER	0000001000	☑	01.01.1000	31.12.9999	
Becker AG	0CUSTOMER	0000001050		01.01.1000	31.12.9999	
Phundix KG	0CUSTOMER	0000001100		01.01.1000	31.12.9999	
I.D.O.C. GmbH	0CUSTOMER	0000001110		01.01.1000	31.12.9999	
P.S.G. GmbH	0CUSTOMER	0000001111		01.01.1000	31.12.9999	

Copyright by SAP AG

Customer 1000 is linked at the lower-level nodes. Another series of parameters that we need to address involve the Hierarchy Attributes button. If we click this button,

Setting in the Duplicate Node Dialog Box	Description and Functionality
Do Not Copy Duplicate Node	This setting will not copy over duplicate nodes. Therefore, you will not be able to include this in your grouping.
Copy Duplicate Node	This setting will copy over duplicate values within the same hierarchy in different nodes. The only issue here is that the rollup of these values is not controlled; therefore, you will be getting incorrect information at upper-level nodes.
Transfer the Duplicate Node as Link Node	This setting will transfer the duplicate nodes and will also link them. Thus, during the rollup of data from lower nodes to the upper nodes, the posting for these two linked values will not get double stated. Therefore, once the hierarchy levels intersect, the duplicate values will be eliminated.
Execute Action for All Duplicate Nodes	This setting will automatically execute the same option for all duplicate nodes without manual prompts.

TABLE 6-3   Settings in the Dialog Box for Duplicate Nodes

we will see this pop-up shown next. These indicators will have an effect on the display of the hierarchies.

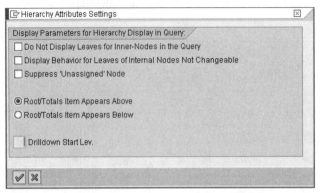

Table 6-4 details the parameters in this dialog box and their functionality. The initial two options are a bit tricky, but the remaining options are straightforward. In the first two options, the concept is that you have a hierarchy that has postable nodes that are nested so that one postable node is positioned as a lower-level node, so the display is not as clear as might be required—for example, if you had a hierarchy that had one cost center nested under another cost center. The hierarchy processing the lower-level values roll up to the

Setting	Description and Functionality
Do Not Display Leaves for Inner-Nodes in the Query	This display option for an inner, postable node is to *not* display the inner nested node but rather to hide it and roll up the results to the upper node.
Display Behavior for Leaves of Internal Nodes Not Changeable	You can determine whether the user is able to change the display for the runtime of the query. If you leave this blank, you cannot change the display in the query. If you check this box, you can change the display in the query.
Suppress "Unassigned" Node	Here you can determine whether to suppress the node under which all postable characteristic values that do not appear in the hierarchy display are positioned.
Roots/Totals Item Appears Above	You can determine whether the root and the total items are displayed at the end or the start of the query and whether the leaves appear above or below.
Roots/Totals Item Appears Below	You can determine whether the root and the total items are displayed at the end or the start of the query and whether the leaves appear above or below.
Drilldown Start Lev.	This is the setting for the initial default level to which the hierarchy is drilled down when you call your query.

TABLE 6-4   Settings for Hierarchy Settings

upper-level node, but if the upper-level node is also a postable value, you will not see the actual value of the upper node but rather the rollup of the lower nodes *and* the value of the upper node, together as one.

The final parameter to be discussed—Maintain Level—is for display purposes only. This option allows you to change the display of the level text in the query. The following illustration shows the screen you will see after you access this option. You can update the text and save.

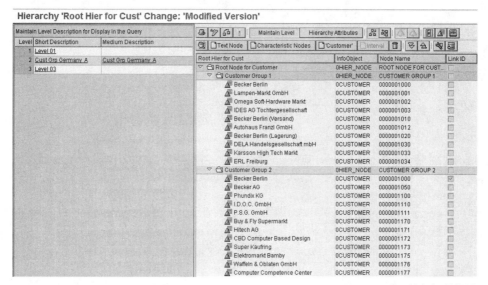

Copyright by SAP AG

We have now completed the build of one hierarchy. This hierarchy has two Text nodes and one characteristic included and therefore is classified as a Text hierarchy. We will go through the process of creating another hierarchy with two characteristics. The process is no different from the previous one, except that we will use the Characteristic Node button to get to the other characteristic we assigned to the root characteristic (that is, 0REGION). The following illustration shows the process of setting up the hierarchy. We access the Hierarchy Create screen as we did previously. We create the Text root node, but then use the Characteristic Nodes option to get to 0REGION and add it to the list. As you can see, the coloring of the node is different.

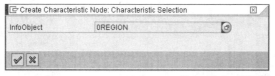

Copyright by SAP AG

The first of the following illustrations identifies the customer value 1000 as a linked node. In this particular case, customer 1000 was in one region for a portion of the time and in another for the rest. Therefore, we use the option for setting From and To dates to eliminate the "linked" issue, as shown in the second illustration.

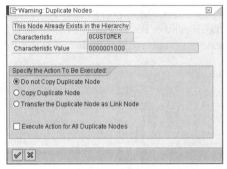

Copyright by SAP AG

Copyright by SAP AG

Notice that the dates for the customer 1000 are broken up between 01.01.1000 and 31.12.2001 in the group Lower Saxony and between 01.01.2002 and 31.12.9999 in the group Bavaria. This will eliminate any collisions between the groups. As a final configuration view of these two hierarchies, the next illustration shows the view of these two hierarchies attached to the InfoObject 0Customer.

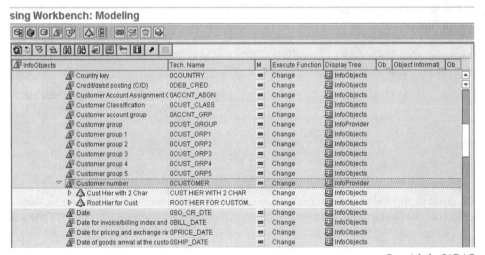

Copyright by SAP AG

Once these tasks are complete, we move into the BEx Query Designer and take the hierarchies that we have defined and use them in the query. The following illustration shows the initial view of the query we are working with to display the hierarchies.

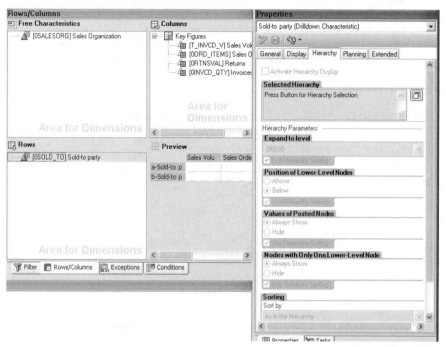

Notice that the 0SOLD_TO PARTY characteristic has been chosen, and we have switched to the Hierarchy tab under Properties for this characteristic. Using the suggestion "Press Button for Hierarchy Selection," we see the dialog box shown here. The options here are fairly straightforward:

- **Hierarchy Name**   From the drop-down you see the different hierarchies you can choose from (the two hierarchies we just created are available).

- **Hierarchy Variables**   If you were using a hierarchy variable (we will set one up later in this chapter), you would choose it here.

- **Default Date from the Query**   If the hierarchy is time-dependent (ours is time dependent), the date to identify the correct node values can be derived from this date.

- **Hierarchy Date**   Used to identify the date for the hierarchy specifically.

- **Date Variable**   If the requirement is to have a flexible date value for the hierarchy, you can identify a variable for the date here.

As you can see, the parameters listed under Properties for the hierarchies are very similar, if not the same, as the attributes we talked about in the configuration of the hierarchy directly on the InfoObject. These items are described in Table 6-5.

As you can see, we chose to use the root hierarchy for Customer. Notice that an additional indicator has been attached to the InfoObject 0SOLD_TO—the small tree like icon that is assigned to the view of the InfoObject. The following illustration shows all these settings.

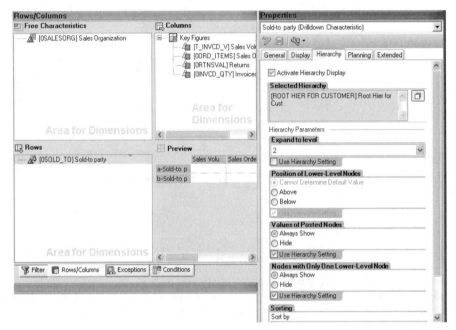

Copyright by SAP AG

Setting	Description and Functionality
Expand to Level	Used to determine the hierarchy level that the initial view of the hierarchy will have.
Position of Lower-Level Nodes	Choose whether the subordinate nodes are positioned above or below a superior node.
Value of Posted Nodes	Choose whether you want to always show or hide the values of posted nodes.
Nodes with Only One Lower-level Node	Choose whether you want to always show or hide nodes with only one lower-level node.
Sorting	Within the hierarchy you can sort in descending or ascending order by key or name.

TABLE 6-5   Settings in the Hierarchies Tab

Finally, we are ready to execute the query. By opening up the BEx Analyzer and executing the query, we see the results as shown in the following illustration. We see that the hierarchy has been used to format and structure the values of the sold-to party, and they appear in the same list as we configured in the system. This gives the information a structure, and the business user will see the same view each and every time they access this query. The "unassigned" list that appears at the lower level of the hierarchy can be left to display, or in the attributes of the hierarchy you can indicate that you do not want to see the "unassigned" node.

Table

Sold-to party		Sales Volume EUR	Sales Order Item	Returns	Invoiced quantity
Overall Result		263,522,452.72 EUR	6,760	347,600.00 EUR	653,302.520 MIX
▼ ROOT NODE FOR CUSTOMER	Root Node for Customer	75,933,687.29 EUR	1,770	0.00 EUR	179,665.370 MIX
▼ CUSTOMER GROUP 1	Customer Group 1	37,871,839.90 EUR	796	0.00 EUR	68,446.370 MIX
1000	Becker Berlin	3,626,032.70 EUR	19	0.00 EUR	1,842 PC
1001	Lampen-Markt GmbH	20,925,966.84 EUR	268	0.00 EUR	52,477 CAR
1002	Omega Soft-Hardware Markt	271,921.21 EUR	62	0.00 EUR	321.760 MIX
1012	Autohaus Franzl GmbH	79,577.48 EUR	3	0.00 EUR	3 PC
1030	DELA Handelsgesellschaft mbH	0.00 EUR	0	0.00 EUR	0 PC
1033	Karsson High Tech Markt	12,949,765.35 EUR	442	0.00 EUR	13,765.070 MIX
1034	ERL Freiburg	18,576.32 EUR	2	0.00 EUR	38.000 MIX
▼ CUSTOMER GROUP 2	Customer Group 2	41,687,880.09 EUR	993	0.00 EUR	113,061.000 MIX
1000	Becker Berlin	3,626,032.70 EUR	19	0.00 EUR	1,842 PC
1171	Hitech AG	1,892,543.42 EUR	42	0.00 EUR	963.000 MIX
1172	CBD Computer Based Design	8,552,122.87 EUR	567	0.00 EUR	46,370.000 MIX
1175	Elektromarkt Bamby	27,553,643.37 EUR	361	0.00 EUR	63,681.000 MIX
1177	Computer Competence Center	63,537.73 EUR	4	0.00 EUR	205.000 MIX
▶ Not Assigned Sold-to party (s)		187,588,765.43 EUR	4,990	347,600.00 EUR	473,637.150 MIX

Now that you have a bit more understanding of what a hierarchy can do in a query, let's go back and make some adjustments to the query and see the functionality of the hierarchy structure. We will go back and use the other hierarchy we built—the one with the two characteristics and one Text node. We will also add 0DIVISION to the rows list and have the hierarchy for the customer be a second level to the individual characteristic. The following two illustrations display these changes to the format of the query.

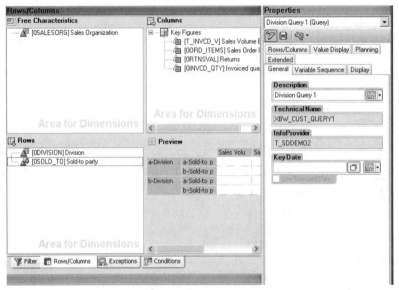

Executing the query produces the results shown in the first of the following illustrations, which demonstrates that the query can use different combinations with any hierarchy. Again, remember that this is the initial screen for the query and not the finished product. We have yet to include numerous bells and whistles before the queries are finished products. An additional change to the query moves the key figures to the same position as the characteristics. Therefore, nothing is in the columns, everything is in the rows. The second illustration shows the changes to the query. Notice that in this configuration of the query, we have expanded the hierarchy to show the level down to the "key figures" (see the properties of the hierarchy). The third illustration shows the results of this change. It always amazes me when executing a query that by switching the view of the data around, we can see a very different view of the query results.

Table

Division		Sold-to party		Sales Volume EUR	Sales Order Item	Returns	Invoiced
00	Cross-division	▶ Not Assigned Sold-to party (s)		4,780.57 EUR	8	0.00 EUR	
01	Pumps	Result		41,299,064.23 EUR	332	0.00 EUR	1
		▼ ROOT NODE FOR CUST W 2 CHAR	Root Node for Cust w 2 char	3,612,933.99 EUR	17	0.00 EUR	
		▼ DE/07	Rhineland Palatinate	5,341.24 EUR	1	0.00 EUR	
		1171	Hitech AG	5,341.24 EUR	1	0.00 EUR	
		▼ DE/09	Bavaria	3,607,592.75 EUR	16	0.00 EUR	
		1000	Becker Berlin	3,607,592.75 EUR	16	0.00 EUR	
		▶ Not Assigned Sold-to party (s)		37,686,130.24 EUR	315	0.00 EUR	1
02	Motorcycles	▶ Not Assigned Sold-to party (s)		53,843,011.68 EUR	409	0.00 EUR	18
04	Lighting	Result		67,452,686.20 EUR	908	0.00 EUR	167
		▼ ROOT NODE FOR CUST W 2 CHAR	Root Node for Cust w 2 char	47,190,530.98 EUR	598	0.00 EUR	114
		▶ DE/03	Lower Saxony	20,926,658.96 EUR	290	0.00 EUR	52
		▶ DE/09	Bavaria	26,263,872.02 EUR	308	0.00 EUR	62
		▶ Not Assigned Sold-to party (s)		20,262,155.22 EUR	310	0.00 EUR	52
07	High Tech	Result		98,647,763.21 EUR	5,081	347,600.00 EUR	28
		▼ ROOT NODE FOR CUST W 2 CHAR	Root Node for Cust w 2 char	1,760,913.25 EUR	131	0.00 EUR	
		▶ DE/03	Lower Saxony	271,229.09 EUR	40	0.00 EUR	
		▶ DE/07	Rhineland Palatinate	171,071.14 EUR	34	0.00 EUR	
		▶ DE/09	Bavaria	1,318,613.02 EUR	57	0.00 EUR	
		▶ Not Assigned Sold-to party (s)		96,886,849.96 EUR	4,950	347,600.00 EUR	28
08	Service	Result		1,851,569.35 EUR	17	0.00 EUR	
		▼ ROOT NODE FOR CUST W 2 CHAR	Root Node for Cust w 2 char	1,769,267.05 EUR	10	0.00 EUR	
		▶ DE/07	Rhineland Palatinate	1,716,131.04 EUR	7	0.00 EUR	
		▶ DE/09	Bavaria	53,136.01 EUR	3	0.00 EUR	
		▶ Not Assigned Sold-to party (s)		82,302.30 EUR	7	0.00 EUR	
10	Vehicles	▼ ROOT NODE FOR CUST W 2 CHAR	Root Node for Cust w 2 char	79,577.48 EUR	3	0.00 EUR	

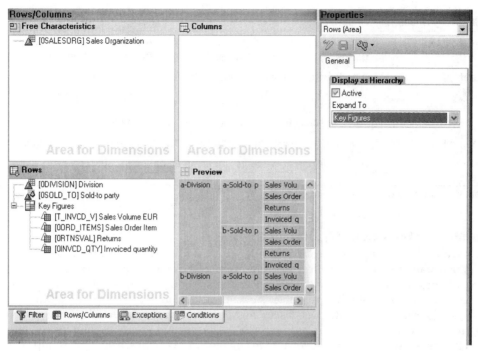

Copyright by SAP AG

Copyright by SAP AG

In addition to the user-defined hierarchies, uploaded hierarchies, and others, there are SBC hierarchies for many InfoObjects and also for all the time characteristics. These "virtual hierarchies" for time characteristics act differently and can be activated in the IMG. We will discuss these in Chapter 14. Some additional terminology concerning hierarchies can be found in Tables 6-6, 6-7, and 6-8.

Hierarchy Nodes	Description
Root (nodes)	A node that is not assigned under any node and has no parent node (predecessor). A hierarchy can have more than one root node.
Leaf	A node without lower-level nodes (successors). Leaves are postable, but are not postable nodes. Leaves are always characteristic values for the hierarchy basic characteristic. Value specification: The value is moved from the InfoProvider.
Interval	A quantity of leaves that are indicated by their lower and upper limits.
Inner nodes	A node having successors, meaning all nodes except for leaves.

TABLE 6-6 Special Hierarchy Nodes

Variables in the BEx Query Designer

We have worked through the back-end configuration for both the navigational attributes and the hierarchies, and you've seen how they impact the architecture and structure of the basic BW objects. Now we move to the front end to see how we can help the business user make queries more flexible and reusable. We will work through the setup, configuration, and use of variables for the queries, discussing their functionality in detail. We will focus on the creation and use of the variables in the BEx Analyzer settings and we will follow this up with the web-based variable functionality in Chapter 15. You will see enough examples of the variable screens that you will feel comfortable once you access them in your systems.

A variable is a parameter of a query that you define in the Query Designer that is filled with values when you execute the query or web application. Variables serve as placeholders for characteristic values, hierarchies, hierarchy nodes, texts, and formula elements, and they can be processed in different ways. This is one of the remaining configuration options you can't get to via the executed query (for example, you can create an exception either in the BEx Query Designer or after you have executed the query). We use variables to make a query reusable—for example, creating one query with variables so that we can use it as a rolling 12-month report; therefore, regardless of the month we enter at execution, we will see a 12-month analysis. Suppose you have a query you would like to give to all your divisional managers. To do this you will create a query with a variable for the division and have the divisional managers either manually enter their division(s) or have the system confirm what divisions they can see and automatically default those values into the variable for the

Grouping	Description
Hierarchy level	A hierarchy level consists of all nodes with the same depth. Root nodes have depth (level) 1. The depth of a node corresponds the number of parent or grandparent nodes up to the root node +1 (increased by one). A hierarchy can have a maximum of 98 levels. Each level can have a name.
Subtree	A subtree includes a node (root node of the subtree) with its lower-level or subnodes. Nodes that are on the border of a subtree are called *border nodes*.

TABLE 6-7 Grouping of Hierarchy Nodes

Postability	Description
Postable nodes	A node that corresponds to a characteristic value for the hierarchy basic or root characteristic. (Please read this slowly: A node that corresponds to a characteristic value for a characteristic that references the hierarchy basic or root characteristic. This definition includes the basic or root hierarchy characteristic.) In contrast to a leaf, additional nodes or leaves are assigned under a postable (inner) node.
	Value specification: The value of a postable node is specified by the aggregation of the values of its lower-level nodes and of its value in the InfoProvider.
	Note: Hierarchies can act differently depending on where we are using them. For example, if we use this type of hierarchy in the BW-BPS (BW-Business Planning and Simulation) process, the ability to post to a characteristic value at any level can be changed or affected by parameters set in the Planning Layout setup (specific to BPS). This is just a heads-up that the use of hierarchies for any other component of BW rather than reporting must be reviewed and not taken for granted.
Not postable nodes	A node that does *not* refer to a hierarchy basic characteristic and is *not* a postable node.
	Value specification: The value of a node that is not postable is specified by the aggregation of the values of its children nodes.
Text nodes	*Text node* is a new artificial term. Text nodes are special characteristic nodes for the artificial characteristic 0HIER_NODE.
External characteristic nodes	A node that is identified by any specification of any InfoObject is an external characteristic node. In order to use a characteristic in the hierarchy as an external characteristic node, you have to explicitly select it in the InfoObject Maintenance for the hierarchy basic characteristic.
Not assigned	The system automatically creates a root node, REST_H, under which all characteristic values reside. These characteristic values exist in the master data, but are not explicitly arranged in the hierarchy. The node Not Assigned guarantees that no data is lost when a presentation hierarchy is activated. In the query, this node is always collapsed first and also does not react to Expand to Level. However, it can be explicitly opened.

TABLE 6-8   Postability of Nodes

managers (via authorization settings). There are many uses for variables, and I can't remember one query that I've either seen or created that didn't have a variable or two included. It just makes sense to cut down on your maintenance and have something available and useable for long periods of time. You will see a number of different uses for variables in this chapter, but this is not anywhere near the total uses of variables in queries.

The variables defined in the Query Designer are available for all InfoProviders that have the specific InfoObject included. Therefore, the variables are linked to the InfoObject— characteristic—and not the InfoProvider.

Types of Variables

The different types of variables depend on the object for which you want to define them. These types specify where you can use the variables. Variables enable you to customize queries flexibly (that is, parameterize the queries). If you use variables in the Query Designer, do not select any fixed characteristic values, hierarchies, hierarchy nodes, texts, or formula elements in the configuration. Instead, set up variables as placeholders. These are then filled with values during query runtime (when you insert the query into a workbook, when you refresh the workbook, or when you execute the query on the Web). You can also use one query definition as the foundation for many different queries if you use variables. Here are the five types of variables:

- Characteristic values
- Hierarchies
- Hierarchy nodes
- Texts
- Formula elements

Figure 6-2 shows a list of the different variable types and the matrix of the intersection between the variable types and the process types. The variable types are the different objects we can create a variable for, whereas the process types determine how the variable is filled at the time of execution.

The important idea to remember when you are creating variables is that you create the variable where you use that particular type of variable. Therefore, if you create a characteristic variable, you will be working in the characteristic screens. Text variables will be created

| | Variable Type: | | | | |
Processing Type:	Characteristic Value Variables	Hierarchy Node Variables	Text Variables	Formula Variables	Hierarchy Variables
Manual Entry / Default Value	X	X	X	X	X
Replacement Path	(X)*		X	X	
Customer Exit	X	X	X	X	X
SAP Exit	X	X	X	X	X
Authorization	X	X			

* Only in conjunction with the replacement path 'Query Result'

FIGURE 6-2 Processing types for the different types of variables

wherever you use text—column headings, query headings, and so on—and the same with the other variables. The hierarchy variables are the tricky ones. For hierarchy node variables, you have to be in the hierarchy node screens, and for the hierarchy variables you have to be in the screens used for accessing the entire hierarchy. You will find out quickly enough if you have set these types up correctly—for example, if you can't get to a hierarchy node and you thought you created one for that node, you will realize you actually created one for the overall hierarchy instead. To explain this in another way, if you have to set up a hierarchy node variable, then you need to have a hierarchy to get the node from. Thus, the two are connected in this manner.

The Variables Editor is available in the Query Designer for designing and changing variables. The Variable Editor is the toolset used for creating variables.

You make the settings on tabbed pages. These are context sensitive and are adjusted according to the combination of variable and processing types used. This means that the Variables Editor only offers the selection options permitted for a particular combination of variable and processing types. This is nice because you are guided through the steps based on the variable type you have chosen to create. Numerous components use variables in BI, such as Integrated Planning, Web Application Designer, and others, but in some of these areas variables take on a different flavor. We will discuss variables and their specific functionality in each of the different areas.

Characteristic Variables   Characteristic value variables represent characteristic values and can be used wherever characteristic values can be used in a query. You also create them directly in the same area where the characteristic values are shown. Therefore, you can go to the characteristic itself on the InfoProvider side of the Query Designer and open up the lower nodes and you will see the node for variables. You can create the variables there or you can create them from the Restrict dialog box. This process is better explained via an example of this type of variable. We will work through this example in detail, but as we work our way through other variable types, we will just be looking at the specific portions of the configuration that are unique to those types of variables. In the following illustration, you can see that we are going to create a variable for 0DIVISION.

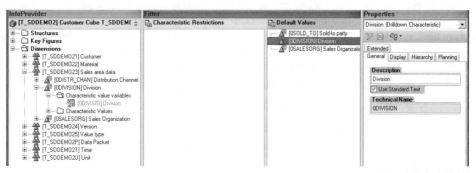

Copyright by SAP AG

Either from the characteristic itself (using the Selection option, then accessing the variables with the context menu drop-down from the selection screen) or from the area included in the InfoProvider section, we can start the process of creating the variable. We'll use the InfoProvider area to create the variable because the creation process will probably be managed by authorizations for creation-specific objects—namely, variables. The illustration at right shows the initial New Variable option from the context menu at the variable node level.

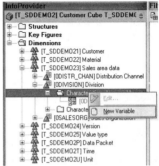

Once the new variable is chosen, you will see that the system creates a technical name automatically. You can use the suggested one or change it based on your naming convention. The next illustration shows this step in the process.

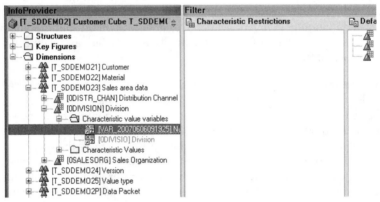

You will then choose the placeholder and in the context menu click Edit to continue the process. The first of the following two illustrations shows this step. Once you execute the Edit function, you will be presented with a dialog box for the creation of your variable. This dialog box has a series of tabs associated with the different parameters for the type of variable you are creating. The second illustration shows the Change Variable dialog box. The initial tab is General, and its series of options are detailed in Table 6-9.

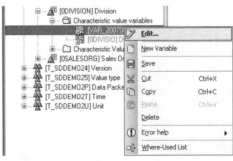

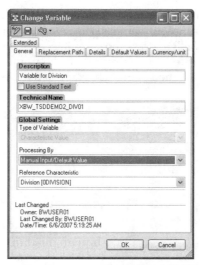

Copyright by SAP AG

Setting	Description and Functionality
Description	Description of the variable.
Technical Name	Technical name either change to a user defined technical name or leave the system generated one for storing the variable in the system table.
Global Settings	For this setting, the type of variable is set. It is grayed out and you can't change it. Again, you are in the characteristic value section of the Query Designer and therefore you are creating a characteristic variable.
Processing By	Five different processing types can be used: • **Manual Input/Default Values** This option allows the business user to manually enter the values they are interested in viewing. Alternatively, a default value has been set and therefore this is the initial value that shows up in the entry field. • **Replacement Path** This is used for specific cases. I explain this option in more detail later in this chapter. • **Customer Exit** If you need to create a company-specific exit program to generate a list of values that are not generally used, you would create an ABAP program and assign it using this type of processing. • **Authorizations** If you have created, configured, and set up your authorizations within BW against the specific characteristic you are reporting on, you can use that authorization process within the variable. • **SAP Exits** SAP offers SBC user exits delivered with the system for certain variables, mostly in the area of time characteristics. These can be accessed using the transaction code CMOD. Then go to the Utilities|SAP Enhancements option to view the SAP exit for variables. Alternatively, you can use the transaction code SMOD to go directly to the SAP exits.
Reference Characteristic	If a reference characteristic is involved, you will be able to identify it from this section. For example, the reference characteristic for Sold-To Party is Customer.

TABLE 6-9   Settings for the General Tab of the Change Variable Dialog Box

We will use the Manual Input/Default Values option; therefore, the Replacement tab will not be available and will not show any settings. However, this functionality will be covered a bit later in this chapter and we'll address those settings at that time. For now, we will be looking at the Details tab. The following illustration shows this tab and the parameters available. In the Basic Settings section of this tab, you will find several options.

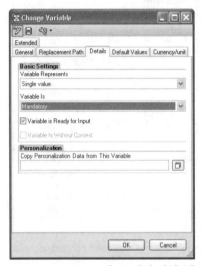

Copyright by SAP AG

This tabbed page from the Variables Editor is required for almost all variable types. Only those variables with the processing type Replacement Path do not require this tabbed page. If the tabbed page is not required, the fields on the Details tabbed page are not input-ready. On the Details tabbed page, you have the following options for the settings:

NOTE *The individual options for the settings vary, depending on the variable type and processing type. All the possible settings are listed here. The Variables Editor automatically displays only those settings that are appropriate.*

- **Variable Represents**
  - **Single Value** The variable represents one value only.
  - **Multiple Single Values** The variable represents a number of single values. This setting is useful in hierarchy nodes, for example, to allow you to enter several single nodes.
  - **Interval** The variable represents a specific "from" value and a specific "to" value, thus the interval.
  - **Selection Option** The variable represents any combination of single values and intervals. In the variable screen where you select values for variables, you can also work with operators (>, <, =, and so on), search by specific criteria (for example, search for all values that begin with *A*), and exclude certain values (by specifying the values for which you do not want to search).

- **Precalculated Value Set**   The variable represents a set of values that were precalculated with a query by the BEx Broadcaster. The available values are those that were precalculated for the characteristic of the variable (such as 0SOLD_TO *Sold-To Party*) or its basic characteristic (such as 0CUSTOMER *Customer*). Such a variable can also be input-ready. You can select various value sets in the variable screen at runtime.

NOTE   *For technical reasons, you cannot use variables that represent a precalculated value set in restricted key figures or in selection structure elements.*

- **Variable Is**
  - **Optional**   If you select this setting, the variable does *not* have to be filled with a value at runtime.
  - **Mandatory**   If you select this setting, at least one value has to be specified for the variable at runtime. The initial value (#) is permitted explicitly. The initial value # means "unassigned" (that is, you can use it to explicitly select all data records in which this characteristic has no instances).
  - **Mandatory, Initial Value Not Allowed**   If you select this setting, at least one value has to be specified for the variable at runtime. The initial value (#) is *not* permitted. You must enter one or more concrete values in the variable screen to be able to execute the query.
  - **Variable Is Ready for Input**   Using this option, you specify whether the variable is to be ready for input when the query or web application is executed. If the Variable Is Ready for Input option is selected (this is the default setting delivered with the initial set up), when you execute the query or web application, a dialog box appears (the variable screen). You can either specify the value(s) you want to use, confirm the default value(s), or change the default value(s). You can deactivate the Variable Is Ready for Input option if you want to assign a value to the variable beforehand. When you execute the query or the web application, it is filled automatically with a value.

NOTE   *If you set the variable as being not ready for input, but have set the variable value as mandatory and have not specified a default value, the system cannot execute the query and an error message is displayed.*

The Variable Is Ready for Input option is available for the processing types Manual Input/Default Value, Customer Exit, SAP Exit, and Authorization.

- **Variable Is Without Context**   If you select the Variable Is Without Context option, you are specifying that the variable can be filled with values independent of an executed query. Examples are Current Day and Current Year. You can set this indicator for exit variables only. This indicator is generally not set for all other variable types; the field is therefore deactivated (that is, all other variables are treated as context specific).
- **Copy Personalization Data from This Variable**   Users can personalize variable values for input-ready variables. The personalized values are saved for each variable and each user.

If you want to use the same personalization data in more than one variable, enter the names of the variables under which the personalization data is stored in this input field. Setting up a template variable with the specific personalized data is a good idea because you can use this in all the queries and manage it from one variable.

- **Length of Input Field**   For text variables, the option Length of Input Field also appears on the Details tab page. Specify a number here. This specifies the number of characters of text the user can enter for the variable.

In the Default tab, you have the option to enter default value(s) for the initial view of the variable. To access this option, choose Button Change Standard Values and you will get a pop-up screen, shown next, that enables you to choose the default values. The final tab on the Change Variable dialog box is Currency/Unit, and as you might expect this is for use in the creation of a formula variable to be used for key figure calculations. Formula variables usually represent numbers without dimensions. You can select a dimension indicator so that the formula variable represents a dimension such as amount, quantity, or price. Depending on the dimension, you can determine a currency or a unit. The following dimensions are available:

- **Amount**   If you choose Amount as the dimension, you can select a currency.
- **Quantity**   If you choose Quantity as the dimension, you can select a unit.
- **Price**   If you choose Price as the dimension, you can select a currency and a unit (Price = Currency/Unit).
- **Number (=default setting)**   If you choose Number as the dimension, you do not need to make any further entries.
- **Date**   If you choose Date as the dimension, you do not need to make any further entries.

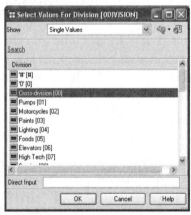

Copyright by SAP AG

Once you're done with the parameters in the Variable settings, move the variable to the right side of the screen and click OK. This will take you back to the Query Designer screen, as shown in the following illustration.

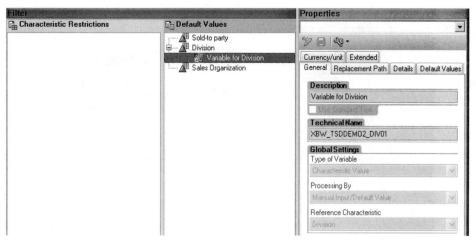

We can now go back and execute the query with the Division variable assigned. The first of the following illustrations shows the execution screen for the BEx Analyzer. Upon execution, the initial screen is a pop-up that requests a division to be entered into the field. You can pick from a drop-down list if this is the initial execution, or you can use the option to pick from a list of divisions, as shown in the second illustration. A number of other important fields are shown here, and we will talk about them a bit later. Once you have identified the value for the variable, you can execute the query and confirm that the list of information is specific to the division (in this case, the division is Pumps).

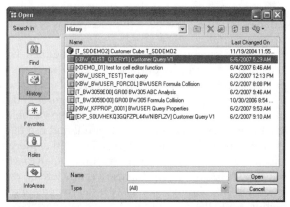

The next two illustrations show the final views of this information. We will now expand on this functionality to show both the use of the characteristic variables and the text variables.

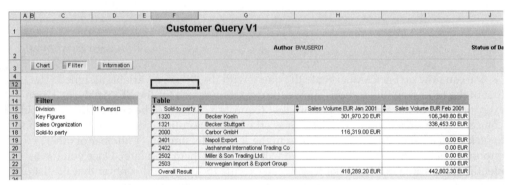

Text Variables   Text variables represent text used in descriptions of queries, calculated key figures, and structural components.

You can use text variables when you create calculated key figures, restricted key figures, selections, and formulas in the description of these objects. Therefore, you can find text variables anywhere text can be replaced or used. In our particular situation, we will be using a text variable to help with the heading of the columns for key figures and calendar months. This scenario is a bit long and complex because we are using two variables at the same time, so be sure to follow along with the screen shots, which you'll find useful. We will be looking to help a query with the columns and column headings. The initial query view is shown in the first of the following illustrations. As you can see, the columns are RKFs for the months and the key figure Sales Volume. Therefore, we need to use a characteristic value variable for the months and a text variable for the column headings. We start by creating the characteristic variable for months. Stepping into the RKF for months, we can start the creation of the characteristic variable, as shown in the second illustration.

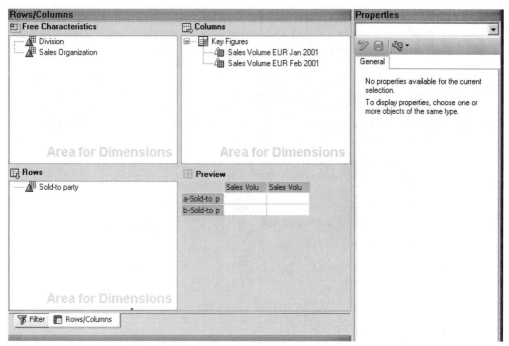

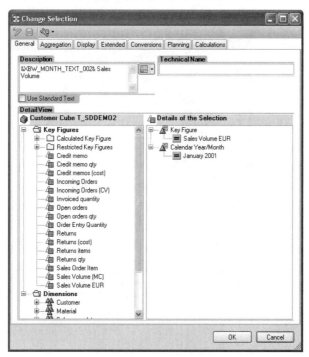

NOTE *When the system is replacing text variables, if it finds no values or multiple values for the reference characteristic and is unable to determine a unique value, the technical name is output as the result, and &<technical name of the text variable>& will appear.*

The first of the following illustrations shows the location where we create the variable for month. Choose Variable from the drop-down list and go through the dialog box to create the month variable BWX_MON_CHAR_001. Notice the settings for this variable, shown in the second illustration. Once we are finished, we can select this variable from the list, as shown in the third illustration.

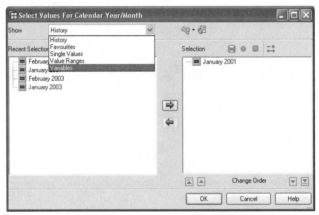

Copyright by SAP AG

Copyright by SAP AG

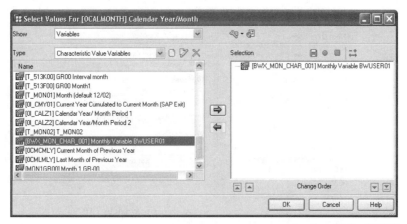

Now we can start creating the text variable. The first of the following illustrations shows the initial view of the variable. Notice the variable symbol next to the Text field for the column heading. We are going to use this to create the text variable. The second illustration shows the variable-creation process, which is very similar to what we have gone through before. The difference here is that we will be using the Replacement Path option so we can link the text variable to the InfoObject 0CALMONTH and use the text saved at the InfoObject level to fill the column heading. The third illustration shows the information used in the dialog box.

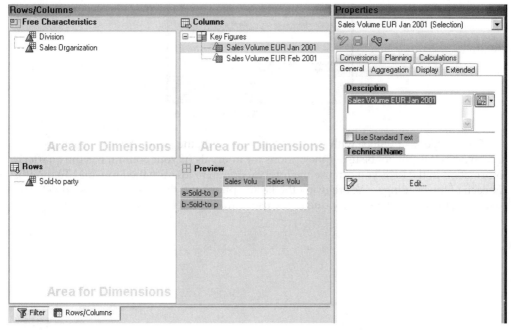

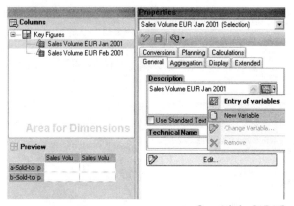

Copyright by SAP AG

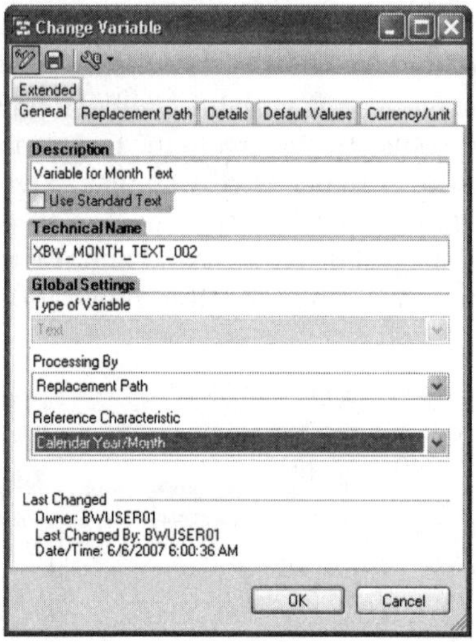

Copyright by SAP AG

The replacement will be with the InfoObject and with the key of the InfoObject, as shown next. We will not be using the options for intervals (if your column has the quarterly information in the RKF, you can use the Interval option to identify the From and To months for each of the headings). We are using the From option, and there is no offset start yet. The remaining tabs are not necessary due to the use of the replacement type.

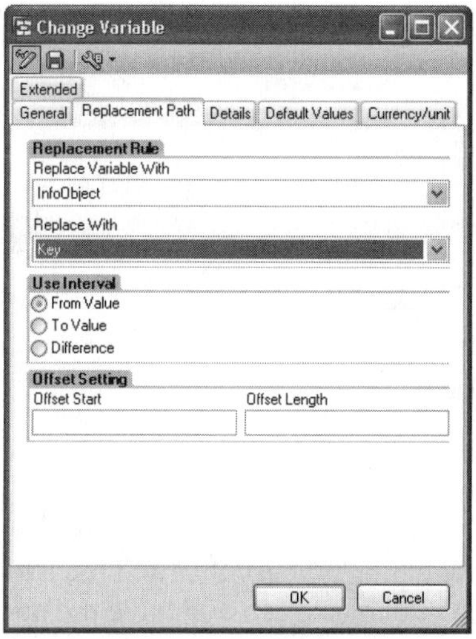

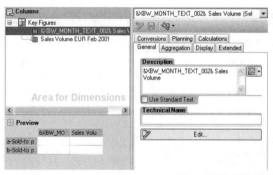

Copyright by SAP AG

The first of the following illustrations shows the final view of the finished text variable. We are ready to execute this query and see what the results are in the BEx Analyzer. The second illustration shows the initial variable screen for data entry. This still has the available division variable, but it also has the variable for the month. We don't see anything for the variable for the text because that variable will be filled based on the replacement process. Using January of 2001, we see that the data in the first column is showing the information for 01/2001. Also, the column heading is showing the month/year of this information, which was defaulted automatically, as shown in the third illustration.

Copyright by SAP AG

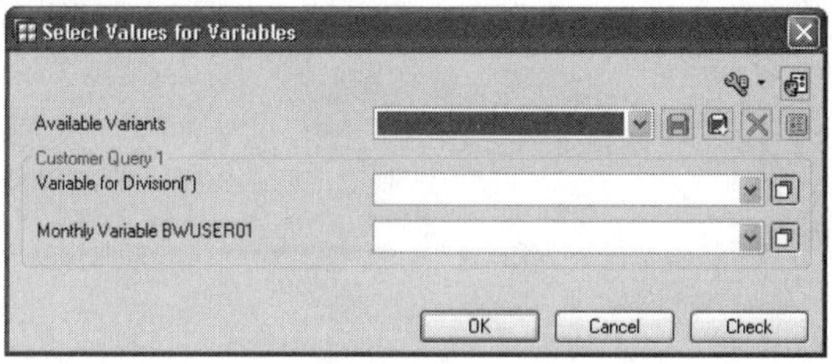

Copyright by SAP AG

Customer Query 1			
Author BWUSER01			Status of Data 2/28/2003 11:27
Chart	Filter	Information	

Table

Sold-to party		200101 Sales Volume	Sales Volume EUR Feb 2001
1320	Becker Koeln	301,970.20 EUR	106,348.80 EUR
1321	Becker Stuttgart		336,453.50 EUR
2000	Carbor GmbH	116,319.00 EUR	
2401	Napoli Export		0.00 EUR
2402	Jashanmal International Trading Co		0.00 EUR
2502	Miller & Son Trading Ltd.		0.00 EUR
2503	Norwegian Import & Export Group		0.00 EUR
Overall Result		418,289.20 EUR	442,802.30 EUR

As you can see, we are developing a query that will have long-term use because we can enter any month/year into the variable screen and have the query adjusted based on that information. Now, we can take this one step further. Let's go back into our query and set up the other column with variables. Thus, we will have a query with a series of variables in it controlled by just one variable that the end user sees. We are looking to go back and add these variables to the second column and upgrade the query for all of the data. The first of the following illustrations starts the process. Stepping into the column for Feb, we can use the same variable we used for the initial column, but we will use the Offset option to add 1 to the variable. Thus, at time of execution, it adds one month (in this case) to the month entered by the business user. The second illustration shows that we have now included the text variable as well as the characteristic variable. We now need to include the option for the offset. The final illustration shows the steps included in this process.

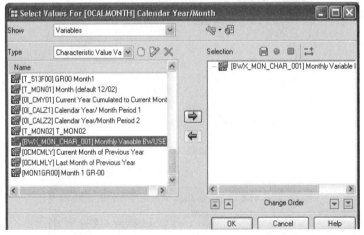

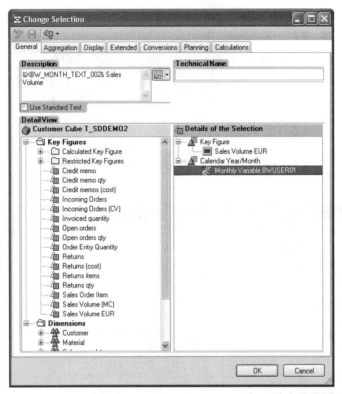

Copyright by SAP AG

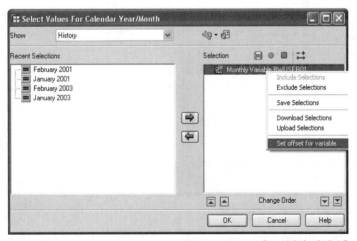

Copyright by SAP AG

Right-click the variable and choose Set Offset for Variable. A dialog box appears in which you can increase or decrease the offset, as shown in the first of the following illustrations. Once that is complete, choose OK and you will be sent back to the initial screen. The second illustration shows the final result. Execute the query, and you can see that there is only one variable to fill in.

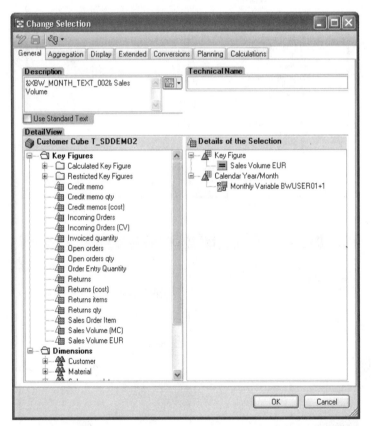

The result of the query is that *both* columns are filled in with the appropriate information and the columns are filled in with the appropriate months. The next two illustrations show the results in the query. You have now created the initial columns of a rolling forecast report, and all the business user sees is *one* variable that will control the entire query. As you can see, this is a very powerful option that helps decrease the maintenance of the variables and queries.

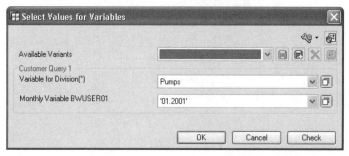

				200101 Sales Volume	200102 Sales Volume		

Customer Query 1

Author BWUSER01   Status of Data 2/28/2003 11:27

Chart   Filter   Information

Table

Sold-to party		200101 Sales Volume	200102 Sales Volume
1320	Becker Koeln	301,970.20 EUR	106,348.80 EUR
1321	Becker Stuttgart		336,453.50 EUR
2000	Carbor GmbH	116,319.00 EUR	
2401	Napoli Export		0.00 EUR
2402	Jashanmal International Trading Co		0.00 EUR
2502	Miller & Son Trading Ltd.		0.00 EUR
2503	Norwegian Import & Export Group		0.00 EUR
Overall Result		418,289.20 EUR	442,802.30 EUR

Formula Variables   The next variable we will review is the formula variable, which is specifically used in the calculations with key figures. Formula variables are used for additional analysis for "what-if" statements: What if the revenue was 10% higher? What if my costs were 5% lower? What are the average costs for my divisions? You can use the formula variable to fill in the number of stores, and including a formula variable in the CKF configuration will provide it to your business user. This is a very powerful tool to use for analysis purposes. Formula variables represent numerical values. Numerical values are also used for calculating exceptions and conditions, and you can use formula variables there as well. The following illustration shows the initial view of where we start to create formula variables.

Copyright by SAP AG

As you can see, we are accessing the CKF screens to start this process. Once you execute this option, you access the CKF screen, where you can create a formula variable in the lower section of the screen, as shown in the following illustration. Now we are going to use one of the available months and multiply that with the formula variable. The creation of the formula variable is not much different from the others we have discussed.

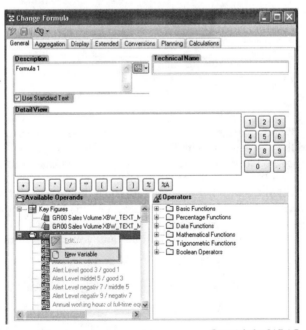

Copyright by SAP AG

The next two illustrations take us through the screens we will see. The General tab is no different from what we've seen before, and we are going to use a manual input approach to this variable. The one thing that is different is the identification of a UOM or currency. In this case, we are looking at a number so that if there are different currencies, we can execute this without having to deal with the different currencies. We will discuss the currency conversion and UOM conversion in Chapter 13.

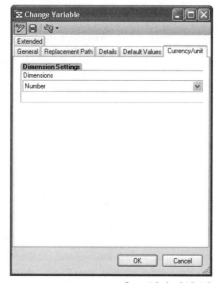

Copyright by SAP AG

Copyright by SAP AG

Once complete, your formula would look similar the basic calculations shown in the first of the following illustrations. The final configuration view is shown in the second illustration. Now we can execute the query and review the results.

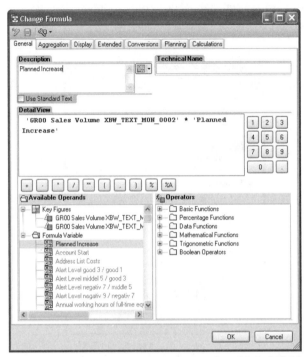

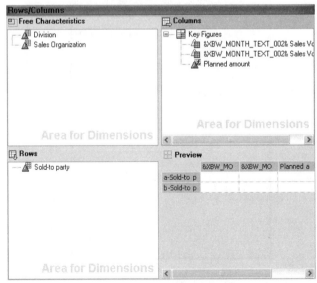

The first of the following illustrations shows the initial screen upon execution, and we indicated a planned increase of 2. If the calculation is correct, we should see that the planned increase will be two times the sales volume for the last month. In the second illustration, we see that this is exactly the outcome from the query. Using formula variables opens up an entirely new area for the business users and allows for the interactive processing of data. You should realize that with this functionality, the calculations are not saved to the BW system. However, having a display of results is better than nothing. We will be looking at the functionality of Integrated Planning in Chapter 17. This process does allow for data posting and input to the BW system. Therefore, we can turn these types of activities into actual values in the InfoCubes possibly assigned to a version for managing the types of data in one InfoCube.

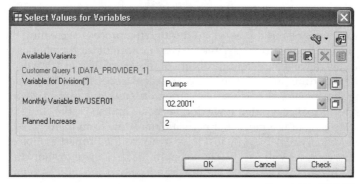

Copyright by SAP AG

				Customer Query 1				
					Author BWUSER01			Status of Data 2/28
	Chart	Filter	Information					
Filter			**Table**					
Division	01 Pumps		Sold-to party		200102 Sales Volume	200103 Sales Volume	Planned amount	
Key Figures			1000	Becker Berlin		0.00 EUR	0.00 EUR	
Sales Organization			1032	Institut fuer Umweltforschung		3,185.40 EUR	6,370.80 EUR	
Sold-to party			1320	Becker Koeln	106,348.80 EUR	233,301.90 EUR	466,603.80 EUR	
			1321	Becker Stuttgart	336,453.50 EUR			
			2000	Carbor GmbH		0.00 EUR	0.00 EUR	
			2401	Napoli Export	0.00 EUR	194,950.00 EUR	389,900.00 EUR	
			2402	Jashanmal International Trading Co	0.00 EUR	215,450.00 EUR	430,900.00 EUR	
			2502	Miller & Son Trading Ltd.	0.00 EUR	218,950.00 EUR	437,900.00 EUR	
			2503	Norwegian Import & Export Group	0.00 EUR	343,950.00 EUR	687,900.00 EUR	
			Overall Result		442,802.30 EUR	1,209,787.30 EUR	2,419,574.60 EUR	

Copyright by SAP AG

Hierarchy Variables   We've covered characteristic, text, and formula variables, and we have worked with different processing types—namely, the manual entry and replacement type. The last grouping of variable types is the hierarchy variables—both the hierarchy itself and the hierarchy node variable. The setup of these variables is very similar to what we just finished with the other three types of variables, so we will not dwell on the setup too much but rather on the functionality and differences in the setup. Hierarchy variables represent hierarchies and can be used wherever hierarchies can be selected. If you restrict characteristics to hierarchies or select presentation hierarchies, you can also use hierarchy variables. Hierarchy node variables represent a node in a hierarchy and can be used wherever hierarchy nodes can be used. The important thing to remember here is to make sure you create the hierarchy variables—whether they are the nodes or the actual variables—from the correct location. Keep the following points in mind:

- Hierarchy node variables are created from the Restrict screen of the InfoObject (make sure that the type is set to Hierarchy so that you can see the hierarchy node variable screen).

- Hierarchy variables are created from the Properties screen of the InfoObject or from within the restriction of the node variable.

You will better understand this as we go through the process of creating the variables. Conceptually, the use of these two variables is very important for the queries. They can very easily help with the management and flexibility of the query displays. We use hierarchies quite a bit in the reporting process. The ability to access a specific node or a particular hierarchy using this functionality is very user friendly. Also, due to the size of some of the hierarchies, its performance is aided if we don't execute and show the entire hierarchy but rather just execute and show a particular node and navigate from there.

To create a hierarchy variable, you just have to access the Properties tabs of the InfoObject. In this case, we will use the characteristic 0MATERIAL to show the creation of the variable for a hierarchy. The following illustration shows the initial screen for the hierarchy variable.

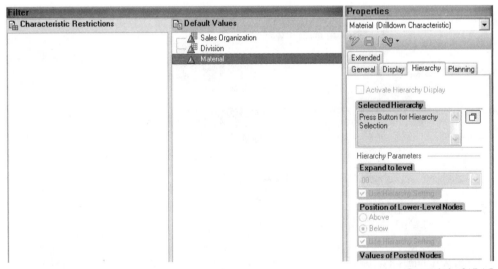

Copyright by SAP AG

Notice that we are in the Hierarchy tab in the Properties section for 0MATERIAL. If you click the Select icon, the dialog box for the hierarchy setup will appear. If the hierarchy is time dependent, you will see options for From and To dates. Otherwise, you will view just the options for the hierarchy or variable. The following illustration shows this information.

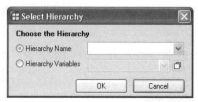

Copyright by SAP AG

Choosing the Hierarchy Variables option opens another dialog box for the creation of hierarchy variables. Notice the grayed out section confirming that we're in the right place to create hierarchy variables, as shown in the first of the following illustrations. The second illustration shows the initial Create New Variable option.

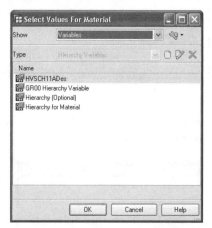

Copyright by SAP AG

Copyright by SAP AG

The following illustration shows the configuration of the hierarchy variable. Again, notice the grayed out field indicating we're creating a hierarchy variable.

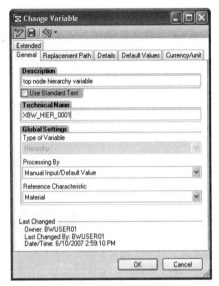

Copyright by SAP AG

Finally, after all settings are complete, we click OK and revert back to the initial screen with the variable defaulted, as shown here.

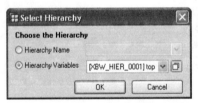

Copyright by SAP AG

The next illustration shows the final view from the Query Designer for the hierarchy variable for 0material. We are now ready to execute the query and display the variable's usage.

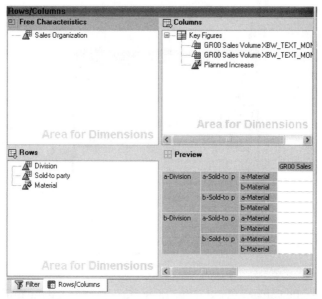

Copyright by SAP AG

The next illustration shows the initial view of the variable pop-up.

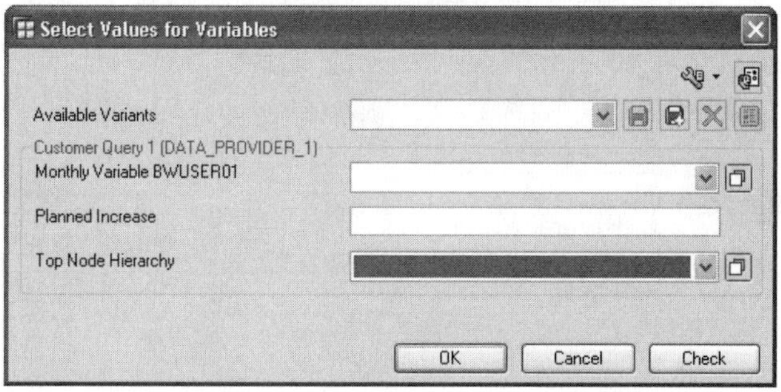

Copyright by SAP AG

The next illustration shows the list of hierarchies available for use by the InfoObject 0MATERIAL.

Copyright by SAP AG

Notice that the only values offered to the query for selection are the full hierarchies. After filling in the hierarchy we are interested in viewing, we can see that this hierarchy is displayed in the query, as shown next.

	Material		200102 Sales Volume	200103 Sales Volume	Planned amount
	Overall Result		3,660,820.93 EUR	5,975,835.70 EUR	11,951,671.40 EUR
▼	-ROOT	Product hierarchy	3,107,142.05 EUR	5,025,313.77 EUR	10,050,627.54 EUR
▼	00100	Machines	442,802.30 EUR	1,209,787.30 EUR	2,419,574.60 EUR
▶	0010000100	Pumps	442,802.30 EUR	1,209,787.30 EUR	2,419,574.60 EUR
▼	00105	Vehicles	606,672.41 EUR	981,275.76 EUR	1,962,551.52 EUR
▶	0010500100	Motorcycles	606,672.41 EUR	981,275.76 EUR	1,962,551.52 EUR
▼	00115	Lighting	1,203,562.10 EUR	1,180,255.82 EUR	2,360,511.64 EUR
▶	0011500100	Bulbs	1,203,562.10 EUR	1,180,255.82 EUR	2,360,511.64 EUR
▶	00125	Hardware	853,240.38 EUR	1,653,130.03 EUR	3,306,260.06 EUR
▶	00140	Services	864.86 EUR	864.86 EUR	1,729.72 EUR
▶	Not Assigned Material (s)		553,678.88 EUR	950,521.93 EUR	1,901,043.86 EUR

Customer Query 1

Author BWUSER01   Status of Data 2/28/20C

Filter: Division, Key Figures, Material, Sales Organization

Copyright by SAP AG

In the case of the Hierarchy Node variable, there is only a minor difference in the process of creating the variable but the issue is with the starting point for the creation process and this is a large part of the issue with creating these variables. The key is that we start out in the Restrict screen for the characteristic. The next illustration shows this step. Once this screen has been accessed, you will be able to identify the hierarchy used to create a hierarchy node variable by choosing the correct hierarchy from this screen.

Copyright by SAP AG

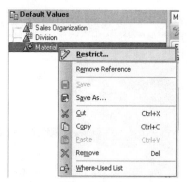

The next illustration shows the dialog box you will see. Notice at the very bottom of the dialog box you have the ability to choose a hierarchy. If you change this setting, you will be creating a hierarchy node variable for that specific hierarchy. We have decided to stay with the Material Class hierarchy as the root for this variable. The process of creating this type of variable is not any different from creating the variable for a hierarchy. Therefore, we will not go through each step. The end result is that we have a hierarchy node variable that is tied to the Material Class hierarchy, and we can identify a node to report on from the execution of the query.

Copyright by SAP AG

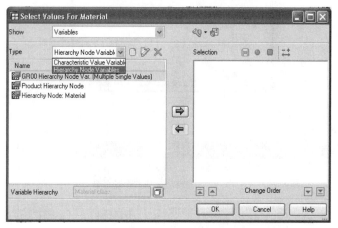

The next three illustrations show the steps for executing the query: Choosing the variable hierarchy node, identifying the actual node, and executing the query.

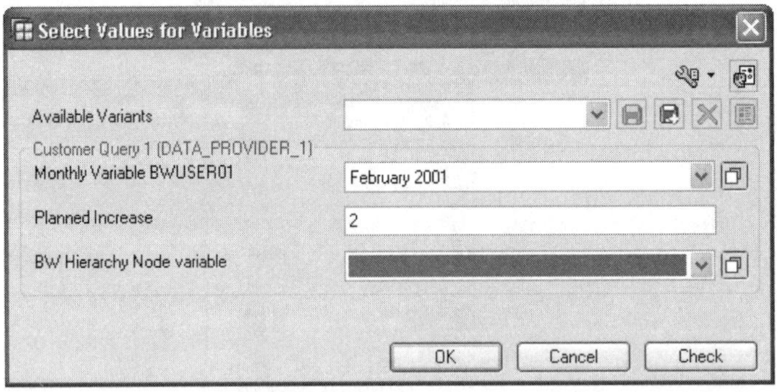

Copyright by SAP AG

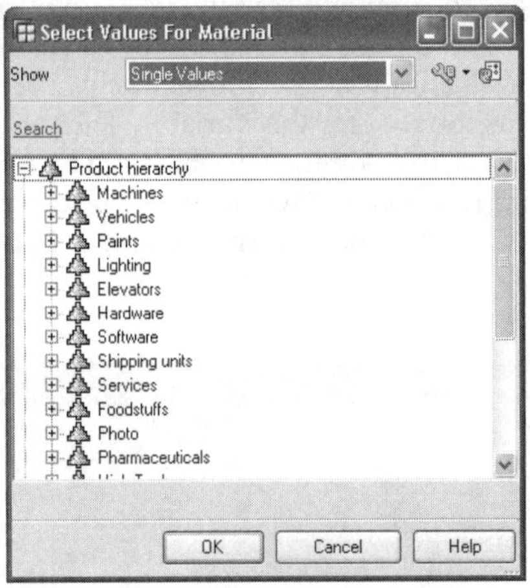

Copyright by SAP AG

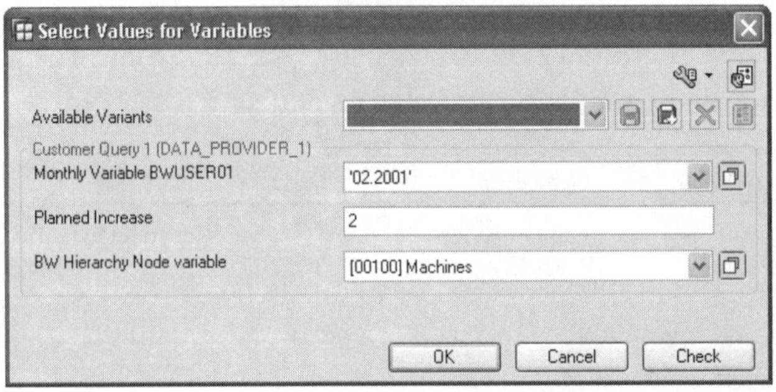

Copyright by SAP AG

The results are that the query displays just that node of the hierarchy we are interested in viewing, as shown here:

	Material			200102 Sales Volume	200103 Sales Volume	Planned amount
	00100	Machines		442,802.30 EUR	1,209,787.30 EUR	2,419,574.60 EUR
	0010000100	Pumps		442,802.30 EUR	1,209,787.30 EUR	2,419,574.60 EUR
	001000001000000110	Special pump		442,802.30 EUR	1,209,787.30 EUR	2,419,574.60 EUR
	P-101	Pump PRECISION 101		0.00 EUR	0.00 EUR	0.00 EUR
	P-102	Pump PRECISION 102		21,259.70 EUR	345,059.70 EUR	690,119.40 EUR
	P-103	Pump PRECISION 103		106,348.80 EUR	403,795.60 EUR	807,591.20 EUR
	P-104	Pump PRECISION 104		92,215.80 EUR	457,746.60 EUR	915,493.20 EUR
	P-402	Pump standard IDESNORM 100-402		222,978.00 EUR	3,185.40 EUR	6,370.80 EUR

Customer Query 1 — Author BWUSER01 — Status of Data 2/28/2003 11:27

Process Types   We have reviewed several of the process types, but we haven't used two of them in a demo. Therefore, a bit more information on the Customer Exit and SAP Exit and Authorization process types is in order. The SAP Exit processing type is contained in variables delivered within the BI Content framework. You can find the delivered variables in the Metadata Repository if you search for variables using the search function.

NOTE   *The technical names of delivered SAP objects always begin with a number.*

You must activate the delivered variables before you can use them. SAP delivers a number of variables. Some variables are processed via automatic replacement using a predefined replacement path (SAP Exit processing type). A large majority of these are in the area of time characteristics. In the Variables Editor, choose the processing type SAP Exit from the General tabbed page. Once you have identified the SAP Exit, you should not have to set up any further parameters in the variable screens.

You have the option of using a Customer Exit to set up a processing type for variables that is tailored specifically to your needs. The Customer Exit processing type for variables enables you to determine values for variables by means of a function module exit. The standard function module used is EXIT_SAPLRRS0_001. You create a project in transaction CMOD by selecting the SAP enhancement RSR000001 and assign this to the enhancement project. Activate the project. Another processing type Authorization enables variables to be filled with values automatically from the authorization of a user. The processing type Authorization can be used with characteristic value variables and hierarchy node variables. You first must maintain the authorizations in transaction RSSM or the new Analysis Authorization. If you choose Process with Authorization when you create a variable, the variable is automatically filled with the values of the user's authorization. When the user opens a query, the data is selected automatically according to their authorizations.

> **NOTE** *Note that when variables are filled automatically, they do not have to be ready for input, which means a variable screen does not need to appear when you execute the query or web application. The user opens the query with the authorization variable, and only the data that corresponds to their authorizations is displayed.*

Pre-query/Result Query There are a number of other uses for variables—too many to elaborate on in this book. However, we should discuss some additional functions before we finish off variables. One of the ones used quite frequently is the pre-query or result query. There is no function in the query process that states specifically that a particular query is a pre-query or a result query. This naming convention is only due to the use of the specific query. The concept here is that you have a list of, say, divisions that you are interested in seeing on an ongoing basis. These are the divisions you are responsible for and maintain. Now, if you have authorizations set up, you don't have to go through this process. However, if you need to, it's a good process to be aware of for variables.

We will be using two queries. The first query is the "control" query, and the second query is the display query. The first query will be used as a filter in a variable for the second query. This is accomplished by using the characteristic variable with a process type of Replacement. In this process type, the only source of information has to be a query—thus, the use of two queries for the execution of this concept. The setup is not complex, but rather just a bit unusual. Therefore, set up a query with a limited number of divisions—your divisions. Then use the main query and set up a variable on the characteristic division with the Replacement Path process type and use the control query as the source of information. Once you execute the main query, the control query will be executed first. Then you can fill the main query with the selections used in the control query. This will generate a final view of the query with the desired divisions. The following illustrations show the steps involved. The first shows setting up the "control" query with a limited number of divisions, and the second is the view of the control query.

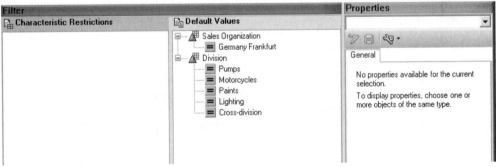

Copyright by SAP AG

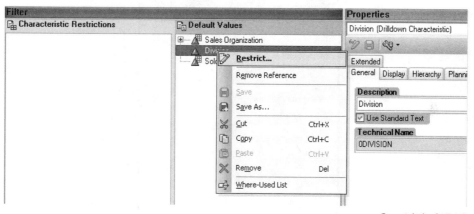

The first of the following illustrations shows setting up the variable on the characteristic Division in the main query. The second shows setting up of the variable with Replacement Path used for the Processing By option. The final illustration shows the use of the query in the replacement process.

The first of the following illustrations shows the final view of the variable in the configuration of the Query Designer, and the second shows the results of the query. There is no pop-up for changing the control query; therefore, you will always get the expected results.

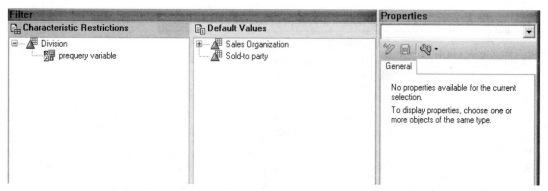

Copyright by SAP AG

Division		Sold-to party		Sales Volume EUR	Sales Order Item	Returns	Invoiced quantity
00	Cross-division	1172	CBD Computer Based Design	4,780.57 EUR	1	0.00 EUR	17 AU
		1400	A.I.T. GmbH	0.00 EUR	1	0.00 EUR	0 PC
		T-S11A00	CompuMax GmbH	0.00 EUR	2	0.00 EUR	0 PC
		T-S11A01	CompuMax GmbH	0.00 EUR	2	0.00 EUR	0 PC
		T-S11B00	PC-World Stuttgart KG	0.00 EUR	1	0.00 EUR	0 PC
		T-S11B01	PC-World Stuttgart KG	0.00 EUR	1	0.00 EUR	0 PC
		Result		4,780.57 EUR	8	0.00 EUR	17 AU
01	Pumps	1000	Becker Berlin	3,607,592.75 EUR	16	0.00 EUR	1,287 PC
		1030	DELA Handelsgesellschaft mbH	0.00 EUR	0	0.00 EUR	0 PC
		1031	Global Trade AG	0.00 EUR	0	0.00 EUR	0 PC
		1032	Institut fuer Umweltforschung	8,341,978.84 EUR	68	0.00 EUR	2,719 PC
		1171	Hitech AG	5,341.24 EUR	1	0.00 EUR	1 PC
		1200	Minerva Energieversorgung GmbH	284,022.63 EUR	4	0.00 EUR	97 PC
		1320	Becker Koeln	5,386,763.33 EUR	49	0.00 EUR	1,722 PC
		1321	Becker Stuttgart	10,999,518.15 EUR	87	0.00 EUR	3,566 PC
		1350	NSM Pumpentechnik AG	2,812.11 EUR	1	0.00 EUR	1 PC
		1390	Technik und Systeme GmbH	46,248.44 EUR	6	0.00 EUR	14 PC
		1400	A.I.T. GmbH	523,051.59 EUR	4	0.00 EUR	186 PC
		1410	PILAR am Neckar	616,618.00 EUR	2	0.00 EUR	220 PC
		2000	Carbor GmbH	11,447,453.13 EUR	90	0.00 EUR	3,802 PC
		4999	Hallmann Anlagenbau GmbH	30,664.02 EUR	3	0.00 EUR	10 PC
		CUSTOMER00	Becker 00	7,000.00 EUR	1	0.00 EUR	2 PC
		Result		41,299,064.23 EUR	332	0.00 EUR	13,627 PC
02	Motorcycles	1174	Motomarkt Stuttgart GmbH	15,390,904.26 EUR	92	0.00 EUR	32,351 PC
		1900	J & P	17,488,544.32 EUR	92	0.00 EUR	35,245 PC
		1901	Motor Sports	12,614,125.37 EUR	104	0.00 EUR	50,420 PC

Table /

Copyright by SAP AG

This is a perfect example of using the Replacement Path option in queries. You may also find that this is a good solution if you are looking to use two conditions (details later in Chapter 8) in one query. If you are using more than one condition in a query, you may find that depending on how you drill down in the query, your conditions will become confused and give you incorrect answers. Using the pre-query/result query option will help in organizing your conditions and make sure that during the drilldown you always get consistent results.

Other Settings for Variables   To complete this portion, we need to round out the discussion concerning the use of selection settings in the variable. Table 6-10 provides a list of the selection options.

To show some of this functionality, we'll go through a couple of examples. In the first of the following illustrations, we have defined a variable with the Multiple Single Selection option. The second illustration shows this option in action in a query execution. Using the selection

Setting	Description and Functionality
Single Value	This variable represents one value only.
Multiple Single Values	The variable represents a list of single values. You can use this setting with hierarchy nodes.
Interval	The variable represents a From and To value.
Selection Option	The variable represents a combination of single values and intervals of your choice.
Precalculated Value Set	The variable represents a number of values that are stored in a database table by the reporting agent (3.x functionality).

TABLE 6-10   List of Selection Options in the Change Variable Dialog Box

box, you have a list of divisions available to you to choose a series of single values, as shown in the third illustration. Thus we can have a list of values to use in our query. In the fourth illustration, we take this one step further with the ability to use the context menu in the field, which offers us the ability to upload, download, and save the selections. The final illustration shows the end result, where the three single values are included in the selection field.

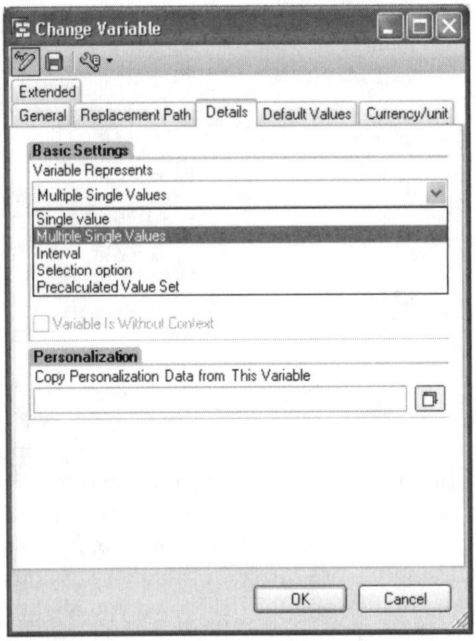

Copyright by SAP AG

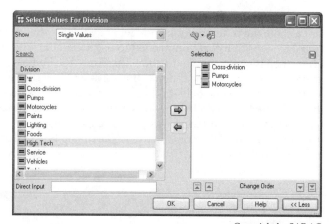

Copyright by SAP AG

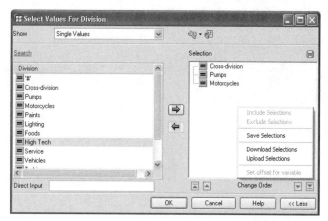

Copyright by SAP AG

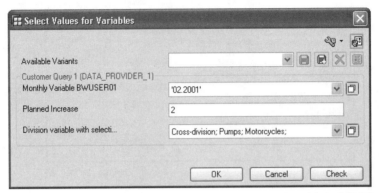

It is also important to note the different look and feel of a variable that use the option Interval. In the previous versions of BW, if you needed to use a variable with the ability to enter a range or interval, then the pop-up would show the From and To fields for entering the values. In the current version, a variable that has this setting will *not* show the interval but rather will initially show just the one field, and you need to access the interval view via the F4 help input option. The first of the following illustrations shows the initial screen with a variable for Division. The parameter Interval was used to create this variable. In the second illustration, the F4 help input indicator was used. The dialog box that appears now has the interval From and To fields available. Therefore, don't be surprised by this functionality in the 7.0 BW version.

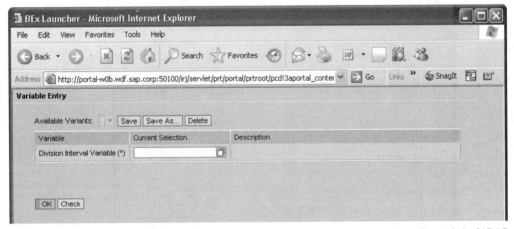

Select values for Division (INTER_VAR   0003)

Show view: Value ranges ▾

Value ranges

Sign: Include ▾
Operator: between ▾
From: *
To: *

Enter an interval for Division:

OK   Cancel

Note   *If you use transaction code RSRT to do any performance analysis, the Interval variable will show up as an interval and not as a single-value field, then using the F4 input option to access the values. If you decide to use the transaction code RSRT first before executing your query online you would not realize that there is a difference between the old view and new view of the variable with a range.*

Variants   We'll close out this section with a comment about the use of variants. We do have the availability to create variants for queries. Variants are user-defined groups of values defined at the time of execution of the query. You can save a variant and be able to use that variant in the future for fast-and-easy access to a set list of values. A minor twist to this process is that you fill in the values you want to have in your variant and then you execute the Save process. The first of the following illustrations shows the initial steps for this activity. Here, the division Pumps is to be saved as a variant. You click the selection button to execute the Save operation. Once you execute this process, a dialog box appears and you fill in a technical name for the variant and then click OK. The second illustration shows the Save process, and the third shows the drop-down displaying the saved variant.

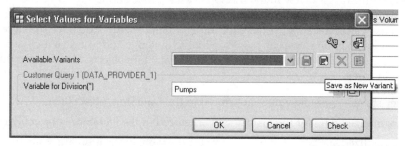

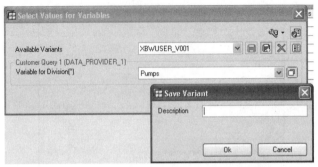

Copyright by SAP AG

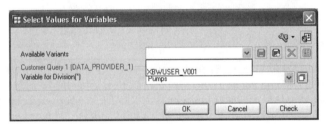

Copyright by SAP AG

> **NOTE** *Variants are available in both the BEx Analyzer and the Bex Web Analyzer in the current version.*

Personalization in the BEx Query Designer

You can use a number of options to help with business user access to the correct information or settings. You have the use of authorizations, which is probably the best option, but if you don't have that to work with, you have the ability to use *personalization* in your queries. This function allows users to fill variables with user-specific values, to save user-specific accesses to BI objects for the history view in the BEx Open dialog box, and to save user-specific starting views for web applications (you will see this in the web applications a bit later in the chapter). To use personalization, you must complete a bit of setup. You have seen a portion of this in a previous chapter, so we can reference that knowledge and just do a review of these screens. The personalized data is stored in different DataStore objects, according to the personalization area:

- User-specific variable values are stored in the DataStore object 0Pers_VAR.
- Personalized data for the history view is stored in the DataStore object 0Pers_BOD.
- Personalized start (bookmarks) views for the web application are stored in the DataStore object 0Pers_WTE.

We have already looked at the personalization for the history view in the Open dialog box for finding objects you have been working with. The one we are interested in is the user-specific variable values stored in the DataStore object 0PERS_VAR. The following illustration shows the view of the DataStore objects in the Administration Workbench.

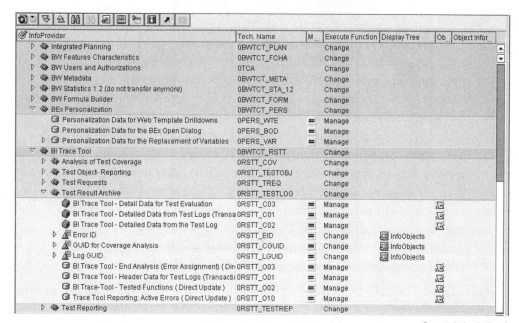

InfoProvider	Tech. Name	M..	Execute Function	Display Tree	Ob..	Object Infor..
▷ ◈ Integrated Planning	0BWTCT_PLAN		Change			
▷ ◈ BW Features Characteristics	0BWTCT_FCHA		Change			
▷ ◈ BW Users and Authorizations	0TCA		Change			
▷ ◈ BW Metadata	0BWTCT_META		Change			
▷ ◈ BW Statistics 1.2 (do not transfer anymore)	0BWTCT_STA_12		Change			
▷ ◈ BW Formula Builder	0BWTCT_FORM		Change			
▽ ◈ BEx Personalization	0BWTCT_PERS		Change			
⬚ Personalization Data for Web Template Drilldowns	0PERS_WTE	=	Manage			
⬚ Personalization Data for the BEx Open Dialog	0PERS_BOD	=	Manage			
▷ ⬚ Personalization Data for the Replacement of Variables	0PERS_VAR	=	Manage			
▽ ◈ BI Trace Tool	0BWTCT_RSTT		Change			
▷ ◈ Analysis of Test Coverage	0RSTT_COV		Change			
▷ ◈ Test Object- Reporting	0RSTT_TESTOBJ		Change			
▷ ◈ Test Requests	0RSTT_TREQ		Change			
▽ ◈ Test Result Archive	0RSTT_TESTLOG		Change			
⬚ BI Trace Tool - Detail Data for Test Evaluation	0RSTT_C03	=	Manage		🖼	
⬚ BI Trace Tool - Detailed Data from Test Logs (Transa	0RSTT_C01	=	Manage		🖼	
⬚ BI Trace Tool - Detailed Data from the Test Log	0RSTT_C02	=	Manage		🖼	
▷ 🔠 Error ID	0RSTT_EID	=	Change	🔳 InfoObjects		
▷ 🔠 GUID for Coverage Analysis	0RSTT_CGUID	=	Change	🔳 InfoObjects		
▷ 🔠 Log GUID	0RSTT_LGUID	=	Change	🔳 InfoObjects		
⬚ BI Trace Tool - End Analysis (Error Assignment) (Dir	0RSTT_O03	=	Manage		🖼	
⬚ BI Trace Tool - Header Data for Test Logs (Transacti	0RSTT_O01	=	Manage		🖼	
⬚ BI Trace-Tool - Tested Functions (Direct Update)	0RSTT_O02	=	Manage		🖼	
⬚ Trace Tool Reporting: Active Errors (Direct Update)	0RSTT_O10	=	Manage		🖼	
▷ ◈ Test Reporting	0RSTT_TESTREP		Change			

Copyright by SAP AG

NOTE *As mentioned before, you have to activate personalization in Customizing (the Implementation Guide) before you can use it. In the SAP Implementation Guide (IMG), see SAP Reference IMG | SAP NetWeaver | Business Intelligence | Settings for Reporting and Analysis | General Settings for Reporting and Analysis | Activate Personalization in BEx. Also, after you have activated personalization in the Business Intelligence IMG, you can no longer deactivate it.*

In many cases, the use of personalization is a bit restrictive. When personalizing variables, you assign a permanent user-specific value to them that cannot be changed in query navigation. You can personalize variables directly in the variable-creation screen or by loading files to the DataStore object with specific values for users. The user can personalize variables at runtime.

The following illustration shows where in the variable-creation process you can identify either a specific value or a variable with personalization assigned to it to be used in the query process.

The next series of illustrations show the use and setup of personalization against a query. This is all from the business user side. If you are concerned with the business users assigning themselves personalization values, you will need to deactivate personalization or not turn it on in the first place. The first illustration shows the execution of personalization based on the variable screen that appears prior to query execution.

The next illustration shows the initial screen after accessing the personalization button.

Copyright by SAP AG

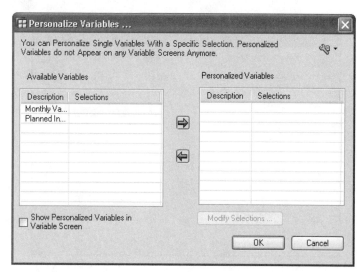

This illustration shows the month/year variable moved to the selection side.

Copyright by SAP AG

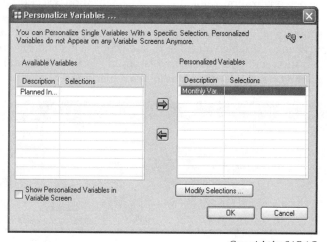

And the following illustration shows the assignment of the value for the month/year 200102.

Copyright by SAP AG

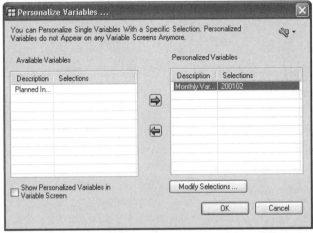

The next illustration shows the execution of the query with personalization turned on. As you can see, the variable field Month/Year doesn't appear on the screen because it has been filled with the personalization value. In the Personalization Selection dialog box, you *must* select the option Show Personalized Variables in Variable Screen. Otherwise, the variable will not show up on the screen and the business user might get confused with the process of trying to change variable values. If this selection is not chosen, you will have to reset your personalization settings in the Administration Workbench for the variable to be active again or you must create another variable as a replacement.

Copyright by SAP AG

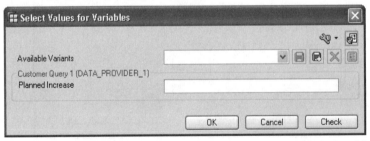

As shown here, the query is executed and is using the value 200102 to drive the columns values rather than having the variable show up with the default values of 200102 through 200103.

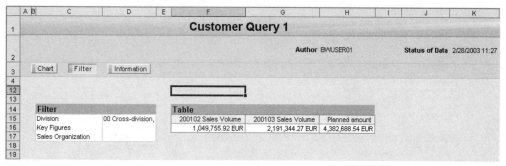

Exceptions

In the process of identifying the uses of the queries and the information generated by the queries, you need to understand what information the business user really is interested in reviewing. Having all the information available is good to a certain point. If we can offer the business user specific information and identify some components that can be highlighted, the information becomes more useable and understandable. This moves the business user from a reviewer of information into a proactive position where they can act on the information quickly and effectively. If we use the exception functionality available in BW, we can move closer to developing this level of information and strategic analysis. Exception functionality allows us to pinpoint information, whether good or bad, and act on it quickly. It allows the business user to notice and make more responsible decisions and to identify events that deviate from expected values. This can be an initial warning system within a report. In exception reporting, you select and highlight objects that are in some way different or critical. Results that fall outside a set of predetermined threshold values (exceptions) are highlighted in color or designated with symbols. This enables you to identify immediately any results that deviate from the expected results.

Exception reporting allows you to determine the objects that are critical for a query, both online and in background processing. The following illustration shows the view of a query with an exception assigned to the results rows for each of the key figure–Sales Volume–by customer and material. This allows the business user to identify the total sales at a glance of each of customers in each type of material and see if there are any variances. This can have numerous applications, such as discount agreements that either your company is assigned to or that you are tracking for your customers. If you know that ordering additional material you will need in the future generates a 10% discount for all the material purchased during the quarter, you might decide to post the order and get the additional discount. Perhaps you have a customer you have offered a discount to if they purchase a certain amount of product from you, and you are tracking their progress through the quarter to see if they are on course to be eligible for that discount.

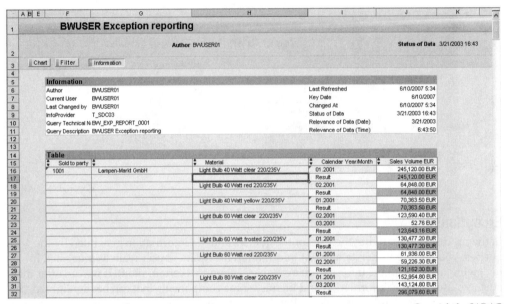

Creating an Exception

Once you have identified the areas where you can use exception reporting, you can then start the process of creating the exceptions in the BEx Query Designer. There are numerous points at which we can create exceptions, such as directly in the workbooks, on the Web, directly in the Web Application Designer, and so on, but we will focus on the functionality in the BEx Query Designer for now. When we get to the other areas, you can go through the configuration process knowing that you are comfortable with the concepts. We'll start out with the initial query screen. The following illustration shows the location for accessing the exception-creation screens.

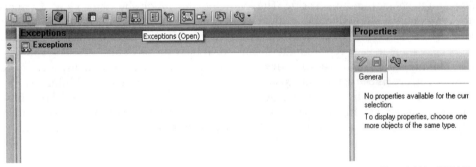

Once you have accessed the Exceptions screen, you can then create the exception by using the Create function on the context menu, as shown here.

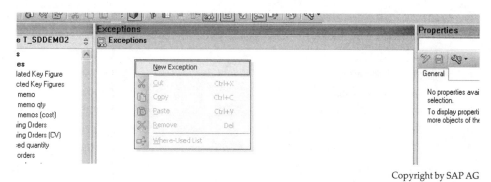

Copyright by SAP AG

The New Exception option creates a placeholder for exceptions. Then select this option and use the context menu–Edit, as shown next to access the Exception tabs.

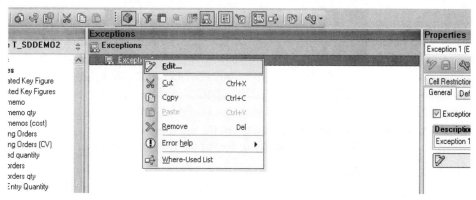

Copyright by SAP AG

The dialog box for creating exceptions appears, as shown next. The dialog box has a series of tabs for each of the parameters. General, Definition, Display, and Cell Restriction.

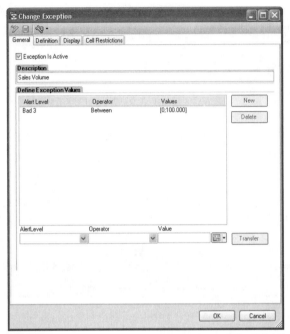

Table 6-11 explains the functionality of each of the parameters.
You can define exceptions in the following area of the Business Explorer:

- BEx Query Designer
- Web applications
- Web Item List of Exceptions
- Context menu
- BEx Web Analyzer

You can evaluate the exceptions online when executing the query or the web application.

If you want to evaluate exceptions for a large number of queries, you can do this in the background with the BEx Broadcaster. Exceptions for a query that you define in the Query Designer are globally valid for that query in all workbooks and web applications. Exceptions for a query view that you define in a web application are globally valid for that query view in all web applications based on the query view.

You have the following options for displaying exceptions in the table:

- **Background Color**   The exception is displayed with the background color of the data cell or characteristic cell. The color shading ranges from dark green for the alert level "Good 1" through yellow for the alert level "Critical 1" to dark red for the alert level "Bad 3." There are a total of nine color shades, corresponding to nine different levels of priority.

Tab	Setting	Description and Functionality
General (Note: The New, Delete, and Transfer buttons located on this tab are used to set up the exception.)	Exception Is Active	Here you can activate or deactivate the condition with Activate Exception.
	Description	Here you can change the description of the exception.
	Define Exception Values	Here you enter your values (use New to access data-entry fields). Alert-level rows are available at the bottom of the screen, and you identify the alert level, operator, and value fields for the exception. You can also use a variable for your exception and allow the business user to define the exception at the time of query execution.
	Alert Level	There are nine alert levels: Bad 1, 2, 3 (shades of red), Critical 1, 2, 3 (shades of yellow), and Good 1,2,3 (shades of green). These levels are internally numbered and ranked. These colors can be modified. It is not required that you use all nine colors; you can use as many or as few as you require.
	Operator	Operators for the assignment of ranges or single values. These operators are Equal To, Not Equal To, Less Than, Greater Than, Less Than or Equal To, Greater Than or Equal To, Between, and Not Between.
	Value	The values assigned by the business users. Depending on the values—percentages, absolute numbers, and so on, this will change.
Definition	Exception Is Defined On	You can select to evaluate the exception against one or all of the key figure elements of the structure, all structure elements, or a specific key figure.
	Time of Evaluation—Before List Calculation	Determines whether this exception is evaluated before or after any local calculation within the query, such as standard deviation or averaging.

TABLE 6-11   Settings for Exception Definition in the BEx Query Designer

Tab	Setting	Description and Functionality
Display	Data Cells/Key Figures	The option Exception Affects Data Cells has the follow settings: **Evaluate Structure Elements** The default on the Definition tab is used against the color levels. **All Structure Elements** All structure elements will receive the color assigned to the alert levels. **Following Structure Elements** You can evaluate one structure element but apply the color of the alert to a different structure element.
	Characteristic Cells – Exception After Characteristic Cells – Rows, Columns, Rows and Columns	The alert level is assigned to the characteristic values in the rows, columns, or both, where the exception occurs.
Cell Restrictions (The New, Delete, and Transfer buttons are used to assign the exception values.)	Standard Operator for All Characteristics That Are Not Listed	You can specify whether the exception applies to both detail and result values or to only the result values. This is used for any characteristic that is not in the Define Cell Restriction section.
	Define Cell Restrictions	Choose New to define an operator for each characteristic in the query definition and a value for each operator.
	Characteristics, Operator, Value	The settings are Everything, Totals Only, Everything Except Totals, and Fixed Values. Here you can filter the exception to a specific cell in the query. Values assigns a specific value of the characteristic to which you want the exception to be applied.

TABLE 6-11   Settings for Exception Definition in the BEx Query Designer (*continued*)

- **Symbol**   The exception is displayed as a symbol.
- **Symbol and Value**   The exception is displayed with a symbol and the value of the data cell or characteristic cell.
- **Value and Symbol**   The exception is displayed with a value and the symbol of the data cell or characteristic cell.

The following illustration shows the view of the properties of the exceptions. In the General tab, we have identified three levels for exceptions—Bad 3, Critical 3, and Good 1—and we have used the "between" operator to identify ranges of values for the use of the exceptions. The basic process is to use the New button to open up a line at the bottom of the dialog box to enter information. Then choose Transfer to send your settings to the screen. Use the same process until all your settings are complete.

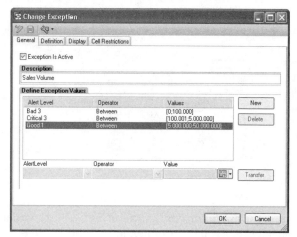

NOTE   *Remember to cover all the ranges possible, especially at the bottom and top of the ranges.*

The additional information for the creation of the Exception includes the Definition Tab. In the Definition tab, shown below, we have decided to filter to the key figure Sales Volume EUR, and none of the other options have been chosen.

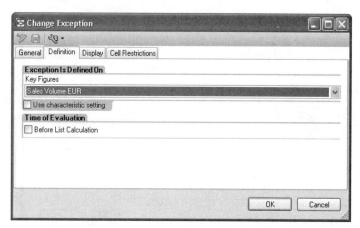

Next we go to the BEx Analyzer to execute this process and see the results. The following illustration shows the query executed and the three exception levels displayed. As you can see, the values are in the three color ranges, and we need to go back into the exception process and remove the exception from the results row.

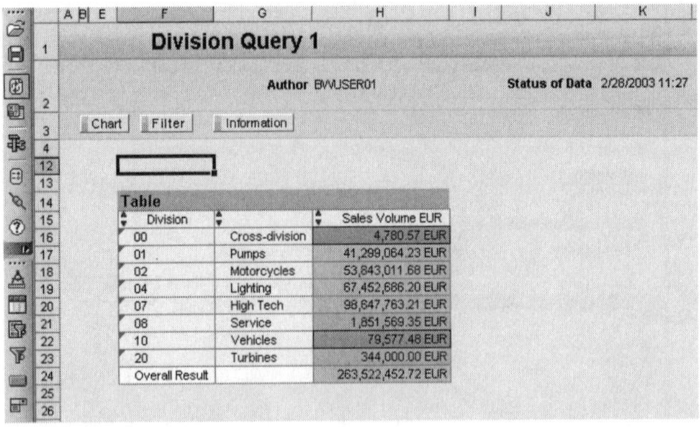

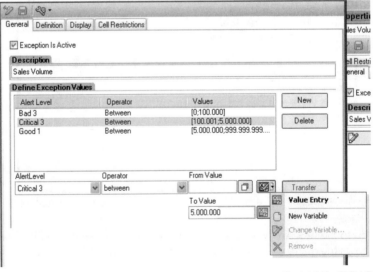

Copyright by SAP AG

We now go back into the exception configuration and set up a variable to offer the business user additional flexibility in determining the exception levels at time of execution. The first of the following illustrations shows the initial step in changing the exception. From the Change Exception dialog box, click to the variable button and use the New Variable option to start the setup. We define the variable as Manual Input and provide a technical name and text, as shown in the second illustration. The end result is that upon execution, the variables for the From and To values are offered as manual entries. This allows the business user to adjust their ranges for Bad, Critical, and Good as the year goes on or at the beginning of each year. The final illustration shows the initial pop-up for the variables upon execution of the query.

Copyright by SAP AG

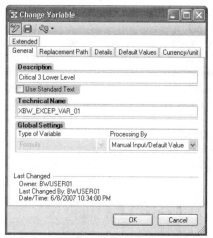

Copyright by SAP AG

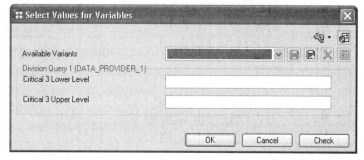

Copyright by SAP AG

Conditions

We have the ability to create *conditions* as partners to exceptions. The functionality of a condition is very useful in the overall analysis of queries and reports. A condition is defined as the use of threshold values and ranking lists in the Query Designer to increase the usefulness of the query results and make data analysis more efficient. In the results area of the query, the data is filtered according to the conditions so that only the part of the results area you are interested in is displayed.

If you apply conditions to a query, you are *not* changing any numbers. Instead, you are just hiding the numbers that are not relevant to you. For this reason, conditions have no effect on the values displayed in the results row. The results row of a query with an active condition corresponds to the results row of a query without this condition. You can define multiple conditions for a query. Conditions are evaluated independently of each other. Thus, the results quantity for the evaluation sequence is independent. The result is the intersection of the individual conditions. Multiple conditions are linked logically with AND. A characteristic value is only displayed when it fulfills all (active) conditions of the query.

In this discussion, we will only be working with the conditions in the Query Designer and in the BEx Analyzer. We will discuss the use of the Conditions Wizard in the WAD in

Chapter 15. With the use of conditions, we are only seeing the information that is of importance to us, whereas with an exception, we are seeing all the data, but the information that is important is highlighted. Using a condition should enable a more efficient analysis of data when large amounts of data are analyzed. By defining a condition, you have the option of analyzing the query results in more detail. You can analyze combinations of characteristics using ranked lists (for example, displaying the Top N% or Bottom 5 customers). Another example is the ability to show key figures that are above or below a certain threshold.

Conditions can be accessed and created in the Query Designer or after execution in the BEx Analyzer. During the creation of the condition, you need to decide whether it will be active or deactivate (in which case the business user will have to activate it after execution of the query). The following illustration shows the initial screen for creating a condition in the Query Designer.

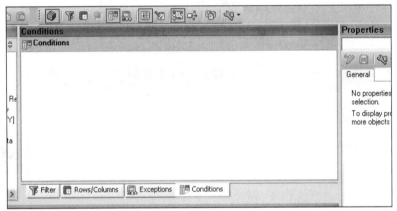

Copyright by SAP AG

After activating the use of the condition (via the icon in the toolbar at the top of the Query Designer, along with the exception), you will then use the context menu and choose New Condition. The following illustration shows this option.

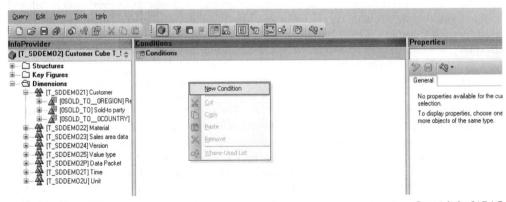

Copyright by SAP AG

Once you execute this option, you will see that a placeholder is created for you to edit, as shown in the first of the following illustrations. Finally, the Change Condition dialog box appears, where you create the parameters for the condition, as shown in the second illustration. The top part of the General tabbed page is straightforward—fill in the description of the condition and whether or not it should be active once created. In the Define Condition Parameter section, you have additional options for creating the condition. The final illustration shows this section with information filled in. To start configuration, click the New button to access a line at the bottom of the page. Table 6-12 details the settings and the functionality of the options on this page.

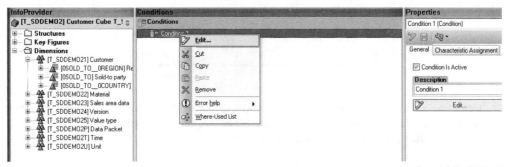

Copyright by SAP AG

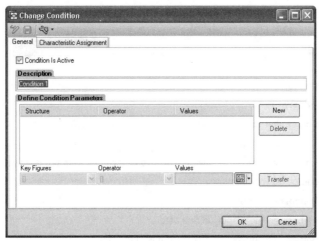

Copyright by SAP AG

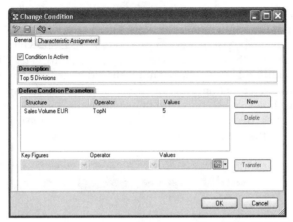

Copyright by SAP AG

Once you have finished creating the condition, click the OK button to confirm it. Before you leave the dialog box, you need to go to the other tab, Characteristic Assignment (shown next), and confirm the parameters for the characteristics to be affected. Here, you define how

Settings	Description and Functionality
Key Figures	Identify the key figure you are going to assign the condition. This will control the level and positioning of the condition against the data.
Operators	**Equal To**
	Not Equal To
	Less Than
	Greater Than
	Less Than or Equal To
	Greater Than or Equal To
	Between
	Not Between For example, sales revenue from/to is excluded from the display.
	Top N Top number of values.
	Bottom N Bottom number of values.
	Top % Top percentage you identify in this field.
	Bottom % Bottom percentage you identify in this field.
	Top Sum The calculation of this value uses the highest amount of a given object/value (for example, highest revenue of a specific customer). The system then sums up the other customers until the threshold of the highest amount is surpassed; at that point those customers are listed and displayed. Note that the summation goes from the highest level downward. Therefore, the top customers, in this example, are used in the calculation.
	Bottom Sum The same calculation as Top Sum, but the weakest customers are used in the calculation first.

TABLE 6-12   Settings for the General Tab of the Change Conditions Dialog Box

the condition will work in conjunction with the characteristics in the query. If the query contains a number of drilldown characteristics, it is easy for the condition to be out of context and/or produce invalid results. Therefore, be aware of assigning the condition to the appropriate characteristics so that the results can be consistent.

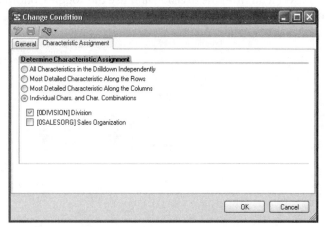

Copyright by SAP AG

NOTE *When you initially execute the query, your results row will display the overall results of the query. You need to adjust this result by using the properties or the key figures via the Properties | Calculations | Calculate Result As | Summation. This will control the results row, and the display will be specific to those values shown.*

The options available on the Characteristic Assignment page are:

- **All Characteristics in Drilldown Independently**   This setting allows you to apply a condition in a very general way. Depending on which characteristics you use in the drilldown, you will obtain varying results. This option is optimized for ranked list conditions, but can also be used for threshold conditions with relative values.

- **Most Detailed Characteristic Along the Rows**   This option is optimized for threshold values. The condition is applied to the most detailed characteristic of the rows.

- **Most Detailed Characteristic Along the Columns**   This option is optimized for threshold values. The condition is applied to the most detailed characteristic of the columns.

- **Individual Characteristics and Characteristic Combinations**   This setting allows you to evaluate the condition only for characteristics or characteristic combinations defined for certain drilldowns only. You can select any characteristic (of the characteristics used in the query in rows or columns or in the free characteristics) or a characteristic combination. This is a very good example of managing a specific customer based on discount agreements, or discount agreements for a certain amount of business.

Let's continue by viewing the results of the condition. We defined the condition to view the top five divisions by sales volume. This condition has been deactivated so that we can start by seeing the total results of the query and then drill down using the condition. The following illustration shows the initial screen of the query, where eight divisions are listed. We then use the context menu from the division and use the Toggle Condition State | Condition 1 option to activate it.

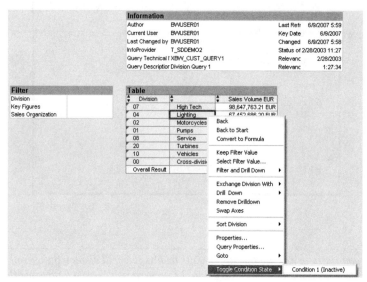

Copyright by SAP AG

After we execute this condition, we see that the list of divisions has been reduced to the top five by sales volume, as shown next.

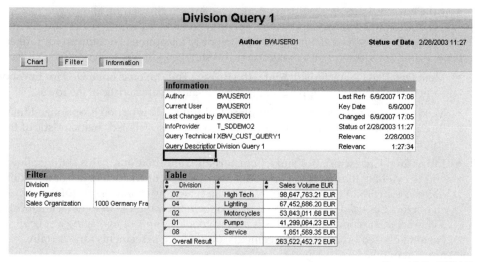

Copyright by SAP AG

The following illustration shows that the condition is, in fact, active. We can toggle the condition to active it or deactivate it.

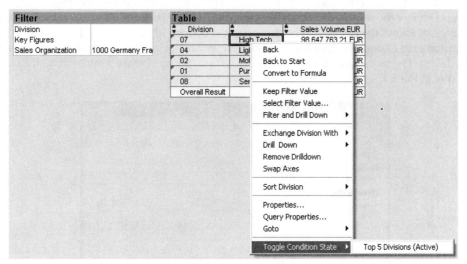

Another option for creating conditions on the fly is Create Condition in the context menu. If you use this, you will be able to execute a standard condition based on the key figure you have highlighted. In this case, we are using the key figure for Division 04—Light—and the amount is 67,452,686.2. The system is offering the conditions based on that amount. The following illustration shows us this option.

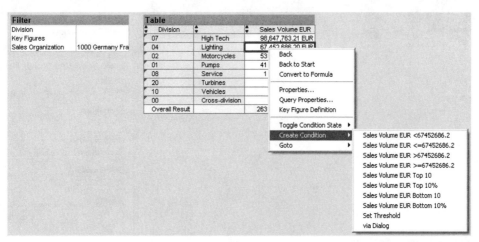

We will now create another condition with the % functionality. In the first of the following illustrations we have started the process of creating a condition for the *bottom* percentage, and identify this as 10%. We are leaving the Characteristic Assignment tab as it is. We are also deactivating the condition before clicking the OK button. The second illustration shows the final view of this condition in the Query Designer. The third illustration shows the results of these two conditions in the query. As you can see, the conditions are inactive. We will execute each and review the results. The final illustration shows the Bottom 10% option, and the list that appears shows the customers that make up the bottom 10%. You should realize that the last customer goes over the total bottom 10%, but we are not going to remove this customer from the list. The business user will review the information and make a decision on the last customer in the list.

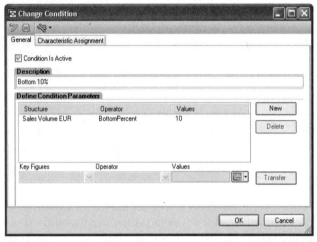

Copyright by SAP AG

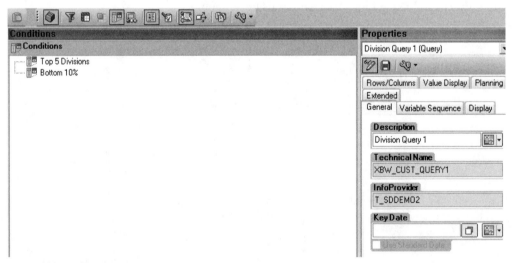

Copyright by SAP AG

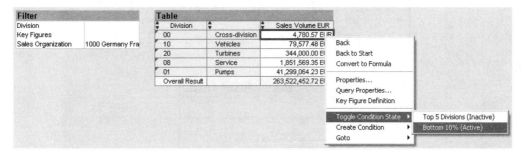

NOTE *Remember to deactivate each of the conditions as you execute another. The reason for this is that conditions are cumulative, and therefore you may generate results that are not consistent.*

In this next series of illustrations, we will use a variable in the creation of a condition. We will use the Top % as an operator and create a variable for the value of the condition. The variable-creation process is very similar to the variable process explained earlier, and therefore we will just view the final result. Once we have assigned the variable to the condition, we will execute the query and verify that the variable will allow the business user to execute conditions based on a variable what-if process. The first of the following illustrations shows the initial process of creating the condition and the variable. The second shows us the variable-creation process with the technical name and text being assigned to the variable. The third shows the final result of the variable assigned to the condition. The fourth shows the query execution showing the variable entry screen for the value of Top %, and the fifth shows the results of the Top 10%. As you can see, the results row shows a total of all the values, not a total of the ones displayed in the query. To fix this, use the properties parameter Calculate Results As – Summation. The final illustration shows the results of this calculation. The results row shows the actual results of the query.

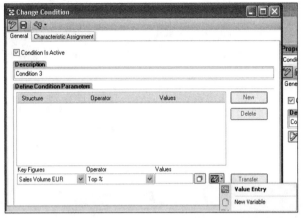

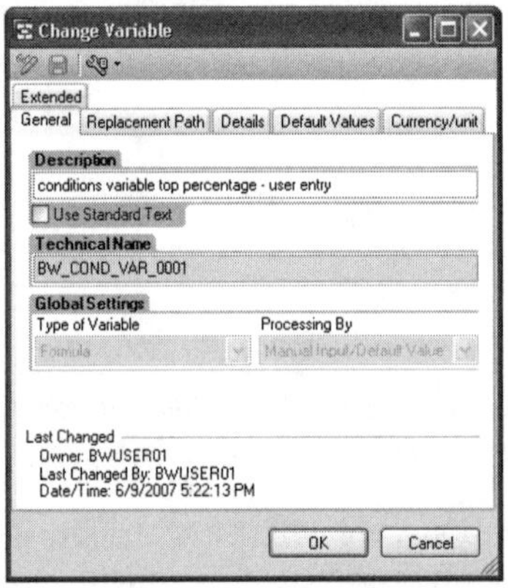

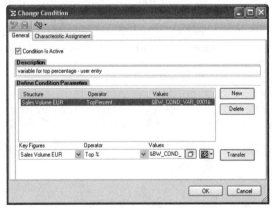

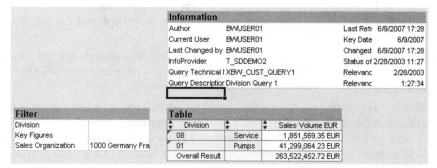

Copyright by SAP AG

Copyright by SAP AG

Copyright by SAP AG

You can have numerous combinations of conditions, and you can see how useful conditions and exceptions can be for proactive reporting. Also, these two functions can be used to execute and distribute information via the BEx Information Broadcaster. Therefore, it would be prudent to review all the options available for conditions.

The system processes conditions according to a set of rules. The following is a short list of the rules and the effects on the conditions. If you are using hierarchies with conditions, you need to also understand some of the particular issues with hierarchies. For example, if one of the lower-level nodes has a condition that applies, then all the upper-level nodes will be displayed, thus not breaking the hierarchical view. There are several rules similar to this for hierarchies.

- **Rule 1**   If you apply conditions to a query, you are *not* changing any numbers. Instead, you are just hiding the numbers that are not relevant for you. This means that conditions do not affect results rows. The results row of a query with an active condition corresponds to the results row of the query without a condition.

- **Rule 2**   Multiple conditions in a query are logically linked by means of AND. Conditions are evaluated independently of each other. In doing so, the results quantity for the evaluation sequence is independent. The intersection of conditions is displayed in the query. A characteristic value is only displayed if it fulfills all (active) conditions of the query.

- **Rule 3**   The condition rows for a condition are logically linked with OR. The union of conditions row results is displayed in the query. A characteristic value is displayed if it fulfills at least one of the condition rows.

- **Rule 4**   The setting All Characteristics in Drilldown Independent means that each characteristic of the drilldown has a condition (identical) defined for it These conditions are linked with AND according to Rule 2. The setting All Characteristics in Drilldown Independent enables you to use a condition in a general way. It is especially useful for threshold value conditions with relative key figures and ranked list conditions.

- **Rule 5**   If the condition for All Characteristics in Drilldown Independent is active in a query and results row suppression is active for some characteristics, the system still generates all results and applies the condition(s) to each of these results levels according to Rule 4.

- **Rule 6**   With several characteristics, the setting Single Characteristics and Characteristic Combinations always stands for the combination of these characteristics and not for a set of (independent) characteristics. A condition on a combination of characteristics is only applied when the following prerequisites have been fulfilled:

  - Both characteristics are in the drilldown.
  - Both characteristics are on the same axis.
  - The two characteristics are next to one another.
  - The axis upon which the two characteristics are drilled down has no hierarchical display.
    - If one of the two characteristics has an active presentation hierarchy, only one threshold condition can be applied for the characteristic combinations, but not a ranked list condition.

  The system attempts to adapt the list display to these prerequisites by automatically activating results row suppression.

- **Rule 7**   Ranked list conditions cannot be applied to characteristics with active presentation hierarchies.

- **Rule 8**   In a cross-classified table (meaning characteristics are not only in the rows, but also in the columns), conditions are only applied to the axes. The axes span across the border of the matrix and all cells are displayed for which both the rows and the columns correspond to the active conditions.

- **Rule 9**   If there are several characteristics in the drilldown and if a results row on this multilevel drilldown list does not fulfill the conditions and is then filtered out, then all the associated detailed rows and detailed (interim) results rows disappear.

- **Rule 10**   If a threshold value condition is applied to a characteristic with an active presentation hierarchy, a node that actually does not fulfill the condition and would normally be filtered out is shown anyway if at least one of the subordinate nodes fulfills the condition.

Summary

In this chapter, we covered a ton of material and developed a number of methods and functionalities to help with your development of queries and reports. Including the navigational attributes, variables – all different types, exceptions, and conditions. I have included as many screen shots as necessary to give you a reasonable display of the screens so that you can use this information as a reference in the configuration and development of your reporting strategy. Depending on your authorizations and responsibilities, you may have to get additional support to develop the necessary navigational attributes and hierarchies you need. Getting your power users and SMEs involved with the overall architecture of the BW system and in discussions of these two components would be a good thing. Get into the system and work through some of these options to get a better feel for the functionality. You should be very comfortable and excited about the process and outcome.

Double-teaming the Attachments

In this chapter, we will look at two different components that enhance the capabilities of your BW queries: attaching documents to the query, and drilling through from one query to another. The correct terms for these components are Document Integration and Report-to-Report Interface (RRI). First, we will discuss RRI functionality in detail—how useful is it, what options we have, and the setup of this component. Up to this point in time, we have discussed the use of the drilldown functionality within the query itself. Depending on the current strategy of reporting, the business user may have or require additional functionality. The use of RRI can help resolve this issue. Setting up the query with free characteristics and other options to help the business user with the granularity of the data needed for decision making might not be enough, and due to the performance of the queries against the InfoProvider, you probably don't want additional data to be stored in the InfoProvider. Therefore, you can use the RRI component to help in this situation.

The second topic of discussion is the concept of Document Integration and the Knowledge Management (KM) system. In many situations, we need to attach a comment or document to the query for justification, analysis, or even just as a reminder for other users of the query. Document Integration allows us to do just that at different levels in the query. We will work through the options and also discuss how the KM system can help in this area.

Report-to-Report Interface

Up to this point, we have worked through the options of using the context menu (BEx Analyzer) and the drag-and-drop functionality (BEx Web Analyzer) to navigate through queries and workbooks. This is known as the ability to "drill down" in the query. The ability to perform RRI is known as "drilling through" into another query or another system for information. This enables us to use additional information from another InfoProvider or even another system to get what we need for business decisions. Figure 7-1 is an overview

FIGURE 7-1
Overview of the
Report-to-Report
Process

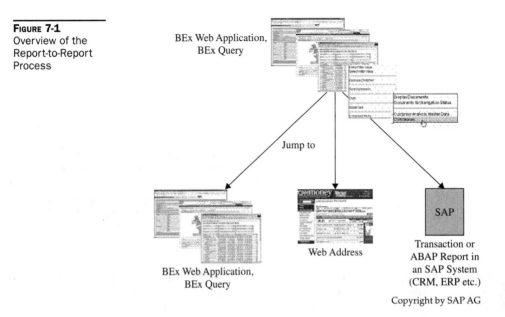

BEx Web Application,
BEx Query

Jump to

BEx Web Application,
BEx Query

Web Address

SAP

Transaction or
ABAP Report in
an SAP System
(CRM, ERP etc.)

Copyright by SAP AG

of the results using RRI. This is a very powerful function that can help in a number of ways with the query process and the reporting strategy for your company. The following illustration shows an example of a question that may be resolved by RRI functionality.

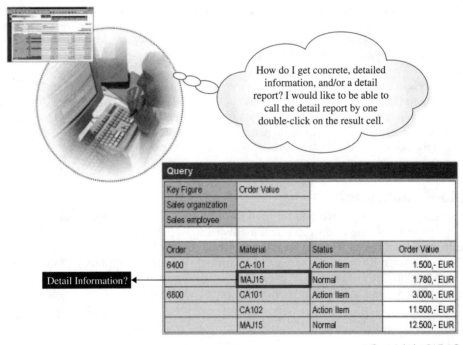

How do I get concrete, detailed information, and/or a detail report? I would like to be able to call the detail report by one double-click on the result cell.

Query			
Key Figure	Order Value		
Sales organization			
Sales employee			
Order	Material	Status	Order Value
6400	CA-101	Action Item	1.500,- EUR
	MAJ15	Normal	1.780,- EUR
6800	CA101	Action Item	3.000,- EUR
	CA102	Action Item	11.500,- EUR
	MAJ15	Normal	12.500,- EUR

Detail Information?

Copyright by SAP AG

If we think about the amount of data that could be used for reporting purposes, we might very well be talking terabytes of data. In terms of performance for the queries, this will definitely slow down execution (unless you have implemented BIA to help with query performance).

NOTE *Report-to-Report Interface (RRI) has a number of names, such as query jump targets, drill-through functionality, and the RRI naming convention. All address the same functionality in BI.*

Therefore, using the RRI functionality gives you the option to avoid these issues. Rather than storing all your data in one InfoProvider and trying to execute on all this data, you can separate the data and store it in a number of InfoProviders and the perform RRIs from one InfoProvider to another for detailed information. You also have the option to perform an RRI from one system to another, which would let you "jump," for example, from a BW system to an ECC system for details. Therefore, depending on the reporting strategy, you can upload the data that, let's say, 90 percent of your business users need and leave 10 percent back in ECC and just execute the RRI functionality to get to those queries. Another aspect of this functionality is the ability to layer your data. Having the summary data available in one InfoProvider and more detailed data in another InfoProvider can help with the performance, authorizations, and flexibility of the queries.

The setup of RRI is straightforward and therefore can be completed very quickly, but you should take additional time to formulate the process of the drill-through of the data by discussing with the business users how they execute their queries and how they look at the data. This will help you organize your RRI architecture. In the setup of RRI, you will normally drill through from a higher level of data to a more granular level of data—for example, from the summary of a plant, to the production order level of that plant, or from the analysis of sales data at the regional level to the analysis at the customer level. In these cases, using a "link" characteristic can be very useful for this analysis. This link characteristic allows you to jump from one query to another and filter the information coming from the next query by that value. Therefore, if you are jumping from a high-level report for Sales by Region and you have set up your detailed query to have the characteristic Region included, you can click directly on the specific region in your query and use that as a filter for the next query. You will see this in the examples in this chapter. This 'link' is not necessary for the RRI functionality to be used, but it is a best business practice to have this option available and give the more detailed query some based on the characteristic that is the 'link' help during the initial execution. This will make more sense to your business users because they will be looking for the detailed analysis by region and to jump to the next level query without the filtering process of a characteristic value, then have to drill down on that query to get to the specific view of the data would be time-consuming and inconsistent with the reporting strategy. Therefore, whatever characteristic you are expecting to drill through, you should have it in all the queries. RRI is not limited to just one query jump; you can drill through as many levels as makes sense. However, realize that drilling through multiple levels will make the rollup or reversing of your process more difficult. Therefore, you might want the query to jump one or two levels and use the functionality to reverse that drill-through to allow yourself to get back to the original query. With one or two jumps, the setup and execution are standard, but if you drill through five, six, or more layers, the ability to reverse all these levels and get back to the original query view may be more difficult.

Technically speaking, the RRI makes the parameterized call of programs from another program. This enables you to link to other queries, other queries from different application areas, other systems (reports and transactions), and to the Internet. We will review the setup and all the functionality available for both the query-level RRI and the InfoProvider-level RRI. Figure 7-2 shows the details of the query-level and the InfoProvider-level options. We will discuss the options for the use of RRI for internal and external program calls. When it is called, RRI first collects the following information from the cells of the sender query:

- The global filter (the rows and columns of the query definition)
- Variables
- The dynamic filter (the values in the navigation block of the query, including hierarchies and any other filters)
- The filter from the selected RKF
- The filter from the selected drilldown characteristics

The RRI provides this information to the receiver as valid selections.

Query-Level RRI and InfoProvider-Level RRI

To start the process, we have to create a series of queries or conceptually identify the jump process so that we can have the information for our "jump targets." These are basically the objects we will be using as receivers in the sender/receiver process. Once we have defined these parameters and objects, we can start the setup of the RRI. In this example, we have set up two queries. One, shown in the first of the following illustrations, has Division as one of the characteristics. The other has Division and Sold-To Party identified, as shown in the second illustration. To get to the start of the RRI setup, from the initial screen select SAP

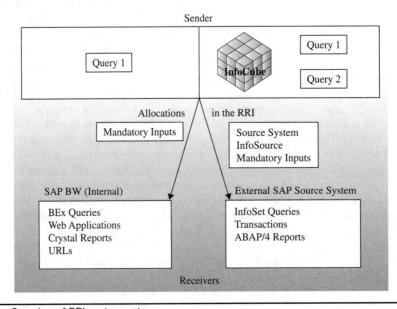

FIGURE 7-2   Overview of RRI system setup

Menu|Business Explorer|Query|Maintain Sender-Recipient Mapping. This is where you set up all the connections for the RRI to work.

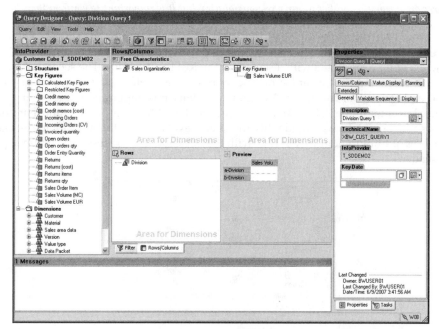

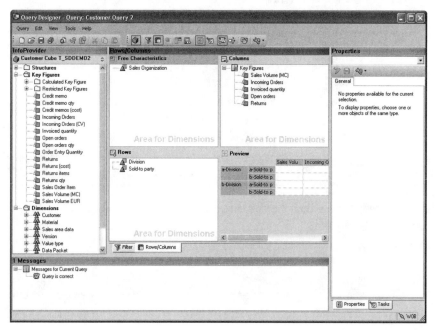

NOTE *Some additional components, such as the appropriate authorizations in all the different systems and the RFC (Remote Function Call) connections, we need to make sure are configured. These are normally another group's responsibilities, but it is important to confirm that the connections between systems will work.*

The first of the following illustrations shows the menu view. Once you execute this option, you will be presented with a screen for the RRI functionality. The second illustration shows the screen and parameters. A number of buttons are self-explanatory, such as Create, Change, and Delete. For the option Assignment Details, it is important to understand what is required to enter in the fields. We'll come back to that at the appropriate time. For now, if we look at the other tabs we can identify the query-level RRI and the InfoProvider-level RRI (All Queries of InfoProvider). We'll start with the "One Query" process and choose a query as the sender.

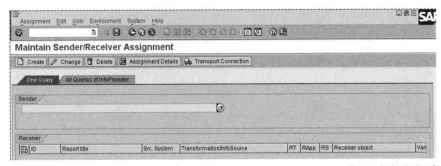

Copyright by SAP AG

Copyright by SAP AG

NOTE *The setup of the InfoProvider-level RRI is exactly the same as the setup of the query-level RRI. The only difference between the two is that you choose an InfoProvider rather than a query as the sender.*

To do this, use the F4 input help to view all the queries in the system. In this example, we will choose a query with just Division assigned and thus use this as the root query or starting point for this process (technical name is XBW_CUST_QUERY1). Next, we execute the Create option, and we will see the screen shown in the following illustration. Notice the entry for the sender query behind the pop-up Maintain Sender/Receiver Assignment. The sender/receiver relationship has a number of choices. Initially, we will choose a report type. The report types are described in Table 7-1.

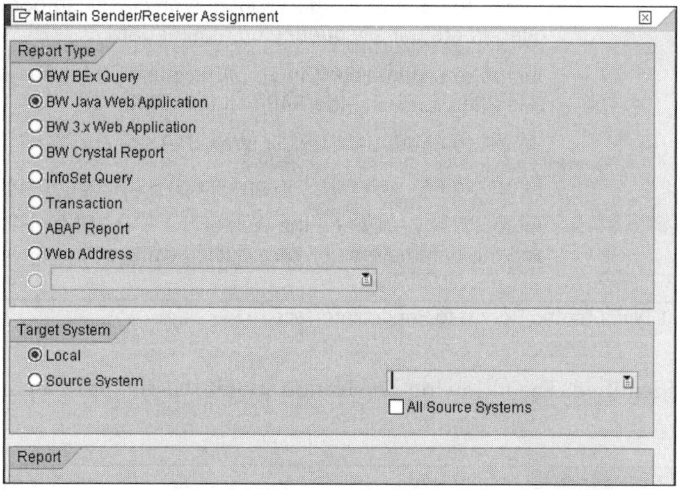

Copyright by SAP AG

NOTE *If you want to jump from a web application to a transaction or ABAP/4 report using the RRI, first you need to install an Internet Transaction Server (ITS) for the target system. The transaction or ABAP report is then displayed in the SAP GUI for HTML, which is part of the ITS. The ITS is also used for jump targets within the BI server. However, this does not have to be installed separately because it is automatically included in a BI system. The URL for starting a transaction in SAP GUI for HTML is generated by the BI server.*

Next, the "target system" needs to be confirmed. We have the option of the local system or source system, and we would then identify the source system this object is associated with for processing. At the very bottom of this pop-up is the field Report. In this field we execute an input help option to review the different types of reports that are possible for the

Report Type	Description
BEx Query	Jumps to a query that was created using the BEx Query designer
BEx Web Application (SAP NetWeaver BI 7.0)	Jumps to a BEx Web Application that is an executed Web Template created using the BEx Web Application Designer. This requires the Java-based runtime of SAP NetWeaver BI.
BEx Web Application (SAP BW 3.x)	Jumps to an ABAP-based BEx Web Application (SAP BW 3.x) that was created using the BEx Web Application Designer (version SAP BW 3.x).
Crystal Report	Jumps to a formatted report in Crystal Enterprise. You can also use a BEx report for formatted reporting.
InfoSet query	Jumps to an InfoSet query (queries on classic InfoSets). InfoSet queries are usually queries on master data.
Transaction	Jumps to a transaction in an SAP system. The transaction must be classified for using the SAP GUI for HTML.
ABAP Report	Jumps to an ABAP/4 report in an SAP system.
Web Address	Jumps to any web address and passes the parameters in the URL.
Own Report Type	Jumps to any target on the Web or the SAP GUI for HTML. The call and the parameters can be modified using customer-specific coding.

TABLE 7-1   Report Types for the Report-to-Report Interface

report type we identified. The following illustration shows the details of a particular list of parameters.

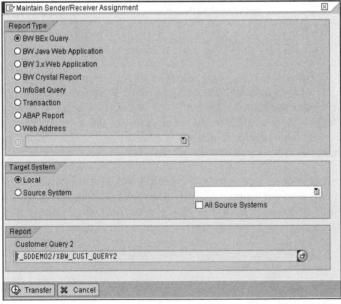

In our example, we have identified the BW BEx query. It will be executed against the local system, and the query we will be using as a target is the one set up with both Division and Sold-To Party included as characteristics (technical name XBW_CUST_QUERY2). As you can see, we can use whatever system can be identified as being recognized by the BW platform. Therefore, you can go against other BW systems, web addresses, other systems such as Crystal Enterprises, and ECC or R3 systems. Remember that the purpose of a BW system is to relieve the source system of reporting processes, and if you decide to go against the source R3/ECC system, you are pushing the reporting requirements back onto a system that may not be tuned for this purpose. Again, this is all discussed and reviewed in the reporting strategy process. If you decide to access the R3/ECC systems for your reporting process, you would choose one of the other options in the list. For example, if you chose ABAP Report as the report type, you would then choose the source system from the list. Once that has happened, a series of screens will prompt you to the ECC/R3 system. In the following illustration, we have done just this, and we are ready to review the options offered in the field Report.

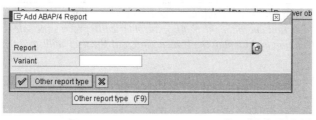

Copyright by SAP AG

Once we choose the dropdown option, the dialog box in the next illustration shows up, and you will use the button at the bottom of the screen labeled Other Report Type first before using the input help for the actual report. This will filter the type of report offered in the next screen.

Copyright by SAP AG

The following illustration shows the next screen that will require a choice. Once you click the Other Report Type button, your options are:

- **Report Portfolio** Reports available via the EIS reporting system.
- **BW Query** Choose this option if you decide to use this approach to get to additional BW queries.
- **SAP Query** Choose this option if you decide to use SAP queries generated from the operating system.
- **Drilldown Reporting** Choose this option if you decide to access reports found in applications such as Profitability Analysis, Consolidations, and Finance.
- **ABAP Report Program** Customized reports in the source system.
- **Report Writer** Reports created using report writer or report painter functionality. These reports can be from numerous applications, such as CO, SD, MM, and so on.
- **Transaction** Allows the execution of a transaction found in the source system via the BW query that is the sender.

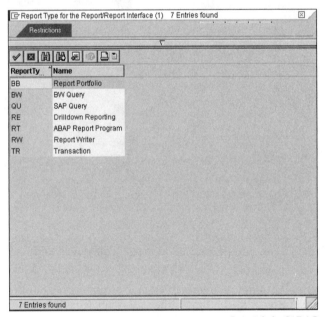

Copyright by SAP AG

NOTE *Transactions that can be used will not execute a process. For example, you can't execute a sales order transaction and have the posting automatically process the sales order. You can execute the transaction and display the transaction, but the user will need to process the activity.*

Once we have identified the other report type, the next screen shows a list of the different applications. Finally, we will identify the actual report we want to assign and use as the jump target. Once these activities are complete, click OK button to close the other screens and return to the original screen to confirm that the sender and receiver are correct. The following illustration shows the final screen in this series. As you can see, the receiver is filled in with all the required information, but there are still some other fields that can be filled in. In some cases, these need to be filled in to make sure the data being read is consistent with what the business user requires. These fields are Src. System and Transformation/InfoSource. They confirm that information being read is coming from the correct source. For example, if the query being used is built on a MultiProvider or if multiple feeds are uploading into the InfoCube, you can assign the source system and the transformation/InfoSource object to these fields to identify exactly what information will be read by the query. Sometimes it is desirable to maintain the field allocations individually for the parameter transfer of the transmitter to the receiver. For this, there are two exits:

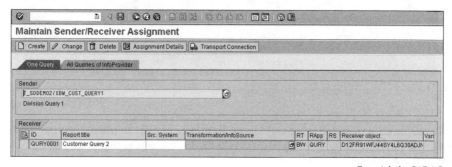

- **EXIT_SAPLRSBBS_001**   Here, the field allocation to the datasource in the source system can be adapted.
- **EXIT_SAPLRSBBS_002**   This function module is called before the jump to an ECC source system.

The last field in this row is for the entry of a variant. This way, if the query has a variable, the RRI can execute the query using the variant to fill in the variable values and then execute the query. In BI, you can prevent a called report from starting when jumping if it does not fulfill certain conditions you specify as mandatory input. These parameters are accessed via the Assignment Details button. We passed by this button earlier in the process because we couldn't set up the parameters at that time. Now that we have a query as a receiver, we can review the settings. Choose a query in the Receiver screen (left-side box) and click the

Assignment Details button. If you choose this option, a Field Assignments dialog box will appear, as shown next.

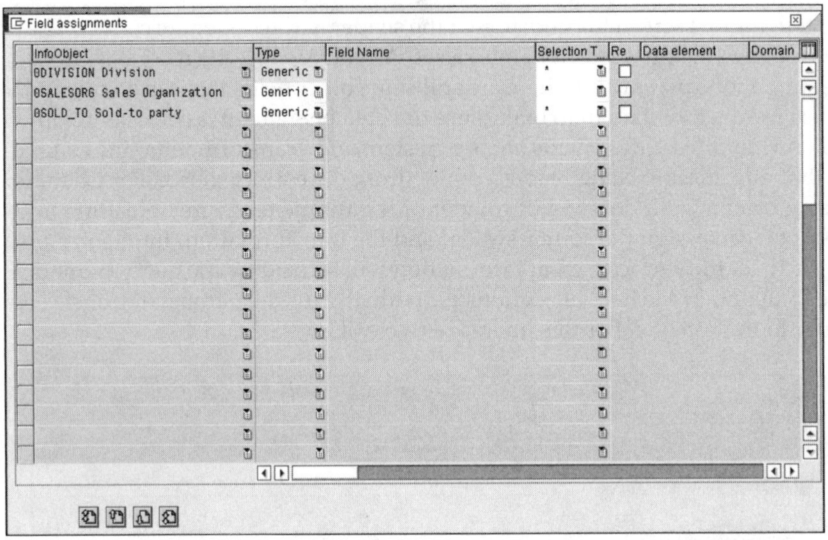

The conditions will be via the parameters. To make changes to the individual fields, choose the required settings from the dropdown list for the respective cells. Here are the options in these fields:

Description	Default Settings	Alternatives
Type	Generic	V – Variable
		I – InfoObject
		3 – Table field
		P – URL Parameters
		X – Delete
Selection Type	*	P – Parameter
		E – Individual Values
		I – Interval
		S – Select option
		H – Hierarchy
Mandatory Entry	Empty	Yes (indicator set)

When the system calls up the receiver, the settings made in the Field Assignments dialog box are set. We have finished configuring the necessary settings for the RRI to work. Jump targets that have been assigned to a BEx query can be selected in Web Applications and in the BEx Analyzer. You access them from the context menu under the Goto function.

Here are some additional notes about the information transferred during the RRI process for specific receiver objects. For Crystal Reports, when the RRI is called with a Crystal Report as the receiver, only the variables are filled. There is no transfer of filters as with BEx queries. When the RRI is called with a transaction or an ABAP/4 report as the receiver, it's done with the RRI from the SAP NetWeaver Application Server. This is possible in an ERP system, a CRM system, or within the BI system. The selections are prepared by the BI system, but the BI system does not recognize the transaction or the report. The assignment is transferred from the RRI of the SAP NetWeaver Application Server using inverse transformation rules. There must also be a complete chain from the datasource of the source system to the InfoSource, through transformations up to the InfoProvider. This does not mean that data absolutely has to be loaded using this chain, only that this chain is consistent with the upload of the data. Calling the RRI for ABAP reports only works for fields with a dictionary reference. For transactions, this means that the DynPro has to have a dictionary reference. Not every transaction can be called with the RRI of the SAP Application Server. For some transactions (such as SV03), you need to program a utility program if you still want to call it using the RRI. In terms of the InfoSet query, the same process applies as described for transactions and ABAP reports. When the RRI is called with a web address as receiver, the assignment details have to be maintained. You have to specify the name of the input field in the field name column. URL variables cannot be used.

Before we review the results of the RRI process, let's add some additional jump targets to this process. We will add two additional jump targets to the query XBW_CUST_QUERY2. In this case, we will add a query and a URL so that we can review that setup process. The assignment of the additional query is exactly the same as what has been described earlier, except for the fact that the sender is the query XBW_CUST_QUERY2. The only difference is in the assignment of the URL for the jump to the Internet site. The following illustration shows the configuration for the website for SAP.com. As you can see, the configuration is similar except for the fact that you can enter a value into a grayed-out field. The choice of Web Address is correct. We'll leave Target System as Local but then enter the URL into the field for Report. This field shows as being grayed out, but you can enter a value here. Now the reporting strategy is to jump two query levels.

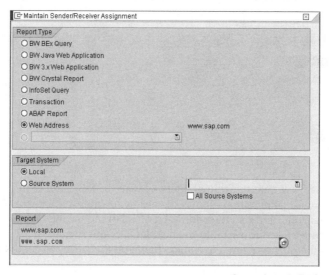

Copyright by SAP AG

Now for the results. The following illustration shows the execution of the initial query. Once that query has been executed, we choose a Division (in this case, Division 02) and use the context menu option Goto | Customer Query 2. This is the result of the initial setup of the query jump. Notice that another query can be executed—Customer/Sales Volume.

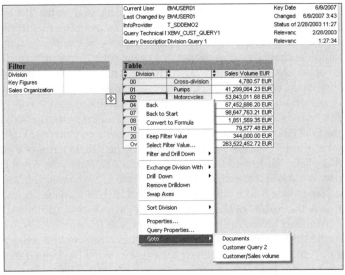

Copyright by SAP AG

This query has been assigned based on the use of the InfoProvider-level RRI. The following illustration shows the setup of this configuration. There is no difference between the setup of a query-level and a InfoProvider-level RRI. In the InfoProvider-level RRI, you have the ability to link any query to any of the InfoProviders—InfoCubes, DSO, MultiProviders, InfoSets, and so on. There are no restrictions for the types of InfoProviders.

Maintain Sender/Receiver Assignment

| Create | Change | Delete | Assignment Details | Transport Connection |

One Query / All Queries of InfoProvider

Sender

T_SDDEMO2
Customer Cube T_SDDEMO2

Recipient

ID	Report title	Src. System	Transformation/InfoSource	RT	RApp	RS	Receiver object	Vari
CUBE0001	Customer/Sales volume			BW	QURY		A4F2DX3392A3Y9850Z0CVSV4?	

Copyright by SAP AG

Now that we have executed the initial query, we can drill through to the next level query. The first of the following illustrations shows the next level query. Notice that Division has been filtered to Division 2 and that the additional detail of the second layer is now available. Now, we can execute the drilldown into the next level of query analysis. The second illustration shows the process using the context menu on this query to get to the additional query jump targets.

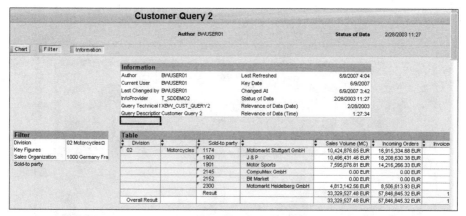

Copyright by SAP AG

Now the Customer Query 2 has become the sender and the query for the formula collision has become the receiver. You can also see that the query assigned at the InfoProvider level shows up for use. Finally, you see the link to the website for SAP.com. The results for the drill-through to the BWUSER collision query and the query jump to the website are shown in the following two illustrations. Also notice that the query jump to the collision query doesn't have any relationship to the root query. This demonstrates the fact that even though it is a best business practice to link the two queries based on a characteristic value, it's not a requirement.

BWUSER Query Formula Collision

Author BWUSER1

Chart | Filter | Information

Filter

Key Figures
Quarterly Comparison

Table

	Sales Volume EUR	Incoming Orders	Sales Volume % Share of Incoming Orders
Quarter 1/2000	10,489,607.18 EUR	9,475,772.10 EUR	110.69923 %
Quarter 2/2000	15,699,854.92 EUR	14,898,941.58 EUR	105.37564 %
Half Year 1/2000	26,189,462.10 EUR	24,374,713.68 EUR	107.44521 %
Percentage Variance of Quarters 1 and 2/2000	49.67057 %	57.23195 %	-4.80906 %

Copyright by SAP AG

Document Management

In most cases when you execute a query, you are reviewing information based on events that have happened and information that comes from a database system. This information is required to make strategic decisions, but it is only 40 percent of the picture. As many business articles and journals have pointed out for over the last 30 years, much of the information required to make informed decisions and guide a corporation through the business world comes from "soft" sources of information—information generated from the market, surveys, journal articles, the worldwide economy, and other stakeholders. This information is not stored in a company database, and reports are not generated with a list of this information. However, the reports that are created are an outcome of this soft information, so it is important that we make sure we capture this information somewhere in the reports to be able to review and understand why the corporate statistics are what they are.

BW's Document Management System can be used to accomplish this task. With this functionality, we can attach documents, charts, graphs, drawings, files, pictures, and many other types of documentation objects to the queries. Examples of this can be seen in any discipline: In logistics we need to attach drawings and documents to the material information. Finance involves the analysis and review of the effects of different market and world economic factors that need to be captured for the profit and loss statements. For planning and forecasting, accessing and creating documentation is valuable and required against the planned data for the corporation. Finally, HR requires pictures, documents, and information assigned to a person's file.

In BW 7.0, Document Integration has been significantly improved over prior versions. Because of the close integration of BI and Knowledge Management (KM), users have more choices of where and how documents can be accessed. Enterprise Knowledge Management provides central and role-based access to the information in your company and creates a connection between structured business data and unstructured documents. The Document Browser can create and edit all types of documents—an improvement over previous versions. In additional, all the common services provided by KM can be assigned to these documents, which can enhance the degree of collaboration on important documents in your organization.

In the Document Browser, you can display the column name, content, assignment, and author/change date. The columns can be switched on and off, either online or in the configuration. Documents can be assigned either online via the query itself or directly in configuration for use in the query. If configured, the document can be edited directly in the Document Browser. The user can upload new documents, add links to documents, and add comments about the documents. These comments are not embedded in the documents but rather are references to the documents. Figure 7-3 shows some of the functionality available via the KM and Collaboration Services.

Notice that this functionality offers the ability to generate feedback information, add subscriptions to a service, and download additional information and documentation. KM integration makes all the KM services available for BI documents, such as text search (something that everyone has been asking for from BW), text mining (the user enters a search text name, and the system pulls all documents based on that search name), rating, personal documents, and other options. Some of the areas that benefit from this are increased user productivity due to closer communication among teams, reduced costs though shortening the different cycles of business, and accelerated problem-solving processes and other components of the business cycle. The first of the following illustrations shows the link in the BEx Analyzer used to access the Document Browser. The second illustration shows the outcome of clicking that link and the initial view of the Document Browser.

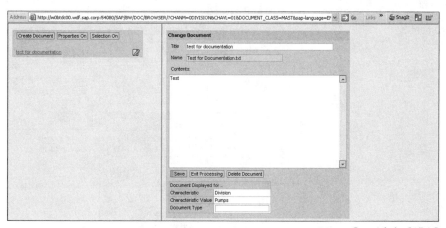

Copyright by SAP AG

Copyright by SAP AG

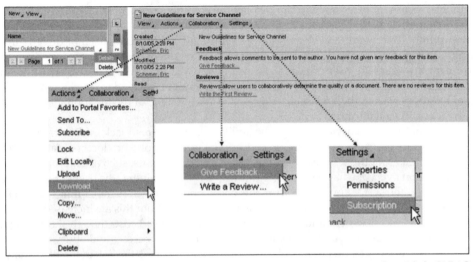

FIGURE 7-3   Overview of Knowledge Management and Collaboration Services

In BW 7.0, three different levels of document attachments can be configured. Document Integration can occur at the metadata, master data, and transactional data levels. You can define and link one or more documents to each of these different objects in different formats, versions, and languages. In the SAP document management process, each document is identified uniquely and is linked to BI objects using attributes and physical documents. These attributes and physical documents will belong to a specific logical document as individual characteristic values and that present meta-descriptions for individual files using their attributes. You can store the individual files either on an SAP database or on an external content server using an HTTP interface. Figure 7-4 shows an overview of all the components of KM and Document Integration.

FIGURE 7-4
Component view
of the Knowledge
Management
system

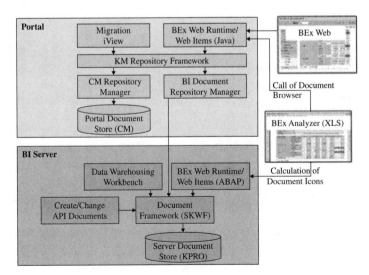

You can use documents for metadata, master data, and InfoProvider data in Web Applications, in Knowledge Management (KM), in the Data Warehousing Workbench (BEx Web runtime, ABAP), and in the BEx Analyzer. Table 7-2 provides an overview of the available tools and options.

Document Classes

A *document class* is made up of the documents from one of the following categories of BI objects: metadata, master data, InfoProvider data. Documents in a document class are characterized by particular logical document properties. Table 7-3 shows you the BI objects you can choose from and the corresponding document classes. For each document class, examples are provided of where the different documents are typically used.

Area	Description
Data Warehousing Workbench	In the Data Warehousing Workbench (BEx Web runtime, ABAP), you can only access and edit documents that are on the BI server and have not been migrated.
	The Administration functional area is available for the editing of documents, BI Metadata Search and BI Documents. The Documents screen is available for maintenance transactions for metadata and master data. The same functions for creating, importing, editing, exporting, and displaying documents are available on both interfaces. In the Administration functional area (Administration/ BI Metadata Search/BI Documents), you can display and edit documents from all document classes using various search criteria. You can also branch to document administration.
Web Applications	In Web Applications, you can access documents on the BI server and in the portal. Using the Single Document, Document List, and Analysis Web items, you can insert context-sensitive documents into the data used in the Web Applications and display the related properties.
Knowledge Management	In the BEx Web runtime (Java), you can integrate BI documents into portal-based Knowledge Management using the BI Document Repository Manager, the BI Metadata Repository Manager, and migration. You can access documents on the BI server and in the portal. All KM services are available for working with BI documents.
BEx Analyzer	In the BEx Analyzer (BEx Web runtime, ABAP), you can display, create, and edit documents created in the Data Warehousing Workbench, in master data maintenance, or in a Web Application.
	The BEx Analyzer only uses the BI server to store documents. Migrated documents are not available in the BEx Analyzer. Only migrate documents if they do not use the BEx Analyzer or do not use it in connection with documents.

TABLE 7-2 Access Options for Documentation

BI Object	Document Class
Metadata Aggregate Transformation rule InfoCube InfoObject InfoPackage InfoSet InfoSource DataStore Object Query (including variables, structures, restricted and calculated key figures) Reporting Agent scheduling package Reporting Agent settings Web item Web template	**META** Example of documents for metadata: Documentation Explanations ("characteristic ABC means ...") History/changes The user can select a document they want to display in the online documentation.
Master data Characteristic value	**MAST** Example of documents for master data: Screens for personnel numbers Descriptions and technical specifications of materials Original documents for order forms Version documentation (target/actual budget)
InfoProvider data Combination of characteristic values It is not possible to assign documents to navigation attributes. Neither is this possible if the attribute is a document-relevant characteristic. If this is the case, you have to model all the characteristics you want to use for assigning documents as direct characteristics in the InfoProviders and not as navigation attributes.	**TRAN** Example of documents for InfoProvider data: Comments on various characteristic values ("Sales for material 4711 in Germany were poor in May because ..." or "In May the following key figures were interesting: Delivery quantity – Explanation ..., Outstanding payments ....")

TABLE 7-3   BI Objects and Associated Document Classes

Document Class	Document Properties
META	You can set *one* value for each of the following document properties: Object Type and Object Name
MAST	You can set *one* value for each of the following document properties: Characteristic and Characteristic Value
TRAN	You can set *one* value for each of the following document properties: InfoProvider and Query You can set *more than one* value for the Key Figure document property. The characteristics that have been maintained as properties of documents are also displayed (sorted alphabetically). You can set *more than one* value for each document property for these characteristics. Important: You have to activate any characteristics you want the system to display in the maintenance screens for InfoProvider data documents. You do this in the maintenance screens for characteristics on the General tabbed page (Characteristic Is Document Property).

TABLE 7-4   Document Classes and the Properties Available for Each

During the configuration of the document object in BW, you will need to assign a document class to each document. Table 7-4 shows you the document classes you can choose from and the corresponding document properties.

Metadata Level

As we go through the process with a metadata-level document, keep in mind that the steps involved are very similar in each of the different groups. Therefore, we will highlight the differences between each document class and try not to be too redundant during the examples. We start the configuration of the documents by going into the Data Warehousing Workbench and choosing Documents from the left side of the screen, as shown here.

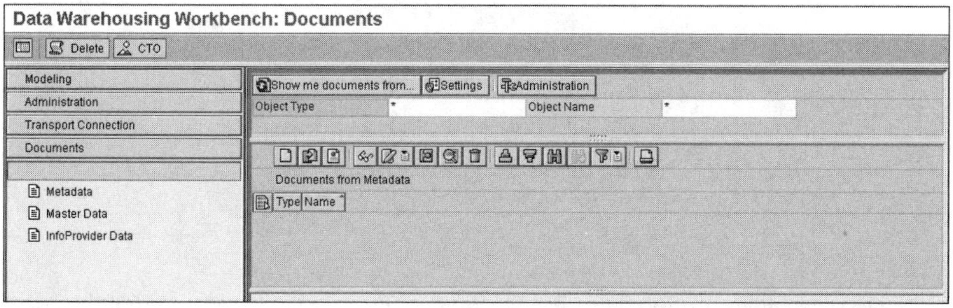

Copyright by SAP AG

For the metadata level, you can assign documents to a total of 35 different objects, including InfoObject, InfoCube, InfoSet, Aggregate, and Workbook. The first of the following illustrations shows a partial list of the metadata objects available for document assignment.

You identify the object class and then identify the object—for this example, we'll choose 0MATERIAL. The second illustration shows the result of our assignment.

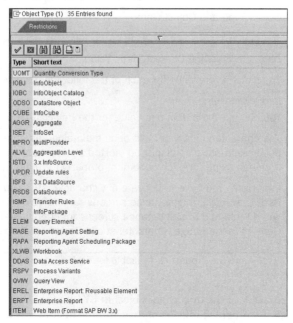

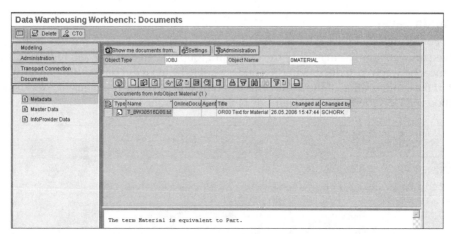

When we execute the option Show Me Documents From, a list is generated of the current documents attached to this object. We can execute the document by double-clicking it to show us the display of the text message. Once we have positioned the object in the Object Name field, we can start the process of creating a document by choosing the icon for Create (blank sheet of paper). Once that is confirmed, the Create New Document dialog box appears, as shown here. We continue by providing the required information—name, description, and Mime type.

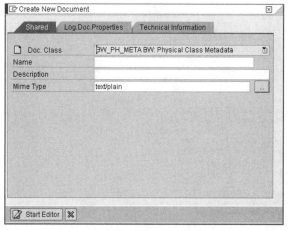

The first of the following illustrations shows the filled-in screen, and the second shows all the Mime types to choose from. You can choose from over 40 different Mime types, including Microsoft Word, Microsoft Excel, audio files, and BMP map files. After choosing Microsoft Word, we then execute the Start Editor process, and the Word document appears. After this process, the document will appear wherever the InfoObject 0CUSTOMER is used in a query. On the Log Doc Properties tab, we can decide whether the document is created as an online documentation. The logical document properties for metadata include the object name, object type, and whether or not it is an online document.

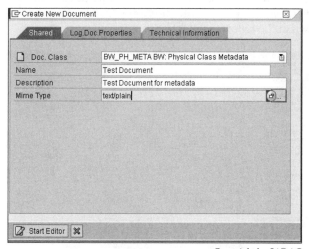

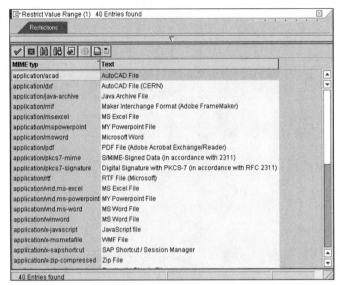

NOTE *If you define several documents for a metadata object with the property Online Documentation, only the last created document displays as an online link; all other documents display as a link reference and are therefore pulled from the database at the time of execution versus at the time the query executes.*

In addition to the Data Warehouse Workbench, you can configure documents from the Query Designer (see Chapter 4 for comments on this functionality). Once the documents are assigned to the object, you have to set up the functionality to view the documents from the query. To do this, you need to go back into the Query Designer and access the parameters from there, as shown in the following illustration.

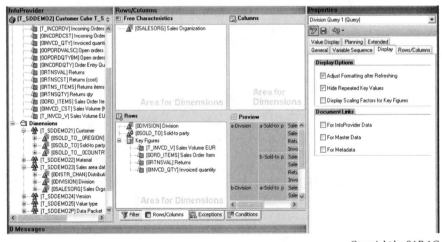

In the Query Designer, choose the InfoObject for which you would like to activate this functionality. In the Properties tab, you can turn on the display of the documents under the Document Links area. Once this is set up, execute the query and you will see the icon identifying what values have documents attached. The following illustration shows this step. Notice the small paper icon next to the customer numbers 1172 and 1000. This confirms that documents are assigned to these two values.

Division Query 1

| | Author BWUSER01 | | | | Status of Data | 2/28/2003 11:27 |

Chart | Filter | Information

Table

Division	Sold-to party		Sales Volume EUR	Sales Order Item	Returns	Invoiced quantity
00	Cross-division	1172	CBD Computer Based Design	4,780.57 EUR	1	0.00 EUR	17 A
		1400	A.I.T. GmbH	0.00 EUR	1	0.00 EUR	0 F
		T-S11A00	CompuMax GmbH	0.00 EUR	2	0.00 EUR	0 F
		T-S11A01	CompuMax GmbH	0.00 EUR	2	0.00 EUR	0 F
		T-S11B00	PC-World Stuttgart KG	0.00 EUR	1	0.00 EUR	0 F
		T-S11B01	PC-World Stuttgart KG	0.00 EUR	1	0.00 EUR	0 F
		Result		4,780.57 EUR	8	0.00 EUR	17 A
01	Pumps	1000	Becker Berlin	3,607,592.75 EUR	16	0.00 EUR	1,287 F
		1030	DELA Handelsgesellschaft mbH	0.00 EUR	0	0.00 EUR	0 F
		1031	Global Trade AG	0.00 EUR	0	0.00 EUR	0 F
		1032	Institut fuer Umweltforschung	8,341,978.84 EUR	68	0.00 EUR	2,719 F
		1171	Hitech AG	5,341.24 EUR	1	0.00 EUR	1 F
		1200	Minerva Energieversorgung GmbH	284,022.63 EUR	4	0.00 EUR	97 F
		1320	Becker Koeln	5,386,763.33 EUR	49	0.00 EUR	1,722 F
		1321	Becker Stuttgart	10,999,518.15 EUR	87	0.00 EUR	3,566 F
		1350	NSM Pumpentechnik AG	2,812.11 EUR	1	0.00 EUR	1 F
		1390	Technik und Systeme GmbH	46,248.44 EUR	6	0.00 EUR	14 F
		1400	A.I.T. GmbH	523,051.59 EUR	4	0.00 EUR	186 F
		1410	PILAR am Neckar	616,618.00 EUR	2	0.00 EUR	220 F
		2000	Carbor GmbH	11,447,453.13 EUR	90	0.00 EUR	3,802 F
		4999	Hallmann Anlagenbau GmbH	30,664.02 EUR	3	0.00 EUR	10 F
		CUSTOMER00	Becker 00	7,000.00 EUR	1	0.00 EUR	2 F
		Result		41,299,064.23 EUR	332	0.00 EUR	13,627 F
02	Motorcycles	1174	Motomarkt Stuttgart GmbH	15,390,904.26 EUR	92	0.00 EUR	32,351 F

Copyright by SAP AG

Master Data Level

The process at the master data level is very similar to that at the metadata level. Once you have chosen the master data button in the Data Administration Workbench, you will see that the screen is very similar to the screen that you viewed for the Metadata but the fields required are looking for an InfoObject and the other field will be for the characteristic value of the InfoObject that the documents will be assigned. We will use the InfoObject 0CUSTOMER and customer 1172. The following illustration shows this view of the screen.

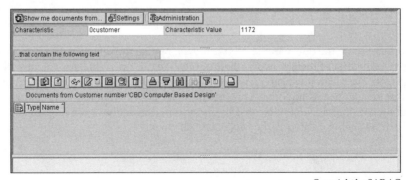

Copyright by SAP AG

Now we click the Create button and fill in the required fields for the name, description, and so on, and we create a document using the Mime type **Text**, as shown in the first of the following illustrations. Notice that the Document Class setting is now MAST (master data). Next, we click the Start Editor button to post some text to this document. The second illustration shows the view of the text document. At this point, we save the document and exit the configuration screen.

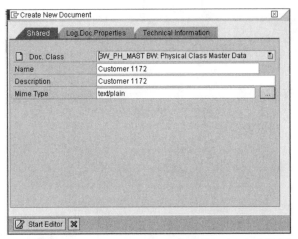

Copyright by SAP AG

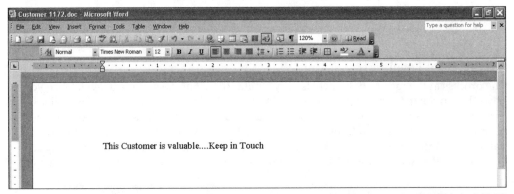

Copyright by SAP AG

We'll now execute the query in the BEx Analyzer. Notice the document icon on customer 1172, shown in the first of the following illustrations. We can open this document with a single click of the icon. We see that we can view current documents as well as create additional documents and change existing ones. This functionality is shown in the second illustration. Notice that the original document created in the system doesn't have the flag for change/edit, but the one that is being created in the BEx Analyzer does.

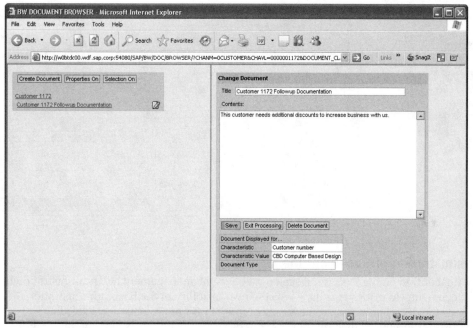

Copyright by SAP AG

Copyright by SAP AG

InfoProvider Level

The last Document Integration level is for the InfoProvider. The configuration for this level is no different from the other two in so far as the mechanics of the process are concerned, but in terms of the requirements and the use of this level of documentation, one additional component is needed. To set up your system to support InfoProvider-level documentation, you need to turn on the Characteristic Is Doc Attributable setting on each of the InfoObjects in the InfoProvider you would like to assign documents. Therefore, if you are using five characteristics from the InfoProvider in the query, those five characteristics, at least, must have this indicator turned on. You can identify the characteristics set for this by using the InfoProvider-level view from the Document screen in BW Data Warehouse Adm.

To start this process, you execute the option for documentation against the InfoProvider. Then you enter an InfoProvider into the InfoProvider field. In the Setting function, identify whether *all* the InfoObjects from this InfoProvider should be viewed or just the *available* InfoObjects, meaning only those with the indicator turned on. In the following illustration, only those available for assigning the document are shown. You can see that numerous documents are assigned to cells in the query. The placement of these documents can be identified by the intersection of the characteristic values and key figures. To create another document, fill in the value fields of those characteristics that will be used in the query. Go through the process of assigning and creating the document, as described previously, and display it in the query.

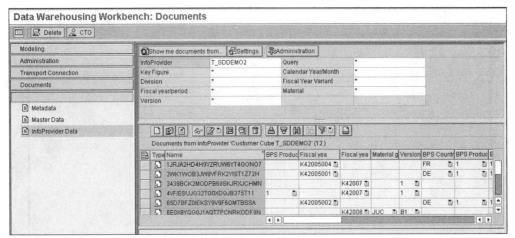

Administration of Document Management

The final option on the Document screen involves the management and administration of the documents. In prior versions, it was the responsibility of the Basis administration to manage the documents and monitor the volume of information being collected and developed. With the availability of the series of tabs shown in the following illustration, the Application BI Manager can monitor and support the Basis team in this process. A number of activities can be accomplished from this component, such as additional indexing of the documents, monitoring of the total number of documents, managing the deletion process, monitoring the volume of data being stored, and other functions. In general, much of this falls under system administration, and it would be wise to coordinate all these activities with your Basis department.

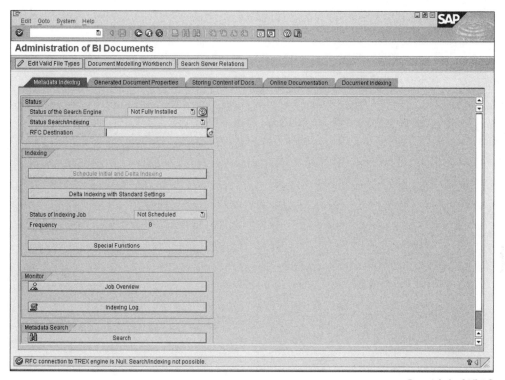

Copyright by SAP AG

Summary

With the incorporation of these two additional functions within the system, the arsenal of available tools continues to grow. We have gone from using basic queries to being able to create numerous calculations, make queries automated for long-term use, and format the queries, among other activities. The last two components we discussed in this chapter didn't have an impact on the BEx Query Designer or the BEx Analyzer, per se, because the queries were already available for us to integrate into the RRI, and the documents, in some cases, were being developed in the configuration process and being assigned and therefore were available for the business user to view within the query. Therefore, it's safe to say we have worked through about 60 percent of the basic functionality within the reporting component of BW everything that has been discussed in Chapters 2–7. We will expand on this using different front ends, such as the WAD and the Report Designer, but these tools are going to help with the flexibility and formatting, not with additional functionality.

It can never be overstated that you should review your reporting strategy, and once you have the business user requirements, you should architect the system around these functions. You can save yourself and your users a lot of frustration down the road in terms of performance by using some of these processes.

Using the Functionality
of the BEx Analyzer

In this chapter we will expand on the information from Chapter 3 concerning the functionality of the BEx Analyzer. This is new functionality in BW for the 7.0 version. We will investigate the options in more depth for Analysis mode and move into the Design mode for this user interface. We will look at the functionality of not only the query in this environment but also the workbook. In the past, the workbook has been considered a stepchild of BEx analysis, but in this recent version of BI the workbook has become much more flexible and useable, in part due to the enhancements of the Analysis and Design modes in the BEx Analyzer. This discussion also introduces new functionality accessed via Excel spreadsheets in the BI environment.

Functions Within the BEx Analyzer—Navigation Within the Design Mode

Before we get into the configuration of the Design area of the BEx Analyzer, a discussion of the results of this toolkit is important so that you can position it within the reporting strategy of your corporation. For a full discussion of the functionality of the Analysis toolbox, refer to Chapter 3. This chapter goes through all the drilldown functionality and the use of the navigation process in the BEx Analyzer. Figure 8-1 shows the results of using the Analysis functionality of the BEx Analyzer. A number of components are used here, including Excel functions to change the background colors, font size, and formatting. Also, a picture was added to the header area of the workbook. The BEx Analyzer design functions include the use of radio buttons, dropdown groups, pushbuttons for the execution of different functions, a graphic grid for the display of the report data, a chart item for the display of the information (with the use of a 3D chart), and finally a text item for the display of information about the data and the filters or variables in the workbook.

NOTE *Notice that we are not talking about queries but workbooks. A workbook is a collection of queries and/or other items that may be collected together for display purposes such as in documents, graphs, or comments.*

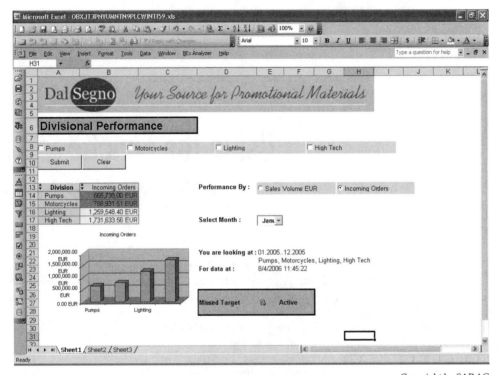

FIGURE 8-1   Use of the Design Functionality of the BEx Analyzer

With the use of the Design mode functions, you can take control of the user interface to produce highly customized workbooks that are flexible and easy to use and that meet the needs of the business users that analyze and review the information. The following illustration shows the Design mode toolbox. We will work through each of the options within the toolbox. This toolbox also provides business users a display that's similar to Excel formatting—something they are very used to seeing. The use of all these functions is based on the BEx workbook. Without the BEx workbook, the ability to save all the formatting and customizing in the BEx Analyzer would be impossible. As in all choices, there are some tradeoffs, and in this case the tradeoff is based on the business users' needs. For example, in Figure 8-1 the workbook is not set up for navigation via the context menu based right-clicking any items within the chart. Not to say that this approach wouldn't work. It's just that the workbook is set up so that users can navigate with radio buttons, dropdown lists, and pushbuttons. Therefore, this set of components satisfies the business users' need for additional bells and whistles without having to add significant enhanced functionality to the query results. Review the needs of your users, and if the BEx Analyzer is the front-end delivery tool of choice, then you can use the BEx Analyzer Design mode option with very good results. Looking at the workbook in Figure 8-1 more closely, we can summarize the navigation process as follows:

- Divisions can be navigated based on a set of radio buttons. Drilling down can be done based on the choice of a division, not via the context menu, then a filter, then a choice of division.

- Performance By can be navigated based on another set of radio buttons, so the specific key figures can be shown using this functionality.

- Select Month uses a dropdown box option, and the different months can be changed in the query by picking the required month from the list.

- The chart item changes based on the filtering of the graph.

- Finally, the exception can be changed by clicking the Exception button.

This approach offers a more direct view of all the navigation options rather than the business user using the context menu for analysis. In the next illustration, however, both options are available for use by the business user. For the navigation of the distribution channels, two radio buttons are used, and for the division a function button is used to drill down by division. There is also a function button for the months for drilldown processing. Looking at the graph in the lower portion of the workbook, you'll see there are no additional dropdown or function buttons to help with navigation. Therefore, to navigate this query, the user needs to be familiar with the context menu.

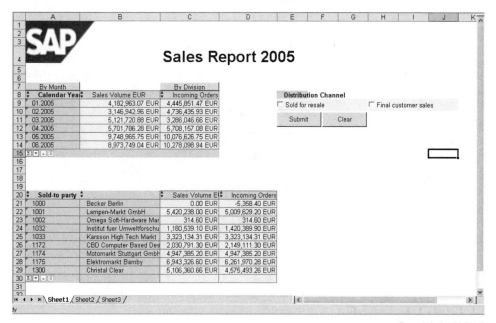

Copyright by SAP AG

The Design mode toolbox is the focus of this chapter, along with some additional functionality within the workbook using specific Excel features. If you take any query developed in the BEx Query Designer and open it in the BEx Analyzer, you will be able to enhance and manipulate the structure by just using the Design mode option on the toolbox.

The following illustration shows the basic query we've been working with for the past several chapters.

Information			
Author	BWUSER01	Last Refreshed	6/30/2007 21:49
Current User	BWUSER01	Key Date	6/30/2007
Last Changed by	BWUSER01	Changed At	6/30/2007 19:02
InfoProvider	T_SDDEMO2	Status of Data	2/28/2003 11:27
Query Technical Name	BWUSER_CUST_Q001	Relevance of Date	2/28/2003
Query Description	BWUSER Customer Query 1	Relevance of Date	1:27:34

Distribution Channel		Division		Order Entry Quantity	Sales Volume (MC)
10	Final customer sales	00	Cross-division	15 PC	0.00 EUR
10	Final customer sales	01	Pumps	14,897 PC	9,068,944.49 EUR
10	Final customer sales	07	High Tech	231,477 PC	30,447,344.75 EUR
10	Final customer sales	20	Turbines	2 PC	0.00 EUR
10	Final customer sales	Result		246,391 PC	39,516,289.24 EUR
12	Sold for resale	00	Cross-division	30 PC	0.00 EUR
12	Sold for resale	02	Motorcycles	195,279 PC	33,329,527.48 EUR
12	Sold for resale	04	Lighting	168,239 CAR	38,351,184.73 EUR
12	Sold for resale	07	High Tech	62,028 PC	38,129,496.48 EUR
12	Sold for resale	10	Vehicles	3 PC	3,003.23 EUR
12	Sold for resale	Result		425,578.600 MIX	109,813,211.92 EUR
14	Service	00	Cross-division	0 AU	0.00 EUR
14	Service	07	High Tech	27 PC	5,176.83 EUR
14	Service	08	Service	0 AU	0.00 EUR
14	Service	Result		27 PC	5,176.83 EUR
16	Factory sales	07	High Tech	0 PC	0.00 EUR
16	Factory sales	Result		0 PC	0.00 EUR
Overall Result				671,996.600 MIX	149,334,677.99 EUR

Copyright by SAP AG

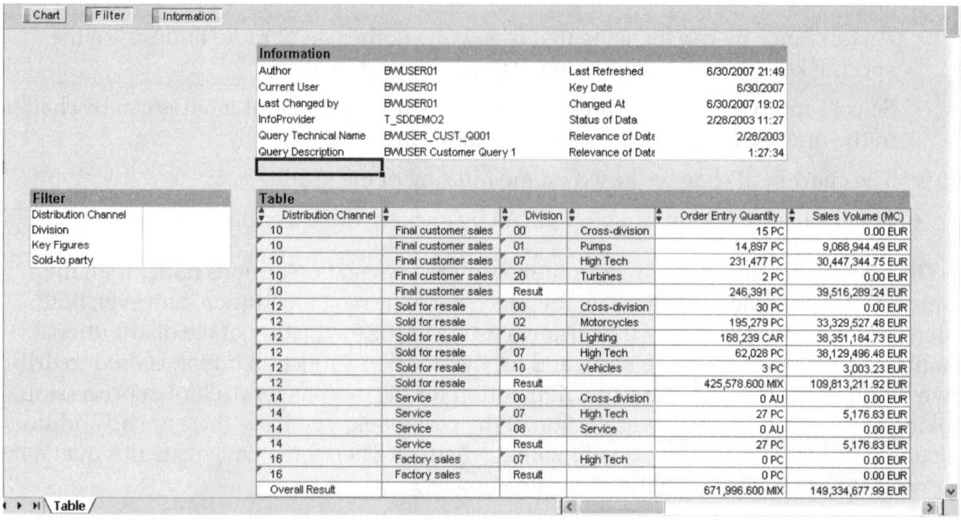

We've opened up the query in the BEx Analyzer to see the work that was done in the BEx Query Designer. Using the Design Mode icon, we can change the view of the query to allow the Query Designer to add any of the options in the Design Mode toolbox to this query. The next illustration shows the position of the Design Mode icon in the BEx Analyzer.

Division		Distribution Channel	
00	Cross-division	10	Final customer
		12	Sold for resale
		14	Service
		Result	
01	Pumps	10	Final customer
		Result	
02	Motorcycles	12	Sold for resale
		Result	
04	Lighting	12	Sold for resale
		Result	
07	High Tech	10	Final customer
		12	Sold for resale
		14	Service
		16	Factory sales
		Result	
08	Service	14	Service
		Result	

Copyright by SAP AG

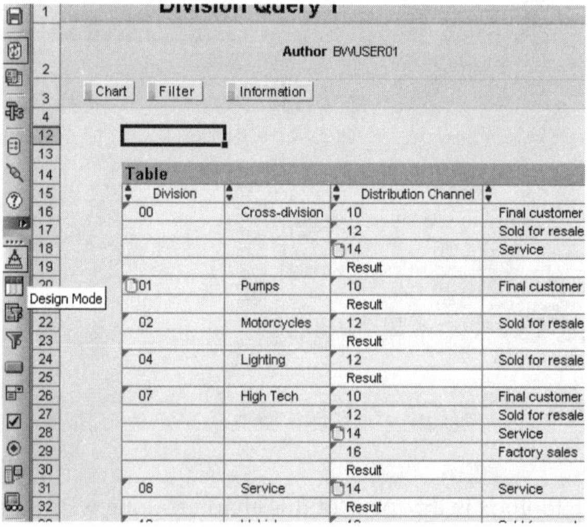

We'll use the Save As Workbook command once we're finished. The next illustration shows the view of the same query, but using the Design Mode icon. If we take a basic technical approach to this, everything in the BEx Query Designer tool that is developed is essentially a complex set of select statements and can be used as objects to support some other views of the results. In Design mode, the workbook appears as a collection of design items represented by their specific icons. In this mode, the additional features can be included to help with the specific display and navigation options required.

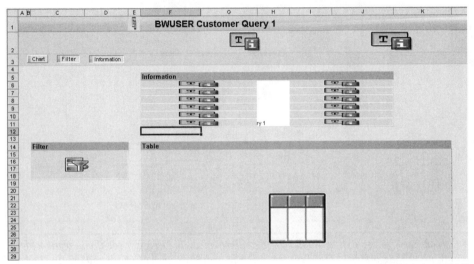

Again, you're not losing the original navigational options, but rather adjusting them to the needs of the users. If you use the Analysis Grid to display the results of the query, it will still have the context menu options that were available in the original query process. In addition, the editing functions in Microsoft Excel are available. You can format the workbook, set up the printing parameters for the results area, insert additional worksheets, embed formulas, change fonts and sizes, and create graphics and charts. The functions of both the Analysis mode and Design mode are typically active, and BEx Analyzer switches automatically to the right mode when you choose a function. For example, if you are in Analysis mode, and you select a tool on the Design toolbar in order to insert a design item, the Analyzer will switch automatically to Design mode and turn on the design items and their representative icons. Thus you can continue your work in Design mode. Once any changes have been made, use the Exit Design Mode icon to leave the design process and go back to the Analysis mode to review the changes. You use the Design Mode icon to enter and exit the design screens. This process has used an existing query that was executed and then we went into Design mode to start designing. Once that is complete, we use Save Workbook As (if we're creating a new workbook) or Save Workbook (if we're adding to an existing workbook) to save the changes and formatting. The other option, Save View, is used for saving the current settings and positions of the objects in the workbook. The following illustration shows the process to complete this task via the Analysis toolbox. The workbooks you create in Design mode are therefore complete query or BI applications. In Analysis mode, you can then save these queries in your Favorites folder or in your role on the BW server for someone else to open and work with in Analysis mode. You can also save the workbook locally on your computer.

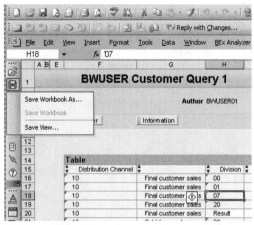

NOTE *Make sure you switch manually from Analysis mode to Design mode if you want to design anything in the workbook. This is a good habit to get into, especially once you are finished with your changes and want to save them. If you have very complex components and you select Save Workbook while still in the Design mode, you may receive a critical error and get knocked off the server. Once that happens, in most cases, all your unsaved configurations will be lost. Once you are finished in Design mode, use the Exit Design Mode option to move to Analysis mode.*

This is one approach to accessing the BEx Analyzer workbook functionality. Another approach is to open the BEx Analyzer and use the New function in Excel (top portion of the Excel screen) to start the creation of a workbook from scratch, as shown next.

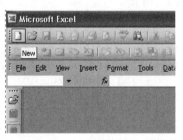

A final approach to entering the BEx Analyzer workbook is to use the BEx function Open | Open Workbook in the Analysis Mode toolbox. This allows you access to existing workbooks you have the authorization to change. The following illustration shows this process.

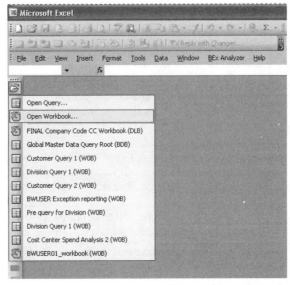

Copyright by SAP AG

Design Toolbox Functions

A set of design items are available for use in enhancing the front-end interface for the query. These design items are all based on the use of a Data Provider, except for the Message design item. A short definition of each design item is included in Table 8-1.

As we go through these different analysis items, keep in mind their use and positioning within the reporting process. These are new functions, and in the correct situation they will be a lifesaver. But used in the wrong situation, they will look good but make the end user frustrated.

The process of inserting a design item is pretty much the same no matter which item you are working with. Use design items in BEx Analyzer to provide controls, an interface, and functionality to your worksheet, turning it into a query application. After you insert a design item into your workbook, you configure the Data Provider and other properties relevant for the particular item. Design items are represented by icons while in Design mode. When in Analysis mode, properly configured design items return data as configured from the Data Providers upon which they are based.

NOTE *To add a dropdown box, radio button group, checkbox group, or button to your workbook, you must enable Microsoft Excel's Trust Access to Visual Basic Project setting (in Tools | Macro | Security | Trusted Sources). If you omit this step, you will see an "Access to Visual Basic Project Failed" error when you attempt to insert or access these design items in Analysis mode.*

Design Item	Icon	Description
Analysis Grid		Displays the results of a query. The Analysis Grid is the main design item in which you can navigate and perform OLAP functions.
Navigational Pane		Provides access to all characteristics and structures in the query for use in navigation and analysis.
List of Filters		Lists all currently active filters.
Button		Allows execution of a customized command on your results.
Dropdown Box		Allows the user to set a filter via a selection from a dropdown box.
Checkbox Group		Allows the user to set a filter via a checkbox selection.
Radio Button Group		Allows the user to set a filter via a radio button selection.
List of Conditions		Lists existing conditions and their status. Lets you activate and deactivate these conditions.
List of Exceptions		Lists existing exceptions and their status. Lets you activate and deactivate these exceptions.
Text		Displays text elements for the query.
Messages		Displays messages associated with the application (the workbook itself).
Workbook Settings		Allows the user to adjust settings specific to the workbook and the format. Allows changes in the themes that control the fonts and format, lists the items and Data Providers and their properties, and the ability to change the macro processing to name a few of the options.

TABLE 8-1   Options in the Design Toolbox for the BEx Analyzer

To insert and configure design items if you are not already in Design mode, you first must use the Design Mode function to enter Design mode. Select a cell (or cells) in the worksheet where you want your design item to appear. This positions the design item in the appropriate location on the workbook. You only need to select one cell to insert a design item, and this will correspond to the item's upper-left coordinate. You don't need to worry about selecting a range of cells large enough to accommodate query results. Once you switch to Analysis mode and the design items are populated with results, they expand to fill the space required by the results. The upper-left coordinate remains fixed, and the lower-right coordinate expands to accommodate the data returned.

With a design item such as a dropdown box or a button, you can adjust the format and size using the properties of the object. Alternatively, you can simply move or drag the object, to the required size once in the BEx Analyzer spreadsheet, then Save, and it will incorporate that size and position into the worksheet. Choose Insert [Design Item] from the Design toolbar, or choose BEx Analyzer|Design Toolbar|Insert [Design Item] from the menu bar. If you scroll over the different design items, the Insert [Design Item] option will be available. An icon representing the design item appears in the workspace. You can access the Properties dialog box for your design item to configure its properties. To access the item's properties using your mouse, click the icon that represents the item with the left (or primary) mouse button. You may also click with your right (or secondary) mouse button and choose Properties.

Another way to access design item properties with the menu option is to choose BEx Analyzer|Design Toolbar|[Item Name] from the menu bar. The follows illustration shows this approach. Once you access the Properties dialog box, only one activity is generic among all design objects—the configuration of the Data Provider. Each design item has properties specific to their respective functionality, but the configuration of the Data Provider is essential to all design items.

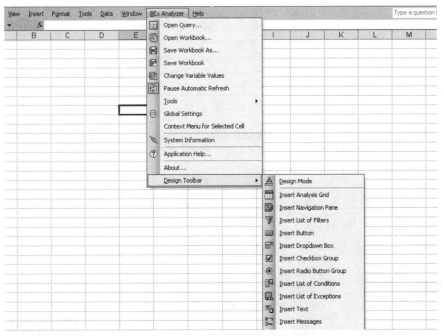

Copyright by SAP AG

Analysis Grid

The Analysis Grid is one of the most popular design items since it supports the actual graph and report for display purposes. The Analysis Grid is the design item that provides the main analysis functionality in BEx Analyzer. It displays the results of a query in a table where you can navigate and perform OLAP functionality. Use the Analysis Grid as the central design item in your worksheets. The grid displays query results in data cells, and it displays characteristics and structures in either the rows or columns of a table. When designing a workbook, you can use the grid together with the Navigation Pane and other design items to create a query application with full access to the range of OLAP functionality. In Analysis mode, you can navigate in the grid in different ways—via the context menu, drag and drop, or the icons. You can configure various settings via the Properties dialog box that affect the way the grid behaves and displays items. The following illustration shows the Properties dialog box for the Analysis Grid. Three specific tabs are available in the Analysis Grid Properties dialog box:

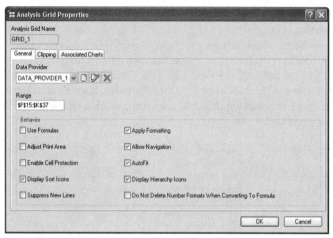

Copyright by SAP AG

- **General** Here you can configure the Data Provider cell range (not that you will change this, but it is available for use with other functions).

- **Clipping** Here you can configure whether the grid display is to be clipped or scrolled.

- **Associated Charts** This allows you to associate Microsoft Excel charts with the Analysis Grid.

Table 8-2 provides the details of each of the available settings.

Setting	Functionality
Analysis Grid Name	Displays the unique name of the grid, which is generated automatically. This name is used in the BEx Analyzer Design toolbar menu to refer to a particular instance of the Analysis Grid.
General Tab	
Data Provider	Used to assign an existing Data Provider to the Analysis Grid, create and assign a new one, or change or delete a Data Provider. The initial view of the Data Provider corresponds to the query view.
Range	This can be manipulated to accommodate different sizes for a cell or cells. These changes are done in this field. The object can also be moved or resized using this functionality.
Use Formulas	Select this checkbox to replace each cell in the Analysis Grid with a Microsoft Excel formula. This property of the Analysis Grid design item is set by the context menu function Convert to Formula.

TABLE 8-2 Options Displayed in the Analysis Grid Properties Dialog Box

General Tab	
Adjust Print Areas	Adjusts the Microsoft Excel print area automatically to the size of the Analysis Grid, and also repeats the header rows and header on every page.
Enable Cell Protection	Locks (protects) all cells that are not defined in the query as input ready, and unlocks all input-ready cells. This prevents you from changing data in any cells other than input-ready cells. This is mainly used with planning functions and prevents you from entering data where inappropriate.
Apply Formatting	Deselect this checkbox to switch off the display of formatting, including icons and background color. Displaying formatting during navigation can be time-consuming. You may therefore want to switch this off for performance reasons—for example, if you are navigating to achieve a result that you want to export to a text-based file. Scroll bars and scrolling icons are not affected by this setting.
Allow Navigation	Deselect this checkbox to deactivate the context menu and drag-and-drop functions in Analysis mode. A similar option is available for the Navigation Pane. This prevents you from analyzing and navigating in the query.
AutoFit	When this option is selected, the width of the cells in the Analysis Grid expands as required to fit the context. If this option is selected, after you navigate and the Analysis Grid is rendered, the columns are resized horizontally to the minimum size needed to render the whole content of the column.
Display Sort Icons	The icons for sorting characteristics and key figures in ascending and descending order are displayed in a report only when this option is selected.
Display Hierarchy Icons	The icons for expanding or collapsing a hierarchy are displayed in a report only when this option is selected.
Suppress New Lines	In BI applications that use Data Providers that are assigned an input-ready query, the system allows you to manually enter data in new input-ready rows. Select this checkbox to suppress the option of creating new input-ready rows.
Do Not Delete Number Formats When Converting to Formula	Number formats are deleted by default when you convert data in cells for the results set into formulas. Select this checkbox to retain the unit when you work in Formula mode.
Clipping Tab	
	Use the clipping options to specifically define the size of the Analysis Grid that use clipping or scroll bars. Clipping settings work together with cell coordinate settings in the range field. You can independently configure horizontal or vertical clipping using the options found on this tab.

TABLE 8-2   Options Displayed in the Analysis Grid Properties Dialog Box (continued)

Clipping Tab	
Horizontal – Clip	The Analysis Grid can only extend as far to the right as the rightmost column defined in the range field. The horizontal display beyond this is clipped and not displayed.
Horizontal – Full Size	The Analysis Grid is displayed starting from the leftmost column defined in the range field, but expands to the right to be as wide as required to display the results.
Horizontal – Scroll	The Analysis Grid displays within the right and left coordinates configured in the range field, and a scroll bar allows you to scroll to the right or to the left within the results. The scroll functionality can use the following icons in the scroll bar: scroll full left, scroll left, scroll full right, and scroll right.
Vertical – Clip	The Analysis Grid can only extend as far down as the lower-most row defined in the range field. The vertical display beyond that is clipped and not displayed
Vertical – Full Size	The Analysis Grid is displayed starting from the topmost row defined in the range field, but expands down as many rows as required to display the results.
Vertical – Scroll	The Analysis Grid displays within the upper and lower coordinates configured in the range field, and a scroll bar allows you to scroll up or down within the results. You can scroll using the following icons in the scroll bar: scroll to bottom, scroll down, scroll up, and scroll to top.
Associated Charts Tab	
Associated Charts	Use this function to associate Microsoft Excel with the Analysis Grid so that the charts always represent the results of the query. The name of any chart you have inserted on any sheet in the workbook appears in the Associated Charts list. Select the checkbox next to the chart or charts that needs to be associated with this Analysis Grid. When you're associating a chart with a grid, the chart is automatically updated with the cell ranges and values in the grid, even if the grid resizes and the values within it change when you navigate. When you create charts for your Analysis Grid using Microsoft Excel, you can leave the data range (cell coordinates) blank. Associated charts will automatically update with the appropriate data range in the current navigation state. Worksheets are automatically protected in Design mode. You can temporarily unprotect the sheet to insert the chart (Tools|Protection|Unprotect Sheet on Microsoft Excel's menu bar) or switch to Analysis mode first.

TABLE 8-2 Options Displayed in the Analysis Grid Properties Dialog Box (*continued*)

The following two illustrations show the configuration options in the Clipping and Associated Charts tabs of the Analysis Grid Properties dialog box.

Copyright by SAP AG

Copyright by SAP AG

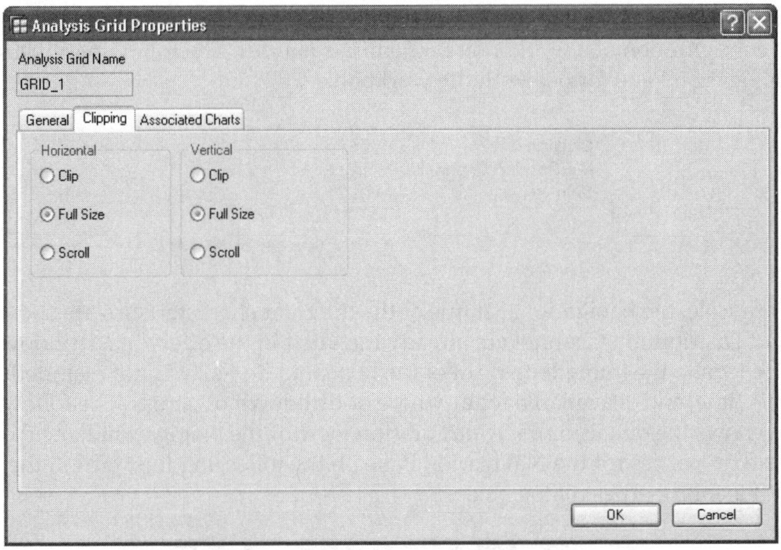

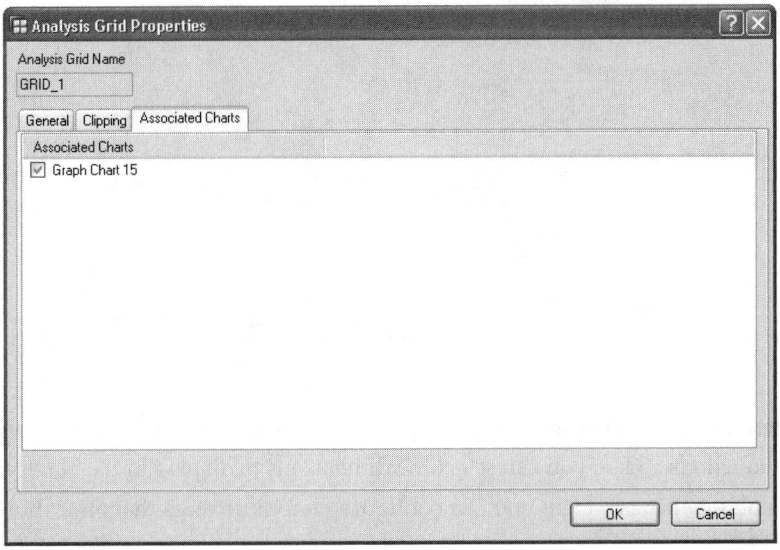

Navigation Pane

The next most popular design item is the Navigation Pane. With the addition of this design item to your workbook (along with the Analysis Grid) it will be very close to what most people will need for about 75% of their requirements. The Navigation Pane design item offers access to all the objects within the query, including characteristics, key figures, and structures. All these items can be used in the process of navigation and analysis. The Navigation Pane is the location of the free characteristic from the BEx Query Designer. The Navigation Pane and the Analysis Grid are the design items you will probably use the most during the configuration of a workbook in the BEx Analyzer. The following illustration shows a Navigation Pane for use with the workbook.

In the example, the navigational status of the different characteristics are shown. Division and Distribution Channel are already included in the query in a drilldown state based on the icon to the immediate right of the text. Sold-To Party is not included in the query, at this time, and is available for any type of drilldown or across. The following illustration shows the details of the configuration view of the Navigation Pane. You configure the properties for the Navigation Pane on the following four tabs in the Navigation Pane Properties dialog box:

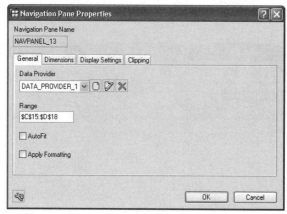

- **General**   Here you can configure the Data Provider, cell range, and AutoFit options.
- **Dimensions**   Here you can select the dimensions to display in the Navigation Pane.
- **Display Settings**   Here you can configure various settings that affect how the pane displays.
- **Clipping**   Here you can configure whether the Navigation Pane display is clipped or can be scrolled.

Table 8-3 details the functionality of the settings on each tab.

Setting	Functionality
Filter List Name	Displays the unique name of the filter item pane, which is generated automatically. This name is used in the BEx Analyzer Design toolbar menu to refer to a particular instance of the filter item Navigation Pane.
Display Technical Names / Do Not Display Technical Names	Located at the bottom of each tab page, this setting allows the display of the technical names per tab. Execute this function for each tab where you want the technical names to display.
General Tab	
Data Provider	Used to assign an existing Data Provider to the Navigation Pane, create and assign a new one, or change or delete a Data Provider. The initial view of a Data Provider corresponds to a query or query view.
Range	You can manipulate coordinates for a cell or cells in this field to move or resize the Navigation Pane.
AutoFit	When this option is selected, the width of the cells in the Navigation Pane (except the third column) expands as needed to accommodate the contents. When the pane is set to AutoFit, the columns are resized horizontally to the minimum size needed to render the whole content of columns. This setting does not apply to the third column (the filer area) because filter values can be very long.
Apply Formatting	Applies the standard formatting for the Navigation Pane to the design object.
Dimension Tab	
Available Dimensions	Lists all the available dimensions in the query. Select a dimension in this list and choose the Add the Selected Dimensions to the Displayed Dimensions button to transfer it to the Selected Dimensions list. You determine in this way which dimensions to display in the Navigation Pane. By default, all dimensions are displayed.
Selected Dimensions	Lists the dimensions you have chosen to display in the Navigation Pane, and allows you to reorder them. By default, all dimensions are displayed, although this list is empty. Select a dimension in this list and choose the Remove Selected Dimensions from the Displayed Dimensions button to remove it, or click the Move the Selected Displayed Dimension Up or Move the Selected Displayed Dimension Down button to reorder it.
Display Settings Tab	
Display Filter Texts	Deselect this checkbox to turn off the display of the filter area of the Navigation Pane. In this case, the whole third column of the pane disappears.
Allow Navigation	Deselect this checkbox to deactivate the context menu, drag-and-drop, and icon functionality in Analysis mode. A similar option is provided for the Analysis Grid. This prevents you from analyzing and navigating in the query.

TABLE 8-3   Options in the Navigation Pane Properties Dialog Box

Display Settings Tab	
Display Icons	Deselect this checkbox to turn off the display of icons in the Navigation Pane. Scroll bars and scrolling icons are not affected by this setting.
Show Dimensions on Rows	If this option is selected, the dimensions that appear on the rows in the current navigation state of the Analysis Grid are displayed in the Navigation Pane.
Show Dimensions on Columns	If this option is selected, the dimensions that appear on the columns in the current navigation state of the Analysis Grid are displayed in the Navigation Pane.
Show Dimensions on Free Characteristics	If this option is selected, the dimensions that appear in the free characteristics in the current navigational state of the Analysis Grid are displayed in the Navigation Pane.
Number of Dimensions Per Row	If you have selected the Display Dimensions Horizontally property, use this field to select the number of dimensions to display on each row of the Navigation Pane, horizontally across the sheet. This effectively shortens your Navigation Pane vertically.
Display Dimensions Horizontally	Select this option to display multiple dimensions per row of the Navigation Pane, and then configure the number of dimensions with the Number of Dimensions Per Row property.
Clipping Tab	
	Use the clipping options to specifically define the vertical size of the Analysis Grid using clipping or scroll bars. Clipping settings work together with cell coordinate settings in the Range field. You configure vertical clipping using the options Clip, Full Size, and Scroll.
Clip	The Navigation Pane can only extend as far down as the lower-most row defined in the Range field. The vertical display beyond that is clipped and not displayed.
Full Size	The Navigation Pane begins display from the top-most row defined in the Range field, but expands down as many rows as the results dictate.
Scroll	The Navigation Pane displays within the upper and lower coordinates configured in the Range field, and a scroll bar allows you to scroll up or down within the results. You can scroll using the following icons in the scroll bar: Scroll to the Bottom, Scroll Down, Scroll Up, Scroll to the Top.

TABLE 8-3   Options in the Navigation Pane Properties Dialog Box (*continued*)

The following three illustrations show the settings on the Dimensions, Display Settings, and Clipping tabs, respectively.

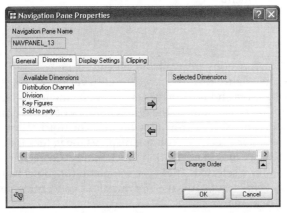

Copyright by SAP AG

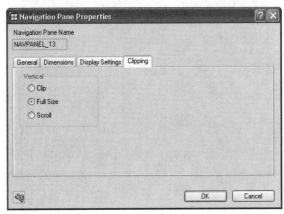

Copyright by SAP AG

Copyright by SAP AG

In Analysis mode, you can navigate with the Navigation Pane in different ways:

- Using the context menu
- Using drag and drop
- Using icons

Different navigation functions are available depending on whether you have selected a cell in a dimension or key figure row. You can configure various settings that affect the way the Navigation Pane behaves and is displayed. When referring to the Navigation Pane, we use the following terminology to refer to the different types of rows: dimension row (characteristic) and structure member row (key figure). The third column of each row in the Navigation Pane is the Filter Area. This column displays the values for any filters that have been configured. Different types of navigation functionality are available depending on which type of row you have selected. These context menu functions were discussed fully in Chapter 3. Refer to that chapter if you have any questions concerning navigation in the Analysis mode of the BEx Analyzer.

List of Filters

The List of Filters design item lists all currently active filters set on selected dimensions in the query results. This item simply displays a list of active filters for one or more dimensions. Because the Navigation Pane also displays currently active filters, this item might be useful if you have suppressed the display of filters in the Navigation Pane (by deselecting Display Filter Texts in the Navigation Pane properties) or if you don't display a Navigation Pane at all in your workbook and yet you want to display the current status of filters. You configure the properties for the list of filters on the following two tabs (see Table 8-4) in the Filter List Properties dialog box:

- **General**   Here you configure the Data Provider, cell range, and characteristic text display.
- **Dimensions**   Here you select the dimensions for displaying filters.

The following illustration shows the Filter List Properties dialog box.

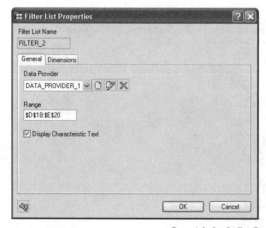

Copyright by SAP AG

Setting	Functionality
Filter List Name	Displays the unique name of the Filter List, which is generated automatically. This name is used in the BEx Analyzer Design toolbar menu to refer to a particular instance of the Filter List.
Display Technical Names / Do Not Display Technical Names	Located at the bottom of each tabbed page, this option allows the display of the technical names of the items on each tab. Execute this function on each tab for which you want the technical names to display.
General Tab	
Data Provider	Used to assign an existing Data Provider to the list of filters, create and assign a new one, or change or delete a Data Provider. The initial view of a Data Provider corresponds to a query or query view.
Range	Manipulate the coordinates for a cell or cells in this field to move or resize the list of filters.
Display Characteristic Text	Select this checkbox to display the name of the dimension in a field next to the list of its selected filters. This acts as a sort of label for each selected dimension in the filter list.
Dimension Tab	
Available Dimensions	Lists all the available dimensions in the query. Select a dimension in this list and choose the Add the Selected Dimensions to the Displayed Dimensions button to transfer it to the Selected Dimensions list. You determine in this way the dimensions for which to display a list of filters. By default, all dimensions are displayed.
Selected Dimensions	Lists the dimensions for which you have chosen to display filters, and allows you to reorder or remove them. By default, all dimensions are displayed, although this list is empty. Select a dimension in this list and choose the Remove Selected Dimensions from the Displayed Dimensions button to remove it, or click the Move the Selected Displayed Dimension Up or Move the Selected Displayed Dimension Down button to reorder it.
Presentation Style	Determines how the filter values are displayed in the list. Select from the following values: • **Key** Displays the technical key • **Key and Text** Displays the technical key, followed by text • **Text and Key** Displays text, followed by the technical key • **Text** Displays text

TABLE 8-4   Options in the Filter List Properties Dialog Box

Button

The Button design item lets you execute a customized command against the query results. Use the button to customize a specific command or sequence of commands. In the syntax, based on the Web API Reference, all Data Provider-specific commands and parameters are accepted, except Export to Microsoft Excel functions. Anything you can do when you manually navigate a query via the context menu, you can also customize with a button. When you click the button, you execute the command or commands, and the query results update accordingly in the Analysis Grid. You configure properties for the button using the Button Properties dialog box.

Button properties have been enhanced in current support packs; therefore, there is a vast difference between the button functionality available five to six months ago and what is available now. The button properties are broken down into several options. With each option chosen, different components will be available. The options available for the initial configuration of the button are:

- **Workbook-Specific Commands**   This option offers functionality specific to the actual workbook, such as activating the drag-and-drop options.

- **Planning-Specific Commands**   This option offers all the functionality to use the planning functions and activities in the BEx Analyzer workbook. This function automatically creates the command language for these functions.

- **Data Provider–Specific Commands**   This option offers the configuration of the Data Provider to be used in the process of supporting the reporting activities and automatically creates the command language for these functions. For example, it is possible to use one Analysis Grid item but swap in and out various queries.

The first of the following illustrations shows the configuration of this initial step. With the Button item, it is better that we cover an example of setting up a button first and then discuss the additional functionality available with the Button option. The steps taken for any option on the Button item are the same—the only difference is the executable you are configuring the button to process. The second illustration shows an example of the final setup of a Button item.

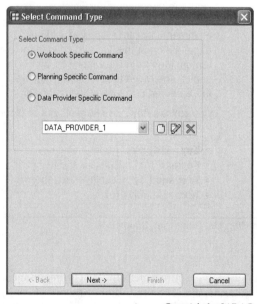

Business Driver Planning Process

Version CG2/Planned Data
Cost Center A
Company Code 1000

| Calculate 2007 Budget | | Distribute to Months | | Save Budget Data | |

CG GL Accounts		CG Business Driver		CG Bus Driver Rate	Actuals 2006	Budget
300100	Revenues	1001	Growth Rate - Rev	2 %	-$ 2,500,000.00	-$ 2,55
430100	Salaries	1002	Staffing Based Sal		$ 903,600.00	$ 92
430200	Benefits	1003	HR Calculation - Ben	3 %	$ 180,720.00	$ 18
430300	Payroll Taxes	1004	Payroll Tax Rate	1 %	$ 56,023.00	$ 5
474100	Travel Expenses	1005	Travel Expense	1 %	$ 200,000.00	$ 20
406002	Office Supplies	1006	Office Supplies	1 %	$ 50,000.00	$ 5
406006	Postage	1007	Postage - Growth Rat	1 %	$ 60,000.00	$ 6
406007	Shipping	1008	Shipping - Growth	1 %	$ 50,000.00	$ 5
416200	Electricity	1009	Overhead allocat	1 %	$ 35,000.00	$ 3
417100	Depreciation	1010	F&A Calculation	1 %	$ 10,000.00	$ 1
428200	Communications	1011	Communication	1 %	$ 76,000.00	$ 7
Overall Result				13 %	-$ 878,657.00	-$ 89

As you can see, this workbook has a series of buttons that execute different planning functions, including calculating the 2007 budget for the company, distributing these amounts to the months, and finally saving the budget data. In this case, behind each of these buttons is a planning function that executes a calculation of some sort that is consistent with the naming convention of the button. These calculations could be anything from a basic multiplication to a customized distribution process to post data to individual months from yearly information. The functionality of the Button item is excellent and can be used for basic reporting and planning. Now, for the process involved in setting up a button, we will use the workbook-specific commands. The first of the following illustrations shows the initial screen after the button has been assigned to the workbook and the configuration screen has been accessed via a single click on the object tag. Using the Next button at the bottom of the screen, we can access the more detailed options of the workbook-specific commands. The second illustration shows this information.

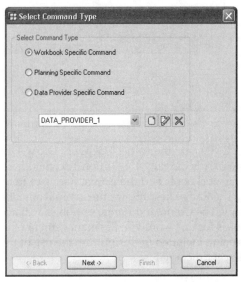

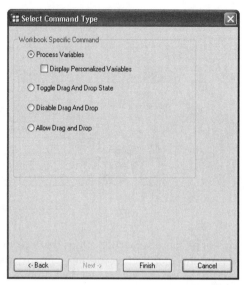

Choosing the option Toggle Drag and Drop State then clicking the Finish button at the bottom of the page causes the dialog box to move to the final view of the technical command that allows the drag-and-drop state to be executed from this button. The following illustration shows the final results.

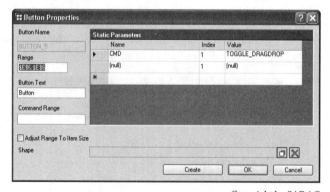

Notice that the name, CMD, and the value, TOGGLE_DRAGDROP, have been filled in automatically by the system. Additionally, the Button Text field has the naming convention the end user will see in the workbook, and the Adjust Range to Item Size Shape option is available to be activated. The Range field allows the manual adjustment of the range of cells that this button will occupy. The Command Range option is available for a number of possibilities. One of the uses for this would be the management of a variable entry. If this were a variable that was being included in this button, the use of the Command Range option can enhance the Excel functionality.

The row and column setting is used to obtain the necessary values to fill a variable. Therefore, rather than having a pop-up for variable entry, the user can just enter the values for the variables in a specific range of cells and this will fill the variable and execute the report. Finally, the option at the bottom of this screen is used to identify the button functionality with a specific shape—for example, a JPEG file with the symbol of the Save icon can be assigned here. Once this process is complete, you can include additional commands under one button by using the Create button at the bottom of the screen—for example, executing a planning function and also saving the information after the calculation is complete.

NOTE *Because the object can be expanded by use of Excel's functionality, after the completion of a configuration I normally use the Excel functions rather than the Button functions. Either work well for this purpose, though.*

Once the third screen has been configured, the button is complete. In every option—whether you're working with a workbook-specific, planning-specific, or data provider–specific command—the steps and fields are the same. The only difference, as mentioned, is the final technical command that is being configured.

Table 8-5 shows the details of each of the options, starting with the second screen.

NOTE *Because there hasn't been any discussion of the use of planning objects, such as functions and sequences, we will defer the discussion of the use of the button for planning objects until Chapter 17.*

Command Type	Specific Commands by Type	Description and Functionality
Data Provider Field	Create/Change	This option is used to identify the Data Provider used as the basis of the commands. The option to create or change the existing Data Provider is available. There is also the option to offer the results offline and reference the view.
	Turn On the Technical Names / Turn Off the Technical Names	This is a toggle setting at the bottom of the dialog box for turning on the technical names of the objects.
Workbook-Specific Commands	Process Variables – Display Personalized Variables	**SHOW_VARIABLE_SCREEN** If this button is executed, the variable screen is displayed. Also, the personalized variable values will be displayed.
	Toggle Drag and Drop State	**TOGGLE_DRAGDROP** With the execution of this button, drag-and-drop functionality can be activated or deactivated.
	Disable Drag and Drop	**DISABLE_DRAGDROP** This button disables the drag-and-drop functionality in the workbook.

TABLE 8-5 Settings for the Command Types Used in the BEx Analyzer Design Mode

Command Type	Specific Commands by Type	Description and Functionality
	Allow Drag and Drop	**ALLOW_DRAGDROP** This button allows the drag-and-drop functionality in the workbook.
Planning-Specific Commands	Save	**SAVE_AREA** This button saves the data posted to the InfoCube.
	Transfer Values	**VALUE_CHECK** This command executes a check on all the values posted in an input-ready workbook and confirms the consistency of the entries.
	Execute Planning Function	This command executes a planning function that has been assigned to a button. Additional explanation of this command is included in Chapter 17.
	Execute Planning Sequence	This command executes a planning sequence that has been assigned to a button. Additional explanation of this command is included in Chapter 17.
Data Provider-Specific Commands	Edit	**SET_INPUT_MODE** This command allows the use of the input functionality in the workbook.
	Display	**SET_INPUT_MODE – X in the ACTIVE Command** Using this function for a button will not allow any data input but only the display of the data. This will allow the business user to set information to display only.
	Filter Commands	**REMOVE_FILTER** This command allows the control of the filters in the workbook by use of the button.
	Assign Query / Query View	**RESET_DATA_PROVIDER** This command allows the user to change the Data Provider for a specific view or table based on the execution of this button. In this case, the configuration requires that a Data Provider be filled into the field for use in this command.

TABLE 8-5   Settings for the Command Types Used in the BEx Analyzer Design Mode (*continued*)

Table 8-6 shows the options that are standard for all of the command types. The final property—Static Parameter—is found on the final dialog box for the button's setup, as shown in the following illustration.

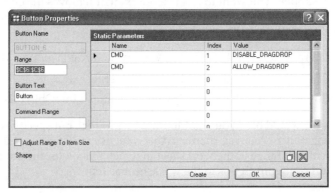

Property	Description
Button Name	Displays the unique name of the button, which is generated automatically. This name is used on the BEx Analyzer | Design Toolbar menu to refer to a particular instance of the button.
Range	Manipulate coordinates for a cell or cells in this field to move or resize the button.
Button Text	The text (caption) you want to display on the button. You can use this to describe the command the button executes.
Command Range	(Optional) Specify a three-column range of cells in the worksheet that contains command parameters. In these cells, you provide the same parameters (Name, Index, and Value) as for Static Parameters (shown next), but in the worksheet these can be variable, changing during navigation based on query results or on a value you manually specify. When the button is clicked to initiate the command, all values in Static Parameters are evaluated first, then all the parameters in Command Range are appended.
Static Parameters	You configure the command or commands to execute by supplying name-value pairs to send to the server. A command can consist of multiple name-value pairs; configure one per row in this table. Any Data Provider–specific command in the Web API Reference (except Export to Microsoft Excel functions) is accepted. • **Name** The name of the command. • **Index** The order in which the command should be executed, starting with 0. You can configure as many commands as you want. • **Value** The value for the command.

TABLE 8-6   Standard Options on the Button Properties Dialog Box

As you can see, the Button command is a very powerful option that can help tremendously in the configuration of the BEx Analyzer workbook. Work with all these options to decide which ones will be useful for your end users. As an example of the use of the filter function, suppose you want to create a button that removes the currently configured filter. Just enter **Remove Filter** in the Button Text field and configure the following three rows in the Static Parameters section:

- Name = DATA_PROVIDER; Index = 0; Value = [name of Data Provider]
- Name = CMD, Index = 0, Value = REMOVE-FILTER
- Name = FILTER_IOBJNM, Index = 0, Value = [name of InfoObject Data Provider]

Another example would be if you want to filter by product, but specify which product while you are navigating in Analysis mode. In this case, use the Command Range field to specify the three-column range in the worksheet in which to look for the parameters. For example, you could configure all this in the worksheet as follows:

Column E	Column F	Column G	Column H
			Filter to the following product:
Row 8	FILTER_VALUE	0	PRODO0001

Set the Command Range field to F8:H8. Now, you can provide dynamic input for the value in column H, labeled "Filter to the following product:" in the worksheet. You can also hide columns F and G so that the static parameters of the command remain hidden.

As mentioned, the use of the Button item for planning functions will be discussed in detail in a later chapter, but buttons can be quite useful within the context of planning functions, which aren't executed in the context of a Data Provider, but rather within a workbook. For example, in a reevaluation scenario, suppose you've created a planning function on the back end in which you get a raise and make your calculations increase by 1%. You can add a button to the worksheet to execute this planning function. In addition, although planning functions are modeled on the back end, they can have variables—which you can also supply in the worksheet using the Command Range field.

Dropdown Box

The Dropdown Box design item lists the values of a dimension and lets you filter it by selecting a value from the list. Use a dropdown box to easily filter a selected dimension. Because filtering is a function also provided in the Navigation Pane, you might not want to use a Navigation Pane in the same worksheet as a dropdown box. You might use the dropdown box if, for example, you don't want to offer the whole range of navigation that the Navigation Pane provides, but you want to be able to conveniently set filters.

The Checkbox Group and Radio Button Group design items provide similar functionality, except that the checkbox group allows you to select multiple filter values at once. Also, with the checkbox and radio button groups, the number of values needs to be taken into account because both items create a list for all values identified. Therefore, the use of a checkbox or radio button group may not work as well as a dropdown box for something like customer lists. In the Dropdown Box Properties dialog box, you configure the values for the dimension to appear in the dropdown list. An example of a dropdown box is shown in the following illustration using the characteristic Division as the dimension. When you select a value from the dropdown box in Analysis mode, the dimension is filtered by your selection, and the query results in the Analysis Grid update accordingly. You configure properties for the dropdown box on three different tabs in the Dropdown Box Properties dialog box:

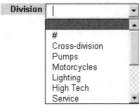

Copyright by SAP AG

- **General**   Here you configure the Data Provider, cell range, and label display.
- **Dimensions**   Here you select and configure the dimension you wish to filter.

NOTE *To add a dropdown box to the workbook, you must enable Microsoft Excel's Trust Access to Visual Basic Project setting (in Tools | Macro | Security | Trusted Sources). If you omit this step, you will see an Access to Visual Basic Project Failed error when you attempt to insert or access the drop-down box in Analysis mode.*

- **Target Data Provider**   Here you select multiple Data Providers for which you wish to apply a filter.

Table 8-7 shows the parameters required by the dropdown option.

Property	Description
Dropdown Box Name	Displays the unique name of the dropdown box, which is generated automatically. This name is used on the BEx Analyzer's Design toolbar menu to refer to a particular instance of the dropdown box.
Display Technical Names / Do Not Display Technical Names	Use this button on any tab to toggle the display of technical names.
General Tab	
Data Provider	Used to assign an existing Data Provider to the dropdown box, create and assign a new one, or change or delete a Data Provider. The initial view of a Data Provider corresponds to a query or query view.
Range	Manipulate coordinates for a cell or cells in this field to move or resize the dropdown box.

TABLE 8-7   Parameters of the Dropdown Box Properties Dialog Box

General Tab	
Display Label	Select this checkbox to display the name of the dimension to be filtered next to the dropdown box.
Adjust Range to Item Size	Automatically adjusts the range used in the workbook to the item's size.
Input Mode	Allows manual data entry in the field for the dropdown box. Therefore, if the user knows the characteristic value, they can manually enter rather than picking from the dropdown list.
Display All Entry	This option generates a list of all the values of the characteristic. This will not be used if a setting on the Dimension tab is used.
Keep Filter Value on Axis	With this option, if the characteristic used as the filter is also in the query, the filtered value of the dropdown list will be held in the body of the query rather than moved to the header of the query.
Dimensions Tab	
Dimension	Select the dimension you wish to filter.
Text Type	Determines which text type to display for the values of the dimension: • **Default Text** Uses the shortest available text to display the values • **Short Text** Uses the short text to display the values • **Middle Text** Uses the medium text to display the values • **Long Text** Uses the long text to display the values
Read Mode	Determines the method of retrieving the list of filter values: • **Posted Values (Q)** Performs a SELECT on the fact table to list filter values that actually return data. Values that return no results when filtered are not displayed in the list. This calculation can be time-consuming, but it yields only usable values in the list. • **Dimension Table (D)** Performs a SELECT on the dimension table to retrieve the list of filter values. This calculation is less time-consuming than Posted Values, with better chances of yielding results than Masterdata Table. • **Masterdata Table (M)** Returns all members of the selected dimension that appear in the masterdata table. Because InfoCubes may be quite sparsely populated, this method yields many selections that show no results when filtered ("No applicable data found"). However, the logic involved is simple and hence the performance is optimal.

TABLE 8-7   Parameters of the Dropdown Box Properties Dialog Box (*continued*)

Dimensions Tab	
Display	Determines how the filter values are displayed in the list. Select from the following values: • **Text** Displays text • **Key** Displays the technical key • **Key and Text** Displays the technical key, followed by text • **Text and Key** Displays text, followed by the technical key
Target Data Provider Tab	
Data Provider Name	The query results of a Data Provider can be filtered by the value of a dimension for which a dropdown box is designed. This filtering is not applied in other Data Providers within a workbook, even though the same dimension is reused. That means you need to create individual filters for the same dimension, which is used in different Data Providers. However, the target Data Provider feature allows you simplify the preceding scenario. In this tabbed page, you can view all Data Providers being used in the workbook. You can select the required Data Providers or all Data Providers to apply the same filtering for specific Data Providers or all Data Providers used in a workbook.

TABLE 8-7 Parameters of the Dropdown Box Properties Dialog Box (*continued*)

The following illustrations show the options for the General, Dimensions, and Target Data Provider tabs, respectively.

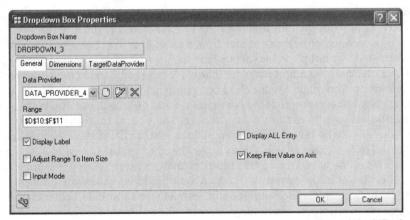

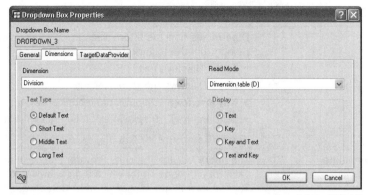

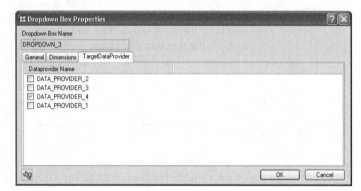

Checkbox Group

The Checkbox Group design item lists the values of a dimension and lets you filter that dimension by selecting one or more values from the list. Use the checkbox group to filter a selected dimension by multiple values at one time. Because filtering is a function also provided in the Navigation Pane, you might not want to use a Navigation Pane in the same worksheet as the checkbox group. You might use the checkbox group if, for example, you don't want to offer the whole range of navigation that the Navigation Pane provides, but you want to be able to conveniently set a group of filter values at once. The significant difference between the Dropdown Box and Radio Button Group design items and the Checkbox Group is that they restrict filter selection to one value at a time. In the checkbox group's properties, you configure the values for the dimension you wish to filter. In Analysis mode, each value appears next to one of the checkboxes in the group, and any currently filtered values are checked. The two buttons at the bottom of the list, Submit and Clear, let you submit and clear checked filter selections, respectively, upon which the dimension filters are updated according to your selection. The query results in the Analysis Grid are then updated. You configure properties for the checkbox group on the following tabs in the Checkbox Group Properties dialog box:

- **General**   This tab allows you to configure the Data Provider, cell range, AutoFit, and horizontal display settings.

- **Dimensions**   This tab enables you to configure the dimension you wish to filter.

NOTE *As with all of the design items it is important to make sure that the security on the Excel Workbook is set to accept information and entries into each of the object. For example, for the Checkbox Group design item to work correctly make sure that the Excel Trusted security requirements are reviewed and the appropriate level of security is assigned to the Visual Basic Project.*

- **Target Data Provider** This tab allows you to select multiple Data Providers for which you wish to apply a filter. (This tab has similar properties and assignments for all the design items, so refer to the previous discussions of the Target Data Provider tab for details.)

Table 8-8 details the parameters for the Checkbox Group design item's configuration.

Property	Description
Checkbox Group Name	Displays the unique name of the checkbox group, which is generated automatically. This name is used on the BEx Analyzer's Design toolbar menu to refer to a particular instance of the checkbox group.
Display Technical Names / Do Not Display Technical Names	Use this button on any tab to toggle the display of technical names.
General Tab	
Data Provider	Used to assign an existing Data Provider to the checkbox group, create and assign a new one, or change or delete a Data Provider. The initial view of a Data Provider corresponds to a query or query view.
Range	Manipulate coordinates for a cell or cells in this field to move or resize the checkbox group.
Display Label	Select this option to use the labels for the checkbox values.
Display Dimensions Horizontally	Select this option to display the values of the checkbox group horizontally, in one row across the sheet.
Dimensions Tab	
Dimension	Select the dimension you wish to filter.
Text Type	Determines which text type to display for the values of the dimension: • **Default Text** Uses the shortest available text to display the values • **Short Text** Uses the short text to display the values • **Middle Text** Uses the medium text to display the values • **Long Text** Uses the long text to display the values

TABLE 8-8 Parameters of the Checkbox Group Properties Dialog Box

Dimensions Tab	
Read Mode	Determines the method of retrieving the list of filter values: • **Posted Values (Q)** Performs a SELECT on the fact table to list filter values that actually return data. Values that return no results when filtered are not displayed in the list. This calculation can be time-consuming, but it yields only usable values in the list. • **Dimension Table (D)** Performs a SELECT on the dimension table to retrieve the list of filter values. This calculation is less time-consuming than Posted Values, with better chances of yielding results than Masterdata Table. • **Masterdata Table (M)** Returns all members of the selected dimension that appear in the masterdata table. Because InfoCubes may be sparsely populated, this option yields many selections that show no results when filtered ("No applicable data found"). However, the logic involved is simple and hence the performance is optimal. This would be a good option if you are looking to display a full set of master data in your queries.
Display	Determines how the filter values are displayed in the list. Select from the following values: • **Text** Displays text • **Key** Displays the technical key • **Key and Text** Displays the technical key, followed by text • **Text and Key** Displays text, followed by the technical key
Maximum Number of Displayed Values	Use this selector to set the maximum number of values to display in the checkbox group.

TABLE 8-8 Parameters of the Checkbox Group Properties Dialog Box (*continued*)

The following illustrations show the options for the General and Dimensions tabs, respectively.

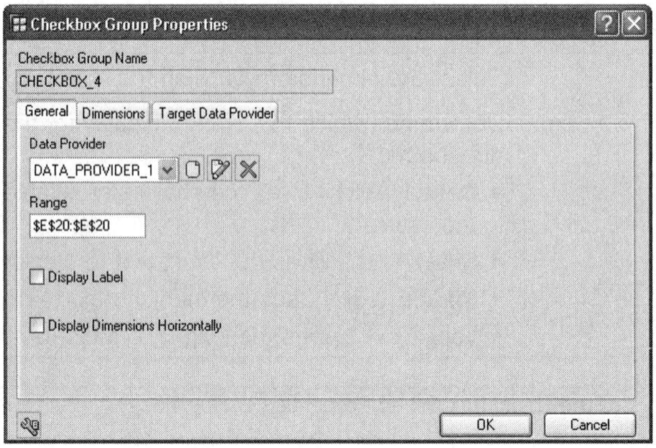

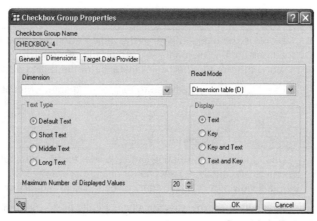

Radio Button Group

The Radio Button Group design item lists the values of a dimension and lets you filter by selecting a value from the list. Use the radio button group to easily filter a selected dimension. The dropdown box and checkbox group provide similar functionality, except that the checkbox group allows you to select multiple filter values at once. In the radio button group's properties, you configure the values for the dimension you wish to filter. In Analysis mode, each value appears next to one radio button in the group. When you then select one of the radio buttons, the dimension is filtered by your selection, and the query results in the Analysis Grid update accordingly. You configure the properties for the radio button group on the following tabs in the Radio Button Group Properties dialog box:

- **General**   Allows you to configure Data Provider, cell range, AutoFit, and horizontal display settings.

- **Dimensions**   Allows you to select and configure the dimension you wish to filter.

- **Target Data Provider**   Allows you to select multiple Data Providers for which you wish to apply a filter. (This tab has similar properties and assignments for all the design items, so refer to the previous discussions for the Target Data Provider tab for details.)

Table 8-9 provides a detailed review of the parameters required for the Radio Group design item.

The illustration at right shows the options for the General tab.

List of Conditions

The List of Conditions design item lists all conditions defined in the query and lets you activate and deactivate them using the context

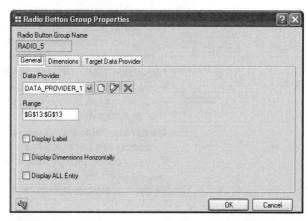

Property	Description
Radio Button Group Name	Displays the unique name of the radio button group, which is generated automatically. This name is used on the BEx Analyzer's Design toolbar menu to refer to a particular instance of the radio button group.
Display Technical Names / Do Not Display Technical Names	Use this button on any tab to toggle the display of technical names.
General Tab	
Data Provider	Used to assign an existing Data Provider to the radio button group, create and assign a new one, or change or delete a Data Provider. The initial view of a Data Provider corresponds to a query or query view.
Range	Manipulate coordinates for a cell or cells in this field to move or resize the radio button group.
Display Label	Select this option, and the display of the label for the characteristic used for the radio button group will be visible.
Display Dimensions Horizontally	Select this option to display the values of the radio button group horizontally, in one row across the sheet.
Display All Entry	Select this option to display all entries for the characteristic values for the radio button group. Depending on the settings in the Dimension tab, this option may be overridden.
Dimensions Tab	
Dimension	Select the dimension you wish to filter
Text Type	Determines which text type to display for the values of the dimension: • **Default Text** Uses the shortest available text to display the values • **Short Text** Uses the short text to display the values • **Middle Text** Uses the medium text to display the values • **Long Text** Uses the long text to display the values
Read Mode	Determines the method of retrieving the list of filter values: • **Posted Values (Q)** Performs a SELECT on the fact table to list filter values that actually return data. Values that return no results when filtered are not displayed in the list. This calculation can be time-consuming, but it yields only usable values in the list. • **Dimension Table (D)** Performs a SELECT on the dimension table to retrieve the list of filter values. This calculation is less time-consuming than Posted Values, with better chances of yielding results than Masterdata Table. • **Masterdata Table (M)** Returns all members of the selected dimension that appear in the masterdata table. Because InfoCubes may be quite sparsely populated, this option yields many selections that show no results when filtered ("No applicable data found"). However, the logic involved is simple and hence the performance is optimal.

TABLE 8-9   Parameters of the Radio Button Group Properties Dialog Box

Dimensions Tab	
Display	Determines how the filter values are displayed in the list. Select from the following values: • **Text** Displays text • **Key** Displays the technical key • **Key and Text** Displays the technical key, followed by text • **Text and Key** Displays text, followed by the technical key
Maximum Number of Displayed Values	Use this selector to set the maximum number of values to display in the radio button group.
Target Data Provider Tab	
Target Data Provider Name	The query results of a Data Provider can be filtered by the value of a dimension for which a radio button is designed. This filtering is not applied in other Data Providers within a workbook, even though the same dimension is reused. That means you need to create individual filters for the same dimension, which is used in different Data Providers. However, the target Data Provider feature allows you simplify the preceding scenario. In this tabbed page, you can view all Data Providers being used in the workbook. You can select the required Data Providers or all Data Providers to apply the same filtering for specific Data Providers or all Data Providers used in a workbook.

TABLE 8-9   Parameters of the Radio Button Group Properties Dialog Box (*continued*)

menu or an icon. If conditions have been defined in the query, you can use the List of Conditions design item to display them in rows in the worksheet. The description of each condition appears in a cell, and its status (Active or Inactive) and an icon (Activate/Deactivate) displays in the cell next to it. In Analysis mode, you can click the icon to toggle the active status. Alternatively, you can evoke the context menu and choose Activate (to activate a selected inactive condition) or Deactivate (to deactivate a selected active condition). Conditions filter the results so that only the part of the results you are interested in is displayed, so when you activate or deactivate a condition, the navigational state of the Analysis Grid updates accordingly. The following illustration shows the configuration of this design item.

Property	Description
Condition List Name	Displays the unique name of the list of conditions, which is generated automatically. This name is used on the BEx Analyzer's Design toolbar menu to refer to a particular instance of the list of conditions.
Data Provider	Used to assign an existing Data Provider to the list of conditions, create and assign a new one, or change or delete a Data Provider. The initial view of a Data Provider corresponds to a query or query view.
Range	Manipulate coordinates for a cell or cells in this field to move or resize the list of conditions.
AutoFit	Select this option to allow the table to automatically fit the conditions being used.

TABLE 8-10   Parameters for the Condition Button in the BEx Analyzer Design Mode

You configure properties for the List of Conditions design item using the Condition List Properties dialog box. Table 8-10 details the parameters that need to be set for the Condition button.

List of Exceptions

The List of Exceptions design item lists all exceptions defined in the query and lets you activate and deactivate them using the context menu or an icon. If exceptions have been defined in the query, you can use the List of Exceptions design item to display them in rows in the worksheet. The description of each exception appears in a cell, and its status (Active or Inactive) and an icon (Activate/Deactivate) displays in the cell next to it. In Analysis mode, you can click the icon to toggle the active status. Alternatively, you can evoke the context menu and choose Activate (to activate a selected inactive exception) or Deactivate (to deactivate a selected active exception). Exceptions set the background color of data cells in the results, alerting you to exceptional values. Therefore, when you activate or deactivate an exception, the background color of relevant data cells in the Analysis Grid updates accordingly. You configure properties for the List of Exceptions design item using the Exception List Properties dialog box. The configuration of the List of Exceptions design item is very similar to that of the List of Conditions design item, so refer to the illustration in the preceding section. Table 8-11 shows the details of the parameter configuration.

Property	Description
Exception List Name	Displays the unique name of the list of exceptions, which is generated automatically. This name is used on the BEx Analyzer's Design toolbar menu to refer to a particular instance of the list of exceptions.
Data Provider	Used to assign an existing Data Provider to the list of exceptions, create and assign a new one, or change or delete a Data Provider. The initial view of a Data Provider corresponds to a query or query view.
Range	Manipulate coordinates for a cell or cells in this field to move or resize the list of exceptions.

TABLE 8-11   Parameters for the List of Exceptions Button in the BEx Analyzer Design Mode

Text

The Text design item displays text elements associated with the query. Use the Text design item to display text-based information saved with the query, such as author, query description, and any global filters configured in the query. You configure which text elements you want to display, and then display them in a list in your worksheet. You configure properties for the Text design item on the following tabs in the Text Properties dialog box:

- **General** Lets you configure Data Provider, cell range, AutoFit, and caption display settings
- **Constants** Lets you select from a list of text constants to display
- **Filters** Lets you select from a list of global filters to display

Quite a few items are displayed in the Text design item, so a detailed review of the parameters is in order. Table 8-12 details the parameters available for the Text design item.

Property	Description
Text Name	Displays the unique name of the text item, which is generated automatically. This name is used on the BEx Analyzer's Design toolbar menu to refer to a particular instance of the text item.
General Tab	
Data Provider	Used to assign an existing Data Provider to the text item, create and assign a new one, or change or delete a Data Provider. The initial view of a Data Provider corresponds to a query or query view.
Range	Manipulate coordinates for a cell or cells in this field to move or resize the text item.
AutoFit	When this option is selected, the width of the cells in the text item expands as needed to accommodate the contents.
Display Caption	Select this checkbox to display the name of the text element in a field next to the text itself. This acts as a sort of label for each selected text element.
Display Formats	Select this checkbox to use the formats of the text element from the system. This acts as a label for each selected text element.
Constants Tab	
	After you have selected a Data Provider on the General tab, the list of available constant text elements appears on this tab, including the following: • **Author** The user who defined the query. • **Last Changed By** The user who last changed the query definition so that the query has been regenerated. Small changes made via navigation are not real definition changes. • **InfoProvider** The InfoProvider with the data reported on in the query.

TABLE 8-12   Parameters of the Text Properties Dialog Box

Constants Tab
• **Query Technical Name**   The technical name you enter for the query when you save it. • **Query Description**   Description of the query. • **Key Date**   The key date is the date for which time-dependent master data is selected. You determine the key date in the query definition (query properties) or supply the value using a variable. If the key date has not been defined, the system date is automatically made into the key date. • **Changed At**   This time tells you when the query definition was last changed. • **Current User**   The user who has this query open or has inserted it into a workbook. • **Last Refreshed**   When the query data was last refreshed. This is the point at which you display the text elements, because refreshing the query is necessary for displaying the text elements. • **Status of Data**   The point in time when data for the latest request that can be used for reporting was posted to the InfoProvider. For MultiProviders, the current InfoPackages are determined from the individual basic cubes, and from these, the basic cube with the oldest data validity date is called. This shows a date and a time (in the local time zone). • **Relevance of the Data (date)**   The date of the Status of Data text element. • **Relevance of the Data (hour)**   The time of the Status of Data text element. • **Status of Data From**   (MultiProviders only.) • **Status of Data To**   (MultiProviders only.) Select the checkbox next to the text elements you wish to display. You may also choose: **Select All**   Selects all checkboxes and hence all constants **Deselect All**   Deselects all checkboxes and hence all constants
Filters Tab
If global filters have been configured in the query, the dimensions for which they are configured are listed on this tab. Select the checkbox next to the ones you wish to display. Current filter values configured for the selected dimension are then displayed in the text element. Your options are: • **Select All**   Selects all checkboxes and hence displays all filters • **Deselect All**   Deselects all checkboxes and hence disables the display of all filters • **Display All Global Filter Values**   Displays all the static filter values • **Display All Global Variable Values**   Displays all the static variable values

TABLE 8-12   Parameters of the Text Properties Dialog Box (*continued*)

The following illustrations show the options for the General, Constants, and Filters tabs, respectively.

Copyright by SAP AG

Copyright by SAP AG

Copyright by SAP AG

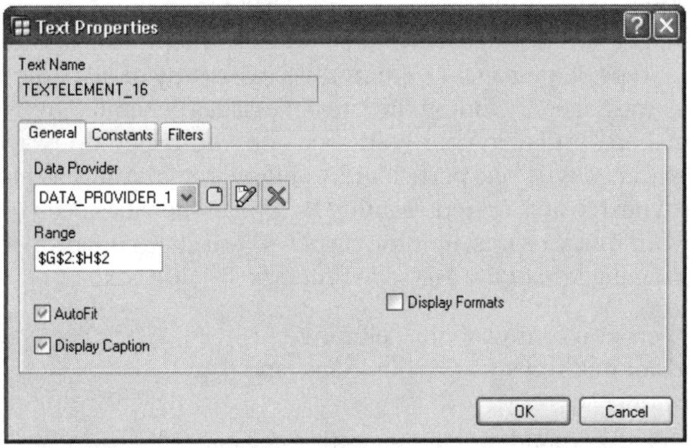

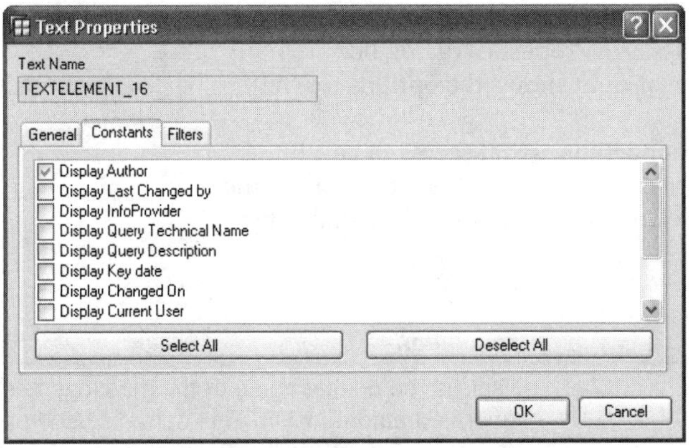

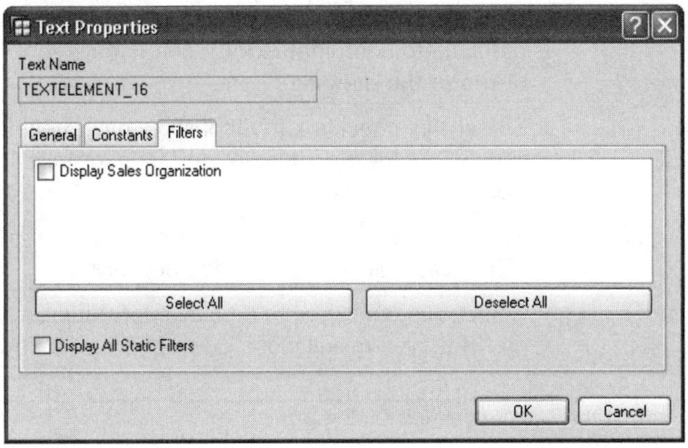

Message

The Message design item displays messages associated with your workbook, such as messages generated by BEx Analyzer as well as messages generated from the system to which you are currently connected. Use the Message design item to reproduce messages in your worksheet. You configure which type of messages (warning, success, or any or all of the others) you want to see. BEx Analyzer messages, including the latest messages generated from the system to which you are logged on, display in your worksheet for your review. Messages are unique, in that they are not associated with one particular Data Provider. In Analysis mode, the messages display in a list, each next to an icon representing its type. If there has been no message since you last refreshed your query results, nothing displays. You configure properties for the messages on the following tabs of the Message Properties dialog box:

- **General**   Lets you configure the cell range, which kinds of messages you'd like to see, and AutoFit options
- **Clipping**   Lets you configure whether the message display is clipped or can be scrolled

Table 8-13 details the parameters you need to configure in the Message Properties dialog box.

The illustration at right shows the options for the General tab.

One of the minor activities that seems to be a bit tricky and confuses everyone at least one time or another is the process of deleting design items. You can delete a

Copyright by SAP AG

Property	Description
Message Name	Displays the unique name of the message item, which is generated automatically. This name is used on the BEx Analyzer's Design toolbar menu to refer to a particular instance of the message item.
General Tab	
Range	Manipulate coordinates for a cell or cells in this field to move or resize the message item.
Display Warnings	Select this checkbox to display warning messages, such as "The value for the variable 'def' is incorrect; Access to Visual Basic project failed."
Display Success Messages	Select this checkbox to display success messages, such as "The query 'abc' was successfully saved."
Display Information	Select this checkbox to display informational messages, such as "The system will close down at 6 P.M. today."

TABLE 8-13   Parameters of the Text Properties Dialog Box

Property	Description
AutoFit	When this option is selected, the width of the cells in the message item expands as needed to accommodate the contents of the message. This is a good option to check because in some situations messages can be a bit long, thus causing the data columns to be pushed out far to the right.
	Clipping Tab
	Use the clipping options to specifically define the vertical size of the message item using clipping or scroll bars. Clipping settings work together with cell coordinate settings in the Range field. Configure vertical clipping using the following Vertical options: • **Clip** The message item can only extend as far down as the lowermost row defined in the Range field. The vertical display beyond this is clipped and not displayed. • **Full Size** The message item begins display from the topmost row defined in the Range field, but expands down as many rows as the results dictate. • **Scroll** The message item displays within the upper and lower coordinates configured in the Range field, and a scroll bar allows you to scroll up or down within the results. You can scroll using the following icons in the scroll bar: Scroll to Bottom, Scroll Down, Scroll Up, and Scroll to Top.

TABLE 8-13   Parameters of the Text Properties Dialog Box (*continued*)

design item when you are in Design mode by using its context menu, which you can access with a right click or with the BEx Analyzer menu. Click the design item with your right mouse button (secondary mouse button) and from the context menu, choose Delete. To delete a design item using the keyboard, you can navigate using the keyboard to any cell that is part of the design item and from the menu choose BEx Analyzer Context Menu for Selected Cell. Then, from the context menu, choose Delete. Make sure you are in Design mode. Another approach to this is to use the Excel functionality by just clicking the design item and then pressing the DELETE button on your computer keyboard.

Workbook Settings

Use the Workbook Settings dialog box to configure general functionality or apply themes to individual workbooks. You configure general properties for the workbook on the General tab, and configure themes on the Themes tab. In the Exits tab, you can also attach the macro necessary to use BEx Analyzer's API. The following settings are available on the General tab and are shown in the following illustration:

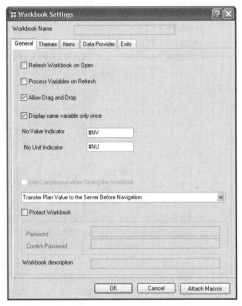

- **Refresh Workbook on Open**   If this option is selected, when you open a workbook from the server, the query is automatically refreshed with values from the server. If this option is not selected, or if you are opening a workbook from your local file system, you must manually refresh the query after you open it to retrieve the latest results from the server.

- **Process Variables on Refresh**   If any query in your workbook contains variables, current values set for the variables are part of the query view definition and are therefore stored in the workbook. If you refresh the workbook, these existing values will be used when fetching the data. If you want to enter new variable values anytime the workbook is refreshed, select this checkbox. Then, whenever you refresh your query, the Change Variable Values dialog box is also evoked and you may set new values for the variables in the query at that time.

- **Allow Drag and Drop**   This option is selected by default. If it's deselected, you will not be able to use drag-and-drop functionality to navigate your query in the Analysis Grid and Navigation Pane.

- **Protect Workbook**   If this option is selected, BEx Analyzer password-protects all the sheets in your workbook against any changes you make with Analyzer functions. When you attempt to change your workbook by inserting a design item, for example, Analyzer requests the password you configured here and allows the changes only if you provide the correct password. When BEx Analyzer protects your workbook, you can still navigate in Analysis mode, but you can't enter data. Cells that are not locked via cell protection are not protected. Activate the Enable Cell Protection option in the Analysis Grid properties to protect the cells in the Analysis Grid as well.

Analyzer's workbook protection is similar to Microsoft Excel's workbook protection (Tools|
Protection). However, you cannot navigate around your query if you protect your workbook
using Excel's protection. When the Protect Workbook option is selected, the Password and
Confirm Password fields activate. Enter a password in the Password field, and reenter the
same password in the Confirm Password field. In Design mode, worksheets themselves are
protected by default to prevent you from unintentionally deleting design items. You can
temporarily disable sheet protection (Tools|Protection|Unprotect Sheet on Microsoft Excel's
menu bar) or switch to Analysis mode before formatting your workbook.

- **Transfer Plan Values**   In a planning workbook, when you change the value of an
  input-enabled cell and perform navigation, the changed value is stored in the buffer
  on the BI server. However, you can change this behavior by selecting the appropriate
  option:

  - **Transfer Plan Value to the Server Before Navigation**   The changed value will
    be transferred automatically when you perform navigation. You need not
    perform the Transfer Plan Values function explicitly from the context menu when
    you change data in an input-enabled cell.

  - **Confirm Transferring Plan Values to the Server Before Navigation**   A message
    pop-up prompts you to confirm whether or not the changed value needs to be
    transferred. You need not perform the Transfer Plan Values function explicitly
    from the context menu when you change data in an input-enabled cell.

  - **Do Not Transfer Plan Values to the Server Before Navigation**   The changed
    value will not be transferred automatically when you perform navigation. You
    must perform the Transfer Plan Values function explicitly from the context menu
    when you change data in an input-enabled cell.

- **Use Compression when Storing the
  Workbook**   Use this option to reduce
  the space required by your workbook
  if your workbook includes a large
  amount of information and metadata.
  Select this checkbox to compress the
  data in the worksheet upon saving.
  You can use this option if, for example,
  you are working in Formula mode and
  want to view the data in your results
  set without having to connect to the
  server. To do this, you must save the
  results set in the workbook. If you do
  not do this, the data is not available in
  the cells the next time the workbook is
  opened, and only the formulas are
  displayed.

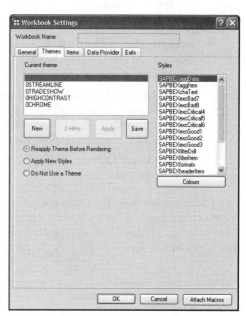

The next tab on the Workbook Settings
dialog box is Themes, which is shown in the
illustration.

Copyright by SAP AG

- **Themes** BEx themes, based on NetWeaver Portal styles, are shared services across the Business Explorer suite. In BEx Analyzer, themes are delivered as a set of Microsoft Excel style definitions for your workbook. Themes provide formatting information such as background color, font, and font size. To see the set of style definitions associated with a particular workbook, choose Format | Style from Microsoft Excel's menu. Those provided by Business Explorer are prefixed with SAPBEX*. Themes are content objects that are stored on the server, and you can choose to activate them. They are similar to stylesheets in that you can make a central change to a theme and all workbooks that use the theme will update accordingly.

- **Current Theme** Displays the list of available BEx themes. The BEx theme that is currently applied to your workbook, if any, is selected.

- **New/Delete/Apply/Save** If you have the following special authorization under your username, you can change and save themes on the server:

  ```
  AUTHORITY-CHECK OBJECT 'S_RS_TOOLS' ID 'COMMAND'  FIELD 'THEMES'
  ```

  If you have this authorization, the following buttons appear:

  - **New** Create a new theme with the New button.

  - **Delete** Select a theme from the Current Theme list, and choose Delete to delete it. This first deletes your theme locally.

  - **Apply** Select a theme from the Current Theme list, and choose Apply to apply currently configured styles to it. When you do this, BEx Analyzer reads the Microsoft Excel definitions of all the styles in the workbook prefixed with SAPBEX* and stores them into the selected theme. This allows you to edit the styles in Microsoft Excel and then create a theme with these customized styles.

  - **Save** To save all the themes to the server, choose Save.

- **Reapply Theme Before Rendering** Because BEx themes are saved on the server, they may be changed on the back end. Select this radio button if you wish to retrieve the most up-to-date definition of the style from the server and apply it again.

- **Apply New Styles** Select this radio button to update the current workbook with any style that has been added to the theme on the server since the theme was originally applied. If, for example, new styles have been added to a theme during a patch release, you can retrieve them from the server with this option.

- **Do Not Use a Theme** Select this radio button to stop using the selected theme in your workbook.

The Items tab is the next one available (see the following illustration), and it provides a convenient method for reviewing the configuration completed in the workbook for the design items. All design items that are inserted in the selected workbook appear in the Items tab. You can view or modify the properties of a design item, if required.

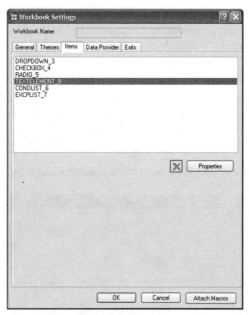

All Data Providers configured for the design items of the selected workbook appear in the Data Provider tab, shown next. You can create a Data Provider or modify an existing Data Provider, if required.

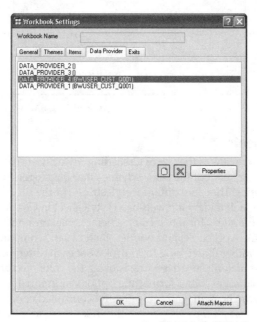

To use BEx Analyzer's API, you need a particular macro as well as references to the type libraries. Instead of manually maintaining the macro and references, you can do this using the following Attach Macros / Delete Macros toggle button, available on any tab in the dialog box. Choose Attach Macros to attach the macro and references you need to use Analyzer's API. Choose Delete Macros to remove the references.

NOTE *If you attach macros to your workbook and then save it locally, when you open the workbook again, you will receive a security pop-up. For this reason, macros are not automatically attached to workbooks. Simply choose Delete Macros to discontinue their use and the pop-ups.*

The following illustration shows the configuration details of the Exits tab.

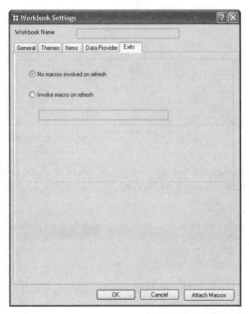

Cascading Style Sheets

One area we still need to review is the use of Cascading Style Sheets (CSS). CSS is one approach to helping with the management of the color schemes that developers use for completing their workbooks and/or queries. There are different stylesheets for the BEx Analyzer and the BEx Web Application. So, we will review the web-based stylesheet in Chapter 15. CSS is a standard structure that stores all the styles for fonts, color schemes, background colors, and other formatting options for the workbooks and queries. It allows the company to manage the use of certain colors and fonts rather than trying to control what each different developer is doing with each query, such as making sure everyone is using the colors red and green correctly. You can change the fonts, colors, and other formatting options individually, one query at a time, but using CSS this task can be managed centrally and controlled companywide. The Standard CSS delivered with BW has all the cells within the BEx Query identified and a specific color or font assigned. This CSS is being stored either locally or centrally on a shared server.

The following illustration shows the CSS that is delivered and used to support the BEx Analyzer process.

Business Explorer Analyzer Style Sample

This sample contains all the styles used in BEx release 2.0

Current cell has style: Normal

This row contains the title	**Selected Sales Figures**		Note that rows can be normal rows, total or remainder rows, while columns car
These rows contain header informati	Access time	Jan, 2nd	
	InfoCube	MBCUBE03	

These rows contain filter information	Product	**TBT-2000**	Also, there are three by three styles to denote exceptions on key figures: Good1
	Customer		The display of exceptions is independent of the other two attributes, emphasis
	Region		In the SAP Standard, all the Good, Bad, and Critical styles are rendered similar.
	Division		

			Incoming Orders	Inc.Orders (planned)	Inc.Orders curr. quar
This row contains a dimension					
This row contains scaling information	Region	Customer	US $	US $	
	South	**Carson Consulting**	10,219.65	n.a.	18,
These rows contain detail data		**Grover & York**	328,301.84	311,000.00	45,
		Plainsdale	21,777.65	22,300.00	3,
This row contains totals		Result	360,299.14	**403,300.00**	67
	SouthEast	**Gianni Vannini**	278,081.30	270,000.00	46,
These rows contain detail data		**The Wainright Institute**	11,337.43	15,000.00	3
		SonoWave	120,443.42	200,000.00	33,
		Tecto	114,934.22	117,300.00	22,
This row contains totals		Result	**524,796.37**	**602,300.00**	105,
	NorthEast	**Grover & York**	320,166.21	502,000.00	69,
These rows contain detail data		**Hamish Dartmouth**	41,654.54	46,400.00	13,
		SonoWave	123,180.76	180,000.00	52,
		AG & T	24,120.89	24,500.00	3,
This row contains totals		Result	509,122.40	752,900.00	**139,**
	West	**Gianni Vannini**	46,590.07	55,000.00	12,

Copyright by SAP AG

Notice that depending on the cell that is chosen, the naming convention changes—this is the connection between the BEx Analyzer and the Excel process. The next two illustrations show the different cells and the font and formatting that goes with them.

Selected Sales Figures		Note that rows can be normal rows, total or remain
Access time	Jan, 2nd	
InfoCube	MBCUBE03	

Product	**TBT-2000**	Also, there are three by three styles to denote excer
Customer		The display of exceptions is independent of the oth
Region		In the SAP Standard, all the Good, Bad, and Critica
Division		

		Incoming Orders	Inc.Orders (planned)
Region	Customer	US $	US $
South	**Carson Consulting**	10,219.65	n.a.
	Grover & York	328,301.84	311,000.00
	Plainsdale	21,777.65	22,300.00
	Result	360,299.14	**403,300.00**
SouthEast	**Gianni Vannini**	278,081.30	270,000.00
	The Wainright Institute	11,337.43	15,000.00
	SonoWave	120,443.42	200,000.00
	Tecto	114,934.22	117,300.00
	Result	**524,796.37**	**602,300.00**
NorthEast	**Grover & York**	320,166.21	502,000.00
	Hamish Dartmouth	41,654.54	46,400.00
	SonoWave	123,180.76	180,000.00
	AG & T	24,120.89	24,500.00
	Result	509,122.40	752,900.00
West	**Gianni Vannini**	46,590.07	55,000.00

Copyright by SAP AG

				Incoming Orders	Inc.Orders (planned)
			Division		
This row contains a dimension					
This row contains scaling information	Region	Customer		US $	US $
	South	Carson Consulting		10,219.65	n.a.
These rows contain detail data		Grover & York		328,301.84	311,000.00
		Plainsdale		21,777.65	22,300.00
This row contains totals		Result		360,299.14	403,300.00
	SouthEast	Gianni Vannini		278,081.30	270,000.00
These rows contain detail data		The Wainright Institute		11,337.43	15,000.00
		SonoWave		120,443.42	200,000.00
		Tecto		114,934.22	117,300.00
This row contains totals		Result		524,796.37	602,300.00
	NorthEast	Grover & York		320,166.21	502,000.00
These rows contain detail data		Hamish Dartmouth		41,654.54	46,400.00
		SonoWave		123,180.76	180,000.00
		AG & T		24,120.89	24,500.00
This row contains totals		Result		509,122.40	752,900.00
	West	Gianni Vannini		46,590.07	55,000.00

The first illustration shows the current cell has the style SAPBEXstdItem. Notice that the cursor is placed on the cell with the customer Grover & York. This has a bold font, the background is a shade of blue, and a specific lettering format is used. This is what will show up in the BEx Analyzer for these specific cells. The other illustration shows the current cell has the style SAPBEXexcBad7. Notice that the cursor is placed in the cell that has the key figure for Incoming Orders (360,299.14). This identifies the exception format and coloring for that specific exception level. Bad7 shows a darker red color for the background, a standard font for the key figure, and no bold or formatting changes. Over 50 different formats are delivered with the BEx Analyzer and used in the queries. To demonstrate the use of this CSS, we'll use a completed query and choose a specific cell and see what the Style option connected with Excel offers us. In the following illustration, the query has been executed and the cursor is placed on the header of the column for Division. Once this is identified, we then choose in the Excel spreadsheet Format | Style and the dialog box in the illustration shows up.

As you can see, this is connected to the style SAPBEXchaText, which is assigned the specific formatting associated with the header Division. If the company method for controlling the formatting is central management, the modification of the format would be done directly from here. Let's suppose a decision has been made to change the format of this specific style. Realize that these styles are linked with many of the cells within a query.

Because there are numerous header positions on a query, any changes will affect all the cells. The next illustration shows the dialog box that appears after the option Modify was chosen on the previous screen.

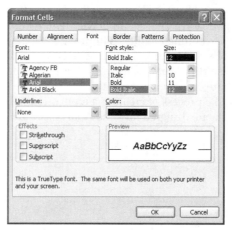

This should look very familiar to many of us—it's basically an Excel dialog box for altering the formatting of the Excel spreadsheet, but in this case we are modifying a template that controls many cells. We have made some minor changes in terms of the bold italic and increase size to identify that something has been changed on this template. Click OK to leave the dialog box. The result is shown in the following illustration. Notice that all the header information has been adjusted to reflect the different font and format modified with the stylesheet indicator. Therefore, both Division and Distribution Channel have been changed for the header of the columns as well as the headers for the dropdown boxes. This can come in handy for larger corporations to help with their management of colors for marketing activities and material that will be distributed either via hard copy or the Web.

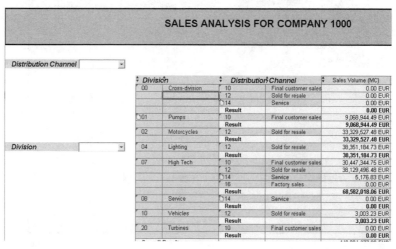

Reviewing All the Steps

A ton of material has been incorporated into this chapter, and having a complete example is a good approach to reviewing all the functionality. This basic example is a good step-by-step process of setting up a basic workbook with many of the designs from the list of 11 design items discussed in the preceding sections. This example will demonstrate the use of several design items and the use of some Excel functionality to improve the look and feel of the workbook.

For this example, the BEx Analyzer has been started and the logon process is complete. Because we are looking at starting from scratch, we'll use the Excel function for a new worksheet to get us to square one. Then we use the Design mode to set up the Excel worksheet for us to use in the process of creating a report. The following illustration shows the initial blank screen with one design item—the Analysis Grid.

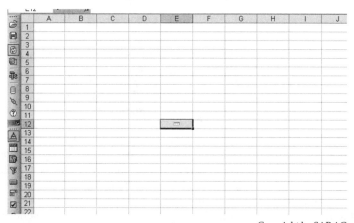

Using the Analysis Grid Properties dialog box, we assign the Data Provider on the General tab. The following two illustrations show the steps to incorporate this into the workbook.

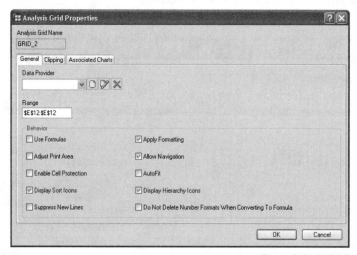

Copyright by SAP AG

We'll leave all the properties at their default settings, and nothing is required in the Clipping and Associated Charts tabs. Click OK several times to get back to the initial worksheet. We have now set the Analysis Grid with a Data Provider (query) for the workbook. Next, we'll add to this workbook a Dropdown design item. The following illustration shows the addition of the Dropdown item to the workbook in cell B8.

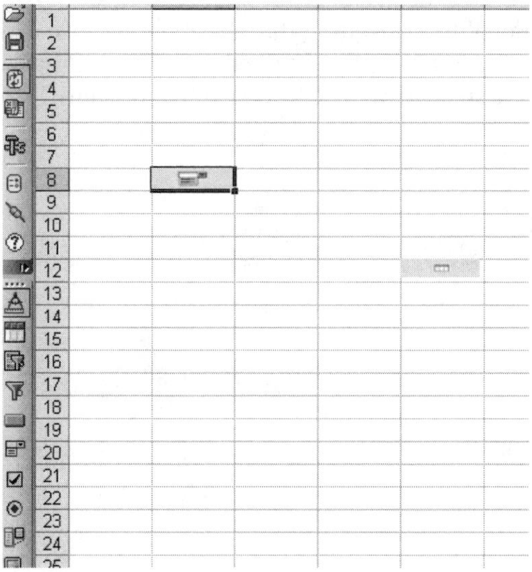

Copyright by SAP AG

Notice that everything is a combination of the BEx Analyzer functionality and the Excel functions. You need to understand the positioning of the objects in the Excel spreadsheet because much of the processing will be tied to the specific cells. We will run into this more in the next section of the chapter. The following illustration shows the setup of the properties for the Dropdown item.

We leave everything else alone except for the Dimension tab, where the assignment of the Distribution Channel (characteristic in the Data Provider) is included in the properties. The default text and the text will be displayed. Click OK several times will get us back to the original worksheet. Because we need a bit more space for the design item in the workbook, we'll use the Excel functionality to just drag the object to what size it needs to be in the workbook. We could use the Range option in the design item's Properties dialog box, but we have more control over the sizing if we use the Excel functionality. The next illustration shows the results of the change.

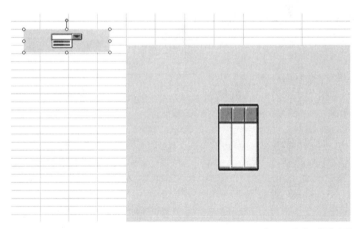

We are ready to execute the workbook and observe the results of our work. The following illustration is a basic view that shows the ease with which you can create something with the integration of Excel and the BEx Analyzer functions. Many things can still be done to improve the overall look and feel, but this shows that you can get to this point comfortably without having to configure much on the tabs. Just allow the default settings to do their job, and the process is much faster.

			Division		Distribution Channel		Sales Volume (MC)
		00	Cross-division	10	Final customer sales	0.00 EUR
				12	Sold for resale	0.00 EUR
				14	Service	0.00 EUR
				Result		**0.00 EUR**
		01	Pumps	10	Final customer sales	9,068,944.49 EUR
				Result		**9,068,944.49 EUR**
		02	Motorcycles	12	Sold for resale	33,329,527.48 EUR
				Result		**33,329,527.48 EUR**
		04	Lighting	12	Sold for resale	38,351,184.73 EUR
				Result		**38,351,184.73 EUR**
		07	High Tech	10	Final customer sales	30,447,344.75 EUR
				12	Sold for resale	38,129,496.48 EUR
				14	Service	5,176.83 EUR
				16	Factory sales	0.00 EUR
				Result		**68,582,018.06 EUR**
		08	Service	14	Service	0.00 EUR
				Result		**0.00 EUR**
		10	Vehicles	12	Sold for resale	3,003.23 EUR
				Result		**3,003.23 EUR**
		20	Turbines	10	Final customer sales	0.00 EUR
				Result		**0.00 EUR**

Distribution Channel [▼]

The next illustration shows that we have started to use the Excel functions to adjust the size of the columns and the format of the dropdown box. Remember to save each time changes are made, just to be sure everything is being controlled by the system. Now, we'll add another design item to the workbook. Return to the Design mode, choose a cell, and then click the design item Radio Button Group.

Distribution Channel [▼]

#			Division		Distribution Channel		Sales Volume (MC)
GM store		00	Cross-division	10	Final customer sales	0.00 EU
Sold for resale				12	Sold for resale	0.00 EU
Final customer				14	Service	0.00 EU
Service				Result		**0.00 EU**
Internet Sales		01	Pumps	10	Final customer sales	9,068,944.49 EU
Direct Sales				Result		**9,068,944.49 EU**
		02	Motorcycles	12	Sold for resale	33,329,527.48 EU
				Result		**33,329,527.48 EU**
		04	Lighting	12	Sold for resale	38,351,184.73 EU
				Result		**38,351,184.73 EU**
		07	High Tech	10	Final customer sales	30,447,344.75 EU
				12	Sold for resale	38,129,496.48 EU
				14	Service	5,176.83 EU
				16	Factory sales	0.00 EU
				Result		68,582,018.06 EU

The first of the following illustrations shows the inserting of the design item into the screen and accessing the properties of the object. Everything is left at the default setting except on the Dimensions tab. The second illustration shows the assignment of Division as the characteristic for the radio button group. Again, accept the default text and display text and then click OK to exit the dialog box. Now, execute the workbook to see the results, shown in the third illustration.

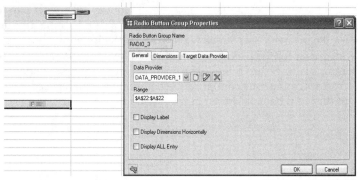

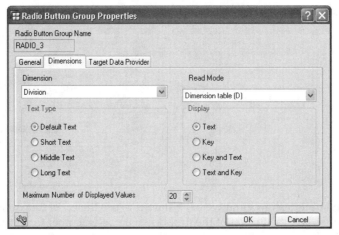

Distribution Channel					

	Division		Distribution Channel		Sales Volume (MC)	Invoi
	00	Cross-division	10	Final customer sales	0.00 EUR	
			12	Sold for resale	0.00 EUR	
#			14	Service	0.00 EUR	
Cross-division			**Result**		**0.00 EUR**	
Pumps	01	Pumps	10	Final customer sales	9,068,944.49 EUR	
Motorcycles			**Result**		**9,068,944.49 EUR**	
Lighting	02	Motorcycles	12	Sold for resale	33,329,527.48 EUR	
High Tech			**Result**		**33,329,527.48 EUR**	
Service	04	Lighting	12	Sold for resale	38,351,184.73 EUR	
Vehicles			**Result**		**38,351,184.73 EUR**	
Turbines	07	High Tech	10	Final customer sales	30,447,344.75 EUR	
Retail			12	Sold for resale	38,129,496.48 EUR	
Foods			14	Service	5,176.83 EUR	
Paints			16	Factory sales	0.00 EUR	
Services			**Result**		**68,582,018.06 EUR**	
	08	Service	14	Service	0.00 EUR	
			Result		**0.00 EUR**	
	10	Vehicles	12	Sold for resale	3,003.23 EUR	
			Result		**3,003.23 EUR**	
	20	Turbines	10	Final customer sales	0.00 EUR	
			Result		**0.00 EUR**	
	Overall Result				**149,334,677.99 EUR**	

As you can see, the workbook is starting to come together, but we need to review the display to make sure the combination of the radio button group and the dropdown box work together for the business user. Now, we'll work on the Excel functions to get the workbook looking better for the user. The first of the following illustrations shows the use of the Excel Options dialog box to remove the grid-like look of the workbook for a better display. As you can see, numerous configuration components can be used for this purpose. The final view of this workbook is shown in the second illustration.

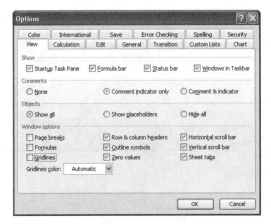

Copyright by SAP AG

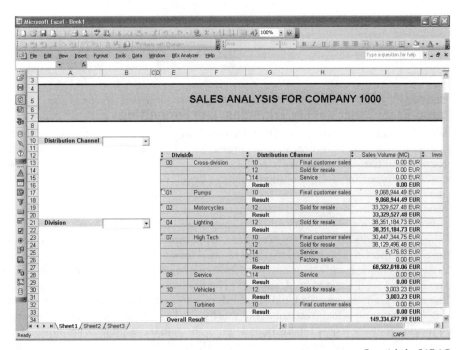

Copyright by SAP AG

Here, we added some header information and introduced additional background colors to enhance the look and feel of the workbook. These are all Excel functions for changing the font, color, and borders of the cells.

Now let's suppose the decision has been made that the combination of the radio button group and dropdown item is not working. Therefore, Division has also been added as a dropdown item. In this situation, the navigation within the actual report is still intact and therefore the context menu approach for the key figures and characteristics is available. However, the use of the dropdowns for Division and Distribution Channel will help the user navigate the characteristics without the context menu. You may at this point want to take advantage of protection for the workbook (located in the Workbook Setting item) so that no one else can change the formatting. Once you have done this, save your work, as shown in the next illustration. Not bad for about 15 minutes of work.

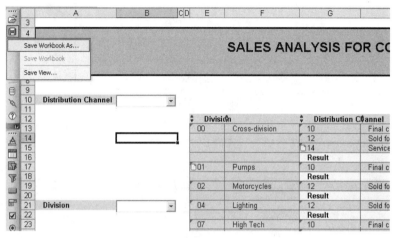

Integrated Excel Functionality, Formulas, and Formatting

With all the business users working with Microsoft Excel, it was time that much of the Excel functionality for formula building be incorporated into the BEx Analyzer and workbook. The integration of Excel formulas with the BEx Analyzer allows the business user to use all the formulas for reporting and planning they have developed over time in Excel with the BEx functionality.

When you insert the Analysis Grid design item, the BEx Analyzer creates a link between the cells in which the results appear and the data on the BW server. The Analyzer controls the formatting of the results cells, applying standard formatting every time the query is refreshed and results are retrieved. This means that any manual formatting you apply to these cells while in Analysis mode is only temporary. For example, if you select a row of results in the Analysis Grid and set the text to bold, and then you navigate the results by selecting a filter value, the results are then refreshed, the standard formatting for the result cells is restored, and the bold formatting is lost. You can avoid this by working in Formula mode. This changes the way the link to the server is established, deleting the actual design item and instead retrieving the results on a cell-by-cell basis using a Microsoft Excel function. You then have complete freedom to format any cell as you wish, and the formatting is retained when you refresh the query.

Formula mode can only be used with queries that have the following structure: one structure in the rows, one structure in the columns, and all other dimensions, if any, in the free characteristics. Configure the Data Provider for the Analysis Grid to provide the results offline, in order to see the data in your results set without having to establish a connection to the server. Otherwise, you may see formula errors in the workbook when you open it. When you're working in Formula mode, the cell results are presented using standard Excel formulas. This means that the presentation of the results cells, including their formatting, can be completely handed over to standard Excel settings rather than being handled by the Analyzer. This allows you access to the results of the query by referencing the characteristic values along with the key figures.

There are two approaches to this functionality. The first would be to use the basic Excel formulas within the BEx Analyzer to reference cells within the query. The second, more powerful function is to use the new BExGetData process discussed previously. This opens up numerous options concerning the structure of the workbooks and the functionality available. Now, it is possible to create and manage the data directly in the Excel screen by referencing the characteristic values and key figures. In the past it has been a common request to develop a workbook of queries and have the first worksheet reference the others and be updated based on the other worksheets. Although this was possible, it involved a complex workaround and normally required a bit of maintenance. With the new BExGetData functionality, it is very straightforward to link data from different worksheets and/or directly from the queries to create a summary worksheet for a series of worksheets in the BEx Analyzer workbooks. The following illustration shows an example of the use of the new BExGetData functionality.

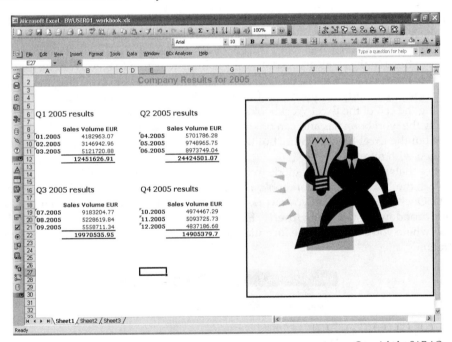

Copyright by SAP AG

This type of workbook, where the format of the workbook is the overriding concern, has been addressed with this new functionality. As you can see, to create this type of workbook before it took a series of smaller queries with specific structures positioned in an exact view. Now, with the new Excel functionality, we can create this type of workbook format quickly and easily. This is a combination of both the BExGetData and Excel formulas all in one workbook. The format, coloring, fonts, block structure, and results (quarterly results, summary formula) all involve basic Excel functions. The actual amounts by month use the

BExGetData functionality. As you can see, this offers increased formatting capabilities. The following illustration shows the configuration behind the monthly amounts.

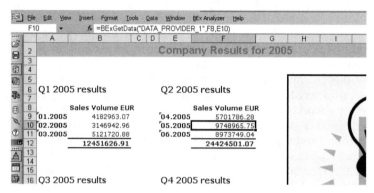

In the workbook, the cursor is on the cell for the total sales volume in Euros for May of 2005, which equals 9748965.75. Notice in the formula BExGetData("DATA_PROVIDER_1", F8,E10) in the Formula bar. The Excel workbook is getting data from Data Provider 1, which is defined in the Analysis Grid. F8 directs the calculation to Sales Volume EUR, and E10 directs the calculation to the 05.2005 cell. Therefore, the system is pulling the data directly from an underlying query and finding the information located in a specific cell and filling the cell of the Excel Workbook. This adds a significant increase in the amount of flexibility the workbook has and can offer to the business user. The quarterly totals are nothing but the Excel function Sum, but that's the great thing. Everything can be saved and reexecuted with refreshed data.

Notice that we are in Design mode in this example, so all of this will be saved and reusable in the BEx Analyzer workbook. The formula process is a basic setup of an Excel call for data. Once you have set up your workbook access, the formulas from the standard Excel formula dropdown list by using Insert | Function are available for your use. A dialog box appears where you can choose the formula function required, as shown in the following illustration.

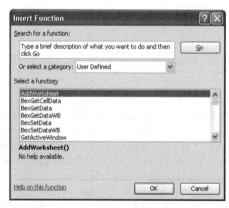

Notice that a number of standard BEx functions are available, but the one we will be using is BExGetData. We will have at least three parameters to complete: Data Provider, Key Figure, and Characteristic(s). As mentioned, multiple characteristics may be needed in the formula, depending on the number of characteristics being referenced. If there are more than one, continue to add characteristics in sequence, separated by a comma. The following illustration shows an example of multiple characteristics involved in one formula. In this case, Data Provider 1 is being used, along with Sales Volume EUR, and all three months in the formula. This is an example of using either the basic Excel formula for Sum to get the quarterly total or using the new BExGetData functionality to arrive at the quarterly total. Therefore, several components are involved, and there is a direct relationship between the InfoProvider, the query results, the formula, and the results in the workbook for all of this to work.

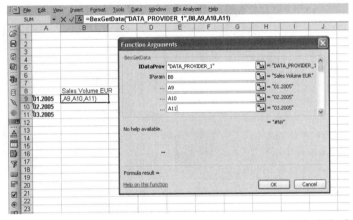

Copyright by SAP AG

We can use several approaches to incorporate the Formula mode into the BEx Analyzer workbook. To switch to Formula mode, you can click the BI results cell and then use the menu option Convert to Formula in the context menu. This converts the results to Excel formulas and also deletes the number formats and deactivates navigation using drag and drop, as shown in the following illustration.

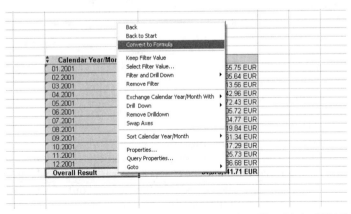

Copyright by SAP AG

Another approach is to insert an Analysis Grid item into the workbook and then select the checkbox Use Formulas in the Analysis Grid Properties dialog box. The next illustration shows this approach. However, the Use Formulas and Convert to Formula functions are not the same. Both functions generate the BExGetData formula in the data cells of the Analysis Grid, but the Use Formulas function relates to a property of the Analysis Grid design item. This function is automatically switched on when you use the Convert to Formula function from the menu.

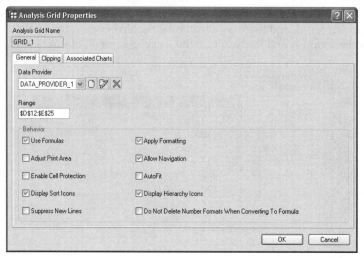

Copyright by SAP AG

Note that the Use Formulas property is just one part of the functions provided by the Covert to Formula context menu functions. It does not delete the Analysis Grid design items, and access to the context menu functions for the Analysis Grid as well as drag-and-drop functionality remain active. When you set the Use Formulas property, the standard formatting is also not overwritten. Therefore, when the workbook is refreshed, the standard formatting is restored. The Convert to Formula context menu function enables all these activities in one step and therefore is the preferred approach. Another alternative to converting results cells to formulas is to simply define a Data Provider using the Settings icon in the Design toolbar for Workbook Settings and then type the formula directly into the cell (or use the menu option Insert | Function). Then you can supply the formula parameters manually. The following illustration shows the initial steps in this process.

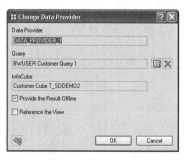

Copyright by SAP AG

Open a new workbook and then access Workbook Settings. Click the Data Provider tab to get to the Change Data Provider dialog box. Having inserted our basic query for the Data Provider of our workbook, we can click the OK button to back out of the screen to the Workbook Settings dialog box. The following illustration shows the Data Provider inserted into the Workbook Settings dialog box.

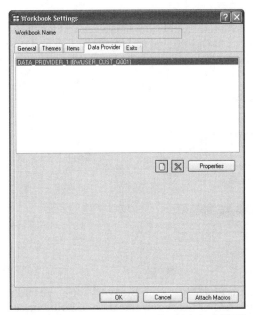

Now, we simply go back to the workbook itself and manually type in the technical names of the characteristics and key figures in the positions we would like to format them. Therefore, in the following illustration, Sales Volume EUR and the months 01.2001, 02.2001, and 03.2001 are positioned in the specific cells B8, A9, A10, and A11, respectively.

Once we have completed this step, we access the formula functions of the Excel workbook and enter the appropriate information. In this case, the intersection of the cells is the total sales volume for each month. Notice that the specific information text in the dialog box for the formula calculation points directly to the characteristics and key figures in the workbook. The following illustration shows the additional activity of cutting and pasting the formula into other cells and making the necessary changes to direct the data to the appropriate month.

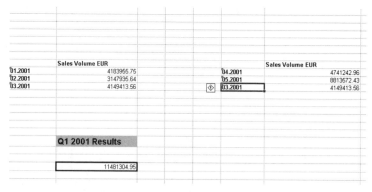

After adding some bells and whistles to the workbook, we end up with a finished workbook that took much less time to complete than it would have in the past. The next illustration shows the finished product. Finally, we save the workbook to either a role in the BW server or to a position in the Excel folder that is detached from the server.

NOTE   *In the example, the option Provide the Results Offline has been checked. This can be of some help to the user during the process of accessing the workbook. When the workbook is open, the cell values may contain the symbols #NV. This happens because the formula has failed to find the Data Provider in the workbook. Therefore, to avoid this problem, you can save the results offline with the workbook by turning on the Provide the Results Offline option in the Workbook Settings dialog box. This allows access to the workbook offline with the current view of the data still available. Once the workbook is accessed, the user can log onto the server and reconnect the workbook to the system so that the data will be refreshed upon execution. If you don't set this property, the query must be executed in the Refresh mode of the workbook to reestablish the link between the Data Provider and the query results.*

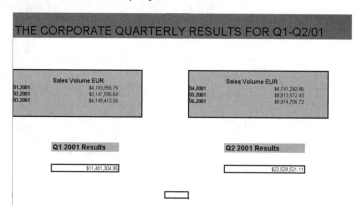

Summary

A tremendous amount of information has been offered in this chapter, basically completing our discussion of the functionality of the BEx Analyzer, both for queries and workbooks. Using this functionality will open quite a few new doors for you during the creation of your reporting strategies. All the information presented in this chapter involves new BW 7.0 functionality that has enabled the BEx Analyzer to keep pace with the functionality offered by web-based queries—both web queries and Web Application Template queries. This new functionality has offered the business user who is working with the BW system much of the requested upgrades for front-end flexibility and usability in the Excel process. With these capabilities and the use of the Report Designer functionality, the user can develop any type of formatted reporting via the BEx Analyzer.

Formatted Reporting— SAP Report Designer

The Report Designer is another new component of the BI Front-end Strategic Reporting Tools. This is one item that has been lacking in the BI environment for quite some time. With the combination of the BEx Analyzer functionality and the Report Designer toolset, the ability to create customized reports has been completely revamped, and the increased functionality for the BEx Analyzer, the web-based query, and printing should come as a pleasant surprise to business users. In this chapter the focus is on the initial setup and process of using the Report Designer. We will begin by reviewing the results of a report using the Report Designer functionality and discuss the positioning of the Report Designer in the corporate reporting strategy. Then we'll move into the basic settings and configuration process within this toolset. Finally, we'll work through a basic Report Designer process to create a basic formatted report.

Introduction to the Report Designer

One of the common questions I've heard during my consulting and instructional activities is, "When will the formatted reporting capabilities that are in R3/ECC be available in the BI environment?" This question has finally been answered. With the functionality in Report Designer and the BEx Analyzer, the formatted report is available and in full force. The Report Designer is in its first incarnation within the BI 7.0 environment, but the functionality is quite good and can offer many different options when it comes to creating formatted reports for printing or execution on the Web.

As we all know, sometimes the format and the look and feel of a report can make or break a project. The one report that the key business user sees is critical to the success of the project and the final signoff of the results. If this is the situation you are currently involved in, using the Report Designer might just help you get over that hump and complete the project. With the use of BW and the queries and reports, which are being generated from the consolidated data stored in the BW InfoProviders, you can develop reports for external use, such as for reporting the corporate profit/loss and balance sheet statements. The formatting and display of the information has become more and more important. Many times a specific "report book" is required to be developed at period end for the corporate headquarters, and with the other versions of BW this process was not easy—and in some cases impossible. The creation of a report that is visually appealing and professional in format is essential for the corporate image. It is also important to position the information in the report in a well-thought-out and consistent manner for review. Some reports that are generated look like the exam questions on an SAT test, and the effort it takes to understand the information will result in too many questions and comments. Ideally, all reports should be easily understood and interpreted in under 7 seconds by a reasonable person. The following illustration shows two different views of information. On the left the information is presented in a raw format and with no consistency or logic. This would take the average person some time to understand, and a number of questions would definitely be asked. Now review the formatted report on the right—the results are easily understood and can be analyzed and reviewed in seconds with very few questions asked.

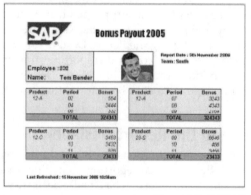

The Report Designer is a component of the Enterprise Reporting strategy in SAP BI. The Enterprise Reporting component is composed of the Report Designer, the Web Item Report (found in the WAD), PDF reporting (printed views of the reports), and the basic formatting of the reports (called *row patterns* or *BI patterns*). The BEx Report Designer and the Web Item Report enable simple integration of Enterprise Report Design and Web Application Design, and the results are displayed in the BEx Web as well. The following illustration shows the positioning of the Report Designer functionality within the overall reporting architecture.

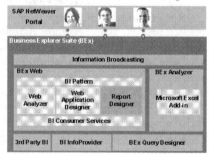

NOTE *The reports created with the BEx Report Designer are optimized for presentation and printing, and have only limited navigation options for data analysis (such as setting filter values). You can use the BEx Analyzer, the Web Application, and the Web Analyzer for the Business Explorer for free multidimensional data analysis.*

With the Report Designer, SAP provides a user-friendly design tool that you can use to create formatted reports that are optimized for presentation and print. You can also access a number of formatting and layout functions. Reports created in the BEx Report Designer can be converted to PDF documents using the connected Adobe server and then printed. You can also use the information-broadcasting functions and broadcast reports. The following illustration shows an overview of the Report Designer, including the PDF and Web functionality.

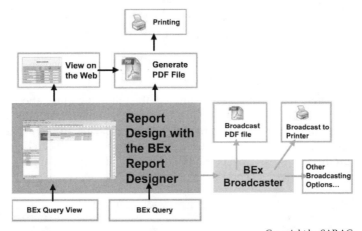

Copyright by SAP AG

The Final Results of a Report Designer Report

I normally like to start with a review of the final results when using the specific component of the SAP reporting process. In the following illustrations, the formatting will be the primary concern and the navigational capabilities will be secondary. The next illustration shows a basic report that has been developed in the Report Designer. The basic setup of a Report Designer report is discussed a bit later in this chapter. For now, just know that one of the requirements to work in the Report Designer is to have an existing query for an InfoProvider. Initially only four options appear at the top of the report—Information, Send, Print Version, and, last but not least, Filter. The functionality in each of these items is discussed later, but as mentioned, the navigational capabilities of the other components of the BEx Web Analyzer are not available (standard) with the template for the Report Designer. In this report, a basic formatting process is used to move the months to a more balanced view for the end user. Therefore, rather than having the full year straight down the left side of the query/workbook, we have moved the last 6 months to the right side for a balanced view of the data. The color scheme and the additional enhancements in the font size and coloring are also options in the Report Designer. Now we are faced with the same situation as with the BEx Analyzer and the BEx Query

Designer—where to turn on what functionality—because the font and color can be managed either by the Report Designer or the Web Application Designer.

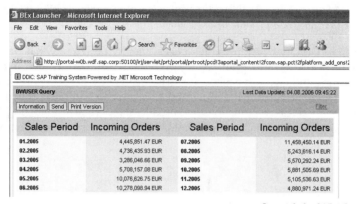

Because the navigational capabilities are limited, the following illustration shows the use of an additional formatting process to bring in a breakdown of the information by product line and channel (see the lower portion of the screen). The coloring and font sizing have been adjusted to meet the needs of the business user, the results rows have been deleted from the report, and the product lines are used as headings for the channels that appear below them, with the total for incoming orders and sales volume.

DDIC: SAP Training System Powered by .NET Microsoft Technology

BWUSER Query View 2   Last Data Update: 04.08.2006 09:45:22

Information | Send | Print Version   Filter

Sales Period	Incoming Orders	Sales Period	Incoming Orders
01.2005	4,445,851.47 EUR	07.2005	11,458,450.14 EUR
02.2005	4,736,435.93 EUR	08.2005	5,243,616.14 EUR
03.2005	3,286,046.66 EUR	09.2005	5,570,292.24 EUR
04.2005	5,708,157.08 EUR	10.2005	5,881,505.69 EUR
05.2005	10,076,626.75 EUR	11.2005	5,105,536.63 EUR
06.2005	10,278,098.94 EUR	12.2005	4,880,971.24 EUR

Breakdown by Product Line and Channel

	Incoming Orders	Sales Volume EUR
Final customer sales		
Cross-division	28,788.26 EUR	3,023.08 EUR
Pumps	19,731,587.80 EUR	15,512,112.40 EUR
High Tech	10,778,271.72 EUR	10,310,549.95 EUR
Turbines	0.00 EUR	344,000.00 EUR
Sold for resale		
Motorcycles	15,429,350.93 EUR	15,429,350.93 EUR
Lighting	15,376,585.35 EUR	16,999,417.87 EUR
High Tech	13,500,612.48 EUR	13,500,612.48 EUR
Service		
Cross-division	0.00 EUR	1,687.26 EUR
Service	0.00 EUR	4,160.82 EUR
GM store		
Retail	0.00 EUR	6,499,251.94 EUR
Services		
Services	1,826,392.37 EUR	0.00 EUR
	76,671,588.91 EUR	78,604,166.73 EUR

Another view of the same report data might involve the use of a hierarchy in the report. In the following illustration we see that the hierarchy is used in the Report Designer and presented on the Web with the additional enhancements of color, font sizing, formatting adjustments, and different color schemes for each of the hierarchy levels. Also, notice that the fonts for the levels changes at level 4 (the lowest level node). Therefore, the font can be managed at each level of a report.

BWUSER Query Hierarchy 03	Last Data Update: 04.08.2006 09:45:22

| Information | Send | Print Version | | Filter |

	Sales Volume EUR
▽ Product hierarchy	571,640,425.24 EUR
▽ Machines	130,111,492.54 EUR
▽ Pumps	130,111,492.54 EUR
▽ Special pump	130,111,492.54 EUR
Pump PRECISION 100	5,929,908.56 EUR
Pump PRECISION 101	14,490,083.58 EUR
Pump PRECISION 102	25,141,577.42 EUR
Pump PRECISION 103	24,162,448.26 EUR
Pump PRECISION 104	31,374,655.12 EUR
Pump cast steel IDESNORM 170-230	9,890,739.76 EUR
Pump standard IDESNORM 100-402	19,122,079.84 EUR
▽ Components (Pumps)	0.00 EUR
▷ Discharge cover	0.00 EUR
▽ Vehicles	110,039,089.04 EUR
▽ Cars	159,154.96 EUR
▷ Car (complete)	159,154.96 EUR
▽ Motorcycles	109,879,934.08 EUR
▷ Motor-cycle (compl.)	93,211,426.82 EUR
▷ Components	7,278,161.40 EUR
▷ Accessories	9,390,345.86 EUR
▽ Paints	0.00 EUR
▽ Gloss paints	0.00 EUR
▽ Opaque	0.00 EUR
Coating Matt Green RAL 6014/10 Liter	0.00 EUR
▽ Lighting	134,905,372.40 EUR
▽ Bulbs	134,905,372.40 EUR
Light Bulb 40 Watt class 220 (225U	20,757,159.46 EUR

Finally, the next illustration shows the end result of the use of the Report Designer. Here, the addition of the corporate logo and information about the report adds the final touch. This report would be well received by any external group and can be easily understood and navigated. Again, remember that our goal is to have a report that can be understood in a very timely manner and with the appropriate focus.

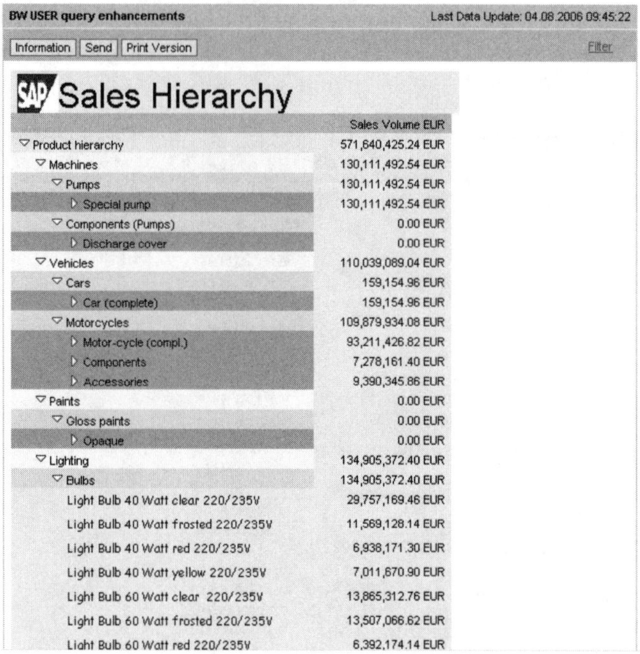

Although the navigational functionality in a Report Designer report can be limiting, do not count out the components of the "filter." When you display a report in the portal (Web), it is automatically embedded in the standard Web template for reports. The report is displayed in a table on the Web. In addition, a date in the upper area of the Web template indicates how current the data is. Using the standard pushbuttons provided (Information, Send, and Print Version) as well as the Filter link, you can access the most common functions for navigating within and further editing your report. When you have created and saved a report in the Report Designer, click Execute to display the report automatically in the portal using the standard Web template for reports. From a technical perspective, the standard Web template for reports is based on the 0REPORT_DEFAULT_TEMPLATE Web template. This Web template is set as the default for displaying reports from the Report Designer in the SAP Customizing Implementation Guide under SAP NetWeaver | Business Intelligence | Reporting-Relevant Settings | BEx Web | Set Standard Web Templates | Enterprise Report. You can copy this Web template to make changes and set it as your new standard Web template for reports in the IMG. The functions of the individual pushbuttons and the Filter link are as follows:

- **Information** You use this pushbutton to display information about the Data Provider, such as the technical name and description, the name of the person who last changed it, and the key data for the Data Provider. You can also document the Data Provider. This pushbutton was discussed in detail in Chapter 8.

- **Send** You use this pushbutton to navigate to the Broadcasting Wizard, from which you can precalculate and distribute your report. The first of the following illustrations shows the initial step in the wizard. Here you identify the output type—either Online Link to Current Data or PDF File. Then, depending on your choice, in step 2 you will identify the e-mail address and additional documentation for the broadcaster. The second illustration shows this step. In the next step (step 3) you identify the technical name and description, and in step 4 you identify the scheduling process for the Information Broadcaster. For more information on the Information Broadcaster, see Chapter 11.

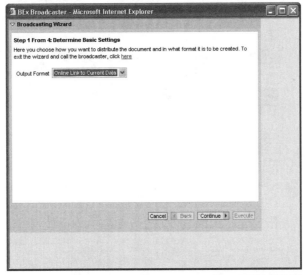

Copyright by SAP AG

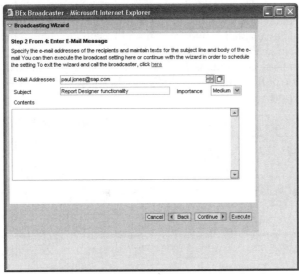

Copyright by SAP AG

- **Print Version**   You use this pushbutton to create a PDF version of the report directly, which you can then print, as required. The following illustration shows the results of clicking the Print Version button. The report is immediately embedded into a PDF document for printing and display. Now there are options when working with the PDF functionality in BW reports. It is not completely necessary to execute the reports and have the Adobe Services system available for reporting. With functionality delivered in SP12 (support package stack 11) in BW 7.0 you can direct your reports to be printed either as a PDF file or a standard word document via the Print button.

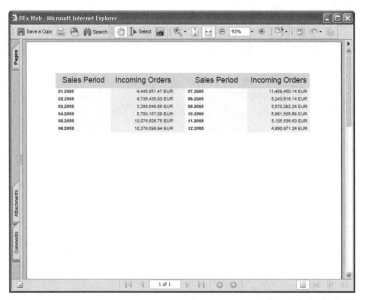

- **Filter**   You use this link to display a filter pane above the table in the report. In this filter pane, characteristic values for the characteristics used in the Data Provider are displayed and available for filtering. This allows you to change the view of the report and use certain analysis options. The following illustration shows the Filter options in the Report Designer process. Be careful with this option since this is a formatted report, the use of filtering characteristics could create a unexpected change to your formatted report.

As you can see, the navigational process in a Report Designer query is limited, especially in the static format (versus the dynamic format). These concepts will be discussed later in this chapter.

Accessing the Report Designer

The Report Designer is a standalone desktop application. You can open the Report Designer directly from the Start menu (Start|Programs|Business Explorer|Report Designer). Alternatively, you can call it directly from the BEx Analyzer (BEx Analyzer|Tools|BEx Report Designer), as shown in the first of the following illustrations, or you can access it in the Web Application Designer using the context menu for the Report Web item, as shown in the second illustration.

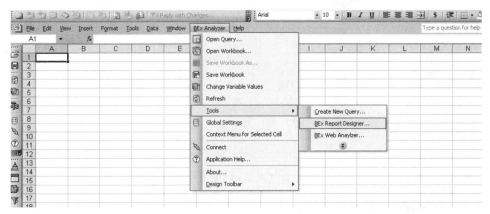

Copyright by SAP AG

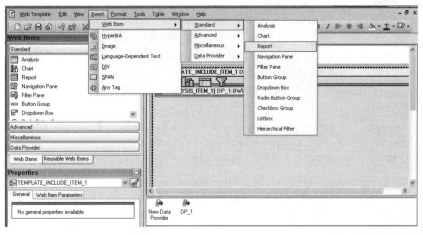

Copyright by SAP AG

Once the Report Designer has been opened, you'll see that the screen is divided into several sections, as shown next. Basically the Report Designer is divided into five different areas. In addition to the menu bar and application toolbar, the BEx Report Designer consists of the following screen areas:

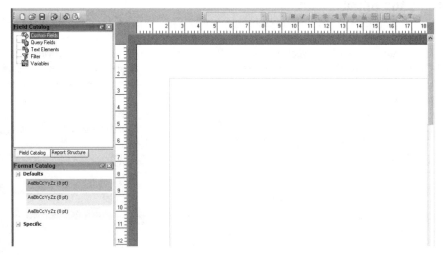

Copyright by SAP AG

- **Design area**   The most important area of the Report Designer is the design area, where you design the layout of your report and format it to be schematically displayed. A report is usually composed of the following elements: page header, report body, and page footer. The page header and footer (if there are any) are repeated on every page of the report.

- **Field Catalog**   The Field Catalog lists all query fields and text elements for the query or query view being used, along with free texts created by the user.

- **Report Structure**   In the Report Structure, the report is displayed with the associated group levels and row patterns.

- **Format Catalog**   The Format Catalog provides an overview of the formats used in the report.

- **Properties**   In the Properties area, you set the properties of the individual report elements (rows or cells). This allows you to determine the format and position of text fields, for example.

All the functions required for creating, formatting, and designing your report are in the menu bar and toolbar of the Report Designer. These items are discussed in detail a bit later in this chapter. The menu bar and toolbars also contain some additional functionality that can be of use to the developer. From the menu bar and toolbars in the Report Designer, the developer can access all the functions you need to create or edit a report.

Report

The first menu choice is Report, which is shown in the following illustration. Table 9-1 details all the options under Report.

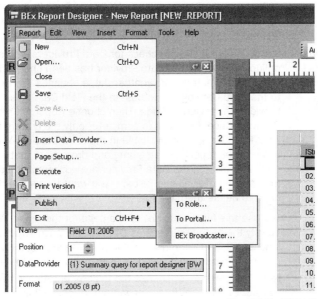

Copyright by SAP AG

Menu Option	Description
New	You use this function to create a new report. This function will offer a new template screen for the configuration of a formatted report.
Open	This function displays the BEx Open dialog box. From this dialog box, you can open a report from History, Favorites, or Roles, or by using the search function, and then edit that report.
Close	You use this function to close a report. If you have edited a report and want to keep the changes, save the report before you close it.
Save	You use this function to save any changes you have made to an existing report. When you create a new report and choose Save, the BEx Save dialog box appears. You can then save your report in Favorites or Roles.
Save As	This function displays the BEx Save dialog box, where you can save your report with a different name in Favorites or Roles.
Delete	When you choose this function, the report is deleted permanently.

TABLE 9-1   Options on the Reports Menu in the Report Designer

Menu Option	Description
Insert Data Provider	You use this function and the Open dialog box to choose a Data Provider for a report section. The Data Providers for a report section can be queries or query views. Once you have made your selection, the Data Provider is automatically inserted into a report section and displayed in the design area.
Check Data Provider	You use this function to check for Data Providers with a static drilldown, whether the Data Provider has been changed since the report was created, and whether these changes are to be applied to the Field Catalog. To do this, in the Field Catalog select a Data Provider under Query Fields. Then choose Report I Check Data Provider. Once the check is complete, only the current fields for the Data Provider are still available in the Field Catalog. You can add new fields to the report by using drag and drop. Note that any fields that no longer exist in the Data Provider are not removed automatically from the list of available fields. If you want to remove these fields, you need to delete them manually.
Page Setup	You use this function to set up the page for the report: You can specify the page size (such as DIN A4), the page structure (portrait or landscape), and the margins. Note that the setting for the page margins applies to reports generated as PDFs only and not to the Web display. Note that you cannot change the page orientation within a report. If you want to have different page orientations within a report, you must use several Report Web items in the BEx Web Application Designer.
Execute	You use this function to execute the report in the Web. The report is displayed in the standard Web template for reports. You set the standard Web template for reports in Customizing for the Standard Web Templates at SAP NetWeaver I Business Intelligence I Settings for Reporting and Analysis I BEx Web I Set Standard Web Templates I Enterprise Report.
Print Version	You use this function to convert the report directly into a PDF document that you can later print.
Publish	**To Role** You use this function to publish reports to roles. The system saves a link to the current report in the selected role. **To Portal** You use this function to publish reports as iViews in the Portal Content Directory. **BEx Broadcaster** You use this function to open the BEx Broadcaster to precalculate and broadcast the report.
Exit	You use this function to close the Report Designer.

TABLE 9-1   Options on the Reports Menu in the Report Designer (*continued*)

Edit

Here you get an overview of the functions provided in the Report Designer's Edit menu. Table 9-2 shows the options available via the Edit menu.

Menu Entry	Description
Delete	You use this function to delete rows or fields, for example, in the report.
Delete Section	You use this function to delete sections of rows or fields, for example, in the report.

TABLE 9-2   Options on the Edit Menu in the Report Designer

View

This section provides an overview of the functions in the View menu, shown here. These options primarily provide the business user a view of the components. Table 9-3 details each option's functionality.

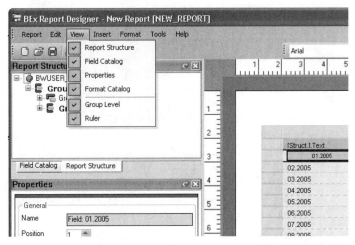

Copyright by SAP AG

Menu Option	Description
Report Structure	You use this function to show and hide the Report Structure screen area.
Field Catalog	You use this function to show and hide the Field Catalog screen area.
Properties	You use this function to show and hide the Properties screen area.
Format Catalog	You use this function to show and hide the Format Catalog screen area.
Group Level	You use this function to show and hide the display of group levels in the design area.
Ruler	You use this function to show and hide the ruler in the design area. Using the context menu (secondary mouse button), you can choose from Points, Pixels, Centimeters, and Inches for the unit of measure for the page format.

TABLE 9-3   Options on the View Menu in the Report Designer

Insert

The Insert menu, shown here, is fairly self-explanatory. These options offer the developer the ability to insert items into the Report Designer, such as headers and footers. Table 9-4 details each option's functionality.

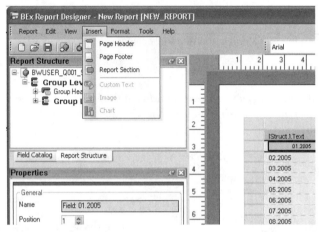

Copyright by SAP AG

Menu Option	Description
Page Header	You use this function to insert a page header into the report, which you can then change according to your needs.
Page Footer	You use this function to insert a page footer into the report, which you can then change according to your needs.
Report Section	You use this function to insert a report section into the report. The inserted report section has no data binding.
Custom Text	You use this function to insert custom text into a cell of the report. In the Properties area, you can specify whether the custom text is to be language independent or language dependent. Language-dependent texts are stored in the BEx Texts table. They can be translated and reused.
Image	You use this function to insert images or logos from the Mime Repository into reports. In the Properties area, you can also specify the properties for the image (such as the size).
Chart	You use this function to insert a stand-alone chart into a report. You can assign a Data Provider already used in the report or a new Data Provider to the stand-alone chart. You can configure the chart using the Chart Designer. You can insert the chart anywhere. It is not related to the group levels. It displays all data for the assigned Data Provider. You need to manually adjust the cell size to fit the chart size.

TABLE 9-4   Options in the Insert Menu for the Report Designer

Format

The Format menu, shown here, has many different items under it used for enhancing the look and feel of the report. This menu also covers much of the formatting that is available via the Excel toolbar, so we won't cover all the options in this section. We will be using many of these options during the creation of our Report Designer report. Under Format | Edit Format, you can change the settings shown in Table 9-5 on the Cell, Font, and Borders tabbed pages. These options are also found under Format.

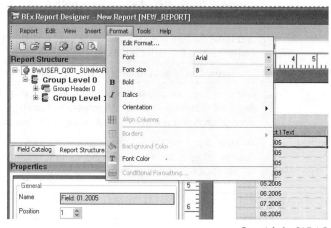

Copyright by SAP AG

Menu Option	Description
Orientation	You use the following settings for text or elements located in a cell of the report: Left Align, Centered, Right Align, Align Top, Vertically Centered, and Align Bottom.
Background Color	You use this function to color a cell.
Field Wrapping	If you choose this function, a line break is automatically inserted between fields of a cell when the length required by all fields exceeds the cell length.
Font	You use this function to specify the font.
Font Size	You use this function to set the font size for text.
Bold	You use this function to format text as bold.
Italic	You use this function to set text as italic.
Font Color	You use this function to color text.
Text Background Color	You use this function to color the text background independently of the background color for the cell.
Word Wrapping	If you choose this function, a line break is automatically inserted at a space within a field with multiple words when the field length is not sufficient.

TABLE 9-5   Features in the Format Menu of the Report Designer

Menu Option	Description
Borders	You use this function to specify a border for each cell. Border settings include solid borders, dashed borders, dotted borders, no borders, border width, and border color. To apply your border settings to the selected cell (in the area to the left), you need to select the relevant side or sides of the cell to which the settings are to be applied. The border type is additive, which means settings are added to the existing border. If you choose No Borders, all borders are deleted.
Padding	You use this function to specify the gap between the cell contents and the cell boundaries.
The Following Functions Are Available Only in the Format Menu	
Align Columns	You use this function to align the columns for multiple report sections with one another. Alignment is based on the report section that you are currently working on in the design area.
Conditional Formatting	You use this function to set a design that deviates from the design for selected characteristic values, hierarchy nodes, and so on, that is set by the default row patterns.

TABLE 9-5   Features in the Format Menu of the Report Designer (*continued*)

Tools

The Tools menu, shown here, offers access to the different BEx components needed to customize the Report Designer. Table 9-6 details the options and their functionality.

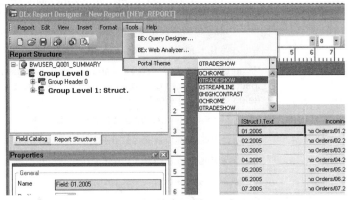

Copyright by SAP AG

Help

The final menu item, Help, is for SAP help and application help. This offers the developer access to additional information if there are questions around the functionality. With this being a completely new reporting tool within BW you will probably need some helpful tips if an error would occur. There will be times where the specific query may just not be configured correctly to be used in the Report Designer and the ability to check on some documentation at that point in time would be very helpful.

Menu Entry	Description
BEx Query Designer	This function calls the BEx Query Designer, where you can create new Data Providers of the type query.
BEx Web Analyzer	This function calls the BEx Web Analyzer, where you can create new Data Providers of the type query.
Settings	You use this function to make settings for the Report Designer. In this way, you can change the theme for displaying the report on the portal, for example. The available themes include Tradeshow, Chrome, Streamline, and High Contrast. Themes are the objects that took the place of the CSS—cascading style sheets

TABLE 9-6   Features of the Tools Menu in the Report Designer

Initial Report Designer Functionality

Before we go into the details of each area of the Report Designer, its important to comment on the initial setup and format of the Report Designer. This will give you some additional information about the functionality, positioning, and objective of the Report Designer. Two areas of the Report Designer will be discussed here: the static and dynamic sections of a report and the use of row patterns in the Report Designer.

Static and Dynamic Sections in Reports

A report can include static and dynamic sections. The distinctive feature of static sections is that query fields can be positioned freely. You do not specify the type of section in the Report Designer. However, the section type is automatically set depending on the type of Data Provider you are using. In the case of a static section of a query (or a query view), the architecture of the query contains two structures—one structure in the rows and one in the columns. A static section is unique because you can freely position all the fields within the section. This is possible because each field is unique in a static section, which in turn is possible because each cell of the result is uniquely defined, so the formatting and positioning of information is related directly to an individual cell. Therefore, the initial view in the Report Designer corresponds to the executed query (query view). Each row in the executed query has one row pattern. The following illustration shows an example of this structure. A static section can also be a report section without a data connection—that is, without a Data Provider. Such sections include the page header and page footer, as well as the report section (for example, for inserting gaps in the report or your own text and comments), which you can integrate into your report using the Insert menu in the Report Designer.

[Structure] Text	[Q1 2004	[Q1 2003	[Delta %] Text
[Software Revenues] Tex	[Software Revenues] Val	[Software Revenues] Val	[Software Revenues] Val
[Total Revenues] Text	[Total Revenues] Val	[Total Revenues] Val	[Total Revenues] Val
[Operating Income] Text	[Operating Income] Val	[Operating Income] Val	[Operating Income] Val
[Income before Income T	[Income before Income T	[Income before Income T	[Income before Income T
[Net Income] Text	[Net Income] Val	[Net Income] Val	[Net Income] Val
[Earnings per Share (in $	[Earnings per Share (in $	[Earnings per Share (in $	[Earnings per Share (in $

Copyright by SAP AG

A dynamic section in a query (or query view) is formed using one or more characteristics in the drilldown and one structure in the query or query view. This means that one or more group levels are designed for the initial view in the Report Designer. There is one group level for each characteristic. Within a dynamic section, query fields can only be taken from external group levels into internal ones. For example, you can move a cell from group level 1 to group level 2, but you cannot move it the other way. The cell-repositioning options are limited with a dynamic section because the cells are not all uniquely defined. Therefore, in dynamic sections, the number of rows varies at runtime, whereas the number of columns is fixed. For example, in the following illustration there are three levels and a dynamic section view. Group level 1 and level 2 are related to the two characteristic: Level 1 is related to Country and level 2 is related to Sold-To Party. Group level 0 relates to the header information.

Group Level 0

Group Level 1

Group Level 2

NOTE   *There will always be a group level 0.*

If a query (or query view) contains two structures and also one or more characteristics, a dynamic section will be used. The dynamic section generates individual cells for each intersection of the two structures, which means you will be able to reposition these cells freely. You cannot use a query or query view that contains more than one structure in the columns. This discussion leads us directly into the details of row patterns.

Row Patterns

A central component of the Enterprise Report Design is the concept of a row pattern. It enables the creation of reports with dynamic sections. With reports of this type, the number of characteristic values in the drilldown is not set at the time of report creation. It becomes visible during runtime. In order to be able to understand the row pattern concept, you need to look at the structure of a report with dynamic sections. The following illustration shows an example of this structure.

In this illustration, you can see that a number of row types can be identified in a report. For example, a specifically formatted row type can be applied to column headers or results values. There are three row types for each group level: Header, Details, and Footer. For each row type, a template, called a *row pattern,* describes the color, font, height, and width of the rows and so on. The following illustration shows the group level concept. It shows the structure of a query in a report with characteristics, structures, and hierarchies. The layout of a query is defined in the drilldown of the structure elements in the columns and rows of the query. Every structure element in the rows of the query corresponds to a group level in the row pattern concept. Thus, the number of possible group levels in a report depends on the drilldown status of the query.

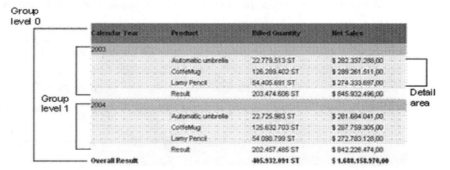

Additionally, the detail area itself can represent a group level (with a header and footer and a detail area). This is how group levels can be nested in each other. The innermost group level of a report has detail rows that contain key figures. The Report Designer generates a row pattern for each area of a group level. Row patterns are the smallest unit of the BEx Report Designer not divided by page boundaries. Row patterns comprise cell grids whose cells can have specific properties. The Report Web item uses the row pattern and data to generate the header, detail, and footer areas of a report. Using the properties of the row pattern, you specify the format of cells and the entire cell grid. These properties are applied when the report is executed. The row pattern and its properties enable you to design reports in the Business Explorer. The Report Web item uses these row patterns to display reports. SAP delivers a pool of standard row patterns. You can change these according to your needs in the BEx Report Designer. You can also create new row patterns by setting the properties of the cells for a cell grid. These options will be demonstrated in more detail in the next chapter, which discusses the functionality of the Report Designer. The cell grid, and therefore every cell in a cell pattern, has the properties detailed in Table 9-7.

In the Report Designer, you can specify or change these properties for each cell in the Properties window. A cell can have a corresponding associated format that has the properties described in the preceding table. The format set can be applied to multiple cells and does not have to be set for each individual cell separately. In the Report Designer, you make these settings in the Properties window. At runtime, the row pattern is applied to the relevant rows of the report. In addition to the cell properties listed in the table, you can also use text properties to format the contents of a cell. You also use them to set or change the cell properties in the Report Designer. Table 9-8 details these properties.

Property	Description
Background Color (BackgroundColor)	This property sets the background color of the cell.
Left Border (BorderStyleLead)	This property sets the border type for the cell boundary used as the start direction for the cell contents.
Right Border (BorderStyleTrail)	This property sets the border type for the cell boundary used as the end direction for the cell contents.
Top Border (BorderStyleTop)	This property sets the border type for the upper boundary of the cell.
Bottom Border (BorderStyleBottom)	This property sets the border type for the lower boundary of the cell.
Left Border Color (BorderColorLead)	This property sets the border color for the cell boundary used as the start direction for the cell contents.
Right Border Color (BorderColorTrail)	This property sets the border color for the cell boundary used as the end direction for the cell contents.
Top Border Color (BorderColorTop)	This property sets the border color for the upper boundary of the cell.
Bottom Border Color (BorderColorBottom)	This property sets the border color for the lower boundary of the cell.
Left Border Width (BorderWidthLead)	This property sets the border width for the cell boundary used as the start direction for the cell contents.
Right Border Width (BorderWidthTrail)	This property sets the border width for the cell boundary used as the end direction for the cell contents.
Top Border Width (BorderWidthTop)	This property sets the border width of the upper cell boundary.
Bottom Border Width (BorderWidthBottom)	This property sets the border width of the lower cell boundary.
Field Wrapping (Wrapping) and Word Wrapping	You use this property to insert text wrapping at the end of the cell. Word wrapping is applied to a line break within a field; field wrapping is applied to a break between the fields of a cell.
Width (Width)	This property specifies the width of the cell.
Height (Height)	This property specifies the height of the cell.
Vertical Alignment (VerticalAlignment)	This property specifies the vertical orientation of the contents of a cell (top, centered, bottom).
Horizontal Alignment (HorizontalAlignment)	This property specifies the horizontal orientation of the contents of a cell (top, centered, bottom).
Horizontal Merging of Cells (Colspan)	You use this property to merge two cells that are next to each other.
Vertical Merging of Cells (Rowspan)	You use this property to merge two cells located above one another.

TABLE 9-7   Properties of the Cell Patterns

Property	Description
Text Color (TextColor)	This property specifies the color of the text.
Background Color (BackgroundColor)	This property specifies the background color of the text.
Font (FontFamily)	This property specifies the font (for example, Arial or Times New Roman).
Bold (FontWeight)	This property specifies the font weight.
Font Size (FontSize)	This property specifies the size of the font.
Italic (FontStyle)	This property specifies the font style (italic or normal).

TABLE 9-8   Text Properties in the BI Patterns

Here are some other items of importance you need to know about navigation and the Report Designer: You have the ability to use the drag-and-drop functionality to move report elements from the Field Catalog, Report Structure, and Format Catalog screen areas to the design area of the report. You can also use drag and drop to move cells and fields within the design area. Finally, the context-sensitive menu in the design area, Report Structure, and Format Catalog can be used to access various functions for creating reports.

Screen Areas of the Report Designer
With these options as our backdrop, we can now fully discuss the different areas of the initial screen of the Report Designer.

Design Area   This is the screen area of the Report Designer and is a principal interface element of the Report Designer. You use it to create reports and display them schematically. The design area displays report elements such as the page header and footer as well as report sections with and without a data connection. You can use the context menu in the design area and the various functions provided by the menu bars and toolbars as well as by the other screen areas of the Report Designer to edit report elements and design your report. The following illustration shows the design area of the Report Designer. We will be using this area of the Report Designer in the follow-up portion of this chapter to create a basic report.

Copyright by SAP AG

Field Catalog   The Field Catalog displays all the query fields and text elements of the Data Provider (query or query view) that provide the basis for the report. The Field Catalog also contains the list of free texts created by users (inserted into the header area of the report, for example). Using the Field Catalog, you can insert or reuse query fields or text elements from the Data Provider that were deleted from the report, for example, at any time with drag and drop. You can also work with free texts the same way. The following illustration shows this area and some examples of the activities involved. As you can see, the free texts Incoming Orders and Sales Period have been created by the user, and the characteristics and key figures are displayed in this section. In the lower portion of this section (not shown) are the additional objects—variables, text, and information—that were part of the query and also displayed for use in the Report Designer.

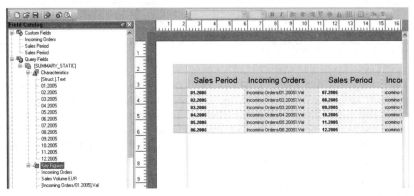

The following elements are listed in the Field Catalog:

- Free texts
- Query fields
- Text elements for the Data Providers, such as Last Changed By, Due Date, Query Description, and so on

Report Structure   The Report Structure hierarchically illustrates the report and all its visible and hidden components. As in the design area, the Report Structure also has a context menu with which you can work. In contrast to the design area, where you cannot select objects such as group levels, in the report structure you *can* select and edit these types of objects. Depending on the structure of a report, the following elements can be displayed hierarchically:

- **Page header and/or page footer**   A static section with the associated row patterns and their cells, which can also contain various fields such as free text and query fields.

- **Report section without data connection**   A static section with the associated row patterns and their cells, which can also contain various fields such as free text and query fields.

- **Report section with data connection**   The static and dynamic report sections are displayed with a hierarchical structure. The name of the Data Provider with the associated row patterns is displayed for every group level (only for dynamic reports), along with the individual elements. Every group level is listed in its structure with the associated header, detail, and footer areas. Each area of a group level is displayed with the associated rows and their cells, which can also contain query fields and free text.

The following illustration shows this integration between the Report Structure and the design area.

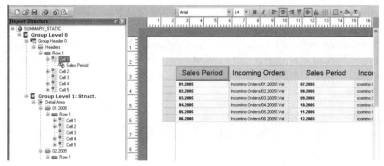

Notice that group level 0 is related to the initial header group of the report. Therefore,

- Row 1, Cell 1 = Sales Period
- Row 1, Cell 2 = Incoming Orders
- Row 1, Cell 3 = Blank Column (notice that cell 3 doesn't have anything under it)

and so on, through to the group level 1 structure and the row, cell combinations displayed. Because this is an example of a static display, it would stand to reason that this format is very rigid and limited.

Format Catalog   The Format Catalog provides an overview of the formats used in the report. Both standard formats and user-defined formats are displayed. You can transfer the formats to report elements (rows or cells) using drag and drop. This is shown in the following illustration. Notice that all the formats being used in the Report Designer are listed here. Once additional formats are either used or customized, they will be available from the Format Catalog.

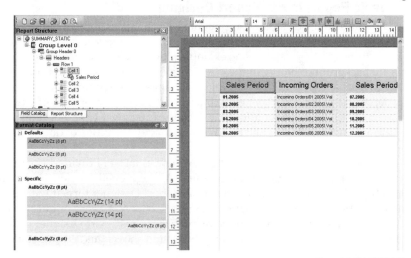

Properties   In the Properties area of the Report Designer, you can specify the properties of the individual report elements (fields, rows, and cells). To do this, you must first select the required row or cell and then make the required settings in the Properties area. This allows you to determine the format and position of text fields and the height and width of rows and columns. For example, in the following illustration, the Sales Period field is highlighted, and the Properties area shows the different options available to be reviewed and changed. In this case, Sales Period is set up as a 14-point Arial font, with a standard font color. Also, field wrapping is on, the cell background color is FF80, and the alignment and other settings are configured.

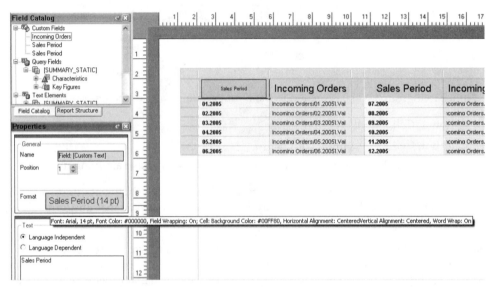

Copyright by SAP AG

Building a Basic Report in the Report Designer

This section combines all the different components we just talked about in an example of building a Report Designer report. Now, this is one of those times when there are too many options to work through all of them in one example. For instance, the process of adjusting the font or color background (or any of the other cosmetic activities) on a report contains too many options to be able to cover. This example will demonstrate some of the options, but it would be better if you as the developer experiment a bit during the process of creating the Report Designer report. If you are comfortable with the functionality and options available in the Excel formatting toolset, you will be comfortable with the range of options during the creation process.

To create a report, you need a query or a query view as a Data Provider. The query or query view must contain a structure in the columns. As mentioned previously, depending on the architecture of the query, the outcome of the Report Designer format will be predetermined—either it's static or dynamic. Therefore, choose a query or query view by using Report | Insert Data Provider from the menu bar of the Report Designer or by using the button Insert Data Provider. The following illustration shows this screen details.

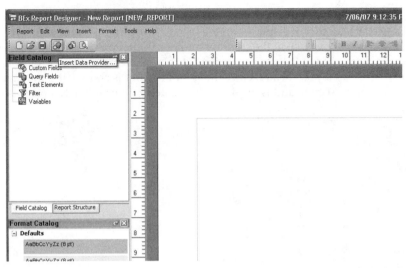

This screen shows the initial view after you have gained access to the Report Designer. Once you click the Insert Data Provider button, the dialog box shown in the following illustration will appear. This dialog box is used for accessing the BEx Query Designer information and other activities.

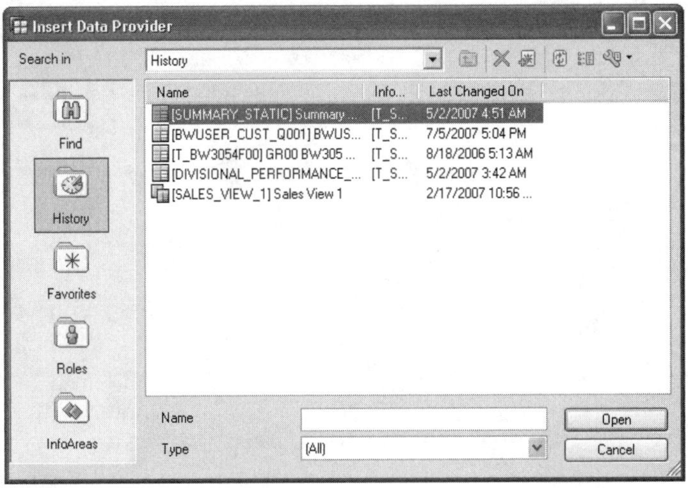

Choose the specific query or query view that you are interested in using for the creation of the Report Designer report so that the information and data that will be used for this example is apparent and you can set up a similar example in your system. The first of the following illustrations shows the query we will use for the Data Provider. It is very basic but will do for our Report Designer process demonstration. Also, the configuration of the query via the BEx Query Designer is displayed in the second illustration. Notice that two structures are being used—one in the columns and one in the rows. Based on the definitions that have been developed in the earlier portions of this chapter, this query will result in a static Report Designer report format. Once the Data Provider is chosen, it is automatically embedded in a report section and is displayed in the design area of the Report Designer.

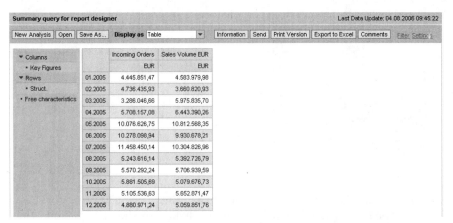

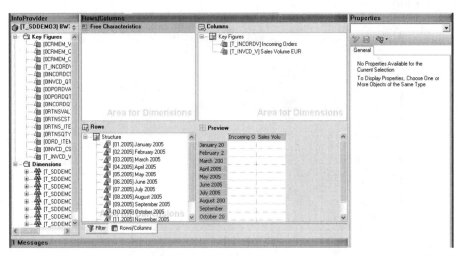

NOTE *You can create a new Data Provider from the Report Designer. To define a new Data Provider, in the menu bar choose Tools|BEx Query Designer (to define a new query) or BEx Web Analyzer (to define a new query view).*

You can use various options to design your reports. Because the design process varies from case to case, only the basics of the procedure are described here. (The entire range of options is left to you to explore.) You can use standard formatting functions, including color, font, and border selections for individual report elements (cells or fields).

If you want to add color to a cell, select the cell and in the menu bar choose Format|Fill Color. The color selection dialog box appears, where you can choose the required color. The options available for changing the layout of a report include:

- **Changing the height and width of rows and columns**   To increase the width of a column, select the outer-right border of the column header and drag it along the length of the ruler displayed in the design area until you reach the required width. The same process would be used to increase or decrease the height of the rows.

- **Inserting free texts into the report**   To insert free text, proceed as follows:

  1. Select the cell or field into which you want to insert the text. Then choose Insert Free Text in the context menu for the cell, or Insert|Free Text in the menu bar of the Report Design

  2. Double-click the selected cell. The cell is now input ready.

  3. Insert the text and use the design functions as required, such as applying a special font type or size to the text.

- **Rearranging fields (query fields, text elements, or free texts) and deleting them**

  - To move a field displayed in the design area within the report, select it and drag it to the required cell using drag and drop.

  - To delete a field displayed in the design area, select the field and choose Delete Field in the context menu.

  - If you have deleted a field from the design area and want to insert it again later, or if you want to reuse a field in the page header or page footer for the report, choose the field from the field catalog and drag it to the required cell in the design area using drag and drop.

- **Inserting additional report sections**

  - You can insert additional report sections (to insert comments or footnotes, for example) as well as a page header and footer into your report. To do this, in the menu bar for the Report Designer choose Insert|Report Section, Insert|Page Header, or Insert|Page Footer.

  - To insert a report section that is directly connected with data, in the menu bar of the Report Designer choose Report|Select Data Provider. The selected Data Provider is inserted directly into a report section and is displayed in the design area.

- **Changing the format of rows**

  - To change the format for a row, you can use the standard formatting functions available in the menu bar and toolbars, or you can use the Format Catalog.

  - In the Format Catalog, choose a format from the standard formats or the specific formats (that you created) and drag it to the row whose format you wish to change.

- **Creating conditional formatting**   To reformat certain characteristic values (such as customer XY), you can use conditional formatting.

- **Saving the Report**
  - In the menu bar for the Report Designer, choose Report|Save. The BEx Save dialog box appears.
  - Enter a suitable description and a technical name for the report and save it in your favorites or roles.
  - You can open the saved report in the Report Designer at any time (to change it, for example). You can also insert the report into a web application using the Report Web item.
- **Executing the report in the portal and printing the report**   In the menu bar for the Report Designer, choose Report|Execute. The report is displayed in the standard Web template for reports in the portal (Web). In the menu bar for the Report Designer, choose Report|Print Version. The report is automatically converted to a PDF document, which is then displayed. You can print this document as required.

You have created and saved a report to suit your requirements. You can display and print this report as a PDF document or execute it in the portal.

With these basic rules, we can continue with the example. As you can see in the following illustration, the query components are indeed embedded into the Report Designer tool. Now, we need to set up the report in the format that the business user is requesting. Such formatting activities will become second nature to you as a developer after a short time of navigating and working with the Report Designer.

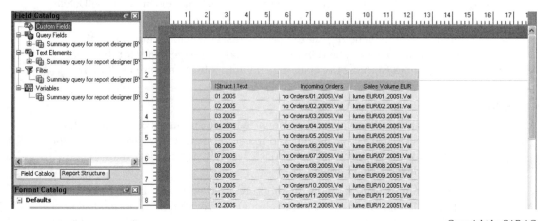

Copyright by SAP AG

In the first of the following illustrations, the third column—Sales Volume EUR—is not required, so the deletion process is used to get rid of the whole column. The next illustration shows the Delete function on the context menu. Once this deletion is carried out, the query format is down to just Incoming Orders. To change the report and make it work for the business user, we will balance the report format rather than having everything going directly down the left side of the report.

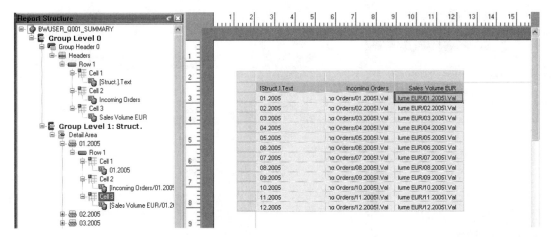

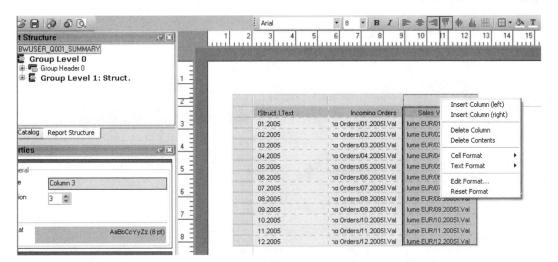

The first of the following illustrations shows the context menu for the current column. We'll use Insert Column (Right) and then drag and drop the cells into a balanced format. The second illustration shows the creation of the two columns to the right of the last column.

Now we can drag the cells for the months and key figures from the left cells to the right cells and fill the top six positions for both the months and the key figures (Incoming Orders).

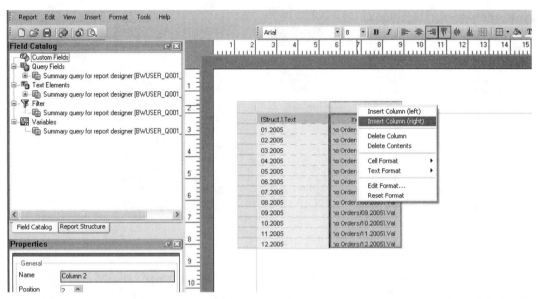

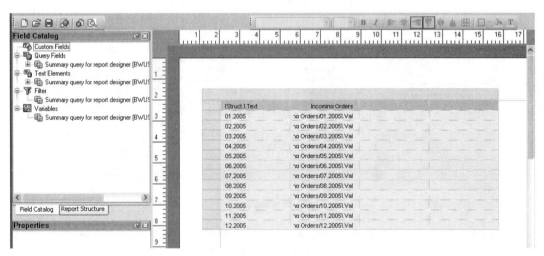

The first of the following illustrations shows the initial drag-and-drop process. Make sure this procedure is followed closely until you get the hang of this process. Position the cursor directly on the cell you are moving to highlight it. This is a sign that the item is ready to be moved. The next illustrations continues with a view of the final drag-and-drop process, where all the characteristics and key figures are in their appropriate positions. After all of the cells have been moved, we can delete the remaining rows. The third illustration shows the use of the context menu's Delete Row option to accomplish this task.

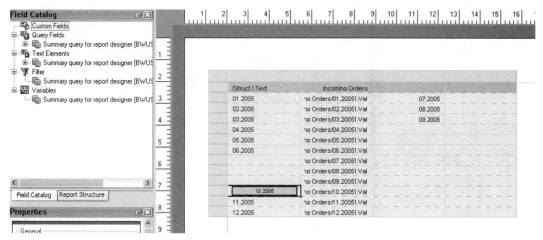

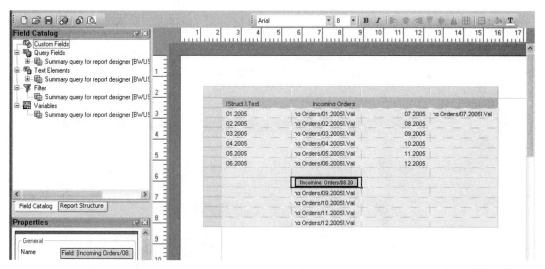

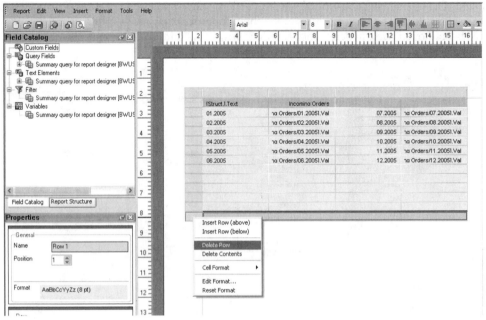

Next, the format and color of the background cells need to be refreshed. The following illustration shows the formatting being completed for the cell with 01.2005 assigned. Via the context menu selection Cell Format | Background Color, you can access the pallet of colors to change the background of cells on an individual level.

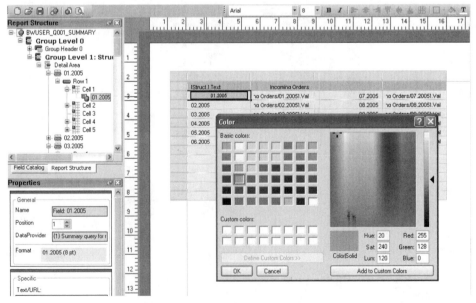

The first of the following illustrations shows the completed background setup for the one cell. Notice in the bottom-left portion of the screen that the exact format that has been developed is now available for use. The Properties area will store any formatting done to the columns and rows so that it can be used in the future. In the next illustration, the format is being dragged from the Properties area to each cell in the left column. You simply click the particular format in the Properties area and drag that format onto the target cell. In this example, the entire column will have the same display format.

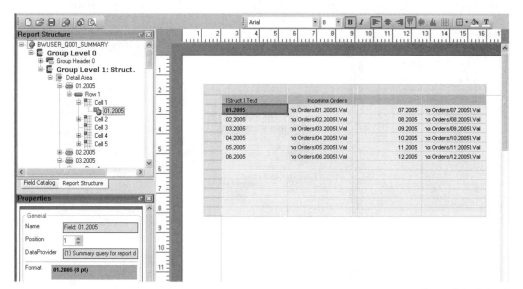

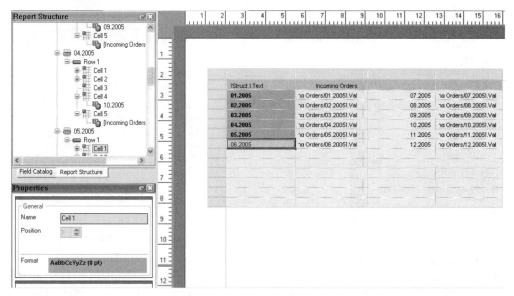

Next, because the headings on the different columns are not quite correct, we will use the Report Designer functionality Delete Contents for the cell showing "Structured Text." We can then use the Insert Custom Text option to manually enter text for that specific column. The first of the following illustrations shows the deletion of the contents of that cell, and the second illustration shows "Sales Period" typed in the column heading. Now the rest of the headers can be changed to reflect what is in the columns. The Field Catalog entries are available for this purpose. Notice that the newly created naming conventions are listed in the Field Catalog and can be dragged to the appropriate heading sections.

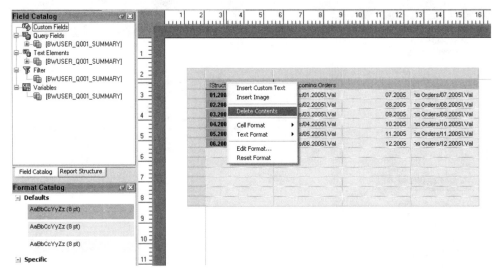

Copyright by SAP AG

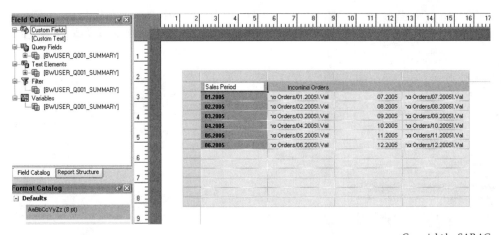

Copyright by SAP AG

The first of the following illustrations shows the use of this functionality to complete all the headings. To continue the formatting process, we change the headings to enlarge the font and adjust the background color for emphasis. Also, a column has been embedded into the center of the two lists to give more definition to the report. The second illustration shows the results of these changes. Also notice that additional color was added to the center column and the font was changed for the column headings. Finally, the background color of the other sales periods was changed.

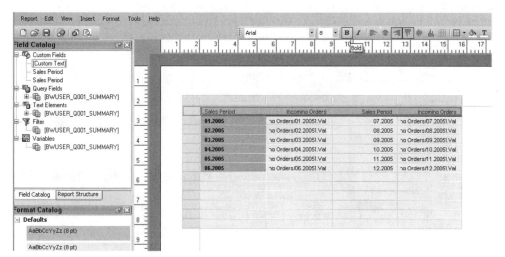

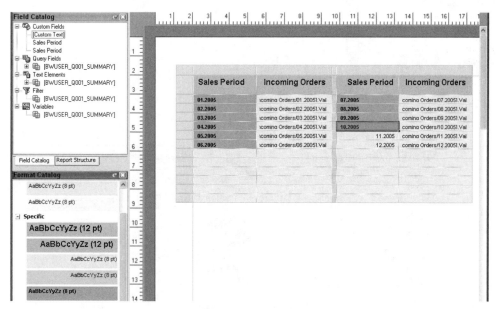

We could work through each of the cells in the report structure but rather than finishing up the formatting per specific cells, we will use the initial cells as a formatting object for the rest of the cells. In the first of the following illustrations the use of the Report Structure and the specific row that we want to copy to complete the additional changes for the fonts and the sizing of the text. Finally, the query can be executed and reviewed. You can always revisit formatted object and change their attributes. The second illustration shows the final results of the Report Designer report view. Some changes should still be made—specifically, adjusting the color for the dividing column and, if required, adding a results row to the report. Now let's enhance the Report Designer report a bit by making it a more "dynamic" report. To do this, exit the Report Designer report on the Web and go back into the Report Designer. Before starting this process, however, let's review the query.

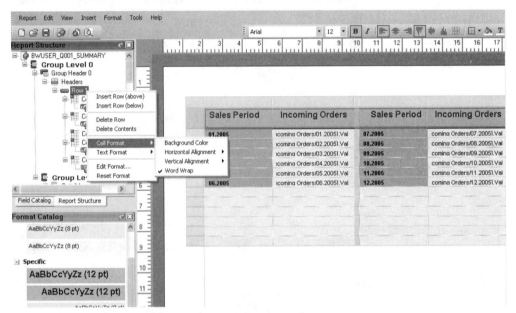

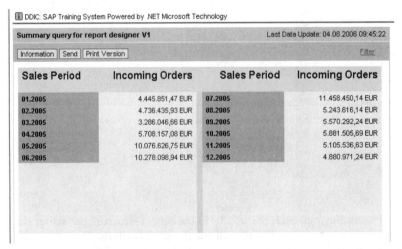

The first of the following illustrations shows the configuration of the query that will be used for this part of the example. As you can see, this query doesn't have a structure in the rows as the last one did. Therefore, it will develop into a "dynamic" view of the information. This means that there is no way to manage the rows or how many will show up for the final report. Back in the Report Designer, another "section" has been added at the bottom of the page, as shown in the second illustration. Notice the dark gray row at the bottom of the illustration. This was achieved via the context menu from the bottom portion of the Report Designer design area.

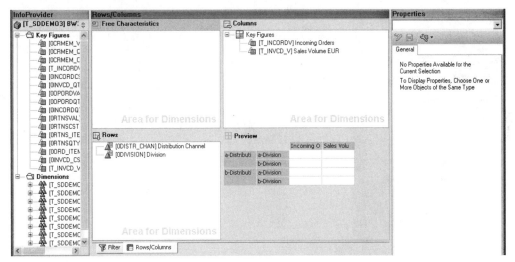

Copyright by SAP AG

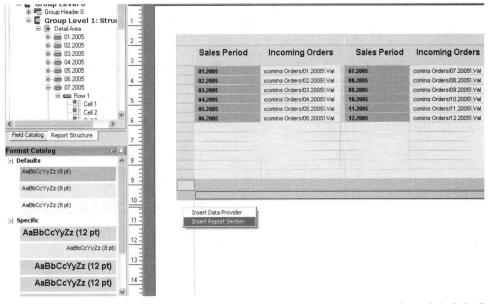

Copyright by SAP AG

The following illustration shows the next step—using the context menu in the lower portion of the screen and choosing Insert Data Provider. The same dialog box appears, from which you choose the required query. Now we can use the same steps as before to enhance the report format.

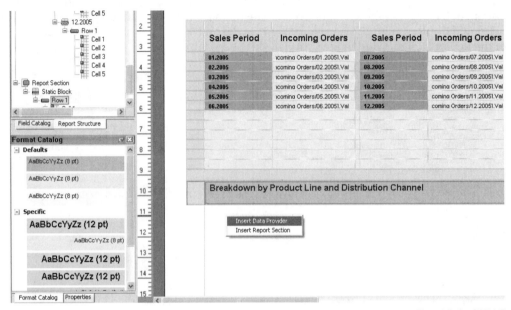

The next illustration shows that all the query properties were defaulted into this Report Designer report. We now take the additional steps of adjusting the format of the report and adjusting the columns and rows to be used. Note that, in this case, the static report is positioned at the top of the report and the dynamic report is in the lower section. This is good to remember because of the limited navigation and flexibility of the report structures using Report Designer. If the dynamic report was on top, this may cause issues with the static report below due to the possible expansion of the total number of rows in the dynamic report.

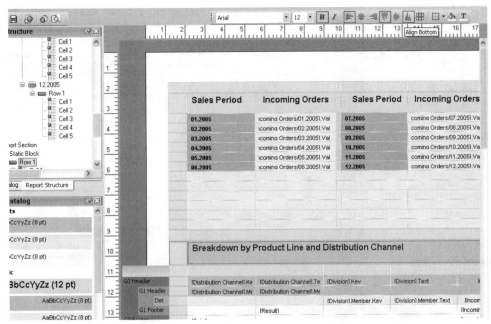

In the first of the following illustrations, the report portion for Division is moved to below Distribution Channel. In the second illustration, the previous column for Division is deleted.

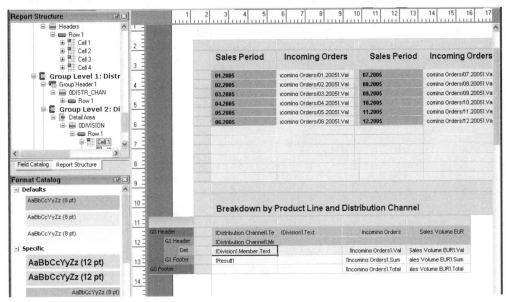

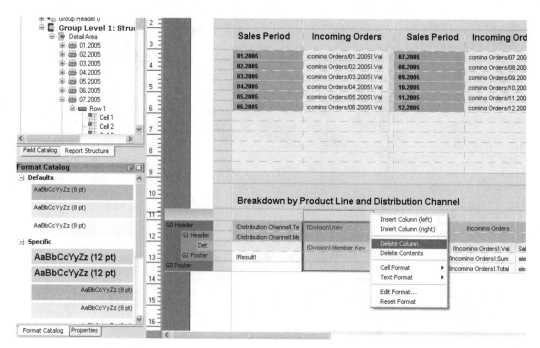

The first of the following illustrations shows some basic enhancements. Fonts, background color, and types of text have been used on the columns for Distribution Channel and Division, and the results rows are accented for Breakdown by Product Line and Distribution Channel with additional color and formatting. The results are shown in the second illustration, with all the changes made to the two reports. The information can be tweaked for additional enhancements and changes, but for the most part the business user will need to get into the Report Designer and review all the options available.

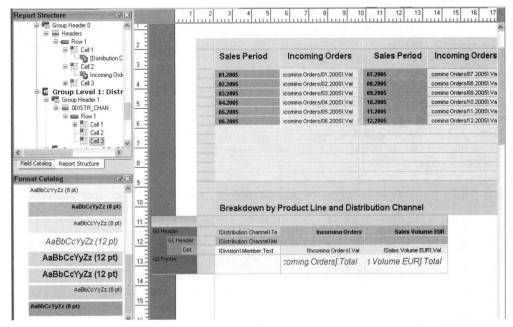

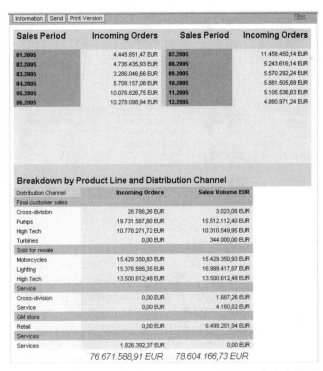

Sales Period	Incoming Orders	Sales Period	Incoming Orders
01.2005	4.445.851,47 EUR	07.2005	11.458.450,14 EUR
02.2005	4.736.435,93 EUR	08.2005	5.243.616,14 EUR
03.2005	3.286.046,66 EUR	09.2005	5.570.292,24 EUR
04.2005	5.708.157,08 EUR	10.2005	5.881.505,69 EUR
05.2005	10.076.626,75 EUR	11.2005	5.105.536,63 EUR
06.2005	10.278.098,94 EUR	12.2005	4.880.971,24 EUR

Breakdown by Product Line and Distribution Channel

Distribution Channel	Incoming Orders	Sales Volume EUR
Final customer sales		
Cross-division	28.788,26 EUR	3.023,08 EUR
Pumps	19.731.587,80 EUR	15.512.112,40 EUR
High Tech	10.778.271,72 EUR	10.310.549,95 EUR
Turbines	0,00 EUR	344.000,00 EUR
Sold for resale		
Motorcycles	15.429.350,93 EUR	15.429.350,93 EUR
Lighting	15.376.585,35 EUR	16.999.417,87 EUR
High Tech	13.500.612,48 EUR	13.500.612,48 EUR
Service		
Cross-division	0,00 EUR	1.687,26 EUR
Service	0,00 EUR	4.160,82 EUR
GM store		
Retail	0,00 EUR	6.499.251,94 EUR
Services		
Services	1.826.392,37 EUR	0,00 EUR
	76.671.588,91 EUR	78.604.166,73 EUR

These are the basic tools available in the Report Designer. Once you have developed your formatted report, you have various output options. You can present the output on the Web. The Report Designer uses a standard Web template to organize the standard features such as the Print and Broadcast buttons. The formatting from the Report Designer is not modified by the template. Another output option is printing. Printing is handled by the Adobe Document Service, as shown in the following illustration. The Printing button allows for the generation of a PDF of the full report. You can click the Print Version button from within the Report Designer or from the Web output. In any case, which ever option you choose you will be presented with a PDF output of the report. You can then decide whether to save the PDF output of the report or to save the PDF to a specific location and print from a specific printer.

Sales Period	Incoming Orders	Sales Period	Incoming Orders
01.2005	4.445.851,47 EUR	07.2005	11.458.450,14 EUR
02.2005	4.736.435,93 EUR	08.2005	5.243.616,14 EUR
03.2005	3.286.046,66 EUR	09.2005	5.570.292,24 EUR
04.2005	5.708.157,08 EUR	10.2005	5.881.505,69 EUR
05.2005	10.076.626,75 EUR	11.2005	5.105.536,63 EUR
06.2005	10.278.098,94 EUR	12.2005	4.880.971,24 EUR

Breakdown by Product Line and Distribution Channel

Distribution Channel	Incoming Orders	Sales Volume EUR
Final customer sales		
Cross-division	28.788,26 EUR	3.023,08 EUR
Pumps	19.731.587,80 EUR	15.512.112,40 EUR
High Tech	10.778.271,72 EUR	10.310.549,95 EUR
Turbines	0,00 EUR	344.000,00 EUR
Sold for resale		
Motorcycles	15.429.350,93 EUR	15.429.350,93 EUR
Lighting	15.376.585,35 EUR	16.999.417,87 EUR
High Tech	13.500.612,48 EUR	13.500.612,48 EUR
Service		
Cross-division	0,00 EUR	1.687,26 EUR
Service	0,00 EUR	4.160,82 EUR

Summary

This chapter laid out the uses for the new 7.0 BW Report Designer functionality As you can see, this is a very powerful formatting tool for Web queries and the PDF process. One area that has been a very sore spot in previous versions has been the printing capabilities of BW. With the Report Designer and other toolsets, you have the ability to print reports in full, and not just what is seen on the page. We will expand on this toolset in the next chapter and get into more complex formatting options and discuss more details of the printing component. We have seen quite a few different reporting tools in BW and as you can see the Reporting Strategy of your company is getting to be more important than ever.

Functionality of the Report Designer

As mentioned in the previous chapter, the Report Designer is completely new to the 7.0 version of BW—and it comes just in the nick of time. The only functionality that the ECC system had over BW was the fact that at the operating system level you were able to create formatted reports that you could execute, display, print and distribute. The ECC environment provided the ability to set up a format for reports so that no matter what drilldown or drill-across process was used, the format of the report (including the print options) was consistent. Therefore each of the Business Users would always see the same structure—columns and rows—no matter how they changed the reporting information. With Report Designer, this gap has been closed in front-end functionality. The previous chapter introduced the Report Designer and many of the basic processes and activities. This chapter covers the enhanced functionality of the Report Designer. As with a number of components in the BW 7.0 version, the Report Designer will be enhanced over the next several versions, and depending on its use and the request for additional options, SAP BW development will move to include other functions in this toolset.

Enhanced Functionality of the Report Designer

In this chapter, the topic of working with the Report Designer will be expanded to include additional functionality. All the components discussed in the previous chapter will now be used in different scenarios and processes to help with the enhanced functionality. The initial topic includes the use of a hierarchy in the Report Designer as well as the use of variables in the process. Then the discussion will move to images and how to set up additional images for use in the Report Designer. We'll also extend our discussion of the use of headers and footers in the Report Designer and then close with the use of themes and conditional formatting. With these features, the Report Designer will become a very integral part of your reporting strategy. As mentioned at the beginning of this book there are components that have so many different options and functions that it would take another book to cover all of them. This is one of those components. We will review numerous areas in the Report Designer but there will always be one more twist to a specific executable that will offer new uses for the Report Designer tools. After working through this chapter look to experiment with a basic query in your Report Designer and see what other interesting and unique formatting options you can develop.

Use of Hierarchies in the Report Designer

The Report Designer is not limited to the use of "flat views" of the data within a query. The use of a hierarchy in a query does not preclude it from additional formatting in the Report Designer. The hierarchy is presented in the normal fashion, as it would be in a query or on the Web, but additional formatting can be applied for each of the levels of the hierarchy. Each of these levels shows up in the Report Designer as a unique node, and you can use all the normal formatting options against each level. The Report Designer can accommodate any of the different versions of the hierarchies—whether it is a text-type hierarchy or a hierarchy with only one text node and all the other nodes are postable, or even if there are several characteristics within one hierarchy. So the use of hierarchies has no limitations (as some of the other components available with BW have). At each level, text colors, text size, font type, bold, italic, cell colors, cell height, and borders are available. To demonstrate this functionality, we will use a basic Material hierarchy off of the InfoObject 0MATERIAL. Figure 10-1 shows the Query Designer with the query we will use.

Notice that the characteristic 0MATERIAL has a hierarchy assigned to it. This is the standard hierarchy for the material levels from an R3/ECC system. Figure 10-2 shows the actual hierarchy from the Data Warehousing Workbench. Notice that this hierarchy has uneven levels (0MATERIAL and 0PRODH3) that occupy the same level. This hierarchy also has text level and more than one InfoObject. Also note that a variable for the hierarchy node is included in this query. Figure 10-3 shows this scenario.

The query is initially inserted into the Report Designer, as shown in the first of the following illustrations. Here, the hierarchy and all levels can be identified in the design area. This is where you can set up unique views of each of the different levels of the hierarchy.

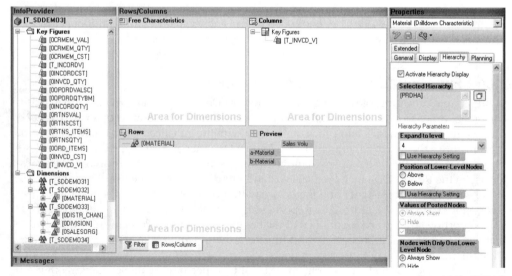

FIGURE 10-1   The Query designer with the Query

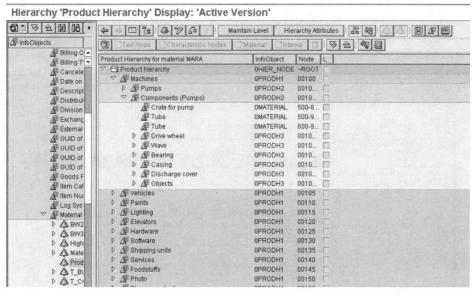

Copyright by SAP AG

FIGURE 10-2 Display of Product Hierarchy—Active Version (top of the figure)

In the second illustration, we begin the process of realigning the format by using the option Edit Format on the context menu of the cell. This opens a dialog box with a number of different options, as shown in the third illustration. The tabs are Cell, Font, and Border.

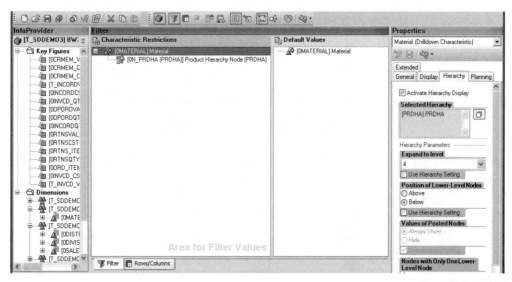

Copyright by SAP AG

FIGURE 10-3 Query Designer Display of Product Hierarchy with a variable for Hierarchy Nodes

Each of these tabs has the same options as those accessed via the dropdown menus in the Report Designer toolbar or the context menu's Cell Format and Text Format options. This allows you to make the adjustments all in one place. We will use the options on the Cell tab to adjust the background color.

NOTE *In a number of the upcoming examples, the details of each step will be minimal because we discussed these details in the previous chapter.*

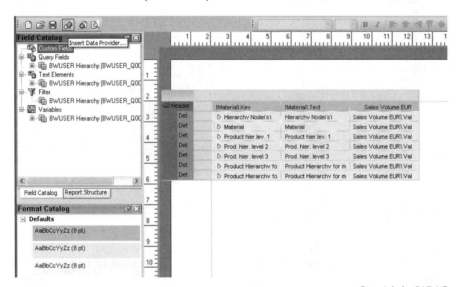

Copyright by SAP AG

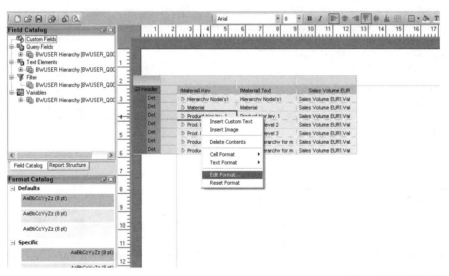

Copyright by SAP AG

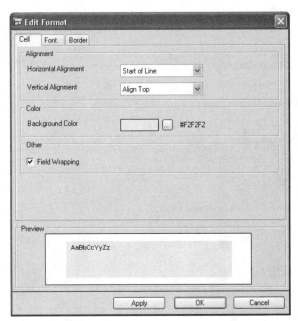

Copyright by SAP AG

Click the small box next to the text Background Color (not the larger field, but the small square) to open up the color pallet, which offers the different colors available as well as the ability to create a customized color for your use (see the first of the following illustrations). Choose any of the different colors to use and then click OK to go back to the Edit Format dialog box. The second illustration shows the end result.

NOTE *In many cases once the query is inserted into the Report Designer the functions such as hierarchies and variables are automatically converted into the Report Designer format.*

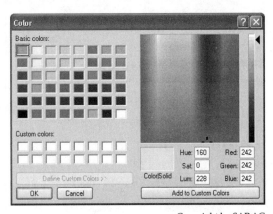

Copyright by SAP AG

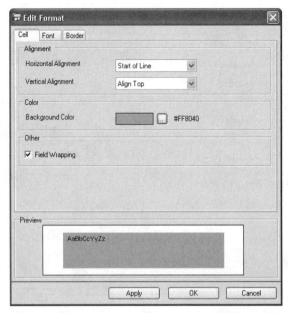

The next illustration shows the second tab, Font, which is used to change the font of the text. Due to the number options, we won't work through them all. Instead, you should experiment with the various options to change the look and feel of your reports to what you want. As you review enough of these options, you'll find yourself only using the ones that are consistent with your corporate colors and formats.

Finally, the Border tab enables you to create borders around any set of cells you need to emphasize, such as cells for certain text or titles. The first of the following illustrations shows these options. To adjust the font of the other levels of the hierarchy, we will use the Format option in the toolbar as well as the Format | Font menu option, as shown in the second illustration.

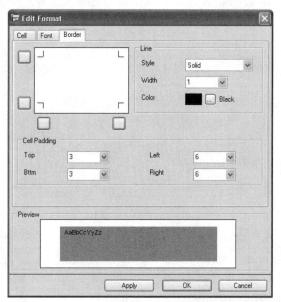

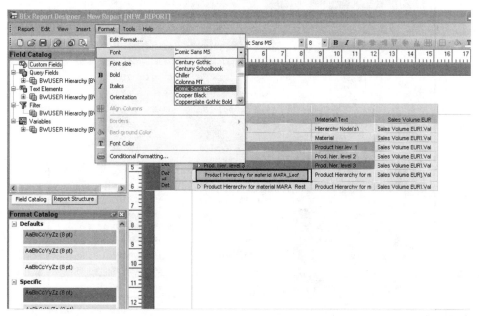

Finally, once executing the report the initial screen that appears offers the field to enter the variable hierarchy node. The first of the following illustrations shows this view. Once the variable is assigned, the results of these changes are shown in the second illustration. Notice that during the process of formatting we included both the text and the technical naming convention with the appropriate background color and font format. The background color for the key figures could have been changed, and other formatting adjustments are available.

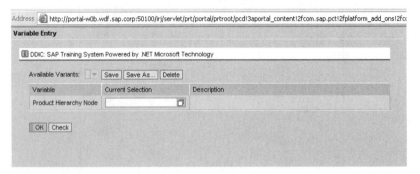

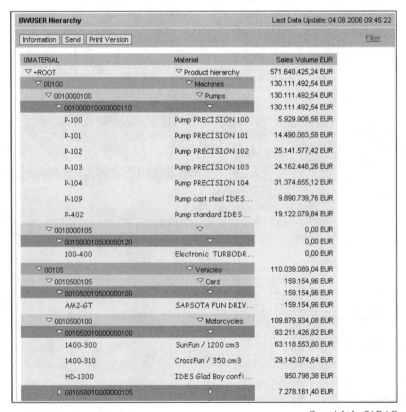

Images

One of the other useful features in the Report Designer is the ability to insert images in reports. This can really help improve the look and feel of your report, especially if it is going to be distributed throughout the corporation. Logos and comments are normally required elements. The graphics available to the Report Designer are stored in the Mime Repository of BI. The Mime Repository is a central storage area for all graphical objects used in BEx as well as in other components linked to BI, such as SEM. The Mime Repository can hold all types of graphical objects, including GIF, JPG, TIF, BMP, and more. It's important to check and test all the different types of graphical objects and their use in the Report Designer. Originally the only image type supported was GIF, but now many more are supported. To access the MIME Repository you have a number of options. You can access this repository with the transaction SE80 from the main screen of the BW system, then choose the Mime Repository or use the transaction code for the Mime Repository directly—SO2_MIME_REPOSITORY. Alternatively, you can use the link from the main menu in Business Explorer.

NOTE *The Mime Repository is used in SEM-BPS and also BW-BPS for storing additional images for icons and corporate logos on the BPS layouts via the Web Interface Builder.*

In the Mime Repository, to identify the exact folder that will store the images for the Report Designer, use the menu path and locate the Custom or Customer folder for the Mime images, or you can go to the Report Designer and use the menu path in the graphic screen for the "image" icon. You will see this later in this section. The following illustration shows the initial screen of the Mime Repository.

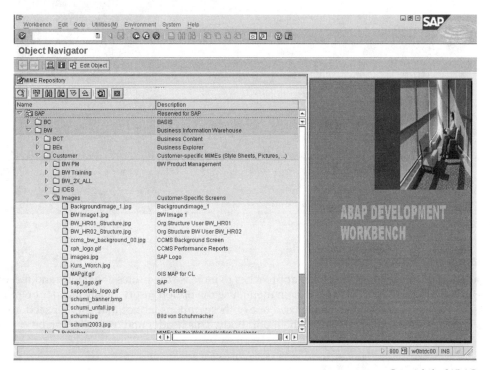

Copyright by SAP AG

From here you can create additional Mime objects, use any of the Mime objects that are currently stored, or import other Mime objects you have available and need to use in the Report Designer. Notice that the logo for SAP is in both the GIF and JPG formats, and both are usable in the Report Designer, as shown in the following illustration. If you need to modify the images available, you can download them using the Download menu option, make any of the necessary changes, and then reload the images by using the Upload/Download context menu option. Images can be assigned to most cells in the Report Designer. Thus, an image can be married with a text or a key figure amount. This can come in handy if you have a series of products in your report and the requirement is to have both the product name and the symbol of the product in the report. This functionality is demonstrated in the next section on headers and footers. Basically, to use the image option, you use the context menu for the cell where the image will be inserted. From the context menu, choose the Insert Image option. A small icon will appear in the cell. If you click that icon, and it will disappear and a gray box with the word "Image" will appear. All the other work is done via the Properties tab for this cell. Go to the lower-left section to see the properties of the image. Once you're there, the menu path for inserting the image is available. Just type in the additional file path to direct the system to the Mime Repository and then the specific image. Adjusting the size and position of the image can also be done in the Properties tab of the Report Designer.

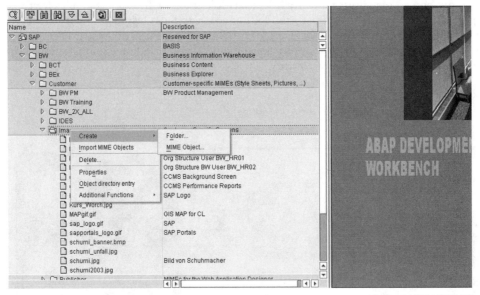

Copyright by SAP AG

Header and Footer Sections

Headers and footers offer additional approaches to increase the professional look and feel of a report. From the Report Designer main menu, use the option Insert | Page Header or Insert | Page Footer. Once you have used one of these options, notice that another section has appeared either above or below the report body. This header and/or footer can be expanded by adding lines or cells. All the options for formatting the text and cells are available, including

- Custom Text
- Images
- Text Fields
- Filter Values
- Query Fields
- Variable Values
- Insert Additional Cells

In addition to inserting a header and footer, you have the ability to insert an additional "section." This allows you to add another Data Provider with other functionality, such as adding another query to the Report Designer format, or simply add additional text and fields.

Field Catalog

From the Field Catalog, you can access any of the objects and text available under the multiple folders. The Field Catalog is where all the elements to drag and drop into the header and footer are stored. In most cases, a report has some type of vital information that needs to be available for the business users to understand what they are looking at and what types of data are available. All these different elements are available in the Field Catalog, including information such as the date of the data refresh, a reminder of the current filter values and variable values, the name of the Data Provider, and other fields. These elements can be inserted into any of the available cells, but are more appropriately positioned either in the header or footer of the report. The best approach to this would be to insert additional fields into the header and footer so that the spacing and formatting can be controlled on an individual basis for these cells and information. The illustration on the right shows the different sections available in the Field Catalog and the different elements available for use in the header and footer sections.

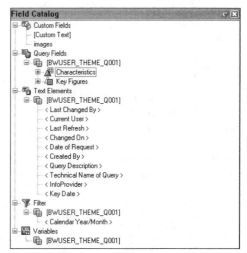

Copyright by SAP AG

Query Fields

The query fields represent all the different characteristics and key figures available in the Data Provider. This means that there is access to every characteristic member description and key as a field. These can be used for numerous sections in the report designer and can also be used in a header or footer. In addition, there is access to every key figure for each member and also the totals of each key figure cumulated to every characteristic. Taking this a step further, you can present the total sales revenue amount in the header of the report before the results have even appeared. It is important to note that restrictions apply to the placement of the individual characteristic members. They can only be placed in a group level of the characteristic. For example, if your report contains Month and Region, you can only place the query fields for Region in the group level for the region. You could not place this in the group level for Month and definitely not in the header and footer sections. The technical reason for this is that the characteristic member and its related key figures are only known at the time of row generation for the group level. All other query fields, such as the final result of the query, can be placed anywhere in the report, including within any group level.

Text Elements
The text elements represent a comprehensive range of informational parameters that can be used to provide the user with useful supporting information about the report. These include items such as date of data refresh, query name, author, and so on. There are no restrictions for the placement of text elements in the report. They can be dragged and dropped anywhere in the Report Designer format to support and add to the information presented.

Filters
The filter fields are used to remind the user of the current filter values applied to the report. This is especially useful if the filters are not obvious (they may be background filters). There are no restrictions for the placement of these filters fields in the report.

Variables
Variable fields are just like filter fields, except they are used to specifically remind the user of the variable values chosen. There are no restrictions for placement of these variable fields in the report.

Custom Fields
Custom fields are automatically generated whenever you create custom text in the report. Every unique custom text that is defined in the report's cells is automatically added to the custom text fields list. These can be reused in any of the other cells in the report via a simple drag-and-drop process.

For an example of this functionality, the previous hierarchy report will be used and enhanced with these different options. The following illustration shows the hierarchy report in the Report Designer with the Page Header and Page Footer options.

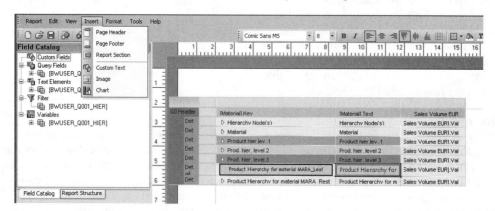

Once the Page Header option is chosen, we use the context menu to identify the option for inserting an image, as shown in the following illustration. Once the image item is assigned to the header field, we double-click it and, as mentioned earlier, the text "image" appears.

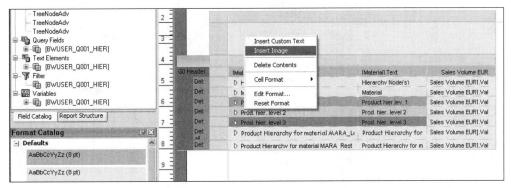

Notice that in the Properties tab, all the different options for inserting the image are available. As you can see, the file path for the Mime Repository is available (sap/bw/mime/ customer/images/...). You can use this to find the appropriate folder to save the images to for use in the Report Designer, as shown in the following illustration.

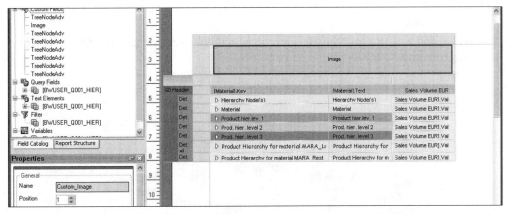

Type the image's technical name (sap_logo.gif), which is available in the Mime Repository, into the filename so that the system can identify the appropriate image to use. Notice that below this field you have the ability to adjust the size of the image. You can choose to "Keep Ratio" and have the width and height stay in the same proportion throughout the process or turn this option off and adjust the size of the image manually, as shown in Figure 10-4.

Once that is complete, we can add another text field to the header to help with information about the report, as shown in the following illustration. This field is used to add a description

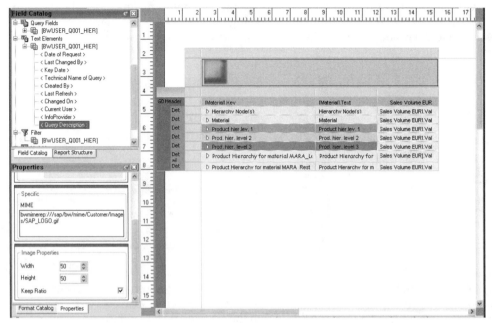

FIGURE 10-4 Options for adjusting the size of the image

of the report, and we can adjust the font and the color of the background. Once this is complete, we turn out attention to the footer.

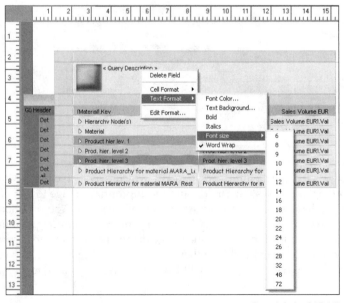

Again we can use the Insert menu to insert the footer into the report, as shown in following illustration. The footer will have additional columns to get some space between the information displayed in the field, which in this case is Created By, Last Refresh, and InfoProvider, as shown in Figure 10-5.

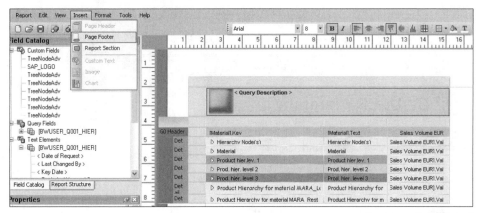

Copyright by SAP AG

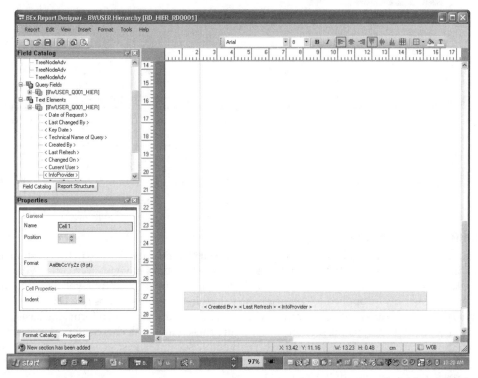

Copyright by SAP AG

Figure 10-5 Display Report Designer Footer with System generated information

Finally, after all these changes, the report is executed and the results are shown in the first of the following illustrations. Notice the image for the logo of SAP and also the enhanced text for the title of the report. In addition, the footer has been inserted, as shown in the second illustration. Notice the use of additional columns to separate the information.

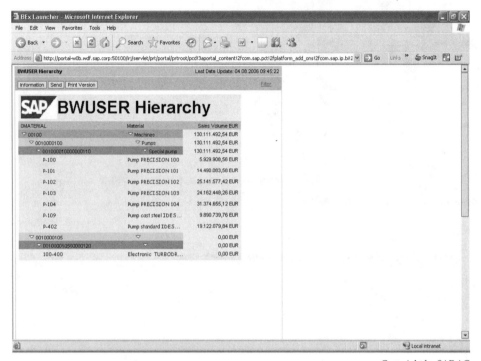

Copyright by SAP AG

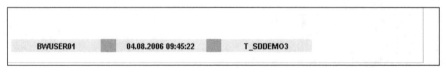

Copyright by SAP AG

Conditional Formatting

Conditional formatting makes it possible to format selected characteristics (such as customer XY) differently. In the executed report, these characteristic values have the formatting you specify and are set apart from the other characteristic values in your group level. Conditional formatting can only be applied to characteristic values in dynamic sections of a Data Provider. A query (or query view) with one or more characteristics in the drilldown forms the basis of a Data Provider with a dynamic section. To configure this component, choose Report | Select Data Provider to select a Data Provider with a dynamic section. The selected Data Provider is automatically embedded in a report section and is displayed together with the associated row patterns in the design area of the Report Designer.

In the design area, select a row in the group level of the characteristic for which you want to apply conditional formatting to its characteristic value(s). Then in the menu bar for the Report Designer, choose Format | Conditional Formatting. Once this has been executed, the BEx input help dialog box appears. In the BEx input help dialog box, select a characteristic value for which you want to create the conditional formatting. In the design area, an additional row is displayed for the selected characteristic value beneath the selected characteristic row. This new row has its own row pattern. Select the new row for the characteristic value and use the formatting functions provided in the menu and toolbars of the Report Designer to apply the required formatting. You can, for example, color the row, left or right align the row, or add borders to the row. Save the report and execute it. This allows you to check the display of your conditional formatting. As an example, we will use the query shown in the following illustration.

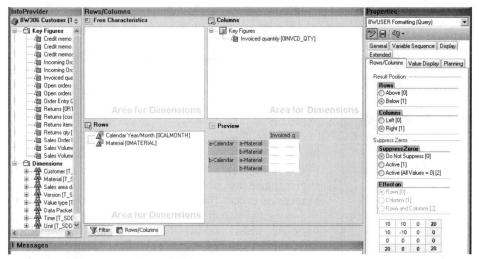

This query has two characteristics (Calendar Year/Month and Material) and one key figure (Invoiced Quantity). This basic query enables us to set up a review of the concept of conditional formatting. Defaulting this query definition into the Report Designer will generate a view of all the elements of the query—including the Material Text. The following illustration shows this view of the information.

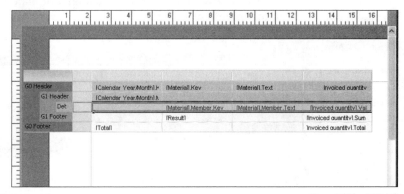

Once the default view of the report is available, use the Format menu to get to the Conditional Formatting option (the last item on the list), as shown in the first of the following illustrations. This causes the interior characteristic Material to appear in the resulting dialog box, as shown in the second illustration.

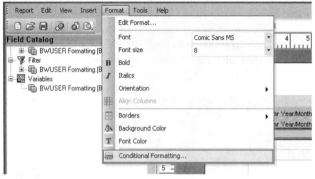

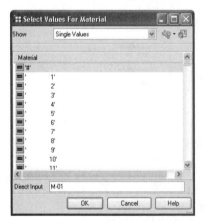

Next, we'll choose a specific value of interest to track or highlight. In this case, we will choose the material number M-01 (Sunny Sunny) for analysis. The following illustration shows the result once the dialog box for the material numbers is exited. The format of the Report Designer area shows the individual material number as a selectable line item. This individual material number is now available for formatting as though it was an actual characteristic or key figure. The illustration on the following page shows the formatting being applied to the material number, and the third illustration shows the results. As you can see, material number M-01 shows up as a highlighted line item for analysis. This is the result of conditional formatting. You can use this to track a specific customer for analysis of a customer agreement or material sales revenue. Instead of having to search for the specific customer or material, you simply highlight it.

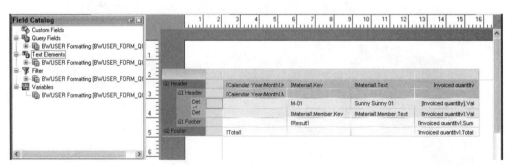

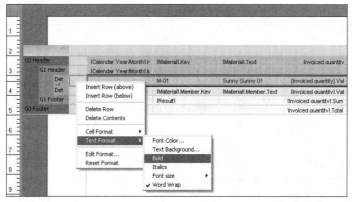

Copyright by SAP AG

Copyright by SAP AG

Use of Themes in the Report Designer

Another feature within the Report Designer is the use of themes for formatting purposes. A theme provides a set of formatting instructions to your report cells. One important point to bear in mind is that the theme formatting supplied by the Report Designer custom settings

Style	Report Designer Area
Standard	Header
SAPBExstdData	Detail
SAPBExaggData	Results

TABLE 10-1 Styles Used in the Report Designer Obtained from the BEx Analyzer

take priority over the default settings supplied by the theme. Themes are supplied by SAP as Business Content objects (themes that start with an zero 0). You can also develop themes yourself in the BEx Analyzer. The workbook styles are passed to the Report Designer via the themes. It is also important to remember that only three of the workbook styles used by the Report Designer, and these are mapped to the areas of the report as shown in Table 10-1.

To create your own customized themes, go to the BEx Analyzer Workbook Settings dialog box, shown in the first of following illustrations. In the workbook, use the Design Item | Workbook Settings option and click the second tab, Themes, to create your own themes to be used in the Report Designer. Notice the four command buttons. To create a theme, click the New button and define a technical name. Then experiment with the different styles to the right, choose those that will be assigned to the theme, and click the Apply button. After you're done, click the Save button. Now, the Report Designer shows the new theme (in this case, BWUSERTHEME01), as shown in the second illustration. This theme can now be applied to the Report Designer report.

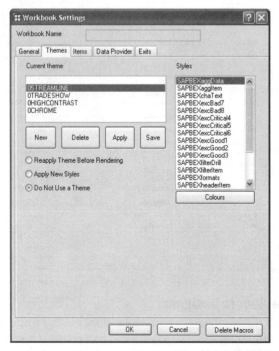

Copyright by SAP AG

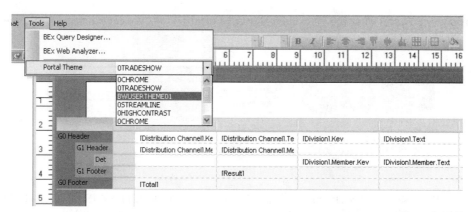

The configuration of themes in the Report Designer is fairly straightforward. The configuration of these themes in the BEx Analyzer workbook, however, can be a bit tricky because the assignment of different styles to themes is manually intense. As an example of this functionality, we'll start by identifying a specific query to use. The following illustration shows the query that will be used for this example.

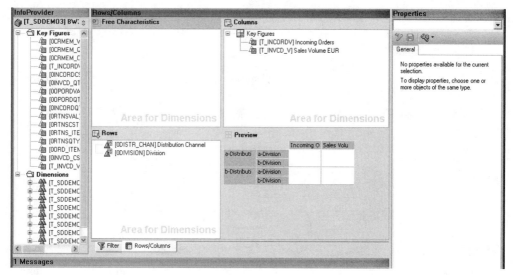

This query has two characteristics and two key figures. We will forgo any changes in formatting and just the review of the use of themes. Once we have identified the query, we'll use the Insert Data Provider option to display all the query elements in the design area, as shown in the following illustration. This illustration also shows the location of the themes we can use. Using the menu item Tools | Portal Theme, we can identify the theme to be used.

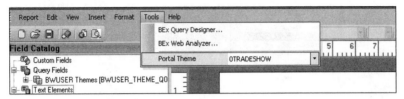

Note that a series of SBC themes is available: 0TRADESHOW, 0CHROME, 0STREAMLINE, and 0HIGHCONTRAST. The theme 0TRADESHOW is used for the report displayed in the first of the following illustrations. Next we'll execute the report using the theme 0HIGHCONTRAST. The second illustration shows the differences between the header information, the results, and the detail sections.

Address http://portal-w0b.wdf.sap.corp:50100/irj/servlet/prt/portal/prtroot/pcd!3aportal_content!2fcom.sap.pct!2fplatform_add_ons!2fcom.sap.ip.bi!2...

BWUSER Themes　　　　　　　　　　　　　　　　　　　　　　Last Data Update: 04.08.2006 09:45:22

Information | Send | Print Version　　　　　　　　　　　　　　　　　　　　　　Filter

0DISTR_CHAN	Distribution Channel	0DIVISION	Division	Incoming Orders	Sales Volume EUR
10	Final customer sales				
		00	Cross-division	28.788,26 EUR	3.023,08 EUR
		01	Pumps	19.731.587,80 EUR	15.512.112,40 EUR
		07	High Tech	10.778.271,72 EUR	10.310.549,95 EUR
		20	Turbines	0,00 EUR	344.000,00 EUR
	Result			30.538.647,78 EUR	26.169.685,43 EUR
12	Sold for resale				
		02	Motorcycles	15.429.350,93 EUR	15.429.350,93 EUR
		04	Lighting	15.376.585,35 EUR	16.999.417,87 EUR
		07	High Tech	13.500.612,48 EUR	13.500.612,48 EUR
	Result			44.306.548,76 EUR	45.929.381,28 EUR
14	Service				
		00	Cross-division	0,00 EUR	1.687,26 EUR
		08	Service	0,00 EUR	4.160,82 EUR
	Result			0,00 EUR	5.848,08 EUR
R1	GM store				
		R1	Retail	0,00 EUR	6.499.251,94 EUR
	Result			0,00 EUR	6.499.251,94 EUR
S3	Services				
		S3	Services	1.826.392,37 EUR	0,00 EUR
	Result			1.826.392,37 EUR	0,00 EUR
Overall Result				76.671.588,91 EUR	78.604.166,73 EUR

As a final note, in the Report Designer's printing functionality is very user friendly and defaults directly to the Adobe PDF format. The printing component for the BEx Analyzer was discussed in Chapter 4, the printing for the Information Broadcaster will be discussed in Chapter 12 and the BEx Web Analyzer, and WAD will be discussed in Chapter 15. The following illustration shows the view of a printed Report Designer report.

Using All the Functionality of the Report Designer

With all of the new functionality for use when formatting your reports or accessing any of the other options such as printing in either the BEx Web Analyzer and the Web Application Designer (we will review the WAD in more detail in the Chapter 15), its very important to understand when to use the Report Designer's toolset and when not to and in turn go directly to the WAD to format your report. In terms of different situations where you would look to use the Report Designer component for formatting one always comes to mind. During a number of projects I have been involved in, requests for these formatted types of reports came from the finance team, and in some cases a "report book" needed to be generated for the corporate headquarters. In some countries, such as Japan, the government requires a specific set of reports in a specific series in a book to be submitted for review. This was difficult to do with BW before, but with the Report Designer this task can be set up just once and then generated on a monthly basis. The Information Broadcaster can be used for distribution over the Web, and the Adobe printing functionality can be used to create the actual "accounting book" for period-end analysis. With this in mind, we will develop a full example by setting up a Balance Sheet report for a corporation using a basic query from BW and the Report Designer.

The first of the following illustrations shows the basic query that will be used for this example. As you can see, the Balance Sheet accounts are listed as a long line of GL accounts and are not in the format we are used to seeing them in (which would be side by side). The second illustration shows the remaining accounts at the bottom of the list for reporting purposes using the basic BEx Analyzer process.

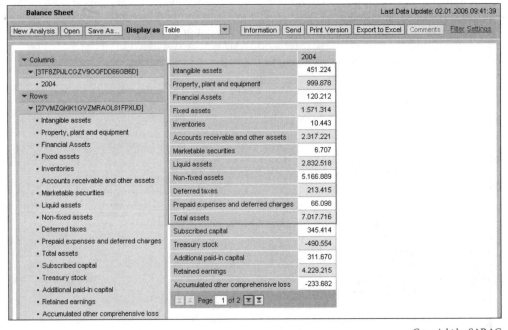

Copyright by SAP AG

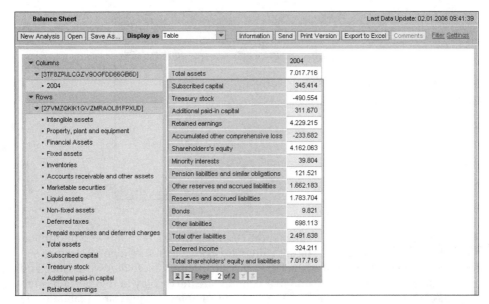

Now, we'll move to the Report Designer to enhance the formatting and functionality of this Balance Sheet statement. The first of the following illustrations shows the initial screen of the Report Designer and the Insert Data Provider button. Clicking this button opens the dialog box to choose the query or query view, as shown in the second illustration. We will choose the Balance Sheet report.

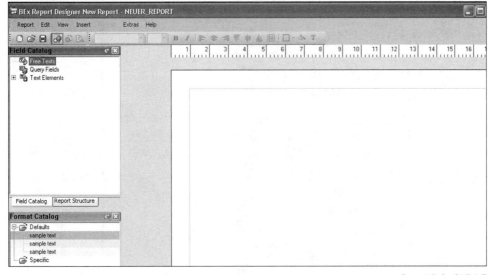

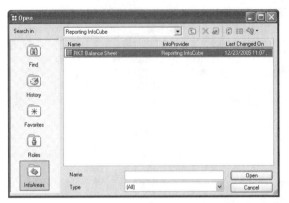

Once this query is inserted into the Report Designer, the GL accounts and information such as the text and the actual key figure values are available in the Report Designer's design area, as shown in the first of the following illustrations. Note that we are also adding columns to the right of the last column to accommodate the display of two portions of the Balance Sheet statement side by side—Assets and Stockholders Equity and Liabilities. The second illustration shows the final addition of the columns required to build this report. Now we will drag and drop the GL accounts from the left side of the query to the right side of the Report Designer design area so that we can format the GL accounts in the appropriate display, as shown in the third illustration.

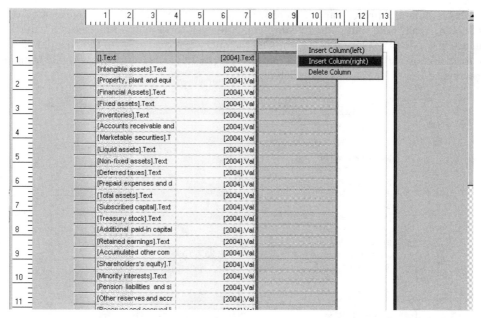

Copyright by SAP AG

Copyright by SAP AG

This is a manual process, and if there are a number of GL accounts to move around on the screen, it may take some time to complete. However, this is a one-time setup for the Balance Sheet display. Once this is complete, the query is refreshed with the new data and the formatted report will reflect the amounts appropriately. The following two illustrations show the additional steps to accomplish this task.

[].Text	[2004].Text	
[Intangible assets].Text	[2004].Val	[Subscribed capital].Text
[Property, plant and equi	[2004].Val	
[Financial Assets].Text	[2004].Val	
[Fixed assets].Text	[2004].Val	
[Inventories].Text	[2004].Val	
[Accounts receivable and	[2004].Val	
[Marketable securities].T	[2004].Val	
[Liquid assets].Text	[2004].Val	
[Non-fixed assets].Text	[2004].Val	
[Deferred taxes].Text	[2004].Val	
[Prepaid expenses and d	[2004].Val	
[Total assets].Text	[2004].Val	
	[2004].Val	
[Treasury stock].Text	[2004].Val	
[Additional paid-in capital	[2004].Val	
[Retained earnings].Text	[2004].Val	
[Accumulated other com	[2004].Val	
[Shareholders's equity].T	[2004].Val	

[].Text	[2004].Text		
[Intangible assets].Text	[2004].Val	[Subscribed capital].Text	[2004].Val
[Property, plant and equi	[2004].Val		
[Financial Assets].Text	[2004].Val		
[Fixed assets].Text	[2004].Val		
[Inventories].Text	[2004].Val		
[Accounts receivable and	[2004].Val		
[Marketable securities].T	[2004].Val		
[Liquid assets].Text	[2004].Val		
[Non-fixed assets].Text	[2004].Val		
[Deferred taxes].Text	[2004].Val		
[Prepaid expenses and d	[2004].Val		
[Total assets].Text	[2004].Val		
[Treasury stock].Text	[2004].Val		
[Additional paid-in capital	[2004].Val		
[Retained earnings].Text	[2004].Val		
[Accumulated other com	[2004].Val		
[Shareholders's equity].T	[2004].Val		
[Minority interests].Text	[2004].Val		

Next we'll move the Total lines to set up the alignment of the totals for the assets and liabilities. The first two of the following illustrations show the movement of the cells, which are lined up directly across from each other. The actual report is coming along nicely, and in the third illustration you can see how this report is being to resemble a normal Balance Sheet report that would be submitted to shareholders and stakeholders for review.

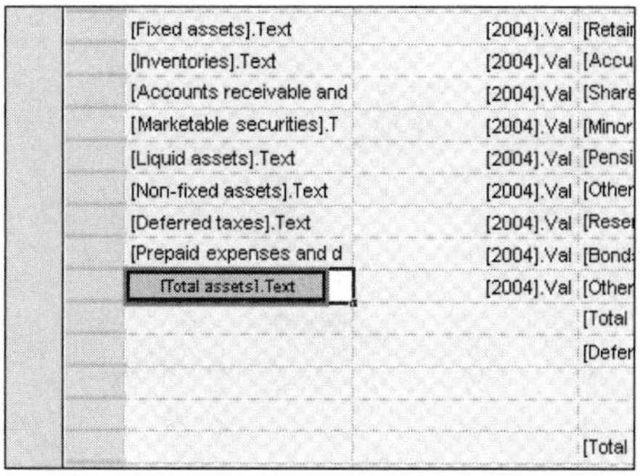

Copyright by SAP AG

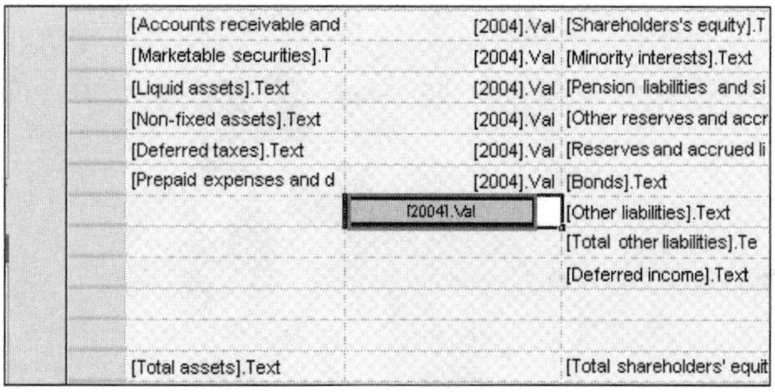

Copyright by SAP AG

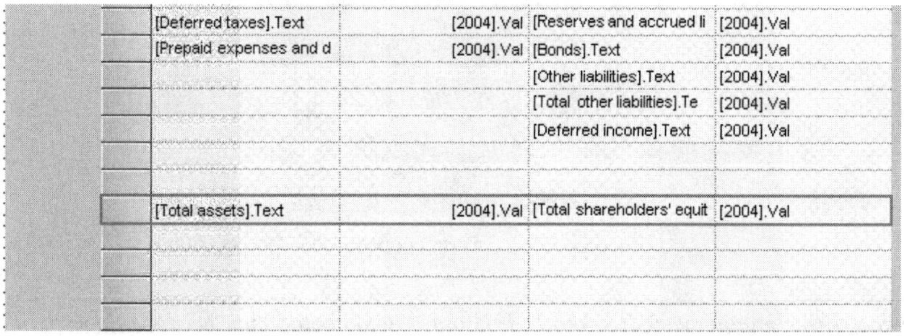

Copyright by SAP AG

Although a number of options still need to be completed, the initial format is visible. Because in many cases this final report will be printed, the format of the print settings is in order. The first of the following illustrations shows the location of the Report | Page Setup option, which opens the Page Setup dialog box. We can use it to configure the margins, height, width, and the view of the report. The second illustration shows the settings in this dialog box.

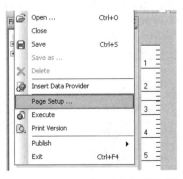

Copyright by SAP AG

Copyright by SAP AG

NOTE *Be sure to save your work frequently if you are new to this tool, because there may be a time when a particular indicator or option is executed but doesn't work like you expected and all your work will be lost. As a rule of thumb, save often when you feel the work you've completed is consistent with the expected outcome.*

Now we will begin the process of setting up the headers and titles for the columns. As shown in the following two illustrations, we are going to "delete" the current text in the cell and change it to "Assets."

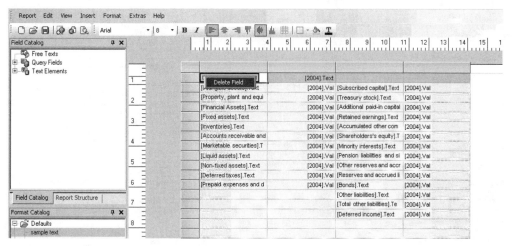

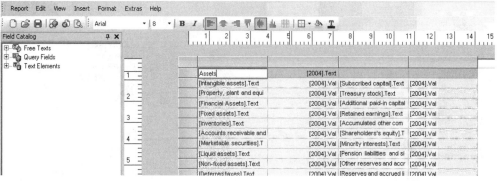

The same approach is taken for "Stockholders Equity and Liabilities." The first of following illustrations shows the final result of the adjustments made with the formatting options for the font, background color, and size of the headings of the columns. As you can see, the report is starting to take shape and looks like something that can be published to the all the appropriate stakeholders of the corporation. The second illustration shows the addition of highlights to the total lines for the subtotals of Assets and Liabilities.

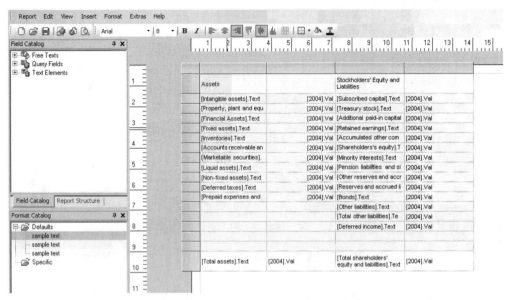

Now, we will realign the columns and add a separator column between Assets and Stockholder Equity and Liabilities. The following illustration shows the end result. To some, this process may not seem that exciting, but for anyone who has been working in BW for the past several years, this one example sums up many different formatting requests from a typical corporate headquarters.

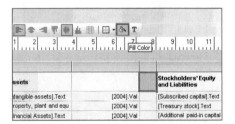

Now, additional work needs to be done on the borders of the headings and also of the report itself. The following two illustrations show the use of the Borders option on the report toolbar. To accomplish this, highlight the cells that are to have borders and use the options either from the toolbar or from the menu Format | Borders to complete this task.

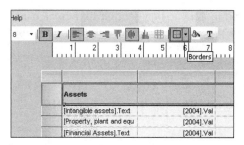

Copyright by SAP AG

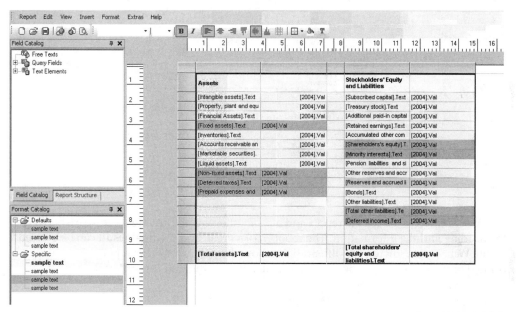

Copyright by SAP AG

By double-clicking the column separator, the columns will automatically "fit" the information in the column. The following illustration shows the results of this activity. Once this is accomplished, the actual report is very close to being completed.

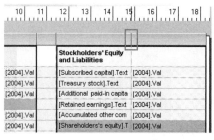

Copyright by SAP AG

The use of a header and footer can be very helpful here. An additional section for the header to show text will be placed here, as shown in the following two illustrations.

Copyright by SAP AG

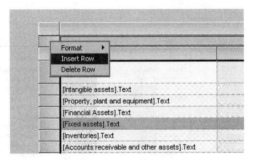

Copyright by SAP AG

We've added a title for the report and also another line to provide some space between the heading and the information. The report looks great, and the final result can be viewed on the Web. The following two illustrations show the end result. This report can now be printed or viewed either in the BEx Web Analyzer or in the Enterprise Portal.

Copyright by SAP AG

Balance Sheet		Last Data Update: 02.01.2006 09:41:39

Information Send Print Version   Filter

2004 Balance Sheet

Assets		Stockholders' Equity and Liabilities	
Intangible assets	451.224	Subscribed capital	345.414
Property, plant and equipment	999.878	Treasury stock	-490.554
Financial Assets	120.212	Additional paid-in capital	311.670
Fixed assets	1.571.314	Retained earnings	4.229.215
Inventories	10.443	Accumulated other comprehensive loss	-233.682
Accounts receivable and other assets	2.317.221	Shareholders's equity	4.162.063
Marketable securities	6.707	Minority interests	39.804
Liquid assets	2.832.518	Pension liabilities and similar obligations	121.521
Non-fixed assets	5.166.889	Other reserves and accrued liabilities	1.662.183
Deferred taxes	213.415	Reserves and accrued liabilities	1.783.704
Prepaid expenses and deferred charges	66.098	Bonds	9.821
		Other liabilities	698.113
		Total other liabilities	2.491.638
		Deferred income	324.211
Total assets	**7.017.716**	**Total shareholders' equity and liabilities**	**7.017.716**

Summary

This chapter completes the review of the configuration and functionality of the Report Designer. This is an invaluable tool in the process of achieving the correct format and view of report data for the business user. Projects often fail due to reports and queries being incorrectly formatted. Therefore, another toolset may be required to get the formatting correct for each level of management. The Report Designer solves many of these issues, and with a little work can be quite easy to format and configure. To see what additional enhancements can be accomplished with the Report Designer, you can take the basic queries you use and add small changes to them and add some bells and whistles for your reports. Most likely, after you start this process someone will notice the formatting changes and start asking for additional enhancements to their reports.

Spreading the Word—
The Information Broadcaster

Now we turn our attention to the component of the BW system we use for distributing data and information. Although it's important we make sure that all the information is consistent and reliable and that we have the proper format set up and the uploading processes are all working correctly, if the information can't get to the appropriate people in the corporation, it's worthless. Therefore, back-end configuration and maintenance, front-end reporting tools and formatting, and finally the methods available for distributing the data must all work together to get the job done. The Information Broadcaster is the component within BW that allows for the distribution of information using multiple methods to any of the different groups and levels of business users required to receive the information. We will highlight the basic Information Broadcaster process in this chapter and will follow up this discussion in a later chapter with an in-depth analysis of the configuration of enhancements within the Information Broadcaster. This chapter provides an overview of the functionality and the basic setup of the Information Broadcaster via the different avenues available. It ends with some additional functionality concerning the distribution of precalculated workbooks.

Introduction to the Information Broadcaster

Information broadcasting is a flexible function of the Business Explorer that provides the ability to distribute reporting results to various audiences, whether or not they are regular SAP BI users or have the ability to access SAP systems. It allows you to make objects within Business Intelligence content available to a wide spectrum of users, according to your own requirements. It also offers functions for optimizing performance and for exception reporting. Broadcasting is not restricted to one method. You can choose the source of the data, the format of the data, the target audience, the broadcast channel, and the timing of the broadcast. Broadcasting can be defined as a one-time distribution or it can be set to distribute result data on a regular basis at predetermined times. The data can be precalculated, or the broadcast can send a link to the online data. If required, the Broadcasting Wizard is available to step you through the process of setting up for the Information Broadcaster. As always the Broadcasting Wizard is a short cut step-by-step process for setting up the Information Broadcaster but remember that in most cases, and in this case, the Wizard doesn't have all of the flexibility that the normal process might offer.

Information broadcasting is a component of the IT scenario Enterprise Reporting, Query, and Analysis. The documentation on information broadcasting is structured according the requirements of users so that you are provided with role-specific guides to support you in performing tasks. The following illustration shows the positioning of the Information Broadcaster in the architecture of the BEx Suite. It is a part of the entire reporting strategy.

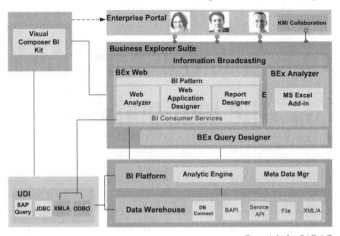

The Broadcaster can offer help and play a critical role in many different scenarios. Broadcasting can be executed as a one-time event, a regularly scheduled event, or used just to alert personnel of any critical situation that may be in need of attention. The uses of the Broadcaster are as many as you want or need. They can be used as updates on queries, as exceptions sent so that the business users only get e-mails about top customers or top product sales or costs, or as portions of a larger query that can be partitioned and then sent to the different users. The following illustration shows some of the newest functionality of the Information Broadcaster.

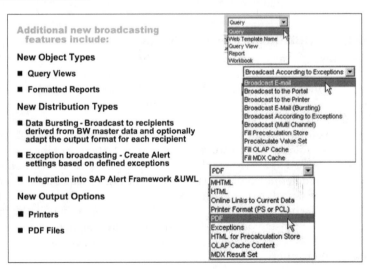

With the BEx Broadcaster, you can precalculate queries, query views, Web templates, reports, and workbooks and broadcast them by e-mail or to the Portal. In addition to the precalculated documents in various formats (HTML, MHTML, ZIP, and so on) that contain historical data, you can also generate online links to the information using the Information Broadcaster. Further broadcast options and functions, specially customized for system administrations, are available. These include the generation of alerts, master-data-based broadcasts via e-mail (bursting), broadcasting in multiple formats with various channels, and precalculation of objects for performance optimization. In many cases depending on the nature of the distribution method these options can be more or less flexible. We will discuss each individually, in detail, a bit later in this chapter.

The basic approach to using the BEx Information Broadcaster (which is a fully web-based tool) is through the Portal or through the BEx Web Analyzer. In the Portal, the ideal way of accessing Business Intelligence information is through a central entry page (for example, BEx Portfolio). This shows the content of the Knowledge Management folder where you published the content. The Broadcasting layout profile displays content especially tailored to the needs of users who work with Business Intelligence content in the Portal. The Business Explorer Portal role illustrates the various options available to you when working with content from BI in the Portal. Once the system has been set up for the Broadcaster you have the ability to access the Portal, and use the full functionality of the Knowledge Management system. This allows the Broadcaster to be used as a strategic tool for feedback information, discussions, ratings, subscriptions, searches, downloads, and collaboration. The following illustration shows some of the functionality of the KM system with the integration to the Information Broadcaster. KM services can be used on any document attached to BI data. The document's physical storage location can be either with the BI server or the CM repository. The repository manager for BI documents and the CM repository manager gives access to documents attached to BI metadata, master data, and transactional data, assuming that the documents are stored in the respective repository.

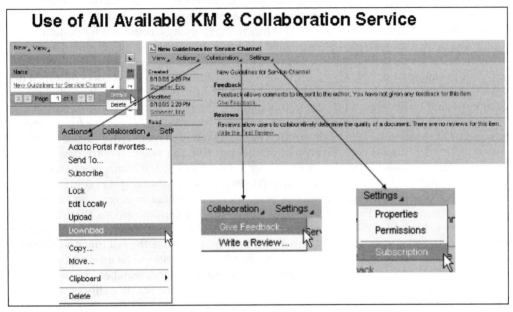

Configuring the System for Information Broadcasting

To use information broadcasting, you must first configure the system in various SAP NetWeaver areas. You have installed the necessary components for information broadcasting. These processes and activities will probably be the responsibility of the NW Basis person at your company or for your project. In any case, we will highlight them so that you are aware of the initial steps to go through before the Information Broadcaster can be used in the different areas of NW. If you want to distribute content from Business Intelligence to the Portal, follow the configuration steps for integrating content from BI to the Portal. This can be found in the Implementation Guide (transaction code SPRO) under SAP Reference IMG | SAP Customizing Implementation Guide | SAP NetWeaver | Business Intelligence | Settings for Reporting and Analysis | Settings for Information Broadcasting | Settings for Integration into the Portal. The following illustration shows the result of accessing this menu path.

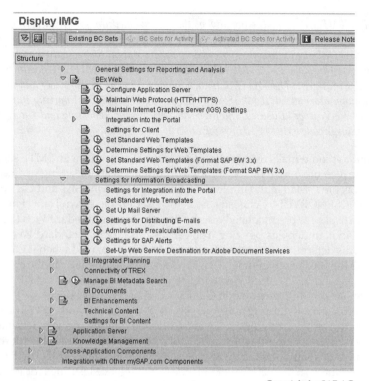

Copyright by SAP AG

If users in the Portal want to use the content from BI to hold discussions, add personal notes, or provide feedback, the corresponding Collaboration Services connected with the Knowledge Management Services can be activated and configured. A number of these settings can also be found in the same location in the IMG as the settings for the Information Broadcaster, just two nodes below. If you want to allow users in the Portal to subscribe to KM folders or individual documents, you can activate and configure the subscription service.

If you want to be able to distribute Business Intelligence content by e-mail, set up the mail server on the application server. Choose node SMTP (Simple Mail Transfer Protocol) under SAPConnect: Administration (transaction SCOT). For more information, see the SAP Reference IMG | SAP Customizing Implementation | SAP NetWeaver | Business Intelligence | Settings for Reporting and Analysis | Settings for Information Broadcasting | Set Up Mail Server. To broadcast by e-mail, you make general settings under Customizing. For example, you define the retention period in days to specify how long send requests are saved after e-mails are sent using broadcasting. You can also specify whether you want to insert a footer into sent e-mails. For more information, see the SAP Reference IMG | SAP Customizing Implementation Guide | SAP NetWeaver | Business Intelligence | Settings for Reporting and Analysis | Settings for Information Broadcasting | Settings for Distributing E-Mails. When documents are broadcast in MHTML format by e-mail, you can make a setting under Customizing to specify that documents in MHTML format are to be sent as attachments when they are broadcast by e-mail.

Note *E-mail in MHTML format is not always the optimal medium for broadcasting content from BI. This is the case, for example, if the recipients' e-mail clients do not fully support the display of MHTML. MHTML is not directly displayed as e-mail content for security reasons. Via the Customizing setting, when MHTML is broadcast by e-mail, the MHTML document is broadcast as an e-mail attachment. The MHTML is then displayed in the web browser and not in the e-mail client. For more information, see the SAP Reference IMG | SAP Customizing Implementation Guide | SAP NetWeaver | Business Intelligence | Settings for Reporting and Analysis | Settings for Information Broadcasting | Settings for Distributing E-Mails.*

If you want to send e-mails using encryption and a signature via an SMTP server, you must first set up a secure e-mail proxy. For more information about setting up and activating this proxy, see Secure E-Mail in the Implementation Guide. Set the SET and GET parameters BCSSIGN and BCSENCRYPT by choosing System | User Profile | Own Data | Parameters. You can modify the display of precalculated queries by defining the standard Web template for query precalculation under Customizing. You can also specify the standard Web template for broadcasting. This determines how the BEx Broadcaster is displayed when it is called from various areas of the Business Explorer. We will review this setting later in the chapter. You specify the corresponding standard Web templates in the BI system under SAP Reference IMG | SAP Customizing Implementation Guides | SAP NetWeaver | Business Intelligence | Settings for Reporting and Analysis | BEx Web | Set Standard Web Templates.

If you want to precalculate workbooks in addition to queries and Web templates, under Customizing you need to specify which precalculation servers are available for the BI system. You make this setting in the BI system under SAP Reference IMG | SAP Customizing Implementation Guide | SAP NetWeaver | Business Intelligence | Settings for Reporting and Analysis | Settings for Information Broadcasting | Administrate Precalculation Server. This discussion is expanded on in the next chapter.

To create PDF files, you must first configure Adobe document services. This is a requirement and the use of additional parameter settings to avoid the Adobe Document Services is not available. To generate and distribute alerts, you have to set up the Alert Framework and execute the following tasks: You define alert categories in the transaction ALRTCATDEF. You select the recipient of the SAP alert. You also maintain the alert container as required. The alert container ensures the exchange between the BI variables and the variables in the central alert server. This procedure is discussed in Chapter 12.

With exception-specific broadcasting, you can specify a Cascading Style Sheet under Customizing. This is used when output is generated in HTML format. The specification is a path in the Mime Repository (for example, /SAP/BW/BEx/StyleSheets/BWReports_ie5.css).

If you do not specify a style sheet, the system uses the standard style sheet /SAP/BW/BEx/StyleSheets/BWReports_ie6.css. You make this setting in the BI system under SAP Reference IMG | SAP Customizing Implementation Guide | SAP NetWeaver | Business Intelligence | Settings for Reporting and Analysis | Settings for Information Broadcasting | Settings for Distributing E-Mails.

You also can assign administrator authorizations for broadcasting. To do this, use authorization object S_RS_ADMWB with the field RSADMWBOBJ = BR_SETTING. After all this setup, you finally have the systems configured according to your needs and can now use information broadcasting. To allow end users in your organization to use the scenarios they require, set up the necessary authorizations in system administration and perform the administrative tasks.

As mentioned, some of these activities (such as the alert process and the exception process) will be discussed in more detail in the following chapter. And as also mentioned earlier, much of this should be the responsibility of the NW Basis person. Check with that person before making any changes or assignments of parameters.

Accessing the Information Broadcaster

The BEx Information Broadcaster can be accessed from a number of the BEx reporting tools. The Broadcaster can also be accessed via the Portal through the delivered BI role. The report developer can create the Broadcaster settings and insert them into BI reports during the development phase. The report user can also create broadcast settings during the runtime of the query or workbook, as needed. There are some minor differences among the reporting tools as to the access of the Information Broadcaster, but all connect to the same server and ultimately look the same after about two steps. As a review, you access the Information Broadcaster from the BEx Query Designer by going to Query | Publish | BEx Broadcaster. The first of the following illustrations shows this view of the menu. Once this option is executed, the system offers a web-based screen for the user to log on to, and then the Information Broadcaster is available, as shown in the second illustration.

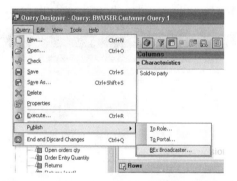

Copyright by SAP AG

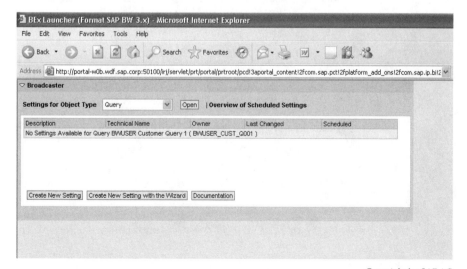

Copyright by SAP AG

From the BEx Analyzer, the Information Broadcaster is accessed via the menu path Tools | BEx Broadcaster, as shown next.

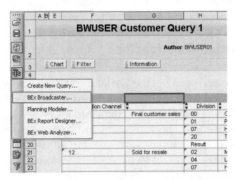

Copyright by SAP AG

From the BEx Web Analyzer, access is via the Send button or the context menu for any selection on the query. Using Broadcast and Export, choose the method you want to use for broadcasting. The following two illustrations show the results of these activities.

Copyright by SAP AG

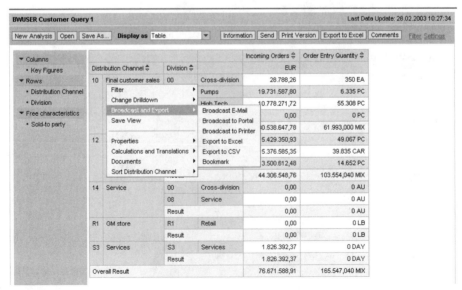

Copyright by SAP AG

From the Web Application Designer, access is via the menu Web Template | Publish | BEx Broadcaster, as shown next.

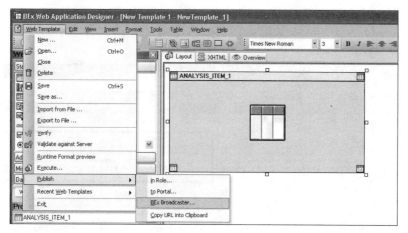

Copyright by SAP AG

Access using the BEx Report Designer is via the menu Report | Publish | BEx Broadcaster, as shown next.

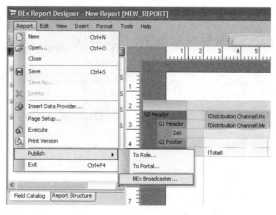

Copyright by SAP AG

Finally, the ability to access this component from the Portal is very direct. From the initial screen, use the link to the BEx Broadcaster. The following illustrations show this process.

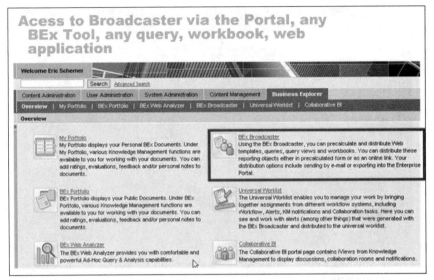

Copyright by SAP AG

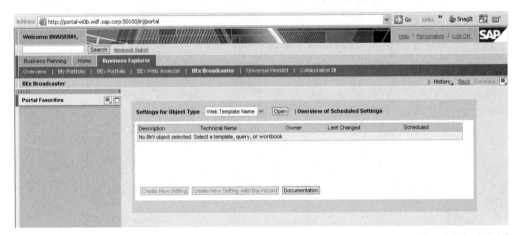

Copyright by SAP AG

Setup and Functionality of the Information Broadcaster

Now that access to the Information Broadcaster has been obtained, we will discuss the different parameters required during the setup of the Information Broadcaster. The initial decision before filling in the parameters is to indicate the Settings for Object Type. This is the source of data for the Information Broadcaster to use for the execution of data. The options are

- Query
- Query View

- Report
- Workbook
- Web Template Name

We have discussed each of these except for Web Template Name, which is a more formatted approach to creating and executing a web-based query. This name is assigned once you save your Web template created in the WAD. The first of the following illustrations shows this initial screen. If you have accessed the Information Broadcaster via a specific query, you can immediately use the query settings. However, if you need use another query, you need to click the Open button (to the left of the object field) to access the dialog box for queries, query views, or any of the other object types. The second illustration shows the result of using the Open button and accessing the Query option. This dialog box is used in all the components of the BEx front end.

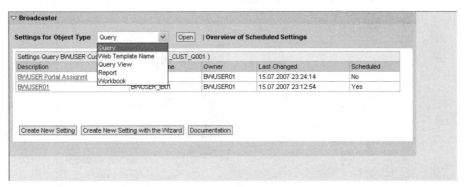

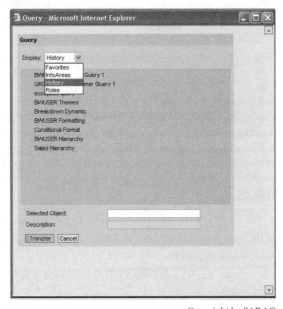

Distribution Types

The next most important setting is Distribution Type. The distribution type identifies the basic methodology used to distribute the information to the business users. The distribution types listed allow users to perform administrative tasks and are therefore only available to users with the appropriate authorization. We will not be reviewing the authorizations process for the Information Broadcaster but it is important to make sure that your Business Users that have authorizations to create the necessary settings are well aware of the process and the distribution methods. . This area will probably be very highly controlled, and it is much better that you review the authorizations with your Securities or Basis person before setting up the Information Broadcaster. The distribution types are detailed next. Depending on the distribution type you choose, the output format will change to suite the type. The output format for a few of the distribution types will be displayed in this section. The following illustration shows the different distribution types with additional information about the output format of some of the types.

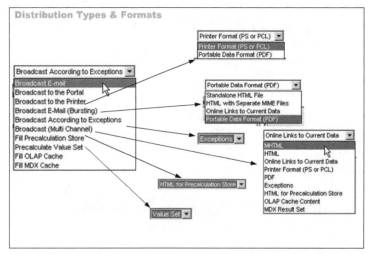

Broadcast E-mail   One of the more popular approaches is broadcasting by e-mail which distributes the BI objects (queries, query views, Web templates, reports, or workbooks). You selected Broadcast by E-mail as the distribution type when you created the broadcast setting. You can send the results of a report or a link for the online report. Your system administrator maintains the possible recipients as communication type E-Mail in user maintenance and enters the e-mail addresses. To broadcast by e-mail, make the following settings on the tabbed pages:

- **Recipients tab**   You can specify recipients using the following settings:
  - **User**   Enter the BI usernames of the recipients manually or choose F4 with the quick info text Selection; usernames must be separated by semicolons.
  - **Users in Role**   Enter the BI roles manually or choose F4 with the quick info text Selection; roles must be separated by semicolons. The e-mail is sent to all users assigned to one of the roles specified here.

NOTE *If an e-mail address for a user you have specified under User or User in Role has not been maintained in user maintenance, the user does not receive the distributed file as an e-mail. Instead, the user receives a message in the Business Workplace (transaction SO01).*

- **E-Mail Addresses** Enter the e-mail addresses of the recipients, separated by semicolons. In order for you to send e-mails to a distribution list, the distribution list must be recognized with a valid e-mail address (SMTP address) on the SMTP server. The e-mail can be sent to the distribution list as soon as the e-mail address has been specified under E-Mail Addresses in the broadcast setting. The SMTP server uses the sender's SMTP address to check whether the sender is authorized to send to the distribution list. In broadcasting, the Internet mail address specified in the user master data is used as the sender's SMTP address.

  For example, your Microsoft Outlook address book contains the global distribution list DL EMPLOYEES. In the properties of the distribution list, the SMTP address is DL_XXXX_EMPLOYEES@exchange.*myCompany*.com. If you specify this SMTP address as the e-mail address in the broadcast setting, the system sends the e-mail to all recipients on the distribution list. E-mails sent using an SMTP server can be signed, encrypted, or both. You must also specify the user settings for the default values for encryption and the use of signatures.

- **Authorization User** If you schedule the broadcast setting for background processing (for example, for a specific time), you can enter a BI username manually or choose F4 with the quick info text Selection. The system generates the document with the settings (for example, date format) and authorizations of the specified user. If you want to distribute the broadcast setting immediately, the system generates the document using the authorizations and settings for the current user who is logged on to the system and is defining the broadcast setting.

- **Language** If you schedule the broadcast setting for background processing (for example, for a specific time), you can select the language in which the document is to be generated. The system displays the languages that are installed on the BI system.

- **User Specific** If you schedule the broadcast setting for background processing, you can specify the document to be "user specific." The system generates the document for each of the specified recipients, using their personal settings (date format, language) and data authorizations. Recipients specified with e-mail addresses only are not included. For these recipients, the system generates the document using the settings for the authorization user. If you want to distribute the broadcast setting immediately, the system generates the document using the settings for the current user.

- **Texts tab** You can specify values for the following settings:

  - **Subject** Enter a subject line for the e-mail manually or use a text variable from F4 Attach Text Variable. The text can contain up to 50 characters.

  - **Importance** Select the importance level for the e-mail (low, medium, or high).

  - **Contents** Enter text for the contents of the e-mail manually or use a text variable by choosing F4 with the quick info text Attach Text Variable. When online links are sent, the system automatically adds a link to the text of the e-mail (if the text does not contain the link) using the PR_ONLINE_LINK variable. This offers the ability to send a static link to the business user with the option to have another link with the refreshed data available.

You can also make settings on the Filter Navigation, General Precalculation, General Link Generation, Layout, and Header/Footer tabbed pages. The tabbed pages are context sensitive and are displayed depending on the selected output format. The following illustrations show the results of each of the data entries discussed previously.

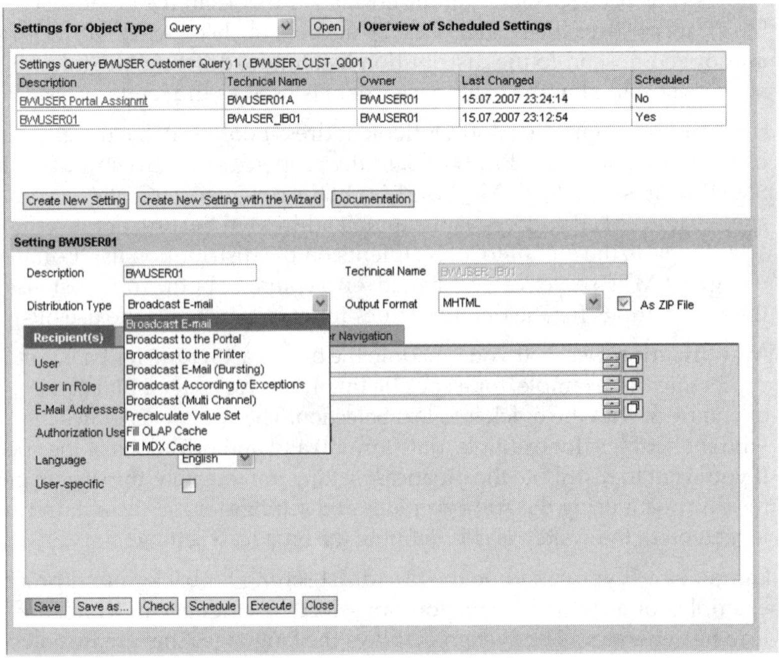

Copyright by SAP AG

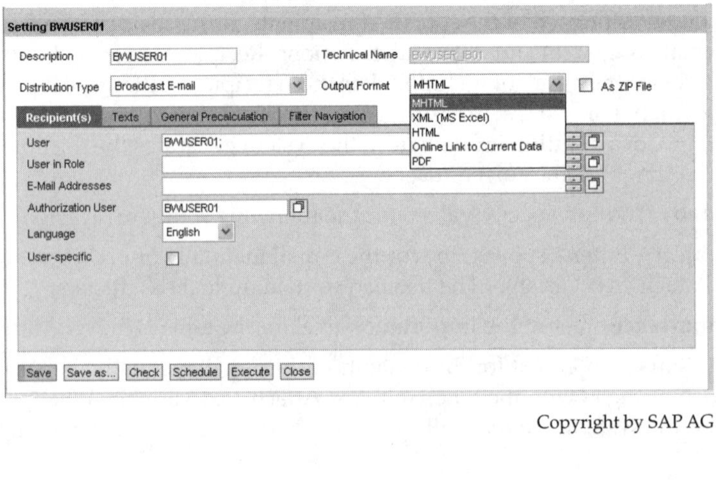

Copyright by SAP AG

Broadcast to the Portal   Broadcasting to the Portal is one way you can distribute BI objects (queries, query views, Web templates, reports, or workbooks). You can put the precalculated documents or online links in a collaboration room or in a KM folder. The Personal Documents and Public Documents KM folders are particularly useful. If you have assigned the Business Explorer role in the Portal, you can access these folders from the My Portfolio and BEx Portfolio iViews. You can use various Knowledge Management functions when you work with documents on the Portal. You can add ratings, evaluations, feedback, or personal notes to documents. If you use the collaboration functions, you can use the precalculated documents or online links to hold discussions with colleagues or work with them in collaboration rooms. Using subscriptions, you can automatically be notified of any changes to a document. To execute this option, you select Broadcast to Portal as the distribution type when you create the broadcast setting.

For the export to the Portal, you make these settings on the following tabbed pages:

- **Target in Portal tab**   You can choose from the following options:
  - **File Name**   Enter the technical name under which the document is to be saved—either manually or using a text variable (by choosing F4 with the quick info text Attach Text Variable).
  - **Authorization User**   If you schedule the broadcast setting for background processing, you can enter a BI username manually or choose F4 with the quick info text Selection. The system generates the document with the settings (for example, date format) and authorizations of the specified user.

NOTE   *If you want to distribute the broadcast setting immediately, the system generates the document using the authorizations and settings for the current user who is logged on to the system and who defined the broadcast setting.*

- **Language**   If you schedule the broadcast setting for background processing , you can select the language in which the document is to be generated. The system displays the languages that are installed for the BI system.
- **Export Document To**   You can store the document in the personal portfolio for selected users or in any other KM folder.
- **My Portfolio**   Enter the BI usernames of the recipients, separated with semicolons, by choosing with the quick info text Selection. The document is stored in the users' personal portfolios. If you schedule the broadcast setting for background processing, for example using a specific time, then you can specify the document to be "user specific." The system generates the document for each of the specified recipients, using their personal settings (date format, language) and data authorizations. This will allow you to distribute the information to multiple users at one time.
- **Other Folder**   Enter the KM folder in which the document is stored in the Portal by choosing F4 with the quick info text Selection. The input help is an iView that displays My Portfolio, CM Repository View, and the Collaboration Room views. With My Portfolio, the system generates a link in Knowledge Management

under the user's personal folder. With CM Repository View, the system generates a link in the KM folder of your choice. The rooms assigned to a user are displayed under Collaboration Room. The system generates a link in Knowledge Management under the selected collaboration room.

NOTE *Your system administrator must set up KM folders and collaboration rooms in the Portal so that you can choose these as the target from the input help.*

- **Texts tab** You can specify values for the following options:
  - **Display Name** Enter the name manually or use a text variable (by choosing F4 with the quick info text Attach Text Variable). The document is displayed under this name in the Portal (for example, in the BEx Portfolio).
  - **Importance** Choose the importance (low, medium, or high) that is to be stored as a property of the document and then displayed in the Portal (for example, in the BEx Portfolio).
  - **Description** Enter a short content-based description of the document or select a text variable (by choosing F4 with the quick info text Attach Text Variable). This description is stored with the document and displayed in the portal (for example, in the BEx Portfolio).

You can also make settings on the Filter Navigation, General Precalculation, General Link Generation, Layout, and Header/Footer tabbed pages. These pages are context-sensitive and are displayed depending on the selected output format. The display of the screen for Distribution to the Portal is similar to the screen for the Distribution via E-mail.

Broadcast to the Printer Printing is a way to distribute BI objects including queries, query views, Web templates, and reports. The BEx Broadcaster generates a spool request and sends it to the chosen output device to print. You can select Broadcast to Printer as the distribution type when you create the broadcast setting. You can choose between the following output formats:

- **Print Format (PS or PCL)** The document is generated in the appropriate format for the output device: PostScript (PS) or Printer Control Language (PCL).
- **Portable Document Format (PDF)** The BEx Broadcaster generates a PDF file.

NOTE *Not all types of web items for a BI object can be exported into the PDF output format.*

You make the settings for printing on the following tab pages:

- **Print Specifications tab** You can specify values for the following options:
  - **Printer** Choose the output device from which you want to print the document. Only devices that support the chosen output format (PS, PCL or PDF) are available for selection.
  - **Authorization User** If you schedule the broadcast setting for background processing (for example, for a specific time), you can enter a BI username

manually or choose F4 with the quick info text Selection. The system generates the document with the settings (for example, date format) and authorizations of the specified user.

- **Language**   If you schedule the broadcast setting for background processing (for example, for a specific time), you can select the language in which the document is to be generated. The system displays the languages that are installed on the BI system.

- **General Precalculation tab**   You can make settings such as variable assignments and exceptions) on this tabbed page.

- **Layout tab**   You make the required settings for the print layout on this tabbed page.

- **Header/Footer tab**   You can define the text for the header and footer for the print version on this tabbed page. You can also use text variables within the text.

- **Filter Navigation tab**   On the Filter Navigation tabbed page, you can specify characteristics or a control query so that the system precalculates several documents with different filter settings from the same query or Web Application. An example might be a query that has 0Material in the rows and 0Division in the free characteristics. This allows for the precalculation of the query results for each 0Division. The results are very different from the actual query and are specific to each division's requirements.

The following illustrations show the parameters for the Print Distribution type.

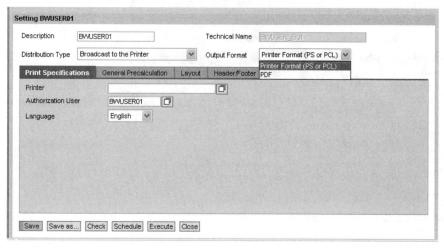

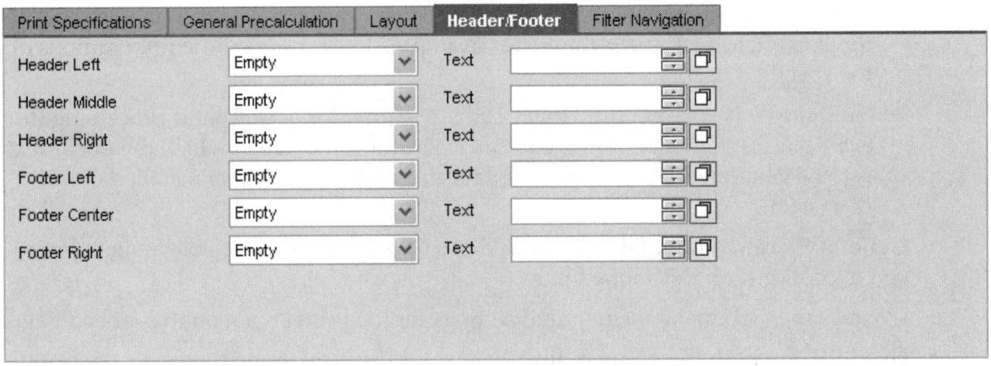

Print Specifications	General Precalculation	Layout	Header/Footer	Filter Navigation

Header Left	Empty	Text	
Header Middle	Empty	Text	
Header Right	Empty	Text	
Footer Left	Empty	Text	
Footer Center	Empty	Text	
Footer Right	Empty	Text	

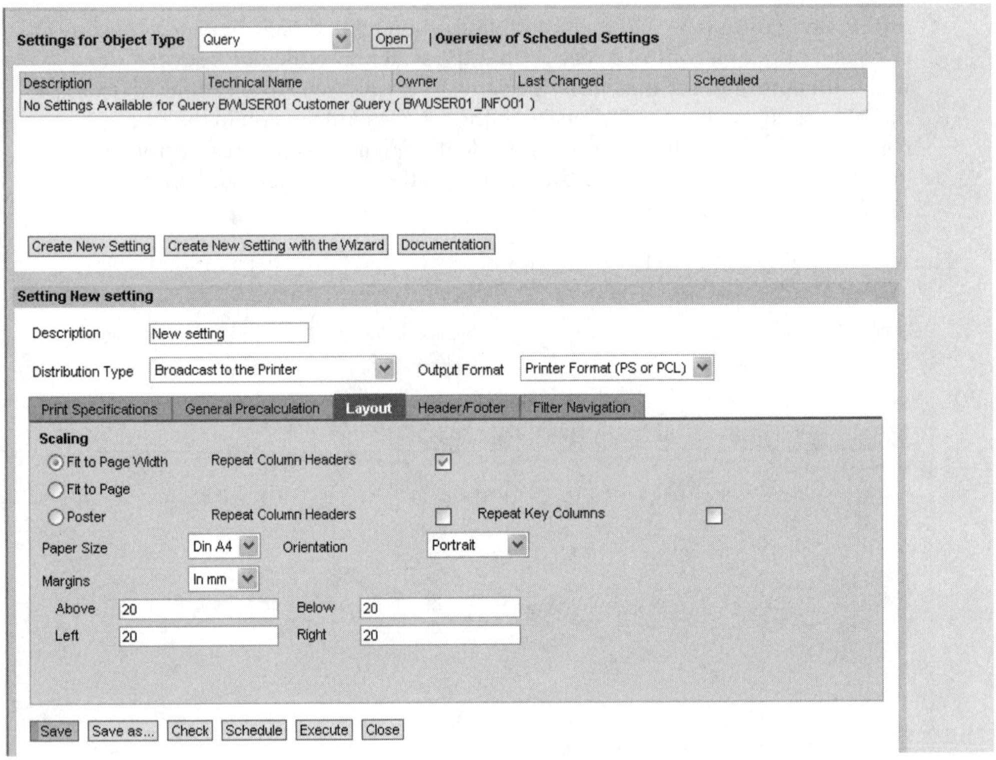

Settings for Object Type Query   Open | **Overview of Scheduled Settings**

Description	Technical Name	Owner	Last Changed	Scheduled
No Settings Available for Query BWUSER01 Customer Query (BWUSER01_INFO01)				

Create New Setting   Create New Setting with the Wizard   Documentation

Setting New setting

Description   New setting

Distribution Type   Broadcast to the Printer   Output Format   Printer Format (PS or PCL)

Print Specifications	General Precalculation	Layout	Header/Footer	Filter Navigation

Scaling

○ Fit to Page Width   Repeat Column Headers   ☑

○ Fit to Page

○ Poster   Repeat Column Headers   ☐   Repeat Key Columns   ☐

Paper Size   Din A4 ▾   Orientation   Portrait ▾

Margins   In mm ▾

Above   20   Below   20

Left   20   Right   20

Save   Save as...   Check   Schedule   Execute   Close

Broadcast E-mail (Bursting)   The distribution type Broadcast E-Mail (Bursting) allows you to broadcast BI objects (queries, query views, Web templates, reports, or workbooks) as precalculated documents or as online links sent via e-mail to recipients you determine on the basis of master data. With this approach we have to do a bit more work in the master data area of the infoobject. It is important that you have have maintained the added e-mail addresses of the recipients in the master data, you can select a characteristic in whose attributes the e-mail addresses or the BI usernames are maintained, and the system can determine the recipients from this information. This type of distribution is known as "bursting."

If required, you can also specify that the document is to be filtered for each recipient by their relevant characteristic values. If you choose to do this, the selected characteristic that you want to broadcast must be contained in the BI object. Every recipient then receives the document with the values that correspond to their area. For example, you can define the broadcast setting so that the monthly sales report is sent to all the branch managers. Every branch manager receives the sales report with the sales data from their branch. You can make settings on the following tabbed pages for the master data–based broadcast as e-mail (bursting):

- **Recipient Determination tab**   You specify the characteristic to use that will determine the recipients and define the characteristic values for each one of the values/receipients which an e-mail message of some sort is to be delivered.

  Under Characteristic for Recipient Determination, you can determine the recipient, choose the characteristic with which the recipient is to be determined, and choose the attribute for which the recipient is maintained:

  - **Send Document Unchanged**   The document is not adapted to suit the recipient. Enter the technical name of the required characteristic for which the recipient is maintained as an attribute—either manually or by choosing F4 Selection. The characteristic can be any characteristic in your BI system and does not have to be contained in the BI object you want to distribute.

  - **Filter Document by Characteristic Value**   The document is filtered by the characteristic value with which the recipient is identified. Each recipient receives the document filtered by the relevant characteristic values. Choose the required characteristic for which the recipient is maintained as an attribute. You can select from those characteristics that are included in the query or Data Provider of the Web Application or the report.

NOTE *With workbooks, you cannot filter the document by characteristic values.*

  - **Generate Document with Variable Value**   The characteristic value for determining the recipient is used as a variable entry when the document is generated. Select the variable you want to use. You can select from those characteristic value variables that are included in the query or Data Provider of the Web Application, the report, or the workbook. The system only displays this setting if the BI object (query, Web template, report, or workbook) contains characteristic values.

  - **Attribute for Recipient Determination**   Choose the attribute for which the recipient is maintained. Under Attribute Value Is, specify whether the recipient is to be identified using the e-mail address or the username.

Under Selection of Characteristic Values, you specify the characteristic values for which an e-mail recipient is to be determined. If you do not make a selection here, an error message is displayed that makes sure the broadcast setting cannot be sent by accident for all characteristic values.

You can create the selection of characteristic values as a list or specify them using a control query:

- **By Following Selection** Specify the characteristic values for which each e-mail recipient is to be determined.

- **By Control Query** Specify the query from which the characteristic values are selected—either manually or by choosing F4 Selection. A document is calculated and broadcast for each characteristic value of the selected characteristic.

Under Variant, you can select an existing variant for a query. Variables of the query that are ready for input can then be filled with values. By using a variant that is already configured helps with the processing of the broadcast since the existing variants will supply the variables with the needed values.

- **User/Language tab** On this tabbed page, you can determine for the background processing of the broadcast setting, the language, authorizations, and user-specific settings with which the scheduled document is to be generated.

- **Texts tab** You can specify values for the following options:

- **Subject** Enter a subject line for the e-mail manually or use a text variable by choosing F4 with the quick info text Attach Text Variable. The text can contain up to 50 characters.

- **Importance** Select the importance level for the e-mail (low, medium, or high).

- **Contents** Enter text for the contents of the e-mail manually or use a text variable by choosing F4 with the quick info text Attach Text Variable. When online links are sent, the system automatically adds a link to the text of the e-mail (if the text does not contain the link) using the PR_ONLINE_LINK variable.

- **Precalculation/General Link Generation tab** If you have chosen a file in a particular format (HTML or PDF, for example) as the output format, you can make various settings here.

  For example, if you have selected an online link as the output format, the settings options on the General Link Generation tabbed page are available to you (for setting relating to variables or exceptions, for example).

- **Filter Navigation tab** On this tabbed page, you can specify characteristics or a control query so that the system precalculates several documents with different filter settings from the same BI objects (query, Web template and so on).

The following illustration displays the details of these settings.

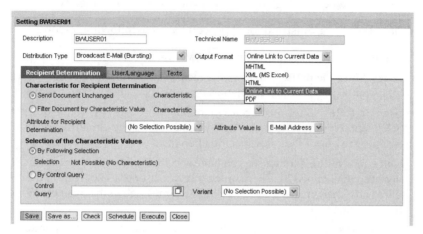

Broadcast According to Exceptions   This option can be very helpful with instituting a proactive approach to using the Information Broadcasting since only the exception or highlighted values are used for the distribution activity. The distribution type Broadcast by Exception allows you to check queries in the background for exceptions. Based on the parameters set, if a threshold value for an exception is exceeded or not reached, the BEx Broadcaster immediately generates a document in accordance with the criteria defined by you and distributes this to the recipients via e-mail, to the Portal, or as an alert (for example, into the central worklist). The query must, of course, have exceptions defined in either the BEx Query Designer or the BEx Analyzer. This distribution type will be configured in detail in the next chapter, but we will briefly discuss the option and process here.

Ensure that the following settings are made for the generation of alerts in Alert Management:

- You have defined alert categories in transaction ALRTCATDEF.

- You have selected the recipient of the SAP alert.

- You have also maintained the alert container, as required. The alert container ensures the exchange between the BI variables and the variables in the central alert server. We will discuss this in more detail in the next chapter.

For exception-specific distribution, make the settings on the following tabbed pages:

- **Distribution Type**   You can define the distribution type you want for each exception. The following distribution types are available for each exception:

  - Broadcast E-Mail

  - Generate Alert

  - Broadcast to the Portal (The system generates a precalculated document format and provides it in Knowledge Management.)

- **Create Parameters**   You specify the parameters for the distribution type. The system opens a new dialog box in which you set the distribution type.

For the Broadcast E-mail distribution type, you have the following options:

- **Recipients**   You can specify recipients in various ways:
  - **User**   Enter the BI usernames of the recipients manually or choose F4 with the quick info text Selection; usernames must be separated by semicolons.
  - **Users in Role**   Enter the BI roles manually or choose F4 with the quick info text Selection; roles must be separated by semicolons. The e-mail is sent to all users assigned to one of the roles specified here.

    If an e-mail address for a user you have specified under User or User in Role has not been maintained in user maintenance, the user does not receive the distributed file as an e-mail. Instead, the user receives a message in the Business Workplace (transaction SO01).
- **E-Mail Addresses**   Enter the e-mail addresses of the recipients, separated by semicolons.
- **Texts**   You can specify values for the following options:
  - **Subject**   Enter a subject line for the e-mail manually or use a text variable by choosing F4 with the quick info text Attach Text Variable. The text can contain up to 50 characters.
  - **Importance**   Select the importance level for the e-mail (low, medium, or high).
  - **Contents**   Enter text for the contents of the e-mail manually or use a text variable by choosing F4 with the quick info text Attach Text Variable. When online links are sent, the system automatically adds a link to the text of the e-mail (if the text does not contain the link) using the PR_ONLINE_LINK variable.

    For the Generate Alert distribution type, you have the following options:

- **Alert Generation**   On this tabbed page, you can select the required alert category that was defined in Alert Management (for example, Book Sold Out). Either the recipient is determined from the alert category (the system distributes the broadcast setting to all recipients specified in the alert category) or you specify additional recipients in the alert category. To do this, you specify BI usernames or roles from the BI system (separated by semicolons) either manually or by choosing F4 Selection.
- **Alert Parameters**   All the parameters are displayed that you have maintained in the alert category. Select the parameters you want to specify with the alert and enter the value for each one to be used to fill the parameter when the alert is generated. You can enter text manually as the value or you can use text variables by choosing F4 Selection.

    The alerts can be displayed in the central worklist. To do this, the central worklist must be correctly configured.

    For the Broadcast to Portal distribution type, you have the following tabs:

- **Target in Portal**   You can choose from the following options:

- **File Name**   Enter the technical name under which the document is to be saved—either manually or using a text variable (by choosing F4 with the quick info text Attach Text Variable).

   You can put the document in the current personal portfolio for selected users or in any other KM folder.

- **Export Document to My Portfolio**

   - **User**   Enter the BI usernames of the recipients using F4 Selection, separated by semicolons.

   - **Users in Roles**   Enter the roles in the BI system (separated by semicolons) by choosing F4 Selection.

      The document is stored in the users' personal portfolios. These users are either determined using the BI usernames or assigned to one of the selected roles.

- **Export Document into Any Folder**   Using F4 Selection, you enter the KM folder in which the document is to be stored in the Portal.

- **Text**   You can specify values for the following options:

   - **Display Name**   Enter the name manually or use a text variable (by choosing F4 with the quick info text Attach Text Variable). The document is displayed in the Portal (for example, in the BEx Portfolio) under this name.

   - **Importance**   Choose the importance (low, medium, or high) that is to be stored as a property of the document and then displayed in the Portal (for example, in the BEx Portfolio).

   - **Description**   Enter a short content-based description of the document or select a text variable (by choosing F4 with the quick info text Attach Text Variable). This description is stored with the document and displayed in the Portal (for example, in the BEx Portfolio).

- **Selection Criteria**   You define the criteria with which you want to select the exceptions to be distributed. You can choose either an exception or a combination of exception and alert level as the selection criterion.

- **Value**   Choose the exception or combination of exception and alert level you want to distribute.

- **Content**   You select the details of the exception to be included in the document (exception details, exception overview).

- **Format**   Choose the format you want for the document (HTML, Text, Text with Technical Name, XML).

- **User/Language**   For the background processing of the broadcast setting, you can determine the language, authorizations, and user-specific settings with which the scheduled document is to be generated.

- **Exception Search**   You define the navigational states that are to be searched for exceptions.

- **Standard Navigational State**   The system searches the navigational state of the query that was produced in the BEx Query Designer when the query was defined (initial view of query).

- **Following Navigational State** The system searches the navigational state of the query that arises if the characteristics given here in the lines are drilled down. Select the characteristic you want under Characteristic and determine the filter values you require.

  You can also specify that the totals row for the characteristics to be added.

- **All Navigational States in Search Path** The system searches all the navigational states that arise if the characteristics specified here in the listed order are included in the drilldown. Select the characteristic you want under Characteristic and determine the filter values you require.

The following illustration shows the initial screens for this distribution type. Due to the value of this particular distribution type and process for the Broadcaster, the initial setup will be discussed in more detail in the next chapter.

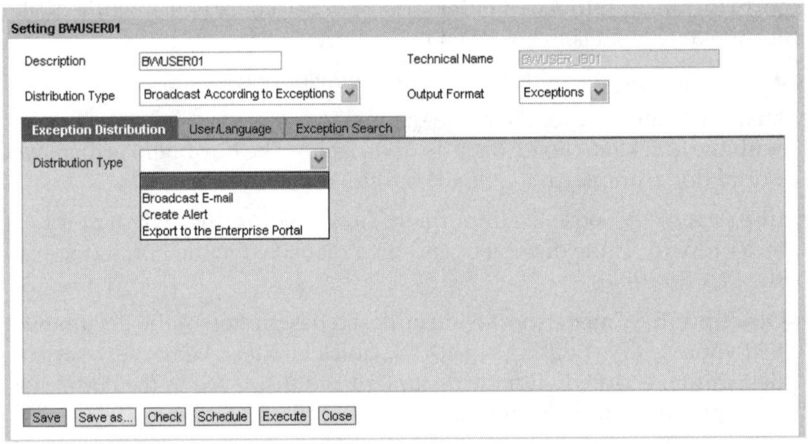

Broadcast (Multi Channel) The distribution type Broadcast (Multi Channel) allows you to distribute a BI object (query, query view, Web template, report, or workbook) with one broadcast setting over multiple channels. Depending on the output format you choose, you can distribute the BI object via e-mail, export it to the Portal, or print it. Basically speaking, this will allow you to do any of the above options for the Information Broadcaster. The following illustration shows an overview of the functionality of this distribution type. This demonstrates the flexibility of this distribution type and the ability to set up numerous broadcast components all at one time. For distribution over several channels, make the settings on the following tabbed pages:

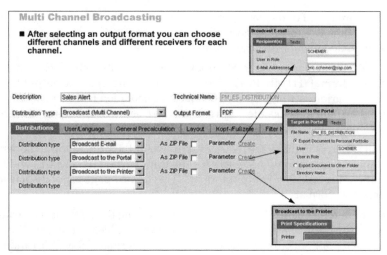

- **Distributions** You choose the required distribution types (Broadcast by E-mail, Broadcast to Portal, or Broadcast to Printer). Depending on the output format you have selected, the BEx Broadcaster provides you with a selection of distribution types. If you want to broadcast the document as a ZIP file, select ZIP File. If you have chosen HTML or MHTML as the output format and want to broadcast the document via e-mail, you have to create the document as a ZIP file. Table 11-1 shows the different "Create Parameters" that you can set depending on the distribution type.

Distribution Type	Parameter
Broadcast by E-mail	You can specify the recipients in different ways on the Recipients tabbed page: • Users • Users in Roles • E-mail Addresses In the Texts tabbed page, enter the subject line, the importance of the e-mail, and the contents of the e-mail.
Export to Portal	In the Target in Portal tabbed page, specify the KM folder the document is to be stored in. On the Texts tabbed page, enter the display name, the importance of the document, and a short description of the contents.
Broadcast to Printer	On the Printer tabbed page, choose the output device you want to print the document on. Only devices that support the chosen output format (PS, PCL, or PDF) are available for selection.

TABLE 11-1   Options in the Distribution Type for Multi Channel Broadcaster

- **User/Language** For the background processing of the broadcast setting, you can determine the language, authorizations, and user-specific settings with which the scheduled document is to be generated.

- **General Precalculation/General Link Generation** If you have chosen a file in a particular format (HTML, PDF, PS, or PCL, for example) as the output format, you can make various settings on the General Precalculation tabbed page. If you have selected an online link as the output format, the settings options on the General Link Generation tabbed page are available to you.

- **Layout** Here you make the required settings for the print layout. The settings on this tabbed page are only necessary for the Print Format (PS or PCL) and Portable Document Format (PDF) output formats. This tabbed page is not displayed for the other output formats.

- **Header/Footer** On this tabbed page you can define the texts for the header and footer of the print version. You can also use text variables in the text. The settings on this tabbed page are only necessary for the Print Format (PS or PCL) and Portable Document Format (PDF) output formats. This tab page is not displayed for the other output formats.

- **Filter Navigation** On this tabbed page you can specify characteristics or a control query so that the system precalculates several documents with different filter settings from the same BI objects (query, Web template, and so on). This tabbed page is not necessary with the Online Link to Current Data output format and therefore is not displayed.

The following illustration shows the settings for the Multi Channel option.

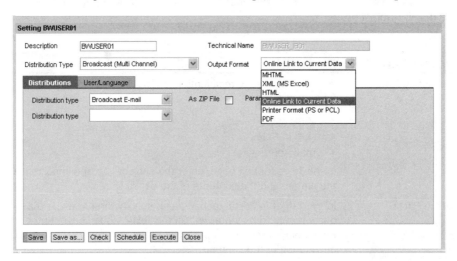

Copyright by SAP AG

Precalculate Value Set The distribution type Precalculated Value Set allows you to fill variables of that type (precalculated value set) with values for characteristic values in the background. The precalculated value sets are then available as variable values in BEx queries. In this case, the query must contain the characteristic that is the placeholder for the variables. The first of the following illustrations shows some of the functionality of the precalculated value set. The second illustration shows the outcome of the Broadcaster for this distribution type.

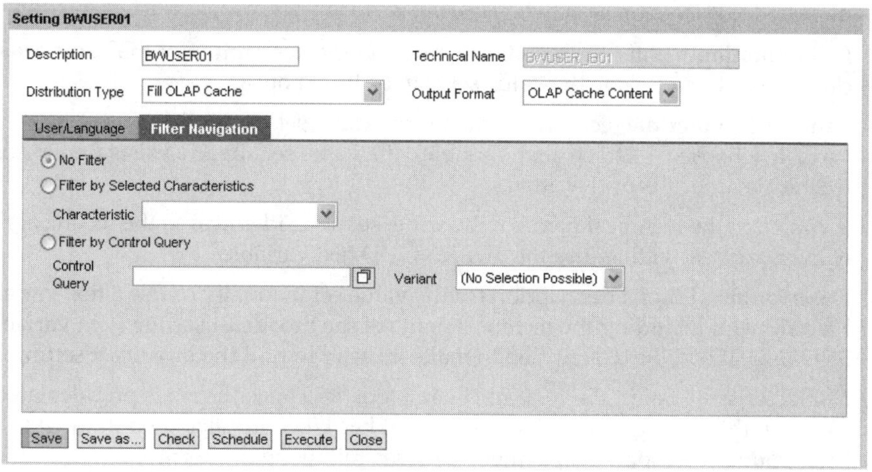

Copyright by SAP AG

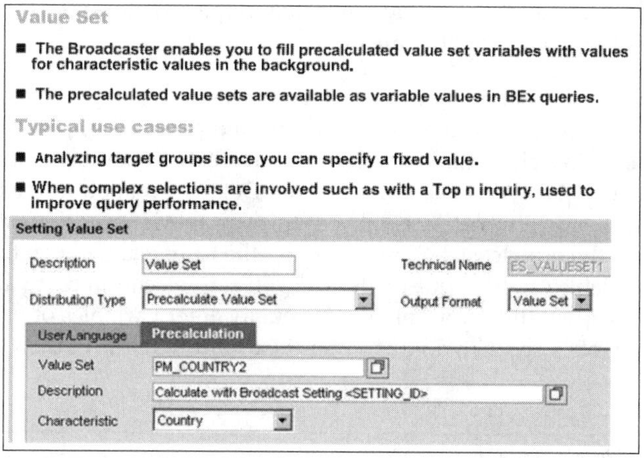

Copyright by SAP AG

The following cases are typical examples of when precalculated value sets in the background are used:

- When you need to identify and analyze target groups, because you can specify a fixed value. For example the top 10 set customers.

- When complex selections are involved, such as with Top N queries. This approach is used to greatly improve query performance.

- Instead of variables that are filled from a query event. Therefore, rather than having a variable filled based on a user exit or a customer exit we can fill them with a list or group of values defined prior to the query being executed.

For the precalculation of value sets, make the settings on the following tabbed pages:

- **User/Language**   Here you can determine for the background processing of the broadcast setting the language, authorizations, and user-specific settings with which the scheduled document is to be generated.

- **Precalculation**   Enter the technical name and the description of the value set and choose the characteristic the value set is to be based on:

- **Value Set**   Enter the technical name for the value set manually or use a text variable (choose F4 Attach Text Variable). If a value set already exists under this technical name, it is overwritten.

  If you want the technical name of the value set to be identical to the technical name of the broadcast setting, use the SETTING_ID text variable.

- **Description**   Enter a description for the value set manually or use a text variable. I recommend including the technical name of the broadcast setting (text variable SETTING_ID) in the description to make it easier to find the broadcast setting.

- **Characteristic**   Select the required characteristic. The value set is precalculated based on this characteristic. A value set that has been precalculated in the background corresponds to a query with the following properties:

  - The key figure structure is in the columns.

  - The characteristic that you have selected in the broadcast setting is in the rows. All the other characteristics are aggregated.

The precalculated value set displays the value of a variable of type Precalculated Value Set from the selected characteristic. As a result of background processing, you can use the precalculated value set in a characteristic variable. You create a characteristic value variable in the Query Designer using the Variable Editor. Under Details, you determine that the variable represents a precalculated value set. The value of this variable is the technical name of the value set specified in the broadcast setting. You enter the technical name in the Default Values tabbed page. The variable can be input-ready, and you can select different value sets in the variable screen at query runtime. You can also manually enter variables of type Precalculated Value Set on the variable screen. To do this, enter the technical name of the value set specified in the broadcast setting.

NOTE   *For technical reasons, you cannot use variables that represent a precalculated value set in restricted key figures or in selection structure elements.*

Fill OLAP Cache   The distribution type Fill OLAP Cache allows you to precalculate queries and to fill the OLAP cache with the generated data. If the users call Web Applications, queries, reports, or workbooks that are based on this data, the access time is significantly reduced and the workload on the application server is considerably less. This is very useful and one of the tools available to increase query performance. Generally speaking there's nothing faster than having your query execute against OLAP Cache. Because the functions of the OLAP cache were designed so that the user does not have to wait any longer than normal when evaluating a query, but it is *not* possible to guarantee the OLAP cache will be completely filled.

It is possible that the expected entry for a query is not stored in the cache. The query must then be completely reevaluated with access to the InfoProvider. This situation is intensified when several attempts are made to access the query at the same time. You make the settings for filling the OLAP cache on the following tabbed pages:

- **User/Language**   Here you can determine for the background processing of the broadcast setting the language, authorizations, and user-specific settings with which the scheduled document is to be generated.

- **General Precalculation**   You make various settings here relating to, for example, variables or exceptions.

- **Filter Navigation**   Here you can specify characteristics or a control query so that the system precalculates several documents with different filter settings from the same query.
  The settings for this distribution type are shown here:

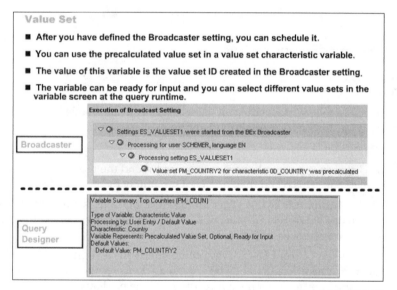

Fill MDX Cache   The Fill MDX Cache distribution type allows you to precalculate BEx queries in the background, which can then be used as Data Providers for external reporting tools such as Crystal Reports. This function is used to improve system performance when executing other third party tools . The output format is specifically MDX Result Set. You make settings for filling the MDX cache on the following tabbed pages:

- **User/Language**   Here you can specify for the background processing of the broadcast setting which language, authorizations, and user-specific settings are to be used to generate the scheduled document.

- **General Precalculation**   You make the settings for the variable assignment here. This tabbed page only appears when the query contains variables.

- **Filter Navigation**   Here you can specify characteristics or a control query so that the system precalculates multiple documents with different filter settings from the same query.

  The settings for this distribution type can be seen in the following illustration:

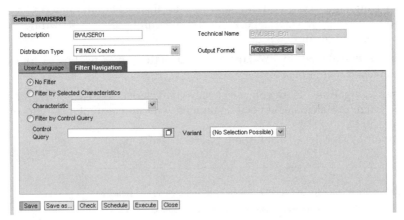

Output Format

Options for output format are dependent on the selection you have made for the distribution type. The various illustrations of the distribution type explanations have shown these different settings. The basic options are:

- **HTML**   Use this option whenever you want to send the report results as a separate file in an e-mail. This could then be saved separately by the user. (very popular).

- **MHTML (Multipart HTML)**   This combines all the objects required for the report together in one single file. Use this option when you want to embed the BEx report within the body of the e-mail (rather than as a separate file).

- **Online Links to Current Data**   The online link sends an e-mail with the URL for the query assigned. This can then be executed whenever the business user is ready to review the information. This option offers all the navigational functionality available in other options.

- **PDF**   Use this option to create a PDF file containing the results of the report, which will be attached to the e-mail.

Recipient(s) Tab

As a follow-up of the information by distribution type, I've organized this section specifically for the information available for the Recipient(s) tab. You have three options to determine who receives e-mails

- On the Recipient(s) tab, one or more SAP users, separated by semicolons, can be selected.

- User in Role sends files to the SAP users associated with the role or roles selected
- E-mail addresses can be entered directly

For the SAP users and "users in roles," their e-mail addresses and the communication type E-Mail are required in SU01 if you would like to use external e-mail addresses. Otherwise, the broadcast is made to the users' SAP Office inbox.

For the background processing, the Authorization User setting can be used to assess date format and OLAP authorizations. Leave the field Authorization User empty if the username is irrelevant to the generation of the document. In this case, the system uses the current user and their authorizations in the execution of the settings.

If the document is created in the foreground, the logon language is used unless you specify differently. If background processing is used, the language in the setting is used.

User-specific settings are selected if you want to generate the document to be user specific. The system generates the document for each of the specified recipients with their personal settings (date, format, language) and data authorizations. Recipients who are only specified with e-mail addresses are excluded from this.

This information is shown in the following illustration, which displays the Recipient tab of the Information Broadcaster.

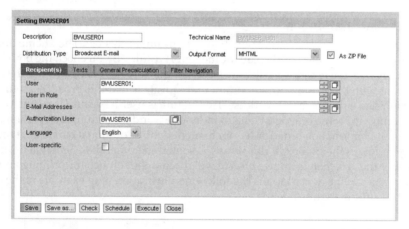

Copyright by SAP AG

Text Tab

The Text tab is for general information for the identification of the Information Broadcaster. Subject is the header of the Broadcaster. You can enter a subject line for the e-mail manually or use a text variable from Attach Text Variable. The text can be up to 50 characters long. Once this is complete, you can set the Importance field of the e-mail—Low, Medium, or High. Additional information can be entered into the Content field for text that you would like to send along with this e-mail. Information can be entered manually or you can use a text variable from the Attach Text Variable. When sending online links, the system automatically adds a link to the text of the e-mail (if it is not part of the text) via the variable PR_ONLINE_LINK. The following illustration shows this information.

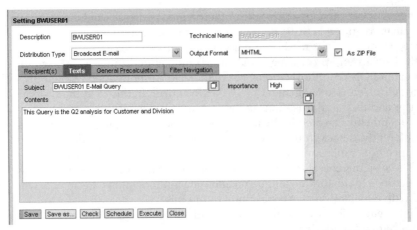

General Precalculation Tab

For broadcasting via e-mail, there are only two options under this tab. The Theme dropdown allows you to choose a preferred display for the report results. If you check the box Only Upon Data Change, the broadcast will only be sent if the data has changed since the last broadcast sent with this setting. An important prerequisite is that this broadcast setting has not been modified since the first broadcast. This feature is useful because it means you can avoid re-sending the same broadcast data to individuals and the redundant creation and execution of the information broadcaster not to mention the additional emails that the business user gets in their inbox. If this setting is something other than Send via E-Mail, the options under this tab change quite a bit. We will discuss the settings for printing and other distribution types in the next chapter. The following illustration is an example of the General Precalculation information.

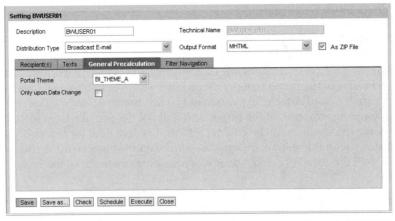

Filter Navigation Tab

For workbooks there are no filtering options. The only Output Format that supports filtering is HTML, and you must use the Zip option. Filtering a query that has sales for six different divisions would result in six separate files by division within the zipped file. Any characteristics in the query but not in the filter can be "filtered on" if Add Unfiltered View is selected; a view will be precalculated that does contain the selected characteristics. Characteristics are either filtered individually or with a control query (predefined query). For each characteristic combination that occurs in the control query, a filtered document is calculated. You should evaluate the number of possible combinations the control query may generate because this could cause a very large number of views to be created. The following illustration shows the information on the Filter Navigation tab.

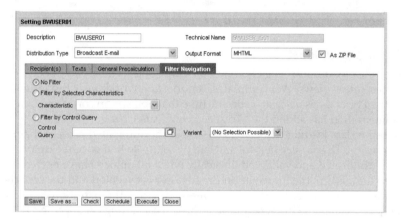

Copyright by SAP AG

Toolbar Functionality

The options found in the toolbar below the parameters of the Information Broadcaster are all basic ones except for the Schedule option. The Schedule option is discussed in detail in the next section. As for the other buttons, their functionality is described in Table 11-2.

Buttons	Description and Functionality
Save	A dialog box appears for you to enter the technical name and description of the Broadcaster settings.
Save As	A dialog box appears for you to enter the technical name and description of the Broadcaster settings.
Check	Confirms that all the settings are consistent and that the information required for e-mails or print settings are complete.
Schedule	Discussed in the "Scheduling the Broadcast" section.
Execute	Immediately executes the Broadcaster settings.
Close	Once you have completed the parameters, this button will close the Create portion of the screen.

TABLE 11-2   Options for the Processing of the Information Broadcaster Settings

Also note that on the dialog boxes for the Information Broadcaster, you have the ability to maintain, change, and delete information via a context menu for the specific Broadcaster settings, as shown here.

Scheduling the Broadcast

You can schedule broadcast settings for all of the same objects that we've been discussing such as queries, query views, Web templates, reports, and workbooks. Broadcasting by e-mail or to the Portal takes place at a specific time that you specify, or when data is changed. System administration has added the "Trigger Event Data Change" process type to the process chains for data loading. This offers the use of the automated process chain to execute a Broadcast process. This is very helpful and can be set up so that once the uploading process of the data are confirmed and validated (basically when all uploads have been confirmed and the green light is on), the Information Broadcaster is executed and the reports are distributed immediately after the data is updated. System administration can define background jobs that enable the scheduling of broadcast settings at specified times.

Once the Broadcaster settings have been defined, there are four main options for the timing of the distribution:

- **Immediately**   This is basically the easiest of all settings. Just use the Execute button to send the broadcast off immediately. Immediate execution works for settings that are saved and also for settings that are not saved—it's basically an *ad-hoc* broadcast.

If you want to schedule a broadcast setting from the list of the available broadcast settings in the upper area of the BEx Broadcaster, choose **Scheduling** in the context menu of the required broadcast setting. You have the following selection options:

- **Execution with Data Change in the InfoProvider**   Select the required InfoProvider. The system distributes the document as soon as data in this InfoProvider is changed. This option is only available if system administration has included the Trigger Event Data Change process type in the process chain for loading data.

- **Execution at a Predefined Time**   Select the required time. The system distributes the document according to your selection. This option is only available if system administration has defined the relevant background jobs. With this option, the business user has the ability to select a specific time for execution of the query distribution, but these times are managed and identified by the system administrator and therefore are set consistent with the overall system activities. In this way, both the business user and the administrator are comfortable with the distribution process.

- **Scheduling in SAP Background Processing**   Select Create New Scheduling and specify the required start date and time. If scheduling is to occur periodically, select Periodic and specify the interval (for example, Every 2 Weeks). The system distributes the document according to your selection. If you have already defined schedules in SAP background processing for this broadcast setting, they are listed here. You can delete them as required. You can only schedule in SAP background processing if you have authorization to create background jobs.

- **Transfer**   The broadcast setting is displayed in the upper area of the BEx Broadcaster and Yes is displayed in the Scheduled column.

If there are multiple broadcast settings, or if there are broadcast settings that require user-specific processing for different users, the scheduled settings are processed in parallel. You can control parallel processing for information broadcasting in BI background management (transaction RSBATCH, process type BROADCAST). You can find and display the scheduled broadcast settings according to various criteria, and you can delete them as required. Choose the option Overview of Scheduled Settings (top portion of the Broadcaster screen) and enter one or more of the following search criteria:

- **Event**   Choose direct scheduling in SAP background processing, the predefined time, or the data change event for which the setting is scheduled.

- **Settings**   Enter the technical name of the broadcast setting manually or use F4 Selection. You can also search within an area.

- **Created By**   Enter the username of the creator manually or use F4 Selection. You can also search within an area.

- **Scheduled By**   Enter the username of the user who scheduled the broadcast setting manually or use F4 Selection. You can also search within an area.

The following illustration shows the settings for this parameter.

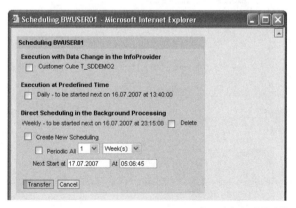

Copyright by SAP AG

Broadcasting Wizard

The Broadcasting Wizard is a good alternative for the business user to create their Broadcast settings during the runtime of the query. The Broadcasting Wizard takes you through a series of prompts where you supply the information (very similar to the generic approach) required to develop a broadcast. It is a bit more straightforward than the "Create" approach, but is supported by the Broadcaster and can be maintained and enhanced in the Broadcaster (fully functional versus the Wizard). Just remember that the Wizard doesn't have all of the functionality of the Information Broadcaster – just the options that make sense for the Business User to be concerned with. The following illustration shows the initial step for entering the wizard. Using the button Create New Setting with the Wizard, the business user can gain access to the Broadcaster settings.

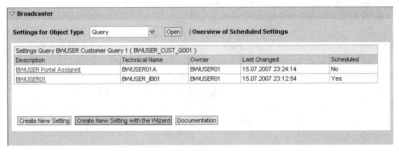

The next illustration shows the initial screen for the wizard. Notice that there are only three options for the distribution type: Broadcast E-mail, Broadcast to the Portal, and Broadcast to the Printer. All output formats for these three options are supported.

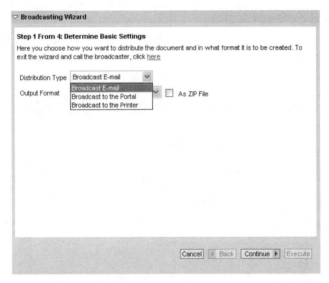

The next illustration shows step 2 in the wizard. The normal required fields are available based on the request for the Broadcaster to support the E-mail process.

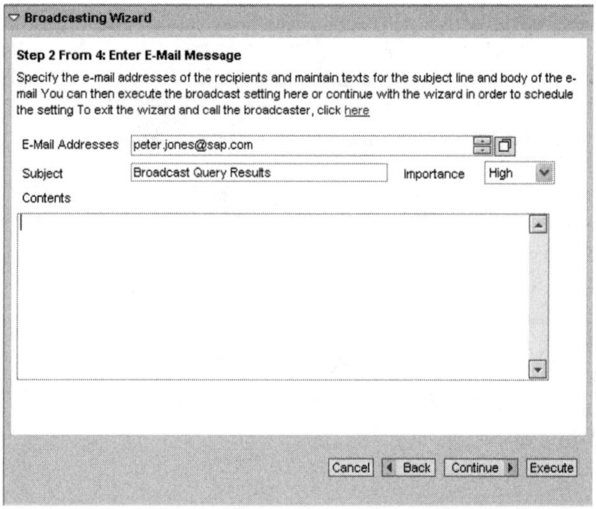

Copyright by SAP AG

The next illustration shows step 3 in the wizard. The technical name and description are required.

Copyright by SAP AG

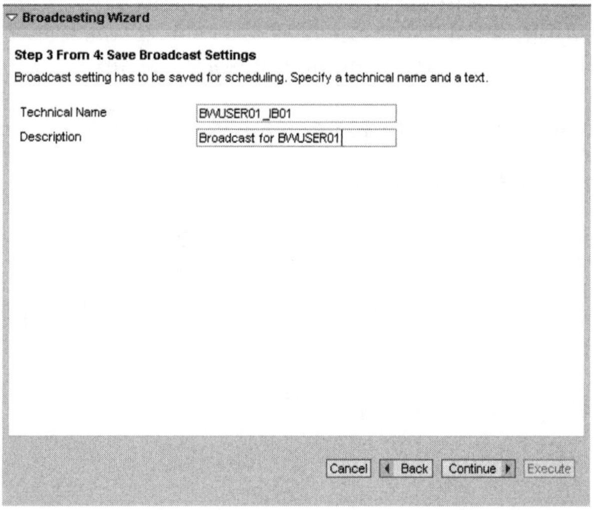

Finally, the next illustration shows step 4 in the wizard. The Scheduling process is available to be configured. These settings are exactly the same as described previously in this chapter.

Workbook Precalculation Service

During this discussion, we will evaluate the precalculation of the workbooks. In the next chapter, we will review the precalculation of the Web Queries, query views, templates and reports. Several administrative activities are necessary in the BI system for precalculating and distributing workbooks, including the following:

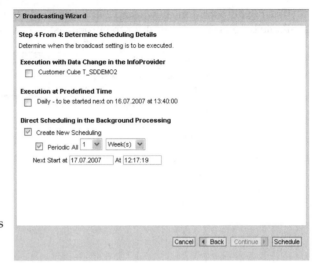

- Install Microsoft .NET Framework. (This should have been installed with other SAP front-end functionality.)

- Install SAP GUI 6.40 or above. (This should also have been installed at this point.)

- Install SAP NetWeaver BI Frontend 2004s (BI add-on). (This should have already been installed, but check the service pack level you are on. It should be the latest service pack.) The following illustration shows this setup.

- Install Microsoft Excel 2000 or higher. (It may be a good idea to have a version of Microsoft Excel higher than 2000 because many of the front-end functions are not compatible with Microsoft Excel 2000.)

NOTE *SAP recommends that you install the Precalculation Service on a server. You can install it on a client PC.*

The Precalculation Service is a separate component with its own installation and is available on 6.40 Final Compilation CD4. After finishing the installation, go to the Services window of your operating system and search for a service called SAP BW PRECALCULATION SERVICE 7.0. The following illustration shows this process.

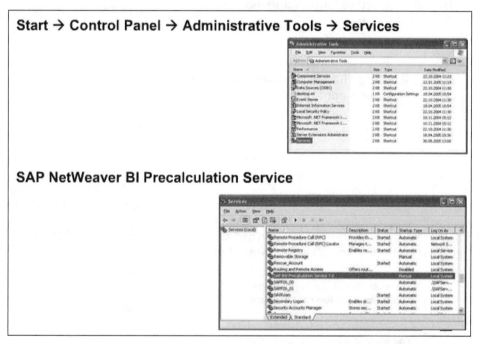

Enable Automatic as the Startup type, as shown next.

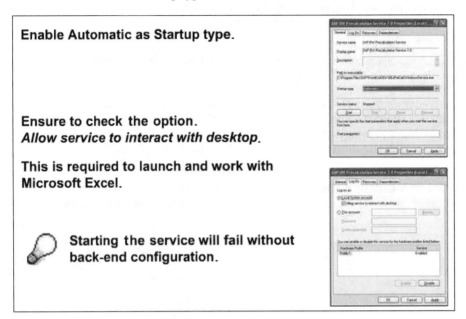

During installation, the management console for the Windows Precalculation Service appears. Log on to the BI system on the PC where the precalculation service is installed and navigate to Customizing (transaction SPRO): SAP Reference IMG | SAP NetWeaver | Business Intelligence | Settings for Reporting and Analysis | Settings for Information Broadcasting | Ad ministrate Precalculation Server. The following illustration shows these steps.

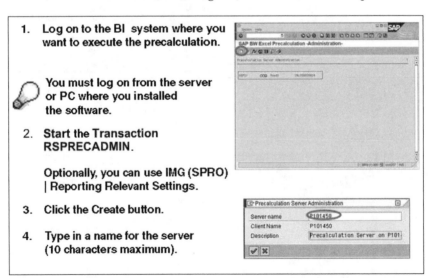

Choose Create Precalculation Server and enter the technical name of the server (maximum 10 characters) and a description. The description is language dependent and appears in the BEx Broadcaster when you select a special precalculation server. The precalculation server, which is an RFC server from a technical viewpoint, appears in the list. When the precalculation server is ready, the status display of the precalculation server shows a green light. The following illustration shows these steps.

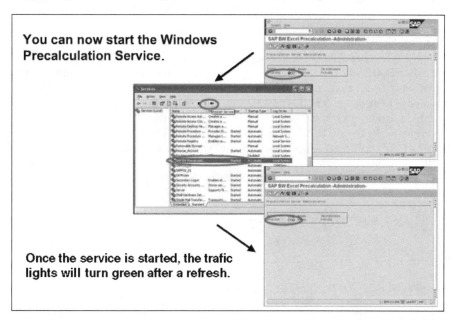

Copyright by SAP AG

You can perform maintenance on the precalculation server from this location. You can use Edit Precalculation Servers to change the description of the server, you can use Delete Precalculation Server to remove servers you no longer need, and you can use Restart Precalculation Server to restart the Windows Precalculation Service.

NOTE *If you restart the BI system, you have to restart the Windows Precalculation Service too.*

Finally, the option Refresh View will refresh the list of precalculation servers, and the status display is available from this location. You can use Information on the Server to open a dialog box where you can see the technical name, the description, and current information (that is, the current instances and the status of the server—either online or offline). In addition, you can display or delete the front-end log. The front-end log is a log file that displays errors that have occurred.

You can use Test of Precalculation to test the precalculation of workbooks and their distribution via e-mail. Follow these steps:

1. Enter the appropriate workbook.

2. If the workbook contains variables, you can specify the variant that determines which variable values will be used to precalculate the workbook.

3. Specify the precalculation server.
4. Specify a Web template that will determine the contents of the e-mail.
5. Specify the e-mail addresses for the distribution.

The precalculation is started from the BEx Broadcaster, and you can test the function.

You can use Display Current Queue to display a list of processed precalculations. You can also determine the average runtime here.

Workbook Precalculation Process

You can use the BEx Broadcaster to precalculate and distribute workbooks. The system generates Microsoft Excel workbooks with historic data. You determine the time at which precalculation is performed: You can have workbooks precalculated at a predefined time or precalculated whenever data in the underlying InfoProvider changes. You can have the precalculated workbooks broadcast via e-mail or you can broadcast them to the Portal, where you can make them available to employees within your company.

The broadcast setting is created from a saved workbook (not a temporary workbook) from the Tools menu. On the analysis toolbar in the BEx Analyzer, choose Tools | BEx Broadcaster. The following illustration shows this step in the process.

Distribution Channel		Division		Incoming Orders	Order Entry Quantity
	Final customer sales	00	Cross-division	28,788.26 EUR	350 EA
		01	Pumps	19,731,587.80 EUR	6,335 PC
		07	High Tech	10,778,271.72 EUR	55,308 PC
		20	Turbines	0.00 EUR	0 PC
		Result		30,538,647.78 EUR	61,993.000 MIX
12	Sold for resale	02	Motorcycles	15,429,350.93 EUR	49,067 PC
		04	Lighting	15,376,585.35 EUR	39,835 CAR
		07	High Tech	13,500,612.48 EUR	14,652 PC
		Result		44,306,548.76 EUR	103,554.040 MIX
14	Service	00	Cross-division	0.00 EUR	0 AU
		08	Service	0.00 EUR	0 AU
		Result		0.00 EUR	0 AU
R1	GM store	R1	Retail	0.00 EUR	0 LB
		Result		0.00 EUR	0 LB
S3	Services	S3	Services	1,826,392.37 EUR	0 DAY
		Result		1,826,392.37 EUR	0 DAY
Overall Result				76,671,588.91 EUR	165,547.040 MIX

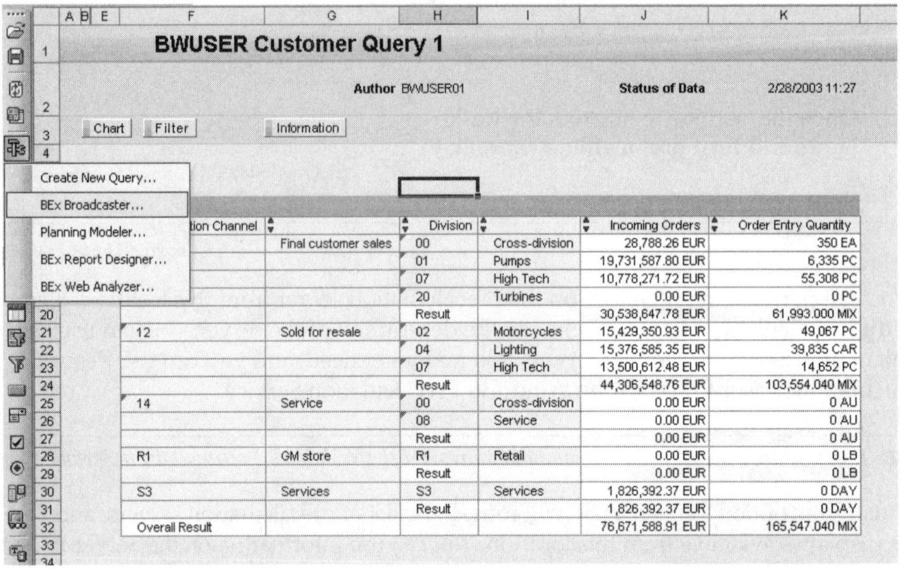

Copyright by SAP AG

NOTE *The Tools | BEx Broadcaster option is only visible when a workbook is open. If you've only opened a query in the BEx Analyzer, this broadcasting option is not available.*

You can also call the BEx Broadcaster from other areas and then select the appropriate workbook for broadcasting: Under Settings for Object Type, choose Workbook. This will execute the Broadcaster. The user then selects a workbook and creates a new setting.

Choose whether you want to send the precalculated workbook as an e-mail or publish it in the Portal. If you want to distribute the workbook as a Zip file, select ZIP File. The following illustration shows the initial screen from the Broadcaster. Notice that the difference is the object type—Workbook.

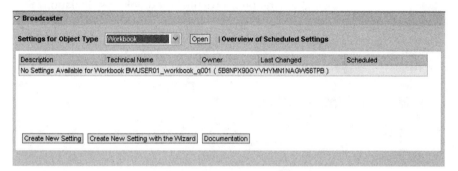

NOTE   *If you want to work with the Broadcasting Wizard, which provides step-by-step instructions for creating the broadcast setting, choose Create New Setting with Wizard.*

Enter a description for the broadcast setting. Then choose the Workbook Precalculation tabbed page.

If the workbook contains variables, you can also set variable assignments in the Variant field. You can also create the values for input-ready variables in the workbook. The workbook is precalculated with these variable values. The following illustration shows this information. Notice that the distribution types have been limited to just four options.

You can enter the required variant in the Variant field. The workbook is precalculated with the data for this variant. The field will be described as—Take from Variant.

You also need to specify which precalculation server is to be used. But first, you have to set up a precalculation server. If you want the system to use the first available precalculation server from the precalculation servers set in Customizing, choose Select Automatically. If you want the system to use a special precalculation server, choose Special Server and specify the server. The following illustration shows the Workbook Precalculation tab and the parameters available.

If this special server is not available, the system terminates. If necessary, check your settings using the Check button and then choose Save. Enter a technical name for the broadcast setting and choose Transfer. The new setting appears in the overview in the upper area of the BEx Broadcaster. If you want to distribute the broadcast setting for the workbook immediately, choose Execute. A new browser window appears; it displays the processing status for the broadcast setting. If you want to close the window, choose Cancel. If you want to distribute the broadcast setting for the workbook at a specific time or whenever changes are made to the data, choose Schedule. You have to precalculate a workbook and distribute the selected setting accordingly. If you have not precalculated the workbook as a Zip file, when the recipients open the file, they have a formatted workbook in which they can navigate further. The recipients of the file need a local installation of the BI front end to log on to the BI system and navigate within the data. The broadcast setting is listed in the upper area of the BEx Broadcaster screen. Here you see all the broadcast settings that were created for this workbook. If you want to edit or delete the broadcast setting, choose Edit or Delete in the context menu for the setting. To view traces of the executed workbook, use transaction code SLG1; object BW_XLWB; subobject PREC. The following illustration shows this information.

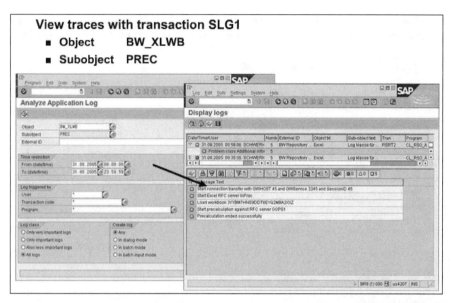

Example of the Information Broadcaster

To complete this chapter, a basic example of the setup of the Information Broadcaster will develop the logical flow of this process. This example will start from the BEx Query Designer, but it could start from any of the other components. Having identified a query and ready to configure the parameters in the Information Broadcaster, we choose the Create New Settings option directly in the Information Broadcaster, as shown in the following illustration.

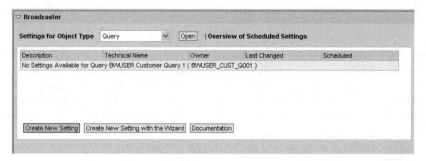

Once we execute the Create option, we have all the tabs discussed in the previous sections. The first of the following illustrations shows us the initial screen. We will be entering some basic information, such as an additional user (BWUSER02), the distribution type (Broadcast via E-Mail), and the output format (MHTML). We will also turn on the option to execute the Zip file format. This information is shown in the second illustration.

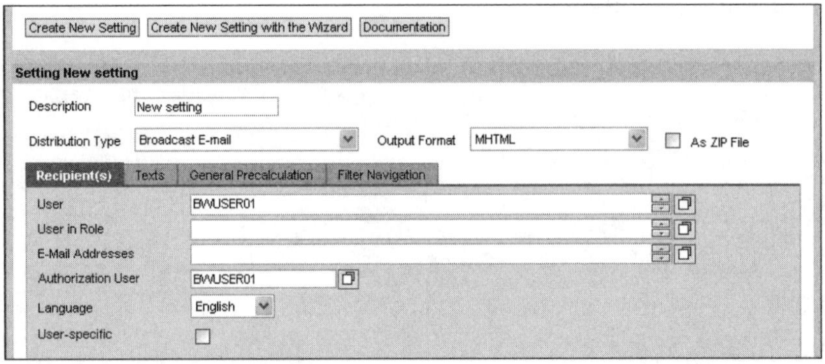

Copyright by SAP AG

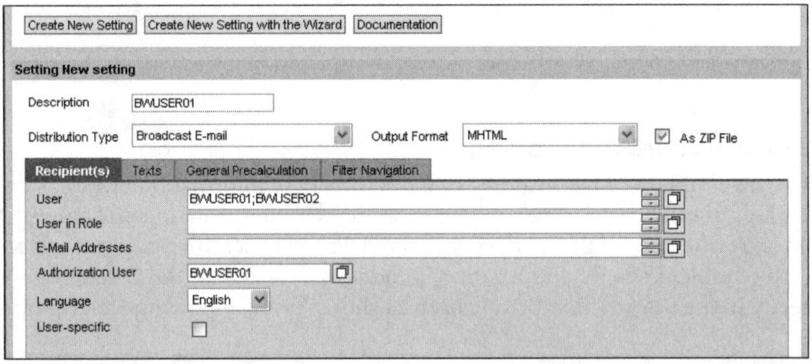

Copyright by SAP AG

Moving to the Text tab, we enter additional information such as the subject (BWUSER01 E-Mail Query) and change the importance to (High). In addition, we include some comments about the query and its significance, as shown in the first of the following illustrations. At this point, because we are not required to fill in any additional information, we can "execute" this broadcast and see an immediate distribution of the information to the SAP Outlook box in the SAP system. Because we identified this as the distribution target, we would then look in the Inbox of the SAP system to find the broadcast available for us to review. The second illustration shows the message that is generated once the process is executed, which indicates that the process of distributing the query information has begun.

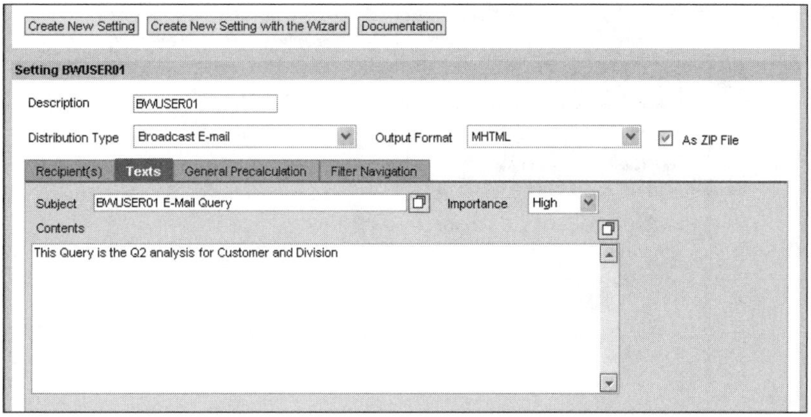

Copyright by SAP AG

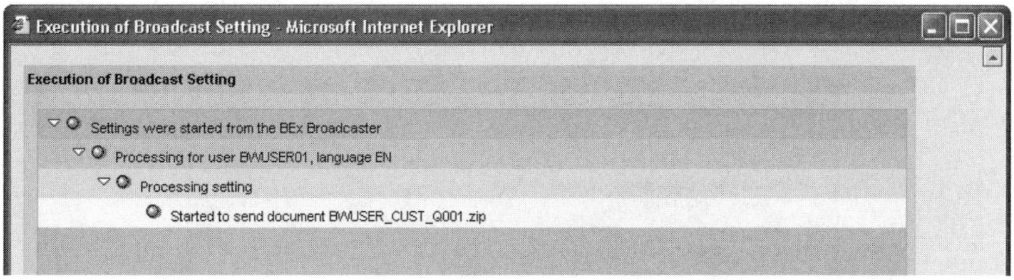

Copyright by SAP AG

If we were to decide to set up a scheduled run of this specific broadcast, we would have to first save the parameters and then set up the scheduled run of the information. The first of the following illustrations shows the pop-up we get when we execute the Save process. We then click the Schedule button to access the Scheduling dialog box for the information about the timing of the broadcast. The second illustration shows this option and the information required.

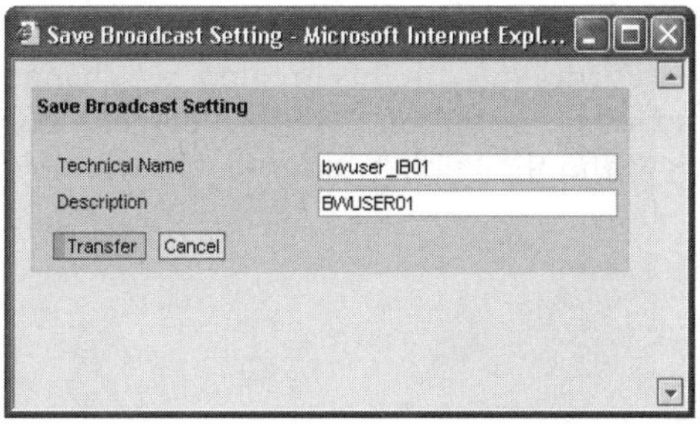

Copyright by SAP AG

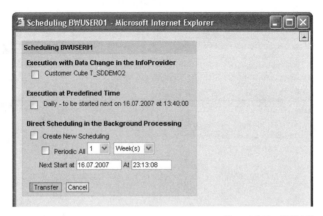

Under the Direct Scheduling in the Background Processing section, we choose the option Create New Schedule and set the timing to periodically once a week, as shown here.

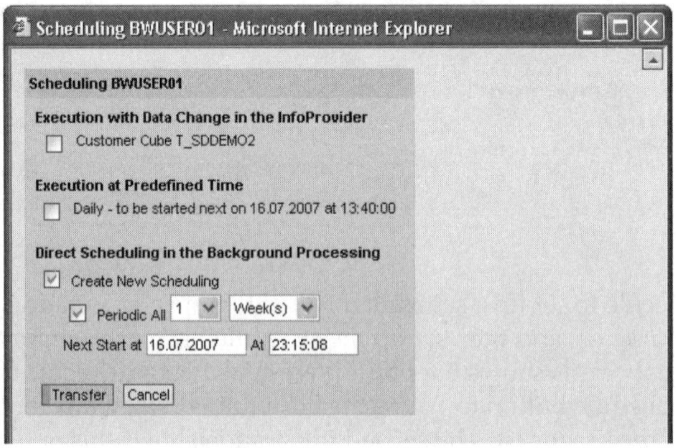

Now, we will change the settings so that the information can be collected and reviewed in the Portal under the BEx Portfolio. With this in mind, we change the distribution type to Broadcast to the Portal and select the option Export Document to Other Folder. We'll also use the CM Repository View and the Public Folder that is available in this section, as shown next.

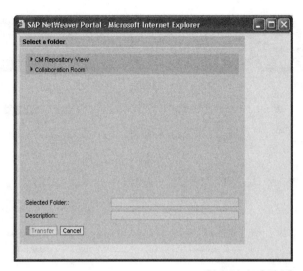

The first of the following illustrations shows the final view of this setup. Notice the use of the Public Documents folder in the KM area. This information will be available in the Portal using the BEx Portfolio. The second illustration shows the access point for the Portal and the BEx Portfolio link.

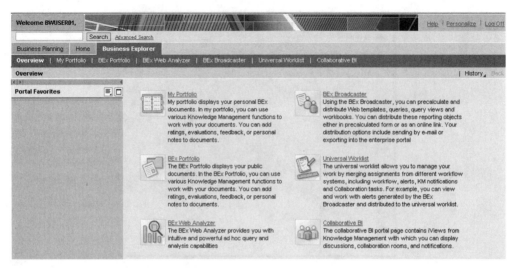

Summary

This chapter introduced the Information Broadcaster component, along with some of the setup of the basic system as well as the Broadcaster itself. A number of the available options are reasonably straightforward, and the users can work through them with only basic training on the system and BW. In other cases, such as the Exceptions and OLAP processes, additional information is needed. In this chapter, the importance and functionality of the Broadcaster is emphasized. As part of the overall reporting strategy and enterprise reporting process in BW, it's important to map out the architecture and uses of this component early on in the project. Due to the additional setup of the Basis portion of the Broadcaster, it is important to get the Basis system maintenance person involved. This will help alleviate any system issues down the road for your corporation. I can't emphasis enough the flexibility and uses of the Information Broadcaster with the distribution of your data and information to multiple users. This is definitely a component that you will use for getting information to your sales force quickly so that additional information can be available for sales activities, distributing critical operational information immediately so that production lines can be effected and run more efficiently, and analysis of customer needs can be done with the most recent information. In this business environment when information is the key to success getting it to the people that need it is the difference that makes or breaks companies.

Advanced Configuration of the Information Broadcaster

In this chapter we will expand on the different distribution types we discussed in the last chapter. The distribution types Data Bursting, Precalculated Value Sets, Multi Channel Distribution, and Exceptions, to name a few, are components of the Information Broadcaster that fit nicely into your information reporting and distribution process. As we get into the details a bit more, we will make sure a clear process exists for configuring these distribution types and that you can work through this process as easily as possible. Setting up distribution by e-mail is a typical process. However, there are some gotchas with the other types that you should be aware of so that the implementation process can be a smooth one.

Advanced Functions of the Information Broadcaster

We covered the basics of the Information Broadcaster in the previous chapter. However, we still need to work through the advanced functionality and options of the Information Broadcaster. For example, to set up of the Exception option of the Broadcaster, you set up the exception in the query, configure the settings in the Information Broadcaster, and, if interested, set up the Alert categories in the Implementation Guide of the BW system. In each case, we will cover the options in detail, including a lot of screen shots. Although it's helpful to have a menu path or a series of steps to understand where you are going, seeing a picture of what the system should look like once you get there is invaluable. In this chapter, I may cover some of the same information discussed in the last chapter in the course of explaining these processes, but a little bit of review isn't a bad thing.

Precalculated Value Set

The distribution type Precalculated Value Set allows you to fill variables of this type with characteristic values in the background. The precalculated value sets are then available as variable values in the BEx queries. Precalculated value sets can be scheduled to run in the background. This helps improve system performance by ensuring complex selections take place offline and possibility in a more convenient time frame versus during a more high volume and active time of the day. When the broadcast is triggered, the query specified in the broadcast is executed. Then, depending on your choice of characteristic in the broadcast, every value is captured and saved to a permanent storage table known as the *value set*. A value set contains exactly one characteristic, but you can define a separate broadcast for each characteristic you wish to capture. Every time a broadcast is executed for a value set, the characteristic values are simply overwritten in the value set each time; there is no recording of historical values. If you wanted to keep a value set, you would simply make sure you do not reexecute the same one. A value set is not tied to a particular query. This means you can reuse the value set as the input selection to any number of queries, and the query can be based on any InfoProvider. For example, you could select the top three products by calculating the results from the DataStore object, and use these results as the filters for a query based on the InfoCube. Another example might be the use of a set of nested conditions. This involves the same query with a set of conditions. For example, the first condition might be to filter on the top five customers, and then the second condition might be to filter the top five materials based on the top five customers. This can be set up and the initial query can be run in the background prior to the required execution of the final query.

This approach—using precalculated value sets—is similar to the concept of the pre-query or result query. However, in the case of the pre-query or result query, the query is executed in real time, whereas with a precalculated value set the initial query (filter) is stored and executed beforehand, based on a set of parameters set up in the Information Broadcaster. Thus, the precalculated value set may be set up to execute and store the values every day at 8:00 A.M., for example. Then, when the business user executes the query and needs to select the variable value, which is the value set, the value is all ready to filter the current query. To help you visual this, the following illustration shows the initial query that is built for the precalculated value set. In this case, the query has 0MATERIAL in the rows and a key figure of Sales and the Calendar Year/Month in the columns. The month is limited to a specific month, just to reduce the amount of data.

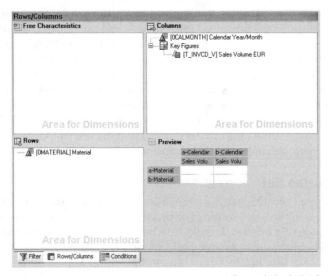

The first of the following illustrations shows the condition that has been applied to this query. The materials are limited to the top five values based on total sales. The second illustration shows the results of this query. Notice that there are only five material values: 1400-300, L-40C, 1400-310, L-80C, and L-60F.

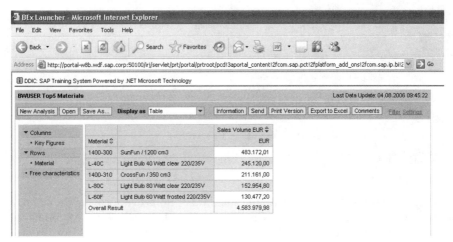

Copyright by SAP AG

Now, we'll step into the Enterprise Portal to set up the Information Broadcaster with the necessary settings for the precalculated value set. The first of the following illustrations shows this scenario. Accessing the Information Broadcaster via the BI Portal, we can access the broadcaster view, as shown in the second illustration. Notice that when we access the

Broadcaster this way, the query is empty and requires that you use the Open button.
Therefore, we use the query as the "object type" and access the Open option.

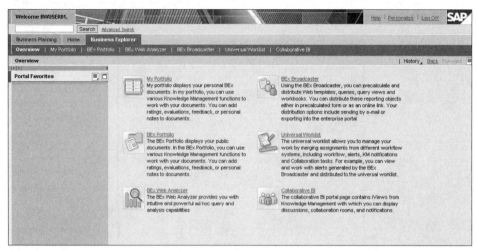

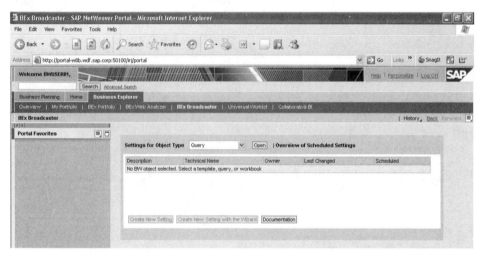

This action causes a dialog box with the standard options to appear, as shown in the
first illustration on the following page. Choose the query BWUSER Top 5 Materials and then
click Transfer. This takes us back to the original screen of the Information Broadcaster, and
the query is set as the source. Then click the Create New Settings button to access the details
of the settings process, which is shown in the second illustration on the following page.

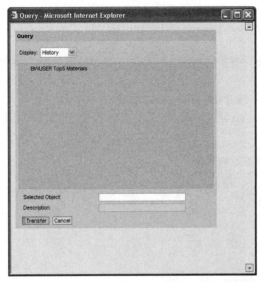

Copyright by SAP AG

Copyright by SAP AG

Once you have accessed the Settings screen, enter a description and then change the Distribution Type setting to Precalculate Value Set. This causes the Output Format setting to default to Value Set. The Authorization User setting will default to the current user, and then the language can be set. The following illustration shows all these settings.

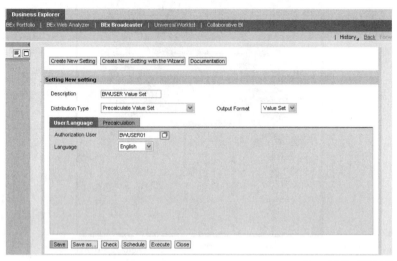

Move to the Precalculation tab and enter the settings necessary. You can review the fields and use the F4 help to use some of the system parameters that are standard settings on the system. The Value Set field will be filled with the Setting IDs. In the Description field, you can include a description, possibly using some system parameters. Finally, the most important setting is Characteristic. Make sure this setting is based on the characteristic that will be used in the query as a variable. In our case, we will be using the characteristic for 0MATERIAL. The first of the following illustrations shows the initial screen for these settings. The second illustration shows the use of some system parameters to automatically fill the fields with set information. Notice that over ten different settings can be used, including User, Language, Date, Time, Calendar Week, and Technical Name of the Settings. The final illustration shows the use of the Time ID as well as the Setting ID for the value set's technical name.

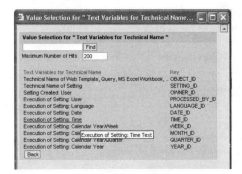

Copyright by SAP AG

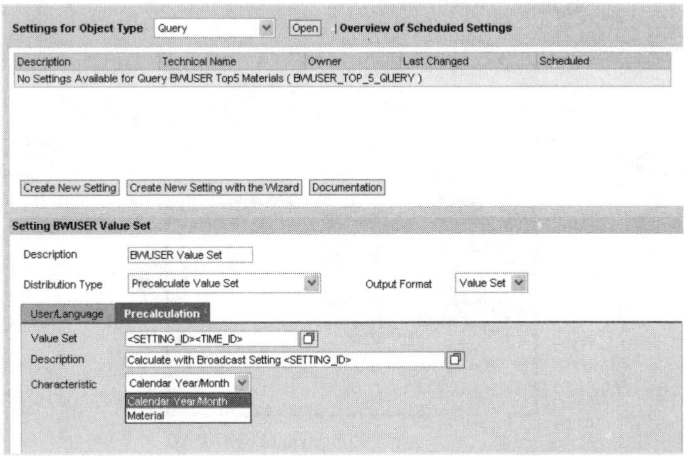

Copyright by SAP AG

The first of the following illustrations shows the identification of the characteristic 0MATERIAL as the set InfoObject for this precalculated value set. Saving these parameters takes us to second illustration, where a technical name and description can be entered. These settings can be scheduled for execution, but for our case using the Execute option will be the quickest approach to see the results. The third illustration shows the outcome once the precalculated value set is executed. Notice the technical name of the value set—TEMP_DC372322F5EECCF1B1C60014. This will come up a bit later.

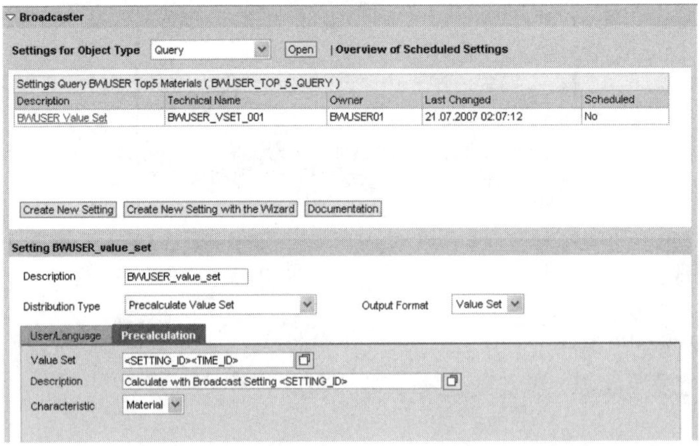

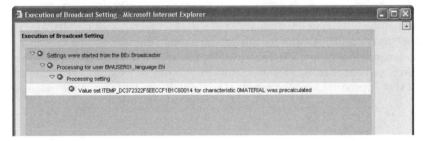

Copyright by SAP AG

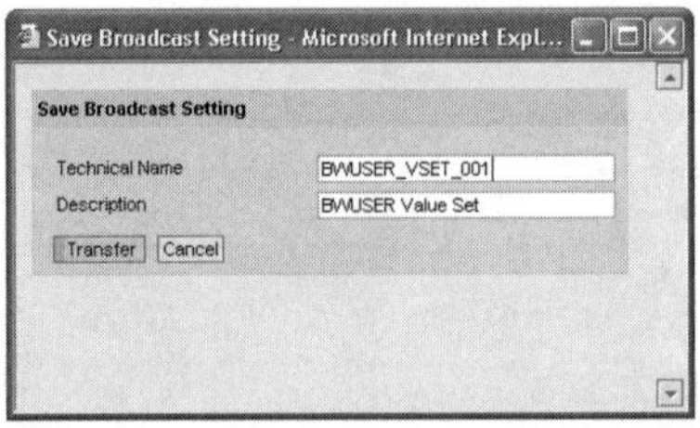

Copyright by SAP AG

Copyright by SAP AG

Now we need to create another query to use the precalculated value set. We'll go back to the BEx Query Designer and set up the query with the characteristic 0MATERIAL and an extra characteristic, 0SOLD_TO PARTY, to be used in the process of extending the information available when using the value set. The important item in this process is setting up the variable correctly to be able to access the precalculated value set. The first of the following illustrations shows the initial screen of the Query Designer. The variable setup is shown in the second illustration. Notice the Processing By setting for this variable (Manual

Input/Default Value). Nothing else on the General tab is different from normal. The important settings are found on the Details tab, where Variable Represents is set to Precalculated Value Set and Variable Is is set to Mandatory. Now we can save the variable. The third illustration shows this information. Once these settings are complete, we can then execute the query.

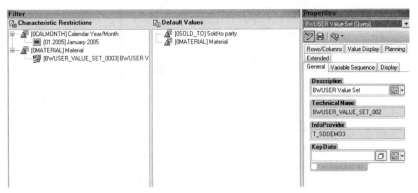

Copyright by SAP AG

Copyright by SAP AG

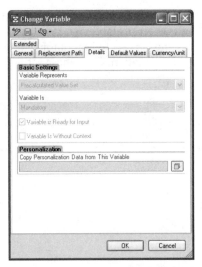

The first of the following illustrations shows the initial screen for the variable of the precalculated value set. The initial screen requires the entry of a precalculated value set. Using the F4 input help, we can see that the only options available are those executed via the Information Broadcaster and available for that specific characteristic (in our case, 0MATERIAL). Therefore, as mentioned, these value sets are available for the assigned characteristics and therefore are available for all queries using that specific characteristic. Notice that the technical name of the precalculated value set is the same as the one we identified earlier. The second illustration shows the final results of the query execution. The results show that the original five materials of the query we used in the precalculation are in the initial column, followed by the customer assigned to them with their specific values for sales.

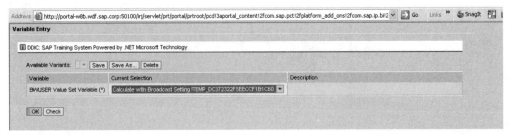

Copyright by SAP AG

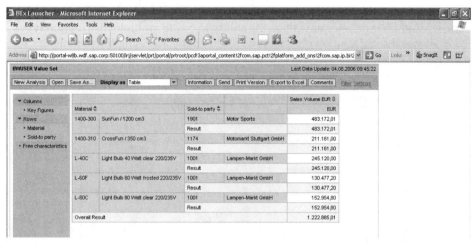

NOTE *In the query, make sure the Precalculated Value Set characteristic is in the first column or the first position in the rows to ensure the results look consistent.*

Multichannel Distribution

The distribution type Broadcast (Multi Channel) enables the use of multiple methods for distributing information to the business users. This offers a much more enhanced option in the Information Broadcaster for flexibility and functionality. Depending on the output format, the reports can be distributed by e-mail, exported to the Portal, or printed. Once the distribution type has been selected, the appropriate tabs will appear, where you can fill in the details of the broadcasting process. An example of this is shown in the following illustration.

Copyright by SAP AG

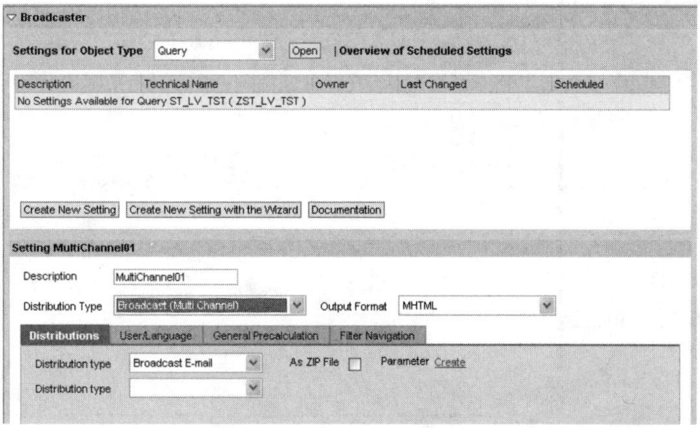

Having accessed the Information Broadcaster and assigned the distribution type as Broadcast (Multi Channel), we now have the ability to create multiple distribution types. In this case, we use the distribution type Broadcast E-mail. By accessing the parameters, we have the ability to add users, roles, and additional e-mail addresses. The following illustration shows this information.

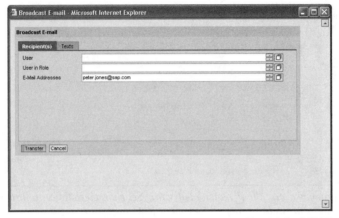

The next distribution type we will use is for the Portal, and the following illustration shows that the options are slightly different from those for the e-mail process. In this case, the options are exporting the results to a personal portfolio and exporting the results to another folder. These settings are confirmed by saving. We can also indicate whether to execute the Broadcaster settings immediately or set up a scheduling process to execute the broadcast of this information periodically.

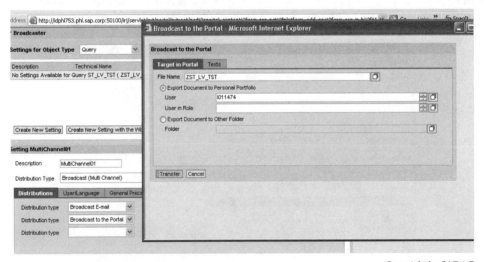

Precalculation of Queries, Query Views, Web Templates, and Reports

This option sometimes gets confused with the precalculated value set, but it is a very different approach to the distribution of information found in the queries, query views, Web templates, and reports. Where you set up a query that you identify as the Value Set – then execute this query before hand and therefore precalculate this specific set of values, the use of precalculation of queries is to execute a program to supply the queries with data that has already been uploaded and sorted so that the data set is available without accessing the database again. You can precalculate queries, query views, Web templates, and reports in various formats or create online links for these BI objects. You can broadcast the information by e-mail, to the Portal, or to a printer. For precalculation and distribution, choose from the following options:

- **For queries**   Query _ Publish _ BEx Broadcaster in the BEx Query Designer.
- **For query views**   Send in the BEx Web Analyzer. The Broadcasting Wizard appears.
- **For Web templates**   Web Template _ Publish _ BEx Broadcaster in the Web Application Designer.
- **For reports**   Report _ Publish _ BEx Broadcaster in the Report Designer.

Next we need to select the object we want to broadcast. Under Settings for Object Type, choose Query, Query View, Web Template, or Report. Click Open, select the required BI object, and choose Apply. Click the Create New Setting button and enter a description for the broadcast setting.

Choose the required distribution type—either Broadcast E-Mail, Portal, or Printer. Then select the output format—MHTML, HTML, XML, Online Link to Current Data, PDF, or Print Format (PS or PCL). We talked about these different types of output formats in the previous chapter, so we will not go into detail again in this chapter. However, it is good to touch on the printing functionality.

The BEx Broadcaster allows you to select from the output formats available for the distribution type you selected. The Print Format (PS or PCL) output format is printer-specific and therefore is only available with the distribution type Broadcast to Printer. The Portable Document Format (PDF) output format is also available for this distribution type. If you want to broadcast the precalculated document as a Zip file, select ZIP File. If you have selected HTML or MHTML as the output format *and* want to broadcast the document by e-mail, you have to create the document as a Zip file. If you selected a particular file format (HTML, PDF, PS, or PCL) as the output format, you can make various settings on the General Precalculation tabbed page. If you selected an online link as the output format, the setting options are available on the General Link Generation tabbed page. If you selected PDF as the output format, you can make the settings for the print version on the Layout and Header/Footer tabbed pages. If you want to create several documents with various filter settings for the same query or Web Application, choose the Filter Navigation tabbed page and make the required settings.

Check your settings, if required, and choose Save. Enter a technical name for the broadcast setting and choose Apply. The new setting appears in the overview in the upper area of the BEx Broadcaster. If you want to distribute the broadcast setting for the query or

Web Application immediately, choose Execute. A new browser window appears; it displays the processing status for the broadcast setting. If you want to distribute the broadcast setting for the query or Web Application at a specific time or when data is changed, choose Schedule.

You have generated and distributed a query, query view, report, or Web Application as an online link or as a precalculated file, in accordance with the selected settings. If you have precalculated and distributed a query, it is displayed as a table with a filter area (according to the filters selected). From a technical viewpoint, the query is embedded in the Standard Web Template for Query Precalculation (0QUERY_TEMPLATE_BROADCASTING70). If you have generated a report (this would be a report created using the Report Designer Functionality) as a precalculated document, the Standard Web Template for Report Precalculation (0REPORT_TEMPLATE_BROADCASTING) is used; this template contains the Report Web item. You can make the setting for the standard Web templates in the Customizing section under SAP Reference IMG _ SAP NetWeaver _ Business Intelligence _ Settings for Reporting and Analysis _ BEx Web _ Set Standard Web Templates (or these templates will be used automatically without specifically identifying them in the IMG). You can also specify another Web template (for example, one containing your company logo) as the Standard Web Template for Query Precalculation or as the Standard Web Template for Report Precalculation. The broadcast setting is listed in the upper area of the BEx Broadcaster screen. It displays all broadcast settings that were created for this query or Web Application. If you want to edit or delete the broadcast setting, choose Edit or Delete in the context menu for the setting.

NOTE *It is important to make sure that several templates are activated and available for use by the Broadcaster. These templates include 0BROADCAST_TEMPLATE, 0BROADCAST_ TEMPLATE70 (found in the WAD template 3.x SBC section), 0BROADCAST_INDEX_PAGE, 0QUERY_TEMPLATE_BROADCASTING70, as well as 0REPORT_TEMPLATE_ BROADCASTING. If unavailable the system will generate an error and therefore require you to activate this SBC.*

General Settings for Precalculation and the Creation of Links

If you selected a particular file format (HTML, PDF, PS, or PCL, for example) as the output format, you can make various settings on the General Precalculation tabbed page. If you selected an online link as the output format, the setting options are available on the General Link Generation tabbed page. Here, you specify the theme you want to use. The theme determines the colors and appearance of the precalculated BI object. Note that the themes available depend on the selected output format. The BEx Broadcaster provides the relevant themes for the output format. As an additional option, the broadcast setting is only distributed when the data displayed in the distributed document has been changed since the last distribution in the underlying Data Provider (such as the query). If the displayed data has not changed, the document is not distributed. You can only make this setting for queries and Web templates. The BEx Broadcaster can only apply this function if the broadcast setting itself has not been changed. If the broadcast setting has been changed, the BEx Broadcaster distributes the document in accordance with your settings, without checking whether changes have been made to the displayed data. The Transfer Navigational State function is only available when you start the BEx Broadcaster from a Web Application (by choosing

Distribute in the context menu) and then navigate to the BEx Broadcaster. Keep the following points in mind:

- If the precalculated document or the online link is to have the current navigational state of the Web Application, choose Apply. The current navigational state is the state from which you called the BEx Broadcaster in the context menu by choosing Distribute.

- If the precalculated document or the online link is to have the initial navigational state of the Web Application, choose Delete. The initial navigational state is the starting view when the Web Application is called (from the Web Application Designer, for example).

Variable Assignment allows the creation of values for input-ready variables of the BI object (Query, Query View, Report, or Web Application). The BI object is precalculated using these variable values. This is a very good example of setting up runtime Variants to be used in this process. If the variables value is "Take from Variant", you can select from an existing BI object – the variant – that was created before hand and can be used for the execution of the Broadcasting process. With this process the values that fill the variables can be managed by the IT department or whomever will be executing the Information Broadcaster program.

Variable assignment from variants is also possible for workbooks. If you selected Online Link to Current Data as the output format, the variable assignment is appended to the URL. When the recipient opens the online link, the BI object is started with these variable values. When you precalculate a file, you can specify one or more variable assignments on the General Precalculation tabbed page. When you generate online links, you can assign only one variable. If the query or Web Application contains exceptions, you can specify whether they are to be considered during precalculation or generation of online links. Here are the available options:

- **No Consideration**   The system precalculates the query or Web Application or generates an online link regardless of whether an alert has occurred.

- **Only Precalculate at Minimum Alert Level**   The query or Web Application is only precalculated or distributed as an online link if an exception occurs within it that has a specific minimum alert level or a worse alert level. Specify the required minimum alert level.

This process is reasonably generic in nature compared to the broadcast settings explained in the other sections. Therefore, we will not go through an example of these options. We will defer to the other examples to fill in the gaps in configuring these specific settings and will review in more detail the Exception distribution type later in this chapter.

Fill OLAP Cache

This distribution type allows the use of OLAP cache, and you can precalculate the queries and fill the cache with the generated query data. If the users call any of the report options that are based on this data, the access time is significantly reduced and the workload on the application server is considerably less. This is because the data is retrieved from the application server memory rather than from the database server, where the reads of the database are required to retrieve the information. This can be a very popular option depending on the amount of time and effort you are expecting to use for performance tuning for your queries. Depending on your reporting strategy for improving performance filling OLAP cache will be the fastest (in most cases even faster than BIA) available option to access your data.

The following illustration shows the initial screen for the Fill OLAP Cache distribution type. Notice that much of the additional tabs are removed from the screen because this process stores the results of the query or other report in the OLAP cache.

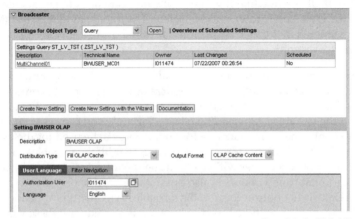

Copyright by SAP AG

The following illustration shows the only other tab, Filter Navigation, and the options available are exactly the same as discussed with other distribution types: No Filter, Filter by Selected Characteristics, and Filter by Control Query with a possible variant. (As you may have noticed, the concept of a control query is very similar to the concept of precalculated value sets for the Information Broadcaster; therefore, the control query filters the initial information for the executed query and again the use of a variant is possible.)

Copyright by SAP AG

Bursting Method of Distribution

This distribution type allows you to broadcast BI information—queries, query views, and other BW objects—as precalculated documents or online links by e-mail to recipients that you determine on the basis of master data. If you have maintained the addresses of the recipients in the master data, you can select a characteristic in whose attributes the e-mail addresses or SAP BI users are maintained, and the system can determine the recipients from this information. This is called *bursting*. The following illustration shows an overview of this concept.

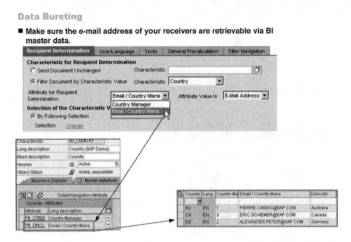

Copyright by SAP AG

Using the master data of the InfoObject to store the e-mail addresses of the recipients of the broadcasting, the Information Broadcaster can access this information and send the appropriate specific information, in this case, to each of the managers. The following illustration shows the differences between the use of Send Document Unchanged and Filter Document by Characteristic Value. This setting is very important depending on the detailed information that you are sending and the fact that this will help in distributing the specific information for that particular region or manager.

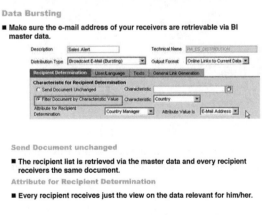

Copyright by SAP AG

The following illustration shows the initial information for this example. In this case, the query is created based on the InfoObject BWCUST01, which has two attributes: 0COUNTRY and PM-EMAIL.

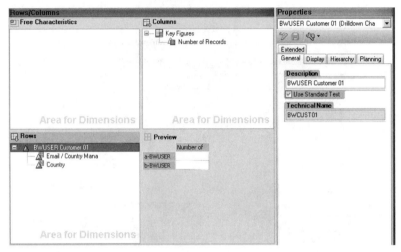

In each of these objects there is master data for two managers. The results are shown in the following illustration. In this case, the query shows the two managers and the ability to report on the e-mail addresses or the SAP addresses.

With the set up of this query complete, we access the Information Broadcaster and configure the initial settings for this type of distribution. The following illustration shows the start to this process. This is the initial Information Broadcaster screen, and the query has already been found and transferred.

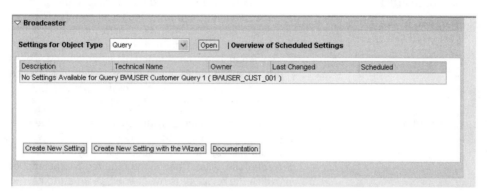

Using the Create New Settings button, we access the next series of screens to complete this activity. The following illustration shows the results of using the distribution type Broadcast E-Mail (Bursting). In contrast to the options with the OLAP distribution type, the Bursting type offers a series of tabs. Each of these tabs and their options are discussed in detail in the following tables.

Information required for determining recipients can be found in Table 12-1.

Parameter	Purpose
Send Document Unchanged	The document is generic and not specific to the individual recipient. Enter the technical name of the required characteristic for which recipient is maintained as an attribute either manually or by choosing the selection icon. The characteristic can be any characteristic in the BI object that you want to distribute. You must also make a selection of the characteristic values for the InfoObject you have chosen.
Filter Document by Characteristic Value	The document is filtered by the characteristic value specific to the recipient that is identified. Each recipient receives the document filtered by the relevant characteristic value. Choose the required characteristic for which the recipient is maintained as an attribute. You can only select from those characteristics that are included in the query or Data Provider of the Web Application or the report. With workbooks, you cannot filter the document by characteristic values.
Generate Document with Variable Values	The characteristic value used to determine the recipient is used as a variable entry when the document is generated. Select the variable you want to use. You can select from those characteristic value variables that are include in the query or Data Provider of the Web Application, the report, or the workbook. The system only displays this setting if the BI object contains variables for characteristic values. The additional use of a variant is possible in this situation
Attribute for Recipient Determination	Choose the attribute assigned to the infoobject that the recipient is maintained. Under "Attribute Values Is", specify whether the recipient is to be identified using the e-mail address or the username.
Selecting Characteristic Values	
Using Following Selection	Under Selection Create, specify the characteristic values that will be used for distributing the information. This will determine each e-mail recipients for the information.
Using a Control Query	The Control Query specifies the query you want the characteristic values to be selected, either manually or by choosing a Selection. A document is calculated and broadcasted for each characteristic value of the selected characteristic. Under Variant, you can select an exiting variant for a query. Variables of the query that are ready for input can then be filled with the values.

TABLE 12-1   Information Broadcasting Settings for Data Bursting by Recipient

Parameter	Purpose
Authorization User	If specified, this user is the basis for the authorization check. Only the result values this user is allowed to see will be presented in the broadcast.
Language	If specified, this language will be used for the broadcast. If this parameter is left blank, the language of the user creating the broadcast will be used.

TABLE 12-2   Information Broadcast Settings for User/Language in Data Bursting

Information required for determining the user/language for this distribution type can be found in Table 12-2.

Information required for the text can be found in Table 12-3.

Information for general precalculations can be found in Table 12-4.

Information for filter navigation can be found in Table 12-5.

In our example, the decision is made to use Filter Document by Characteristic Value and the characteristic BWCUST01, which has as attributes the Country and the PM E-mails for the managers (being used for Attribute for Recipient Determination). The following illustration shows the results of these settings.

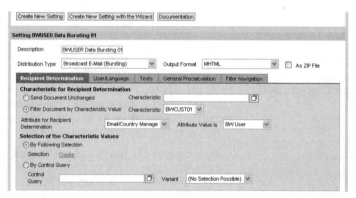

Copyright by SAP AG

Parameter	Purpose
Subject	Enter a subject line for the e-mail manually or use a text variable by choosing with the quick info text Attach Text Variable. The text can contain up to 50 characters.
Importance	Select the importance level for the e-mail (low, medium, or high).
Contents	Enter text for the contents of the e-mail manually or use a text variable by choosing with the quick info text Attach Text Variable. When online links are sent, the system automatically adds a link to the text of the e-mail (if the text does not contain the link) using the PR_ONLINE_LINK variable.

TABLE 12-3   Information Broadcast Settings for Text in Data Bursting

Parameter	Purpose
Portal Theme	Choose the theme which will be used to format the results. Themes can be maintained in the Theme Editor within the Portal.
Only Upon Data Change	If this box is checked, the broadcast will only be sent if the data has been changed since the last time the broadcast was sent based on the data in the source infoprovider
Exceptions	
No Include	Do not use the exception in the query or query view for checking whether to send the broadcast.
Only Precalculate at Minimum Alert Level	If the broadcast is based on a query or query view that contains exceptions, you can specify that the broadcast should only be sent if the alert level (exception level) has been met. You specify that alert level here. This is very popular since it will only send information that may require attention.

TABLE 12-4   Information Broadcast settings for General Precalculation in Data Bursting

Parameter	Purpose
No Filter	Broadcast the report unfiltered.
Filter by Selected Characteristic	Enter the characteristic from the query to use as the filter and select a characteristic. You will then see a link to create the values for filtering. You will also have the option to create an unfiltered view for each recipient.
Filter by Control Query	Enter the name of a query that will be used to determine the characteristic values for filtering the broadcast result. For example, this query might select the worst performing sales regions on the basis of the condition in query A. These regions will then be sent a detailed breakdown of their results in the broadcast based on query B.

TABLE 12-5   Information Broadcast settings for Filter Navigation in Data Bursting

The next step in the process is to access Selection of the Characteristic Values. In this case, these values are the master data values of BWCUST01. This distributes the information to the selected values, so in this case we choose all values except for the # sign. The following two illustrations show these results.

Copyright by SAP AG

Copyright by SAP AG

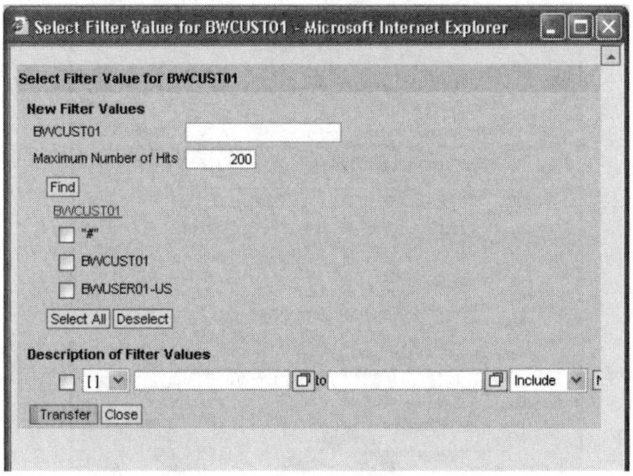

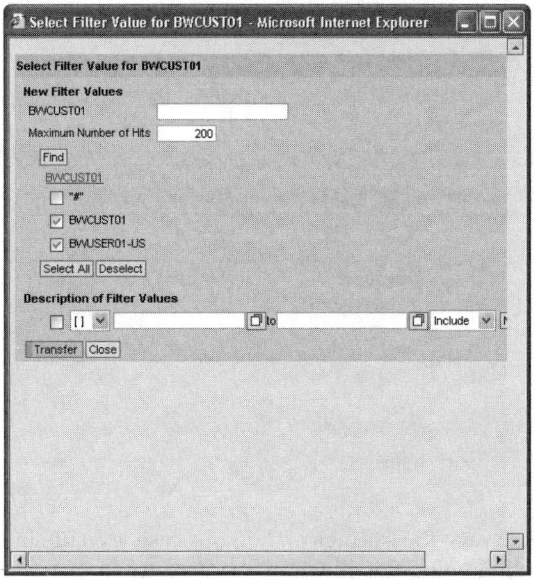

In the next step, we use some of the standard system-delivered variables to help with the Text field. We will use two system variables—one for the object description and the other for the date created. The following two illustrations show the results of this process.

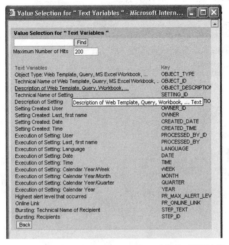

Copyright by SAP AG

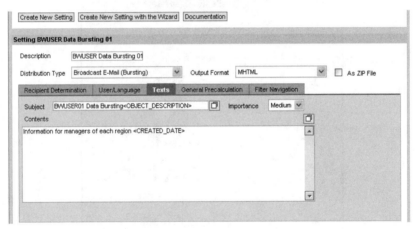

Copyright by SAP AG

The final process is to save the settings and, in our case, execute immediately to see the results, as shown in the following two illustrations. Because in this case there was only one SAP user to go to, we see only one step in the results process.

Copyright by SAP AG

Copyright by SAP AG

If required, specific documents can be filtered to each recipient by their relevant characteristic values. Thus, every recipient receives the document with the values that correspond to their areas. For example, each division manager gets distributed the information only they require and are responsible for, not all the information available for the company. This is useful when you need to distribute business results to a large number of recipients. As you have seen, some of the distribution types are very similar to others, and the Bursting type is very similar to the Broadcast E-mail, except with bursting the recipient addresses are stored externally from the broadcast setting as master data attributes. The final result is shown in the following illustration. The result was e-mailed to the user, showing the query with the different managers who were alerted.

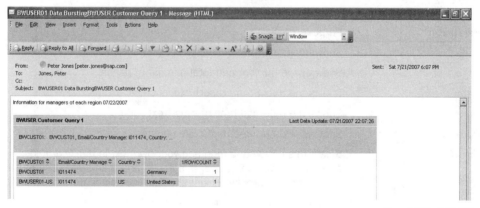

Copyright by SAP AG

Parameter	Purpose
Fit to Page Width	The BI application is adjusted to fit the width of the page in the print version.
Fit to Page	The BI application is adjusted to fit to the size of the page.
Poster	The BI application is printed in the form of a poster, in which individual areas of the BI application are printed on different pages. You can repeat lead columns and column headings.
Theme	Choose to use either the SAP default theme or black and white.
Paper Format	Choose between DIN A4 format and letter format.
Orientation	Choose between portrait format or landscape format.

TABLE 12-6   Parameters in the Layout Tab of the Print Settings Dialog Box

Printing Process

If you need hard copies of the reports and they are scheduled to run at a specific time of the day and week, then use the distribution type Printing. A spool request is automatically generated for the required report. You have two output format options to choose from for the printing process:

- Printer Format (Printer control language or PostScript Language)
- PDF

NOTE *Before the PDF option can be used, the settings for this specific printing process have to be set up.*

This option was not as popular in the previous versions of BW broadcasting since the functionality of printing was not as robust as many would have needed but in this version of BW you should not overlook this option since you will see a significant improvement in the Printing component. When you are selecting your printer device, you will be prompted with the supported devices and the available formatting options. The print parameters on the Layout tab are detailed in Table 12-6.

On the tab Header/Footer, you can choose to display various parameters such as those in Table 12-7.

Parameter	Purpose
Page 1	Shows page number.
Page 1 of ?	Shows page number and total number of pages.
Date	Shows the date of the report execution.
Date, Time	Shows the date and time of report execution.
Date Time Page 1 of ?	Shows the date, time, and page number.
Free Text	Select this option and then add your own text in the Text field. Alternatively, you can select this option and then select one of the system parameters by clicking the Text Variable icon.
Time	Shows the time of report execution.

TABLE 12-7   Settings on the Header/Footer Tab of the Print Settings Dialog Box

The first of the following illustrations shows some of the information involved in setting up the printing function. Notice that the Adobe Service is used for the PDF process. Also, to configure the print settings, use the menu path SAP Menu | Tools | CCMS | Print, as shown in the following illustration.

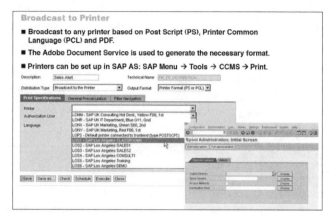

▽ 🗀 SAP menu
  ▷ 🗀 Office
  ▷ 🗀 Modeling
  ▷ 🗀 Administration
  ▷ 🗀 Business Explorer
  ▷ 🗀 Business Planning and Simulation
  ▷ 🗀 Enhanced Analytics
  ▽ 🗀 Tools
    ▷ 🗀 ABAP Workbench
    ▷ 🗀 Customizing
    ▷ 🗀 Administration
    ▷ 🗀 ALE
    ▷ 🗀 Business Communication
    ▷ 🗀 Business Framework
    ▷ 🗀 Business Workflow
    ▽ 🗀 CCMS
      ▷ 🗀 Control/Monitoring
      ▷ 🗀 Configuration
      ▷ 🗀 DB Administration
      ▽ 🗀 Print
        ⬡ SP01 - Output Controller
        ⬡ SPAD - Spool Administration
        ⬡ SE73 - Font Maintenance
        ⬡ SP11 - TemSe Contents
        ⬡ SP12 - TemSe Administration
    ▷ 🗀 Background Processing
  ▷ 🗀 Form Printout
  ▷ 🗀 Hypertext
  ▷ 🗀 Find
  ⬡ SXDA - Data Transfer Workbench
  ⬡ EEWB - Easy Enhancement Workbench

As an example of the setup of the print functions, the first of the following illustrations starts out directly in the Information Broadcaster, where the distribution type has been set to Broadcast to the Printer. Notice the different tabs now available—specifically Header/

Footer and Layout. Using the F4 option beside the Printer field, we get a list of printers available, as shown in the second illustration.

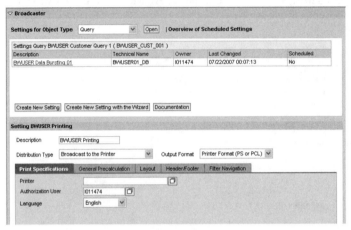

Copyright by SAP AG

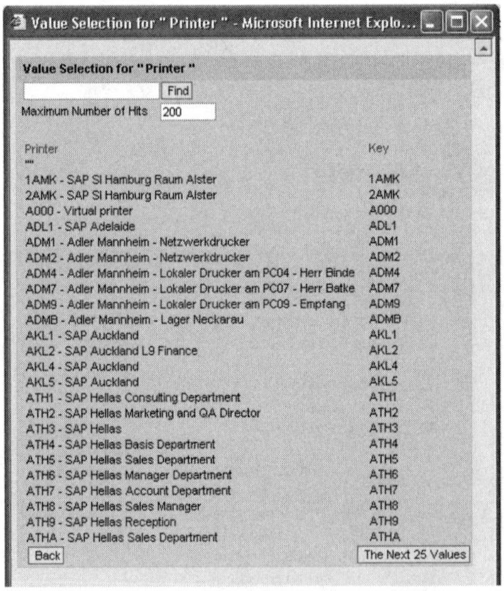

Copyright by SAP AG

Once the specific printer is chosen, the next step is to verify the theme, which is located on the next tab, as shown in the first of the following illustrations. The next two tabs are important in this case because this is where the print settings are configured. The second illustration shows the parameters for the Layout tab. The ability to change or affect the page structure, margins, size, format, and so on, is very useful for business users who need some flexibility during the print process. The third illustration shows the options on the Header/Footer tab, with all the selections discussed in Table 12-7. Again, the ability to format the header and footer is important, and the ability to use system variables to fill in the basic information is effective and efficient.

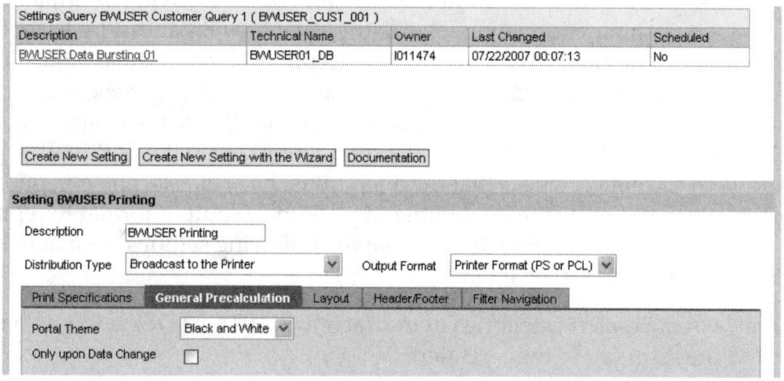

Copyright by SAP AG

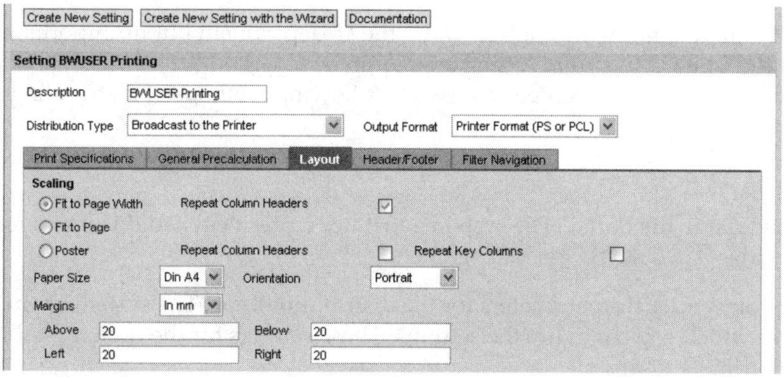

Copyright by SAP AG

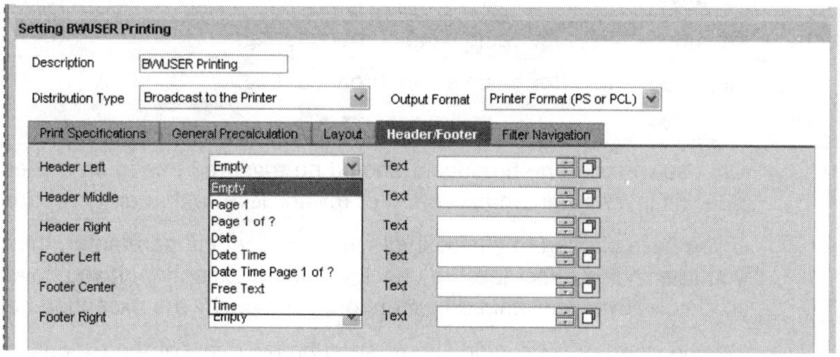

Copyright by SAP AG

NOTE *If your BW version is at SP12 you will have other options available rather than just having the PDF process. This will allow you to use the printing capabilities without the requirement of the Adobe Service.*

Exceptions in the Broadcaster

Broadcast by Exception is one of the most important distribution types because it helps move the reporting strategy of the company from the basic process of receiving information to the proactive process of pushing information. The distribution type Broadcast by Exception allows you to check queries in the background for exceptions. If a threshold value for an exception is exceeded or not reached, the BEx Broadcaster immediately generates a document in accordance with the criteria defined by you and distributes this to the recipients via e-mail, to the portal, or as an alert (for example, into the central worklist in the BI Portal). A perquisite for the Broadcast by Exception type is that the query must have at least one exception. You select Broadcast by Exception as the distribution type with the output format Exceptions when you create the broadcast setting. Ensure that the following settings are made for the generation of alerts in Alert Management:

- You have defined alert categories in transaction ALRTCATDEF and you have selected the recipient of the SAP alert.

- You have maintained the alert container, as required. The alert container ensures the exchange between the BI variables and the variables in the central alert server.

These settings are normally configured by the IT department but its important that you both check and understand what setting are required.

The Exception distribution type can use the following methods of distributing the data:

- Broadcast E-Mail
- Create Alert
- Broadcast to the Portal (The system generates a precalculated document format and provides it in Knowledge Management.)

Finally, you specify the parameters for the distribution type. The system opens a new dialog box in which you configure the settings. These settings for the Broadcast E-Mail type are detailed in Table 12-8.

Parameter	Purpose
Recipient tab options	Generic settings for basic e-mail broadcasting.
Text tab options	Generic settings for basic e-mail broadcasting.
Exception Distribution Tab	
Selection Criterion	Choose whether the broadcast should be triggered based on a check of a specific level within an exception or for any level within an exception.
Value	If you have chosen to check levels in the preceding parameter, then here you specify the exact level to check within an exception. If you have chosen to check any level within an exception, you specify the exception here.
Contents	Decide whether you would like to send an overview of the exceptions or a detailed report.
Format	Specify the output format of the broadcast. You can choose between HTML, XML, and text.

TABLE 12-8   Settings for the Distribution Type Broadcast E-mail for Exception Broadcasting

You can specify recipients in two ways:

- **User** Enter the BI usernames of the recipients manually or choose F4 with the quick info text Selection; usernames must be separated by semicolons.

- **Users in Role** Enter the BI roles manually or choose F4 with the quick info text Selection; roles must be separated by semicolons. The e-mail is sent to all users assigned to one of the roles specified here.

If an e-mail address for a user you have specified under User or User in Role has not been maintained in user maintenance, the user does not receive the distributed file as an e-mail. Instead, the user receives a message in the BW business workplace (transaction SO01).

The next distribution type for exception broadcasting is Export to the Enterprise Portal. This allows the exceptions to be sent to the Portal to either the Personal Portfolio of a user or the shared portfolio within the Portal. Based on the selection of this distribution type, the settings will be different than in the preceding table. These settings are detailed in Table 12-9.

On the User/Language tabbed page, for the background processing of the broadcast, you can determine the language, authorizations, and user-specific settings with which the scheduled document is to be generated.

For Exception Search you define the navigational states that are to be used for identifying the specific state for the exceptions:

- **Standard Navigational State** The system searches the navigational state of the query that was produced in the BEx Query Designer when the query was defined (initial view of query).

Parameter	Description
File Name	Enter the technical name by which the file will be saved to the Portal or use text variables to generate the name (or append the text).
Export Document to personal portfolio	Enter the user IDs or the role of the users who should receive this broadcast in their Personal Portfolio in the Portal.
Export Document to Other Folder	Enter the name of the Portal folder where this broadcast should be saved. Any user who has access to this folder will be able to open the report.
Text (tab)	Same generic settings as the general e-mail broadcast, including the Importance settings of Low, Medium, and High.
Exception Distribution Tab	
Selection Criterion	Choose whether the broadcast should be triggered based on a check of a specific level within an exception or for any level within an exception.
Value	If you have chosen to check levels in the preceding parameter, then here you specify the exact level to check within an exception. If you have chosen to check any level within an exception, you specify the exception here.
Contents	Decide whether you would like to send an overview of the exceptions or a detailed report.
Format	Specify the output of the broadcast. You can choose between HTML, XML, and text.

TABLE 12-9 Settings for Distribution Type Export to the Portal for Exception Broadcasting

- **Following Navigational State**   The system searches the navigational state of the query that arises if the characteristics given in the lines are drilled down. Select the characteristic you want under Characteristic and determine the filter values you require.

You can also specify that the totals row for the characteristic is to be added.

- **All Navigational States**   The system searches all the navigational states that arise if the characteristics specified in the listed order are included in the drilldown. Select the characteristic you want under Characteristic and determine the filter values you require.

The last distribution type is Create Alert, which is used to send details of the exception to the universal worklist in the Portal. Once this option has been selected, you'll see that the parameters are, yet again, different. The parameters involved are detailed in Table 12-10.

Parameter	Description
Alert Generation (tab)	On this tabbed page, you can select the required alert category that was defined in Alert Management.
Alert Category	Choose the alert category (which you should have already defined). The alert category combines a number of parameters that determine how the alert will be managed in the Central Alert Framework (CAF).
Alert Recipient (using Alert Category)	The recipients will be determined from the alert category recipients list.
Alert Recipients | Export Additional Alert Recipients	In addition to the recipients determined from the alert category, you can add more users or roles here.
Alert Parameters	All the parameters are displayed here that you have maintained in the alert category.
Parameters of the Alert Category	If the alert category has been defined with containers, you will see them appear here. You can select them via their checkboxes and then specify the text variable that will fill them.
Exception Distribution Tab	
Selection Criterion	Choose whether the broadcast should be triggered based on a check of a specific level within an exception or for any level within an exception.
Value	If you have chosen to check levels in the preceding parameter, then here you specify the exact level to check within an exception. If you have chosen to check any level within an exception, you specify the exception here.
Contents	This parameter is not required.
Format	This parameter is not required.

TABLE 12-10   Settings for Distribution Type Alert Generation for Exception Broadcasting

Alerts

A critical connection exists between the Broadcaster settings and the Central Alert Framework. All the comments and information we discuss concerning setting up alerts are managed and configured in the Central Alert Framework. One of the components that needs to be confirmed before any activity in the Information Broadcaster is the alert category. The CAF is a component that would be set up with a combination of business user input and the IT department configuration.

An alert category contains various properties and other specifications that define the alerts within that category. The category defines the conditions when a specific alert is sent to someone. Alert categories can be defined by applications or customers using the alert category definition environment, which is accessed in transaction ALRTCATDEF. You can define an alert category to suit your business requirements. When the critical situation defined in the alert category arises, the system recognizes this and sends an alert instance of this category to the recipients you determined. The alert also can be directed to the users' UWL (Universal WorkList) in the BI Portal and can then be processed as a task. An alert category can be assigned to a specific alert classification. Alert classifications help to organize and group alert categories. If you do not assign a category to a specific classification, it will be stored in the classification folder Unclassified.

An alert category is defined by the following:

- Technical key (language independent) for identification purposes.
- Description (language dependent).
- Classification.
- Priority.
- Maximum number of deliveries. (This applies to delivery to a destination other than the alert inbox.)
- Expiry time (in minutes) after which the alert is deleted.
- Escalation recipient to whom the alert is sent if it is not confirmed by any of its recipients.
- Tolerance time before escalation.
- Short text, long text, and title. The title is used as mail title, fax subject, and alert title in the inbox. The long text is used as the mail/fax body and the long text view in the inbox. The short text is used for pager messages and SMS.
- Container for variable definition if variables are to be used in the text, or for other application-specific attributes.
- Subsequent activities in the form of URLs.

You can perform the logical administration of alerts by defining alert categories. During alert category definition, you specify the alert text, expiry time, escalation, and all other conditions related to the sending of this kind of alert. Before setting up the alert category, you should be familiar with the business aspects for which the alert category is to be defined. In addition, the authorization activities should be assigned to your SAP user as described in the authorization concept section of the alert category configuration. The following illustration shows the connection between the Broadcaster and the Alert Framework.

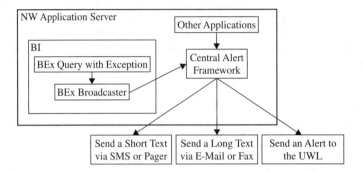

The procedure to set up the alert category is defined in the following paragraphs. During the example of an exception broadcast, this process will be demonstrated directly in the system so we will not use any screenshots here since these will be seen in the example.

NOTE   *These steps are only necessary to manage the Alert Management process so if you are looking to use any of the other Information Broadcasting types this process is not required.*

In the initial process make sure that you are in change mode in the alert category definition environment (transaction ALRTCATDEF). Execute "Create Alert Category" and in the Alert Category column, enter a technical key. Choose a key based on your company defined naming convention. This should describe the situation that triggers the alert and have some business logic to it. This key is language independent and identifies the alert category. A standard namespace convention can apply to the key, which means keys Z* und Y* belong to the customer namespace. In the Description of Alert column, enter a description of the alert category.

On the Properties tabbed page in the Description field, enter a description for the alert category. The description can be of your choice but having something that is consistent with what the alert category is assigned to would be more helpful. The description is language dependent therefore you can have a number of different languages used to fill this field. If required, you can select a classification in the Classification field. If you do not choose a specific classification, the category is stored in the classification folder - Unclassified.

In the "Max. No. of Dels" field, specify a maximum number of times that an alert of this category is to be delivered if it is not confirmed. Therefore, the number of times that you would be willing to wait on a response from the recipient before having to move to either a more proactive alert or a different level of management. This process refers to delivery using a communication channel other than to the recipient's display program (Univeral WorkList, application-specific program, or alert inbox). Then select "Dynamic Text" options if the texts of the alert category cannot be defined at this stage. This refers to situations in which the texts are not known until runtime (for example, when CCMS alerts are forwarded to ALM).

NOTE   *No translation can be performed for alerts with dynamic text. System messages can be entered manually in several languages.*

Once these activities are complete we move to the "Expiry Time in Min" field, you can enter a specific length of time for alerts of this category if the alerts will no longer be relevant after a specific period of time. If the expiry time elapses, the alert is removed from the alert inbox and is no longer delivered using any other channel. All of these options are very important in the Alert Management Process since this will be the company strategy to proactively distribute critical information to either sales or management users.

NOTE *Expiry times can be derived from various sources. Priority is given first to the data provided by the triggering application, second to the BAdI ALERT_EXP_DATE, and third to this field in the alert category definition. If none is found in any of these sources, the default expiry of 31.12.2099 applies.*

In the Rule-Based Recipients field, enter the eight-digit number of the rule to be applied. Select Process Data Flow and find a list of the corresponding alert and rule containers. Then, in the second part of the window assign an element of the rule to each element of the rule container. Finally, select the binding instructions and confirm your input. If you wish to specify an escalation recipient, select Escalation Active and enter the escalation recipient. Additionally, as in the initial set up process you can specify a tolerance time in minutes. When escalation is active for an alert category, an alert is escalated if none of the alert recipients has confirmed the alert after this tolerance time. The escalation recipient is also informed that he or she has received the alert because of an escalation. The escalation function is based on the administrator report RSALERTPROC. This report has to be scheduled as a regular job.

Now you can continue configuring settings on some of the other tabs in this process. On the Container tabbed page, define any variables you may want to use in the short text or long text. You can also define other application-specific variables, such as cost centers, divisions, or sales organizations. These variables are then replaced at runtime with values from the application. On the Long and Short Text tabbed page, enter the texts for the alert category. You can include text variables referring to elements of the alert container or system symbols. In the case of a container element, the variable must be defined in the alert container. The entry in the text must be in the form &<ElementName>&.

NOTE *The title is used as mail title, fax subject, and alert title in the inbox. The long text is used as mail/fax body text and the long text view in the inbox. The short text is used for pager and SMS messages.*

On the Optional Subsequent Activities tabbed page, you can enter URLs for subsequent activities. If you trigger your alerts by calling a function module, you can also specify dynamic subsequent activities. Finally, save your entries.

The next component that should be set up in this process is the alert container, which is a container for the exchange of (application-specific) variables, such as divisions or sales organizations, between the local systems (alert providers) and the central alert server. As you can see this is the interface between the application that triggers the alert and the Central Alert Framework. When you use application-specific variables in your container definition, you supply the values for these variables by writing them into the container as name-value pairs. These are supplied to the Alert Framework on the central system and an interpretation is executed. When the container is filled, no validation check is performed on the elements entered and the data types of their values are in accordance with the container definition. You must ensure that the element names and the data types that you use are in accordance with the definition.

NOTE *Due to technical restrictions between the Workflow Container and SAPscript, only the first 80 characters of a container element are taken into account, when the variables are replaced during runtime.*

The Alert Framework uses the alert container not only for the exchange of application-specific variables, but also for the exchange of internal information. Table 12-11 provides a list of variables used for this purpose.

Be careful if you define your own variables and ensure that no naming conflicts arise. The names of the variables used internally by the Alert Framework all start with an underscore. It may sometimes be appropriate to write variables used internally directly into the container. If, for example, you want to pass URLs to the Alert Framework as subsequent activities, you could instead fill an internal table of the structure SALRTSACTI and write the table into the container with the element name _ALERT_ACTIVITIES. Constants for standard elements in the alert container can be found in the Include statememt <ALRT01>.

Triggering Alerts   An application triggers an alert of a particular alert category based on the business needs and importance of a particular situation. This can be either a business or technical aspect that would trigger an Alert. The alert recipients are determined either by the application, by an administrator, or via a subscription procedure. An Alert outlining the situation is delivered to the recipients on a timely manner based on the parameters in the Alert Category. Depending on the configuration, the alert can be viewed by the recipients in the UWL, in application-specific display programs, or in the alert inbox. In addition, the alerts can be delivered using other channels as well, if the recipients have made the appropriate settings and the communication method is configured in SAPconnect (for example, to the user's e-mail address).

Name	Meaning	Typing
_ALERT_RECIPIENTS	Recipient list	type salrttrcp
_ALERT_ACTIVITIES	Subsequent activities	type table of salrtsacti
_ALERT_EXPIRATION	Expiry date/time (timestamp)	type timestamp
_ALERT_DYNAMIC_SHORTTEXT	Short text	type salrtdcatd (CHAR60)
_ALERT_DYNAMIC_LONGTEXT	Long text	type table of CHAR255
_EVT_OBJECT	Triggering object	type BORIDENT
_ALERT_LOGICAL_SYSTEM	Logical system in which the alert is triggered	type RFCDEST

TABLE 12-11   List of Variables Used in the Alert Framework

NOTE *Alert Management does not incorporate feedback to the triggering application. However, it is possible to model feedback to the application, such as confirming that a subsequent activity has been executed, using SAP Business Workflow and merging of alerts that are related from a content perspective.*

The Alert Container is the main component of the interface between the alert provider (triggering application) and the central alert server. When Alerts of a particular category are used, they must be triggered by an application at runtime. This can be done in a variety of ways. You can call a function module directly or use middleware components that trigger alerts. Some examples of this process might be the use of the Business Object Repository triggering events in case certain changes occur in an event linkage activity. For example, an alert is to be triggered if a Sales Order is changed, a Post Processing Framework (PPF) checking certain conditions and triggering alerts if the conditions are met. This could also be the use of an SAP Workflow activity such as alerting the Finance Department that a specific activity within the Closing Process has been completed or finally the use of the CCMS to trigger alerts if the corresponding activity was assigned in CCMS.

To trigger alerts, the Central Alert Server must be maintained as an RFC destination in transaction SM59 in the local system (similar to setting up a source system RFC to execute transactions or data loads for BW). This central alert server must also be selected as the RFC destination in transaction SALRT1 or in Settings | RFC-Destination of Alert Server. (This constitutes the unique entry in table TALRTDST.) If the central alert server is running on the local system in the same client, you do not have to maintain an RFC destination. In this case, you can simply enter **NONE** in transaction SALRT1. If the alerts are to be sent from the central alert system additionally with an external communication method, the chosen external communication method (e-mail, SMS, fax) must be correctly configured in SAPconnect. During SAPconnect configuration, the communication data (for example, e-mail address) has to be customized in the user settings of the recipient in transaction SU01. As mentioned you can trigger an alert by using any of the following:

- **Triggering by calling a function module directly** The function module SALRT_ CREATE_API is called directly by the application in the local system and passes the data to the central alert server via RFC. The alert category (IP_CATEGORY) is the only mandatory import parameter. You can also add non-SAP user addresses to the Central Address Management.

- **Triggering by calling a function module in the Workplace plug-in** With the SAP Workplace plug-in, it is possible to use the alert management in SAP Web AS 6.10 or older SAP Basis releases. The function module for triggering an alert is SALERT_ CREATE_API. This function module possesses an interface analogous to described SALRT_CREATE_API.

- **Triggering with an event linkage** An alert can also be triggered by the occurrence of an event defined in the Business Object Repository (BOR). In transaction SWE2 in the local system, you enter the alert category as the receiver type and the function module SALRT_CREATE_VIA_EVENT as the receiver function module for the event. The Alert Framework receives your alert category from your entry in the event linkage table.

- **Triggering with the Post Processing Framework (PPF) or Message Control (MC)**
  Using PPF/MC to trigger alerts enables you to define general conditions and initiate
  output, such as printing, sending an Internet mail, or starting a workflow. The
  triggering of an alert can be modeled as a method call (PPF) or by writing a processing
  program for the medium "special function" (MC). You should only trigger alerts using
  PPF/MC if you already use PPF/MC in your application.

- **Triggering from a workflow**   You can define the triggering of an alert as a step in a
  workflow definition, although you would usually only do this as an extension to an
  existing workflow. Elements in the workflow container can be used as attributes.

- **Triggering from CCMS with autoreaction**   CCMS offers the autoreaction method
  CCMS_Send_Alert_to_ALM. If this method is assigned to a monitoring node, the
  monitoring architecture sends the alerts of this node to ALM.

Recipient Determination

Alert Management must know who the recipients of alerts of a particular category are so
that it can inform the correct parties. There are various ways of determining the recipients
of alerts. The various options for determining recipients are detailed here, and they can be
combined to create a more specific recipient analysis.

- **User subscription**   The user chooses the alert categories that are relevant for him
  or her. Subscription is implemented as the Business Server Page (BSP) application
  ALERTSUBSCRIPTION. A user can only subscribe to alert categories for which he
  or she has the authorization. This authorization is assigned to roles using
  Subscription Authorization in the alert category definition environment (transaction
  ALRTCATDEF).

- **Administrator Determines Recipients**   A system administrator determines the
  recipients of a particular alert category in the definition environment (transaction
  ALRTCATDEF). The administrator can define individual recipients (using Fixed
  Recipients) or roles (using Recipients Via User Roles).

- **Application Determines Recipients**   For recipient determination during runtime,
  applications can pass specific recipients to the alert server in the API. If the application
  knows precisely who is to receive a particular alert instance, the application can
  pass the specific recipients to the alert server in the API. This could be on the basis
  of the organization hierarchy model or application customizing. The application
  must ensure that the recipients are authorized to receive the particular alert. These
  recipients will receive the alert regardless of whether they have subscribed to the
  relevant alert category.

Now, with all this information, you're likely wondering how you will be able to work
through the system comfortably and consistently to get everything to work. It's time to go
through an example of setting up an exception broadcast and discuss all the different parts.
Our example starts out with developing an exception in a query. We discussed this process
at length in a previous chapter, so we will work through this portion by just looking at the

end result. The following illustration shows the BEx Query Designer with the formatted query. This is a basic query, so the process can be more focused. The only InfoObjects involved are one key figure (Incoming Orders) and two characteristics (Sold-To Party Country and Calendar Year/Month).

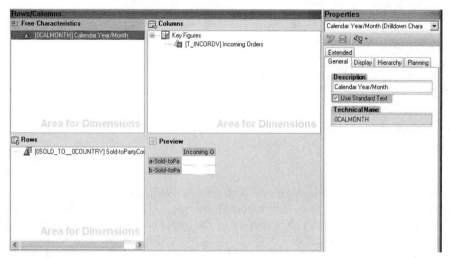

The exception we have created has two levels to it: BAD (less than 3,000,000) and CRITICAL (between 3,000,000 and 5,000,000). This is shown in the first of the following illustrations. The outcome of the query is shown in the second illustration. Notice that some results use both of the exceptions.

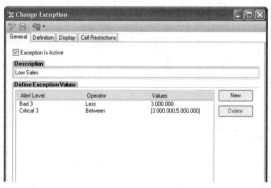

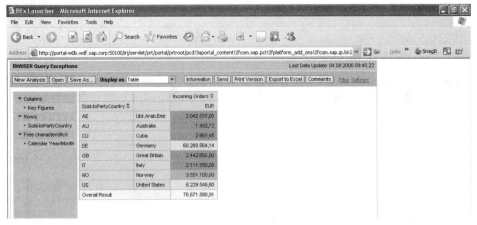

Before heading into the Information Broadcaster to configure the settings, we have some work to do in the Alert Categories component. Therefore, we'll head into the system and use either the transaction code ALRTCATDEF or the Implementation Guide (SPRO) | SAP NetWeaver | Business Intelligence | Settings for Reporting and Analysis | Settings for Information Broadcasting | Settings for SAP Alerts. The following illustration shows the results of this activity.

We then choose the folder the alert will be assigned, which is shown in the Classification field in the first of the following illustrations. Once the folder is chosen, we can create the alert category. The second illustration shows the Create Alert Category icon on the screen. Once this option is executed, we can enter the technical name and description of the alert category. The BWUSER01 and BWUSER alert categories are entered. As you can see, the description of the alert category defaults into the screen, as shown in the illustration on the.

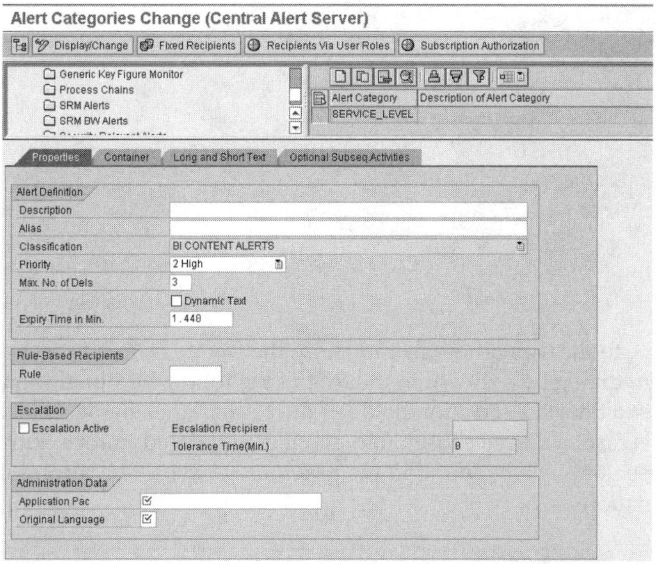

Copyright by SAP AG

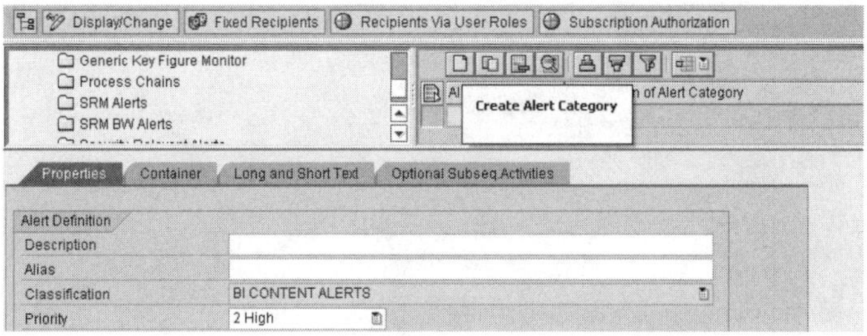

Copyright by SAP AG

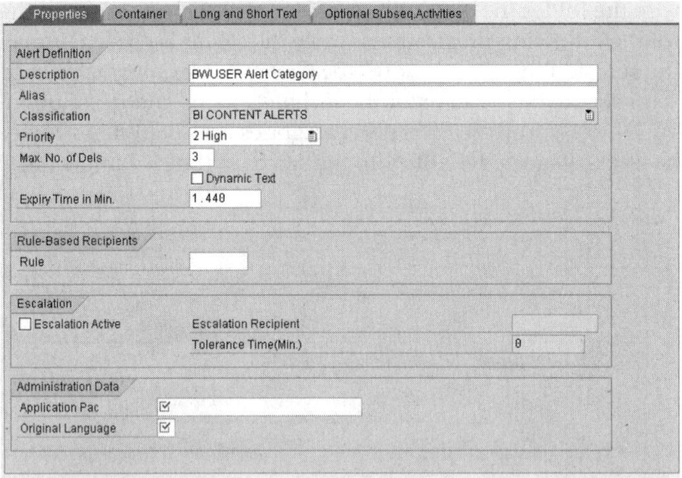

Copyright by SAP AG

Next, we move to the Container tab and chose the Create button to access the Create Container Element dialog box, shown in the first of the following illustrations. Fill in the Element, Name, and Short Description fields of the container element. Also, identify the object type. In this case, we have chosen to make this undefined (information on the definitions of these items can be found in the previous section). The second illustration shows this information.

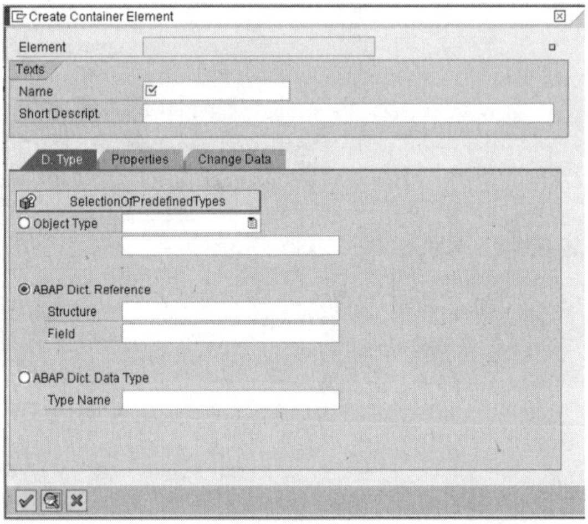

Copyright by SAP AG

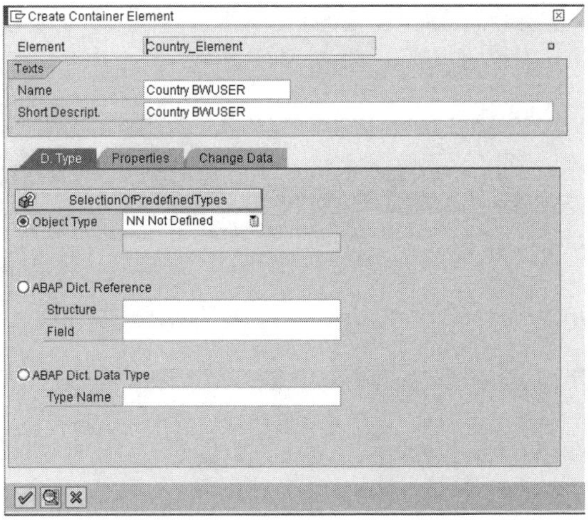

Copyright by SAP AG

On the Long and Short Text tab, we provide the text that will be used for the distribution of the information. In this case, we enter some basic text but will use the system variables to help. Also, notice that the container that was just configured can also be used to fill in some text for the broadcast, as shown in the first of the following illustrations. The result of this setup step is shown in the second illustration.

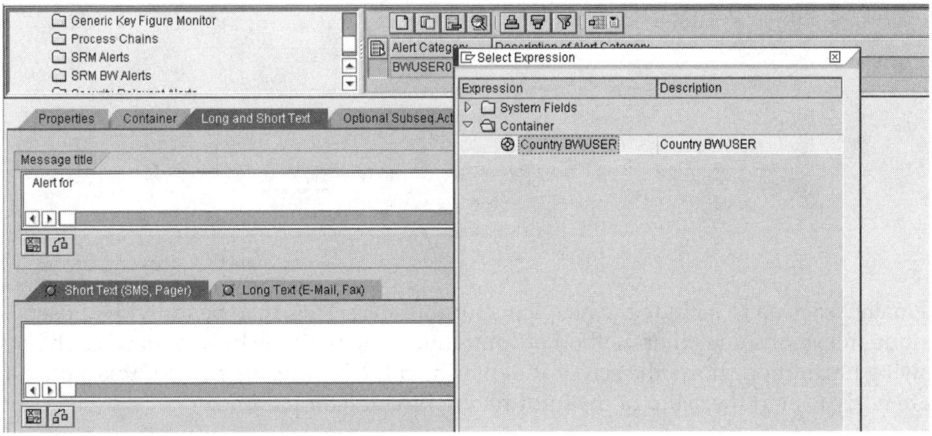

Copyright by SAP AG

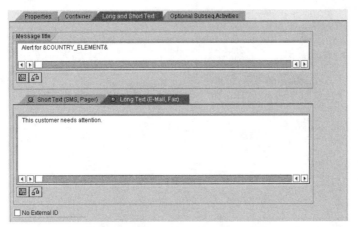

In addition to this, the Optional Subseq Activity tab is available to include the URL of another report or additional information for the business user, as shown next.

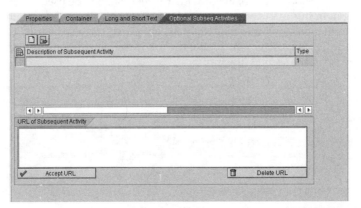

Finally, we need to include the recipients for this alert. These can be individual users, a distribution list, or some other method of communicating with the business users. The following illustration shows the screen for entering the "fixed recipients" for this alert. Now we are ready to start the setup of the Information Broadcaster parameters.

Since we have accessed the Information Broadcaster quite a few times now, we will start directly in the Broadcaster and with the required query inserted in the Object Type area of the screen, as shown in the first of the following illustrations. To begin, click the Create New Setting button. Notice that we can now use the distribution type Broadcast According to Exceptions. The second illustration shows this initial step.

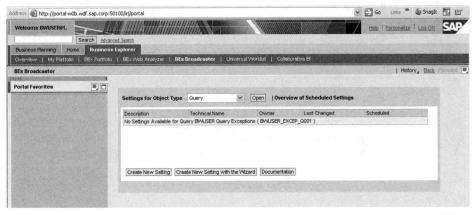

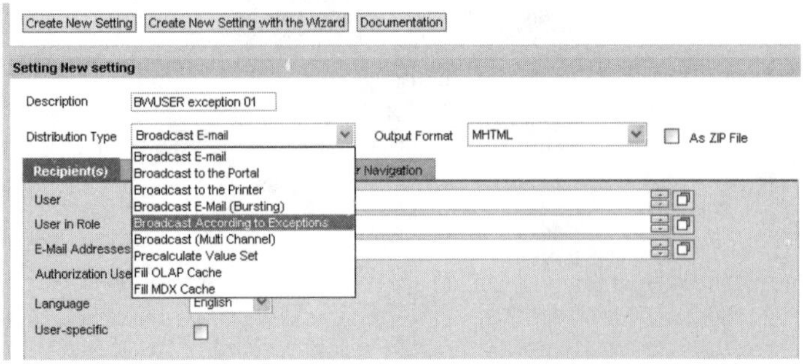

Copyright by SAP AG

Once we have identified the distribution type, the parameter fields appear. They are very different from the others we have encountered so far. The distribution type that is chosen is Create Alert. Notice the option to the right of the Create Alert field: Parameters. Click the Create option, which moves us to the next step of setting up the parameters for the alert: the Alert Generation tab. The first of the following illustrations shows the initial step of choosing the distribution type, and the second illustration shows the dialog box that appears for setting up the alert generation. In the field Alert Category, notice on the dropdown list that the alert category set up prior to this is available for use. Therefore, all the settings and information assigned to the alert category are available for this alert.

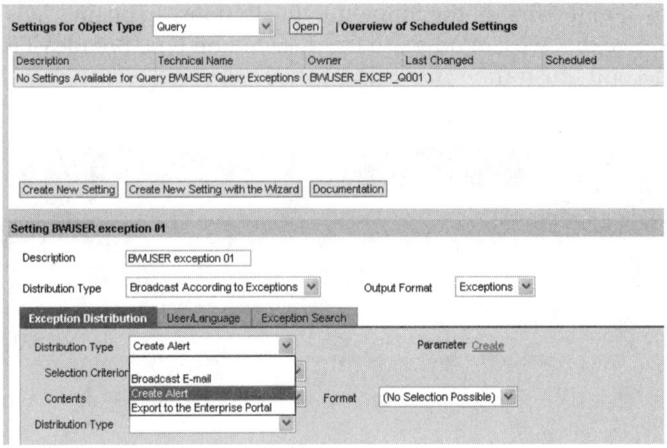

Copyright by SAP AG

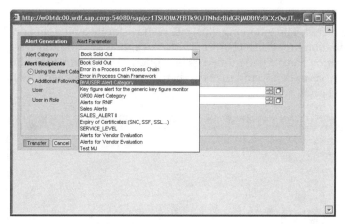

The first of the following illustrations shows the options on the Alert Parameter tab. On this tab, we have the option to turn on the indicator to identify the alert category parameters to the InfoObject, and we can use these parameters to add some additional text to the message. The second illustration shows that we have decided to use some of the system variables and have the text default based on the characteristic value of the Sold-To Country values.

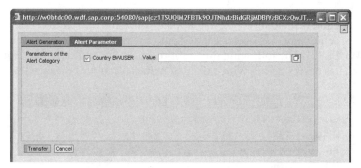

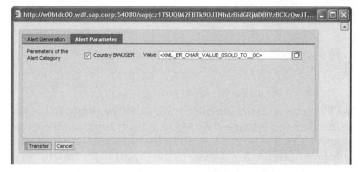

The next step shows the completion of the initial alert by using the levels to identify what will be delivered. The following illustration shows quite a bit going on. If you look at the actual Information Broadcaster screen for the exception distribution type Create Alert, the selection criterion has been identified as Exception/Alert Level, the value has been identified as Low Sales/Bad 3, and the next distribution type has been identified as Export to the Enterprise Portal.

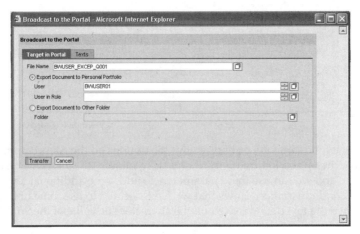

Above this section is the dialog box that appears once the option to create parameters has been chosen. A filename has been assigned, and the results are to be sent to the Personal Portfolio of BWUSER01. The following illustration shows the additional information on the Texts tab, which has been filled in with a display name and an importance level.

The following illustration shows the final result of both settings. In the Create Alert distribution type, the decision is to use the exception/alert level and the value of Low Sales/Bad 3. Therefore, this will be at a Low Sales level analysis of the exception, and the exception will only broadcast the Bad 3 level. In the Export to the Enterprise Portal distribution type, the decision is to use the exception and the value of Low Sales. Therefore, this will be an exception at the Low Sales level of the report and not just at the Bad 3 level, and the exception will be broadcast at all levels of Low Sales.

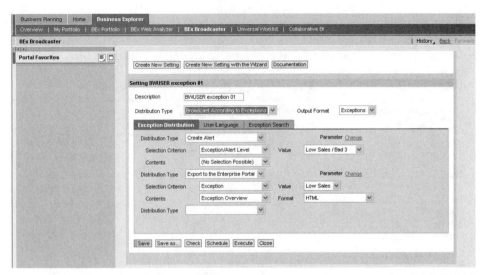

The final step is to execute this broadcast and review the results. The following illustration shows the results of this process. Notice that two steps were executed—one to generate an Exception with Alert, and the second to execute an exception distributed to the Portal. We need to review the results in the Portal to see the outcome of this process.

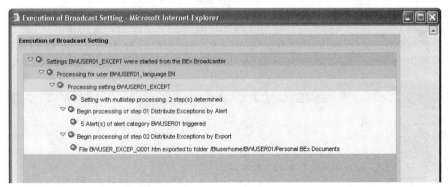

The following illustration is an example of the results by opening the Portal to the Business Explorer | Universal Worklist. Five alerts were sent by country, as requested.

To access the information, click on each of the countries' names (this is the link to the report information).

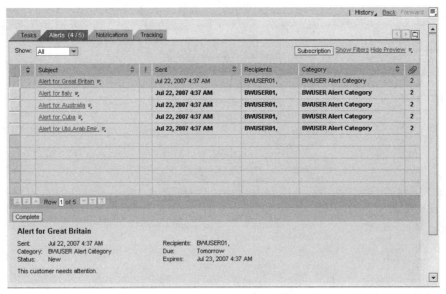

Moving to My Portfolio, we see that another alert has been sent, and the report can be executed to see the results. Notice the options below the Modified By item. The business user can download the information, subscribe to the information, and Send To the information – basically Send the Information to another Business User. Also, under the More link are other options for saving and executing the results. The first of the following illustrations shows the result. Once the report is executed, the view shows the total of all the exceptions generated for the specific report, as shown in the second illustration.

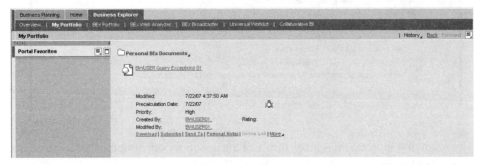

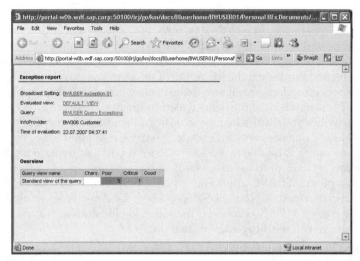

This completes our discussion of the Information Broadcaster distribution type of Exceptions. As you can see, the setup can be quite involved, but the results and benefits for a one time setup can be significant. Before settling on a specific view of the results, take a sampling of the business users who are your customer base and see what types of detailed information they might be interested in receiving via e-mail or the Portal. Keep in mind that having too many e-mails is as bad as having too little.

Alert Management

Our discussion of the Alert category, the Central Alert Framework, and other components in the alert process are all incorporated into the Alert Management (ALM) component. The ALM controls all alert processes within the NetWeaver Framework and comes into play when situations in the business process are critical enough to require immediate attention and have to be acted on immediately. Within ALM, conditions for critical situations are predefined. When an alert is triggered in ALM that meets these conditions, responsible or interested parties are determined and informed immediately. Examples of critical situations might be an important customer terminating a contract or a customer exceeding their credit limit. The alerts are polled from the UWL of the Enterprise Portal, application-specific display programs, or the alert inbox. These display programs can be personalized according to the users' needs. In addition, the users can receive alerts as e-mail or other methods both internal and external, if these external methods of communication are configured in SAPconnect. End users can personalize their alert notifications (for example, they can create notification variants or determine a substitute). Alert Management helps prevent delays in the processing of critical situations, because the time between discovering and responding to such situations is reduced considerably. This can also be used for other areas such as Period End Closing processes where a specific group or individual would need to be alerted once a particular activity is complete – such as alerting the Finance Department that the Costing allocations have been completed to the appropriate accounts. Alert Management (ALM) is an ideal solution if you can identify specific business or technical situations that are critical and could jeopardize efficient operation, and you want specific parties to be informed if these situations arise. The ALM server has to be a SAP Web AS as of release 6.20. The local application systems can be a SAP Web AS as of release 4.6C.

The Alert Framework is provided as part of the SAP Web Application Server. The application that wants to trigger alerts must define its own alert categories, assign them to alert classifications, and implement the triggering of the alert instances to connect to the Alert Management component. Alerts are all sent to the display program (UWL, application-specific program, or alert inbox) of the defined alert recipients. There are a number of administration activities you must schedule according to your requirements. For example, report RSALERTPROC must be executed in order to enable escalation. Also, you can configure alert processing to be able to send alerts to third-party systems, to be able to confirm alerts by SMS/Internet mail, or to have logs written. If you want to send alerts not only to the recipient's display program (UWL, application-specific program, or alert inbox), but also via external communication methods (e-mail, SMS, and fax), the chosen communication type must be correctly configured in SAPconnect. The following illustration is a good diagram of the integration between all the different areas that use ALM.

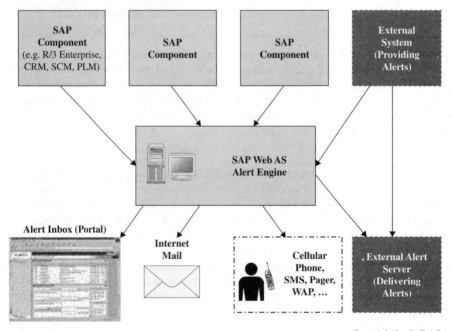

Copyright by SAP AG

Alerts to the Universal Worklist

The Universal Worklist (UWL) of the Enterprise Portal can poll for ALM alerts in the ALM system and display these alerts. This could be the central location for all the different alerts and messages that a business user might get. It would have to be configured to receive all the information, and the broadcast information can be directed to this list.

The following describes the basic steps necessary to view ALM alerts in the UWL. Quite a bit of this information and what was discussed in the last several pages will probably be completed by the BW Basis team, but it's a good idea to be aware of these components just in case the responsibilities of validating that all is configured that is required would be yours.

1. The ALM system has to be made known to the Portal (System Configuration | Portal Content | alertsystems).

2. The UWL system has to be determined in the UWL administration with the connector AlertConnector.

3. Finally, the users between the Portal and the ALM system have to be mapped in the user mapping so that the Portal users know under which user the ALM alerts can be found in the ALM system.

Scheduling of the Information Broadcaster

Once the information broadcaster settings have been created, the scheduling options can be reviewed. There are three methods for scheduling broadcasting settings:

- Using predefined timepoints
- On the change of data in the InfoProvider
- Using user-defined time settings

Each of these scheduling methods causes the Broadcaster's settings to be triggered, which means the assigned report option is executed in the background. The results are then processed according to the broadcast settings. Each of these can normally be found on the last dialog box pop-up during the configuration of the Information Broadcaster. We have been executing the Broadcaster immediately in many of the examples we have encountered and these options are always available, if required. Scheduling information broadcast settings can be helpful in avoiding system performance problems and allowing users to choose timepoints that don't interfere with critical system activities or heavy workloads (i.e., – during the end of period processing. It is important to remember that scheduling broadcast setting is not something that you would want every user to be able to do. To help control who is able to work with scheduling options, you need to take a look at the authorization object S_RS_BCS. With this object, you can determine which user is allowed to register broadcasting settings for execution and in which way.

Use of the Data Change in the InfoProvider Option and the Process Chain for Broadcasting

With this method of scheduling, you can ensure that broadcast setting are only triggered when there is a change in the information of the underlying InfoProvider to the assigned query, query view, report, Web template, or workbook. The InfoProvider can be any of the objects that can generate a query, such as an InfoCube, InfoSet, MultiProvider, and others. If the InfoProvider is a virtual object, the check of the data change is made on the underlying physical InfoProvider. For example, if the broadcast setting was based on a query that receives its data from a MultiProvider, and the MultiProvider is assigned to numerous InfoCubes and InfoObjects, it would only be necessary for a change to be made to one of the underlying objects for the broadcast to be triggered. This is a very popular approach to distributing the information even though the Business User has to become comfortable with the approach that they will not be getting this information as a specific time during the week or period but that it will be distributed once a change has been made and therefore an email will alert them that there is additional information that is available. Also, this method will depend on when the updating occurs – if this is on a daily basis and there is normally a change during that time the business user may not be interested in seeing this all of the time but on a set time frame and therefore this method will not be used.

To achieve this, a process chain is used. The process type that controls this activity is called the Trigger Event Data Change (for Broadcaster). In the process chain, this process type allows the loading of data to broadcast settings when data is changed. The Trigger Event Data Change (for Broadcaster) process type is added to the data-load processes. In this process type, you can choose the changed InfoProvider for which information broadcasting can be triggered. The end users who have created settings for precalculation and distribution in the BEx Broadcaster can specify when scheduling their broadcast settings that the precalculation and distribution be executed whenever there is a data change in the InfoProvider on which the scheduled BI object (query, query view, Web template, report, or workbook) is based. You can specify multiple InfoProviders within this process type, either directly by entering the InfoProvider's name or indirectly by specifying the name of the variant based on one of the following process types.

- Execute DTPs—Data Transfer Process (LOADING)
- Activate DataStore Object Data
- Update DataStore Object Data (Further Updating)
- Read PSA and Update Data Target

This is a new option in the Process Chain and is being used very successfully in a many companies. The process to set this scenario in motion involves calling Process Chain Maintenance (transaction RSPC). On the left side of the screen, navigate to the required display component for the process chain in which you want to include the Event Data Change and select it by double-clicking it. The system displays the planning view of the selected process chain in the right screen area. To include the Event Data Change process type, choose Process Types on the left side of the screen. The system displays the available process categories. Expand the Load Process and Post-Processing process category and drag the Trigger Event Data Change (for Broadcaster) process type to the process chain in the right screen area using drag and drop. The Insert Trigger Event Data Change (for Broadcaster) dialog box appears. In the Process Variant field, enter an existing variant using the input help or create a new variant. If you are creating a new process variant, select Create. Enter a description in the dialog box that appears and choose Continue. The Process Maintenance: Trigger Event Data Change (for Broadcaster) dialog box appears. The system displays information about the variant at the top of the screen such as the Variant (technical name), Description (this field is input ready), Last Changed By, and Changed On (date of last change). At the bottom of the screen, you can specify for which InfoProvider the Event Data Change is to be triggered. You can specify the InfoProvider as follows:

- Use the process chain to determine the InfoProvider by selecting the variants of the process chain that are to be included. This is possible for variants based on the preceding list. For the Execute InfoPackage process type, you should explicitly specify the InfoProvider. Otherwise, it is possible that the Broadcaster does not recognize the InfoProvider and does not offer execution when data is changed for this InfoProvider in the Scheduling dialog box.

- Another option would be for InfoProviders without a physical data store (MultiProviders, InfoSets, and so on), you can specify the individual InfoProviders directly using the input help for the InfoProvider field. This would be important if there are several InfoProviders and only a specific one would be required to change and therefore execute the broadcaster settings.

If required, make any specific settings for the parallel processing of the current process variant by using the Parallel Processing pushbutton. In doing this, you override the general settings for parallel processing for information broadcasting, which you can make in BI background management (transaction RSBATCH, process type BROADCAST). Save your entries and return to the previous screen. The Insert Trigger Event Data Change (for Broadcaster) dialog box appears. Choose Select. The Process Chain Maintenance Planning View screen appears. You have now completed the Trigger Event Data Change (for Broadcaster) process type in a process chain. You need to activate and schedule the process chain. Now, the Business User responsible for chosing "Execution with Data Change in the InfoProvider" and specify the required InfoProvider when they schedule their broadcaster setting.

To follow this up with some additional information, the first of the following illustrations shows the settings and system view of the process chain. Notice that this particular process type is at the very end of the process chain. This way, we are able to confirm that all the upload processes have successfully been carried out and the data has been completed loaded. The second illustration shows the details of this process type. Here, you can define the particular object that the change will affect. This offers the options for the InfoPackages and InfoProviders (specifically the DataStore objects and the upload from these to the InfoProviders, such as the InfoCubes).

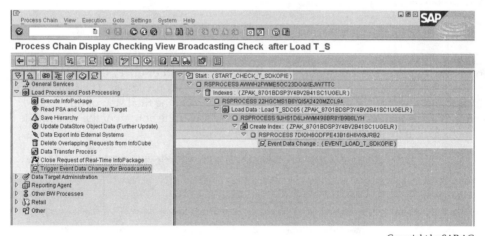

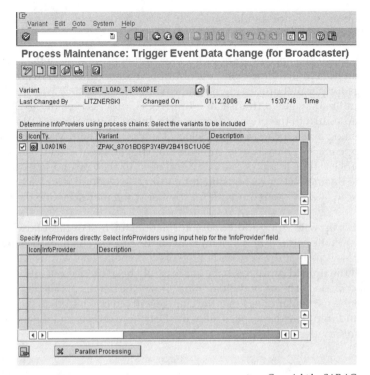

Copyright by SAP AG

Once the process chain is executed and the final step is complete, an event it created. This is the trigger to the Information Broadcaster. Any report or query that has been set up to update based on this Change option will be executed and processed. The following illustration shows the location of the indicator to complete the final step of this setup. Notice that this involves the use of the Schedule button at the bottom of the screen. The first option is Execute with Data Change in the InfoProvider.

Copyright by SAP AG

Scheduling from the Broadcaster Using the Predefined Timepoint

The definition of times for scheduling broadcast settings enables users to select preset times that determine when the precalculation and distribution of BI objects is to be executed. This is a very good approach to ensuring that users are only able to select specific timepoints that are configured with the performance of the system and job scheduling in mind. A *timepoint* is basically a background job that has been predefined by the system administrator. The job name must be prefixed with TP_BROADCAST_XXX, where XXX is additional text that you include to identify the background jobs. The XXX can be basically any length but some identification logic would be good to enter into the title. If you do not use the prefix, the job will not be recognized by the Broadcaster and will be ignored for scheduling. Jobs can be set to run once, but it is usually something that is set up to occur on a periodic basis.

NOTE   *Every timepoint will be seen by everyone who is scheduling a broadcast setting. You can't set up a timepoint specifically for one InfoProvider, reporting object, or specific broadcast setting. Timepoints are shared across the BI system. Therefore a good naming convention process is essential.*

It is possible to use more than one timepoint against a specific reporting object. Therefore, the settings can include the process of running a report both once a week and once a month. The process of setting up a timepoint includes defining the various times for scheduling broadcast settings by defining background jobs as follows:

1. Choose Define Job in the SAP menu, or call transaction SM36. The Define Job screen appears. This is the normal Job Screen that we have been using for quite some time in SAP.

2. Use the following naming convention when entering the job name: TP_BROADCASTING_<ID you select for time>.

3. The options for the Starting event are: Choose Start Condition. The Start Time dialog box appears. Choose Date/Time. The corresponding fields are displayed. Enter the required values and select Execute Job Periodically. Choose Period Values. The Period Values dialog box appears. Choose the required value and save your entries. The Start Time dialog box appears. Or finally the following values are supported for information broadcasting: Daily, Weekly, Monthly and Other Periods.

4. Choose Save. The Define Job screen appears.

5. Choose Step. The Create Step 1 dialog box appears and then choose ABAP Program, and in the Name field, enter the ABAP program (report) RSRD_BROADCAST_FOR_TIMEPOINT, which is to be executed as part of this step.

6. Finally, save your entries.

You can override the general settings for the parallel processing of the report by also entering a variant. A variant contains information about the number of parallel jobs and the job class.

If you want to create a variant, proceed as follows:

1. Start the RSRD_BROADCAST_FOR_TIMEPOINT report in transaction SE38.

2. Specify the number of parallel jobs and the job class.

3. Save the selection screen as a variant.

4. Choose Save in the Define Job screen.

This completes the configuration of the timepoints and defines the various background jobs that trigger scheduling for the broadcast settings at preset times. Once this is complete, at the end of the setup process for the Information Broadcaster when you access the Schedule option, you will see the background job that has been set up via TP_BROADCASTING_XXX. The following illustration shows an example of this final step. Notice the series of background jobs under the Predefined tab.

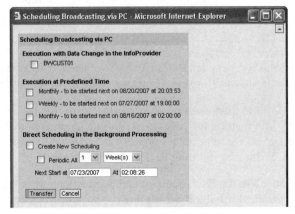

User-defined Settings

It is possible to allow a user to schedule their own broadcast setting. This is normally available in situations where there is no suitable timepoint available or when the broadcast setting should only be limited to a specific number or runtimes. To accomplish this task, you would be defining your own scheduling settings and therefore using the Create New Scheduling option to specify the required start date and time. Once you access the date field, a calendar will appear to allow you to chose a particular date. If scheduling is to occur periodically, select Periodic and specify the interval. The system distributes the document according to your selection. If you have already defined schedules in SAP background processing for this broadcast setting, they will be listed here with scheduling information to confirm what has been set up for scheduled runs. The ability to change and/or delete is available from this location. We actually reviewed and looked at an example of this in chapter 11. Again, as a note of caution, this option should only be used for those Business Users that are very comfortable with the company processes and the workload that the current BW system is under. If this is being done by too many people it may impact your overall BW performance.

Management and Monitoring of the Broadcaster

As we have commented before there can be large volumes of data being distributed via the Information Broadcaster and during the process of setting up the many different options in the Information Broadcaster, it is important to identify the methods of management and monitoring for all these different activities. If this functionality is used, there can be large volumes of data and information moving throughout the e-mail and Internet systems. It is important that a method of management for all this activity is taken into account before too much traffic is generated via the Broadcaster. Various functions are available for you to manage and monitor information broadcasting. You can search for the broadcast settings and their schedules in Broadcasting Administration using various categories. You can edit them and delete settings that are no longer needed. You can also look for error analysis log entries and display them. You are able to monitor and test the distribution of BI content by e-mail in transaction SAPconnect: Administration (System Status) (transaction code SCOT). When information broadcasting is operational, the system automatically generates bookmark IDs and iViews for the online links. You are able to reorganize and delete no-longer-used bookmarks and view IDs with report RSRD_BOOKMARK_REORGANISATION. The following illustration shows the use of this program. Using transaction code SE38, you get to the ABAP Editor and fill in the report name.

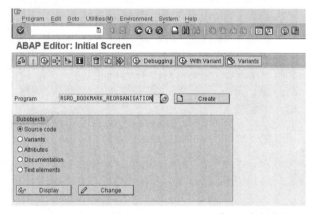

Copyright by SAP AG

The first of the following illustrations shows the results after executing the program. Notice the options that are available for managing the bookmarks. This covers bookmarks and URLs that have both been used in the Information Broadcaster and those that have not. Therefore, this is the administration tool that will help with all the bookmarks and URLs for the system. The second illustration shows the results after the program has run and the different objects that would have been affected. It is very important to keep up on the management of the different objects that are created for processing of information. This will help solve problems concerning the bookmarks and other virtual objects that are being used and not controlled.

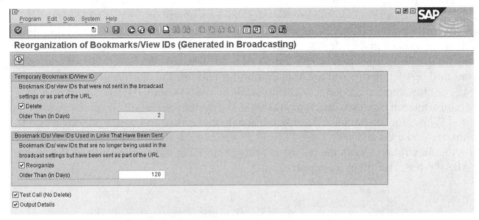

Reorganization of Bookmarks/View IDs (Generated in Broadcasting)

```
Reorganization of Bookmarks/View IDs (Generated in Broadcasting)                                    1

Temporary Bookmark IDs Found (BW3.x)          2
Bookmark ID             Template ID               Last Changed By   Last Changed
DOTO7A6ARUT405WXD9PP2K6UC   ZTPLI_0CDM_C0_Q0001_01    ANA10-35          02.05.2007 22:28:33
DOTOAXJ32BYV6F24X56KN0S6C   ZTPLI_0CDM_C0_Q0001_01    ANA10-36          02.05.2007 22:45:42
Temporary Bookmark IDs Found                  14
Bookmark ID             Template ID               Owner             Last Changed
1BZUPAZEO7RDTBDMME6LX1KKI   APPELT_TEMPLATE          APPELTA           21.11.2006 21:00:35
06TH65UPDHMJEUZ6QLXUMZLLT                            WORCH             18.09.2006 15:15:41
1IA9HN73A352SB3VQDW4RYSJ0                            APPELTA           23.11.2006 10:02:43
2KMJZFC36K5FRDZ4CTQ8WAB9J                            GREEN             03.08.2006 00:35:59
64PXT6IFN79X1SD0G0ZNR5Q0W                            WORCH             19.09.2006 17:03:16
7ZO2OF39QKYC6G5RTNT6X6A4P                            MAYROCK           09.08.2006 17:41:01
8ZU6HBEMF85MRT3SYNGYZQ6DF                            WORCH             19.09.2006 17:10:32
AJLEM0F29WHCQSX1NISVY0BAI                            MAYROCK           09.08.2006 17:37:51
AVEO8N3NNURR4W6X1QV0Y1HLS                            WORCH             19.09.2006 10:08:09
D63GCPL2YH7V7Y3ONLOMBXRHG                            APPELTA           21.11.2006 20:29:36
DR9DVOZQ69FXC8FDVF9ZB4FB5                            WORCH             18.09.2006 18:15:19
ECAZLUQV46ANSQJEKKSB4GNKU                            APPELTA           22.11.2006 18:30:24
EN3HWH22LRHCH47FWVFO4NUNN                            MAYROCK           09.08.2006 17:38:10
F41QF46ET8U6RK6B0PJTQWK1F                            APPELTA           22.11.2006 18:32:59
Temporary View IDs Found                      1
View ID                 Query            InfoProvider   Owner       Last Changed By   Last Changed
3LJO9HUCDHEN4GVK2MJAQEOQP   T_BW306_UNIT_8   T_SDDEMO3      WORCH       WORCH             18.09.2006 15:15:40
Sent Bookmark IDs Found (BW3.x, Not Referenced)       0
Sent Bookmark IDs Found (Not Referenced)              4
Bookmark ID             Template ID               Owner             Last Changed
2D1W2DAEYYCQMEMSG3WPRLCY8                            APPELTA           23.11.2006 10:02:09
2TR6DTA0U327AXSP06QVVWA9P                            APPELTA           21.11.2006 20:32:02
6260X7FEN429D3LELDAA6HVU4                            APPELTA           22.11.2006 09:25:24
B669U7Q6WUVEGCIH6YF8W329H                            APPELTA           22.11.2006 09:22:51
Sent View IDs Found (Not Referenced)          0
Sent and Referenced Bookmark IDs Found (BW3.x)        0
Sent and Referenced Bookmark IDs Found                4
Bookmark ID             Template ID               Owner             Last Changed
```

Another approach to the management of the Information Broadcaster activities is to use the Broadcasting Administration Monitor. You can search for the broadcast settings and their schedules in Broadcasting Administration (transaction code RSRD_ADMIN) using various categories. You can edit them and delete settings that are no longer needed. The following illustration shows the initial screen of the Broadcasting Administration Monitor.

You can also look for error analysis log entries and display them. The following functions are available for the administration of broadcast settings.

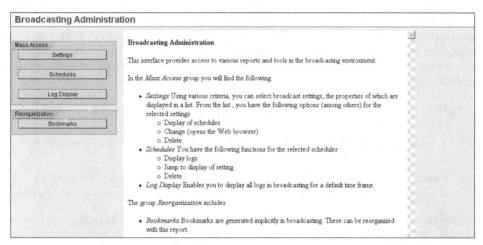

Copyright by SAP AG

Settings

You can select broadcast settings for which the properties are displayed in a list using various criteria (such as the technical name, description, last changed by, changed at, type of object concerned [query, query view, report, Web template, or workbook], distribution type, or output format). You can then select the broadcast settings in the list and you can manage these settings by displaying the schedules for the broadcast settings and navigate into the log display to analyze errors or delete schedules that are no longer required. You can change the broadcast settings that appear with the BEx Broadcaster in the web browser. Finally, you can delete the broadcast settings that are no longer required.

The following illustration shows the initial screen for these activities.

Copyright by SAP AG

Schedules of Broadcast Settings

You can search for and display schedules of broadcast settings using various criteria (such as the technical name of the broadcast setting, the time/date it was created or of the last schedule, and the type of schedule). You can use this type of schedule to find, for example, all the schedules that were generated when data was changed in the InfoProvider, at a given time or date, or as a background job as a result of direct scheduling. The corresponding schedules are displayed in the list. You can select the schedules and work with the following functions:

- **Log display**   You can display the last log of a schedule to, for example, analyze errors.

- **Branch to broadcast setting display**   You can navigate from the schedules to the list of broadcast settings.

- **Delete**   You can delete the broadcast settings that are no longer required. (A very useful option especially if many business users can actual create broadcast settings.)

The following illustration shows the results of the use of the Schedules button.

Selection of Scheduling of Broadcast Settings

General Parameters
Technical Name of Setting				
Scheduling Created by	BWUSER01	to		
Created On		/ 00:00	To	/ 00:00
Last Executed on		/ 00:00	To	/ 00:00
☐ Error During Last Execution				

Type of Scheduling
☑ Data Change in InfoProvider			
Techn. Name of InfoProvider		to	
☑ Default Time			
Techn. Name of Time		to	
☑ Direct Scheduling			

Copyright by SAP AG

Log Display

You can display logs for particular periods and users that were produced in broadcasting to analyze, for example, errors. The following illustration shows this option via the Broadcast Administration Monitor. It is also possible to reorganize the bookmarks that were created implicitly in broadcasting via this screen. This can be seen as the last button on the screen. Therefore, the ability to get to all functionality is available via the Broadcast Administration Monitor.

Broadcasting: Log Display

Selection of Log Entries
Date		to	22.07.2007	
User Name	BWUSER01	to		
Subobject				
Log number				

Copyright by SAP AG

Monitoring the Sending of E-mails

You can monitor and test the distribution of content from BI by e-mail in transaction SAPconnect: Administration (System Status). You set up the mail server and maintain the e-mail addresses of the users in Master Data Maintenance. To do this, access the IMG via SAP Reference IMG _ SAP Customizing Implementation Guide _ SAP NetWeaver _ Business Intelligence _ Settings for Reporting and Analysis _ Settings for Information Broadcasting _ Set Up Mail Server.

To complete this, perform routing tests, as follows:

1. In the BI system, choose transaction SAPconnect: Administration (System Status) (transaction code SCOT).

2. In the menu, choose Utilities _ Routing Test. The SAPconnect: Test Route screen appears.

3. Enter the required username for the BI system as the sender.

4. Choose INT (Internet mail address) as the recipient address type.

5. Enter the e-mail address of the BI user as the recipient address. You can view the address in User Maintenance (transaction code SU01).

6. In the menu, choose Routes _ Explain to test the routing and see explanations.

To monitor send requests in the BI system, follow these steps:

1. Choose transaction SAPconnect: Administration (System Status) (transaction code SCOT).

2. In the menu, choose Utilities _ Overview of Send Orders. You can view the status of sent e-mails. On the Period, Send Status, Sender, and Options tab pages, you can enter the required selection criteria.

If message number 672 (Waiting for Communication Service) is displayed in the status bar, the system is unable to output the send status Transmitted. In this case, check the selected settings in transaction SAPconnect: Administration (System Status) (transaction SCOT) by choosing Settings _ Confirmation of Receipt. Make sure that the option SAPconnect Does Not Expect Receipt Confirm for Internet Mail is selected. If you selected SAPconnect Expects Receipt Confirmations for Internet Mail, the recipients of the sent e-mails may not return a receipt confirmation. The system then displays message number 672.

Summary

As you can see, the functionality of the Information Broadcaster extends the ability of the BW system to distribute information, both structured and unstructured, far beyond the basic BW users and offers just about all the different processes available from both an SAP BW point of view and the company point of view for distributing information. This is one area that in prior versions of BW (3.5) was a bit lacking. However, with the addition of all this functionality in the Information Broadcaster and the use of additional tools such as the Adobe Printing option, as well as access to numerous external methods of distributing information, BW has come a long way toward accommodating just about all the needs of a company in the distribution of information. As you will see in chapter 16 on the Enterprise Portal (EP), along with the EP functionality, the Information Broadcaster can be the solution for much of a company's requirements for the distribution of data.

Advanced Reporting Processes and Functionality

When it comes to the reporting processes within the BI architecture, there are many different advanced options. With all the different toolsets available, you have quite a few avenues of analysis you can take. There's the use of Crystal Reports, which offers an additional third-party user interface for the BW data. In this case, you will need to bolt on some additional hardware to the system and set up the integration between the BW server and Crystal server environment. However, this is another option for the business user when processing the BW data. Within the BW environment, the Analysis Process Designer (APD) in conjunction with data mining offers another completely different user interface for the user and very different functionality. In this case, the APD offers the platform to set up the integration of the BW data to be used for data mining. This process can result in a number of different activities—from filling another attribute of the master data with a scoring or statistical value for reporting purposes, to the use of predictive information for the forecasting of sales or other information that the company would need for business purposes. Figure 13-1 shows the initial screen for the APD process.

In this chapter, we will discuss several topics in detail. These are not related to one another in any way; they simply offer the business user additional information concerning the use of BI data and reporting functionality. We will start by describing the use of the Elimination of Internal Business Volume for a cleaner, more accurate picture of the volumes of information—whether this is sales volume, inventory volume, or any other activity within the company that is involved with the transferring of values. Following this we will work through a discussion of the new Unit of Measure (UOM) functionality for the query. There is also new functionality for the uploading of the UOM, but we will focus on just the query side of the process.

We will continue this chapter with a discussion of two WAD web items. First, we will cover the Map web item and the GIS (Geographical Information System), including the display of this using the WAD. Second, we will discuss the use of the Chart web item. Both of these options use additional functionality from another toolset, but in the case of the GIS, it's a third-party component, and in the case of the Chart web item, it's an embedded use of the Excel chart process. I've decided to present these two WAD items in detail, even though we will not be discussing all the functionality of the BEx Web Analyzer or the WAD in detail.

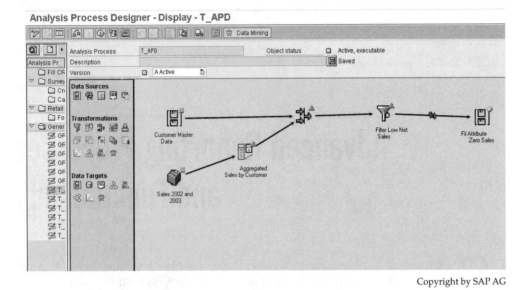

FIGURE 13-1   The Analysis Process Designer's initial work area

The reason is the Chart web item is one of the more popular items to use for displaying information. Also, the GIS and Map web item are a very useful components but a more complex item to set up and use; therefore, all activities involved with this process need to be understood.

Our last section will comment on functionality specific to the display and execution of queries, either for the BEx Analyzer or from the web components of BW reporting. Our initial focus will be on the use of variants. Their functionality has changed quite a bit in the overall architecture of BW 7.0, and understanding them is important because just about everyone I know uses variants for testing purposes on queries or for holding personal settings in queries. Therefore, we will discuss variants to ensure you understand this new functionality. We close this section with a discussion of the use of the Key Date field within the query properties. This can be very useful when looking to display the appropriate information to your end users. Therefore, understanding the use and the set up of the types of data displayed is critical.

Introduction to Advanced Reporting Processes

When it comes to advanced processes in SAP BW, there are so many different topics we can focus on that it is difficult to decide which ones to discuss. If we look at the entire area of BW reporting, we can focus on time dependency in the queries and InfoObjects, Crystal reporting, APD functionality, data modeling in the Query Designer, and the list goes on and on. However, based on the different situations I've been involved in, four areas jump out as being important for the business user and a bit misunderstood in terms of functionality and configuration. Therefore, the Elimination of Internal Business Volumes, the new Unit of Measure configuration for the BEx Query, and the Map and Chart web items are the ones we will discuss. After our discussion, you will better understand the configuration and uses of these four components and their importance and usefulness will be obvious.

Elimination of Internal Business Volume

One of the functions available in the BW system I believe is overlooked is the ability to set up and generate the Elimination of Internal Business Volume. This is a very powerful and useful process in all areas of your business. If you think about it, you can have issues with the management of a number of different activities in your company that may involve the movement or transfer of values. I'll try to be as general as possible here because as soon as you start to talk about the Elimination of Internal Business Volume, automatically everyone starts to think about financial activities. Not just financial information needs to be eliminated. What about the movement of inventory from one plant to another? What about the sales part of the financial equation, or the movement of employees and their associated cost? There are many different areas of the business process that need this type of functionality for organizing the information being analyzed by the business user. This is not to say that this approach does the same as actual consolidations via ECC or that it comes close to the functionality of the SEM-BCS component. However, it does offer a quick-and-easy approach to tracking activities and costs internally and gives you a good idea whether your current system is being managed well.

Using this functionality requires a little setup in the configuration of InfoObjects (we are going to go back a bit and test your memory) and InfoProviders. But these are one-time activities, and once completed they can be used for the execution of the queries. You can use this function to eliminate the internal business volume when executing a BEx query. In other words, the effect of this function is that revenues made between two entities in one organization are no longer displayed and therefore are not double-counted. This can be of great help for those companies that have distribution plants, sales offices, or any divisions in different countries or regions and are interested in the "true" picture of their inventory, sales, and so on that may involve activities within a corporation.

Several configuration activities need to be completed before we can proceed with the creation of a query to display the results. Initially, you have an InfoProvider that includes two characteristics (called a sender and receiver) that contain the same reference (they are reference characteristics and therefore contain the same master data) and are on the same level within the hierarchy attached to those characteristics. Also included in the InfoProvider are key figures that are classified as "reference" key figures. These reference key figures will build the relationships between the two reference characteristics. We have not run across these types of characteristics or key figures in our discussions so far, so we will review them in detail.

NOTE *You can only create aggregates for InfoCubes that contain both sender and receiver characteristics.*

To eliminate internal business volume in an InfoProvider, you have to create a key figure with a reference. Therefore, the values for these key figures are *not* stored in the InfoProvider but are generated during the execution of the query. The value is kept here after the elimination during the query, but is not included in the fact table for the InfoCube (or in the DataStore object). We will be looking at an example using the combination of profit centers and countries to explain the functionality of Elimination of Internal Business Volume, but you can use any combination that make sense to your company—such as combinations between plants to perform internal inventory elimination between these plants, or combinations between divisions to perform internal sales elimination between the divisions.

Configuration in the BW Data Warehouse Workbench

Before starting to work on the actual query for this process, we need to set up some configurations to support this activity. As mentioned, we need to set up reference characteristics and key figures. These are required components of the elimination process.

We will start by setting up the characteristics because we need the characteristics to help build the key figure. In this case, we will use the InfoObjects Profit Center and Country, which will provide us the ability to eliminate volumes at two levels—Profit Center and Country. For our purposes, we need four characteristics: one standard Profit Center characteristic, and the other a "reference" Profit Center characteristic. The same process is required with the Country characteristic. The twist to this situation is that the second characteristic is built with a reference to the first. The following illustration shows the result. You can see the combination of Country and Partner Country, with a reference built between them. As you'll remember, the link for referencing is done during the creation of the characteristic, with reference.

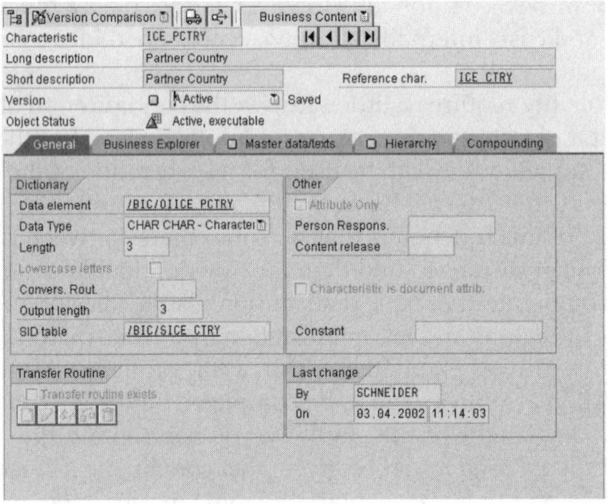

Copyright by SAP AG

Complete the same process for the Profit Center, as shown here. We have now completed the setup for the characteristics.

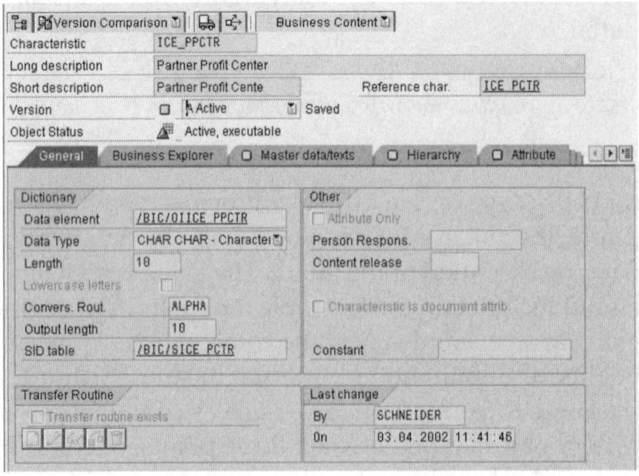

Copyright by SAP AG

Next we need to set up of the key figures. The initial key figure will be a standard key figure with no reference activities, as shown in here. The key figure's technical name is ICE_REV.

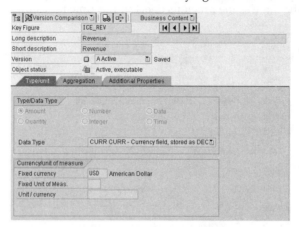

This is the key figure that actually gets uploaded to during the collection of the data for elimination activities. Next, the additional reference key figures need to be created. When creating these key figures, select Key Figure with Reference. In the InfoObject maintenance, you have an additional tabbed page, Elimination. Enter one or more characteristic pairs here regarding the key figure to be eliminated. In doing so, always choose a "sending" characteristic and a "receiving" characteristic. A typical example for such a pair of characteristics is Sending Profit Center and Receiving Profit Center. The characteristics of such a pair must have the same reference characteristic. You can also enter the names of the navigation attributes here. You can display permitted characteristics for an elimination characteristic by using the input help. The following illustration shows this result. In our case, we have used Profit Center as the reference characteristics.

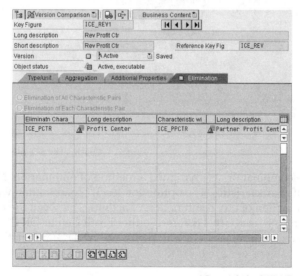

This gets us half way to completing the configuration necessary. Now we will need to create additional key figures. First, we'll set up another pairing for the country. Create the key figure exactly the same as the previous one, but this time for Country, as shown next.

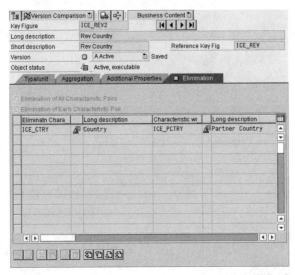

Copyright by SAP AG

We now have key figures that will give us the necessary combinations for the profit centers and countries separately. Next, we'll create the key figures that will give the display of a combination between Country and Profit Center. The only difference is that both pairs of characteristics will be used in the *same* key figure. The following illustration shows this result.

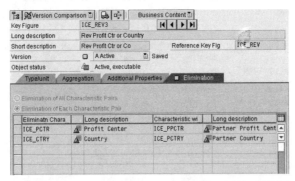

Copyright by SAP AG

In this case, the combination was assigned a method of elimination. Notice the buttons just above the set of characteristics. The option for "each" combination was chosen. This means that the elimination of any combination of activities between the two characteristics would classify as an "OR" activity. Therefore, either Profit Center OR Country will be eliminated. Another key figure is also created with an "AND" combination, which is shown here.

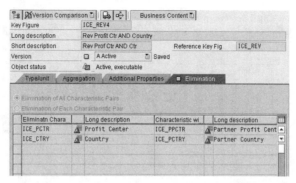

In the final two key figures, we have specified several characteristic pairs. We specify one of the following by using the selection buttons:

- **All characteristic pairs need to be eliminated** In this case, the key figure value is only eliminated if the elimination condition is fulfilled for all characteristic pairs (an "AND" relationship).

- **Each individual characteristic pair needs to be eliminated** In this case, the key figure value is already eliminated as soon as the elimination condition for one of the characteristic pairs is fulfilled (an "OR" relationship).

Once these activities are finished, the system has set up combinations within specific tables to help with the process. Reviewing the table RSDICE, we see that the system has automatically set up the combinations that were configured with the key figures. This shows the types of Boolean logic that have been defined. Notice the combinations of OR and AND as well as the third column for the position of the two pairs of characteristics. As you can see, both the Modified and the Active versions of these key figures are shown (see the following illustration). This table holds the elimination business rules. In this example, four eliminations are being performed:

- ICE_REV1 eliminates revenue between a profit center/partner profit center assigned to the same node of the Profit Center hierarchy.

- ICE_REV2 eliminates revenue between a country/partner country assigned to the same node of the Country hierarchy.

- ICE_REV3 eliminates revenue between a profit center/partner profit center where *either* of the profit centers are assigned to the same node of the Profit Center hierarchy *or* the countries are assigned to the same node of the Country hierarchy.

- ICE_REV4 eliminates revenue between a profit center/partner profit center where *both* the profit centers are assigned to the same node of the Profit Center hierarchy *and* the countries are assigned to the same node of the Country hierarchy.

Data Browser: Table RSDICE Select Entries   12

Table: RSDICE
Displayed Fields: 7 of   7 Fixed Columns: 3 List Width 0250

KYFNM	OBJVERS	POSIT	IOBJNM1	IOBJNM2	BOOLEOP	BOOLEOP2
ICE_REV1	A	0001	ICE_PCTR	ICE_PPCTR		
ICE_REV1	M	0001	ICE_PCTR	ICE_PPCTR		
ICE_REV2	A	0001	ICE_CTRY	ICE_PCTRY		
ICE_REV2	M	0001	ICE_CTRY	ICE_PCTRY		
ICE_REV3	A	0001	ICE_PCTR	ICE_PPCTR	OR	
ICE_REV3	A	0002	ICE_CTRY	ICE_PCTRY	OR	
ICE_REV3	M	0001	ICE_PCTR	ICE_PPCTR	OR	
ICE_REV3	M	0002	ICE_CTRY	ICE_PCTRY	OR	
ICE_REV4	A	0001	ICE_PCTR	ICE_PPCTR	AND	
ICE_REV4	A	0002	ICE_CTRY	ICE_PCTRY	AND	
ICE_REV4	M	0001	ICE_PCTR	ICE_PPCTR	AND	
ICE_REV4	M	0002	ICE_CTRY	ICE_PCTRY	AND	

Another table that gets populated during this process is RSDIOBJCMP. This table holds all the information for all the InfoObjects that are compounded. In this case, the key figures are compounded, so notice that REV1 through REV4 are compounded to REV, as shown next.

Hierarchy 'Country' Display: 'Active Version'

Maintain Level   Hierarchy Attributes

Text Node   Characteristic Nodes   'Country'   Interval

Country	InfoObject	Node name	L
Country	0HIER_NODE	ROOT	
Europe	0HIER_NODE	EUROPE	
AT	ICE_CTRY	AT	
DE	ICE_CTRY	DE	
UK	ICE_CTRY	UK	
Asia	0HIER_NODE	ASIA	
SGP	ICE_CTRY	SGP	
Americas	0HIER_NODE	AMERICAS	
CDN	ICE_CTRY	CDN	
US	ICE_CTRY	US	

Next, we need to set up the hierarchies that we will use in the query to recognize the combinations and assign the correct values to the report. Two hierarchies will be configured in this case: one for the Profit Center combinations and another for the Country combinations. The two hierarchies are shown here. Notice the combinations of the profit centers in a specific node and that they are rolling up to Text nodes for subsection summaries. This will be the final driver to execute the elimination of revenues.

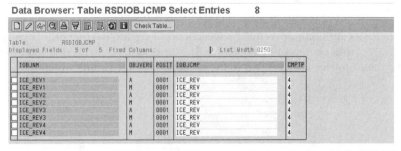

Data Browser: Table RSDIOBJCMP Select Entries   8

Table: RSDIOBJCMP
Displayed Fields: 5 of   5 Fixed Columns: ╠ List Width 0250

IOBJNM	OBJVERS	POSIT	IOBJCMP	CMPTP
ICE_REV1	A	0001	ICE_REV	4
ICE_REV1	M	0001	ICE_REV	4
ICE_REV2	A	0001	ICE_REV	4
ICE_REV2	M	0001	ICE_REV	4
ICE_REV3	A	0001	ICE_REV	4
ICE_REV3	M	0001	ICE_REV	4
ICE_REV4	A	0001	ICE_REV	4
ICE_REV4	M	0001	ICE_REV	4

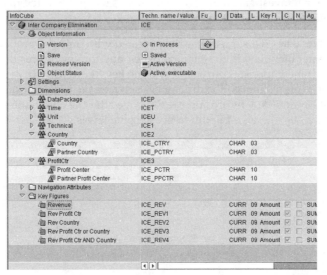

Hierarchy 'Profit Center' Display: 'Active Version'

Profit Center	InfoObject	Nod	L
Profit Center	0HIER_NODE	ROOT	
PC01	0HIER_NODE	PC01	
PC0102	ICE_PCTR	PC0...	
PC0103	ICE_PCTR	PC0...	
PC0104	ICE_PCTR	PC0...	
PC0105	ICE_PCTR	PC0...	
PC0181	ICE_PCTR	PC0...	
PC02	0HIER_NODE	PC02	
PC0201	ICE_PCTR	PC0...	
PC0202	ICE_PCTR	PC0...	
PC0203	ICE_PCTR	PC0...	
PC0204	ICE_PCTR	PC0...	
PC0205	ICE_PCTR	PC0...	
PC03	0HIER_NODE	PC03	
PC0301	ICE_PCTR	PC0...	
PC0302	ICE_PCTR	PC0...	

Finally, the InfoCube is created. There is nothing unusual about the InfoCube. All the different characteristics and key figures are included. The following illustration shows the results of this process.

InfoCube	Techn. name / value	Fu	O	Data	L	Key Fi	C	N	Ag
Inter Company Elimination	ICE								
Object Information									
Version	In Process								
Save	Saved								
Revised Version	Active Version								
Object Status	Active, executable								
Settings									
Dimensions									
DataPackage	ICEP								
Time	ICET								
Unit	ICEU								
Technical	ICE1								
Country	ICE2								
Country	ICE_CTRY			CHAR	03				
Partner Country	ICE_PCTRY			CHAR	03				
ProfitCtr	ICE3								
Profit Center	ICE_PCTR			CHAR	10				
Partner Profit Center	ICE_PPCTR			CHAR	10				
Navigation Attributes									
Key Figures									
Revenue	ICE_REV			CURR	09	Amount	✓		SUM
Rev Profit Ctr	ICE_REV1			CURR	09	Amount	✓		SUM
Rev Country	ICE_REV2			CURR	09	Amount	✓		SUM
Rev Profit Ctr or Country	ICE_REV3			CURR	09	Amount	✓		SUM
Rev Profit Ctr AND Country	ICE_REV4			CURR	09	Amount	✓		SUM

Once the data is uploaded into the InfoCube, the query can be built and reviewed for the results. Even though the InfoCube has a total of five key figures assigned, only one key figure will be used to physically hold data in the InfoCube—the key figure ICE_REV, as shown next.

Therefore, the uploaded data are records with all four characteristics but only one key figure assigned. The other key figures will generate the appropriate values at query runtime.

ICE_CTRY	Partner Country	Profit Center	Partner Profit Center	Revenue
DE	DE	PC0181	PC0102	100,00
DE	DE	PC0203	PC0103	200,00
DE	AT	PC0201		100,00
DE	UK	PC0201	PC0301	300,00
DE	CDN	PC0201	PC0201	200,00
DE	US	PC0201		80,00
DE	AT	PC0201	PC0201	500,00
SGP	DE	PC0302	PC0203	150,00
UK	DE	PC0301	PC0102	50,00
UK	US	PC0302	PC0203	250,00

Now we can move on to the analysis of the information to see what this functionality can do for us. We will investigate a total of four queries using the different hierarchy and key figure combinations to shows the results.

Query 1: Profit Center Only   This query has been created with only the profit center assigned and the Profit Center hierarchy in the characteristics, and for key figures there will be Normal Revenue (for comparison purposes) and the key figure ICE_REV1, as shown next. Once the query is executed, notice the differences between the basic information received from the Normal Revenue key figure and the Revenue after the elimination of internal volume. As you can see, there's a big difference at some levels.

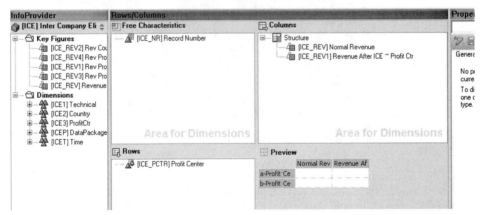

Let's investigate this in more detail. Notice that PC0181, PC0203, PC0301, and PC0302 have exactly the same values, but PC0201 shows a definite difference between the two key figure results. Reviewing this, we see that in two cases, PC 0201 had transactions that were internal volume sales of $200 and $500. Therefore, these sales were eliminated because they were internal to the specific node. All other sales were from node to node and not internal to the specific node, so all those sales are counted. If you look at the actual total, you'll see a difference there also. At the root level, the Normal Revenue key figure has a total of $ 1,930.00 in sales, but the Elimination key figure only has $180.00. Looking at the actual data, notice that only two transactions are not within the Profit Center hierarchy and they total $180.00 (sales from PC0201 that have no partner profit center) and these are the only ones that count at that level. The following illustration shows these results.

Profit Center ⇕	Normal Revenue ⇕ $	Revenue After ICE ~ Profit Ctr ⇕ $
▼ROOT	1.930,00	180,00
▼PC01	100,00	
• PC0181	100,00	100,00
▼PC02	1.380,00	680,00
• PC0201	1.180,00	480,00
• PC0203	200,00	200,00
▼PC03	450,00	450,00
• PC0301	50,00	50,00
• PC0302	400,00	400,00

Query 2: Country Only   This query has been created with only the country assigned and the Country hierarchy in the characteristics, and for key figures there will be Normal Revenue (for comparison purposes) and the key figure ICE_REV2. The following illustration shows this information. Once the query is executed, notice the differences between the basic information received from the Normal Revenue key figure and the Revenue after the elimination of internal volume.

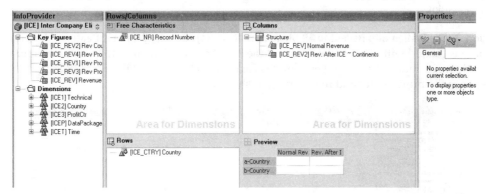

As you can see, there's a big difference at most levels, and at the top level there's a dramatic difference. It is important to mention that the business user will need to be very clear about what they are looking at in terms of analysis because executing and delivering this information may be very confusing if the user is not completely aware of what is involved in the results. We can review this in more detail. Notice that countries UK and SGP have exactly the same values, but DE and the total of that node have definite differences between the two key figure results. Reviewing this, we see that in the case of DE, two sales of a total $300.00 occurred within that country and were therefore were eliminated from the REV2 key figure total.

Looking at the total for Europe, we can see that the difference is significant. Therefore, if we just look to see the records that actual make up the total of $530.00, we can identify the information that qualifies. Only two records will count at the very top node for Europe—the sale from DE to the U.S. for $ 80.00, from the UK to the U.S. for $250.00, and the sale from DE to CDN for $200.00. All the other sales were within the countries internally and were therefore eliminated. At the root level, the Normal Revenue key figure has total of $1930.00 (same as before), but for the REV2 key figure, the total is $0.00. Reviewing the results, you'll notice that no sales were initially driven from outside of the Europe and Asia levels (therefore none of the sales were driven from left to right by the U.S.). Therefore, the Root node shows $0.00 in sales. The results are shown here.

T_ICEQ2 Countries within Continents			Normal Revenue ⇕	Rev. After ICE ~ Continents ⇕
	Country ⇕		$	$
▾ROOT	Country		1.930,00	
▾EUROPE	Europe		1.780,00	530,00
• DE			1.480,00	1.180,00
• UK			300,00	300,00
▾ASIA	Asia		150,00	150,00
• SGP			150,00	150,00

The next two examples are a bit more complex, and the Boolean logic starts to get more involved. These queries show the results of a combination of Country and Profit Center characteristics.

Query 3 (Elimination with Regard to All Characteristic Pairs): Country OR Profit Center   Here the query is created with the profit center and the country included and the Normal Revenue key figure included. The other key figure is REV3, which holds the Boolean OR logic between the profit center and the country, as shown next.

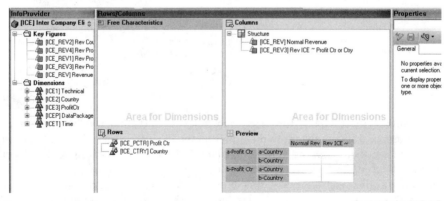

The result shows that the Normal Revenue is the same, as it should be, and a total of $1,930.00 in sales for the total hierarchy. Now we can look to the column with the combination of Profit Center or Country to see some interesting information. For someone who doesn't understand what they are looking at, this would make absolutely no sense, so some additional investigate will help.

Let's look at the node for PC02 and drill down on the information offered for the country node Europe, and below that the node for DE. The total of $480.00 is a combination of three postings: from DE to AT and from DE to the U.S. ($180.00) and the posting from DE to the UK ($300.00). This is due to the combinations of profit centers or countries. Now, if we go to the next node up, we see that the total is only $80.00. The only record that will count is DE to U.S. (and from PC0201 to a blank field), because this is the only record outside the countries and also outside the profit centers. Therefore, the $80.00 is assigned, as shown here.

T_ICEQ3 Profit Ctr or Ctry					
New Analysis	Open	Save As...	Display as Table ▼	Information	Send	Print Version	Export to E			
▼ Columns				Normal Revenue ⇕	Rev ICE ~ Profit Ctr or Ctry ⇕
• Structure	Profit Ctr ⇕	Country ⇕		$	$
▼ Rows	▼ROOT	▼ROOT	Country	1.930,00	
• Profit Ctr		▼EUROPE	Europe	1.780,00	80,00
• Country		• DE		1.480,00	180,00
• Free characteristics		• UK		300,00	
		▼ASIA	Asia	150,00	
		• SGP		150,00	
	▼PC01	▼ROOT	Country	100,00	
		▼EUROPE	Europe	100,00	
		• DE		100,00	
	• PC0181	▼ROOT	Country	100,00	
		▶EUROPE	Europe	100,00	
	▼PC02	▼ROOT	Country	1.380,00	
		▼EUROPE	Europe	1.380,00	80,00
		• DE		1.380,00	480,00
	• PC0201	▼ROOT	Country	1.180,00	
		▶EUROPE	Europe	1.180,00	80,00
	• PC0203	▼ROOT	Country	200,00	
	Page 1 of 2				

Query 4 (Elimination with Regard to Each Individual Characteristic Pair) Profit Center AND Country   Here, the query is created with the profit center (initially in the free characteristics) and the country included and the REV2 key figure included. The other key figure is REV4,

which holds the Boolean AND logic between the profit center and the country. The following illustration shows this result.

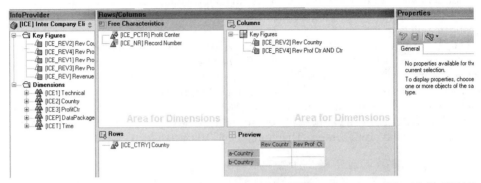

We are now looking at two virtual key figures that generate their values during the time that the query is being executed. These results are even more confusing to the layman, and this type of report will be almost always used internally (versus external use as a formal report). In this case, we will focus on the lower portion of the hierarchy and see how to break down the results. The following illustration shows the results of the query. We will focus on the node for profit center group PC03. Now, looking at the key figure Rev Country, we see that Asia is easy to understand because it shows $150.00 for all levels because there is only one posting that being between profit centers and countries.

ICE_QUERY4 ProfitCtr and Country

| New Analysis | Open | Save As... | Display as Table | ▼ | Information | Send | Print Version |

Columns	Profit Center ⇕	Country ⇕		Rev Country ⇕	Rev Prof Ctr AND Ctr ⇕
• Key Figures				$	$
▼ Rows	▼ROOT	▼ROOT	Country		180,00
• Profit Center		▼EUROPE	Europe	530,00	630,00
• Country		• DE		1.180,00	1.180,00
▼ Free characteristics		• UK		300,00	300,00
• Record Number		▼ASIA	Asia	150,00	150,00
		• SGP		150,00	150,00
	▶PC01	▼ROOT	Country		
		▼EUROPE	Europe		
		• DE			
	▶PC02	▼ROOT	Country		680,00
		▼EUROPE	Europe	280,00	880,00
		• DE		1.180,00	1.360,00
	▶PC03	▼ROOT	Country		450,00
		▼EUROPE	Europe	250,00	300,00
		• UK		300,00	300,00
		▼ASIA	Asia	150,00	150,00
		• SGP		150,00	150,00

Moving up a group, we see that the combinations of results need some additional documentation, and based on the results of the last two queries, I would definitely attach comments or a document. Getting back to the query, in the Rev Country column, the lower amount is $300.00, and this comes from the postings between the UK to both DE and the U.S. Once the totals roll up to the next level, we see that the amount has changed to $250.00, which comes from the fact that one of the postings ($50.00) is between the UK and DE within the same hierarchy node and therefore is eliminated. Moving to the next column, we see that the lower level amount matches but the upper node is still at $300.00. When this is calculated, it holds the extra $50.00 because both the profit centers *and* the countries are not consistent and therefore can't eliminate the extra $50.00 from the node.

Based on this explanation, take a look at the other nodes and work through the records that have been posted to understand the posting process and the elimination process. We've only been using about 20 records so that the overall discussion can be focused and so that we don't have to search through large volumes of records to discuss the concepts. Just think of the company that has large volumes of records processing through this scenario. You definitely want to understand the functionality of Elimination of Internal Company Volumes and how the results come about, rather than trying to work through large volumes of records to figure out all the postings. As you can see, this component of the BW reporting system can be very useful in the appropriate situation.

Unit of Measure Conversion

Well, it's finally here—the standard ability to create a method to perform Unit of Measure conversions both in the query and in the upload process. This has been a thorn in the side of many companies during the last several years, and there has been numerous home-grown options developed out of the need to do this. If I had a nickel for every time I created a query with quantity and the results were the infamous "*" wildcard or MIX (identifying to the business user that there are mixed UOM in the column and that the results are not consistent), I would be a millionaire. Now, we can avoid that entire conversation and just say, "Yes, we do support that functionality as a standard part of our process."

This is a very helpful component to understand and be able to configure. I have already used it in all the implementations for the 7.0 version of BW that have quantities. We will focus on the BEx Query conversion and not the upload conversion, but the two do intersect in terms of the setup of the InfoObjects to support this process. Quantity conversion allows you to convert key figures with units that have different units of measure in the source system into a uniform unit of measure in the BI system. This function enables the conversion of updated data records from the source unit of measure into a target unit of measure (or into different target units of measure) if the conversion is repeated. In terms of functionality, quantity conversion is structured similarly to currency translation. In part, it is based on the quantity conversion functionality in SAP NetWeaver Application Server. Simple conversions can be performed between units of measure that belong to the same dimension (such as meters to kilometers and kilograms to grams). You can also perform InfoObject-specific conversions— for example, two palettes (PAL) of material 4711 were ordered, and this order quantity has to be converted to the stock quantity *carton* (CAR). Quantity conversion is based on quantity conversion types. The business transaction rules of the conversion are established in the quantity conversion type. The conversion type is a combination of different parameters (conversion factors and source and target units of measure) that determine how the conversion is performed. The quantity conversion type is stored for future use and is available for quantity conversions in the transformation rules for InfoCubes and in the Business Explorer. In the transformation rules for InfoCubes, you can specify for each key figure or data field whether quantity conversion is performed during the update. In certain cases, you can also run quantity conversion in user-defined routines in the transformation rules. In the Business Explorer, you can establish a quantity conversion in the query definition and translate quantities at query runtime. Translation is more limited here than in the query definition. Figure 13-2 shows the positioning of the UOM conversion both in the upload process and in the execution of the query.

NOTE *The new conversion-type approach in BW 7.0 supports the use of the two-tier/step method. Therefore, if you have conversion steps of Pallet-to-Box and then Box-to-Each, the conversion type will be able to convert from Pallet to Each.*

The conversion of units of measure is required to convert business measurements into other units. Business measurements encompass physical measurements that are either assigned to a dimension or are nondimensional. Nondimensional measurements are understood as countable measurements (palette, unit, and so on). You differentiate between conversions for which you only need to enter a source and target unit in order to perform the conversion, as well as conversions for which specifying these values alone is not sufficient. For the latter, you have to enter a conversion factor derived from a characteristic or a characteristic combination (compound characteristic) and the corresponding properties.

- **Measurements of length** Conversions within the same dimension ID (T006-DIMID; for example, length). 1 m = 100 cm is a linear correlation. Both meter and centimeter both belong to the dimension ID LENGTH.

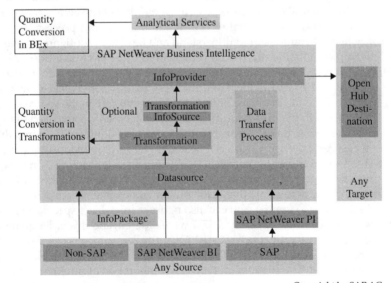

Copyright by SAP AG

FIGURE 13-2 Quantity conversion in the upload process and in the BEx Analyzer

- **Measurements of number associated with measurements of weight**   Conversions involving different dimension IDs (for example, number and weight). 1 unit = 25 g is a linear correlation. Unit has the dimension ID AAAADL, and gram has the dimension ID MASS.

Table 13-1 shows examples of these conversion issues.

Question: How many chocolate bars fit on one europallet (PAL)?

In principle, every characteristic that contains at least one unit as an attribute can be used for quantity conversion. To start this off, we need to do some configuration of the InfoObjects. In our example, we will be using the InfoObject ZMATL18. Within this InfoObject we need to complete the setup of the UOM components. The conversion of units always takes place based on the base unit of measure (as with material management conversion, table MARA R/3). When creating a unit of measure for the characteristic, the system creates a DataStore object for units of measure. You can specify the name of the quantity DataStore object, the description, and the InfoArea into which you want to add the object. The system proposes the following name:

UOM<Name of InfoObject to which the quantity DataStore Object is being added>

With objects of this type, the system generates an SID column in the database table for each characteristic and stores the characteristic attributes in the form of SIDs. Assignments of quantity DataStore objects to characteristics are 1:1. This means that only one characteristic can be assigned to a quantity DataStore object and that only one quantity DataStore object can be assigned to a characteristic.

NOTE *You cannot enhance or change a quantity DataStore object in DataStore object maintenance because the object is generated by the system. You can only display it.*

You can fill the quantity DataStore object with data only by using a data transfer process with transformation; update rules are not supported in this case. If a characteristic that has a quantity DataStore object assigned to it is changed at a later time or date (for example, changes to compounding or to the base unit of measure), you have to delete the quantity DataStore object and regenerate it. In practice, this does not occur after the data model has been finalized.

Table 13-2 shows the structure of quantity DataStore objects.

In our example, ZMATL18 shows the setup of the UOM DataStore object, as you can see in the following illustration. Once you execute the Create process, the system will

Number	Unit		Number	Unit
1	Chocolate bar	=	25	g
1	Small carton	=	12	Chocolate bar
1	Large carton	=	20	Small carton
1	Europallet	=	40	Large carton

TABLE 13-1   Conversion Table with Units in Nondimensional Groups

Key	Object
Key	<Characteristic>
Key	<Compounding for characteristic, where applicable>
Key	<Unit of measure that you can convert into>
	<Base unit of measure>
	<Conversion factor: Counter>
	<Conversion factor: Denominator>
	<SID_Characteristic>
	<SID_Compounding for characteristic, where applicable>
	<SID_Unit of measure that you can convert into>
	<SID_Base unit of measure>

TABLE 13-2   Configuration of the DataStore Object for UOM

automatically generate the technical name of the DataStore object (DSO). In this case, the technical name is UOMZMATL.

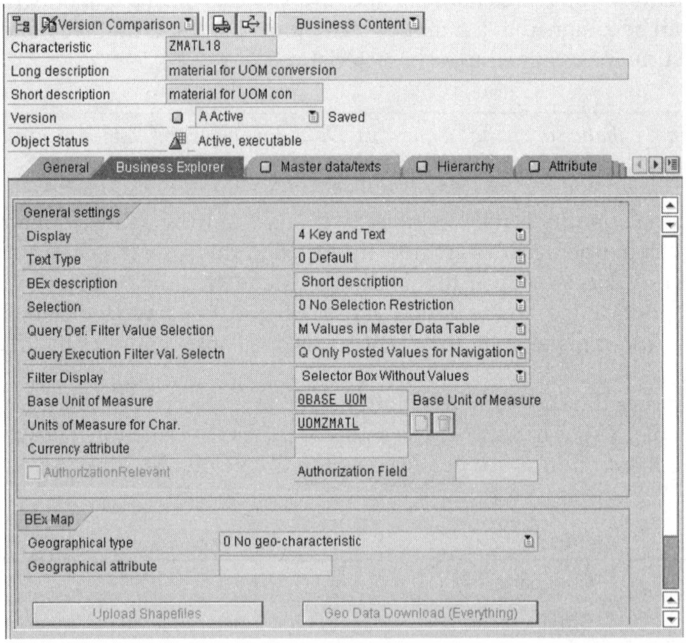

Copyright by SAP AG

Now we can go to the InfoProvider area of the Data Warehouse Workbench and review the configuration of the DataStore object UOMZMATL. The following illustration shows this configuration.

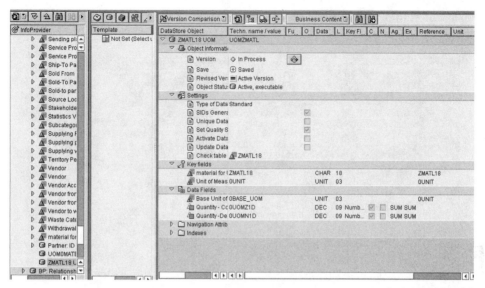

As you can see, the DSO uses the InfoObject ZMATL18 as the key field and also as a check table. In the data fields, the two InfoObjects necessary for conversion purposes are available—0UOMZ1D and 0UOMM1D. These two InfoObjects will hold the conversion amounts for the UOM.

Before going any further, we can review the data that is to be converted. In the following illustration we see the query that generates a set of data that has three different UOMs attached: Pallet, Cardboard Box, and Gram. They are attached to the materials P-100, P-200, and P-300. The result doesn't make any sense at this point. The total of 450,000 MIX confirms that the system can't make out the base UOM that is required to do the conversion.

BW USER UOM Query			Last Data Update: 17.08.2007 21:15:24

material for UOM con ⇕	Base Unit ⇕	Invoiced quantity ⇕
P-100	Cardboard box	100 BOX
P-200	Gram	300 G
P-300	Pallet	50 PAL
Overall Result		450,000 MIX

- Columns
  - Key Figures
- Rows
  - material for UOM con
  - Base Unit
- Free characteristics

Now we need to take care of uploading the conversion table (UOMZMATL) into the DSO so that it can help with the conversion process. Again, this is all setup work that has to be completed. The following illustration shows the setup of an uploading process into the DataStore object for the UOM conversion table. The configuration consists of setting up the transformation rule to link the flat file of data to the DSO component. In addition, the datasource, InfoPackage, and DTP are set up to upload the flat file of conversion information.

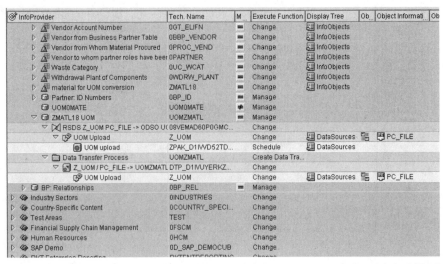

The following illustration shows the transformation rule. This is a basic one-to-one mapping into the DSO.

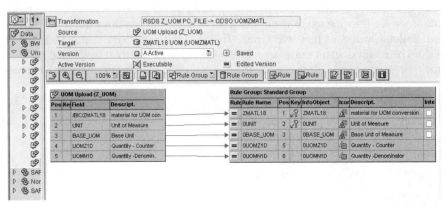

The following shows the flat file with the conversion information to be uploaded. This conversion is going to use Material as the key field. You can set this up with any number of different combinations of characteristics to be used—Plant, Material Group, Division, and so on. It depends on the base characteristic that will be used for conversion.

	A	B	C	D	E	F	G
1	MATERIAL	0UNIT	0BASE_UOM	UOM COUNT	UOM NUMBER		
2	P-100	BOX	EA	240	1		
3	P-200	G	EA	1	25		
4	P-300	PAL	EA	300	1		
5							
6							
7							
8							
9							
10							
11							

Working through a basic uploading process in the 7.0 BI system by execution an upload via the InfoPackage then moving that information from the PSA to the DSO through the use of a DTP (Data Transfer Process) we get the conversion information into the DSO. The results are shown here for uploaded into the active table of the Unit of Measure DSO.

Data Browser: Table /BIC/AUOMZMATL00 Select Entries   3

/BIC/ZMATL18	UNIT	BASE_UOM	RECORDMODE	UOMZ1D	UOMN1D	O__ZMATL18	O__0UNIT	O__0BASE_UOM
P-100	BOX	EA		240,000	1,000	2	1000000235	1000000049
P-200	G	EA		1,000	25,000	3	1000000057	1000000049
P-300	PAL	EA		300,000	1,000	4	1000000193	1000000049

We are now ready to use all the different components in the conversion process.

Quantity Conversion Types

A quantity conversion type is a combination of different parameters that establish how the conversion is performed. The parameters that determine the conversion factors are the source and target unit of measure and the option you choose for determining the conversion factors. Figure 13-3 shows the combinations and positioning of variables, key figures, characteristics, source and target units, central tables, and conversion types that make up this process.

The decisive factor in defining a conversion type is the way in which you want conversion factors to be determined. Entering source and target quantities is optional.

The following options are available for the conversion factors:

- **Using a reference InfoObject**   The system tries to determine the conversion factors from the reference InfoObject you have chosen or from the associated quantity DataStore object. If you want to convert 1000 grams into kilograms but the conversion factors are not defined in the quantity DataStore object, the system cannot perform the conversion, even though this is a very simple conversion.

- **Using central units of measure (T006)**   The conversion can only take place if both the source unit of measure and target unit of measure belong to the same dimension (for example, meters to kilometers, kilograms to grams, and so on).

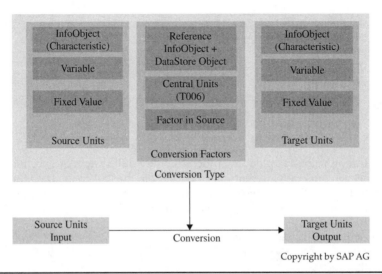

FIGURE 13-3   Conversion process for Unit of Measure

- **Using a reference InfoObject if available, central units of measure (T006)**   The system will initially attempt to use the reference infoobject, if not, the system tries to determine the conversion factors using the quantity DataStore object you have defined. If the system finds conversion factors, it uses these to perform the calculation. If the system cannot determine conversion factors from the quantity DataStore object, it tries again using the central units of measure.

- **Using central units of measure (T006) if available, reference InfoObject**   The system will use the central units of measure and if not, the system tries to find the conversion factors in the central units of measure table. If the system finds conversion factors, it uses these to perform the conversion. If the system cannot determine conversion factors from the central units of measure, it tries to find conversion factors that match the attributes of the data record by looking in the quantity DataStore object.

The following illustration shows this in the system.

Quantity Conversion Type Display

Conversion Type	ZT_CONV1
Long Description	Conversion from BASE_UOM into KG
Short Description	BASE_UOM -> KG

| Hdr data | Conversion Factors | UoM |

Dynamic Determination of Conversion Factor

2 Using Central Units of Measure (T006)

1 Using Reference InfoObject
2 Using Central Units of Measure (T006)
3 Using Reference InfoObject, If Available, Otherwise Using Centr. UOMs (T006)
4 Using Central Units of Measure (T006), If Available, Otherwise Ref. InfoObject

The settings you can make in this regard affect performance, and the decision must be strictly based on the data set. If you only want to perform conversions within the same dimension, the second option is the most suitable. If you are performing InfoObject-specific conversions (for example, material-specific conversions) between units that do not belong to the same dimension, the first option is the most suitable. In both cases, the system only accesses one database table. That table contains the conversion factors. With the third and fourth options, the system tries to determine conversion factors at each stage. If conversion factors are not found in the basic table (T006), the system searches again in the quantity DataStore object, or in reverse. The option you choose should depend on how you want to spread the conversion. If the source unit of measure and target unit of measure belong to the same dimension for 80% of the data records that you want to convert, first try to determine factors using the central units of measure (the fourth option), and accept that the system will have to search in the second table also for the remaining 20%.

The Conversion Factor from InfoObject option (as with Exchange Rate from InfoObject in currency translation types) is only available when you load data. The key figure you enter here has to exist in the InfoProvider and the attribute this key figure has in the data record is taken as the conversion factor.

The Source Unit of Measure is the unit of measure you want to convert. The Source Unit of Measure is determined dynamically from the data record or from a specified InfoObject (characteristic). In addition, you can specify a fixed Source Unit of Measure or determine the Source Unit of Measure using a variable. When converting quantities in the Business Explorer, the Source Unit of Measure is always determined from the data record. During the data load process, the Source Unit of Measure can be determined either from the data record or using a specified characteristic that bears master data. You can use a fixed Source Unit of Measure in planning functions. Data records are converted that have the same unit key as the Source Unit of Measure. The values in input help correspond to the values in table T006 (Units of Measure). You can reach the maintenance for the units of measure in SAP Customizing Implementation Guide _ SAP NetWeaver _ General Settings _ Check Units of Measure.

In reporting, you can use a Source Unit of Measure from a variable. The variables that have been defined for InfoObject 0UNIT are used.

You have the following options for determining the Target Unit of Measure:

- Enter a fixed Target Unit of Measure in the quantity conversion type (for example, "UNIT").

- Specify an InfoObject in the quantity conversion type that is used to determine the Target Unit of Measure during the conversion. This is not the same as defining currency attributes, where you determine a currency attribute on the Business Explorer tab page in characteristic maintenance. With quantity conversion types, you determine the InfoObject in the quantity conversion type itself. Under InfoObject for Determining Unit of Measure, all InfoObjects are listed that have at least one attribute of type Unit. You have to select one of these attributes as the corresponding quantity attribute.

- Alternatively, specify that the Target Unit of Measure is determined during the conversion. In the Query Designer under the properties for the relevant key figure, you specify either a fixed Target Unit of Measure or a variable to determine the Target Unit of Measure.

- Use the setting Target Quantity Using InfoSet. This setting covers the same functionality as InfoObject for Determining Target Quantity. If the InfoObject you want to use to determine the target quantity is unique in the InfoSet (it occurs only once in the whole InfoSet), you can enter the InfoObject under InfoObject for Determining Target Quantity.

You only have to enter the InfoObject in Target Quantity Using InfoSet if you want to determine the target quantity using an InfoObject that occurs more than once in the InfoSet. The InfoSet contains InfoProviders A and B, and both A and B contain InfoObject X with a quantity attribute. In this case, you have to specify exactly whether you want to use X from A or X from B to determine the target quantity. Field aliases are used in an InfoSet to ensure uniqueness. All the active InfoSets in the system can be displayed using input help. As long as you have selected an InfoSet, you can select an InfoObject. All the InfoObjects with quantity attributes contained in the InfoSet can be displayed using input help. The following illustration shows this in the system.

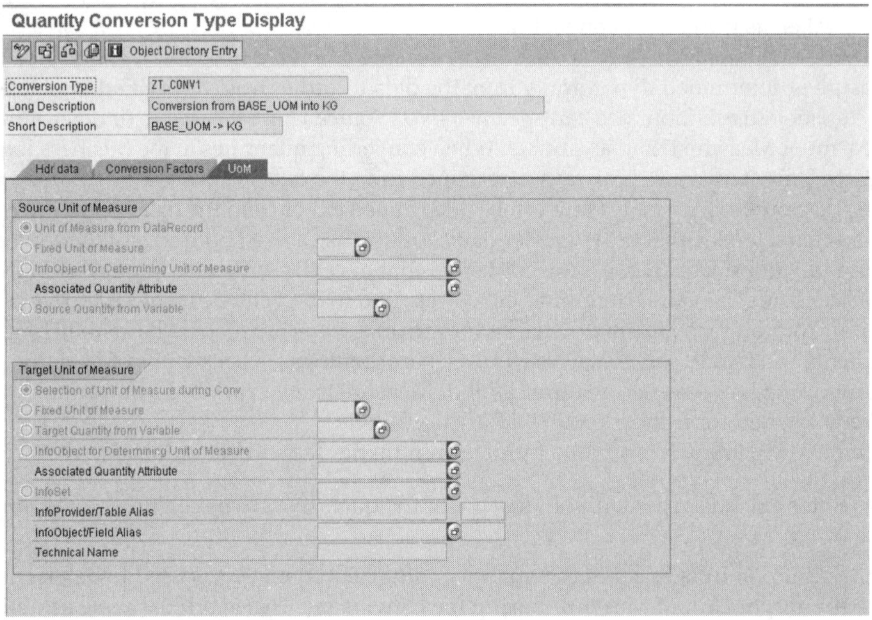

If you want to determine the Target Unit of Measure for quantity conversion using an InfoObject, proceed as follows:

- You require a characteristic that has at least one unit as an attribute. This characteristic (for example, 0MATERIAL) has to contain valid units of measure. Also, the corresponding conversion rates have to be maintained (either specific to an InfoObject or in the central units of measure).

- Define a quantity conversion type in which the Target Unit of Measure will be determined using this InfoObject.

- In Associated Quantity Attribute, set the quantity attribute for the InfoObject you are using to determine the target quantity.

- In the transformation rules for your InfoCube, specify that the values for the corresponding key figures are to be translated in the transformation and enter the previously defined translation type. The InfoObject specified in the quantity conversion type must exist in both the source and the target system and be filled using a rule.

This is very similar to what we are doing in our example. Our next step is to set up the conversion type for our process. The initial transaction code to get to the Unit of Measure Conversion Types screen is shown here.

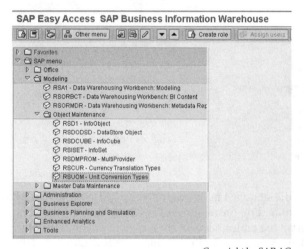

Copyright by SAP AG

Now that we are in the Conversion Types screen, we will be using the dynamic process as well as all the setup we've completed on our DSO and InfoObject. The following illustration shows this result. On this screen, we have identified the reference InfoObject option and the reference InfoObject ZMATL18.

Copyright by SAP AG

In the following illustration, you can see that we have set this UOM to use the Unit of Measure from the DataRecord option and also the Selection of Unit of Measure During

Conversion option. We could also decide to use the Target Quantity from Variable option if we knew that the business user would need a number of different conversions. However, in our case we have only one Target UOM—Each.

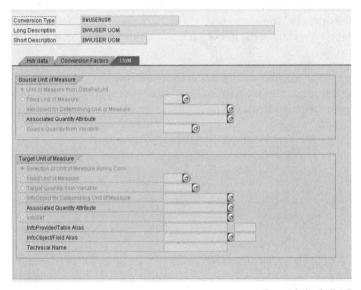

If you are using the standard tables supplied by SAP, you will need to upload them using the standard uploading process from the source system connection. You use this function to transfer all the tables relevant for unit conversion from other SAP systems connected to the BI system. Specifically, this includes the following tables:

T006, T006A, T006B, T006C, T006D, T006I, T006J, T006T

In the Data Warehousing Workbench under Modeling, choose the source system tree. In the context menu of your SAP Source System, choose Transfer Global Settings. The Transfer Global Settings: Selection screen appears. Under Transfer Global Table Contents, select the Units of Measure field. Under Mode you can select whether you want to simulate upload or update, or copy the tables again. With the Update Tables option, existing records are updated. With the Rebuild Tables option, the corresponding tables are deleted before the new records are loaded.

Setting Variable Target Units of Measure in the Query Designer

Depending on how the target quantity determination is defined in the quantity conversion type, you can either specify a fixed target quantity or a variable that the system uses to determine the target quantity. If a variable is used, the system will request the variable when you execute the query. In the Translations tabbed page, we have Currency Translation and Unit Conversion. Also, the Conversion Type is a required entry in this case.

You can set a Target Unit of Measure for a structural component in the Query Designer. Select a conversion type in the Quantity Conversion Type dropdown box. Depending on how the unit conversion type was created, you have the following options:

- **Select the Target Unit of Measure When Converting**   The Target Unit of Measure is not fixed in the conversion type, but can be determined during conversion. Select the required conversion type and enter the required unit in the Target Unit dropdown box. In addition, you can choose the variable icon to call the input help dialog box and select a variable Target Unit of Measure. By choosing the black arrow, you can navigate to the context menu and can then choose New Variable to create new variables or Edit to change existing variables. Both options use the variable editor. When you execute the query, the Variables screen appears, in which you can then choose the Target Unit of Measure.

- **Fixed Target Unit of Measure**   The Target Unit of Measure was specified in the conversion type. Select the required conversion type with the fixed Target Unit of Measure. The fixed Target Unit of Measure (such as Gram) for this conversion type appears in the Target Unit dropdown box.

- **InfoObject Determines Target Unit of Measure**   The Target Unit of Measure is specified in the conversion type so that it is determined from an InfoObject. Select the required conversion type with the Target Unit of Measure from the InfoObject. The text "From InfoObject" appears in the Target Unit field when you select this conversion type.

- **Target Unit of Measure from Variable**   A variable was specified for 0UNIT InfoObject in the conversion type. The text "From Variable" appears in the Target Unit field when you select this conversion type.

For the quantity conversion, you can set a Target Unit of Measure for a structural component in the Query Designer. Select a translation key in the Quantity Translation Key dropdown box. Depending on how the quantity translation key was created, you have the following options:

- **Select the Target Quantity Unit When Translating**   The target quantity unit is not fixed in the translation key but can be determined when translating. Select the required translation key and enter the required unit in the Target Quantity Unit dropdown box. You can also use the variable symbol to call up the input help dialog box and select a variable target currency. You click the black arrow to reach the context menu and can then choose New Variable to create new variables or Edit to change existing variables. Both choices take you to the variables editor. When you execute the query, the Variables screen appears. You can choose the target quantity unit here.

- **Fixed Target Quantity Unit**   The target quantity unit was determined in the translation key. Select the required translation key with the fixed target quantity unit. The fixed target quantity unit (for example, Gram) for this translation key appears in the Target Quantity Unit dropdown box.

- **InfoObject Determines Target Quantity Unit**   The target quantity unit was set in the translation key so that it is determined from an InfoObject. Choose the required translation key with the target quantity unit from the InfoObject. The text "From InfoObject" appears in the Target Quantity Unit field when you select this translation type.

- **Target Quantity Unit from Variable** A variable was specified for 0UNIT in the translation type. The text "From Variable" appears in the Target Quantity Unit field when you select this translation type.

We'll now move back to the example. As the final steps in the process, we need to access the BEx Query Designer and do some additional configuration for the Invoiced Quantity key figure. The following illustration shows this information. As you can see, the Translations tab has been accessed, and we will be using the conversion type BWUSER UOM, which we created. To follow through with the addition of the target unit, based on the initial configuration of the conversion type, we add Each to the Target Unit field.

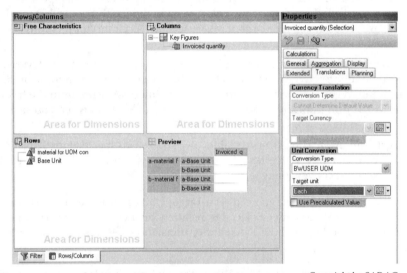

Upon execution of the query, we see that the quantities that were completely mixed are now converted to the based unit of measure (Each (EA), in this case), as shown next. Let's look at the conversion P-300. In this case, the conversion is 300 EA equals to 1 PAL. If we do the math, we see that the original number of pallets is 50, and therefore the total number of EA is now 15,000.

As you can see, this setup process is very straightforward, but if the combination of characteristics gets very complex—compounding and different levels—the table for the conversions may get rather involved. You can see how this will help significantly with the analysis of inventory, sales information, cost of goods sold, and so on, in your company.

Web Application Items: Chart and Map

In this section we look at two unique web items: Chart and Map. Although we will be discussing the BEx Web Analyzer and the Web Application Designer (WAD) in Chapter 15 in the book, now is a good time to take a look at the two web items. We've discussed the WAD a couple of times so far, so accessing it should not be an issue for you at this point. These two web items not only use the functionality of the WAD, they also use significant functionality that's outside of the SAP front-end process. So, in terms of the Chart web item, we will discuss the use of Excel-based chart components. For the Map web item, the use of the Geographic Information System (GIS) is a large part of the configuration. These items definitely are major parts of the WAD. You have probably set up a chart in Excel and will therefore feel very comfortable with this component during out discussion. This area is not specific to SAP or BW. The GIS functionality attached to the Map web item has been around for quite some time, but has only recently started to get more use in the business world. This is one of those tools that was ahead of its time.

Chart Type

What better approach to take than to deliver to your business users a Web Application with a "dashboard" look, where the users receive information in a graphical format that allows them to be able to interpret results quickly, with more understanding? Delivering information similar to what is shown in Figure 13-4 can only help analysts in their position of offering corporate management relevant data. Notice in this figure the use of both graphics and a map to emphasis the results from the chart. This is an excellent example of the power of graphics and of the additional analysis that can be done due to the use of the Chart and Map web tools.

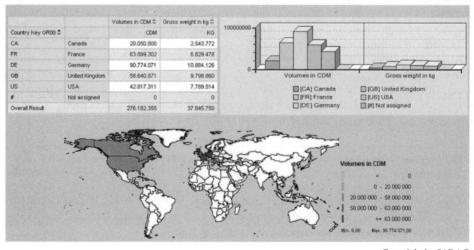

Copyright by SAP AG

FIGURE 13-4   Using charts and maps for analysis

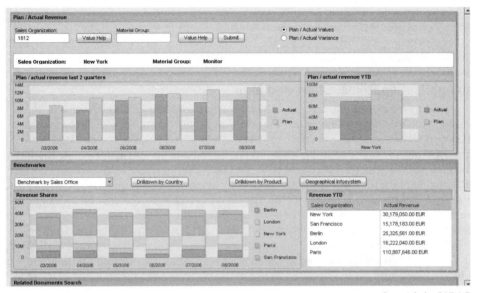

FIGURE 13-5 Plan/Actual Analysis of Sales Organization Revenue

Another excellent example is shown in Figure 13-5. Here, you can assimilate the information very quickly and easily. Notice the graphical layout of the information, starting from the details of the information you need for analysis being identified. Then in the middle of the dashboard we have the plan/actual information broken down by month for a quick review of the historical trend. Moving to the right side of the dashboard, notice the information for the Sales Organization by Material Group cumulative YTD analysis. Finally, at the bottom we can analyze the total revenue and the share that New York has of the total company. If I were to give you this information in a basic report, you would be hard pressed to do this type of analysis at a glance. But with the use of charts, the analysis is easy, fast, and helpful for strategic decision making.

All of this is done with the use of the Chart web item in the Web Application Designer. In the BEx Web Application Designer, the Chart web item is used for any graphical display of data. One key property is the Edit Chart property under the Internal Display property grouping. By using the Edit Chart web item, you call the Chart Wizard, which provides a step-by-step guide to producing useful charts of all types.

NOTE *This functionality is also available in the BEx Analyzer with the use of the Excel functionality.*

The Chart Wizard takes you through a six-step process for choosing the major properties of a chart. The following illustration shows the initial screen for using the Chart web item. As you can see, we have already assigned a query to this web item.

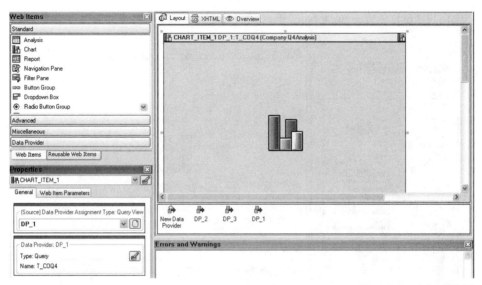

We will work our way through the details of setting up a WAD process in a later chapter. For now, we will only concentrate on the specific items related to the Chart web item. These are found on the Web Item Parameters tab. The following illustration shows this information. This is one of those times when there are so many options available that we will only touch on the basics because going through all the advanced scenarios of chart building would take an additional several chapters.

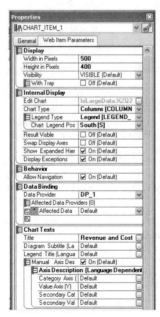

Table 13-3 lists the parameters for the Chart web item.

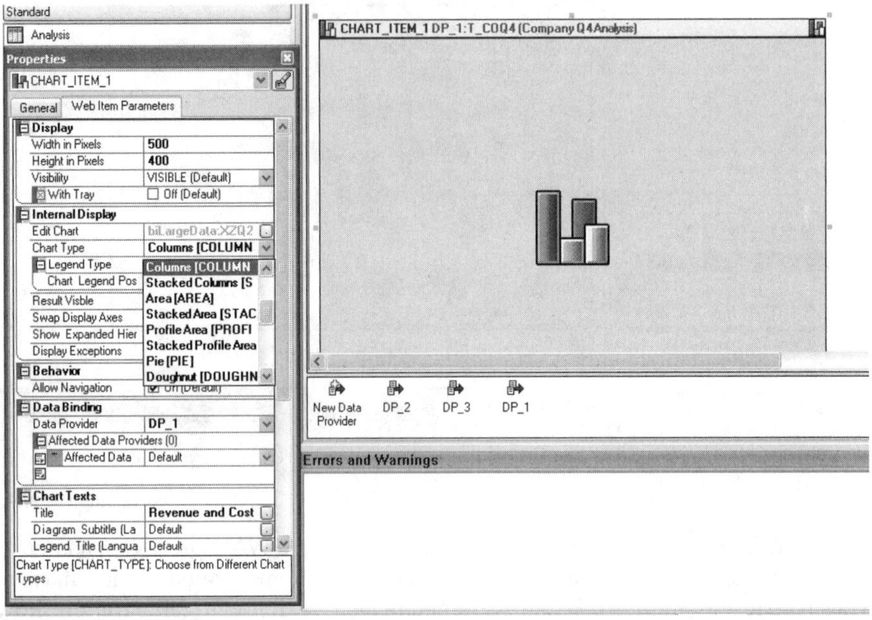

Parameter/Grouping	Description
Display	
Width in Pixels (WIDTH)	You use this parameter to specify the width of the web item.
Height in Pixels (HEIGHT)	You use this parameter to specify the height of the web item.
Visibility (VISIBILITY)	You use this parameter to specify whether the web item is to be visible in the Web Application.
With Tray (WITH_TRAY)	You use this parameter to specify whether the Chart web item is to have a symbol that allows the web item to be expanded and collapsed.
Internal Display	
Edit Chart (CHART_CUSTOMIZING)	You use the button for this parameter to navigate to the Chart Designer. In the Chart Designer, you can make various settings for the chart. We will review this process in more detail in the next section of this topic.
Chart Type (CHART_TYPE) (See the following for this result)	You use this parameter to select the required chart type. The default value is Column Chart.

TABLE 13-3 Parameters for Chart Web Item

Parameter/Grouping	Description
Internal Display	
Legend Type (LEGEND_TYPE)	You use this parameter to make the following settings for the legend:
	Legend (default setting) The legend is displayed. The option Chart Legend Position is also displayed. You can choose from the following options: North (N), East (E), South (S; the default value), and West (W).
	None The legend is hidden.
	Data Table Specifies that the system is to display the data in a table below the chart.
Only Legend (LEGEND_ONLY)	You use this parameter to specify that the legend is to be displayed without the chart.
Result Visible (RESULTS_VISIBLE)	You use this parameter to specify whether the results are to be displayed in the chart or hidden.
	This parameter is deactivated by default and the totals rows/columns for the underlying data provider are not displayed in the chart. This means that you can suppress totals that may affect the chart display adversely without having to change the data provider.
Swap Display Axes (AXES_SWAPPED)	You use this parameter to swap the chart axes in the display without changing the navigational state of the query view.
	You achieve the same effect if you swap two free characteristics with one another in the underlying query view.
Show Expanded Hierarchy Nodes (OPEN_HIERARCHY_NODES_VISIBLE)	You use this parameter to specify whether expanded hierarchy nodes are to be displayed or hidden in the chart.
	If you deactivate this parameter, it is possible to remove the expanded nodes from the chart generation when the display hierarchy is active. This ensures that the total of the values displayed is the overall result.
Display Exceptions (EXCEPTIONS_VISIBLE)	You use this parameter to specify whether exceptions are to be displayed in the chart or are hidden.
	This parameter is deactivated by default and no exceptions are displayed in the chart, even though the data provider on which it is based has exceptions.
Behavior	
Allow Navigation (INTERACTION_ALLOWED)	You use this parameter to specify whether navigation and other interaction is to be possible in the Web Application.
Data Binding	
Data Provider (DATA_PROVIDER_REF)	You use this parameter to assign a data provider to the web item. The web item gets the data and metadata that it needs to generate the output and commands from this data provider. I recommend that you keep to the conventions supported by the Web Application Designer when specifying names: Names can be a maximum of 30 characters and consist of A-Z, 0-9 and the underscore character (_), but cannot start or end with an underscore character. Adhering to these conventions simplifies the upgrade to subsequent SAP releases.

TABLE 13-3 Parameters for Chart Web Item (*continued*)

Parameter/Grouping	Description
Data Binding	
Affected Data Providers (LINKED_DATA_PROVIDER_REF_LIST)	You use this parameter to specify the list of data providers to which all chart commands are sent.
Chart Texts	
Title (TITLE)	You use this parameter to specify the language-dependent text for the title of the chart.
Diagram Subtitle (Language-Dependent) (SUBTITLE)	You use this parameter to specify the language-dependent text for the subtitle of the chart.
Legend Title (Language-Dependent) (TITLE_LEGEND)	You use this parameter to specify the language-dependent text for the title of the legend.
Manual Axis Description (OVERRIDE_AXIS_DESC)	You use this parameter to specify whether or not you want to override automatic axis labeling. If you do not select this parameter, the system creates labeling for the chart axes of simple charts, such as column, bar, line, and profile charts. For example, the name of a key figure appears on the Y axis in a bar chart. If you select this parameter, you can choose between the following options for overriding the automatic labeling of the axes: **Category Axis (X): Title (Language-Dependent)** You use this parameter to specify the language-dependent text for the title of the category axis (X). **Value Axis (Y): Title (Language-Dependent)** You use this parameter to specify the language-dependent text for the title of the value axis (Y). **Secondary Category Axis (X): Title (Language-Dependent)** You use this parameter to specify the language-dependent text for the title of the secondary category axis (X). This parameter is only needed for specific chart types such as histograms or scatter charts. **Secondary Value Axis (Y): Title (Language-Dependent)** You use this parameter to specify the language-dependent text for the title of the secondary value axis (Y).
Manual Axis Label (OVERRIDE_AXIS_LABEL)	You use this parameter to specify whether or not you want to override the automatic display for units and currencies. If the units and currencies in the query and other settings are the same and you do not select this parameter, these units, currencies, and settings are displayed automatically in the chart. If you select this parameter, you can choose between the following options for overriding the automatic display: **Category Axis (X): Unit (Language-Dependent)** You use this parameter to specify the language-dependent text for the unit of the category axis (X). **Value Axis (Y): Unit (Language-Dependent)** You use this parameter to specify the language-dependent text for the unit of the value axis (Y). **Secondary Category Axis (X): Unit (Language-Dependent)** You use this parameter to specify the language-dependent text for the unit of the secondary category axis (X). This parameter is only needed for specific chart types such as histograms or scatter charts. **Secondary Value Axis (Y): Unit (Language-Dependent)** You use this parameter to specify the language-dependent text for the unit of the secondary value axis (Y).

TABLE 13-3   Parameters for Chart Web Item (*continued*)

The texts, such as chart titles and chart subtitles, as well as the titles and units of the axes, are all language-dependent. You can enter the texts in the Chart Designer or in the Web Application Designer using the text input dialog box for the relevant parameters.

Using the button on the right of the Edit Chart item, we get to the Chart Wizard, which offers six steps for developing charts. You could spend days in these six steps (and I'm sure the graphic designers at your corporation do) creating exactly the correct chart format, using the required corporate colors, adding ledgers for additional information, and on and on. There are over 20 different chart types, with subsets of these chart types. For example, the chart type Columns has seven different subsets. The great part about using this wizard is that you really don't have to spend too much time in this process if you don't want to. In our case we will be going through some of the functionality but won't cover all the details. This is one portion of the toolset that you need to work with to get a feel for the functionality.

The following illustration shows the results of step 1 in this process. All types are supported by the Web. Here, you select the chart type from the list of charts. The selection is interactive, and you can see an example of what the chart will look like. You might be tempted to start configuring the information immediately on this screen, but it is just for deciding what chart type is required. You can display variations (for example, a 3D chart) on a chart type by clicking the plus sign in front of the chart type in question and expanding the structure tree.

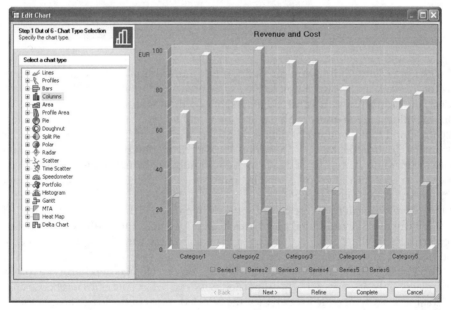

Copyright by SAP AG

In step 2 of the Chart Wizard, the process continues with you setting the various text titles, axis titles, and so on. You can also set the number of data series that will be displayed, as shown here.

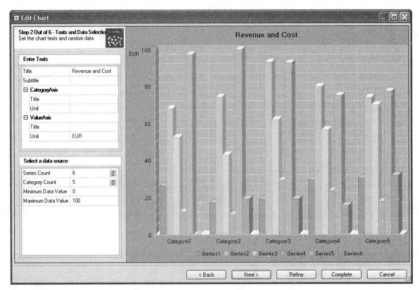

In the upper-left window, you can define a title and subtitle for the chart, determine labels for the axes, and assign a unit to the axes. Enter the following into the lower-left window: the number of series and categories that occur in your data source, and the minimum value and maximum value that correspond to your query. The chart preview will then correspond to the number of data series and categories of the final chart, and you will be able to judge its appearance more easily. The values are determined using random data. Specify the maximum number of data series and number of categories to be displayed in your chart, even if the data source contains more series or categories. The same is true for Minimum Value and Maximum Value.

Step 3 involves realigning the color for the different series that have been identified in step 2. You can also set additional properties in step 3, such as the border color, labels, and any changes to the chart type. In this step of the wizard, you can determine the specific properties of all rows in your chart, or you can define each row individually (for all pie charts' and polar charts' categories). For example, you can change the chart type for just one series or label only one series. In the upper-left window, select All Series or choose an individual series. Change the property for the selected series in the lower area of the window. You can usually change the color and border color here, as well as the labels of a series. The properties available depend on the chart type.

Step 4 enables you to change the properties of various elements such as chart background, the plot area, legends, and titles. The following illustration shows the elements that can be changed.

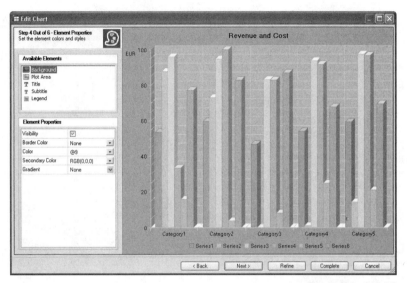

In this step of the wizard, you can set specific properties that affect the background, the drawing area, or the legend. For example, you can set a color ramp in the background. Simply select Background in the upper-left window, enter a color and a secondary color, and then determine a color ramp in the Gradient field. You can also set the same properties for the drawing area, and you can set a transparency by entering a value between 0 and 100 in the Transparency field. If you select Title or Subtitle, you can determine the font, its orientation, size, color, and style. In order to change the properties of the legend, select the legend. Now, in the lower-left window, you can set whether the legend should be visible (Visibility), whether you want to see the legend only (Only Legend), and where the legend should be positioned.

Step 5 offers you the ability to change the different axes properties. You can adjust the grid view and other items such as the text wrap functionality. The following illustration shows this information.

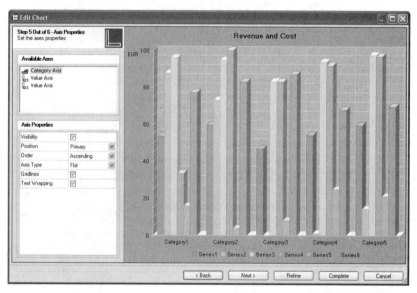

You can format the axes of your chart in this step. The wizard omits this step for chart types without a vertical axis, such as a pie chart. Select the required axis in the upper-left window. Choose the corresponding properties in the lower-left area. If more axes are offered for formatting than are visible in the chart preview, the additional axes do not have the Visibility property. Check the Visibility field beneath the axis in question to make it visible and then format it as required.

The final step is a confirmation that the process is complete. The nice part of this is that at any time you can switch to the chart editor, which provides access to all chart properties at one time and is useful for fine-tuning the design and functionality of the chart. The ability to switch from either toolset is available, so to switch between the editor and the wizard, click either the Refine or the Wizard button. The chart editor is shown here.

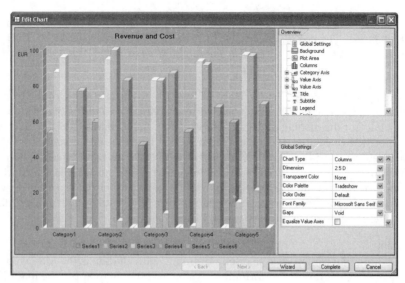

The result of this basic process is shown here. We actually did very little to the default values in this chart process, and even with this basic configuration, the result is good. We could, of course, go back and use the editor to adjust some parameters, but for the initial view of the results, this is not too bad.

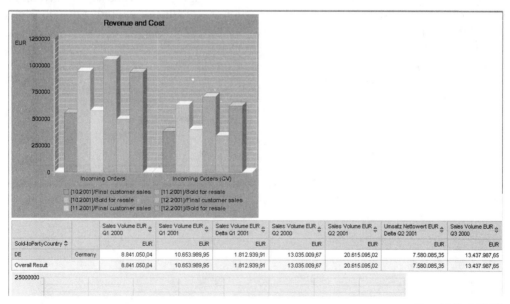

Sold-toPartyCountry		Sales Volume EUR Q1 2000	Sales Volume EUR Q1 2001	Sales Volume EUR Delta Q1 2001	Sales Volume EUR Q2 2000	Sales Volume EUR Q2 2001	Umsatz Nettowert EUR Delta Q2 2001	Sales Volume EUR Q3 2000
		EUR	EUR	EUR	EUR	EUR	EUR	EUR
DE	Germany	8.841.050,04	10.653.989,95	1.812.939,91	13.035.009,67	20.615.095,02	7.580.085,35	13.437.987,65
Overall Result		8.841.050,04	10.653.989,95	1.812.939,91	13.035.009,67	20.615.095,02	7.580.085,35	13.437.987,65

25000000

NOTE *If you want to convert charts that you have used in SAP BW 2.x or SAP BW 3.0/3.1/3.2 to the current format, you need the standalone Internet Graphics Server (IGS) 6.40. Then you need to change to Internet Graphics Server 7.0. You can edit a chart in the Web Application Designer or in the Web Application Wizard of the Business Explorer.*

These are the basics of the Chart Wizard. If we drill down into some of the basic functionality of each area, we find extensive settings available in terms of setting up additional details for the display of the axis information, the formatting of the different chart types, and specific tweaks that developers can use to enhance the end result. This is the area of the Chart web item and the Chart BEx Analyzer item that you would need to investigate for your particular situation. With over 20 different chart types, subsets of each chart type, and different formats you can use to get completely unique properties to configure, you can see that you could spend hours getting your hands dirty. The results can be incredible, and for your business user they can be very useful in analysis and decision making.

Map Web Item

Another web item that can be used to offer a dramatic view of data is the Map web item, with the use of the Geographical Information System (GIS) to help apply the mapping components. In this case, the saying "A picture is worth a thousand words" is very appropriate. The GIS functionality was available in both the BEx Web Analyzer and the WAD in the previous versions of BI, but in the 7.0 version this functionality is only available in the WAD. This component of the BI reporting process is not used as much as I believe it could be. It can be used for analyzing regional sales volumes and the use of sales people in a specific area based on volumes of business, as well as reviewing costs and sales or inventory based on location—and you can see this information in a picture format rather than looking at a report. There's a lot to be said about seeing information in a graphical view—and specifically using the Map web item in conjunction with the GIS. Figure 13-6 shows an

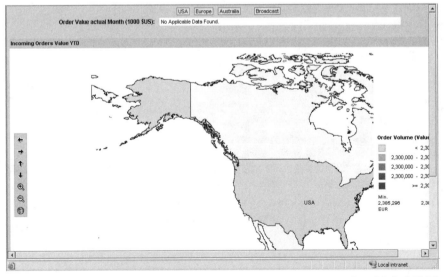

Copyright by SAP AG

FIGURE 13-6   MAP web item with GIS functionality

example of the end result of using the Map web item. As you can see, it offers an excellent view of the total order volume by region/country. The legend offers a display of the details of the color coding and the ranges of order volume per color. We can then drill down on the countries and see additional information.

In the following illustration, you see a map of Australia, the total incoming order value, a breakdown of the regions in this country, and the color coding for the different regions. From here we could broadcast the results to other offices and management.

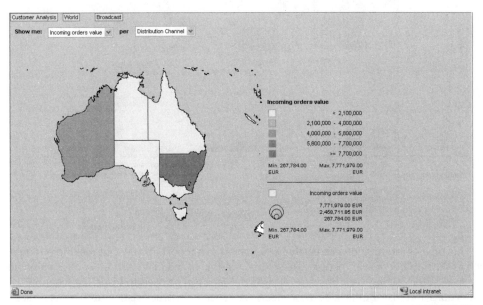

Copyright by SAP AG

A final drilldown to a more detailed view is shown next. In this case, the statistics that support the map are displayed at the bottom of the map for verification of the information.

Now, if we take this a step further and add another characteristic to this, such as sales person, we could visualize the total volume per sales person per region.

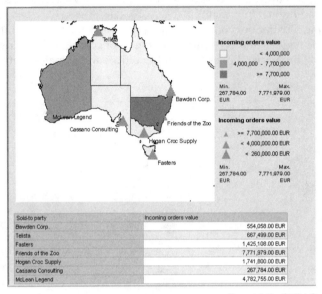

This type of information can easily be delivered in a report format, but picking out data such as the number of sales people versus total volume of sales can definitely offer valuable information for driving your business decisions. Maps can be used to visualize economic connections and distributions. You can clearly see specific characteristic numbers as circles, or bar charts for a country, region, or city. You can also zoom in or out to see detailed or region-specific information. Identifying market opportunities or risks can be done in one view. Within the BEx Map, you can use the following different ways to visualize information:

- Assign different colors to certain areas of the map.
- Add diagrams, such as bar charts, columns, 3D charts, or pie charts.
- Display location information in the form of points, triangles, squares, and other symbols.
- Use any query that contains geo-relevant characteristics for mapping.

Wouldn't it be nice to see all your markets geographically and then drill down with a click into a specific region, and then to a specific ZIP Code? You could recognize opportunities by reviewing information from the top down. Then, once you're into a specific area, you could add information about where your customers are in that area, the number of sales visits for each customer, and so on. This is all possible with the Map web item. Maps of different degrees of detail can be layered on top of each other based on different levels of characteristic values. Connections and correlations between data provide the basis for planning and actions because they are more easily recognizable when visualized on a map. In a nutshell, the Map web item in conjunction with the GIS toolset gives us the ability to look at and analyze information using a geographic view.

Maps help you with reporting geo-relevant data. By using the **Map web item**, you determine a geographical display in the BEx Web Application Designer for your business-oriented data for the Web Application. Geo-relevant InfoObjects are stored and maintained in the **Metadata Repository**. The master data for geo InfoObjects has geo-attributes. The assignment of geographical data to business data (mapping/geocoding) is carried out using an external tool: **ArcView from ESRI** (Environmental Systems Research Institute). Using maps to prepare and evaluate data of a geographical nature (characteristics such as customer, sales region, and country, for example) allows additional detailed analysis. Through the use of enhanced navigation options ("geographical drilldown"), regional information can be evaluated more easily at different levels of detail.

In the initial process of using the Map web item and GIS, we need to do some configuration in the BW Data Warehouse. Therefore, we have some configuration to complete on the InfoObjects (specifically characteristics). Included in this process is work that needs to be done using the GIS toolset. Once this is complete, using the Map web item in conjunction with a query will do the trick. We will start here and work our way through the process, and you will see how easy it is to use this web item.

To begin, we need to do some configuration of an InfoObject. This InfoObject needs to be defined as a geo-characteristic. This is done in the InfoObject Maintenance of the Administrator Workbench. In the listing of the InfoObjects, you need to select one that will be used to identify some sort of area or location. In this case, we will be using an InfoObject that is linked to the areas and regions of the world—Country. With this InfoObject selected, we need to access the Business Explorer tab and indicate the desired type of geo-characteristic in the Geographical Type field, as shown next.

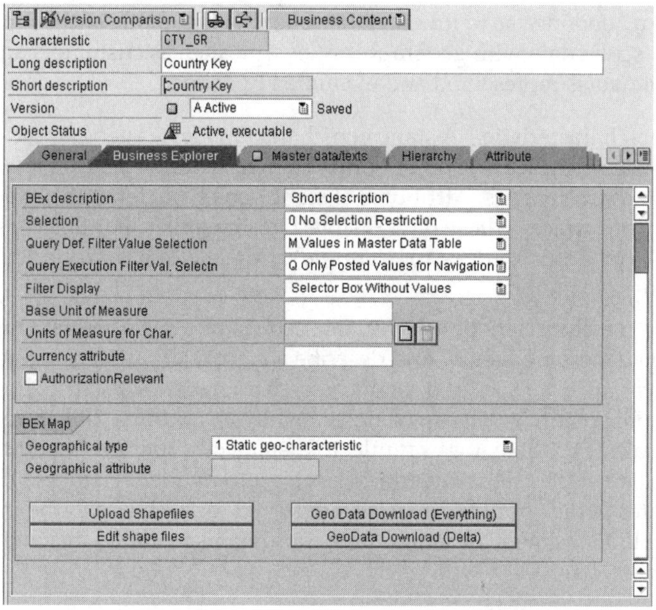

In this scenario we will use a combination of functionality found on this tab. The following illustration shows the different options available for the geo-characteristic type. As you can see, this is identified using the Geographical Type context menu.

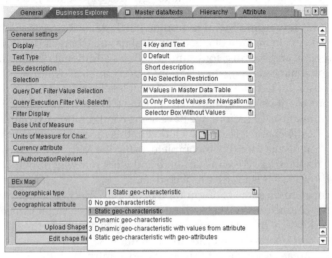

Copyright by SAP AG

The four different types of geo-characteristics are detailed in the following list. Notice that the initial two types and the latter two types are very similar in naming convention, which gives you a good idea as to functionality of each type. Static and dynamic geo-characteristics describe data with geographic relevance such as customers and countries. This geo-relevant data is represented and evaluated by maps.

- **Static geo-characteristic**   A static geo-characteristic has geographic coordinates that describe a surface and do not often change. Country and region are examples of static geo-characteristics. Attributes of static geo-characteristics are defined by the geometry of surfaces whose data is stored in shape files. For this type you can use shape files (country borders, for example) to display the characteristic on a map in the Business Explorer.

- **Dynamic geo-characteristic**   A dynamic geo-characteristic has geographic coordinates that change more frequently and describe a place or location. Customers and workplaces are examples of dynamic geo-characteristics because they are settled at a geographic point, which can be described by an address. Therefore, this type would make it possible, for example, to display customers as a point on a map. The address data of these characteristics is subject to frequent changes. The geographic coordinates of the appropriate object are stored for each line in the master data table. Table 13-4 shows the geographic coordinates included in a geo-attribute.

NOTE   *At present, only the attributes Longitude and Latitude are used. Altitude, PreciseID, and SRCID are reserved for future use. If you change the geographic type of a characteristic to No Geo-Characteristic, these attributes in the InfoObject definition are deleted.*

Technical Name	Description	Data Type	Length
Longitude	Geographic length of the location	DEC	15
Latitude	Geographic width of the location	DEC	15
Altitude	Height of the location (compared to sea level)	DEC	17
Precise ID	ID for accuracy of the data	NUMC	4
SRCID	ID for datasource	CHAR	4

TABLE 13-4 Geo-Attributes of a Dynamic Geo-Characteristic

- **Dynamic geo-characteristic with values from attribute** To avoid the need to geo-code each dynamic geo-characteristic separately, a dynamic geo-characteristic can take its geo-attributes from another geo-coded dynamic characteristic—for example Postal Code. Examples of this type of geo-characteristic are customers and cities. This geo-characteristic is treated in the system like a regular dynamic geo-characteristic, which describes a place or location. On the database level, the master data table is not extended by the geo-attributes specified previously. Instead, the geo-coordinates of a regular attribute of a characteristic are stored in the master data table. Therefore, if you want to set up a dynamic geo-characteristic for a workplace that as a postal code, the geo-coordinates are generated at runtime from the postal code master data table.

- **Static geo-characteristic with geo-attributes** A static geo-characteristic can refer to a geo-characteristic of type 3, which possesses geo-attributes such as length, height, and width. For example, you can use the postal code as an attribute of a dynamic geo-characteristic, and it receives its coordinates from this attribute. Therefore, the map reference for the business partner on its level is stored by the postal code areas.

With Business Content, SAP NetWeaver BI delivers a range of geo-characteristics. Table 13-5 through Table 13-8 show the most important delivered geo-characteristics.

To display BI data geographically, you must create a link between this data and the respective geographical characteristic. This process is called *mapping geo-relevant characteristics*. The geographical information about geographical boundaries of areas that are displayed using static geo-characteristics is stored in shape files. In the shape file, a BI-specific attribute called the SAPBWKEY is responsible for connecting an area on the map with the corresponding characteristic value in BI. This attribute matches the characteristic value in the corresponding

Technical Name	Description
0COUNTRY	Country key
0DATE_ZONE	Time zone
0REGION	Region (federal, state, province)

TABLE 13-5 Static Geo-Characteristics

Technical Name	Description
0APO_LOCNO	Location number
0TV_P_LOCID	IATA location

TABLE 13-6   Dynamic Geo-Characteristics

BI master data table. This process is called *SAPBWKEY maintenance for static geo-characteristics*. You can use ArcView GIS or other software that has functions for editing dBase files to carry out the SAPBWKEY maintenance (Microsoft Excel, for example). With data in point form that is displayed using dynamic geo-characteristics, geographical data is added to BI master data. The process of assigning geographical data to entries in the master data table is called *geocoding*. You can execute the geocoding with the help of the ArcView GIS from ESRI software. As well as geocoding, ArcView also offers a large number of functions for special, geographical problems that are not covered by SAP NetWeaver Business Intelligence. ArcView enables you to create your own maps—for example, a map of your sales regions. When you buy SAP NetWeaver BI, you receive a voucher that you can use to order ArcView GIS from ESRI. The installation package also contains a CD developed specially by SAP and ESRI. The CD contains a range of maps covering the whole world in various levels of detail. All maps on this data CD are optimized already for use with SAP NetWeaver BI. The .dbf files for the maps already contain the column SAPBWKEY, which is predefined with default values. For example, the world map (cntry200) contains the usual values from the SAP system for countries in the SAPBWKEY column. Therefore, you can use the map immediately to evaluate your data geographically. Therefore, you do not have to maintain the SAPBWKEY.

To use the static geo-characteristics, you must use a set of shape files. The structure of the shape files is as follows:

- **.shp**   Geo-data that forms the map
- **.shx**   Geo-index to reduce map access time
- **.dbf**   Attributes for the geo-element, such as countries and regions

These shape files help with the structure of the different shapes and sizing. Static geo-characteristic are connected to shape file map coordinates using the SAPBWKEY. With the integration of this SAPBWKEY and the shape files, the query will show the information transferred to areas on a map.

Technical Name	Attributes	Description
0BPARTNER	0POSTCD_GIS	Business partner
0CONSUMER	0POSTCD_GIS	Consumer
0CUSTOMER	0POSTCD_GIS	Customer number
0PLANT	0POSTCD_GIS	Plant
0VENDOR	0POSTCD_GIS	Vendor

TABLE 13-7   Dynamic Geo-Characteristics with Values from Attributes

Technical Name	Description
OCITYP_CODE	City district code for city and street file
OCITY_CODE	City code for city and street file
OPOSTALCODE	Postal/ZIP Code
OPOSTCD_GIS	Postal code (geo-relevant)

TABLE 13-8   Static Geo-Characteristics with Geo-Attributes

During runtime, BI data is combined with a corresponding shape file. This enables the BI data to be displayed in geographical form (country, region, and so on) using color shading, bar charts, or pie charts. The SAPBWKEY makes sure that the BI data is assigned to the appropriate shape file. Figure 13-7 shows the process of using the shape files and also supporting the SAPBWKEY in those shape files.

In the standard shape files delivered with the ESRI BI map CD, the SAPBWKEY column is already filled with the two-character SAP country keys (DE, EN, and so on). You can use these shape files without having to maintain the SAPBWKEY beforehand.

NOTE *You can use ArcView GIS from ESRI to maintain the SAPBWKEY, or you can use other software (Microsoft Excel or FoxPro, for example) that has functions for displaying and editing dBase files.*

For static geo-characteristics (such as Country or Region) that represent the geographical drilldown data for a country or region, you have to maintain the SAPBWKEY for the individual country or region in the attributes table of the shape file. The attributes table is a database table stored in dBase format. Once you have maintained the SAPBWKEY, you load the shape files (.shp, .dbf, .shx) into BI. The shape files are stored in the Business Document Service (BDS), a component of the BI server. To be able to maintain the SAPBWKEY you have to load the three files for the shape file to your local hard drive, but you only maintain the SAPBWKEY in the DBF file.

FIGURE 13-7
Maintenance of
the SAPBWKEY
for displaying the
locations

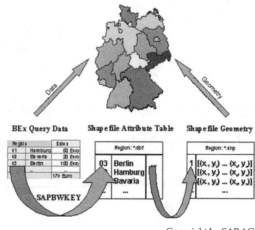

Copyright by SAP AG

Creating a Local Copy of the Shape File   You need a local copy of the shape file before you are able to maintain the SAPBWKEY column in the attributes table of the shape file. To do this, use your file manager (Windows Explorer, for example) to localize the three files cntry200.shp, cntry200 .shx and cntry200.dbf on the ESRI BI map data CD, and copy these files to the C:\SAPWorkDir directory, for example. You must deactivate the Write Protected option before you are able to edit the files. (Select the files and choose the Properties option from the context menu. Then under Attributes, deactivate the Write Protected option.) If you do not have access to the ESRI BI map data CD, the files are already maintained in the BI Business Document Service (BDS). To find them, log on to the BI system and go to the InfoObject maintenance screen (transaction RSD1). This takes you to the Edit InfoObjects: Start screen. Access the InfoObject 0D_COUNTRY (this is a standard delivered InfoObject that is set up as geo-enabled) and choose Display. Choose the Business Explorer tabbed page. In the BEx Map area, 0D_COUNTRY is shown as a static geo-characteristic. Choose Display Shape Files. This takes you to the Business Document Navigator, which already associates three shape files with this characteristic. Open up the shape files completely in the BI Metaobjects tree. Select the .dbf file BW_GIS_ DBF and choose Export Document. This loads all the files to your local SAPWorkDirectory. (The system proposes the C:\SAPWorkDir directory as your SAPWorkDirectory.) Repeat the last step for the .shp (BW_GIS_SHP) and .shx (BW_GIS_SHX) files.

Downloading BI Master Data into a dBase File   To maintain the SAPBWKEY column in the shape file attribute table, you have to specify the corresponding BI country key for every row in the attribute table. Because this information is contained in the BI master data table, you have to download it into a local dBase file to compare it with the entries in the attribute table and maintain the SAPBWKEY. To do this, log on to the BI system and go to the InfoObject maintenance screen (transaction **RSD1**). This takes you to the Edit InfoObjects: Start screen. Once you have accessed the specific InfoObject, choose the Business Explorer tab. In the BEx Map area, choose Geo Data Download (All). Accept the filename proposed by the system by choosing Transfer. The following illustration shows the result of executing the Download option.

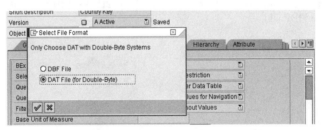

Copyright by SAP AG

The following illustration shows the filename that is automatically created for this purpose.

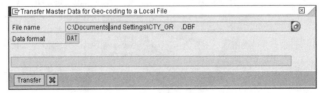

Copyright by SAP AG

NOTE *The proposed filename is made up of the technical name of the characteristic and the .dbf extension. If the Geo Data Download (All) pushbutton is deactivated (gray), there is no master data for the InfoObject. If this is the case, download the texts for the InfoObject manually to get to the SAPBWKEY.*

Maintaining the SAPBWKEY Column   You have now completed the downloading of the shape files to your local drive and have created a copy and downloaded BI master data into a dBase file. The SAPBWKEY is maintained in the dBase file with the extension .dbf. This file contains the attributes table. The process of maintaining the SAPBWKEY involves launching Microsoft Excel and choosing dBase Files (*.dbf) from the dropdown box in the Files of Type field. From the C:\SAPWorkDir directory, open the cntry200.dbf file. The attributes table from the shape file is displayed in an Excel worksheet. Repeat this procedure to show the BI master data file. This file shows you which values from the SAPBWKEY are used for which countries. Use the short description (0TXTSH column) to compare the two tables.

NOTE *ESRI delivers an ESRI BI map data CD. This CD contains the SAPBWKEY (corresponding to the SAP country key) for the Country characteristic. This is why the SAPBWKEY column in the cntry200.dbf file is already filled with the correct values.*

Copy the SAPBWKEY manually to the attributes table in the shape file if you are using a different country key or if you are working with characteristics for which the SAPBWKEY column has not been defined or is filled with invalid values. The following illustration shows a sample of the file you would get from the country shape file, with the areas and perimeters for the countries.

A	B	C	D	E	F	G	H
AREA	PERIMETER	CNTRY299SA	CNTRY299SA	CNTRY_NAME	FIPS_CNTF	SAPBWKEY	REGION
24.667	105.843	1	1	Svalbard	SV		Northern Europe
0.115	2.588	2	2	Jan Mayen	JN		Northern Europe
653.621	673.903	3	3	Greenland	GL		Northern America
62.354	54.747	4	4	Finland	FI		Northern Europe
57.758	177.711	5	5	Norway	NO		Northern Europe
19.750	49.590	6	6	Iceland	IC		Northern Europe
0.071	1.398	7	7	Faroe Islands	FO		Northern Europe
7.050	21.486	8	8	Estonia	EN		Eastern Europe
9.518	18.716	9	9	Latvia	LG		Eastern Europe
78.508	77.938	10	10	Sweden	SW		Northern Europe
28.171	31.273	11	11	Byelarus	BO		Eastern Europe
9.193	16.737	12	12	Lithuania	LH		Eastern Europe
9.401	29.002	13	13	Ireland	EI		Northern Europe
32.896	86.168	14	14	United Kingdom	UK		Northern Europe
5.735	32.860	15	15	Denmark	DA		Northern Europe
40.903	34.814	16	16	Poland	PL		Eastern Europe
0.085	1.295	17	17	Man, Isle of	IM		Northern Europe
73.507	75.633	18	18	Ukraine	UP		Eastern Europe
184.485	83.852	19	19	Mongolia	MG		Eastern Asia
3.918	11.643	20	20	Belgium	BE		Western Europe
4.603	22.936	21	21	Netherlands	NL		Western Europe

Copyright by SAP AG

The following illustration shows the file from the master data of our InfoObject with the SAPBWKEY assignment that we will fill into the column of the country shape file.

CTY_GR	SAPBWKEY	0TXTSH
	#	Not assigned
CA	CA	Canada
DE	DE	Germany
FR	FR	France
GB	GB	United Kingdom
US	US	USA

Copyright by SAP AG

If you are working with compounded characteristics, copy the complete SAPBWKEY—for example, for region 01 compounded with country DE, copy the complete value DE/01.

Do not under any circumstances change the sequence of the entries in the attributes table (for example, by sorting or deleting the rows). If you were to change the sequence of the entries, the attributes table would no longer agree with the index and the geometric files. When you have finished maintaining the SAPBWKEY column, save the attributes table in the shape file.

Uploading Edited Shape Files into BI Systems   The last step is to attach the shape file set (.shp, .shx, .dbf) to the InfoObject by uploading it into the Business Document Service (BDS) on the BI server. To accomplish this in the Business Explorer tabbed page, choose Upload Shape Files. The Business Document Service: File Selection dialog box appears. Select the .shp file and choose Open. The Business Document Service suggests entries for the filename, description, and so on, and allows you to enter keywords that will make it easier for you to find the file in the BDS at a later date. Choose Continue. The system automatically asks you to upload the .dbf and .shx files for the shape file. Once this is complete, you have uploaded the edited shape file into the BI system. You can now use the characteristic in the Business Explorer. Every user who works with a query that contains the geo-enabled InfoObject can now attach a map to the query and analyze the data on the map. The following illustration shows the result of accessing the uploading process from the Business Explorer tab.

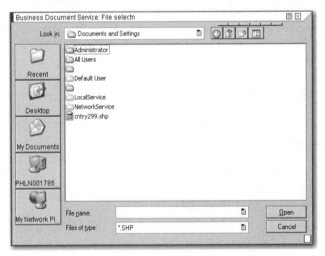

Copyright by SAP AG

Once we have uploaded all three files to the BI master data and the Business Document Storage, we can access all three and confirm that they have been uploaded correctly. An example of the display of all three files is shown here.

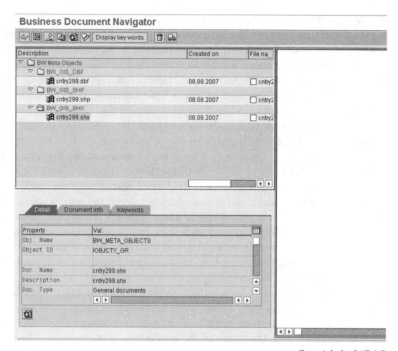

To display dynamic geo-characteristics as points on a map, you have to determine the geographic coordinates for every master data object. The master data table for dynamic geo-characteristics is, therefore, extended with a number of standard geo-attributes such as Longitude and Latitude. The process of loading these attributes to the BI master data tables of dynamic geo-characteristics is very similar to that of the static geo-characteristics. You go through the same downloading of the master data and the mapping process with the SAPBWKEY, although the mapping, in addition to the SAPBWKEY, is for attributes such as Longitude and Latitude.

Downloading BI Master Data into a dBase File The first step in SAPBWKEY maintenance for dynamic geo-characteristics and their geocoding is to download the BI master data table into a dBase file. This process is exactly the same as before, but we are using a different type of InfoObject, such as Customer or Vendor instead of Country or ZIP Code. Once you have executed the Download All option, the process changes.

NOTE *If you only want to maintain those entries that have been changed since the last attribute master data upload, choose Geo Data Download (Delta). The geo-data has to be downloaded in the delta version before you execute the realignment run for the InfoObject. Otherwise, the delta information is lost.*

The system asks you to select a geo-attribute that you want to include in the dBase file. The system only displays those attributes that were defined as geo-relevant, such as Country or Region. The proposed filename is made up of the technical name of the characteristic and the .dbf extension.

Geocoding Using ArcView GIS   Using geocoding, you enhance dynamic geo-characteristics from BI master data with the geographical attributes degrees of longitude and degrees of latitude. To begin, in ArcView GIS you can execute many commands easily from the context menu. To open the context menu, select an element and click it with the secondary mouse button. Then select Programs _ ArcGIS ArcCatalog. Under Address Locators, double-click the entry New Address Locator. Then, in the Create New Address Locator window, select the entry Single Field (File) and click OK. In the New: Single Field (File) Address Locator window, enter the name of the service and the description (for example, Geocoding Service SoldTo). Under Reference data, enter the path for the reference shape file (for example, g_stat00.shp), and from the Fields dropdown menu, select the most appropriate entry (in this case, SAPBWKEY). Under Output Fields, activate the control box X and Y Coordinates. Then in the navigation menu, the new service is displayed under Address Locators. Select Programs _ ArcGis ArcMap and start with a new, empty map in the entry dialog box. Choose OK. In the standard toolbar, click the Add Data symbol and add the corresponding dBase file (for example, SoldTo.dbf) as a new table. The window Choose an Address Locator To Use is opened. All available services are displayed in this window. Choose the Address Locator entry in the Add Address Locator window under Search In and then select the service you created in step 4 (in this example, Geocoding Service SoldTo) and click Add. In the Choose an Address Locator to Use window, select the service again and click OK. Under Address Input Fields, choose the appropriate entry (for example, 1_0D_Region). This is the field that tallies with the reference data. Under Output _ Output Shapefile or Feature Class, enter the path under which the result of the geocoding is to be saved. Choose OK. At this point the ARC view toolset geocodes the information. After you have checked the statistics in the Review/Rematch Addresses window, click Done. The final step is to convert the file to a CSV format for upload into the master data tables. Once you have converted the dBase file into a CSV file with the geo-attribute for the dynamic geo-characteristic, an upload of the master data can be scheduled.

We have now completed the necessary processes in configuring the Map web item to be functional. Once all this is complete, we then go to the InfoProvider that is using that specific InfoObject and create a query with the InfoObject as part of the analysis. In our case, we are using the geo-enabled InfoObject for Country. The query we are using is a combination of Country and Sales Volume. We will use this to configure the Map web item and display a map with information by country. The following illustration shows this query.

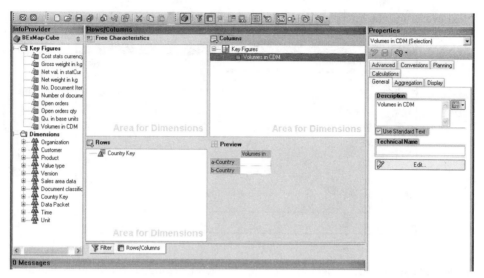

Configuration of the Map Web Item in the WAD Now, we direct our attention to the WAD and the Map web item to display geo-relevant data on a map. The Map web item contains general information on a map such as information on the map layers. You use the map layers to define the different layers in a map that are laid on top of each other in the Web Application. For example, you can use colors to highlight the countries in one map layer and display bar charts for each country in another layer. The parameters you set control how a map and its layers are displayed in the Web Application. The following illustration shows the initial screen with the Analysis and Map web items included.

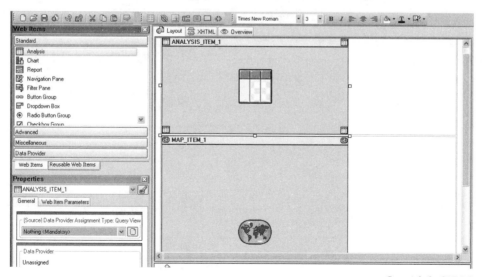

Next, we assign the query to the Analysis and Map web items, as shown here.

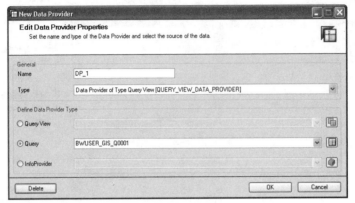

Table 13-9 lists the parameters for the Map web item, arranged according to the various parameter groupings. The following illustration shows the parameters list.

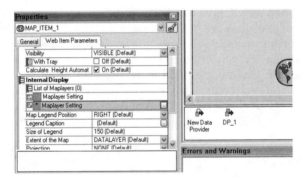

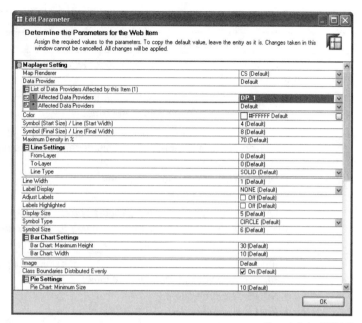

Parameter/Grouping	Description
Display	
Width in Pixels (WIDTH)	You use this parameter to determine the width of the web item.
Height in Pixels (HEIGHT)	You use this parameter to determine the height of the web item.
Visibility (VISIBILITY)	You use this parameter to determine whether the web item is visible in the Web Application.
With Tray (WITH_TRAY)	You use this parameter to determine whether the web item has a symbol that allows it to be expanded and collapsed.
Internal Display	
List of Map Layers (MAPLAYER_LIST)	You use this parameter to create a list of map layers and make settings for each map layer at the same time. The settings for the individual map layers depend on the chosen map renderer. The illustration following this table shows the details of the List of Map Layers option.
Map Legend Position (MAP_LEGEND_POSITION)	You use this parameter to determine whether to display the map legend in the Web Application and where to display it in relation to the map. The following options are available: • **RIGHT** Right of the map • **LEFT** Left of the map • **NONE** No legend

TABLE 13-9   Parameters for the Map Web Item

Parameter/Grouping	Description
Internal Display	
Legend Caption (LEGEND_CAPTION)	You use this parameter to give the map legend a caption using the text input dialog box.
Legend Size (LEGEND_SIZE)	You use this parameter to determine the size of the map legend. You can only specify the values in pixels.
Visible Map Extent (MAP_EXTENT)	You use this parameter to specify which areas of a map are displayed in the Web Application. This depends on the data stored in the application. • **DATALAYER** Data with geography • **DATA** Only data • **LAYER** Data and complete geography available The default setting, DATALAYER, allows you to display data taking the corresponding geographic context into account.
Projection (PROJECTION)	You use this parameter to determine the possible projection of the map. The following options are available: • **NONE** No projection • **FLAT** Flat projection • **MERC** Mercator projection
Background Color (BACKGROUND_COLOR)	You use this parameter to determine whether to display a map background and to specify the color for this background. You select the color from a color selection dialog box.
AXL File (cartography) (CART_AXL_NAME)	You use this parameter to specify the name of an AXL file for the cartography description (stored in the directory for shape files).
Cartography Information On/Off (CART_AXL_VISIBLE)	You use this parameter to define whether additional cartography information stored in an AXL file is to be displayed.
Behavior	
Activate Navigation (INTERACTION_ALLOWED)	You use this parameter to determine whether navigation or other interaction is possible in the Web Application.
Geo Functions (GEO_FUNCTIONS_POS)	You use this parameter to determine whether to display the geo functions bar in the Web Application, and how to display it. The following options are available: • **NONE** Do not display • **TOP** Top • **BOTTOM** Bottom • **LEFT** Left • **RIGHT** Right Note that you modify the long text in the WAD.

TABLE 13-9   Parameters for the Map Web Item (*continued*)

Finally, we execute the WAD template. The result is a graphic of a world map that identifies the areas/countries with different shades of color, depending on the total sales volume, as shown next. Notice that we have both the analysis report and the GIS map results. If you display this within a professionally finished report, the result is impressive.

Country Key GR ⬍		Volumes in CDM ⬍
		CDM
CA	Canada	20.050.800
DE	Germany	90.774.071
FR	France	63.899.302
GB	United Kingdom	58.640.871
US	USA	42.817.311
#	Not assigned	0
Overall Result		276.182.355

Volumes in CDM

The following illustration shows the result with just the map of the world and the legend that is automatically generated with the map. You can see the different countries with shades of blue for the different sales volume levels.

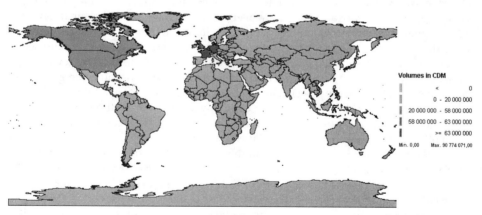

Volumes in CDM

‹	0
	0 - 20 000 000
	20 000 000 - 58 000 000
	58 000 000 - 63 000 000
	>= 63 000 000

Min. 0,00   Max. 90 774 071,00

Components of the Query

In this section we will discuss two items that are handy in the process of using queries and workbooks. The first area involves the use of variants to help with the management of value inputs for variables. This is a popular approach to managing the different values that each business user needs in the execution of their reports, and it offers the business user the option to store their specific value settings. There are a number of different approaches to this, and we've talked about some of these approaches previously, including the process of setting up "personalization" on the variables.

The second area involves the use of the Key Date field in the query or Query Designer and how it impacts the display of data in queries. It is important for the business user to understand the data as well as be comfortable with the data being displayed. Being able to confidently state to the management team of a company that the data being displayed is consistent and is the "true" view of the information is priceless.

Variants

With the new BW 7.0 version, the ability to fill variables with variants and determine how they are used and stored has changed quite a bit. One of the options available for the use of variants in a query is the ability to manage the values that fill the variants via the TVARV table and the global variables included in this table. However, with the BW 7.0 version, this table is no longer available as the TVARV or TVARVC. So if you are looking for your variants, look to the RSRVARIANT or the RSRPARAMETRIZA table; you will find the 3.x version of the variant being stored in the former table and the 7.0 version of the variants being stored in the latter. As a bit of a background, we can talk about the use of this type of approach more in terms of the R3/ECC environment. I use this type of methodology to manage the values for the variables within the operational environment a bit more than in the BW environment, but the approach and concept are the same. Basically speaking, we can manage our input for variables using variants. You have likely used variants at one time or another with reports and queries to save a series of values so that you wouldn't have to manually fill in the values every time you executed the query. This is a good way of saving time and effort. You can give someone else the required values to filter a query without having to repeat every one of the settings. It's much easier to tell someone to use a specific variant in a report execution versus telling them all 10 or 20 values they would have to enter into a query variable screen before executing the query.

This is the initial view of a variant. However, we can manage the values that have been initially assigned to a variant by looking at the table in which the variant resides and changing the values from there. Once the next person uses that variant, they would see the changed values. One reason I would use this approach is to help the auditors reviewing the SAP system, for example. Let's say we set up variants for the external auditing group and would like to reuse them every time the auditors come to our company to review the records. Because the visits from the auditing company are at different times during the course of the year and we would like to manage what they see with variants, we can use the approach of changing the values of the variants in the background. Once the auditors use the variant the next time, the values stored in the variant tables would be updated to the appropriate view. We would give the auditors a list of variants to use with each report, for example directing them to the appropriate company codes, plants, or time frames. This approach can also be used to manage the closing date of a period, if the end of the period is different each time. In other words, rather than always having an exact end of period, it varies from time to time by a day or two. You can manage the variables for many reports via variants and only have to change the ending date once to affect all these variables. In the end, this approach allows you to manage many variables and variants from one table.

The scenario used to be that you would execute a report—basically any report—and be able to assign a variant to that report. The following illustration shows the execution of a financial report in ECC. Once you executed this initial screen with a list of variables,

Selection: Actual/actual comparison for year

G/L account selection
G/L account		to		⇨
Company code	1000	to		⇨

Transaction Figures Selection
Business area	1000	to		⇨
Currency type	10			
Ledger				

Report selections
FIS Annual Rep.Struc	INT	Commercial balance s
Fiscal year	2005	2005

Parameters for special evaluations
☐ P_ALTKT

Output type

Copyright by SAP AG

you could then use Goto | Variant | Save As Variant to save a variant. The following illustration shows this view. Once in the Save as Variant screen, you have the ability to manage

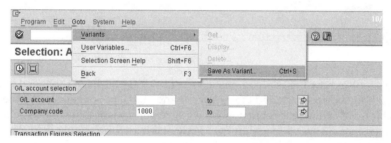

Copyright by SAP AG

the properties of the variables and variable values assigned to the variant, as shown next. The variable values are managed via the Selection Variable field.

Variant Attributes

✐ Copy Screen Assignment

Variant Name	
Meaning	

Scrn Assignm.
Created	Selection Scrns
☑	1000

☐ Only for Background Processing
☐ Protect Variant
☐ Only Display in Catalog
☐ System Variant (Automatic Transport)

Objects for selection screen

Selection Scrns	Field name	Type	Protect field	Hide field	Hide field 'BIS'	Save field without values	Switch GPA off	Required field	Selection variable	Option	Name of
1.000	G/L account	S	☐	☐	☐	☐	☐	☐			
1.000	Company code	S	☐	☐	☐	☐	☐	☐			
1.000	SD_INDEX	P	☐	☐	☐	☐	☐	☐			
1.000	Alternative local currency	P	☐	☐	☐	☐	☐	☐			
1.000	Translation date	P	☐	☐	☐	☐	☐	☐			
1.000	Fiscal Year	S	☐	☐	☐	☐	☐	☐			
1.000	Business area	S	☐	☐	☐	☐	☐	☐			
1.000	Currency type	P	☐	☐	☐	☐	☐	☐			

Copyright by SAP AG

In this field you could use the F4 dropdown, which offers you the ability to use the TVARV table to supply a particular variable with a value based on what is assigned in the TVARV table. The following illustration shows this step. This allows the R3 or BW developer working with the reports to maintain one table (TVARV, via SM30) and affect all variants that use that method to fill the variables.

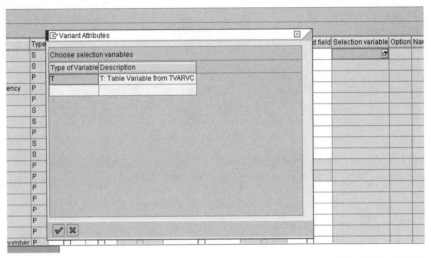

Now let's look at how this is accomplished as of BW 7.0 (this hasn't changed in the ECC systems) and how the approach and tables have changed. We no longer can use the TVARV/ TVARVC tables, nor can we expect that when we save our variant that we will be presented with the screen that allows us to assign the TVARV table to the variable field. This process is different and becomes a critical issue to the customer who needs this for precalculation of data for background execution of reports or for the developer who has used this approach to manage the many variables being used. and finally for use in the Information Broadcaster.

As mentioned, the TVARV and TVARVC tables have been replaced with the RSRVARIANT table in the 3.x version of BW and the process is a bit different. The RSRVARIANT table can't be maintained by using the SM30 transaction code; therefore, we need to set up our own approach to managing the variable values. Initially we need to set up a method of maintaining the RSRVARIANT table. This is accomplished via an ABAP program and can be as complex or as basic as you want. In the basic approach, you will be able to manage one variant and one variable of that variant at one time. Not being able to access all the variables associated with one variant at once can be a bit frustrating, so you may opt to create a more complex front end for the user to so that they can retrieve all the variables to manage for a particular variant. The basic ABAP program we'll set up is reflected in this illustration.

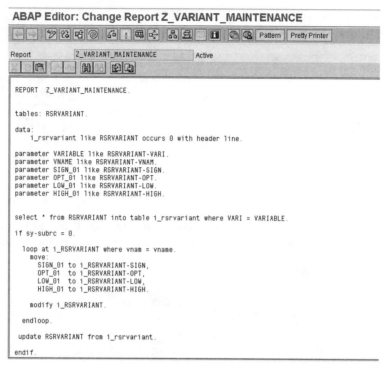

Copyright by SAP AG

The result of this program is that it offers you the ability to maintain the RSRVARIANT table by variant or by variable. The following illustration shows the initial screen for maintenance. The variable and variant technical names are required to work with this program.

Copyright by SAP AG

After filling in the information, you would execute this program to affect the variable values, which will be shown shortly. Now all we need is a variable to use in our process.

The following illustration shows the variable ZDIV01, which was created to use in this example. There's nothing special about this variable, so we will not dwell upon the setup.

Now we need to execute this basic query and have the variable displayed in the BEx Analyzer. The following illustration shows the initial dialog box for selecting variable values.

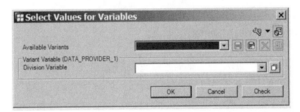

Then we enter a value for the variable (in this case, Division 1000 – Motorcycles) and select Save As New Variant. In this case the technical name for the variant is ZUSER_VAR01. The following illustration shows this information.

Now we can look at the results in the RSRVARIANT table. Here we see that this variant has the variable ZDIV01 and the value assigned to it is 1000 (value in the field titled LOW).

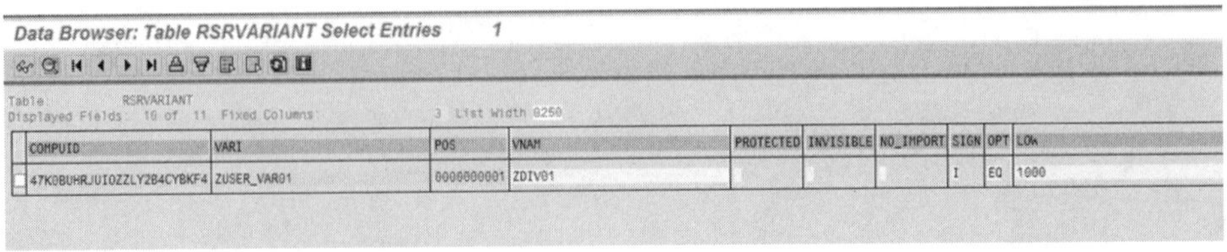

Data Browser: Table RSRVARIANT Select Entries   1

Table   RSRVARIANT
Displayed Fields: 10 of 11 Fixed Columns   3 List Width 0250

COMPUID	VARI	POS	VNAM	PROTECTED	INVISIBLE	NO_IMPORT	SIGN	OPT	LOW
47K0BUHRJUIOZZLY2B4CYBKF4	ZUSER_VAR01	0000000001	ZDIV01				I	EQ	1000

Once we have confirmed this, we can go back into the ABAP program and execute the program Z_VARIANT_MAINTENANCE and fill in the required fields and any additional information. In this case, we are looking to change the value of the division in the variable. Therefore, fill in the value 3000 as the "low" value for the division. The following illustration shows this information.

User screen for variant maintenance

VARIABLE	ZUSER_VAR01
VNAME	ZDIV01
SIGN_01	I
OPT_01	EQ
LOW_01	3000
HIGH_01	3000

Next, we can verify that the value has changed by reviewing the RSRVARIANT table again. As you can see, the value 1000 has been replaced with 3000.

Data Browser: Table RSRVARIANT Select Entries   1

Table: RSRVARIANT
Displayed Fields: 10 of 11 Fixed Columns: 3 List Width 0250

COMPUID	VARI	POS	VNAM		PROTECTED	INVISIBLE	NO_IMPORT	SIGN	OPT	LOW
47K0BUHRJUIOZZLY2B4CYBKF4	ZUSER_VAR01	0000000001	ZDIV01					I	EQ	3000

The final step in this process is to confirm that the actual value in the variable screen has changed. Therefore, we re-execute the query and get a prompt for the variant available (ZUSER_VAR01). We use it to fill in the variable field. Now you can see that the value assigned to the variant has changed to reflect the 3000 division rather than the 1000 division. The following two illustrations show these steps.

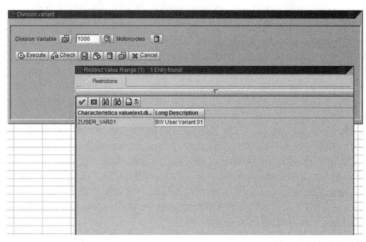

Now let's complete this discussion with the additional information around the 7.0 BI variants and the additional table RSRPARAMETRIZA that holds the variants for this version. The creation of variants in the 7.0 version for either the BEx Analyzer or the Web components will add these new variants to the RSRPARAMETRIZA table and not the RSRVARIANT table. Therefore you may have the two tables that are holding the variants not being in sync. There is a specific SAP ABAP program that will help with that process and make sure that each table has the same variants. So if you are running some queries in the 7.0 and others in the 3.x they will have access to all of the variants whether they were created in either version.

There are a couple of comments around this new table in the 7.0 version that we need to address. The fact that the variants are held in the RSRPARAMETRIZA table in the format of XML is a big difference then what you might have been use to in the former versions. In those versions the values for the variants were held in a table and basically managed using ABAP programs. In this case the values are held in a string of XML language but some of the other values such as the technical name of the variant are being held in the standard format. If you are looking to affect these entries you will need to make sure that you are creating a ABAP program that addresses the need to change values in an XML format rather than just a position in a basic table. Another concern is that in both cases, either BEx Analyzer or the WEB components, when you create a variant these variants are personalized to the individual that created them and are not available for other processes—such as, using them to do any sorts of Information Broadcasting activities. That means that one of the parameters in the variant table is to assign an 'X' to the variant personalization automatically. Therefore you will need to create a program that will effectively remove that 'X' parameter from the RSRPARAMETRIZA table so that everyone can use the variant and not just the creator of that variant.

A final note that is just for your information is that the variants that are created in the BEx Analyzer will be stored with a system generated index and you will see that in the table rather than the technical name that you assigned when you saved it but if you create the variant on the web it will be saved with the technical name that you assigned. Don't get me wrong, you will still be able to use the variant with the system generated index since the technical name that you saved it with is also stored in the table but you will notice that it shows the encrypted index rather than the true technical name. To adjust these variant values you will follow the same approach as you did for adjusting the 3.x variants but you will be looking to make the changes in the RSRPARAMETRIZA table rather than the RSRVARIANT table. Therefore, create a program that will allow the IT department to manage the values of the variants from a central screen rather than having to try to individually manage each variable and variant.

NOTE *To view this table use transaction code SE12 and enter the table name – RSRPARAMETRIZA. Review each of the variants created in 7.0 and notice that the values are assigned to a string of XML language.*

Variant values can now be managed for activities such as the precalculation of queries for background jobs and determining the values that specific people see from the configuration side rather than from the front end. This allows a central process to manage all variants.

Query Key Date Display Options

I decided to incorporate this topic into the book because it is something that many people don't really think about during the configuration process. Then once the system is configured, they realize they would have liked to able to decide on the view of the data being displayed. As mentioned, several views of the data can be offered. They are broken down into two distinct formats, depending on whether you are interested in displaying your information with a current view or a historical view.

Let's discuss this a bit further before we get into the actual system configuration. By *current* view, I mean looking at *all* the data based on the view of that information as defined by the master data. If you take, for example, the two characteristics Material and Material Group, this view would be based on the current links between the values of Material Group and Material and not what would be called the "historical view." If we are interested in displaying the information based on the historical view, we are looking to see the historical truth and therefore want the report to display the information based on how things actually happened. In the case of the two characteristics Material and Material Group, we would be relying on the actual posting of the transactional data that occurred in the table (InfoCube, for example). These are two very different approaches and can deliver two very different interpretations of the data. You want to understand what your options are and what your business user wants before the configuration is complete. Even though the title of this section includes the Key Date field of the query, the source of this information starts way back in the configuration of the InfoObject and the InfoProvider (in this case, we will use the InfoCube as an example of the InfoProvider). Therefore, during your discussions with the end users, you should identify this as a decision point and make sure the delivered format will support your display needs.

Let's say we are looking at data about revenue generated by our salespeople. All the salespeople are assigned regions, and they work those regions for the first half of the year. Then a decision is made to realign the salespeople and the regions. What do you think the request by the salespeople will be in terms of reports to see their bonus calculations? In this case, they would be interested in seeing the historic truth instead the current view. The historic view allows them to see what they did in the first half based on the actual sales as they occurred, and in the same manner as they did in the second half. If we were to configure our system to show just the current view, all the salespeople would see all their data based on the view of the second half, because that was when the regions were realigned. We would then have to generate another report to show what happened in the first half so that we wouldn't lose all of our sales force. These situations are common— perhaps a particular customer changes locations and falls into a different region, or an employee changes location or region and you need to track the costs of that employee. As you review your needs, don't forget to think about the view of the data that makes sense to you. There are definite uses for both approaches to viewing the data, and identifying them initially will save you tons of time during the reporting process.

Now, let's view the data in the InfoCube. The following illustration shows the data stored in the InfoCube, which we will be using for this example. This will be the only data we use during the examples. As you can see, the information is sliced for the periods January 2000 and February 2000, and there are two material groups—Food and Chemicals. Notice that the group for the material BBB changed between January and February from the Food group to the Chemicals group. It therefore has a different posting for each month. We will talk more about the materials in the next section. We will execute some basic queries against this information and look at the differences in the data views.

"ZBWUSER1", List output

0MATL_GROU	ZMAT_01	0CALMONTH	Currency	Amount
FOOD	AAA	01.2000	USD	100,00
FOOD	BBB	01.2000	USD	100,00
CHEMICALS	CCC	01.2000	USD	100,00
CHEMICALS	DDD	01.2000	USD	100,00
FOOD	AAA	02.2000	USD	100,00
CHEMICALS	CCC	02.2000	USD	100,00
CHEMICALS	DDD	02.2000	USD	100,00
CHEMICALS	BBB	02.2000	USD	100,00
CHEMICALS	EEE	02.2000	USD	100,00

Historical View   Now, let's say that the business user design documentation requires that we show the historic view, or the view of the data as it was posted. This is required due to the changes that occur in the relationships between the characteristic values. Therefore, we need to data model our InfoCube to reflect this request. This is done by taking the two characteristics that are required to be used in the historic view and using them in the InfoCube as unique characteristics in the dimension of the InfoCube. This is exactly what we have done to obtain the required results. The following illustration shows this configuration.

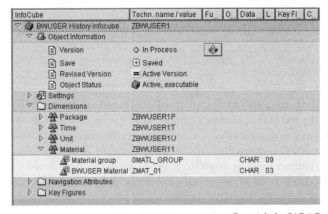

Now that we have created this linkage in the InfoCube, we can view the information in the query and see what it shows us. Remember that we need to show the historic view of the data. Therefore, we need to review the new product EEE and notice the changes between the months of January and February for this new product and the changed material group for material BBB. In the following illustration, you see the initial configuration of the query on this InfoCube. Notice that we have set the key date as 01.01.2000.

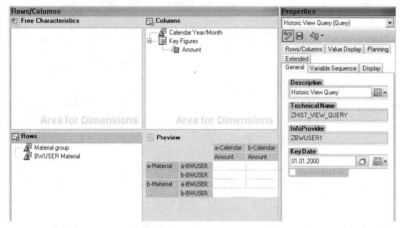

The results of the query are shown in the following illustration.

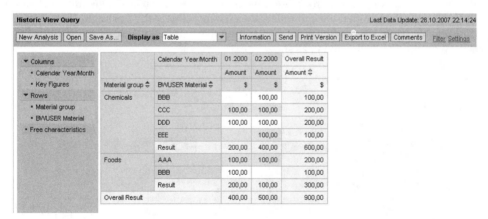

Now, we can go back to the Query Designer and change to key date to 01.02.2000 for February of 2000 and rerun the query. The following illustration shows the Information section of the selections once the query has been executed (notice the Key Date field, which shows 01.02.2000). We can see that the view of the data hasn't changed and that the actual posting process is shown regardless of whether we have the key date set for January or February of that year.

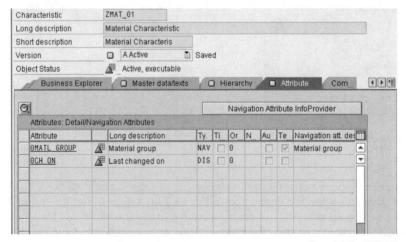

This is one approach to showing the historic view of the data and probably the easiest. Therefore, data modeling the relationship into the dimensions in the InfoCube will offer you the historic view of your data.

Current View   Now, let's assume that the business requirement for viewing the data is based on the current look of the information. We are now faced with a different challenge. We need to be able to show all the transactions based on the current view of the information, so we'll use a different approach to try to get this view. We need to use a navigational attribute for the material group so that we can reflect the current view of the postings. Therefore, we need to step back into the configuration of the InfoObject material and set the attribute Material Group to be navigational, as shown next.

We can accommodate the business user by having the material group as a characteristic in the InfoCube and also setting the same InfoObject as a navigational attribute and collecting the data in that manner, thus fulfilling the business requirements for this view of the data. As you can see, the data in the InfoCube has been enhanced by the addition of the navigational attribute (in dark shaded column) in the view of the record. Notice that material BBB, which was in the material group Food before, is now pointed toward the material group Chemicals for the navigational attribute. Therefore, this will show in the query in the Chemicals group instead of the Food group.

"ZBWUSER1", List output

0MATL_GROU	ZMAT_01	0MATL_GROU	0CALMONTH	Currency	Amount
FOOD	AAA	FOOD	01.2000	USD	100,00
FOOD	BBB	CHEMICALS	01.2000	USD	100,00
CHEMICALS	CCC	CHEMICALS	01.2000	USD	100,00
CHEMICALS	DDD	CHEMICALS	01.2000	USD	100,00
FOOD	AAA	FOOD	02.2000	USD	100,00
CHEMICALS	CCC	CHEMICALS	02.2000	USD	100,00
CHEMICALS	DDD	CHEMICALS	02.2000	USD	100,00
CHEMICALS	BBB	CHEMICALS	02.2000	USD	100,00
CHEMICALS	EEE	CHEMICALS	02.2000	USD	100,00

Copyright by SAP AG

We have configured a query with the navigational attribute for material group instead of the characteristic material group, and the following illustration shows the results. Notice that the Food group has only one entry—the material Foods—and that the material BBB, which was in the Food group, is now showing in the Chemicals group. This is due to the fact that we are executing this query based on the master data configuration versus the transactional posting.

| New Analysis | Open | Save As... | **Display as** Table | | Information | Send | Print Version | Export to Excel | Comments | Filter Settings |

				Cal. Year/Month	01.2000	02.2000	Overall Result
▼ Columns					Amount	Amount	Amount ⇕
• Cal. Year/Month	Material group ⇕		Material Characteris ⇕		$	$	$
• Key figures	CHEMICALS	Chemicals	BBB		100,00	100,00	200,00
▼ Rows			CCC		100,00	100,00	200,00
• Material group			DDD		100,00	100,00	200,00
• Material Characteris			EEE			100,00	100,00
• Free characteristics			Result		300,00	400,00	700,00
	FOOD	Foods	AAA		100,00	100,00	200,00
			Result		100,00	100,00	200,00
	Overall Result				400,00	500,00	900,00

Copyright by SAP AG

Therefore, if we execute this and change the key date to February 2000, we see that the results of this are the same as the results of the query with the key date of January 2000, as shown next.

Therefore, the business requirement for the current view of the data can be accommodated by using the data modeling of this view outside of the InfoCube with the navigational attribute for the characteristic rather than the characteristic as a part of the InfoCube. These are very important concepts because other views of the data can be displayed, and the configuration of these other views is very close to the two situations explained here.

Historical or Current vs. Historical and Current   At face value, these different views might not make sense or be of any interest to you. But in terms of a number of reports you rely on to make critical decisions about your own personal finances, these two views are very important. What I'm alluding to is the analysis you probably go through when picking stocks or making an investment in a corporation. One of the more important reports many companies deliver on a quarterly basis is a year-over-year or quarter-over-quarter comparison report. These types of reports are one of two views—either historic OR current or historic AND current. What's the difference between these two views? Let's take an example of a report generated by a retail company on a quarterly basis. You would normally hear something like "comparison of same-store sales year over year" and feel comfortable that you understand what that really means. In terms of information, they could have reported the "AND" or the "OR" for a view, so you need to dig a bit deeper to see what position the company takes with their data. If they report the "AND," that means only the products in the stores at both times of the year were counted. So if the company has decided to add 50,000 new products to the mix in each of the stores, they would *not* be reporting these changes in their same-store sales numbers. This is a much more difficult way to show growth because you are looking at only those products that are in the store now that were in the store a year ago.

Now, if the company has decided to take the OR position in their reporting analysis, they could take into account *all* the products—both those that were in the stores a year ago and everything in the stores now. That would mean that a store could add 50,000 new products to its store inventory and be able to report growth based on two very different product mixes. Now, generating growth based on this view would be much easier than the prior approach. In this case, *both* approaches could be of interest to the investor and identify the inherent growth of the current products and what the company has done to improve the actual product mix in each of the stores.

The configuration for these two views is accomplished by adding time attributes to the master data of the root characteristic or by using the time dependency as a part of the navigational attribute. As mentioned, these two situations are satisfied by additional enhancements to the two configuration concepts shown previously. In the case showing the historical OR current view, the additional change in configuration involves turning on the time dependency of the navigational attribute Material Group (in this case) so that the combination of *all* the values in *all* the periods can be displayed in the query. This explains the fact that material BBB changed from one material group to another and that material EEE was added in the latter period of time. In the case showing the historical AND current view, the additional change in configuration involves adding two attributes for time—From and To—to the InfoObject Material. This is in additional to using the configuration changes for the view of OR. Using these additional time attributes in the query results in a report that's the AND combination. Therefore, you would not see the materials BBB (changed groups) and EEE (new material) because either they were *not* in the same material group for the entire time or they were added after the timeframe being analyzed. In the last three situations of displaying the data with some connection to the use of time dependency and attributes in the modeling, you can use the option for creating hierarchies to display a similar view of the data. In this case, you would create a hierarchical relationship along the lines of the time dependency, and the results in the queries would be the same as described previously. This can be a bit time consuming because the hierarchies, as well as the master data, have to be updated (via uploading processes) as each of the changes in relationships occurs.

Summary

As you can see, these four advanced components of the SAP BW system—Elimination of Internal Business Volumes, UOM options, GIS and the Map web item, and the Chart web item—are a bit more involved than just using the BEx Analyzer or the Web Analyzer. They include a combination of activities involving functionality and configuration. They offer a very important point of view in terms of the setup and configuration of BW. The reports cannot be developed and implemented in a vacuum without the coordination between the configuration in the workbench and the configuration in the reporting area. This is true in all areas of BW, but for the sake of consistency and the fulfillment of the business user requirements, it is very important to coordinate the configuration with the reporting. To this point, the final section of this chapter covered the use of variants and key dates within a query. As you can see, there are multiple options for offering the business user the ability to "save" their settings/values, as well as multiple options of displaying the data for the "true" view. In both cases, the coordination between functional and technical BW resources is critical. Therefore, during the process of developing the blueprints and architecture of BW, it is important to get someone in from the reporting and analysis side of the company to make sure all requirements for strategic reporting are being met.

Working with SAP BI Standard Business Content

I n this chapter we will review the options for using Standard Business Content (SBC) while developing queries and reporting strategies. Standard Business Content consists of much more than the standard delivered queries, web templates and workbooks and can help you with the overall timelines and processes in your implementation because you can turn on the SBC you need—for queries as well as InfoProviders, datasources, and many other objects within the BI system to increase the ROI on the implementation. You can also turn on the SBC for help with the performance analysis and tuning of your system. There's much more in the area of technical help within the 7.0 BI system versus the 3.x version. You also have available the Administration Cockpit, which is, among other things, a central focal point for all the reports and queries for tracking query and system performance.

Introduction to BI Standard Business Content for Queries

We have worked through quite a bit of information concerning the design, functionality, and creation of queries, workbooks, and web objects. At this point, however, it's important to take a moment and review what it is we are trying to accomplish. As you go through your implementation, your initial discussion will involve trying to understand how you are going to configure your BI system to deliver to your customers—whether they are executive users, business users, or even other systems—the information, both structured and unstructured, that they need in the format they need. This is where Standard Business Content (SBC) comes into play. The idea of Standard Business Content has been discussed in different ways for the last several chapters, and it is important we discuss it here in a more formal manner. Figure 14-1 shows a overview of the different SBC objects. These are not all the SBC objects available. Rather, this is a view of the critical objects you might use for your project.

If you have gone through numerous implementations, you'll know that you have to answer some initial questions about what to configure and how—and getting the answers to these questions sooner is better than later. This is one area where SBC queries, workbooks, and WAD queries can help. If we are going to get business users involved with the project, we need to get their attention and suggestions—and to do that we need to be able to show them something ASAP. That something could be SBC queries. The easiest and

FIGURE 14-1
Overview of the
Standard Business
Content objects

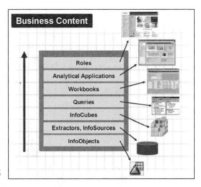

fastest approach to getting information and samples out to your business users is to activate SBC and demo this information for them. This will get them to understand what the possible outcomes could be for the information and how this toolset will work for them.

Another reason for the use of SBC is to increase the speed of an implementation. We are all comfortable with the fact that SBC will not exactly fit our project, but it may fit about 50% to 75% or more of our needs. That's not a bad start, and getting any help to decrease the project timeline and increase the speed in which we can implement this toolset is all good. Therefore, activating SBC to see what it can offer, determine whether it can reduce the amount of customization we need to do, perform gap analysis, and produce a prototype to show the business users is always good and would be a great start.

There are other reasons to get SBC up and running, but these can be specific to a particular project. Needless to say, you should review your requirements and investigate what SBC can do for you before spending time on customized anything in BI. We will cover the activation as well as the deactivation of SBC, but only in terms of queries, even though the other objects' activation processes are very similar. In Figure 14-2 you can see a partial list of SBC objects by object type, and at the bottom of the list (not shown) is an additional item called More Types, which offers additional objects not on the primary list. Once you start reviewing the SBC—either by looking to activate a portion of it to review the standard objects in that specific area, activating the SAP Demo SBC for use in demonstrating functionality, or just using the Metadata Repository to view what SBC you have available—you will see that there are literally thousands of SBC objects for you to use.

I think of SBC not only as what the SAP BI system can offer you in terms of the activation of objects, but also what the system can offer you in terms of standard parameters for your queries. Therefore, I have added to this section the parameters you can set in the IMG for the BEx Analyzer and WAD queries. These components have sometimes been overlooked, and they may offer you some help with your business requirements. We will complete this chapter with a discussion of the Metadata Repository.

Standard Functionality for Query Design

Before we move into the true Standard Business Content in the BI system, we'll cover some of the other parameters that could affect your implementation and display of information via queries. These parameters can be found in the Implementation Guide (IMG) for BI. They are settings that control the display of some of the basic information in your queries. Remember that these parameters are systemwide parameters, and if you change them, you change them for everyone.

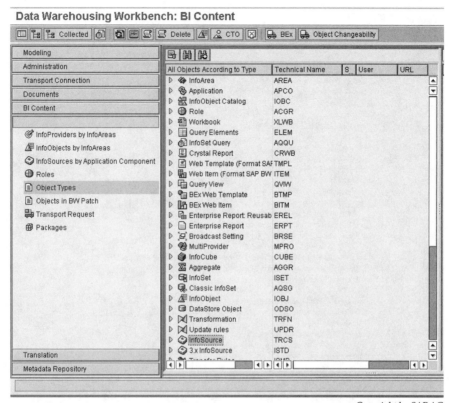

Copyright by SAP AG

FIGURE 14-2 Overview of the Standard Business Content by object type

NOTE *We have used the transaction code SPRO in past chapters to get to the IMG.*

Settings for Reporting and Analysis

Figure 14-3 shows you the menu path in the IMG to the actual parameters we will discuss. These parameters are found under the heading General Settings for Reporting and Analysis and are list next:

- Analysis Authorizations: Select Concept
- Presenting the Numeric Value in the Business Explorer
- Set Alternative Currency Display
- Set F4 Help and Hierarchies for Time Characteristics/OLAP Settings
- Activate Personalization in BEx
- Set BEx Analyzer Version

Analysis Authorization is the new authorization process in BI 7.0 version. In this activity, you can choose whether you want to set up the new analysis authorization concept or the

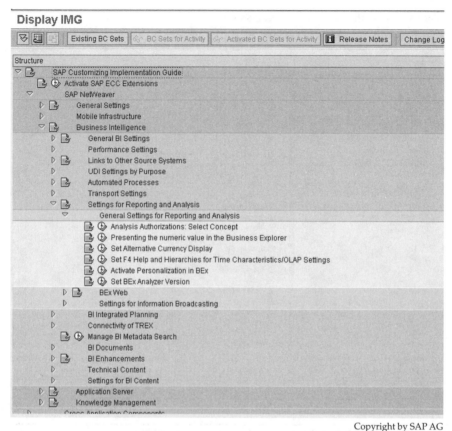

Copyright by SAP AG

FIGURE 14-3 General settings for reporting and analysis

old concept of reporting authorizations. The new concept is active as the default setting. You reach the new infrastructure from transaction RSECADMIN, or you can use SAP Easy Access Menu BI | Business Explorer | Authorizations. Both allow you to restrict how data for authorization-relevant characteristics is displayed in a query. However, the new concept is more user friendly and is better suited to the requirements of the BI system. For this reason, SAP recommends that you use the new concept. Only use the old concept in exceptional cases, and when doing so, make sure you have switched back to the old concept.

Presenting the Numerical Value in the Business Explorer allows you to set text for certain instances in the display of the data in the query. This text is important and for the final display may be critical to the acceptance of the data by the business users. The following illustration shows the different options you have when setting default text for certain situations. In most cases, these items are self-explanatory, but some need a bit of explanation.

Change View "BEx Values": Details

BEx Values	
Division by zero	DIV/0
Does not exist	X
Num. overflow	NUM. OVERFLOW
Mixed values	MIX
No authorization	NOT AUTHORIZED
☑ Mixed values	

Under certain circumstances, numeric values and texts for currencies, or units, in the Business Explorer cannot be determined uniquely. In such cases, predefined texts are displayed instead of the numeric values and currencies, or units. If a division-by-zero arises when a numeric value is calculated, the text DIV/0 is the option. If a numeric value cannot be determined, the text X is output (Does Not Exist). If a numeric value is not calculated due to numeric overlapping, the text NUM OVERFLOW is output. If a numeric value is made up of several currencies, or units, the text MIX is output instead of the currency or unit (Mixed Currencies). If a user does not have authorization to display a particular numeric value for a cell in the executed query, the text NOT AUTHORIZED is output in the cell instead (No Authorization). If a calculated numeric value is made up of different currencies, or units, the numeric value may or may not be output. If you choose Mixed Values, the numeric value is output. If Mixed Values is not active, the text is the output that you entered under Mixed Currencies.

Set Alternative Currency Display is generally used to determine whether the dollar sign ($) or U.S. dollars (USD) is used for display in queries. If you are looking to use USD versus the dollar sign ($), you can set that here. The standard setting is that all currencies are displayed in accordance with the ISO norm, by default, and appear after the numeric value, with the following exceptions:

- DEM is displayed as DM.
- USD is displayed as $ (in front of the numeric value).
- GBP is displayed as £ (in front of the numeric value).

The first of the following illustrations shows the entries you would use to alter the standard setting for USD. The second illustration shows the outcome in the query. As you can see, the $ for U.S. dollars has been changed to USD and appears after the amount.

New Entries: Overview of Added Entries

Alternative Currency Display in BEx

Curr.	Alt. text	bfr/aftr V	
USD	USD	A After value	

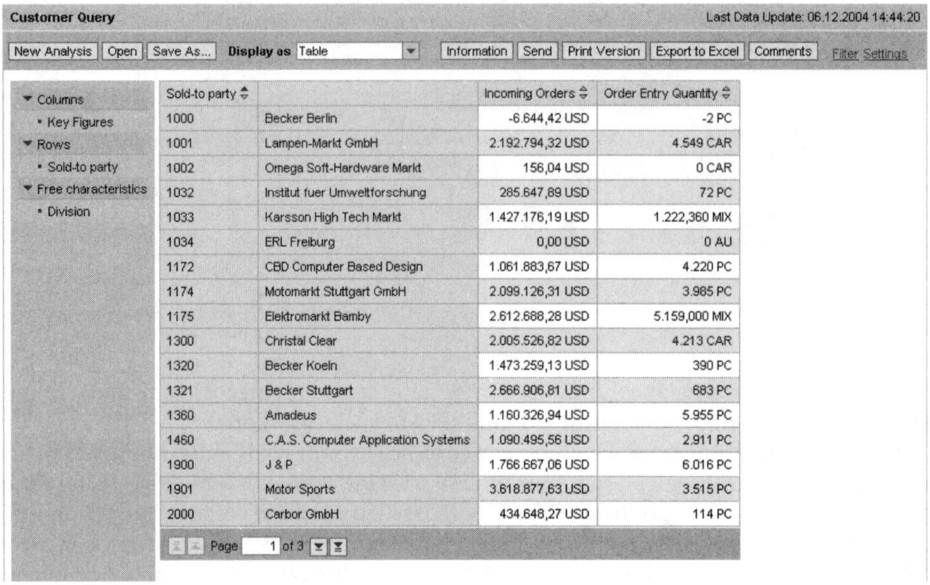

Customer Query			Last Data Update: 06.12.2004 14:44:20	

New Analysis | Open | Save As... | **Display as** Table ▾ | Information | Send | Print Version | Export to Excel | Comments | Filter Settings

	Sold-to party ⇕		Incoming Orders ⇕	Order Entry Quantity ⇕
▼ Columns	1000	Becker Berlin	-6.644,42 USD	-2 PC
• Key Figures	1001	Lampen-Markt GmbH	2.192.794,32 USD	4.549 CAR
▼ Rows	1002	Omega Soft-Hardware Markt	156,04 USD	0 CAR
• Sold-to party	1032	Institut fuer Umweltforschung	285.647,89 USD	72 PC
▼ Free characteristics	1033	Karsson High Tech Markt	1.427.176,19 USD	1.222,360 MIX
• Division	1034	ERL Freiburg	0,00 USD	0 AU
	1172	CBD Computer Based Design	1.061.883,67 USD	4.220 PC
	1174	Motomarkt Stuttgart GmbH	2.099.126,31 USD	3.985 PC
	1175	Elektromarkt Bamby	2.612.688,28 USD	5.159,000 MIX
	1300	Christal Clear	2.005.526,82 USD	4.213 CAR
	1320	Becker Koeln	1.473.259,13 USD	390 PC
	1321	Becker Stuttgart	2.666.906,81 USD	683 PC
	1360	Amadeus	1.160.326,94 USD	5.955 PC
	1460	C.A.S. Computer Application Systems	1.090.495,56 USD	2.911 PC
	1900	J & P	1.766.667,06 USD	6.016 PC
	1901	Motor Sports	3.618.877,63 USD	3.515 PC
	2000	Carbor GmbH	434.648,27 USD	114 PC

Page 1 of 3

One of the more important topics in this area is the next set of parameters: Set F4 Help and Hierarchies for Time Characteristics/OLAP Settings. In this activity, you can make some general OLAP settings for time characteristics. You can also determine hierarchies for the time characteristics you want to use in reporting. The leaves of the hierarchy are then in the time interval you have set. In the parameters of the initial tab, you have some basic settings for the time intervals. Here, you can determine the time interval that appears in F4 help for the characteristic values. This period should be as big as required, but also as small as possible so as to keep F4 help as clear as possible. If the interval is later changed, all aggregates that contain a hierarchy of time characteristics are deactivated. Another entry here is for the factory calendar, where you can select a factory calendar for the calculation of working days. Finally, using Masterdata Texts Time Characteristics, you can choose whether the fiscal year or the calendar year is to appear in the text for fiscal year periods.

On the second tab in this table you have the virtual time hierarchies. Here, you can select hierarchies for a time characteristic you want to work with in reporting. On the left side, the system displays the existing active time characteristics for which hierarchies exist in the characteristic maintenance. You can use these pushbuttons to see lists of hierarchies related to the time characteristic in question. The list is displayed in the upper-right section of the screen. You can select a hierarchy from this list by double-clicking it. The following illustration displays the view and outcome of the activation of a virtual time hierarchy for Half-Year Hierarchy. Selected hierarchies have green tree icons and are displayed as selected in the list below. Here, you can select the start level and a description of the hierarchies. If you do not enter a description, the system generates one for you. Remember that these hierarchies don't show up in the Administration Workbench or under the time characteristic, only in the Query Designer under the specific time characteristic.

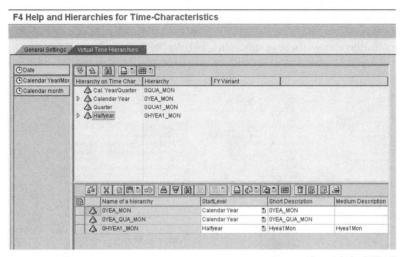

Activate Personalization in BEx is something we have covered before. In this case, we will highlight the other two entries available. The following illustration shows the additional two items. We covered the Active BEx History option before; the Variables Personalization and Web Report Person options are the ones of interest here. You use this activity to activate personalization in the BEx Analyzer. You can personalize variables so that certain ones selected by you are proposed. Thus, you can identify a default value for a variable and execute a personalization against this value. If you do this, that value will be saved in the appropriate DataStore object for use the next time the query is executed. You can change the personalized settings and adjust the values held for use. The other option is for Web Applications, so that report drilldowns are saved. Remember, once personalization is activated, it cannot be deactivated.

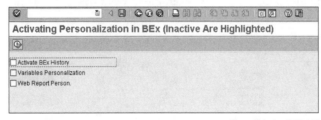

Set BEx Analyzer Version is used for setting the version of the BEx Analyzer (either SAP 3.x or SAP NetWeaver 2004S) that is called in transaction RRMX. Although this can be set, you are better off letting the system identify which version of the BEx Analyzer is available for use.

Configuration Tools for BEx Analyzer

To round out the parameters, that I found to be standard delivered functionality but not SBC objects that we activate from the BW Data Warehouse Workbench, we have several different Excel spreadsheet components we can use to help confirm the configuration of the BEx Analyzer and, more specifically, the Excel spreadsheet used with the BEx Analyzer to help us manage styles within the BEx Analyzer. These can be found either on a shared drive your company has set up and is using for this purpose or directly on your local drive. The following illustration shows these components highlighted in Explorer. If you do a search and use the wildcard *sapbex*, you should be able to locate these items.

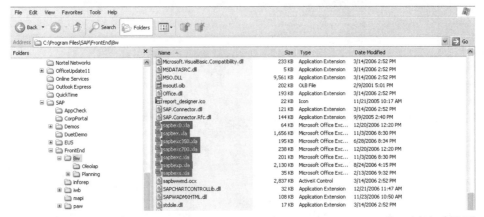

Copyright by SAP AG

Those listed as SAPBEX0.XLA and SAPBEXX.XLA are for the confirmation of the assignment of the current front end for the BEx Analyzer. You may also see SAPBEXC350 or 700.XLA. These are for the same purpose—to confirm the implementation of the Excel front end for the BEx Analyzer. The important ones are SAPBEXS.XLA and SAPBEXC.XLA. Also, SAPBEXC.XLA is a tool that helps in confirming that PC, Server Check, and Version are consistent on your computer. Once you have located this workbook, you can click the Start button to confirm the setup for Excel works consistently with your BEx Analyzer. Executing this each time with the client can save quite a bit of time if you can identify the issues before you work through a query setup and everything short dumps just as you are saving the query. The following illustration shows an example of what this component looks like and what items it tests.

	A	B	C	D	E	F
1	**Check Installation on PC**					See Note 197460 f
2						Version is okay
3	Start	File	C:\DOCUME~1\d020097\LOCALS~1\Temp\sapBEX_PC_0306_175544.xls			Version is higher th
4		Date/Time	06.03.2006 17:55:44			Version is lower th
5		Excel Version	11.0 6355 (049)			Version of non-BI f
6		Windows Version	Windows XP Service Pack 2 (2600)			
7		OSS Note	921921		In case of a problem, please create ar	
8		SAP GUI 6.40	13 or higher		and send this file to **bw.bex.support**	
9						
10	Filename	Version on PC	7.00 Patch 1100	Path	Date/Time	Size
11						
12	BI in SAP NetWeaver 2004s					
13	AxInterop.SHDocVw.dll					
14	BExAddin.dll					
15	BExAnalyzer.exe					
16	BExAnalyzer.xla					
17	BExApi.dll					
18	BExCAControls.dll					
19	BExCommon.dll					
20	BExCommunication.dll					
21	BExControls.dll					
22	BExControls2.dll					
23	BExDialogOpenSave.dll					
24	BExDiffViewer.dll					
25	BExFormulaParser.dll					
26	BExGeneratedAll.dll					
27	BExInstaller.exe					
28	BExMailTrace.dll					
29	BExOpenSaveServices.dll					

Copyright by SAP AG

The final Excel workbook that is offered, SAPBEXS.XLA, is a very important part of your workbook and query strategy. This workbook delivers the Cascading Style Sheet (CSS). The CSS is the worksheet that controls the initial colors and formatting you see in the query. If you were wondering what supported these items in the query, this is it. The CSS stores all fonts, styles, colors, and so on, that you would use in the query and workbook configuration. As you can see in Figure 14-4, this has all the fields your query shows and the formatting used. This functionality was demonstrated in a previous chapter, so it is just mentioned here as part of the standard parameters delivered with the system.

Metadata Repository

With the HTML-based Metadata Repository, you can access information about the metadata objects of SAP NetWeaver Business Intelligence from a central point. This metadata especially includes important object properties and their relationships with other objects. Metadata means "data about data," and this is appropriate for the Metadata Repository. It provides descriptive technical information about the objects used to build your application—in this case, your BI system. For example, metadata about an InfoCube would include the names of the InfoObjects and Dimension tables used in the InfoCube, the date it was designed, the last person who changed the design, and the structures and other objects linked to this InfoCube. It would *not* include the records stored in the InfoCube—that would be transactional data, not metadata. If you were to look at any of the "Create" screens for the objects in BI, you would be looking at the information stored in the Metadata Repository. There are metadata tables for storing information about InfoCubes, InfoObjects, DataStore objects, and all other objects in the BI system. The Metadata Repository is the grouping of all the information collected and stored in these tables. In the new version 7.0 of BI, you have an SBC InfoCube called 0BWTC_C08 that

Copyright by SAP AG

FIGURE 14-4   Sample style for the Business Explorer Analyzer has all the objects included in the SBC available for your review. Thus, you can create a query against this InfoCube and display all the SBC objects in a specific area (for example, all queries attached to an InfoCube).

Options within the Metadata Repository

You access the Metadata Repository from the Data Warehouse Workbench by using the Metadata Repository button on the left side of the screen. Figure 14-5 shows the initial screen for the Metadata Repository.

From the SAP Easy Access screen, choose Modeling | Data Warehousing Workbench. The Metadata Repository is displayed. A navigation area is available on the left side of the Metadata Repository, and a display area appears on the right side. In the navigation area, you can choose the objects for which information needs to be displayed—either activated objects from the local objects of the BI system or objects from all systems. Business Content (SAP-delivered objects) in the display area includes the available object types for the selection. By clicking the link for an object type, you get a list of all objects that belong to this type. By clicking the link for an object, you get detailed, object-specific information. To navigate from page to page in the Metadata Repository, choose Display Previous Page or Display Next Page. Choose Main Page to call up the entry page. Another approach to

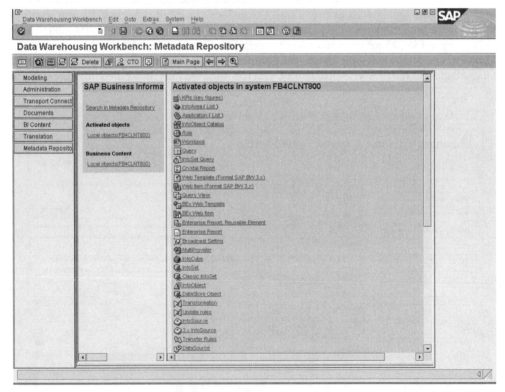

FIGURE 14-5   Initial screen for the Metadata Repository

accessing the Metadata Repository is shown in the following illustration. It offers a view of accessing the file system via the BW Administration Workbench configuration screen.

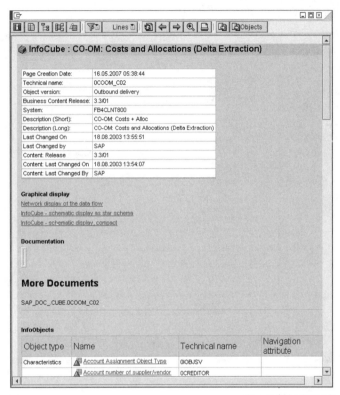

You can start your search by selecting the Search in the Metadata Repository link, as shown in Figure 14-5, or by selecting one of the object icons in the right pane. If you choose to use the right pane, you will see a list of objects. You then use the Find function to look for the specific object that is of interest to you. For example, if you choose the link to the InfoCubes, you can see the list of InfoCubes available in the system, as shown in the following illustration. This list is not only SBC, but also all the InfoCubes available because we didn't identify that specific information before the search. If only the activated objects or business content objects are of interest, then you should start with the left pane and click the appropriate link and filter your search by business content only or activate objects only for a specific system. This will set the right pane to only those objects and help with the search functions.

NOTE *Remember to use the arrows to move back and forth among these screens. Also, use the Main Page button to move to the initial page of the Metadata Repository. You can also use CTRL-F to find objects you are looking for via a search term.*

	Inter Company Elimination	ICE
SAP Business Informa	Interactive Scripting	0CRM_CIC1
	Interactive Scripting Evaluation (IC WebClient)	0CRM_ISE2
Search in Metadata Repository	Internal Data	0CM_C03
	Internal Data: Stock (Month, Quarter, Year)	0CM_C05
	Inventory Management InfoCube Qr00	TR_C00
Activated objects	Inventory Showcase	T_INV00
Local objects(FB4CLNT800)	Liability	0CDM_C2
	Liquidity Planning: Actual Data	0TRLP_C01
Business Content	LIS Cube00	LISCUBW00
Local objects(FB4CLNT800)	Lock 99	LOCK99
	LOCK00	LOCK00
	Logistics	0RT_C54
	MAP: Actual Data Bottom-Up	0RT_C17
	MAP: Actual Data Top-Down	0RT_C16
	MAP: Assortment Planning	0RT_C15
	MAP: Merchandise Planning	0RT_C12
	MAP: Objective Planning	0RT_C10
	MAP: Price Band Planning	0RT_C13
	MAP: Store Group Planning	0RT_C14
	MAP: Store Planning	0RT_C11
	MAT	MAT
	Material Movements	0RT_C35
	Material Movements and Stock	0CP_IC_C1
	Material Stocks/Movements (as of 3.0B)	0IC_C03
	Merchandise Flow (Distribution Center)	0RT_C04
	Merchandise Planning, Plan	0RMP_C05
	Merchandise Planning, POS Sales, Month	0RMP_C01
	Merchandise Planning, POS Sales, Week	0RMP_C02
	Merchandise Planning, Stock, Month	0RMP_C03
	Merchandise Planning, Stock, Week	0RMP_C04
	Merchandise Procurement	0RT_C05
	Migration	T350IC02

Copyright by SAP AG

You can get a ton of information from the Metadata Repository, and initially you should try to take advantage of this as much as possible. It will definitely help with your search in the SBC area. Rather than trying to review the information via the Business Content screen in the system, you can navigate via web-based screens and view the details.

NOTE *Another approach to reviewing SBC is to go to the Help.SAP.com website and use this option to investigate all the SBC available (via the BI content link), but remember, this is not specifically your system, so you need to compare what is available.*

As you review the information in the repository, you can view the details of the specific objects. For example, if we drill down to the InfoCube view, we can choose the InfoCube 0COOM_C02 (SBC, because it begins with a zero). We can see that it offers us information about the initial setup, the last time it was changed, and the content release. Notice in the first of the following illustrations that you have three links in the screen below the heading Graphical Display:

- Network display of the data flow
- InfoCube – schematic display as star schema
- InfoCube – schematic display, compact

Then, below these in the area titled More Documents you have a link to other documents that are assigned to this InfoCube. With the initial three options, you can generate a graphical view of the design of the InfoCube, which will give you a visual of the characteristics and key figures in your InfoCube and how they are set up in the dimensions. This will allow you to analyze the possible performance questions based on the dimension design and also offer you some help with other InfoCubes that you might be creating and the possible dimension design. The second illustration uses the option "InfoCube—schematic display, compact" to show the view of the dimensions and fact table that store the characteristics and key figures. You can identify a number of interesting items on these screens. Every time I review the Metadata Repository, I see something I didn't see before. For example, if you look closely at this illustration, you can see that some of the InfoObjects have a small double arrow figure in front of them. This identifies the InfoObject as a navigational attribute. In addition to this, you can see that some of the InfoObjects are indented a bit—for example, under Network Activity the InfoObject Network is indented. This shows that Network is a compound of Network Activity.

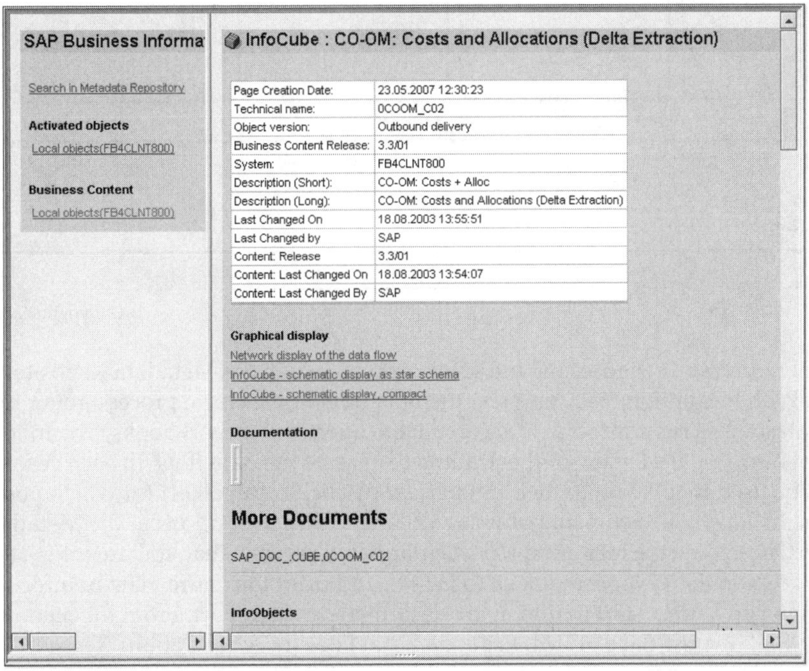

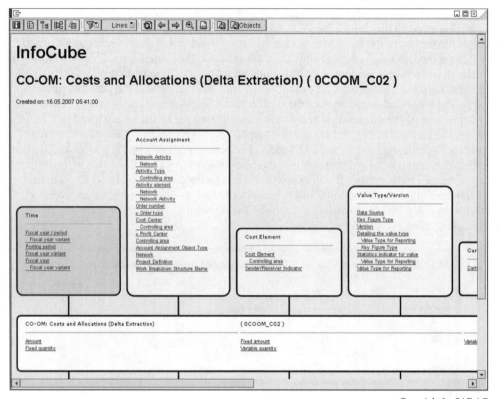

Copyright by SAP AG

The other interesting view of the information available in the Metadata Repository is Data Flow. With this option, you can view the data flow of the entire process going from the different datasources right through to the available queries and workbooks. The following illustration shows a partial view of the graphic display of the data flow. In each case, these objects can be used to link you to their details just by clicking an object for which you are executing a drilldown. This functionality is available for all the options in the Metadata Repository. Once you have identified a particular object or view that you are interested in analyzing, you can then export the page to HTML and print the entire view of information. This will give you a great start to review the information via a chart. From the menu bar, go to Extras_HTML Export_Save HTML Pages as Local Files (or other option). This will allow you to save the entire view and then print it if required. The options in this list are defined in Table 14-1. Just remember that selecting Extras_HTML Export always means that the *entire* HTML document is exported. This may take some time, so you will probably want to export via the context menu of the actual object.

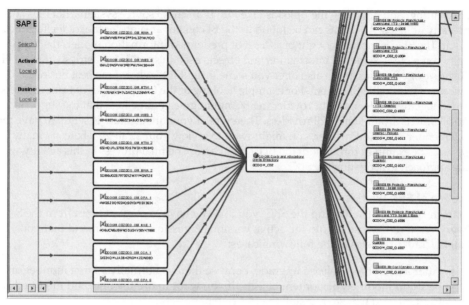

In addition to the options discussed so far, you can also create your own documentation and upload it. You can then connect it to the objects for review and analysis.

Standard Business Content

As you can see in Figure 14-2, a tremendous amount of Standard Business Content is available. SBC covers a number of different aspects of the business process, and more. Some of the SBC we will not really focus on includes all the functionality delivered for the management and analysis of system performance. An entire set of objects is used specifically for the analysis and management of the BI system—how it is performing, how the query is performing

Function	Description
Generate HTML Pages	Generates HTML pages for the metadata objects in the A version (active objects).
Generate HTML Pages (Business Content)	Generates HTML pages for the metadata objects in the D version (Business Content objects).
Save HTML Pages as Local Files	Exports the entire HTML documentation for the metadata objects in the A version.
Save HTML Pages (Business Content)	Saves the entire HTML documentation for the metadata objects in the D version.
Delete Saved HTML Pages	Deletes the HTML pages for metadata objects in the A version generated on the database.
Delete Saved Pages (Content)	Deletes the HTML pages for metadata objects in the D version generated on the database.

TABLE 14-1   Options to Export the Definitions and Detail of the Metadata Repository

and executing, and how long the uploads take into BI from R3 source systems, flat files and third-party uploads. All of this can be found in the BI content area under the folder Technical Content. The SBC is mostly thought of as a set of predefined information models that help identify some of the standard information and objects used in specific industries, different lines of business, or countries. It can also offer you some insight into what some best business practices are within the BI system. For example, looking at the total number of InfoProviders grouped together under a MultiProvider in SBC might give you the idea that the suggested practical limit is around ten InfoProviders. Therefore, if your architecture is set up to have more than ten under an MultiProvider, you might want to review your strategy. There are many of these types of examples throughout the BI Content area. The final process in this activity would be the approach to activating the SBC.

Activation of SBC Queries

To start the process of activating the SBC, you initially have to convert them from the SAP delivery version (D version) into the active version (A version). I recommend that you install BI Content objects in the following cases:

- After a BI Content release upgrade, because there is normally a large number of new and modified BI Content objects. If you want to use the new and modified BI Content, you have to reinstall the BI Content objects.

NOTE   *Please refer to the Release Notes published with the upgrade.*

- After installing a BI Content support package, because this will deliver a large number of new objects. Refer to the SAP Notes that are delivered with each Content Support Package. These SAP Notes contain information on why certain BI Content objects are being redelivered.

Navigating to the Data Warehousing Workbench to Install BI Content

From the main Business Intelligence menu, choose Modeling_Data Warehousing Workbench: BI Content. If you are already in the Data Warehousing Workbench, select the BI Content functional area by clicking the corresponding pushbutton in the left navigation window or by choosing the menu path Goto_Install BI Content.

The Data Warehousing Workbench for installing BI Content has three navigation windows. In the left window you determine the view of the objects in the middle area of the screen. In the middle window, you select the objects you want to activate. In the right window, you make the settings for installing the BI Content. The right window also contains an overview of the objects you have selected, and it is here that you start the installation of BI Content. One of the steps that is often overlooked is assigning a relevant source system (or systems). If you want to assign a source system, select the Source System Assignment function.

The Choose Source System by Default? dialog box appears. Select one or more source systems by setting the corresponding indicators in the Default Assignment column. Figure 14-6 shows the dialog box. If you do not select a source system, *all* the source systems are assigned automatically and therefore you may be activating objects indirectly that you don't need.

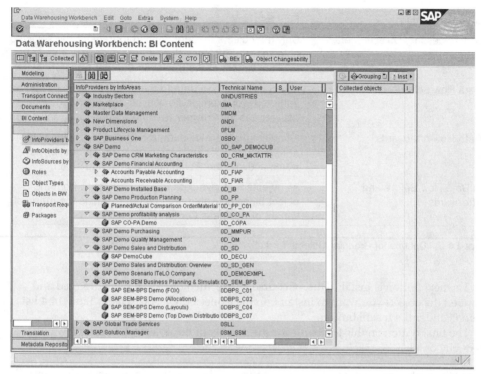

Copyright by SAP AG

FIGURE 14-6   The Dialog Box for Choosing the Source System Default Assignment

NOTE *Some objects may be source system dependent, whereas others are not. Still others may have multiple source system dependence. There may be other concerns with the activation of these objects. Be sure to review the information with these points in mind before activating these types of objects.*

Grouping   Before you drag and drop the objects you are going to activate, we need to review the settings along the toolbar for the activation process. The following illustration shows the toolbar for this process. The first option is for grouping the objects to be included and for determining the mode of collection of these objects.

Copyright by SAP AG

Make the settings you require from the following selection lists on the right side of the screen. For Grouping, choose the objects you want the system to include. The groupings combine the objects from a particular area. Table 14-2 details the available options.

The next option for which we need to select a method is Collection Mode. This indicator is for the method you are using to gather all the objects needed to support the item you are activating. Table 14-3 details the options and functionality.

Grouping Option	Function and Description
Only Necessary Objects (default setting)	Only the objects that are needed to transfer the selected objects from Business Content are gathered. This is the minimal variant of the Business Content transfer.
Data Flow Before	All objects that give data to the object being activated are gathered. For example, to activate the query, you would activate the InfoProvider, Transformation Rule, and so on.
Data Flow Afterwards	All object that receive data from the object being activated are gathered. For example, to activate the query, you would activate the Workbooks, Roles, and so on.
In Data Flow Before and Afterwards	All objects that give data to or receive data from the object being activated are gathered. This is the maximal variant of Business Content transfer.

TABLE 14-2   Options for Grouping Objects for Activation

The next option is Install. This, of course, is executed once you have dragged and dropped the objects you want to install into the Collected Objects screen. Table 14-4 lists the options under the Install button.

The final option on this toolbar is for the display of the objects. You can view either a hierarchy or a list.

Installation   Once you've reviewed and confirmed these settings, you are ready to install and activate Standard Business Content. The first illustration on the next page shows the initial step of choosing the object (in this case, an InfoCube) to be installed. Once you have "transferred" this object to the Collected Objects area, you execute the installation process. The system will start to activate all tables, objects, structures, programs, and dependent components (depending on the settings you have identified) that will allow this InfoCube to be used in the implementation of BI. The Transfer or Collected Object area of the screen has a series of columns that offer information on the installation and activation process occurring.

Collection Option	Description and Functionality
Collect Automatically	The objects are collected automatically after the object has been selected. This is the default setting. Therefore, all the objects required for the setting in the Grouping option would be collected.
Start Manual Collection	The objects to be activated are only collected if you choose the GATHER DEPENDENT OBJECTS (Execute (clock) Icon) function.

TABLE 14-3   Options for the Collection Mode

Type of Install	Description and Functionality
Simulate Installation	The system tests for errors on the critical objects that would be installed. This can be helpful during the initial activations to review the possible issues that may occur. The result of the activation is shown by a green and red icon under the Simulation Results header.
Install	The selected objects are activated directly.
Install in Background	The selected objects are activated in the background as a batch job. This is reasonable if you are activating large numbers of objects.
Installation and Transport	Depending on your transport strategy, this option would activate the objects and then write them to a transport request.

TABLE 14-4   Installation Options

The second illustration shows the column headings in this screen area. Table 14-5 lists the headings their functionality.

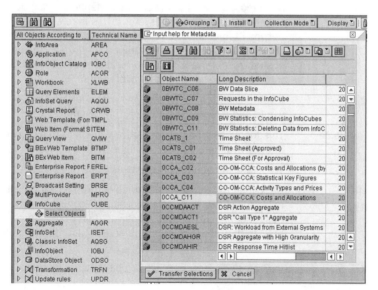

Copyright by SAP AG

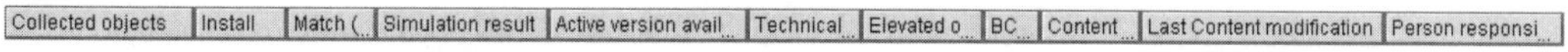

Copyright by SAP AG

Collected Objects Toolbar	Description and Functionality
Collected Objects	In this column is a list of all the objects that have been collected based on the option you've selected. In the context menu of this column is a list of additional options—install all, do not install any below a specific level, merge or copy all, display details, display description (Metadata Repository), display version comparisons, and export HTML documentation.
Install	In the Install column the following business content objects are indicated by default: • Objects transferred for the first time • Objects that have been redelivered by SBC in a more recent version
Match (X) or Copy	If the SAP delivery version and the active version can be matched, a check box is displayed in this column. With the most important object types, the active version and the SAP delivery version can be matched. From a technical point of view, the SAP delivery version (D version) is matched against the M version. As in most cases, the M version is identical to the active version (A version) in a customer system. This is referred to as a match between the D and A versions for reasons of simplification. The use of the "match" option is important if there has been some customizing of the SBC, thus, making sure the customization that has occurred will not be overwritten.
Simulation Result	If you decided to "simulate" the activation and installation, you would see a "color" light below this column.
Active Version Available	This identifies whether the active version of this object is already available via a green light icon.
Technical Name	The technical name of the object.
Elevated Objects Association Type	Describes the criticality of the object to the root object that is being activated. Thus, informational comments such as "is essentially required" and "receives data from" identify the objects that are required to be activated for the root object to be supported.
BC Components	Indicates whether a particular object has a Business Content component.
Content Release	Identifies in what content release this object was initially delivered.
Last Content Modification	Identifies in what content release this object was last changed.
Person Responsible	Because this is SBC, the person responsible is normally SAP.

TABLE **14-5** Options in the Collected Objects Columns

The following illustrations show the sequence of events during activation. In the first illustration you can see that we have executed the activation and installation of the SBC InfoCube 0CCA_C11 and that most of the list of InfoObjects have a green light beside them, confirming that their active version is available. You can also see some of the additional information available in the versioning information. The second illustration verifies that the InfoCube is, in fact, available for use in the Data Warehousing Workbench: Modeling folder for the InfoProviders.

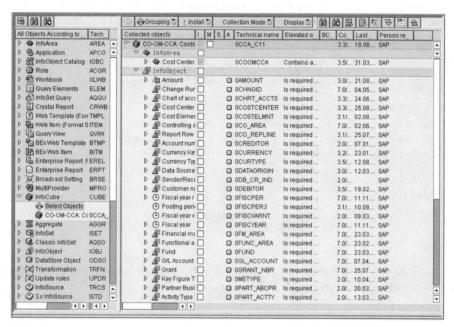

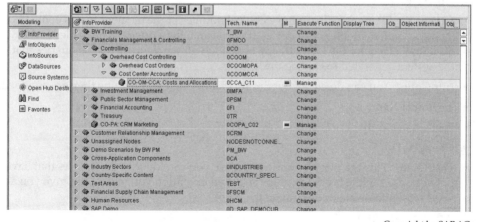

Deletion of SBC Queries

In order to better manage the number of queries and query components being developed and created, you may want to delete some of them over time. If you have activated or installed more SBC than you need, you can use the Deletion option to deactivate some of the SBC queries or the elements that make up the queries. This is one of the areas of SBC that activating more than what you may need or want is not that much of an issue later on in the maintenance process and the deletion is very straightforward. The wording may seem a bit confusing because in reality you are not deleting the SBC of the queries but rather deactivating them. Therefore, they will not be available for use. If you are dealing with queries you have developed that are not SAP naming convention protected, you will actually delete these if you use this functionality. You find this function from the menu Business Explorer | Query | Delete Objects (transaction code RSZDELETE). The following illustration shows the screen you will see if you execute this component.

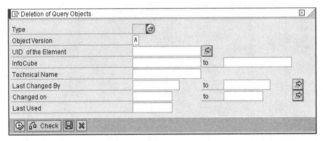

Copyright by SAP AG

In this screen you have a number of methods for deleting/deactivating the SBC queries. Some of these methods are reasonably self-explanatory:

- **Type**   Includes queries, filters, structures, restricted key figures, calculated key figures, and variables. It offers the ability to delete just specific objects or elements of the query or the query itself.

- **Object Version**

- **UID of the Element**   This is the technical number of the element that is generated by the system to identify that object. If you search for a query in the tables of the DataStore object for the Open dialog box, you will see the UID for the queries that the system generated to catalog these items.

- **InfoCube**   You can delete all queries by identifying the InfoCube they are assigned.

- **Technical Name**

- **Last Changed By**

- **Changed On**

- **Last Used**   This is a popular option because you can identify the queries that have not been used in the last 90 days (or any date limitation you feel would give you a good reason to delete or deactivate these queries).

When you execute this process, the system offers another dialog box to ensure you want to delete the specific queries. Finally, once you answer this question, another dialog box appears asking if you are interested in deleting dependent objects such as workbooks, views, and so on from your favorites and roles.

SAP DemoContent

SAP DemoContent comprises additional SBC that is delivered with SAP BI. These are complete data flow processes that are available to be activated and used to demonstrate the functionality of BI. The business processes and areas in the DemoContent are from different lines of business and specifically included in the SBC so that you can have something to display to your business users quickly. This can be done while you are organizing your corporate governance processes, blueprint processes, or overall project activities, and your business users can start to get a feel for the toolsets in BI and their functionality. The SAP DemoContent all begin with 0D_ and are activated the same way as other business content. However, in this case, many of them supply sample transactional data and master data so that you avoid having to waste time setting up flat files or another means of getting the required data into the InfoProviders for immediate use. The sample flat files of data are delivered with the BI system, and during the installation of the server they are uploaded into the application server. Figure 14-7 shows the SAP DemoContent in terms of InfoCubes.

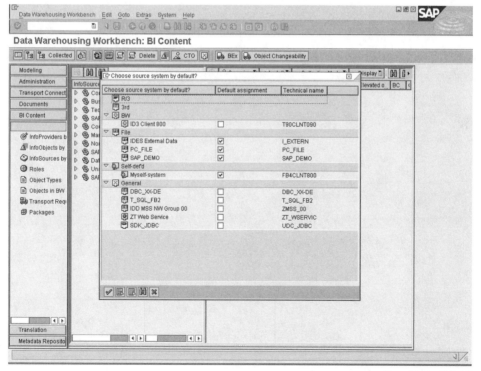

Copyright by SAP AG

FIGURE 14-7   SAP DemoContent viewed from the Data Warehousing Workbench: BI Content

Along with this, of course, are all the structures and objects required to have a viable demonstration of BI within a short period of time.

Summary

SAP delivers thousands of different objects, structures, programs, queries, and other components so that you can quickly and effectively implement BI and use its functionality for reporting and analysis. As SAP continues to deliver additional functionality, the SAP SBC will continue to grow so that customers can take advantage of these standard templates in the business process of implementing BI. Again, too much emphasis cannot be given to the need to review and use the SBC available. This has been a sore point for me in certain implementations—that not enough SBC had been used or the investigation into the possible use of SBC has been cut short, thus causing the need to re-create something already available.

Be sure to include time in your project plan to investigate SBC both before the configuration starts and during the initial process of implementation. This can be very helpful with training as well as developing awareness of how BI works and what additional information, and thus strategic reports, can be developed by BI.

What the Web Can Do for Your Reporting

I will now shift gears on you for this chapter. I have been writing about all the functionality in the BEx Analyzer, and for the past four to six chapters we have worked our way through all the components and procedures. Now a discussion of the functionality, flexibility, and configuration of the Web BEx Analyzer and the Web Application Designer (WAD) template query is in order. As we go through this information, remember that there will be quite a bit of overlap in terms of capabilities and topics between these two front-end options and the BEx Analyzer. I will try to minimize the amount of redundant information, but if it is important to highlight certain areas and to reinforce the functionality of the web front end, I will. In this chapter, the discussion will be driven by the navigational functions within the Web Analyzer and the WAD template query. The advanced configuration and implementation of the web-based front ends will be discussed at a high level. There's so much more that can be discussed about the WAD that we won't cover it all here—enough, in fact, to fill another book. Numerous activities can be executed on the Web via web queries or WAD queries. The usability of this approach to reporting can't be understated. The Web is definitely a user interface within the SAP reporting strategy and enterprise reporting that should be reviewed and discussed as the interface of choice.

Introduction to the BEx Web Analyzer and WAD

The BEx Web Analyzer is the initial web front-end tool offered as part of the Business Explorer Reporting options. The entire navigational and analytical process within the Web Analyzer is structured to be business user friendly. Much of the functionality in the Query Designer is available to the business user from the executed web query. Thus, most of the functionality that can be configured when using the BEx Analyzer can also be done by the business user on the Web. For example, the ability to create exceptions and conditions is available to the business user and not relegated to configuration only. Note that the exceptions and conditions created using this approach are not saved but are available for that particular period of time that you are using them. This web front end has an easy-to-use drag-and-drop functionality that allows the user to navigate intuitively through queries. The web

FIGURE 15-1
Web Analyzer in
the front-end
architecture

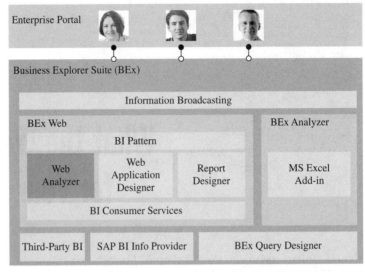

front end holds a very important position in the architecture of the reporting strategy. With a
web-based strategy, the ability to distribute the information from a report increases two-fold.
The business user is given access to information via a thin front end—a web screen—rather
than having to have access to the GUI version of the workbook or query. Access to other
third-party systems (in addition to access to the BW system) via the Web is available and
more easily obtained. Figure 15-1 shows the positioning of the web-based front end in the
reporting strategy of SAP. For the most part, the discussion so far has been about the BEx
Analyzer, but if you look closely when you save a query, you'll notice a web-based query is
created automatically. The following illustration shows the final result of a save operation in
the Query Designer. A query developed in the BEx Query Designer has a format available for
the BEx Analyzer front end (Excel based) and also the BEx Web Analyzer (web based). As
you can see, we have saved this query in the Favorites folder, but we also have the option to
store the query in a role, another folder option. Both options make the query available for
publishing to the SAP Enterprise Portal.

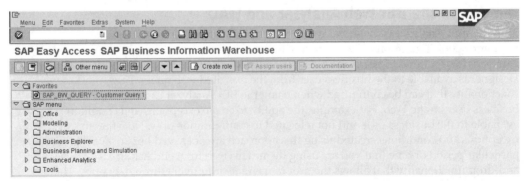

Access to the BEx Web Analyzer

You have several options to access the BEx Web Analyzer. As mentioned, any query created using the BEx Query Designer automatically is saved as a web-based query and is available for reporting using the BEx Web Analyzer. From an existing query that has been executed, you can access any BI data provider via the New button. This will be reviewed in the next section during our discussion of the toolbar buttons. Here are the other options for accessing the BEx Web Analyzer:

- From the BEx Analyzer, the BEx Web Analyzer can be accessed via the menu bar (BEx Analyzer | Tools | BEx Web Analyzer). The following illustration shows this approach.

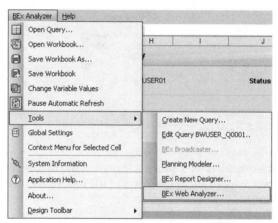

Copyright by SAP AG

 - From the BEx Query Designer, you can access the BEx Web Analyzer from the menu bar (Query | Execute). This will execute the query directly to the Web. The following illustration shows this approach. Access can also be obtained using the Execute icon.

Copyright by SAP AG

The following illustration shows the initial format of the query we will be using. In terms of key figures, the Sales Volume and Incoming Orders will work for the moment. For characteristics, we will use Division and Distribution Channel, as listed in the rows. Sold-to party is used for the free characteristic, and we have a restriction on Sales Organization for characteristic value 1000. This will be all we need to work through the functionality of the BEx Web Analyzer.

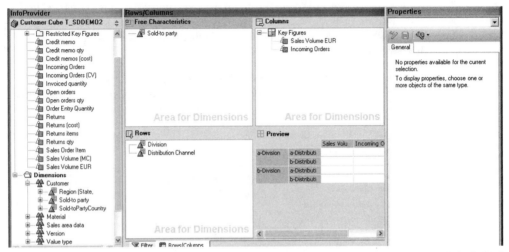

The initial view of the executed web query is shown in the following illustration. Division and Distribution Channel are in the Rows of the report, and the Sold-To Party is in the Free Characteristics area.

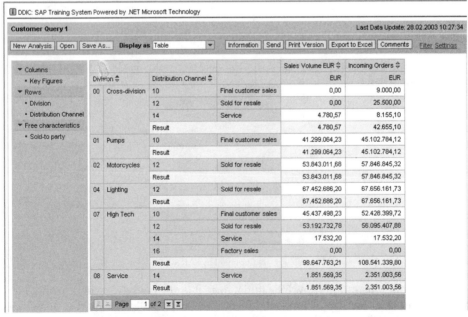

Once the query is displayed on the Web, it is embedded automatically into a standard web template for ad-hoc analysis that corresponds to the Web Analyzer. You can call the standard web template for the ad-hoc analysis from the following BEx tools:

Tools	Path for Call
Query Designer	Choose Display Query on the Web from the menu bar of the Query Designer.
Web Application Designer	Choose Tools I BEx Web Analyzer, or Web Template I Execute.

From a technical viewpoint, the standard web template for ad-hoc analysis and display of the Web Analyzer is based on the template 0ANALYSIS_PATTERN. This template can be set by default for ad-hoc analysis in the SAP Reference IMG under SAP NetWeaver I Business Intelligence I Setting for Reporting and Analysis I BEx Web I Setting Standard Web Templates. You can copy this web template to make changes and set it as your new default web template for ad-hoc analysis in the IMG.

The default web template for ad-hoc analysis is provided in the SAP delivery version (D version). Therefore, you can change it in the active version (A version) as required. However, a recommendation may be that you make changes to and edit the template in a copy unless you will be using the changes for the entire company then change the A version of 0ANALYSIS_PATTERN.

Navigation Options in the BEx Web Analyzer

Navigation in the BEx Web Analyzer is a bit different from its counterpart front end, the BEx Analyzer. In the BEx Analyzer, adding a characteristic or other component to the format involves using the context menu or a dropdown and then inserting the characteristic by drilling down or across with the options offered in the menu or using the Drag and Drop option. With the BEx Web Analyzer, we have the same options. The Drag and Drop option is a user-friendly option that allows you to navigate using your cursor and position the characteristic where you want it. In the BEx Analyzer depending on the option for navigation that you choose, you may have had to take several navigational steps before you could get the characteristic in exactly the correct position. With the ability to drag and drop, you can format the report with one movement—and more intuitively. The following illustration shows the movement of Distribution Channel from within the rows of the query to a position outside of the query in the free characteristics.

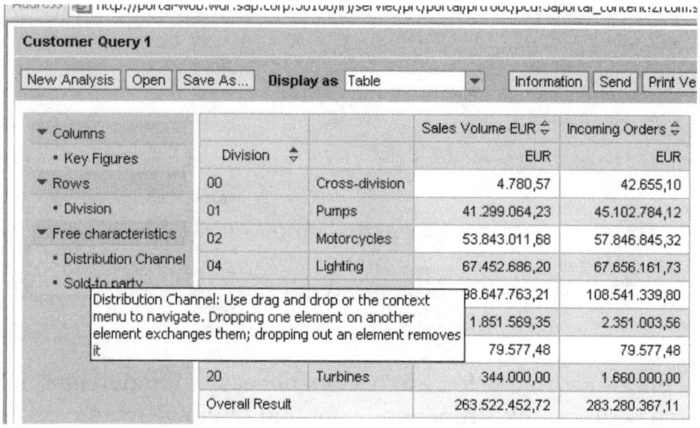

Again, this is done with a drag-and-drop operation and not via a context menu, although both methods are available for use. Specifically, with drag and drop, the user can perform the following actions:

- Drag items from one section of the navigation block to another, such as from rows to columns, or from rows or columns to free characteristics.

- Drag items from the navigational block directly to the rows or columns of the analysis results.

- Drag characteristics to the filter area to immediately perform the corresponding filtering of the results.

- Drag items out of the analysis grid to remove them from the analysis.

This is a similarity between the two front ends. We will find differences between the two front ends and they will become more apparent as we go through the list of navigation functions of the BEx Web Analyzer.

Toolbar Functionality

The best approach to reviewing these options is to move from left to right on the Web Analyzer toolbar. The following illustration shows the initial view of a web-based query. Each option on the toolbar will open up a dialog box with its own specific components. In this list of options, the least conspicuous one is the most useful—that being the Settings link at the far right side of the list.

				Sales Volume EUR ⇕	Incoming Orders ⇕
	Division ⇕	Distribution Channel ⇕		EUR	EUR
00	Cross-division	10	Final customer sales	0,00	9.000,00
		12	Sold for resale	0,00	25.500,00
		14	Service	4.780,57	8.155,10
		Result		4.780,57	42.655,10
01	Pumps	10	Final customer sales	41.299.064,23	45.102.784,12
		Result		41.299.064,23	45.102.784,12
02	Motorcycles	12	Sold for resale	53.843.011,68	57.846.845,32
		Result		53.843.011,68	57.846.845,32
04	Lighting	12	Sold for resale	67.452.686,20	67.656.161,73
		Result		67.452.686,20	67.656.161,73
07	High Tech	10	Final customer sales	45.437.498,23	52.428.399,72
		12	Sold for resale	53.192.732,78	56.095.407,88
		14	Service	17.532,20	17.532,20
		16	Factory sales	0,00	0,00
		Result		98.647.763,21	108.541.339,80
08	Service	14	Service	1.851.569,35	2.351.003,56
		Result		1.851.569,35	2.351.003,56

Copyright by SAP AG

All the other options across the top are reasonably easy to understand in terms of what they will do, but the Settings link's function is not that obvious. In any case, using the pushbuttons available in the BEx Web Analyzer, you can quickly navigate to important functions that perform convenient ad-hoc analysis of your business data. You can also use the navigation pane and context menu to access a variety of analysis functions.

New Analysis   You use this pushbutton to create a new ad-hoc analysis by first selecting a data provider to form the basis of your analysis. You can select data providers from a BI system or from a non-SAP data source. You make this selection in the System dropdown box from the resulting dialog box. Data providers of this type can be queries, query views, or InfoProviders, which you can select from the History, Favorites, Roles, or InfoArea view. In one of these views, select the required data provider and choose OK. The data is displayed in the way you selected in the Display As dropdown box. Non-SAP data providers are query views or InfoProviders, which you can select from the InfoArea view. In this view, select the required data provider and choose OK. The data is displayed in the way you selected in the Display As dropdown box. The following illustration shows these options in the dialog box accessed by clicking the New Analysis button.

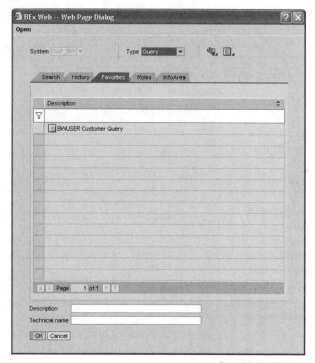

Copyright by SAP AG

Table 15-1 details the options in the dialog box and their functionality.

NOTE   *A query view involves saving a specific view of a query and executing that view rather than executing the entire query. A query view is a version of a basic query. It can be used in the BEx Analyzer, BEx Web Analyzer, and the WAD. To clarify a bit more about the "saved view"— a query view is updated dynamically with new data at the time of execution and the "saved view" refers to the structure of the display.*

Tab	Description	Use and Functionality
Search	Search process	Type in the technical name or description of the query, query view, or InfoProvider (based on the parameter at the top of the dialog box). Use either the technical name or description to find the object.
History	List of queries, InfoProviders, or views	The historical list of queries, InfoProviders, or views that the user has worked with in the past. This relies on the same functionality as the BEx Analyzer—namely the DataStore object that stores the historical activities of the business user.
Favorites	Favorites list	Any query or query view that is stored in the Favorites list during the Save process.
Roles	Roles assigned to the business user	Any role attached to the business user can be viewed from here. This allows access to all the queries, query views, and other objects assigned to the role.
InfoArea	InfoArea list	This option may not be available to all business users due to authorization restrictions. If it's available, the user has access to all the InfoProviders and in turn has access to all the queries and query views in the system or for specific areas allowed.

TABLE 15-1   Functionality in the New Analysis Dialog Box for the BEx Web Analyzer

As the illustration at right shows, in the InfoArea of the New Analysis dialog box, navigation is accomplished by double-clicking each of the specific areas. In this example, the drilldown is InfoArea | Financial Management & Controlling | Financial Accounting | General Ledger Accounting | General Ledger: Transactional Figures. From here you can choose the query required.

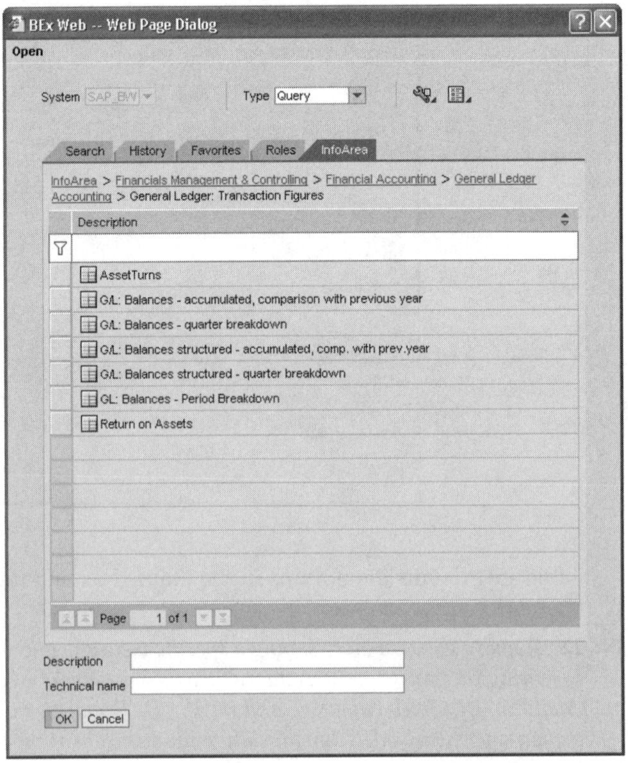

Open   This option allows you to open saved ad-hoc analyses from the Portal Favorites folder, the BEx Portfolio view, or the My BEx Portfolio view. This functionality is similar to the

New Analysis option, but is not as robust. The following illustration shows a view of this function.

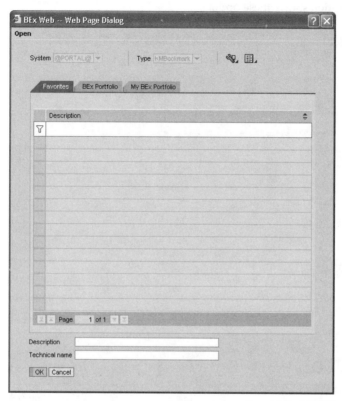

Copyright by SAP AG

Save As   You can save the results of your ad-hoc analysis with an appropriate name in your Portal Favorites folder or in the BEx Portfolio. This operation saves the type of data display (table, graphic, or table and graphic) in addition to the navigational state of the data. To access the saved results of your ad-hoc analysis again, choose Open. To save the navigational and drilldown state of the data as a new query view, choose Save View in the context menu of the Web Application. You can use the query iView created in this way as a data provider for other BI applications. Within the BEx Web Analyzer, you have two options for saving the results of the ad-hoc analyses. The first option permits users to leverage the integration of BI with the NetWeaver Portal to save their results using the Save button in either the BEx Portfolio or the Favorites portion of the Knowledge Management Area. When this option is used, the complete layout of the ad-hoc analysis is saved. Results saved to the Portal can be accessed using the Open button from the Web Analyzer. Using the Save As button, users can store various versions of their analysis in the KM folders on the Portal. The second option allows the users to save their ad-hoc analysis results as a BEx query view via the context menu. These BEx query views can then be used as data providers for BEx Web Applications or BEx reports. The BEx query view contains the navigation status of the analysis, but does not contain information about the layout. This is saved in the BI Metadata Repository. The user can access query views saved on third-party BI data as well as SAP NetWeaver BI data. The following illustration shows these options.

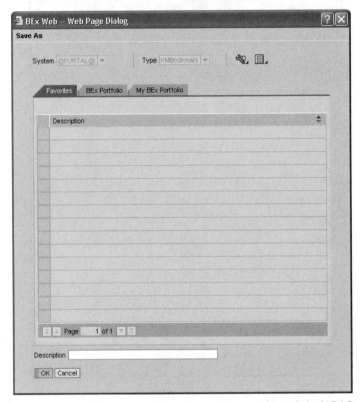

Display As You determine the type of display for the data using the dropdown box next to Display As. You can choose from the following options for displaying the data:

- Table
- Graphic
- Table and Graphic

The following illustration shows these options.

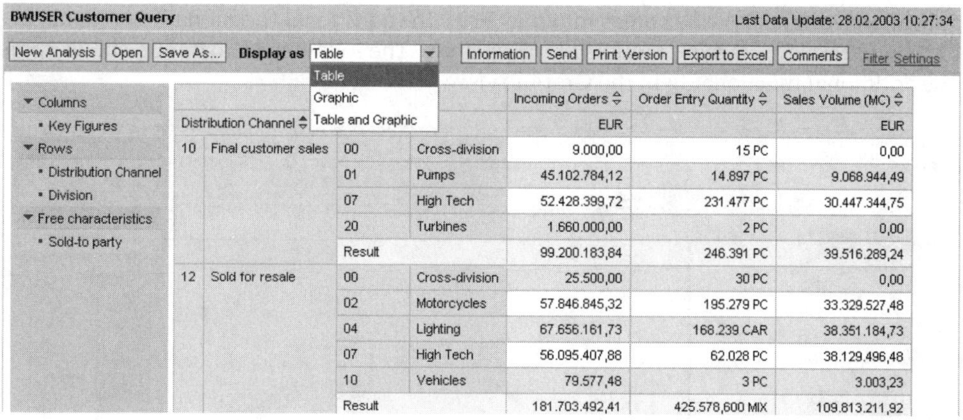

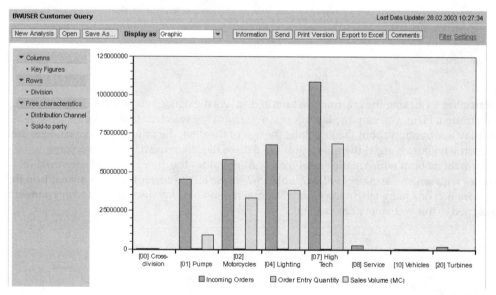

Distribution Channel		Division		Incoming Orders EUR	Order Entry Quantity	Sales Volume (MC) EUR
10	Final customer sales	00	Cross-division	9.000,00	15 PC	0,00
		01	Pumps	45.102.784,12	14.897 PC	9.068.944,49
		07	High Tech	52.428.399,72	231.477 PC	30.447.344,75
		20	Turbines	1.660.000,00	2 PC	0,00
		Result		99.200.183,84	246.391 PC	39.516.289,24
12	Sold for resale	00	Cross-division	25.500,00	30 PC	0,00
		02	Motorcycles	57.846.845,32	195.279 PC	33.329.527,48
		04	Lighting	67.656.161,73	168.239 CAR	38.351.184,73
		07	High Tech	56.095.407,88	62.028 PC	38.129.496,48
		10	Vehicles	79.577,48	3 PC	3.003,23
		Result		181.703.492,41	425.578,600 MIX	109.813.211,92

Copyright by SAP AG

Depending on the amount of information in the table, the use of graphics can be helpful. The following illustration shows the use of a graphic with just the division information displayed.

Copyright by SAP AG

If you were to try to create a graphic with Sold-to party and Division, too much information would be displayed and the graphic would be useless. This is where the use of the Web Application Designer (WAD) comes into play, with the additional functionality of managing the size and format of larger amounts of information. The following illustration shows some of the additional functionality in the Graphic view.

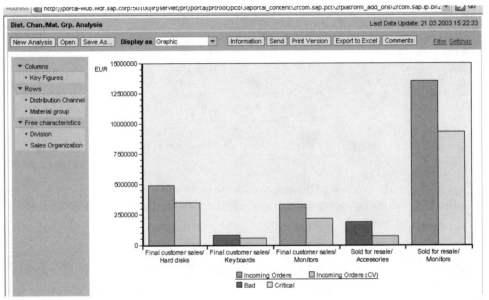

Copyright by SAP AG

Information   Clicking the Information button displays the dialog box shown in the following illustration. Here, you can display information about the selected data provider, as well as display information about the key date, the age of the data, the time of the last change, the person who last changed the query, and the date of the last refresh. You also receive information about which static and dynamic filter values the query has and the variable values with which the query is filled. Table 15-2 shows all the current settings available in the Information on Query tab. In the Query Documentation tab, any documentation or comments assigned to this web query are available.

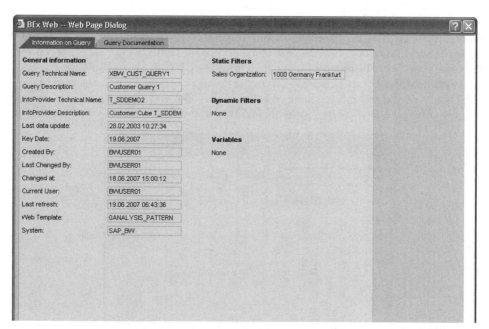

Copyright by SAP AG

Setting	Functionality and Use
Query Technical Name and Description	The saved technical name of the query and current query description.
Last Data Update	The last time the data was uploaded to the InfoProvider.
InfoProvider Technical Name and Description	The technical name of the InfoProvider of this query and the description of the InfoProvider.
Key Date	Key date of the query. This setting controls the view of the characteristic values shown in the query. Depending on the time dependency of the master data, this setting may create different views of the data.
Created By and Last Changed By	The user who created the query and the user who last changed it.
Changed At	The date that the change occurred.
Current User	The current user.
Last Refresh	The date that the query was last refreshed (executed).
Web Template	The technical name of the web template being used.
System	The system identifier.
Static Filters, Dynamic Filters, and Variables	The list of static filters (within the Filter portion of the Query Designer), dynamic filters (free characteristics or other filters in the rows or columns), and variables used in the query.

TABLE 15-2   Information Available on the Information Tab of the Web Analyzer

Send   You use the Send button to open the Broadcasting Wizard and access the information-broadcasting functions to broadcast your ad-hoc analysis. This functionality was discussed in Chapters 11 and 12. The option in this case offers only some of the functionality. The complete distribution process can be found by using the Information Broadcaster (The complete Information Broadcaster can be accessed from the Wizard by using the link assigned to the 'HERE' button on the dialog box, as shown below.). The following illustration shows the initial step in this process. A series of four steps are involved in the setup, and each is self explanatory.

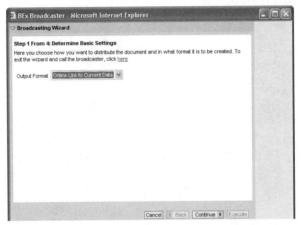

Copyright by SAP AG

Print Version   Using the Print Version button, you can make settings for a print version of your ad-hoc analysis. For example, you can set the format for the print version and define whether a header is to appear on the pages printed. When you have made your settings and have chosen OK, a PDF document is generated, which you can then print. The following illustration shows the dialog box with all the settings available.

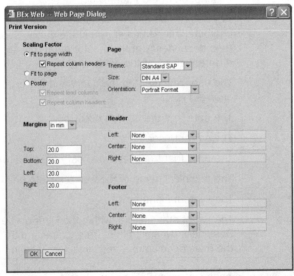

Copyright by SAP AG

As you can see, the settings are basic. Additional functionality can be gained by using the Print function, discussed in the previous chapter. The options here involve margins for the pages, scaling factors, page sizing, header information and format, and footer information and format.

Export to Excel   Using Export to Excel, you can export the query result to Microsoft Excel. The query data is displayed in the same way as queries are displayed in the BEx Analyzer. The filter restrictions and the data in the table are the same as in the Web Analyzer. Exceptions are highlighted in color in the same way as they are on the Web. This allows you to continue to edit the data using the Microsoft Excel functions. As you can see in the following illustration, when the Export to Excel option is executed, the initial prompt is to open, save, or cancel the download to Excel.

NOTE   *In the current Support Package for the Web Analyzer, the Excel version needs to be later than Excel 2000. Although this and other versions of Excel can be used with some additional configuration, doing so is not best business practice.*

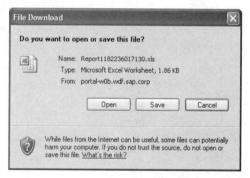

Copyright by SAP AG

Comments   You can use this pushbutton to create comments for the data provider. The options in the resulting dialog box are to create a comment, create a formatted text document, or upload a document from another source. These are the supported document formats available in this function. In the Document function, approximately 25 to 30 different types of documents are supported. The illustration on the right shows this functionality.

The next two items are the Filter and Settings links. These are referred to as *link functions*. Numerous options, specifically in the Settings area, can be very valuable in the analysis and flexibility of the BEx Web Analyzer for the business user. The Settings option offers the ability to adjust the table view, enhance the graphics, create new exceptions and conditions, and adjust the

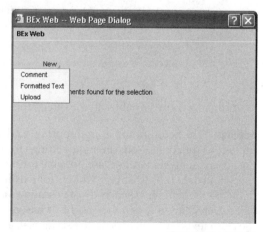

Copyright by SAP AG

format of the query. These are all functions you have seen before with the BEx Analyzer, except for the ability to create conditions and exceptions. We have already discussed, in detail, the configuration of these two options, but in the process of using the Exception Wizard and the Condition Wizard in the BEx Web Analyzer, additional capabilities are available, which we will discuss.

Filter   You use this link to display the Filter pane. The characteristics you can use for filtering are displayed in the Filter pane. You can enter characteristic values to be used for filtering for each characteristic used in the data provider. There is also the possibility of filtering the key figures that appear in the query. This is an excellent approach to manipulating the data all from one screen, rather than having to use the context menu or the drag-and-drop process. The following illustration shows the screen that appears once the Filter link is executed.

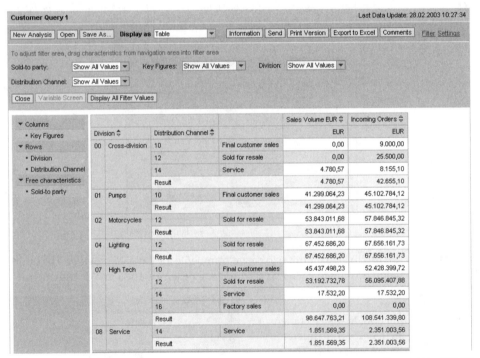

Copyright by SAP AG

If there are any variables in the query, these will also be available from this view.

Settings   The Settings link is an important and useful option. Using this link, you can access numerous functions. You can make settings for the table, graphic, and data provider used for the ad-hoc analysis. Settings are possible for the layout (display alternating styles for table rows) and data cells (display symbols for existing InfoProvider documents). You can also use data-specific settings (such as display scaling factors) for the table. You have settings for the Chart web item on which the graphic is based (such as chart-type selections) and settings for the chart texts (such as overwrite axis labels), as well as data-specific settings (such as swap axes for display) for the graphic. You can make various settings for the data provider at runtime. For example, you can define where the results are to be displayed in the table. You can also display existing exceptions and conditions for the data provider or define new exceptions and conditions in a step-by-step process. When you choose Insert on the Exceptions tab page, you navigate to a new browser window in which you are guided through the process of creating new exceptions step by step. You can display details for existing exceptions, change their status, or delete them. The Condition component is also available from this area in the "setting" screen. When you choose Insert on the Conditions tabbed page, you navigate to a new browser window in which you are guided through the process of creating new conditions step by step. You can display details for existing conditions, change their status, or delete them. Table 15-3 outlines all the options for Settings.

Tab	Description	Use and Functionality
Table (see the first of the following illustrations)	Layout: Alternative Table Row Styles	Used if alternative table row colors are required. This will generate the blue/white format of the rows.
	Cell-Specific Settings: Exception Visualization	Settings include Color, Symbol, Symbol and Text, and Text and Symbol. This option effects the use of the Exception function and manages the format of the exception in the query.
	Cell-Specific Settings: Document Icons for Data, MetaData, and Master Data	Displays the document icon in the web query.
	Data-Specific Settings: Display Repeated Texts	Used if repeated text is needed in the query.
	Data-Specific Settings: Scaling Factors Visible	Allows the display of the scaling factor for key figures.
Graphic (see the second of the following illustrations)	Chart Settings: Chart Type	Web Analyzer supports approximately 30 different chart types, including columns, pie, stacked lines, bar charts. (All the chart types are typically found in Excel.)
	Chart Settings: Legend Type	The following settings are available: **None** None. **DataTable** Displays the information in the legend directly from the database table information from the InfoProvider. **Chart Legend Position** Uses the legend position for the information display. Also generates the view of only the naming convention for the legend. **Legend Only** No chart, only the legend.

TABLE 15-3   Functionality in the Settings Tab for the Web Analyzer

Tab	Description	Use and Functionality
	Chart Settings: Chart Legend Position	In connection with the Chart Legend Position for Legend Type, this option positions the legend on the screen (North, South, East, West, and so on.)
	Chart Texts: Manual Axis Description	This option is used to assign the text to the axis manually for both the primary category and value axis and the secondary category and value axis.
	Chart Texts: Manual Axis Label	This option is used to assign the label to the axis for the primary and secondary category and value axis.
	Data-Specific Settings: Swap Display Axes, Result Visible, Show Expanded Hierarchy Nodes	The following settings are available: **Swap Display Axes** This option swaps the characteristic format for the X-axis. For example, rather than the data being displayed by division, the display would use the key figures for the X-axis and the divisions as columns. **Result Visible** The results for each column are displayed while the user scrolls across them with the cursor. **Show Expanded Hierarchy Nodes** If a hierarchy is used with the Web Analyzer, this option allows the user to manage the display of the levels of the hierarchy nodes.
Exceptions	Access to Exception Wizard	(See the discussion following this table.)
Conditions	Access to Exception Wizard	(See the discussion following this table.)
Data Provider (see the third of the following illustrations)	Data Formatting: Display Columns hierarchically and...	This option offers management at the column level of the initial drilldown for display. If chosen, the additional field to complete the drilldown appears. Fill in this field with the option of whether to drilldown to the key figures or not.
	Data Formatting: Display Rows hierarchically and...	This option offers management at the row level of the initial drilldown for display. If chosen, the additional field to complete the drilldown appears. Fill in this field with the option of whether to drilldown to the specific characteristic or not. It will also create a hierarchical view of the data (additional tabs for lower level characteristics).

TABLE 15-3   Functionality in the Settings Tab for the Web Analyzer (*continued*)

Tab	Description	Use and Functionality
	Number Format: Result Position	Displays the results using one of the following settings: Bottom/Right, Top/Left, Bottom/Left, Top/Left.
	Number Format: Display of +/− signs	Displays the format of numbers as −5, 5−, or (5).
	Number Format: Display of zeroes	Displays zeroes with currency/unit, without currency/unit, as empty cells, as a custom string. (With this option, an additional field appears that allows the business user to enter a symbol.)
	Zero Suppression: Apply Suppression to Rows, Apply Suppression to Columns	Defines the display of zeroes to the columns and rows (the view with zeroes or without).
	Zero Suppression for Structure Key Figures	Zero suppression for key figures within a structure.

TABLE 15-3   Functionality in the Settings Tab for the Web Analyzer (*continued*)

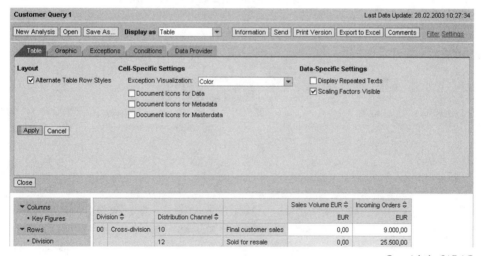

Copyright by SAP AG

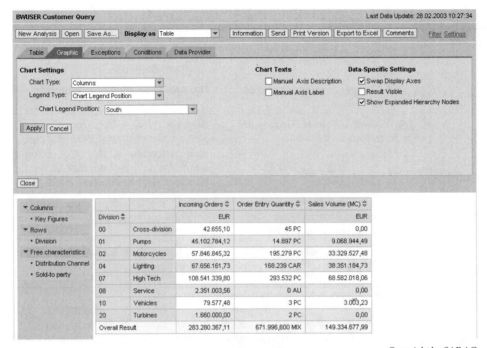

Copyright by SAP AG

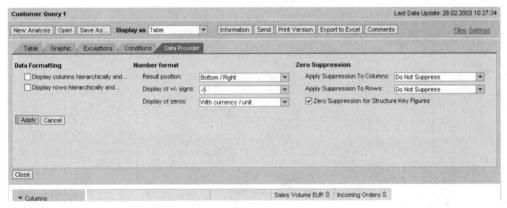

Copyright by SAP AG

The two tabs not explained in detail in Table 15-3 are Conditions and Exceptions. Because some interesting differences exist between the display of the exceptions and conditions in the BEx Analyzer and the BEx Web Analyzer, a more detailed discussion of the options and components of these two wizards is in order. Because we have already reviewed the concepts of both components in a previous chapter, the initial overview can be eliminated. As you can see, both wizards can be launched from their associated tabbed pages in the Settings area. Also, both wizards lead the user through their various steps, and the user can move backward in this process to adjust or correct a previous step.

Let's look at the Exception Wizard first. It has six steps. To create an exception in the BEx Web Analyzer, choose the Settings link and then in the Exceptions tab click the Add button to start the process. The following illustration shows the initial step, which is to choose an exception type—either Status or Trend.

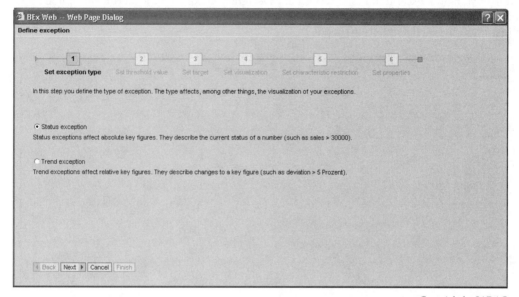

NOTE *Exceptions created via the Exception Wizard can be saved in the KM folder in the Portal or they can be broadcast to other parties. However, exceptions created with the Exception Wizard in the Web Analyzer do not become a part of either the query or the query view definition. The only way to make an exception a permanent part of the query or query view definition would be to create the exception using the BEx Query Designer.*

The Status exception operates on absolute key figures. For example, a status exception is similar to a benchmark identified for Sales Volume – Sales Volume of Greater Than $1,000,000.00. A Trend exception operates on relative key figures. For example, a key figure might be considered a Trend exception if the deviation of the key figure is greater than a 5% variance.

When the exception type is chosen, the subsequent wizard screens adapt to that choice. For example, on the fourth step of the wizard, Set Visualization, the choice for a status exception is a traffic light icon (normal view), whereas the choice for a trend exception is an arrow icon. This arrow icon is very similar to some of the functionality available in the SEM-CPM component Balanced Scorecard, where the trend of the analysis can be highlighted rather than just the position of the process. Thus, analysis can be focused on the trending process, and you can see additional information on the indicator rather than on the absolute position of a specific value.

Step 2 of the wizard is where the setup of the threshold values takes place. The user makes the settings for the key figure threshold values. A key figure is chosen for the exception definition, or all the key figures are involved in the exception. In addition, the timing of the exception evaluation can be before or after any local calculations such as formulas in queries or local calculations created in the BEx web query. The additional setup of the threshold values for the alert levels and the operators is exactly the same as if you were creating the exception in the BEx Query Designer. There are nine alert levels: three in the Good alert, three in the Critical alert, and three in the Defective alert. The following illustration shows the details in Step 2.

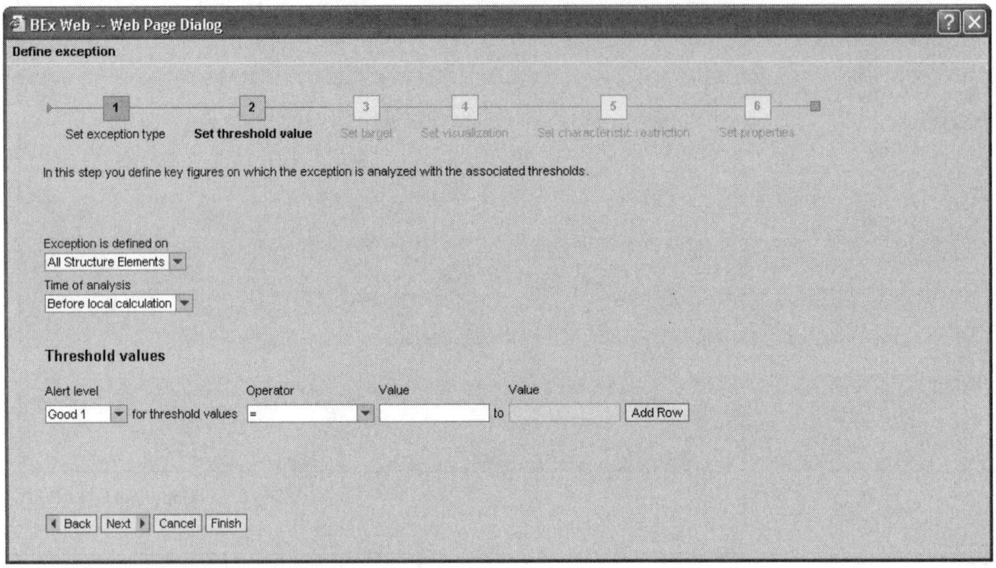

In Step 3 of the Exception Wizard, the user can choose whether the result of the exception is applied to the data cells of an analysis. If this choice is made, the user can make a subsequent choice of which data cells are affected. The choices are shown in Table 15-4.

Define Exception	Description and Functionality
Evaluated structure element	The key figures chosen for a specific exception in the prior step of the wizard. This is the most common setting.
Following structure element	This option allows you to evaluate one key figure but apply the color emphasis to a different key figure.
All structure elements	With this option, the color highlighting from an exception is applied to all key figures in the analysis.

TABLE 15-4 Options for Step 3 in the Exception Wizard

Step 3 is shown in the first of the following illustrations, and an example of the three options listed in Table 15-4 is shown in the second illustration. This is for the initial setting in this screen.

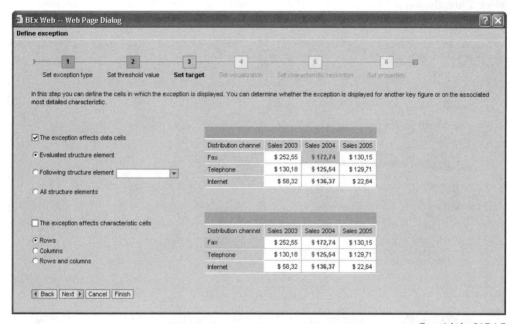

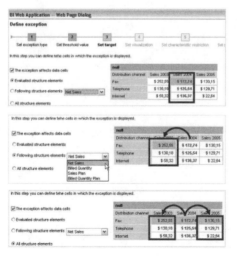

The exception affects the data cells only for the evaluated structure element chosen in step 2 of the wizard.

The exception will be determined from the structure element chosen in step 2 but affects the data cells of another key figure (e.g. the exception will be determined from a deviation but applied for the absolute key figure "Revenue").

The exception will be applied to the data cells for all available key figures.

The Exception Affects Characteristic Cells option has three settings: Rows, Columns, or Rows and Columns. This step is not as involved as the earlier indicator. Depending on what characteristic cell you would like to highlight, you can use either the rows or columns.

Step 4 involves the visualization properties of the exception. The first of the following illustrations shows the options available. The Background Color option is displayed, but there are also the options to have just the symbol in the cell and not the value, to use both the symbol and the value (or the Value and the Symbol). The second illustration shows the option Symbol and Value, just as another example of the outcome.

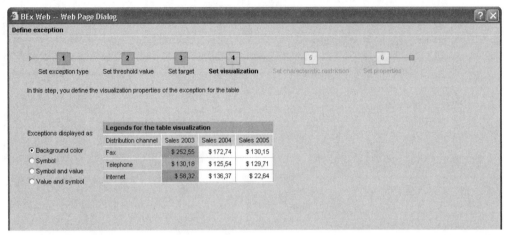

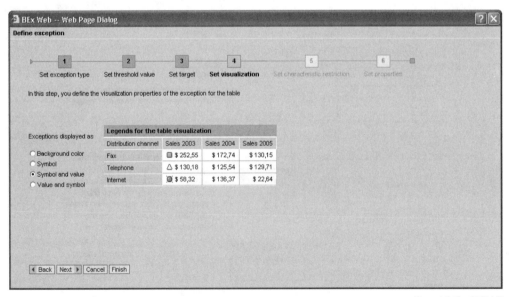

As mentioned, if the setting in Step 2 is Static, the traffic light icon is displayed, but if Trend is chosen, the symbol will be an arrow.

Step 5 is for setting the characteristic restriction against the characteristics in the analysis. This step has several options for the characteristic restriction:

- All values.
- Standard.
- Only the results.
- Everything except the results.
- A fixed value. (With this option, you specify the value that will be used in the exception.)
- A fixed hierarchy level. (With this option, you specify the level that will be used in the exception.)

The following illustration shows this steps detail. Finally, in Step 6, the properties of the exception are assigned. The two settings in this screen are for the Exception Is Active option; therefore, the exception will be immediately applied before the display of the results and the description of the exception.

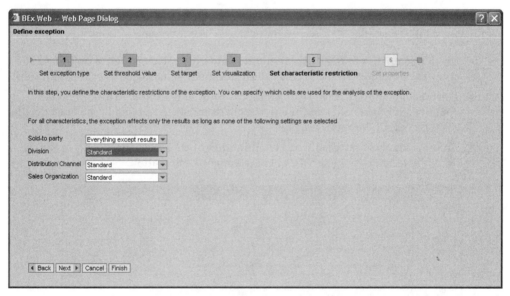

In the case of the Condition Wizard, only four steps are involved. In the first step of the Condition Wizard, the condition type is set—either Ranked List Criterion, Threshold Value Condition, or Mixed Condition. Table 15-5 provides the description and functionality of each setting. As in the Exception Wizard, depending on the setting in this step, the following step—Set Condition Parameters (Step 2)—will change to fit the requirements.

Condition Type	Description	Functionality Required in Step 2
Ranked List Criterion	Use this option to define conditions such as Top %, Top N, Bottom %, and Bottom N.	Required for this type. Identify the key figure to be affected. Operators are limited to TOP and BOTTOM for %, N, and Total. The final field, Value, requires a value for this option.
Threshold Value Condition	Use this option to define threshold values—for example, sales volume between 100,000 and 1,000,000.	Required for this type. Identify the key figure to be affected. Operators are limited to =, <>, >=, >, <=, <, [], and][. Final field, Value, requires a set of values for each option.
Mixed Condition		Required for this type. Identify the key figure to be affected. Operators available include all the ones for the other options. The final field, Value, requires a set of values for each option.

TABLE 15-5 Settings for the Condition Wizard in the BEx Web Analyzer

The following illustration shows step 1 of the Condition Wizard. Once Steps 1 and 2 are set up, you set the characteristic assignment in Step 3. The following options are available:

- **All characteristics in the drilldown independently**   This option is optimized for range list conditions, but can be used for threshold values with relevant values.

- **The most detailed characteristic along the rows or columns**   This option is optimized for threshold conditions. The characteristic is applied to the most detailed characteristic of the specified axis.

- **An individual characteristic or a combination of characteristics**   This option is used to select any characteristic or characteristic combination.

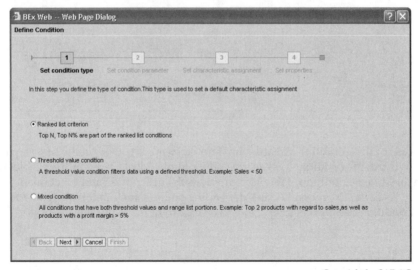

The following illustration shows the details of this step. Under each of the options you'll find an explanation of what the business user will see as an outcome.

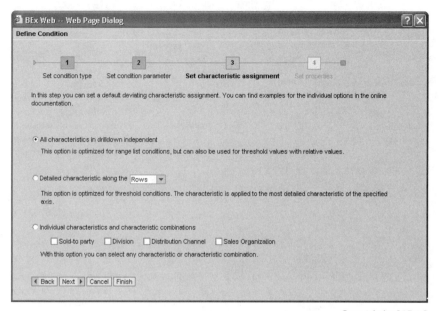

Finally, Step 4 is similar to the final step in the Exceptions Wizard. You identify whether the condition will be immediately active, whether the business user will activate it after execution of the query, and provide a description of the condition. The Toggle State button can be used to switch from an active to inactive state of a condition or exception.

NOTE *If you are working with complex conditions and exceptions, it may be better to deactivate them initially and have the business user activate them as needed. This will result in fewer concerns regarding the information that shows up with the initial processing of the query.*

Functionality in the Navigational Filter Pane

The navigation pane displays the navigational state of the data provider. All the characteristics and structures of the data provider are listed. You can alter the navigational state to analyze your data by dragging characteristics or structures to an axis (rows or columns) of the table (or you can remove them). You can swap axes in the navigation pane using drag and drop, and the table changes accordingly. You can also drag characteristics to the filter pane using drag and drop. Much of the functionality and activities in this section are consistent with the

BEx Analyzer. You can refer to Chapter 3 for a more detailed analysis. The following two illustrations show the details of the context menu options.

Copyright by SAP AG

Copyright by SAP AG

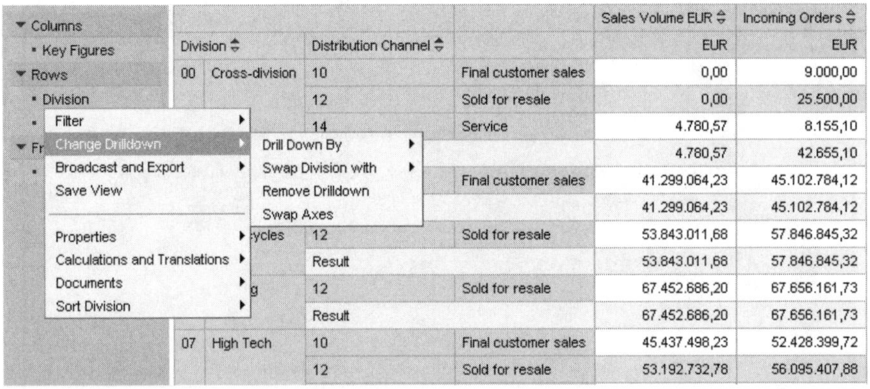

Navigation in a Web Template Query

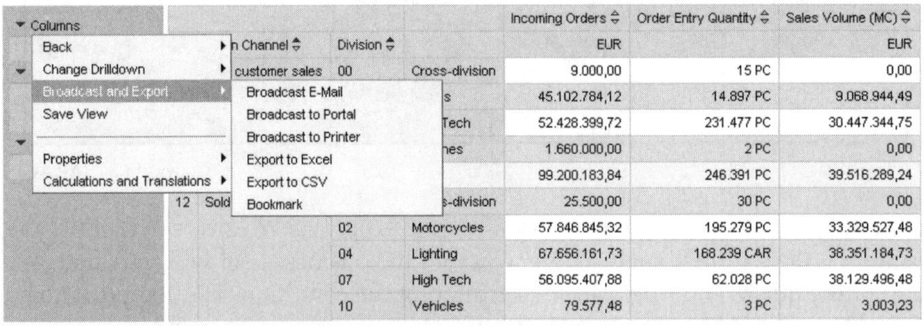

The Web Application Designer (WAD) toolset used to create web-based queries is very powerful. The functionality available in the WAD extends the BEx Web Analyzer well beyond what we have reviewed in the previous sections of this chapter. A full discussion and development of the functionality can be found in the next chapter, but a high-level discussion of some of the functionality is warranted here, specifically concerning the navigational options.

NOTE *Web items are objects in the WAD that are used to support the display of graphs, charts, button groups, maps, and other objects on the Web. They contain the HTML that will support these objects on the Web.*

Over 50 different web items can be used to develop the WAD templates and queries. Therefore, several examples of the use of these functions and the results of their configuration are provided in this section. Again, this is just a sample of the many options available for WAD-supported queries.

The first example is a basic view of a WAD-created query that has a navigation panel, a dropdown box for Sold-to party, and a tab strip with a chart and table supported. The next illustration shows the view of this WAD query. The format and positioning of these objects can be adjusted as the business user's needs change.

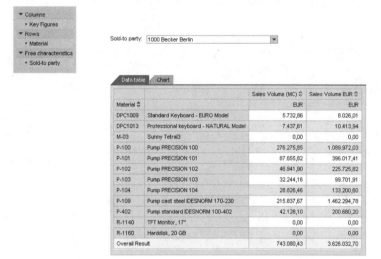

Copyright by SAP AG

The final format of each of the WAD-supported queries depends on the business user and whether they believe that a tab strip with a table and chart is easier and more flexible to use than a dropdown box with a chart and table available. The result will be the replacement of the table with the chart, and vice versa, rather than toggling from tab to tab. The following illustration shows the switch from the table to the chart using the tab strip and the details of the sales volume by Sold-to party.

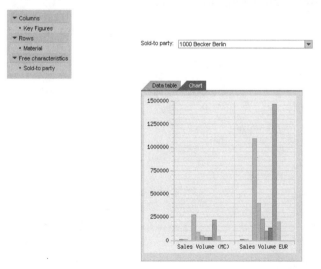

Copyright by SAP AG

In this example, the chart shows the key figures as groupings for Sales Volume and Material. The legend, in this case, should be more clearly defined to tell the business user that the material is the other object on the X-axis. This is an example of some of the additional setup required with WAD queries. Therefore, each color represents a material from the table. The following illustration shows that the drilldown in a WAD query is very similar to that in a BEx web query.

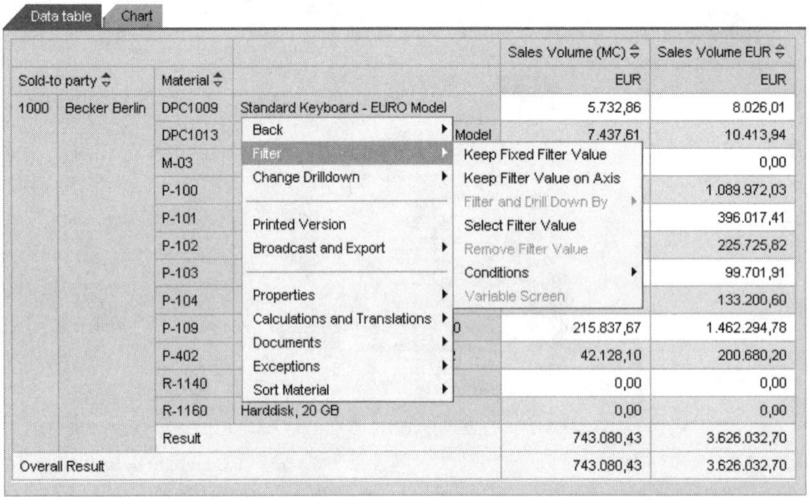

			Sales Volume (MC) ⇕	Sales Volume EUR ⇕
Sold-to party ⇕	Material ⇕		EUR	EUR
1000 Becker Berlin	DPC1009	Standard Keyboard - EURO Model	5.732,86	8.026,01
	DPC1013	Back ▶ Model	7.437,61	10.413,94
	M-03	Filter ▶ Keep Fixed Filter Value		0,00
	P-100	Change Drilldown ▶ Keep Filter Value on Axis		1.089.972,03
	P-101	Filter and Drill Down By ▶		396.017,41
	P-102	Printed Version Select Filter Value		225.725,82
	P-103	Broadcast and Export ▶ Remove Filter Value		99.701,91
	P-104	Conditions ▶		133.200,60
	P-109	Properties ▶ Variable Screen		
	P-402	Calculations and Translations ▶ 0	215.837,67	1.462.294,78
	R-1140	Documents ▶	42.128,10	200.680,20
	R-1160	Exceptions ▶	0,00	0,00
		Sort Material ▶	0,00	0,00
		Harddisk, 20 GB		
	Result		743.080,43	3.626.032,70
Overall Result			743.080,43	3.626.032,70

Copyright by SAP AG

Other functions can be added to the context menu with the WAD query, and other changes can be made as well. For example, the context menu can be split into a basic view and an advanced view, with some of the more advanced functions on a separate view. The next illustration shows additional functionality in one of the context menu options—the ability to use the display attributes of the characteristic 0MATERIAL.

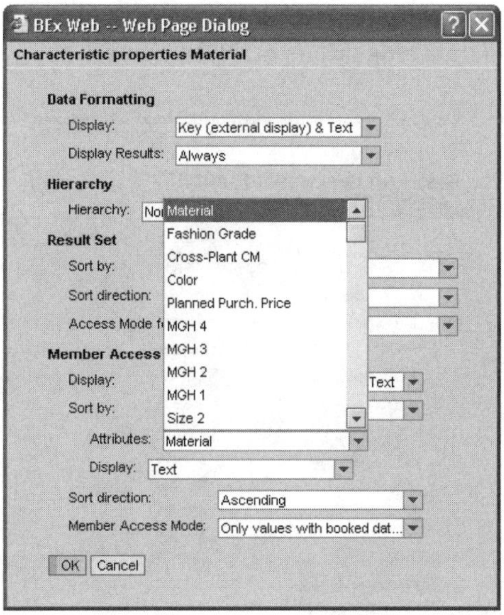

Copyright by SAP AG

This shows the list of attributes available for display purposes, as well as the ability to sort, change the display format, and adjust the drilldown of the specific members of the list. Another example of the functionality of the WAD query is displayed in the following illustration.

Copyright by SAP AG

In this web query, the use of multiple tabs has been enhanced. The tabs have been given more business-oriented naming conventions, and the information important to the business user about the data is displayed at the bottom of the query. Also, a logo is assigned to the web template query. The following illustration shows the second tab and a nicely structured query with information formatted with the months in the rows and the net value of incoming orders and cost of incoming orders in the columns.

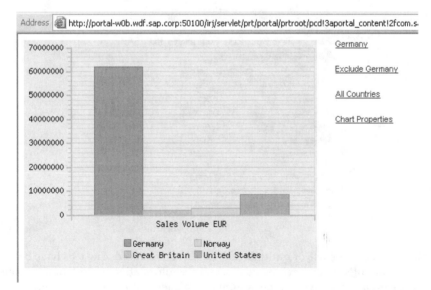

Calendar Year/Month ⇕	Distribution Channel ⇕	Incoming Orders ⇕ EUR	Incoming Orders (CV) ⇕ EUR
10.2001	Final customer sales	550.962	380.003
	Sold for resale	944.337	625.999
	Result	1.495.299	1.006.002
11.2001	Final customer sales	576.969	397.584
	Sold for resale	1.053.835	702.639
	Result	1.630.804	1.100.222
12.2001	Final customer sales	493.215	340.163
	Sold for resale	934.783	617.860
	Result	1.427.999	958.022
Overall Result		4.554.102	3.064.247

Query Description:	Company Q4 Analysis
InfoProvider Description:	Order Cube
Last data update:	21.03.2003 15:22:33

All discussion surrounding the drilldown functionality is available in this query. Another view of a WAD template query is shown in the following illustration. Graphs are used to enhance the business user's analysis of the information displayed.

The navigation process is based on the use of links on the right side of the graph. Therefore, rather than having to drag and drop a characteristic into the table and the graph changing to the appropriate format (or using the context menu to do the same thing), we are using hyperlinks to accomplish this task. The drilldown effect is shown in the following illustration, where the Germany link is used.

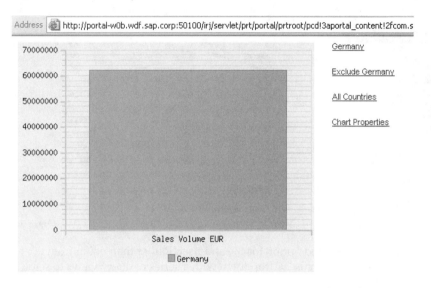

The next illustration shows another view of graphs within the WAD query.

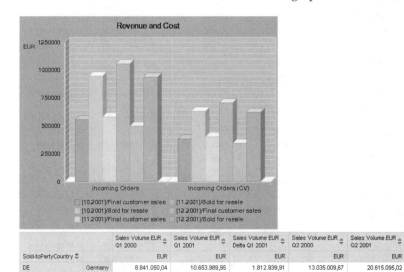

		Sales Volume EUR Q1 2000	Sales Volume EUR Q1 2001	Sales Volume EUR Delta Q1 2001	Sales Volume EUR Q2 2000	Sales Volume EUR Q2 2001	Umsatz Nettowert EUR Delta Q2 2001	Sales Volume EUR Q3 2000
Sold-toPartyCountry		EUR	EUR	EUR	EUR	EUR	EUR	EUR
DE	Germany	8.841.050,04	10.653.989,95	1.812.939,91	13.035.009,67	20.615.095,02	7.580.085,35	13.437.987,65
Overall Result		8.841.050,04	10.653.989,95	1.812.939,91	13.035.009,67	20.615.095,02	7.580.085,35	13.437.987,65

In this format, we incorporate the use of three-dimensional graphics for added value for the business user. As you can see, the format and display is much more dramatic in the 3D view. In addition, query views can be used to help with the performance of the queries. The following illustration shows the use of a set of query views to help with the navigation process in the web query.

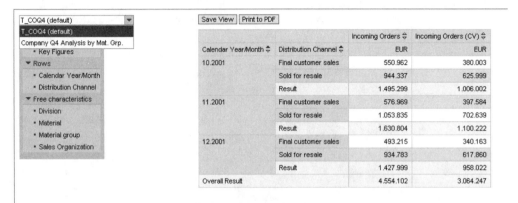

This could be a very good option for the end user. Rather than going from tab to tab to see the other tables, they can use a dropdown with a series of query views to scroll through. In the preceding illustration, the buttons Save View and Print to PDF have been added. Therefore, the business user can create their specific saved views for later analysis and then print them to a PDF format for the hard copy. Another view of WAD query functionality includes the use of the dropdown with additional components for creating a range of values, as shown in the illustration at right. This can be very useful for the analyst because it's faster to use.

Rather than the user having to fill in individual fields for From and To, additional web functionality is used to get them to that point faster by just toggling from month to month. In this case, with the initial choice of month, the From time is fixed, and with the next choice of month, the To time is fixed, thus creating a range of values. Of course, the analyst will need to understand the navigation process, but this is not a difficult task and can be useful for the analysis of month-to-month comparisons. No analysis can be complete without the use of my favorite web item—the Map web item, with the inclusion of the GIS map, as shown next. As you can, see the mapping has been done for several countries in Europe, thus offering a view of the information via a GIS-enabled map of the world.

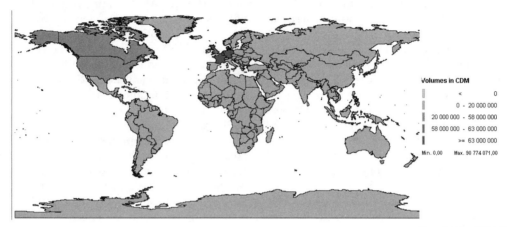

Copyright by SAP AG

Again, more than likely, the same information we have been reviewing is included in this WAD query, but the format and display offers additional analysis information for the company. In this case, the user could highlight a specific country and drill down on that information. There are many more examples of the functionality of the WAD queries, and we could go on for another chapter about the many options. However, this sampling should give you a good idea of the options and results available.

Introduction to the Web Application Designer (WAD)

The Web Application Designer is the toolset at the top of the BW food chain in terms of the different reporting tools SAP offers. This component's list of reporting functionality and options will probably make any customer happy. The WAD offers that finishing touch to all the reports you are ultimately going to deliver to your customer—the management of your company. The end result is a customized and professional report that can be used as a static review of results or a more dynamic drilldown of the information. The WAD is well suited for such tasks.

Design principles must be used while constructing the web template(s) that comprise the Web Application. In addition to this, the developer of the WAD application needs to have a detailed understanding of the sources of the data that will be used. The BI sources that supply data to the Web Applications are BI queries, BI query views, and BI InfoProviders. That being said, the data available to the Web Applications is basically everything in the BI Data Warehouse environment. We will be using mostly BI queries in our discussion and examples because they are the most widely used for supporting the WAD.

The BEx Query is the most used source of data for support of other components in the BI process. The Web Application Designer allows you to use generic OLAP navigation for your

BI data in Web Applications as well as in Business Intelligence cockpits for simple or highly individual scenarios. You can use the Web Application Designer to generate HTML pages that contain BI-specific content such as tables, charts, and maps. Web Applications are based on web templates you create and edit in the Web Application Designer. You can save the web templates and access them from a web browser or a portal. Once they have been executed on the Web, web templates are known as *Web Applications*. The Web Application Designer also allows you to create highly individual scenarios with user-defined interface elements by using standard markup languages and the Web Design API. The BEx Web Applications that are generated are used for data analysis, reporting, and analytical applications on the Web. In addition, the BEx Web Analyzer, which we discussed in a previous section, has been provided as an independent Web Application that can be used to analyze data on an ad-hoc basis. The WAD is another option in the portfolio of reporting tools known as Enterprise Reporting, which allows you to create reports for customized presentation.

The results we are looking for might look something like Figure 15-2, which shows the YTD sales trending process for the current year. Notice that several options are available for reporting and drilling down in the reports. The detailed analysis of the graphic by material is shown at the bottom of the report. This detail goes a step further by showing the sales data by material and by sales organization. This would seem to be a good combination because if we were to try to include the data on the Sales Organization level in the graphic, it may add too much complexity to the screen, thus making the report less effective.

NOTE *The final results from the WAD would probably be delivered a portal, whether in just the BI Portal or some sort of Enterprise Portal (EP), but here we will only be working with the results of the WAD. Chapter 16 will develop the use of the EP.*

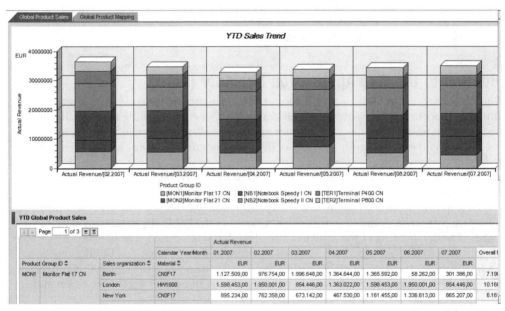

Copyright by SAP AG

FIGURE 15-2 Results of a Web Application Designer report (chart/graphic)

The details concerning the legend are very well spelled out and consistent across the report. The color choices are good, clear, and accurate. As you can see, the final results of WAD reports are not just about the data, but also about the presentation. Many projects encounter issues and setbacks due to the customer not being comfortable with the finished look of the report. A dashboard may not be well received due to issues with coloring or the look and feel. Therefore, this is a good example of a finished product. Finally, the additional tabbed page can be used for detailed reports or other activities such as alerts or documentation.

Another very good example of a finished WAD report is shown in Figure 15-3. In this case, the customer is looking for a more consistent and static reporting view of the data. A number of web items have been used for this display, and as you can see the format has been developed around the sizing of the information and the functionality. Notice that in the upper portion of this report the information is positioned to the left and there are additional activities to the right. The person reviewing this report can immediately execute the process of either printing the data or e-mailing the information to the appropriate individuals. Additional information about the report and comments are listed below the data. The bottom of the report shows the information at a more detailed level with graphs.

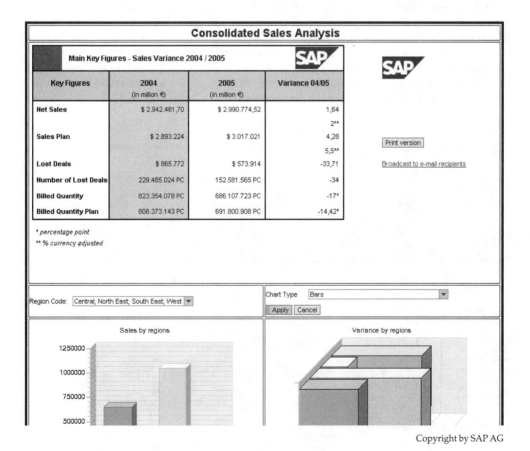

Copyright by SAP AG

FIGURE 15-3   A WAD static report

Alerts

- Sales for COMPUTER 3000 Ltd Down to 450 items
- Invoiced Quantity Product Line 'Promotional Articles' Down 1.0%
- Sales less than 50,000. $ last Month

FIGURE 15-4   A WAD Alerts Monitor report

Notice that the user has the ability to change the view from a bar chart to another type of chart, such as a pie chart. Also, on the left is the option to adjust the display from all the regions to individual ones.

Another example is the basic Alerts Monitor, shown in Figure 15-4. In this case, the customer receives these alerts automatically and executes the link to the reports. They are then able to investigate the detailed information on the alerts.

A final example of a WAD report is shown in Figure 15-5. In this case, the report is broken down into four sections, with navigational capabilities and charts for quick analysis and simulation of the results. The color coding is excellent and spelled out in detail in the legend. A forecast of the billable days and a review of the past billable days are available on the same screen and can be used for additional analysis of the planning process or forecasting process.

A follow-up report is shown in Figure 15-6. We are able to drill down to the lower-level report to see the breakdown by functional group, but the graphs located above are definitely created by a higher-level characteristic combination.

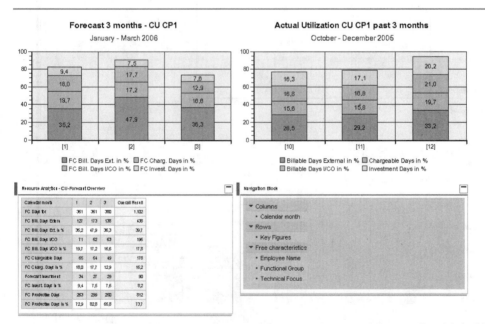

FIGURE 15-5   A WAD navigational report

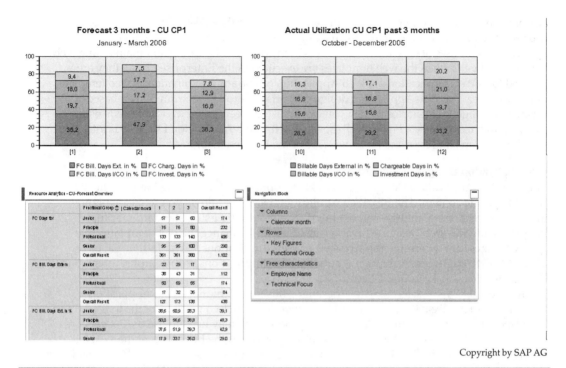

Copyright by SAP AG

FIGURE 15-6   A follow-up WAD navigational report

We could go on forever slicing and dicing the data and views in these reports. You can certainly see that many options and opportunities are available by using the WAD in your reporting strategy.

Overview of the Web Application Designer

In the WAD, the BI sources are linked into the Web Framework through Data Providers. A Data Provider creates a logical connection to the data supplied by a BI source. There is usually a one-to-one relationship between the BI source and the Data Provider. Each Data Provider is independent, so it is possible to use the same BI source for multiple Data Providers if necessary. In general, web items are responsible for formatting the data received from a Data Provider. For example, a Chart web item (explained in Chapter 13) would show the data as a chart, whereas the Navigation Pane web item would list the components of the Data Provider in the format of a navigation window. The assignment of a data provider to a web item is known as *data binding*.

Not every web item formats data for the user of the Web Application. The XML Data Provider Information web item makes the data and metadata of the Web Application available in XML format for use with JavaScript routines. There are other web items, such as Containers and Context Menus, that do not supply data but are used for formatting. Web items serve as the building blocks of the web template due to their ability to represent the Data Provider data in many different formats. A web template is the collection of web items, formatting objects, texts, images, and parameters that define a web page. Web templates can be very basic or customized to the customers' needs. This will depend on their uses in the overall reporting process. Therefore, the main items the user of the WAD needs to be aware of are the applications and uses of each of the web items in the process of creating and maintaining web templates. Finally, when the web templates are executed in the Enterprise Portal, they are referred to as Web Applications. A Web Application can be any combination of web templates linked together. The Web Application design comprises a broad spectrum of web-based Business Intelligence scenarios, which you can adjust to meet your individual needs using standard web technologies. Figure 15-7 shows how the Web Application Designer is integrated into the function landscape and tool landscape of the Business Explorer.

Web Application Designer Components

The BEx Web Application Designer is a desktop application for creating Web Applications with BI-specific content. The BEx Web Application Designer allows you to create highly individual scenarios with user-defined interface elements by using standard markup languages and the Web Design API. You can adjust and enhance the web templates (the XHTML pages that determine the structure of Web Applications) on an individual basis. These XHTML pages are the basis not only for Web Applications with complex interaction, but also for Web Cockpits and iViews.

To access the WAD, select Start | Programs | Business Explorer | Web Application Designer. With NetWeaver 7.0 (2004S) BI, you have access to two versions of the tool—7.0 and 3.x. Depending on your company's migration process, you may need to use the 3.x version rather than the 7.0 version. The path just mentioned accesses the BI version of the WAD. If you want to execute the BW 3.x version of the WAD, you need to select Start | Programs | Business Explorer | Business Explorer (SAP BW 3.x) | Web Application Designer (SAP BW 3.x). The initial screen that is presented to you after logging in to the WAD should be similar to the one shown in Figure 15-8. If you have been working in the WAD, you'll see a list of web

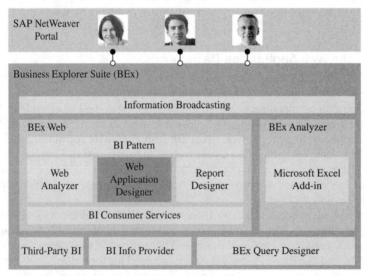

Copyright by SAP AG

FIGURE 15-7 Positioning of the Web Application Designer in the BI Environment

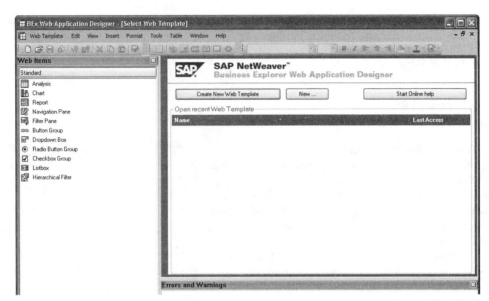

Copyright by SAP AG

FIGURE 15-8 Initial screen for the Web Application Designer

templates you have been using as long as you have that option active in your system. This is a historic list of templates you have worked on before. In this case, we are entering this component of the system for the first time, so we see nothing in the Web Template area.

In order to see all the different sections of the WAD, click the Create New Web Template button to open a new template screen. The following illustration shows this view of the WAD with the New Template screen open.

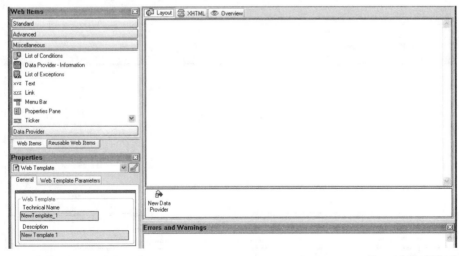

Copyright by SAP AG

The initial view of the BEx Web Application Designer has four different screen areas in addition to the menu and toolbars:

- Web Items
- Web Template
- Properties
- Errors and Warnings

You can adjust the appearance of the Web Application Designer to your requirements. The object on which you are working—namely the web template—is handled differently from the Tools and Help windows. You can show and hide the individual screen areas and toolbars using the View menu option. The location of this option is shown here.

You can move the three toolbars and the Web Items and Properties windows as you require. Depending on where you move an object to, it is anchored or floats freely as a toolbox. The following illustration shows everything in a horizontal position. Because the Web Application Designer is a Multiple

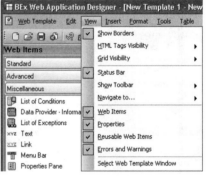

Copyright by SAP AG

Document Interface (MDI) application, you can open and manage different windows with web templates at the same time. You can use the Window menu option to arrange the windows differently: cascading (overlapping), vertically, or horizontally.

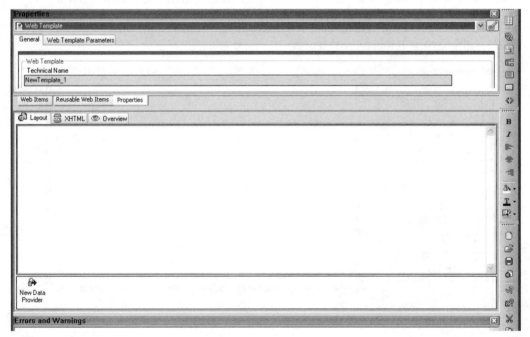

Copyright by SAP AG

Web Item Screen Area   The Web Item screen area provides access to all the available web items and Data Providers as well as a small help section. The web items are segmented into three groupings: Standard, Advanced, and Miscellaneous. Clicking the group heading displays the contents of that group. The following illustration shows the result of choosing the Advanced grouping. Because the web items are the basic building blocks of the web templates, this is a commonly used section and really almost a requirement to get anything to show up in the WAD.

Copyright by SAP AG

NOTE *There are really four sections in this screen area, but the Data Provider section is for assigning, changing, and reviewing Data Providers and doesn't offer additional WAD functionality.*

A web item describes the way in which the data from a Data Provider is displayed, such as in a table (Analysis web item), map (Map web item), or graphic (Chart web item).

Under the Data Provider section, you can create Data Providers of type Filter or type Query View. You can drag the required Data Provider type into your web template. The dialog box for creating Data Providers opens. Underneath the selection for Web Items and Data Provider Maintenance, you see the help area, which provides explanations for the web items and the Data Providers. To display the texts for the respective web item, double-click the web item. To hide the texts, double-click the web item again. Once you have hidden the display of texts and selected a web item by single-clicking, some quick info is displayed for the web item, as shown here.

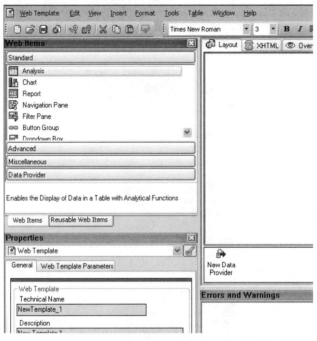

Copyright by SAP AG

Properties Screen Area   The Properties screen area provides access to all the properties of the selected web item or the web template itself. The component you select determines the number of properties associated with the web item. Also, all the parameters are set here. The Properties screen area uses two tabs to segment the properties. The General tab provides access to the Data Provider assignment, if required. The Web Items tab is, in most cases, the more important portion of the screen and shows a listing of the configuration settings of the component. The Properties screen area, which is shown next, is very important to developers. This is where you will spend most of your time configuring the WAD template.

Copyright by SAP AG

In the dropdown box in the header of the screen area, you see the selection for which you want to define properties—for a web template or for specific web items. Depending on your choice in the dropdown box, you can then make various settings for the web template or web items. Once you have selected a web template from the dropdown box, you can set its parameters on the Web Template Parameters tabbed page. Once you have chosen a web item from the dropdown box, you can make settings on the following tabs:

- **General**   Use the Create New symbol next to the dropdown box to create a Data Provider and assign it to the web item.

- **Web Item Parameters**   Here you can set the parameters for the selected web item. Context sensitive help is available in the lower area of the Web Item Parameters tabbed page (or the Web Template Parameters tabbed page). The following illustration shows this information, accessing the Properties section at the web template level.

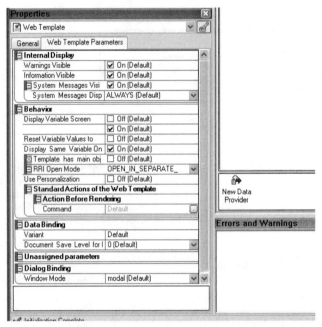

Web Template Screen Area   The Web Template screen area is where the actual web template is constructed. Basically the web items are dragged and dropped into this area, and from here the parameters associated with each web item are configured. In the following illustration, an Analysis web item has been dropped onto the Web Template area.

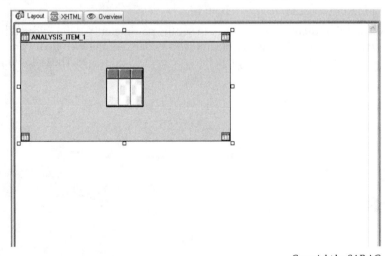

Syntax Element	Color
Comments	Gray
Attributes	Red
Attribute values	Blue
HTML tags	Black
BI-specific content (BI tags) such as web items, commands, and Data Providers	Dark red
Texts	Green
Hyperlinks	Violet

TABLE 15-6   Syntax Elements and the Color Coding

The Web Template area contains the web templates you edit in the design process. These form the basis of your Web Applications. The HTML page published on the Web is called a Web Application. The web template is the HTML page you use to specify the structure of the Web Application. In the upper section of the Web Template screen area are three tabbed pages—Layout, XHTML, and Overview—which you can use to change the view of the web template, in the same way you do in an HTML editor.

In the Layout tabbed page, you have a visual focus and can specify the layout of the Web Application. To do this, you use drag-and-drop operations to insert web items from the pool of web items into your web template. In the lower section of the layout view, you can create Data Providers. When you double-click New Data Provider, the dialog box for creating Data Providers opens. You can also create Data Providers in the Web Items screen area. The Web Template area is not an exact representation of the placement or spacing of the individual web items when the Web Application is executed. Instead, it is a logical grouping of items that enables you to see the relationship of each web item to the other.

The XHTML tabbed page displays the XHTML that corresponds to the layout view. Table 15-6 lists the various elements of the XHTML syntax and the colors associated with them.

In the XHTML view, you can edit the XHTML of a web template directly, as shown next, or you can edit the XHTML using an external XHTML editor. In the XHTML tabbed page's work area, you can see the code that is automatically generated as web items are placed in the web template. You can also see the text that is assigned as well as any options available that can be assigned to the Web Layout screen area.

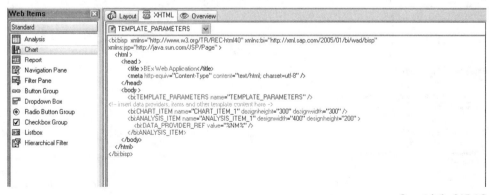

Once the objects are assigned to the layout, you can use XHTML to change the objects by adding code directly in this area. It is important to note that many of the tags used in HTML coding can also be used in the XHTML area, but make sure you are coding in the appropriate area of the tags. As you directly assign code to this area, you will see prompts if there are any issues with the appropriate tags or coding. These prompts appear in the Error and Warnings area. If you are comfortable with XHTML coding, you will find that using industry-standard XHTML to enhance the WAD results definitely comes in handy.

On the Overview tabbed page, shown next, lists all the web items, Data Providers, and commands used in web templates. By selecting or deselecting check boxes, you specify which of these objects is listed. The objects are listed vertically in the Item Name column. In the horizontal alignment of the table, any Data Providers and reusable web items associated with the objects listed are displayed. This area is helpful in verifying that the data binding of the web items is correct. The logical names of the web items as well as their properties can be changed in this work area. Using the Sorting dropdown, you can specify how these objects are to be listed:

- **Grouped**   If you choose this sort order, the objects used are listed by type: Data Providers, web items, and commands.

- **Web Template**   If you choose this sort order, the sequence of the objects used in the web template is displayed as a flat structure.

- **Web Template (Hierarchical)**   If you choose this sort order, the sequence of the objects used in the web template is displayed as a hierarchical structure. You see a hierarchical structure if you nest web items in the web template (for example, when you use the Container web item). You can change the parameters of the associated objects using the context menu for each web item, web template, and Data Provider listed.

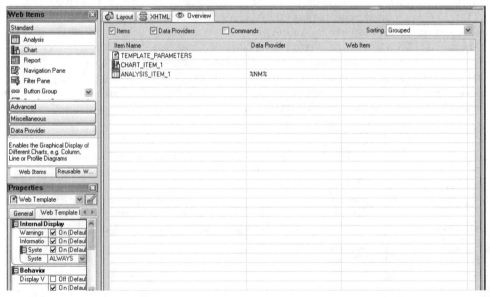

Errors and Warnings Screen Area   The Errors and Warnings screen area is used to display errors and warnings while a web template is being verified. The errors and warnings displayed in this screen area refer to the following possible checks of the web template:

- **Verify**   This check is performed automatically and by default every two seconds. Within the verification, the internal structure of the web template is checked. You can change the refresh time for the verification in the menu bar under Tools | Settings.

- **Verification on the server**   With this verification, which you trigger manually, additional conditions for creating a correct web template are checked on the server side. Here, for example, the system verifies whether a query that is being used as a Data Provider exists. To trigger the verification, on the menu bar for the Web Application Designer, choose Web Template | Verify on Server.

- **Correct and format**   During this verification, which you can trigger manually, the internal structure of the HTML is checked. You can only trigger this verification when you are in the XHTML view. From the Web Application Designer menu bar, choose Edit | Correct and Format.

Reusable Web Items   A final tab that appears on this screen is the Reusable Web Items tab. In most cases, as in the other reporting tools, it may be a good idea to have a "library" of reusable web items that can be shared with other developers. This reduces development and configuration time and allows for the collection of different web templates so that everyone can be using the same parameters, when necessary, and also provide the same look and feel to their objects. The use of reusable web items can help with this process. This option allows the developer to configure web items and save them in roles or the Favorites folder as reusable web items. Once saved, these items can be accessed from the Reusable Web Items tab in the Web Items screen area. It is important to note that not all properties of the web items are saved in the reusable web items. The data binding of a web item, for example, is not retained in the reusable web item. Data binding must be done on an individual basis for each relevant web item in the template where it is used. This can be seen in the illustration at right.

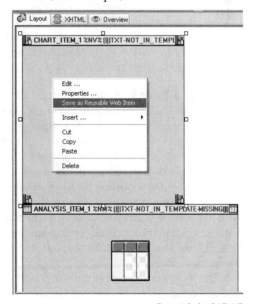

To decrease the total cost of ownership (TCO), you should consider to what extent you can reuse a Web Application you've created. If one Web Application differs from another by only a few objects (for example, a different Data Provider is displayed, a pushbutton does not appear, or another web item is used to display the data), you can create a second web template by only using the Web Template web item there. Drag the Web Template web item into the second web template. You assign the first web template to this web item using the Web Template (TEMPLATE_ID) parameter. Save the web template and open it again. Now you see all the elements that exist in the first web

Copyright by SAP AG

template. Here, you can overwrite individual web items or Data Providers. When you integrate a web item into your web template from the web item groupings in the Web Items screen area and define your settings, you might want to use this web item again in this form in other web templates, without having to define the settings over again. The BEx Web Application Designer enables you to use your own version of a web item as the web template for other items. You store this web item as a template. You can then access your web item from the Reusable Web Items screen area. Any changes that you make to the settings of the reusable web item (as described earlier) have a global effect. This means that the changes are effective in all saved web templates where the web item is used. This does not apply to web templates in which you changed the parameters of a reusable web item locally. In this case, the settings you made locally are effective. If you want to change the settings in a reusable web item locally (that is, in a specific web template where you are using this web item), proceed as follows:

1. Open the web template.
2. Select the reusable web item in the web template.
3. Change the parameters of this web item on the Web Item Parameters tabbed page in the Properties screen area.
4. Save the web template.

The changes you make to the reusable web item apply only in this web template. The parameter settings of the reusable web item are not affected by the changes.

NOTE *If you try to overwrite the parameters of a Chart web item that you have saved as a reusable web item locally, the "Create Local Chart Settings?" dialog box appears. Here, you are told that you are about to overwrite the settings for a reusable web item locally. If you choose Yes, the Edit Graphic dialog box appears. To change the parameters for the chart locally, reset the chart parameters and close the Edit Graphic dialog box by clicking OK. If you close the Edit Graphic dialog box by clicking Cancel, no local chart parameter settings are created. The reusable web item's settings are still effective. If you choose No or Cancel, no changes to the saved chart parameter settings are made.*

Setting Up a Basic Web Application

Now that we have finished reviewing the screen areas within the WAD, we can start to focus on the actual creation of a WAD template. We will start with a basic setup with two different web items and review the process of defining a web template. We will use two of the more popular web items so that you can gain a good basic understanding of the process used for developing a WAD template (keep in mind that there is so much functionality in this component of the reporting toolset that we would need another book to do justice to all the possible options available). We already worked our way through one of the more popular web items—the Chart web item—in Chapter 13 and also covered the more complex Map web item. Here the emphasis will be on the use of the Navigational Pane and the Analysis Grid. Using these web items, you can start constructing a very good WAD template for your business users.

The process used to configure any of the different web items starts basically the same way; the differences don't really come in until the very end when you need to start doing the detailed configuration for the specific web item. So, once we open the new web template and go through this process, we will be looking more intensely at the ending steps instead the beginning ones. My favorite initial step when working with an Analysis Grid, Navigation Pane, or any other object that needs to be managed in terms of space is to insert a table to help me position the object. From the menu bar select Table | Insert (or you can use the toolbar) to insert a table, as shown here. We will create a table with two columns and two rows.

The dialog box for the Table option appears, as shown next. Here, we can determine the use of the columns and rows. Also notice that on this dialog box are two additional tabs to adjust and enhance the attributes and the Cascading Style Sheet (CSS). After positioning the 2×2 table, click Apply and then OK to go back to the original screen.

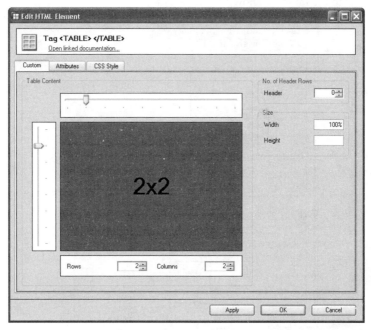

The following illustration shows the results in the Web Application template. The table is available for positioning any web items.

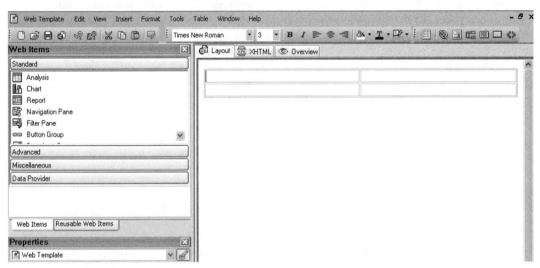

Now, drag and drop the Navigational Pane and the Analysis Grid web items into the appropriate cells in the table, as shown here.

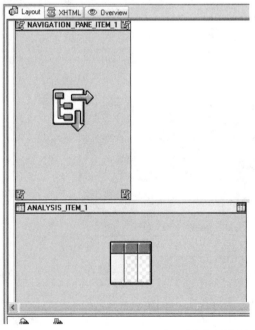

Now we'll turn our focus to the Analysis Grid web item and work through a basic configuration process. In the Properties screen in the General tab, we need to assign a Data Provider, as shown here.

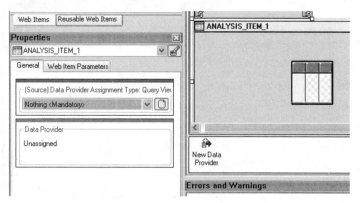

Using the icon for New Data Provider, shown next, we access the dialog box for assigning the Data Provider. We could have also used the object in the Web Designer screen New Data Provider (bottom-right side of the illustration).

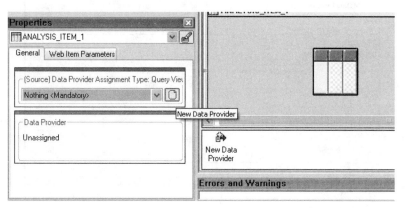

The following illustration shows the dialog box for assigning the Data Provider. You have three different options for the Data Provider type: Query View, Query, and InfoProvider.

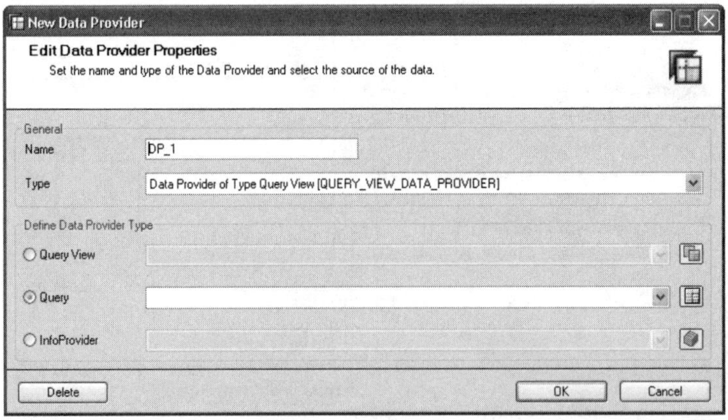

Copyright by SAP AG

We will choose a query to assign as a Data Provider, as shown next.

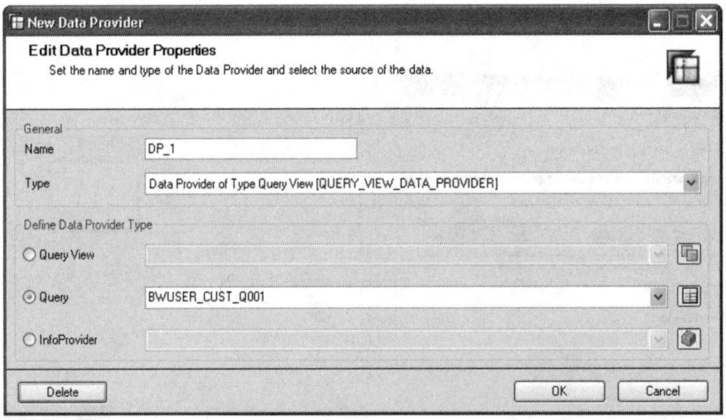

Copyright by SAP AG

In the following illustration, we can see that the query has been assigned after exiting the dialog box by clicking OK.

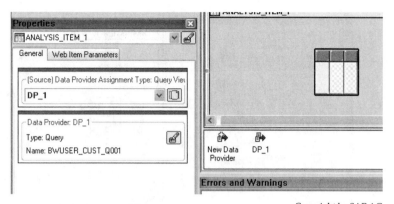

Stepping into the Properties section of the ANALYSIS_ITEM, shown in the following two illustrations, notice that six different areas can be set: Display, Internal Display, Behavior, Data Binding, Paging, and Cell Content. We will go through, in detail, all the different settings a bit later in this chapter. Safe to say, from this Properties section, most of the attributes of the ANALYSIS_ITEM can be altered. For example, the total pixel size can be changed, the color by line can be changed, navigation can be adjusted, and we can alter the Data Provider from here, if required.

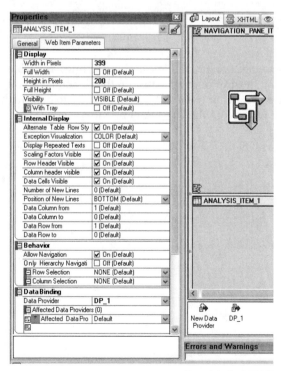

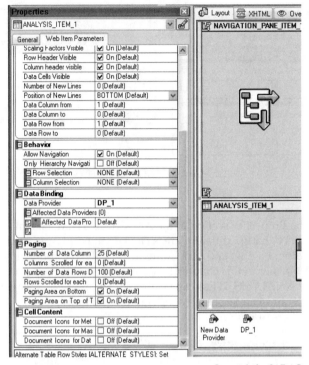

Now we can review the Navigation Pane and the settings available from the Properties section. In the following illustration, notice that on the General tab you must assign a Data Provider. Because we are going to use this Navigation Pane to help with the query in the following sections, we will assign the DP_1 data provider.

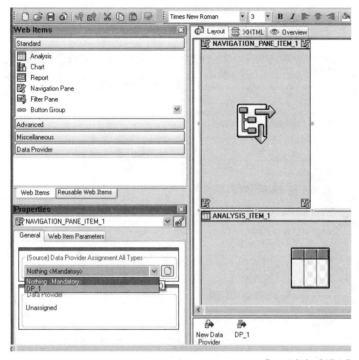

The following illustration shows the Web Item Parameters tab. Here we can adjust a series of attributes for the Navigation Pane, namely Display, Internal Display, Behavior, and

Data Binding. Generally speaking, this is all we need to do for the basic WAD template to be completed, but we will add a few items to the WAD template.

Copyright by SAP AG

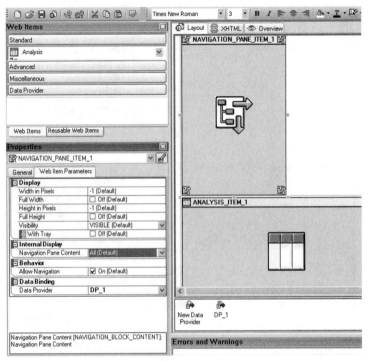

To improve the look and provide additional information, we can easily use the Tray function of the Navigation Pane and add a caption. Notice in the following illustration that we have chosen the On indicator for the tray. This opens a dialog box for adding text.

Copyright by SAP AG

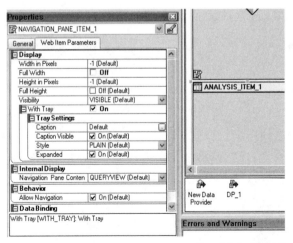

We could instead use a manual approach to adding text. If we were to select another cell in the table and choose Table | Insert | Language-Dependent Text from the context menu, as shown here, another dialog box appears.

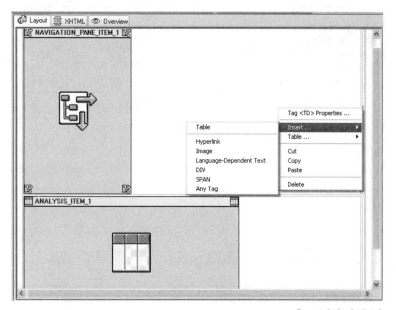

Here is the dialog box that appears for adding text to the WAD template.

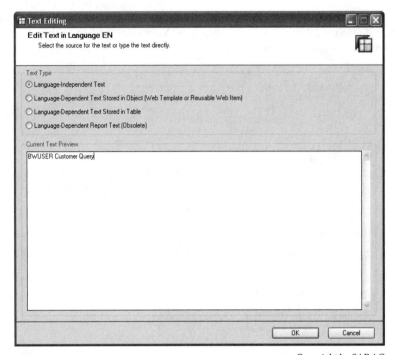

The final result of this entire configuration is shown here.

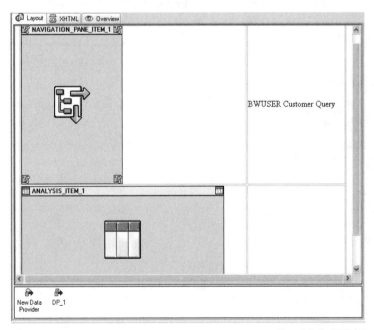

Now we can review all the XHTML that was generated in this WAD template, shown next. Notice in the middle of the XHTML screen that the two different captions are available. One is "Navigational Pane for Customer Query' and the other is "BWUSER Customer Query."

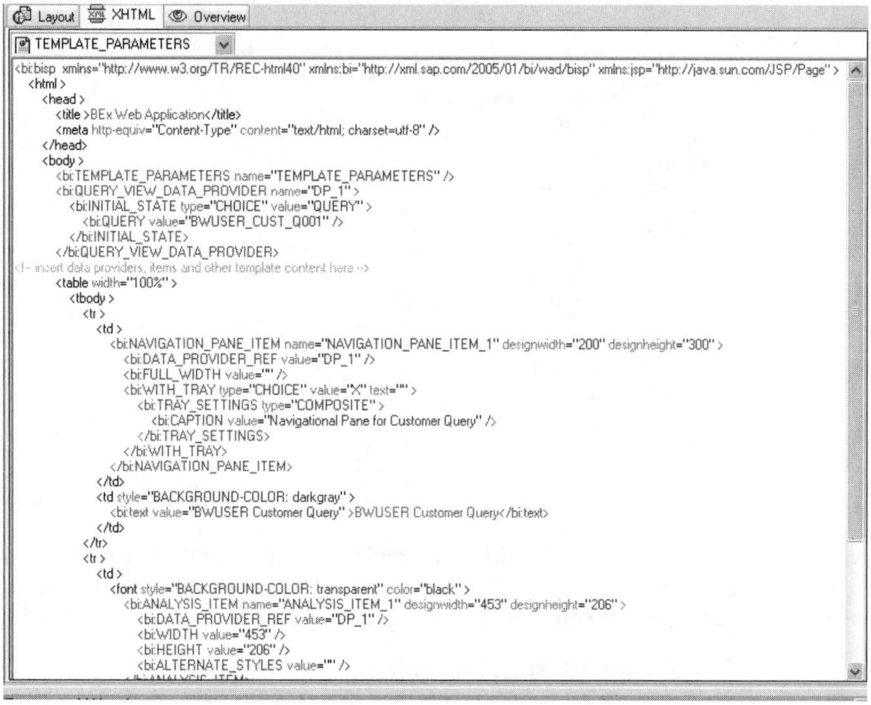

Copyright by SAP AG

Finally, we can execute this example and review the results (see the following illustration). Based on what we've done to this WAD template, it is not ready for prime time yet, but at least we have a basic WAD template in short order as an example of the steps involved.

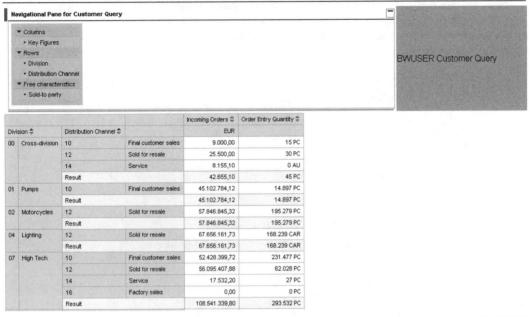

If we head back into the WAD for additional review, we see that the actual template has specific parameters that can be affected directly from here. The General tab shows the technical name assigned, so we can quickly move past this tab. This result is shown here.

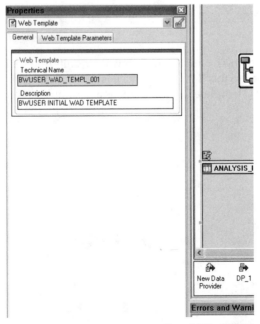

The more important items are on the Web Template Parameters tab, where we can alter the Internal Display, Behavior, Data Binding, Unassigned Parameters, and Dialog Binding settings. The Web Template Parameters tab is something you will be using for each of the WAD templates, and these settings influence the entire web template. The properties themselves are segmented into the groupings just mentioned. Very often, the default values for these properties will be sufficient for proper operation of the Web Application. You may have requirements that differ from the default values, however, and therefore will need to make the necessary changes. Table 15-7 details each group of properties.

In any case if additional documentation is required all you need to do is double-click on the line and you will see documentation show up at the bottom portion of the screen. The following shows the results of this process.

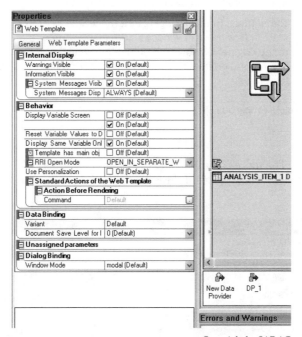

Copyright by SAP AG

As you can see from this example, there are many different parameters for each of the web items, and depending on how complex the Data Provider is, the impact of these settings will be even greater for the WAD template. The Data Provider is something we will run into most of the time during the creation of these web templates. As mentioned, almost every web template will have at least one Data Provider, and possibly most of the web items will have their own Data Provider. A Data Provider can either be a Filter or a Query View. Data Providers of the Filter type usually provide data for web items that are related to filtering data, such as a dropdown box or the radio button group. They cannot be used with web items that display the results of a Query or Query View, such as the Analysis Grid and

Parameters	Description
Internal Display	This property controls which, if any, system messages should be displayed to the user of the Web Application.
Behavior	Properties in this grouping deal with the interaction of the Web Application with the user. The more useful parameters in this grouping include whether the variable screen is shown before the template results, whether the report/report interface launches in a new browser window, and whether personalized values for the template are stored and used.
Data Binding	The two properties in this grouping include the variant, if any, that the Web Application will use and the level (Query level or InfoProvider level) at which InfoProvider data documents are created.
Dialog Binding	The settings in this grouping determine whether or not new dialog boxes start in new browser windows and, if so, whether the user can return to the original window. This would be significant if the Web Application has navigation items such as links or buttons that launch other web templates.

TABLE 15-7   Web Template Properties

the Chart web items. The more common Data Provider is the Query View type, which can reference Queries, Query Views, and InfoProviders. The following illustration shows this information.

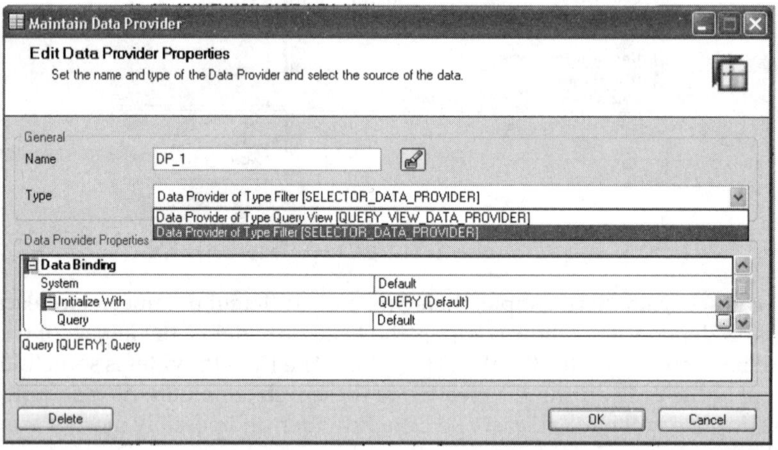

Copyright by SAP AG

The process of assigning a Data Provider is called *data binding*. We did this for both the Analysis Grid and the Navigation Pane in the example. You also saw the two locations for data binding and for the commands. The Data Binding is done directly in the Command Wizard.

As you will see, the majority of the time spent in the process of setting up a web template is not in the identification of the web items we need. Instead, after the items are assigned to the web template, the process of configuring all the settings and parameters for each web item can be quite time-consuming. These parameters can change the overall look of the object if not correctly formatted. For example, if the pixels for different screens are not consistent, you will be viewing reports that are only a portion of the screen rather than sharing the screen equally. So, bear that in mind while reviewing each of the objects. Some are straightforward in their setup, but others will have numerous parameters. Understanding what each one does is very important.

The web items are broken down into the following groupings:

- **Standard**   This grouping includes Analysis, Chart, Report, Navigation Pane, Filter Pane, Button Group, Dropdown Box, Radio Button Group, Checkbox Group, Listbox, and Hierarchical Filter Selection.

- **Advanced**   This grouping includes Web Template, Container Layout, Container, Tab Pages, Group, Single Document, Document List, Map, System Messages, and Information Field.

- **Miscellaneous**   This grouping includes Data Provider, Information, Text, Link, List of Exceptions, List of Conditions, Menu Bar, Properties Pane, Ticker, Context Menu, and Script.

Each web item has a specific set of parameters that control the use and view generated by that item. For example, the one we used—the Navigation Pane web item—shows the navigation status of a Data Provider. All the characteristics and structures of the Data Provider are listed. You can alter the navigation status by dragging characteristics or structures to an axis (rows or columns) of the table, or you can remove them from the axis. You can swap axes in the Navigation Pane using drag and drop, and the table changes accordingly. You can also drag characteristics into the Filter pane. In the Properties section of the Navigation Pane web item, you can use the Internal Display | Navigation Pane Contents property to choose which elements of the assigned Data Provider will be shown in the Web Application. Table 15-8 lists the parameters for the Navigation Pane web item, arranged according to the various parameter groupings.

Formatting Web Template Layouts

One of the most important things you will need to do with your web reports is to format them correctly and offer the business user a view of the data that is consistent and easy to read. It is important that the business user can read, understand, and assimilate the results of the queries. The normal rule of thumb when configuring a report is to make sure that the results can be understood in less than seven seconds. That means the business user should be able to execute the report, and once the information is available be able to walk away from the report with a good idea of the analysis and what was being communicated through the report in less than seven seconds.

This means making sure that there are as few issues with the display of the data as possible. One of the "deal breakers" with a report is the formatting and making sure that all the objects are aligned correctly for display purposes. Creating Web Applications where the content is arranged incorrectly on the screen leads to user complaints, time-consuming analysis, and finally a lack of trust of the data—and in turn a lack of use of the reporting tools.

Parameter/Grouping	Description
Display	
Width in Pixels (WIDTH)	You use this parameter to determine the width of the web item.
Full Width (FULL_WIDTH)	You use this parameter to ignore the specification in the Width in Pixels (WIDTH) parameter. The width will be set to 100% instead. The full width depends on the width of the environment in which the web item is embedded (for example, the width of a tabbed page on a Portal page or iView).
Height in Pixels (HEIGHT)	You use this parameter to determine the height of the web item.
Full Height (FULL_HEIGHT)	You use this parameter to ignore the specification in the Height in Pixels (HEIGHT) parameter. The height will be set to 100% instead. The full height depends on the height of the environment in which the web item is embedded (for example, the height of a tabbed page on a Portal page or iView).
Visibility (VISIBILITY)	You use this parameter to determine whether the web item is visible in the Web Application.
With Tray (WITH_TRAY)	You use this parameter to determine whether the Navigation Pane web item has a symbol that allows the web item to be expanded and collapsed.
Internal Display	
Navigation Pane Content (NAVIGATION_BLOCK_CONTENT)	You use this parameter to determine the characteristics that are displayed in the navigation pane. You have the following selection options: **All** All characteristics are displayed. **Columns** Only the characteristics in the columns are displayed. **Rows** Only the characteristics in the rows are displayed. **Free characteristics** Only the free characteristics are displayed.
Behavior	
Activate Navigation (INTERACTION_ALLOWED)	You use this parameter to determine whether navigation and other interactions are possible in the Web Application.
Data Binding	
Data Provider (DATA_PROVIDER_REF)	(See the previous discussion on data binding.)

TABLE 15-8   Parameters for the Navigation Pane Web Item

We can use a number of objects and options to help us with this process. Some of them were identified in the previous section, such as the Container, Container Layout, and Grouping web items. These web items are definitely worth investigating in order to better understand their functionality. One of my favorites for fast consistent formatting is the use of an inserted table. The HTML table serves as a grid into which web items are placed. This provides an effective method for arranging web items side-by-side or vertically on the web page. It's very easy to get started, and will help format the data so that basic testing results can be more easily read. Once you open the Web Template page, use the Table icon or the Table | Insert Table menu to access the dialog box for inserting a table. Identify the number of rows and columns you need and click Apply.

The table will be inserted into your web template at the current cursor location. At any time, you an use the table's context menu to make changes, as shown next. From the context menu you can do the following:

- Add or delete rows or columns or delete the table itself.

- Edit the properties.

- Split and merge cells.

- Add a URL link to the information, add images, and add objects to help with the sizing of the space between objects (DIV and SPAN).

Copyright by SAP AG

***

NOTE *In order to merge cells, select the text in the cells and choose Merge Cells from the context menu. A similar approach is used for splitting cells.*

In some cases you may need to do a little extra formatting because the web items can only help so much, so manual formatting is required. A number of options are available on the menu and toolbars that can be of some use. You will often need to provide some basic text information to help the user put the data in context, or to provide additional direction concerning the Web Application or the results being displayed. For these purposes, we can easily insert text directly into the web template by just using the context menu of the cell. For example, suppose you need to add some text to make sure that specific directions are to be followed after the user reads the report. Simply type them in, and the XHTML will be automatically generated to support the text. The results are shown here.

ℹ DDIC: SAP Training System Powered by .NET Microsoft Technology

After Reading this Report please contact Mr. Miller with any questions at X3550

Division ⇕		Distribution Channel ⇕		Incoming Orders ⇕	Order Entry Quantity ⇕
				EUR	
00	Cross-division	10	Final customer sales	9.000,00	15 PC
		12	Sold for resale	25.500,00	30 PC
		14	Service	8.155,10	0 AU
		Result		42.655,10	45 PC
01	Pumps	10	Final customer sales	45.102.784,12	14.897 PC
		Result		45.102.784,12	14.897 PC
02	Motorcycles	12	Sold for resale	57.846.845,32	195.279 PC
		Result		57.846.845,32	195.279 PC
04	Lighting	12	Sold for resale	67.656.161,73	168.239 CAR
		Result		67.656.161,73	168.239 CAR
07	High Tech	10	Final customer sales	52.428.399,72	231.477 PC
		12	Sold for resale	56.095.407,88	62.028 PC
		14	Service	17.532,20	27 PC
		16	Factory sales	0,00	0 PC
		Result		108.541.339,80	293.532 PC
08	Service	14	Service	2.351.003,56	0 AU
		Result		2.351.003,56	0 AU
10	Vehicles	12	Sold for resale	79.577,48	3 PC
		Result		79.577,48	3 PC
20	Turbines	10	Final customer sales	1.660.000,00	2 PC
		Result		1.660.000,00	2 PC
Overall Result				283.280.367,11	671.996.600 MIX

By using some of the functionality in the Text toolbar, you can format quite a few items with very little effort. The following shows some basic formatting that was done and some background color added.

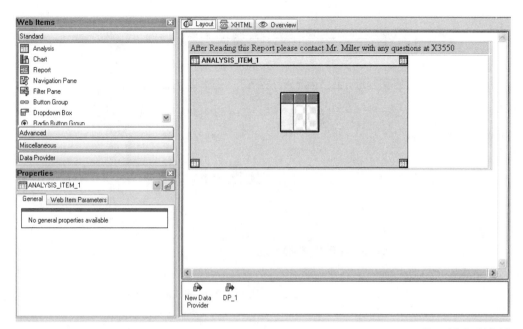

The Text toolbar lets you modify the font and font size, apply bold and italic, change the alignment of the selected text, select a background color for the web template, and change the text color and/or text background color. The <DIV> and <SPAN> HTML tags can also be used to specify properties of textual information. For example, the <DIV> tag is used to specify a container within which you can put text and apply various properties, such as font, color size, and the alignment of the text. This is useful for formatting the different areas of the header of your Web Application.

The <SPAN> tag defines an inline text container and is often used to apply specific Cascading Style Sheet (CSS) styles to parts of a text block. For example, you could use the <SPAN> tag to insert a style to change the color and style of the text if the user hovers over the text with the cursor. These different functions can be used as a quick-and-easy fix for your web reports. For example, suppose we want to realign the web objects within one of our web reports. We can use the context menu options to help, and then we can access the report and tweak the results as we go. To do this, we access an existing web template and use the Table | Edit | Edit Row context menu, as shown next.

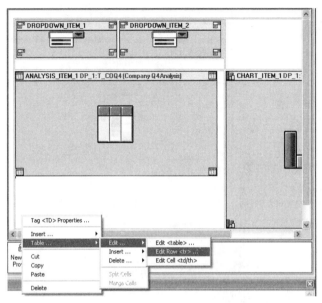

When this is executed, the dialog box for changing the text appears. In this dialog box, we can adjust the format of the report by rows and columns, adjust the sizing, and alter the attributes and add another CSS style sheet, as shown here. In this case, all we do is change the setting for the vertical alignment to Top. This will move all the web objects to the top level of the cells.

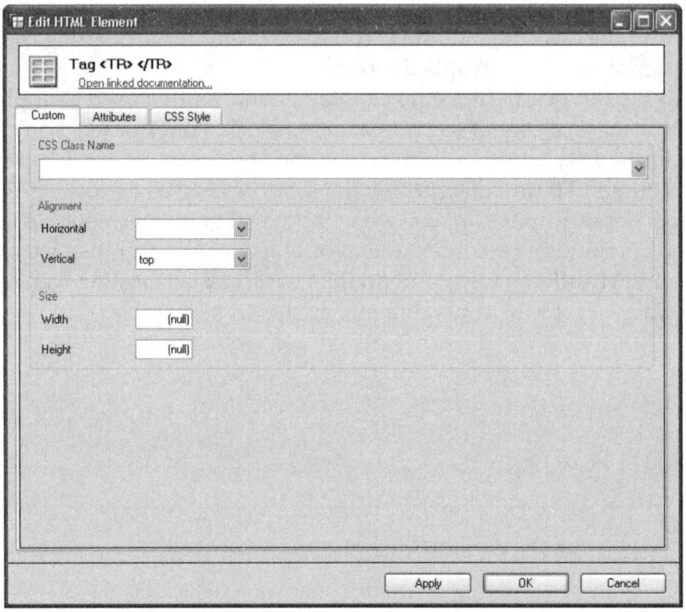

Finally, we can execute the WAD report and see the results, shown next. Notice how much more consistent this looks versus the basic WAD query assembled earlier in this chapter. This improvement was made with just one minor change in a setting. Therefore, you should work with all of the options available and see what they can do for your WAD reports.

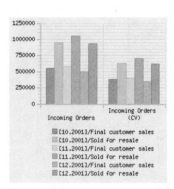

ⓘ DDIC: SAP Training System Powered by .NET Microsoft Technology

Calendar Year/Month: [Show All Values ▼]   Distribution Channel: [Show All Values ▼]

		Incoming Orders ⇕	Incoming Orders (CV) ⇕
Calendar Year/Month ⇕	Distribution Channel ⇕	EUR	EUR
10.2001	Final customer sales	550.962	380.003
	Sold for resale	944.337	625.999
	Result	1.495.299	1.006.002
11.2001	Final customer sales	576.969	397.584
	Sold for resale	1.053.835	702.639
	Result	1.630.804	1.100.222
12.2001	Final customer sales	493.215	340.163
	Sold for resale	934.783	617.860
	Result	1.427.999	958.022
Overall Result		4.554.102	3.064.247

Copyright by SAP AG

If the use of multiple languages is required, you can use language-dependent text in your Web Application. Because the Web Application is executed in the NetWeaver Portal, it is the logon language of the NetWeaver Portal user ID that determines which text language is displayed. The dialog box for working with text offers these choices for text input:

- **Language-Independent Text**   This text will always show in the Web Application regardless of the logon language of the user.

- **Language-Dependent Text Stored in Object (Web Template or Reusable Web Items)**   The text can only be entered in the current logon language of the web template developer. Therefore, if the text is required in two languages, the developer would have to log on twice—once in either language—and enter the text in both languages.

- **Language-Dependent Text Stored in Table**   This option allows the web template developer to enter the text in as many languages as needed in the same session. Each text has a language key to identify it. The text is stored in separate tables (RSBEXTEXTS) and needs to be transported separately from the web template.

- **Language-Dependent Report Text (Obsolete)**   If you need to access another object such as an ABAP report program, you would use this option.

All this can be found in the context menu of the Properties option, as shown in the following illustration. From anywhere in the WAD template you can insert any of these parameters. For example, in the table, use the context menu Insert _ Language Dependent Text.

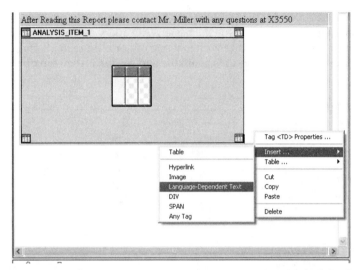

This opens the dialog box for text options. Here, we have the four different options of language-dependent and independent text, as shown next.

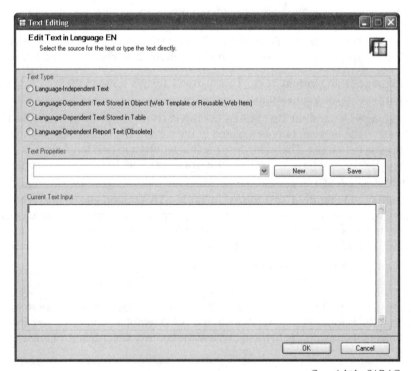

By choosing the option Language-Dependent Text Stored in Table, we can use text in the different languages that have been stored, as shown next.

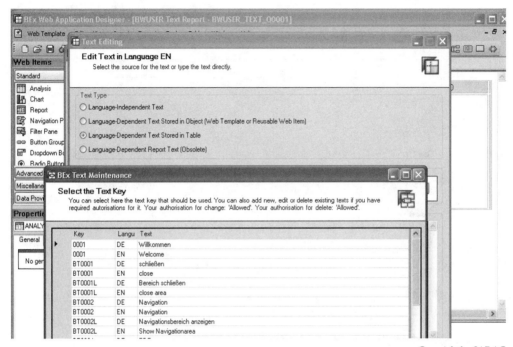

Another easy option we can access from this screen is the ability to insert images. If needed, we can add a company logo or divisional logo, or even just some background color that is specific to the customer. Graphic files with the extensions .bmp, .jpg, and .gif can be used. The initial step is to access the Mime Repository (transaction code SE80) and go to the location where customer images are stored (SAP _ BW _ Customer _ Images). Here, we can insert or upload our images. Once that is complete, we use the context menu again to access the option to insert an image. We will then be able to insert our image in the appropriate location in the WAD template, as shown here.

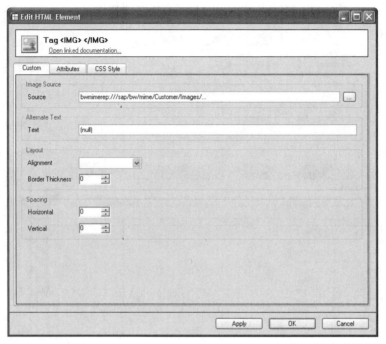

Another available option that will make a big impact on your WAD templates with little effort on your part is the use of themes. Because all BI Web Applications are displayed on the NW Portal, the portal themes are used to apply HTML-like styles to the objects in the Web Application. Prior to NW 7.0 (2004S) BI, a cascading style sheet was assigned to each web template. Therefore, the portal themes are replacing the cascading style sheets. These portal themes serve the same purpose, but are created and maintained with the Theme Editor in the NW Portal. These themes are in turn assigned to a portal desktop, which is a collection of parameters that define the look and feel of the specific portal environment. Portal users are then assigned to the portal desktop, and the appropriate Web Applications, as they are executed, will take on the look defined by the connected portal theme.

In the WAD, it is possible to override the styles from the portal theme for any of the tags in your web template. You can directly assign text a specific font, color, and size using the context menu. Once you access the context menu, choose the Tag <TD> properties to display the Edit HTML dialog box, where you can access any of the CSS styles from the CSS Style tab.

Based on all this configuration that can be accomplished directly from the context menu, it's definitely something that you don't want to overlook while configuring and implementing the WAD component.

Command Wizard

Another new function is the use of commands and the use of the Command Wizard to create web-based activities. I believe that this is an outgrowth of the need to have more flexibility for using the different functions within the WAD and to develop and display some existing components in a different manner while having additional flexibility to develop new functionality. We've seen the command setup process in a number of chapters up to this point. We used something similar to this in the development of the functionality of the BEx Analyzer and the use of workbooks and commands embedded into the dropdown objects and button groups. We will also use this functionality in the process of configuration of the Integrated Planning in the BEx Analyzer. Therefore a basic comment about this functionality is only warranted at this point. As you go through the process of using the Command Wizard, notice some of the overlap of the items that we can create commands for and the fact that they are already in the context menu of a particular Web API or available in the BEx Web Analyzer. Because some of the functionality overlaps, it all comes down to what the business user is more comfortable using—the context menu or a button on the screen. The additional flexibility of the command process allows developers to extend the navigational and processing power of web items without having to immediately go to developing JavaScript programs. This offers much more flexibility for the developers and the business users. The combination of the Web Design API functionality and embedding the command option into it offers the ability to enhance web templates, web items, Data Providers and planning application commands. These commands extend the interaction and capabilities of objects to enhance the integration of web-based analysis objects.

The Command Wizard is the main tool for creating commands from the Web Design API. You can use it to create commands easily by following a step-by-step procedure and include them in your web template. This enables you to create highly individual Web Applications with BI content. In the Command Wizard, all the parameters available for each command are listed so that they can also be set directly there. You also see a description for each command and each parameter directly in the Command Wizard.

The Command Wizard is part of the Web Application Designer and does not require any additional installation. You usually call the Command Wizard in the Web Application Designer from the web item parameter Action (Command Triggered) (ACTION). If you insert a hyperlink into the web template, you can also call the Command Wizard in the dialog box that follows with the button next to the text-entry field.

This functionality is embedded into numerous web items, including Button Group, Dropdown Box, Web Item, Menu Bar, and Group, to name a few. One of the most popular areas for this functionality is the Button Group, which offers individual buttons for each command assigned. The Web Design API enables you to create commands for any Data Providers, planning applications, web items, and web templates. Any context menu navigation can be replaced with a command that offers the ability to develop a step-by-step view of querying on different reports. So rather than having the business user work through a context menu–driven drilldown, they can use a series of buttons from the Button Group with commands executing in the system. Commands can also help with the parameterization of different web items. The Web Design API tool is accessible from anywhere that a command is relevant, and it guides the user through the necessary parameters without the need to master HTML or XHTML syntax.

NOTE *We will be working through some of the planning commands in detail in Chapter 17, where the context is more consistent and understandable.*

Using BI Patterns and Configuring Formatted WAD Templates

Another very helpful functionality in the Web Application Designer is the use of the BI patterns to help with formatting and functionality. BI patterns are Web Applications tailored to the requirements of particular user groups and are used to unify the display of BI content. The user always finds the same function with the same name in the same place. To some degree, the patterns can be configured. The concept of patterns helps to reduce the total cost of ownership because the actual logic for the display and interaction in BI applications for each pattern is stored centrally in only one web template, so any changes only have to be made there. This can be very helpful when it comes to adding any sort of headers or footers to the screen. Building a BI Pattern component can reduce the total cost of implementation immediately. For example, suppose you have a disclaimer that is required on each of your WAD reports. Rather than having to rework the document each time, you can set up a BI pattern and use it whenever you need to include the statement. In the Information Consumer pattern, a button is configured for exporting the data to Microsoft Excel in the main web template of the pattern. When you configure the Information Consumer pattern, you can decide whether you want to see this button.

You can create as complex or as simple a BI pattern as you would like. This could be a BI pattern that's a disclaimer in a footer included in all WAD reports. You can include dropdowns, buttons, filters, variables—all the functionality available on a basic WAD report. Within the Web Application Designer, you can access SAP-supplied BI patterns and maintain them for your own use. Each supplied pattern is a full analysis template designed for a specific purpose. For example, the BI Consumer pattern provides a common analysis workbench complete with filters, buttons, dropdown boxes, variables, and analysis areas. The BI patterns and BI Pattern Wizard are accessed from the Select a Template screen that is displayed when the WAD is started. From the menu bar, go to Web Templates | New, and the BI patterns and BI Pattern Wizard will appear, as shown next. The initial screen is for commonly used BI patterns, and the All Patterns and Web Templates tab houses the standard-delivered content.

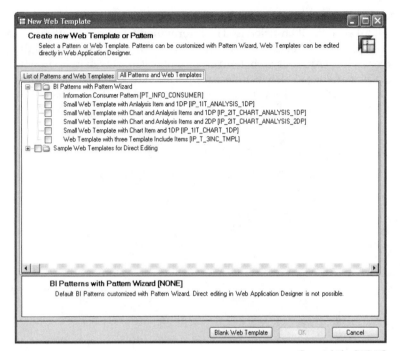

Copyright by SAP AG

The steps for using the BI patterns are straightforward:

1. Copy the BI pattern you would like to change (click OK on the BI screen, which will move you to the BI Pattern Wizard).

2. Choose the style and content of the toolbar.

3. Configure the content and settings for the dropdown boxes using other web items.

4. Identify the characteristics to appear in the filter area.

5. Adjust any of the general settings for formatting as necessary.

Table 15-9 shows the different BI patterns available.

Pattern	Description
Information Consumer pattern	Easy-to-use BEx Web Application for users without specific BI knowledge.
Analysis pattern	BEx Web Application for complex data analysis. The analysis pattern is called the *BEx Web Analyzer* in the Portal.

TABLE 15-9   BI Patterns Available as SBC

These BI patterns are defined as user-friendly BEx Web Applications that are intended for users without specific BI knowledge. The Information Consumer pattern is a template for BEx Web Applications that can be used in different variations. In general, this pattern includes either a table (Analysis web item) or a graphic (Chart web item) in which the data is displayed. The pattern can also include an application toolbar that, depending on the variation of the pattern, includes various pushbuttons and functions. The following is an outline of this template.

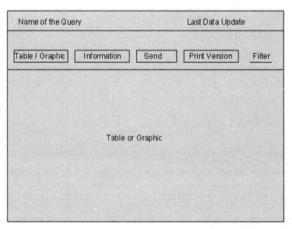

In the upper list, you receive information on how current the data is and can see the name of the query. In the lower area, you see the data either in a table or in a graphic. Here, you can use the arrow keys in the column header to sort the column in ascending or descending order. The context menu for the cells of the table is also available when you right-click. Depending on the variation of the pattern, different functions are included in the context menu. For example, you can jump to another BEx Web Application. In the application toolbar above the table or graphic, several pushbuttons are available, each of which offers a different function. Table 15-10 lists the functions of the pushbuttons on the application toolbar.

The second example, shown here, has changed things a bit. In addition to the functions from the first example, a dropdown box is available in which you can select different views of the data. In this way, you can switch between different navigation views that each show a different aspect of the data.

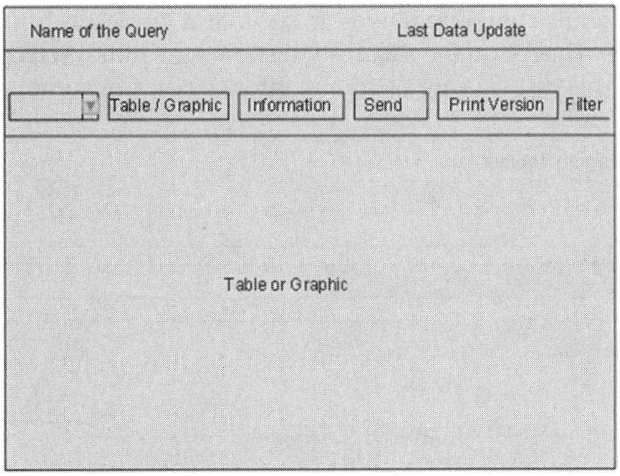

Copyright by SAP AG

For example, the BEx Web Application displays the sales data for a specific product. You can choose between the following views in the dropdown box: Sales for Each Distribution Channel, Sales for Each Region, and Sales for Each Customer.

Pushbutton (or Link)	Description
Table (or graphic)	You use this pushbutton to switch between the display of data as a table or as a graphic. If the data is to be displayed in a table, *Graphic* appears as the text in the pushbutton. When you switch, the data is displayed in a graphic. Now *Table* appears as the text in the pushbutton. With this pushbutton, you go back to the table.
Information	You use this pushbutton to display information about the Data Provider. You can display information about the key date, the "currentness" of the data, the time changed, who last changed the query, and the date of the last refresh.
Send	You use this pushbutton to send the BEx Web Application by e-mail. The Broadcasting Wizard appears and helps you to make the necessary entries with step-by-step instructions.
Print Version	You use this pushbutton to make the settings for a print version of the BEx Web Application. For example, you can set the format for the print version and define whether a header appears on the pages printed. When you have made your settings and have chosen OK, a PDF generation is triggered. You can print out the created PDF document.
Filters	You use this link to display the filter pane. The filter pane is displayed between the application toolbar and the table (or graphic). The characteristics that you can use for filtering are displayed in the filter pane. You can select the characteristic values to be used for filtering for each characteristic that is used in the Data Provider.

TABLE 15-10 Functions of the Application Toolbar

If we look at the actual component, we can see that it guides us through the configuration process. The following illustration shows the initial screen after the BI pattern to copy is chosen. In this case, we are using the Information Consumer pattern.

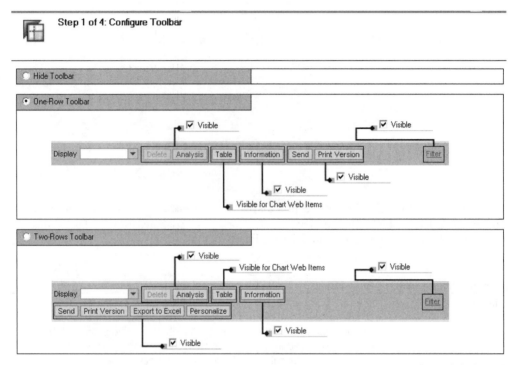

Leaving all indicators turned on, we move to step 2 in the process. Here, we are confirming the functionality of the input field as well as the sorting and filtering process. We will keep the Dropdown Box view and add the Filter view, as shown here.

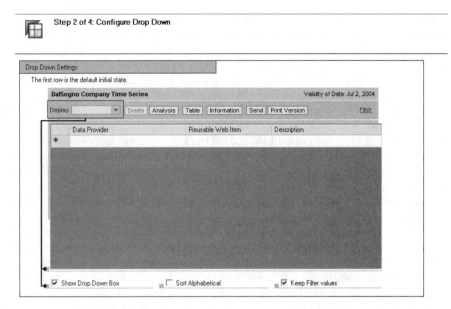

Step 3 in this case is a confirmation of the formatting that was accepted. Finally, step 4 gives us the chance to adjust the formatting and add headers and footers to the BI pattern, as shown next. Once this is complete, perform a Save operation and you have an additional formatted BI pattern available.

Another approach to this process would be to set up different objects that can be reused and combined to make a formatted reporting process. Many companies have different sets of standards for their Web Applications. Doing so helps new users adopt new analysis applications because the learning curve and maintenance process will be shorter if the reports follow the same patterns throughout the company. To assist with this process, you can create Web Application modules that can then be reused wherever needed in producing web templates. Common examples of these Web Application modules might be a corporate header with logo and text, disclaimer statements for corporate reports, standard headers or footers with common text elements, and standard button sets and images for common actions.

Once a module is developed, it can be linked to another template with the Web Template web item, thus creating a template format for all to use. Therefore, the Web Template web item is the basis for this approach. This process is not difficult, and once you understand that this is a series of component WAD templates combined using the Web Template web item, you can probably set this option up—or you may have already done this but didn't realize that the modular approach was the official terminology for this process. Generally speaking, when you set up a template to be used throughout the company, as long as the template stores generic components, there will be no issues with saving. If you are creating a modular application and there's a specific Data Provider, you can delete the Data Provider before saving and reattach the correct Data Provider at the time you use the template. The following illustration shows an example of this approach. As you can see, the header (corporate logo and text) and footer (Query Description, InfoProvider Description, and Last Data Update) can be set up to be consistent across all reports and thus reduce the time to develop queries and WAD templates. These are reusable templates for all companywide reports.

SAP The Best-Run Businesses Run SAP.

Country Analysis	Q4 Analysis		

Calendar Year/Month ⇕	Distribution Channel ⇕	Incoming Orders ⇕ EUR	Incoming Orders (CV) ⇕ EUR
10.2001	Final customer sales	550.962	380.003
	Sold for resale	944.337	625.999
	Result	1.495.299	1.006.002
11.2001	Final customer sales	576.969	397.584
	Sold for resale	1.053.835	702.639
	Result	1.630.804	1.100.222
12.2001	Final customer sales	493.215	340.163
	Sold for resale	934.783	617.860
	Result	1.427.999	958.022
Overall Result		4.554.102	3.064.247

Query Description: Company Q4 Analysis
InfoProvider Description: Order Cube
Last data update: 21.03.2003 15:22:33

Summary

As you can see, the functionality available via the BEx Web Analyzer is a bit different from that of the BEx Analyzer, but there's nothing discussed here that reinvents the wheel, so to speak. There are important differences in terms of navigation and some enhancements in functionality, but nothing that would cause the business user concern. The combination of both of the Analyzers allows the business user to choose between the two or use both, but not suffer any reduction in functionality or flexibility. Both of these front-end tools have come a long way, but it is fairly obvious that the future focus of business is getting information out on the Web and offering business users additional methods of receiving that information and getting to the required data to run their departments and divisions without having to support the heavy infrastructure of GUI-based reporting. Many corporations are putting their efforts behind enhancing the use of the Web and the thin-client format to get data out as quickly and effectively as possible.

There is definitely much more in terms of configuring the options and functionality available within the WAD than was discussed in this chapter. As mentioned, the details of all the components and processes for the WAD would fill another book. There is so much functionality with the additional web items in the 7.0 version, plus the enhanced formatting and the use of JavaScript and XHTML, that creating any sort of web report or dashboard is certainly possible.

Organizing Your Reports— Enterprise Portal

This chapter discusses the uses the Enterprise Portal to organize, display, and structure all the reports generated by your company. This is the SAP-suggested approach to the final display of all the reports and queries that will be built for all levels of management and operational business users. This chapter begins with an overview of the Enterprise Portal and shows some examples of the final display options. You have seen some of these options in earlier chapters—such as the Information Broadcaster and Visual Composer—but we will review all of them here. Then we'll move into a bit more detail surrounding the linkage between the BI system and the Enterprise Portal and what basic steps you need to take to integrate the two components. This chapter doesn't go through all the functionality of the Enterprise Portal, nor is it intended to be a complete discussion of the configuration process for the Portal. We will stick as closely as possible to the portions of this component that deal with the BI system and not get bogged down in the details of the system or the actual application setup. In some areas we may have to go into additional details (for example, when discussing the functionality of the authorization process), but as a whole we will just keep to areas that pertain strictly to the subject matter of this book— specifically the integration with BW. As you can see, this is the theme in chapters that are not directly linked to BI. After this discussion, we will cover the process involved in linking the two components in detail so that you have a good idea of how to get started. The information in this discussion will be broken down into sections that describe the integration from the Portal user's viewpoint as well as the viewpoint of administrators and authors who generate and publish the BI content. You will notice in this chapter's illustrations that a number of fields and indicators are not identified as we configure the Enterprise Portal (EP). There is much functionality available within the EP than we cannot cover here, and all of that is for another book.

Overview of the Enterprise Portal Integration to BW

The Enterprise Portal (NetWeaver Portal) is very tightly integrated with BI in the NetWeaver 2004S version (BI 7.0), and this is one of its strengths. The ability to consolidate all the functionality of the 7.0 BI version into the Enterprise Portal, along with the functionality of the Knowledge Management (KM) component, allows the availability of BI web-based reports to all of the functionality of the web, documentation, and collaboration options within the NetWeaver system. This seamless integration enhances the ability to link documents, reports, and communication processes together and gives the business user all the options in one location. The Portal enables you to access applications from other systems and sources, such as the Internet or an intranet. Using one entry point, you can reach both structured and unstructured information. In addition to content from Knowledge Management, business data from data analysis is available to you from the Internet or an intranet. The integration of BI content into the Portal enables you to work more closely (and promptly) with company colleagues when you need to do so. For example, this integration can help when you need to insert notes and comments for key figures and reports, run approval processes automatically, and take part in decisions within a broad company context. The provision of information is based on user roles in the company. As the role concept is used in the BI system, it is possible to carry out a simple integration of BI content with the Portal. The users see the same BI role content in the Portal. In addition, you can use the iView concept to integrate BI applications and individual Web Applications from BI as iViews in the Portal. You can then display and use them from a page in the Portal, together with other iViews from the BI system or from other systems. All of the front-end components of BI are available to the Portal. For example, the BEx Information Broadcaster allows you to precalculate BEx web applications, queries, and workbooks and to distribute them to the Portal. You can also generate online links to queries and web applications and then publish them to the Portal. The unification concept for the Enterprise Portal enables you to directly relate content from the BI system to content from other systems or from the Internet. With the drag-and-relate function, you can link data together across systems' boundaries in order to obtain additional information.

NOTE *The drag-and-relate functionality identified here is not the same as the drag-and-drop functionality discussed in previous chapters. The drag-and-drop functionality in previous chapters refers to the ability to drag either a characteristic or key figure from a navigational pane and drop it in a report/query. The drag-and-relate functionality here refers to the ability to link different master data in various systems together and review that information on a consolidated level. For example, the same material in two different systems may have different material numbers. In the EP, you have the ability to integrate these two material instances (which are the same but have different values in different systems) and use them interchangeabley in the same report.*

The BEx Portfolio, based on Knowledge Management, forms the central entry point for access to business intelligence information in the Portal. The following illustration shows the positioning of this overall front-end toolset and where it fits into the landscape of the BI system and functionality. As you can see, it encompasses all the different functions we have talked about throughout this book.

In terms of overall changes from the 3.x to the 7.0 versions of BW, the Enterprise Portal or BI Portal represents the most significant change to the Business User. If a company was currently using the BEx Browser for access to all reports, the BI Portal (at the minimum) would be the replacement for this activity and therefore the user would have to get used to the differences in look and feel of the two components. As you will see the BI Portal can offer all of the options that the BEx Browser had and much more.

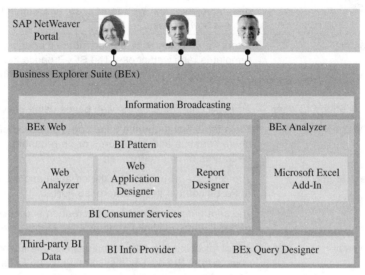

Copyright by SAP AG

NOTE *Before we go any further, let's review what an iView is. An iView is a program that retrieves data from content sources within your company or on the Internet and displays this data in the Enterprise Portal content area.*

To distribute or integrate content from the SAP BI to the SAP Enterprise Portal, you can use the tools described in Table 16-1. Most should be familiar to you; only the EP-specific terms will be new. These terms are discussed later in this chapter.

The Portal Content Studio is the central component in the Enterprise Portal for creating and managing Portal content. It can be used to edit the following types of Portal content: iViews, Portal pages, layouts of Portal pages, folders, Portal roles, and worksets.

As mentioned, there are two different approaches to accessing the Enterprise Portal— from the business user point of view and from the administrator point of view. Each approach is consistent with the needs and requirements of these different groups. To give you an overview of the integration with the BI objects, we can use the business user view. The first of the following illustrations shows the initial screen the business user might see once logging on to the EP. This screen has all the required reports, workbooks, possibility planning objects, documents, communication options, and alerts that the business user will need to perform their responsibilities. We've seen this view in some of the previous chapters. Based on the configuration completed in the EP, this screen can have a different look and feel. For example, the second illustration shows a bit more of the functionality available across the top toolbar. This would be more appropriate for the administrator view

Component	Description and Functionality
BEx Broadcasting Wizard	A wizard/assistant that supports precalculating and distributing queries, Web templates, and workbooks using a flow process.
BEx Broadcaster	A tool for precalculating and distributing queries, Web templates, and workbooks. The BEx Broadcaster offers more extensive options than the BEx Broadcasting Wizard (it's the wizard on steroids).
BEx Web Application Designer	An application for creating web pages using BI content.
BEx Query Designer	Tools for defining queries based on a selection of characteristics and key figures or on reusable structures of an InfoProvider.
Portal Content Studio	The central environment for the creation and management of Portal content in the Enterprise Portal.
KM Content	The central environment for the creation and management of documents and links in Knowledge Management.
SAP Role Upload	A tool for uploading role definitions and the associated objects from the back-end systems into the Enterprise Portal. You can integrate BI content into the Portal using Role Upload. The Role Upload function can be used in the following scenarios: • You want to continue to use existing role definitions for a BI system in the Portal. • You want to use objects from a BI system (for example, Web Applications) as content objects to build your roles in the Portal. This means these objects have to be available in the Portal. • You've uploaded all the relevant roles and objects from the BI system into the Portal, but in the future you want to create and maintain your content objects only in the Portal. • You upload newly created role definitions from the back-end system into the Portal at regular intervals. You mainly do this when you use the BI system as the leading system. In this case, you continue to create your roles in the BI system and only use the Portal as a medium for display and navigation.

TABLE 16-1   Integration Tools for BI Objects in the Enterprise Portal

of the EP. Table 16-2 gives some details about each of the different options possible in the Business Explorer tab.

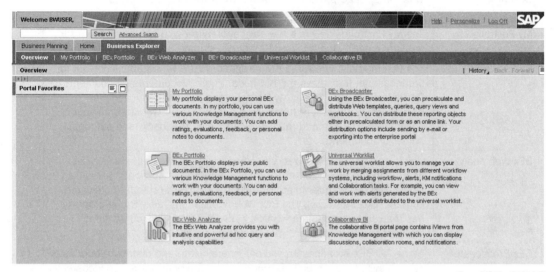

To give these definitions and descriptions a bit more meaning, we will look at a screenshot of each. So, as we work our way across the options in the Business Explorer toolbar, the first is the Overview view of the Portal. The next option is the My Portfolio view, which is configured to provide all business users immediate access to critical

Tab	Description and Functionality
Overview	This initial page provides an overview of the content of this Portal role.
My Portfolio	The My Portfolio iView is a KM navigation iView with a special layout for broadcasting. It displays your KM folder Personal BEx Documents.
BEx Portfolio	The BEx Portfolio iView is a KM navigation iView with a special layout for broadcasting. It displays the KM folder Public Documents (/documents/ Public Documents). Under My Portfolio and BEx Portfolio, various Knowledge Management functions are available for working with your documents. You can add ratings, evaluations, feedback, and personal notes to documents.
BEx Web Analyzer	Using the BEx Web Analyzer, you can navigate in queries and analyze data. With the BEx Web Analyzer iView, a BEx Web Application iView is called with the Web template 0ANALYSIS_PATTERN (standard delivered content WAD template). The BEx Web Application Query String property has the value bi_template =0ANALYSIS_PATTERN. This component replaces the BEx Ad Hoc Query Designer in 3.x.
BEx Broadcaster	Using the BEx Broadcaster, you can precalculate and distribute queries, query views, Web templates, reports, and workbooks. The Broadcaster iView is a BEx Web Application iView for which the command to start the BEx Broadcaster is used.
Universal Worklist	The Universal Worklist (UWL) allows you to manage your work by merging tasks from different workflow systems. These include workflows, alerts, KM notifications, and collaboration tasks. The Universal Worklist is used as a central point of access for tasks, alerts, notifications, and so on. For example, you can view and work with alerts generated using the BEx Broadcaster and broadcast to the UWL.
Collaborative BI	The Collaborative BI Portal page contains iViews from Knowledge Management to display discussions, collaboration rooms, and notifications. Users of the collaboration functions can see the results in these iViews: • **Collaboration rooms** Groups of users can exchange context-related applications and information. Content from BI can also be included. • **Discussions** Enables an exchange of ideas about specific topics using a document in Knowledge Management. Users can hold discussions based on the documents and links that you stored in Knowledge Management using BEx Information Broadcasting. • **Notifications** Users can be automatically informed about any changes to a document (as a result of a new precalculation, for example).

TABLE 16-2   Tab Pages of the Business Explorer Role in the Enterprise Portal

information specific to their needs. This can be configured to have whatever information the business user requires and as a matter of fact can be configured by the specific business user themselves depending on the authorizations. Documents can be uploaded to this view and displayed for reference and used for analysis. This option is shown here.

Copyright by SAP AG

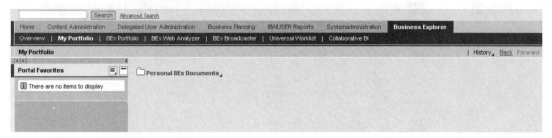

The next option is the BEx Portfolio view. In this view, the user can subscribe to different reports and BW objects to be updated and then sent to the Portfolio. The following illustration shows this view.

Copyright by SAP AG

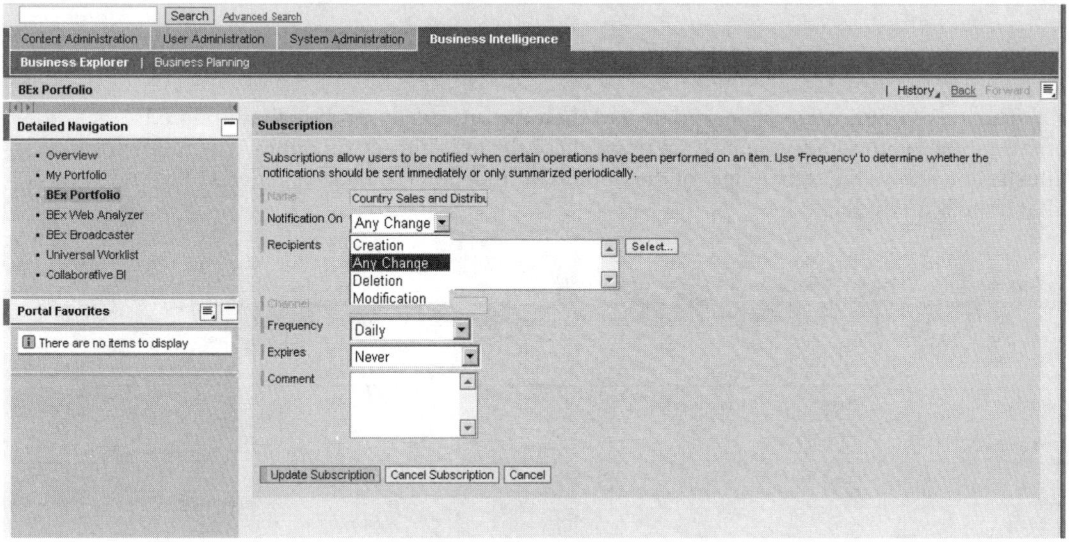

Once the subscription process is complete, different reports and workbooks can be uploaded and linked for the business user. Numerous different objects can be linked to this screen, such as online links to reports, BEx workbooks, Web templates, queries, and iView objects. A list of the different icons is supplied here (see the following illustration). As you can see, the ability to send, download, edit, rate, as well as other functionality, is available from this screen.

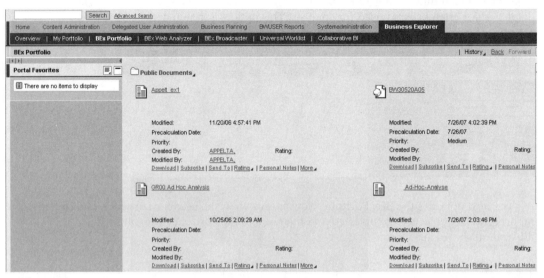

 The initial notification of an update and then the process of sending that updated information to other individuals is an example of the use of these functions. The following illustration shows the initial view of the update notification. The flag is generated to show that there is an update.

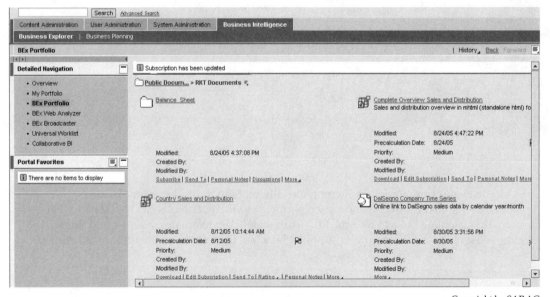

NOTE *The flag icon identifies the "update" of a report or other object, and the yellow light bulb icon indicates that an object is "new."*

Executing the query, we see that the exception shows that the critical threshold for the specific distribution channel (Services) for the country of Canada has fallen below the requirements. The following illustration shows the executed query.

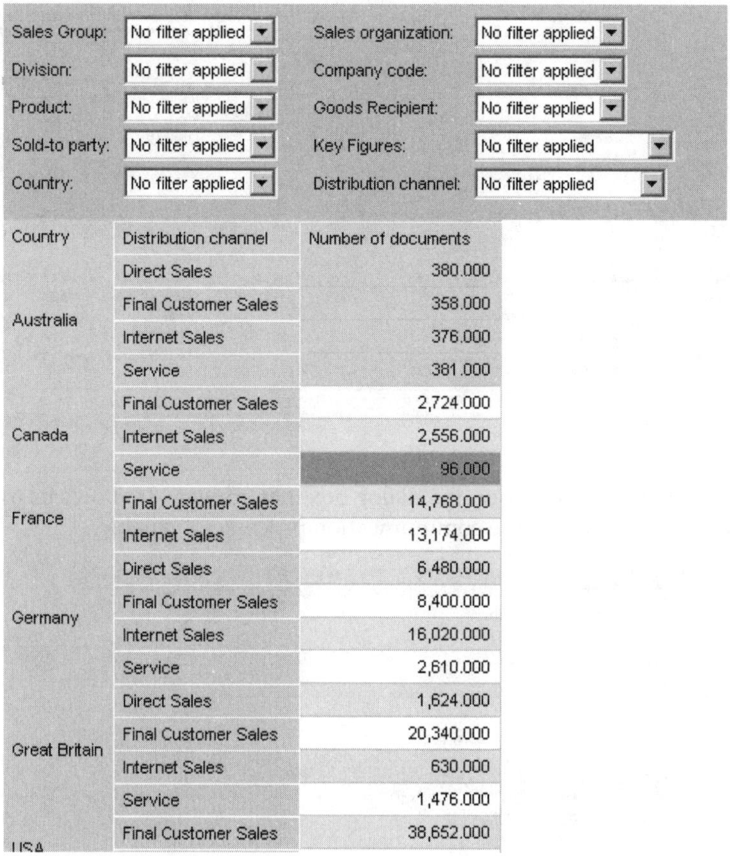

Country	Distribution channel	Number of documents
	Direct Sales	380.000
Australia	Final Customer Sales	358.000
	Internet Sales	376.000
	Service	381.000
Canada	Final Customer Sales	2,724.000
	Internet Sales	2,556.000
	Service	96.000
France	Final Customer Sales	14,768.000
	Internet Sales	13,174.000
	Direct Sales	6,480.000
Germany	Final Customer Sales	8,400.000
	Internet Sales	16,020.000
	Service	2,610.000
	Direct Sales	1,624.000
Great Britain	Final Customer Sales	20,340.000
	Internet Sales	630.000
	Service	1,476.000
USA	Final Customer Sales	38,652.000

Filter panel above table:
Sales Group: No filter applied; Sales organization: No filter applied; Division: No filter applied; Company code: No filter applied; Product: No filter applied; Goods Recipient: No filter applied; Sold-to party: No filter applied; Key Figures: No filter applied; Country: No filter applied; Distribution channel: No filter applied

Seeing this, we can decide to execute the Send To option on this screen. This view is shown here.

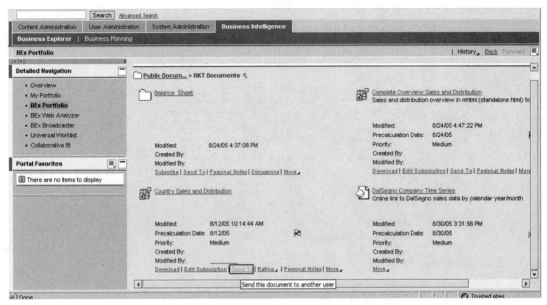

The following illustration shows the dialog box that appears. It allows us to send this report to other users via any of the communication processes available.

The report can be sent either as a static or dynamic report. The following shows the ability to attach a personal note with ratings to this query.

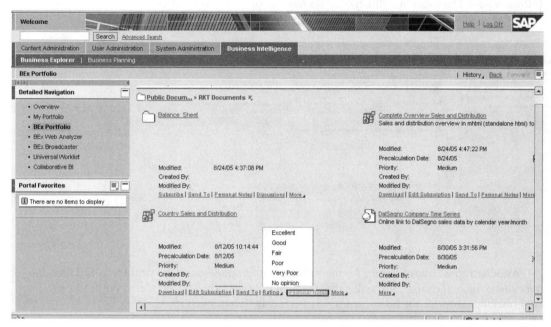

The next option is our old friend, the BEx Web Analyzer. It offers the ability to access any of the queries that have been developed in the BEx Query Designer and then, of course, view them. This view is shown next. Notice that the default template for these queries comes along into the EP.

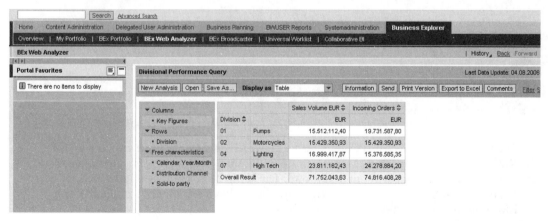

Moving to the next option we run into the BEx Broadcaster. (This has been displayed before in Chapter 12.) This view, of course, allows the use of the Information Broadcaster within the EP. The following illustration shows this option.

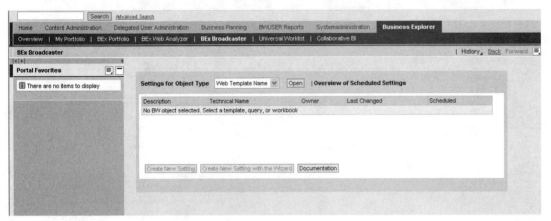

Another repeat from Chapter 12, the Information Broadcaster is the next view, Universal Worklist, which, if configured, will generate a list of tasks, broadcasted alerts, notifications, and tracking items for the business user. This view is shown next.

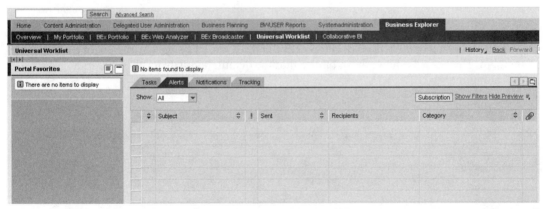

The final option in this list is Collaborative BI, which enables the business user to use the KM to generate information, communicate with other team members, and manage processes within their department and group. The setup of this area is within the EP, but the functionality is not necessarily within BW but rather a combination of the BW and the KM systems. This functionality is shown here.

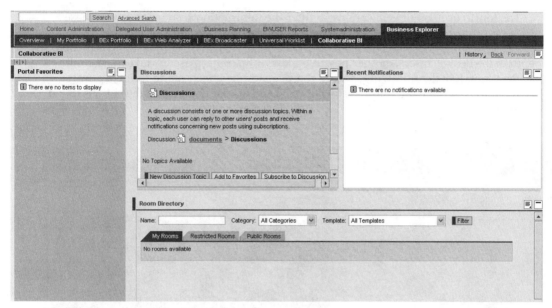

Copyright by SAP AG

The other tab on the screen for business users (Business Planning) offers the ability to work with the Integrated Planning (IP) structures within the EP. The following illustration shows this functionality. We will have a more detailed discussion of IP in the next chapter, but we can identify the different options within EP in this chapter. Looking at this illustration, notice that three different options—Planning Modeler, Planning Wizard, and BEx Web Analyzer—are the basic tools used in the process of setting up the Integrated Planning functionality.

NOTE *Even though the BEx Web Analyzer is mentioned in this list, it is only for viewing data and is used specifically for the definition of the planning screen but is not involved directly in the Integrated Planning process.*

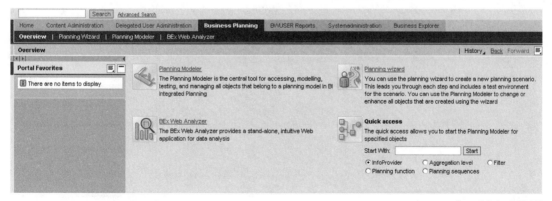

Copyright by SAP AG

The fourth option offers the ability to filter the information seen using any of these different tools to a specific object such as an InfoProvider. This helps focus the planning process to an individual object in the BW system. Again, we will cover these options in more depth in the next chapter. Another possible view of the Enterprise Portal screen could be something like the following, where the decision has been made to incorporate everything under one tab (Business Intelligence) and the user can choose the buttons found under this tab.

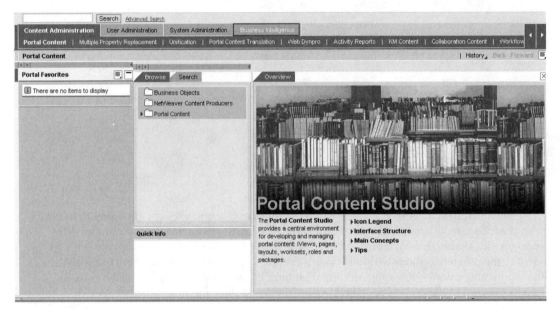

A final view is that of the Administrator. We will be visiting this view later in this chapter and will discuss the different areas of this Portal Content screen. This initial screen is displayed in the following illustration.

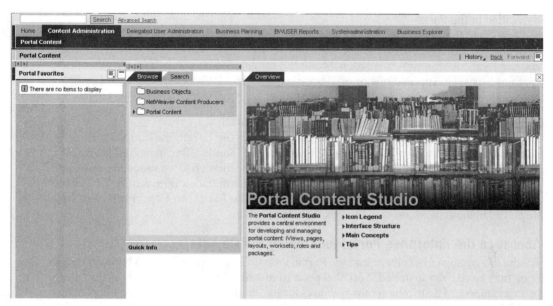

Navigation with BI Content in the Portal

The various options for displaying BI content in the Portal enable you to display BI content in a number of different ways as well as combine it with other content. Navigation with BI content in the Portal involves switching from or to BI content within the Portal. Generally this means that another iView is called or that the content of a portal page has changed. Transfer of information (parameters) between the various types of content in the Portal is especially interesting. There are several methods used for navigation within the Portal.

Eventing in the Portal

Eventing in the Portal involves navigation within a Portal page. The information is exchanged between iViews using JavaScript. The contents of the iView in which the event was triggered remain visible. A BEx Web Application can be both the source and the target of an event. Developers can exchange user-defined events between BEx Web Applications. Some applications in the Portal, such as Manager Self Service (MSS), send and receive their own events, which can also be sent or received from BEx Web Applications. The developer of a BEx Web Application is responsible for the implementation of the JavaScript for sending and receiving. The sending of a Portal event can be displayed as a link or as an extension of the context menu.

Navigation in the Portal

Navigation in the Portal enables the swapping of iViews with other iViews. The initial navigation bar and detailed navigation are adapted accordingly. Within a BEx Web Application, you use JavaScript for implementation. Multiple parameters can be transferred to other iViews (such as BEx Web Applications or SAP transactions in SAP ERP, SAP CRM, and so on). Navigation in the Portal can be displayed as a link or as an extension of the context menu.

Jumping Using the Report-to-Report Interface in the Portal

When the Report-to-Report Interface is used to jump in the Portal, the jump targets are administrated in BI within the transaction Maintaining Sender/Receiver Assignments (transaction code RSBBS). You can define BEx Web Applications, SAP transactions, or external targets on the Web as jump targets. The Report-to-Report Interface automatically transfers all parameters that can be assigned. The jump targets of the Report-to-Report Interface are displayed in the context menu of the BEx Web Application.

Access to the Enterprise Portal for Linking BW Objects

For the integration of BI content into the Portal, it is necessary to configure in both systems once they have been installed. You also need to install a Precalculation Service for the precalculation and distribution of workbooks for information broadcasting (see Chapter 12 on the Information Broadcaster). To complete this process, you can use the Installation Guide. Also, information is available in the system under SAP Reference IMG _ SAP Customizing Implementation Guide _ SAP NetWeaver _ Business Intelligence _ Setting for Reporting and Analysis _ BEx Web _ Integration into the Portal.

Once this process is complete, you should be able to link the BW objects to the Enterprise Portal. Access to linking the different BW objects to the Portal can be found in each of the front ends of the BI system. In all cases, once the Enterprise Portal is accessed, the sequences of steps to assign the BW object to the Portal are the same. Therefore, the initial process will be displayed once and referenced as we go through these different access points.

If we use the BEx Query Designer as the initial example, the process starts once the query itself is ready to be saved. The following illustration shows the initial screen of the BEx Query Designer and the step for accessing the Portal. Access to the Portal dialog box is automatic using the Query | Publish | To Portal command.

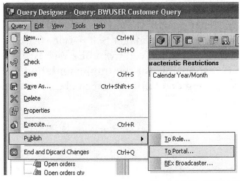

Copyright by SAP AG

Once this is executed, another dialog box appears with certain default information, as shown in the following illustration. The Technical Name and Description fields are already filled in with default values. You can change either of these at this time.

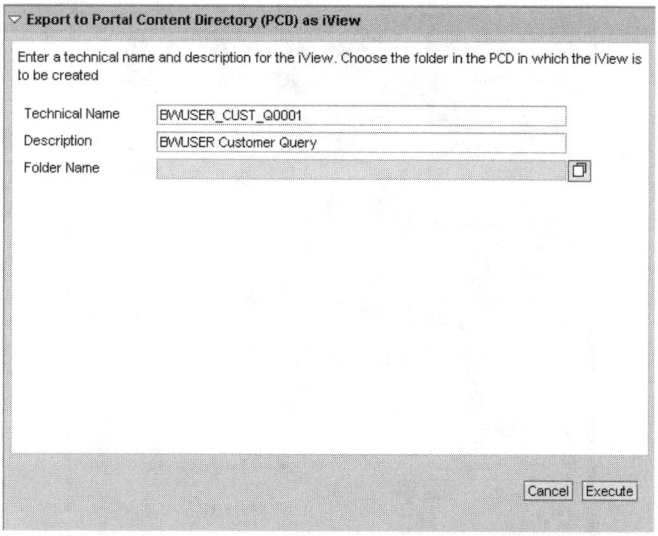

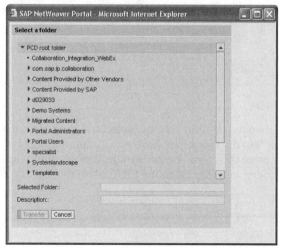

Copyright by SAP AG

Just below these options is the field for the link to the Enterprise Portal. Notice the title of the dialog box: Export to Portal Content Directory (PCD) as iView. Basically, this screen helps link the two objects together. Also, notice that the Folder Name field is grayed out so that information cannot be manually assigned. However, using the F4 dropdown help, we can locate the appropriate folder in the Portal Directory and use this for the connection. The following illustration shows the results of using the F4 dropdown function. This shows the different folder structures available in the Enterprise Portal.

Copyright by SAP AG

Depending on the authorizations assigned, the administrator will be able to assign this particular component to the Portal. Once the appropriate folder is found, use the Transfer button to transfer the folder to the PCD screen. This result is shown here.

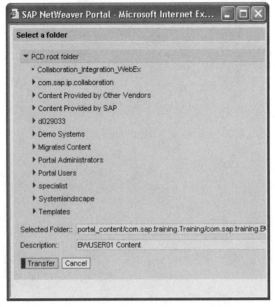

Copyright by SAP AG

Once the folder shows on the PCD screen, use the Execute button to complete the process. The following illustration shows the results.

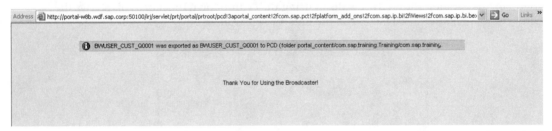

Copyright by SAP AG

A notification is generated to show that the object has been assigned to the appropriate folder in the Portal Content directory. The final verification that this process has worked is to access the Portal Content directory and confirm it. The following illustration shows the results as well as the query we assigned to the EP Content directory.

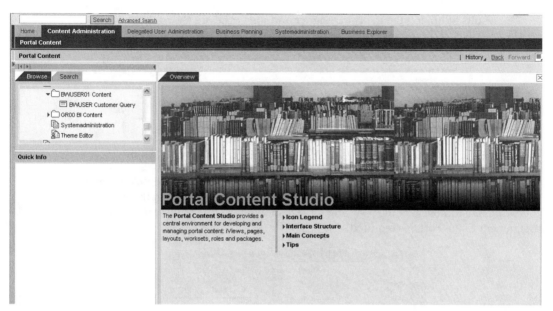

Once this is complete, we begin the process of organizing, formatting, and setting up the administration of the reports.

Access via the BEx Report Designer is very similar. The initial screen from the BEx Report Designer is shown here. Use the Report | Publish | To Portal command to link the Report Designer report to the Portal. Once this is complete, a similar dialog box appears. From here, the process is exactly the same as before.

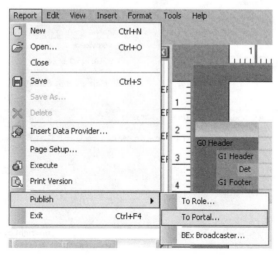

The results of linking the Report Designer and the Portal are shown here.

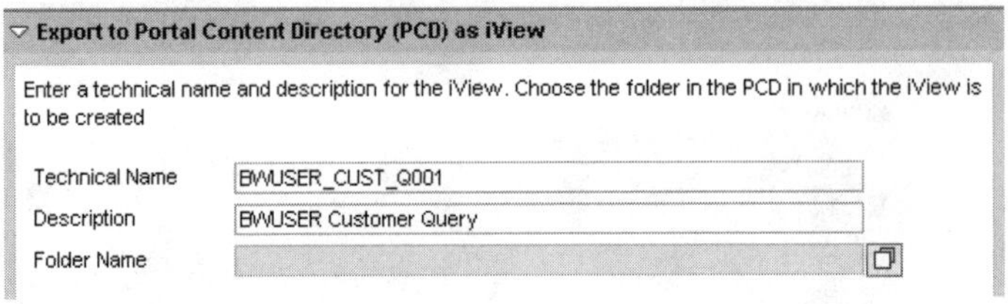

Export to Portal Content Directory (PCD) as iView
Enter a technical name and description for the iView. Choose the folder in the PCD in which the iView is to be created
Technical Name
BWUSER_CUST_Q001
Description
BWUSER Customer Query
Folder Name

The process for the Web Application Designer is the same. From the WAD, use the Web Template | Publish | To Portal command to create the link, as shown in the first of the following illustrations. On the resulting screen, shown next, the request for the folder assignment to the Portal is required.

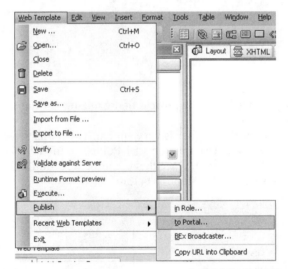

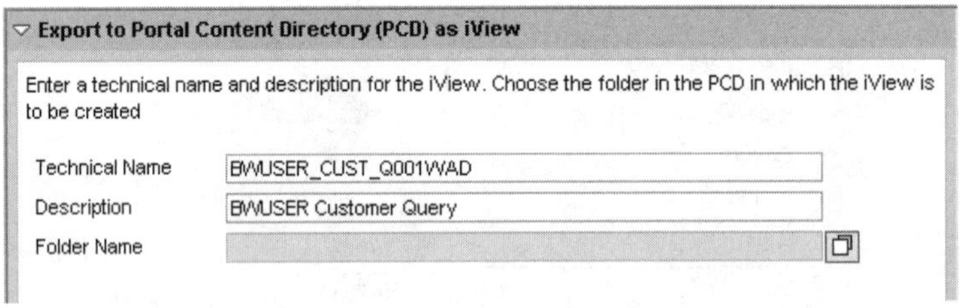

Web Template
Edit
View
Insert
Format
Tools
Table
Window
Help
New ...
Ctrl+M
Open...
Ctrl+O
Close
Delete
Save
Ctrl+S
Save as...
Import from File ...
Export to File ...
Verify
Validate against Server
Runtime Format preview
Execute...
Publish
Recent Web Templates
Exit
Layout
XHTML
in Role...
to Portal...
BEx Broadcaster...
Copy URL into Clipboard

Export to Portal Content Directory (PCD) as iView
Enter a technical name and description for the iView. Choose the folder in the PCD in which the iView is to be created
Technical Name
BWUSER_CUST_Q001WAD
Description
BWUSER Customer Query
Folder Name

Finally, we need to touch on access from the BEx Information Broadcaster. This has actually been detailed in Chapter 12, but as a reminder it is shown in the following illustration. This shows the access point for the Enterprise Portal from the BEx Information Broadcaster. The Distribution Type setting controls this activity.

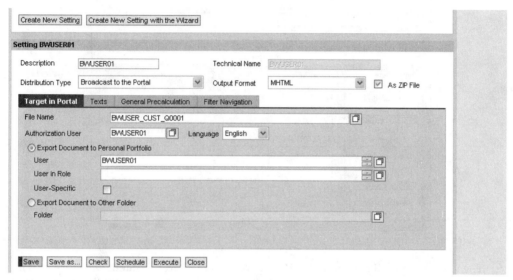

Once this step is complete, the objects for any of the different reporting tools are now available in the Enterprise Portal and can be linked to a Portal page, folder, and/or role to be distributed and displayed in the EP. Each of these reports can be either dynamic or static views in the Portal. Therefore, review with your business user the requirements for each report so that they can be linked using the appropriate connection.

Components of the Enterprise Portal

The Enterprise Portal has numerous components, so we will keep as close to the list of components required by BI as possible.

Business User and the Enterprise Portal

This section explains integration from the Portal user's viewpoint. The Portal desktop is the central complete view of the Enterprise Portal for the business user. It refers to the entire portal screen, including content and layout. As shown in the following illustration, the Portal desktop is divided into three main areas: header area, navigation panel, and content area.

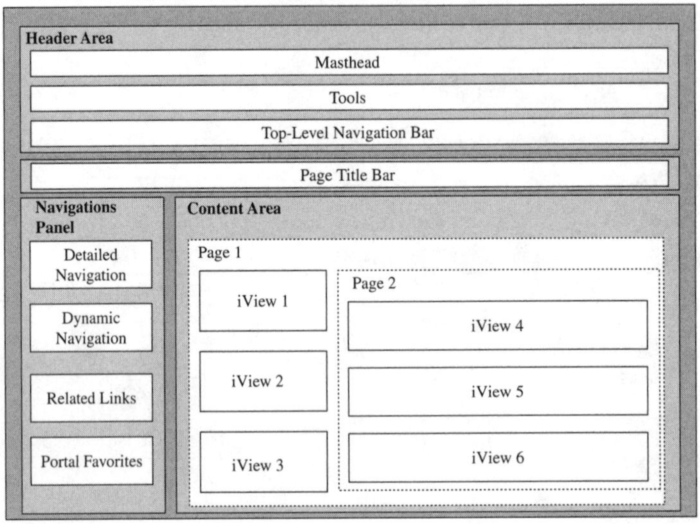

Copyright by SAP AG

The integration of BI content in the Portal involves the Portal Content Directory area in particular. In addition, the navigation panel offers a number of options for the integration of BI content. The BI content objects included in the content area of the Portal are:

- BEx Web Application as an iView
- Precalculated BEx Web Applications as a Document in Knowledge Management
- BEx Web Applications as a Link in Knowledge Management
- BEx Analyzer workbooks
- BI documents
- Web interface (from BW-BPS)

A BEx Web Application as an iView object shows the current data for the BI report. From a technical viewpoint, a direct call of the BEx Web Application occurs in the BI system. You can combine the BEx Web Application as part of a Portal page with other iViews from other systems as an iView. You can change the properties of the iView so that BI bookmarks or BEx queries can be displayed.

With the Precalculated BEx Web Applications as a Document in Knowledge Management object using BEx Information Broadcasting, you can precalculate BEx Web Applications and store them as a document in Knowledge Management. The precalculated BEx Web Applications contain historic data for specific times (static view of the data). These documents can also be displayed in an iView. You can then manage the precalculation (refreshing of the data) for each of the reports.

The BEx Web Applications as a Link in Knowledge Management object can create links to BEx Web Applications in Knowledge Management. These links show current data from the BI report. In contrast to the BEx Web Applications as an iView object, the call takes place indirectly using the Repository Manager for BI metadata. The collaboration functions can be applied to BEx Web Applications as documents and links. Collaboration with the BEx Web Application as an iView object is not possible.

There are several differences between calling BEx Web Application as an iView object from a Precalculated BEx Web Applications as Documents in Knowledge Management object and from a BEx Web Applications as Links in Knowledge Management object. Information on these differences specific to the Portal can be found in the Portal documentation.

In addition to BEx Web Applications as iViews or Documents, BEx Analyzer workbooks maintain a special position. Workbooks can be included in the Portal and can be called from the Portal. Workbooks are opened in a separate Microsoft Excel window. Opening workbooks within the web browser window is not possible for technical reasons. This again is an area where discussions with your business users are required since with the web-based reports the report itself is opened directly in the browser, but with excel based reports they are viewed as a separate pop-up window from the Portal. The documents and metadata created in the BI system (metadata documentation in particular) can be integrated into Knowledge Management of the Portal using the Repository Manager. They are displayed together with other documents for the end user in a directory structure. Furthermore, individual documents can be displayed as an iView.

As a final comment, the web interface (WIB from BW-BPS) is a web-capable planning application in the form of a Business Server Page Application (BSP application) that is created using the Web Interface Builder and can be incorporated into the Enterprise Portal. You are able to combine a web interface as part of a Portal page with other iViews, such as BEx Web Applications, to form an iView. The important thing to remember about this integration process is that the parameters of the Web Interface Builder (in the upper portion of the initial WIB screen) ensure that the First Page field is filled in; otherwise, the EP can't read the URL requirements. The following illustration shows the area we are discussing in the WIB component. At the very bottom of the page, the information for the field First Page should contain default information. If it doesn't, you need to manually enter the required information. The required information is exactly what is visible in this screen (pm_page.htm).

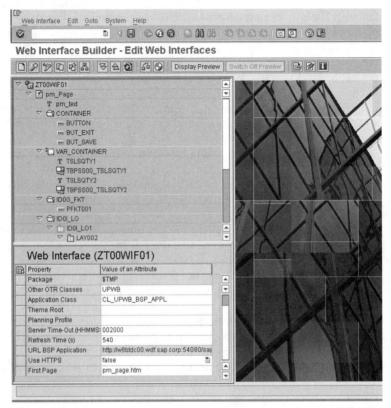

Calling BI Content in the Portal   The Portal desktop is the initial page for calling BI content in the Portal. The header area contains the initial navigation bar, which includes all the initial folders for the assigned Portal roles of a user. The initial entry takes place through the Portal roles. Selecting a folder displays either an iView or a Portal page in the content area of a subfolder in detailed navigation view. You have the following options when you call BI content:

- The BEx Web Applications as iView objects are started directly from Portal roles or Portal pages.

- You can include BEx Web Applications as Documents and Links in Knowledge Management (KM) as iViews.

- You can also display the documents and links that can be selected using the BEx Portfolio or KM Navigation iView. With the KM Navigation iView, a complete Knowledge Management folder is displayed. The KM Navigation iView allows you to execute collaborative functions for these documents and links. The BEx Portfolio provides a special graphical display of the KM Navigation iView.

The fundamental difference between the two options for calling BI content is that when Portal roles are used, navigation using the initial navigation bar and detailed navigation are carried out. In contrast to this, navigation using folders in Knowledge Management takes place via the content area. The various options for including collaboration functions with documents and links are clarified in the Portal role Business Explorer.

BI Content in the Navigation Panel   In addition to detailed navigation, the navigation panel includes iViews for dynamic navigation and related links, which can also contain BI content. Detailed navigation automatically appears as needed if the second level of a Portal role contains a folder with iViews and Portal pages and thus contains further levels. The iViews for dynamic navigation and related links appear in the navigation panel when the displayed Portal page or iViews contain the appropriate links to iViews. You can set up the links to iViews on the Portal page and at each individual iView. All links for the Portal page and the iViews contained are combined in the navigation panel and are displayed as Dynamic Navigation and Related Links. During dynamic navigation, the iViews themselves are displayed in the navigation panel. With Related Links, a list of links is displayed. In addition to the iViews listed previously, the iView Portal Favorites is also displayed in the navigation panel.

Business Intelligence Portal Role   In the Portal, the Portal role Business Intelligence is a main entry point for your work with BI content. It includes analysis and reporting as well as planning. The technical name of the Portal role is com.sap.ip.bi.bi_showcase.

The Business Intelligence Portal role includes content from the two Portal roles Business Explorer and Business Planning. The Business Explorer Portal role, which has been described earlier, provides an example of how users can work with BI content in the Portal to analyze business data and to distribute it while using Knowledge Management and collaboration functions. The Business Planning Portal role, on the other hand, allows business experts to use model planning applications.

Enterprise Portal Administrator and the Enterprise Portal

This section provides a description of the different scenarios for the integration of BI content into the Portal. The explanations contain technical information that will make it easier for administrators to understand and make necessary settings. The prerequisites displayed under Customizing refer to the current scenarios. For more information, see the SAP Reference IMG _ SAP Customizing Implementation Guide _ SAP NetWeaver _ Business Intelligence _ Settings for Reporting and Analysis _ BEx Web _ Integration into the Portal. This information is mostly technical in nature and may be the responsibility of the IT and/ or the Portal group but it is good to have a basic understanding of how each of these different integration portals can be displayed.

The BI content can be displayed in the Portal in different ways. BEx Web Applications can be included as iViews, as precalculated documents, or as links in the Portal. Furthermore, you can display BEx Analyzer workbooks and BI documents in the Portal. You can call these BI objects using Portal roles or with KM folders in the Portal. Various tools support you in generating BI objects in the Portal and integrating them into it. Integrating BI content into the Portal requires experience both in SAP NetWeaver BI and in SAP NetWeaver Portal. To make the necessary settings, close cooperation between administrators of the BI systems and those of the Portal is necessary. Similarly, the authors responsible for the BI content and the Portal content must also work closely together to integrate the BI content into the Portal.

You can integrate the BI content into the Portal using various tools. Depending on the type of integration, you create different objects with different displays in the Portal. You have a variety of options for displaying BI objects in the Portal. The various display types are summarized in Table 16-3.

Display Type	Description
BEx Web Application as an iView	Web-based BI application that is displayed as an iView in the Portal. BEx Web Applications are Web templates executed on the Web that are created using the BEx Web Application Designer.
BEx Web Application as a Document in Knowledge Management	Document stored in a KM folder with historical data for a web-based BI application.
BEx Web Application as an Online Link in Knowledge Management	Link to a web-based BI application with current data in a KM folder.
BEx Analyzer Workbook as an iView	Microsoft Excel workbook with one or more embedded queries displayed in a separate browser window as an iView in the Portal. (This is a very important point to make since the use of the BI Portal replaces the BEx Browser and the Portal can be the central access point for your reporting strategy. Therefore, you can access both the web-based reports and the BEx Analyzer Workbooks in the Portal.)
BEx Analyzer Workbook as a Document in KM	Microsoft Excel workbook with one or more embedded queries stored as a document with historical data in a KM folder.
BEx Query as an iView	Query displayed as a web-based BI application in a standard view as an iView in the Portal. This is a special form of a BEx Web Application.
BEx Query as an Online Link in the Knowledge Management	Link to a query with current data that is displayed in a standard view. The link is stored in a KM folder.
BW Query as a Document in Knowledge Management	Document with historical data for a query that is displayed in a standard view. The link is stored in a KM folder.
Single BI Document in Knowledge Management as an iView	A single document generated in BI (such as documentation on metadata) that is displayed as an iView in the Portal. The document or the link can be available in either Knowledge Management through the Repository Manager for BI documents and BI metadata or a precalculated BEx Web Application in Knowledge Management.
Multiple BI Documents in Knowledge Management as an iView	Multiple documents and/or links from a folder in Knowledge Management are displayed with a KM Navigation iView. The documents and/or links in Knowledge Management can come from the BI system and other sources. The layout of a KM Navigation iView can be adapted using layout sets.
Web Interface as an iView	Web-capable planning application of the BW-BPS that is displayed as an iView in the Portal.
BI Components	Various applications and tools from the BI system, such as the Data Warehousing Workbench, the BEx Query Designer, the BEx Web Application Designer, and the BEx Analyzer.

TABLE 16-3 Options for Displaying BI Objects in the Portal

BEx Web Application or Query as an iView in the Portal The BEx Web Applications and queries displayed on the Web can be displayed as iViews in the Portal. A BEx Web Application or query as an iView can, together with other iViews, be part of a Portal page or can take up the complete content area. At execution there is a direct call of the BEx Web application or query in the BI system with which the current data is displayed. When the Portal cache is used, data updates can appear with a delay. An iView with a BEx Web Application or query can be generated using the BEx Web Application Designer, BEx Query Designer, or Portal Content Studio. The iViews are of the type BEx Web Application iView and have the following code link:

    com.sap.portal.appintegrator.sap.BWReport

The two most important properties, System and BEx Web Application Query String, are set automatically for the BEx Web Application Designer and the BEx Query Designer. You need to enter these properties manually in the Portal Content Studio.

The System property includes the alias on the BI system (see SAP Reference IMG _ SAP Customizing Implementation Guide _ SAP NetWeaver _ Business Intelligence _ Setting for Reporting and Analysis _ BEx Web _ Integration into the Portal _ Create a BI-System in the Portal). Table 16-4 shows the BEx Web Application Query String property values that must be used for SAP BI 7.0.

The <…> entries are placeholders that are to be replaced with the name of the required object.

You can add more URL parameters for BI to the BEx Web Application Query String property (for example, to set filter values). The URL parameters are separated by an ampersand (&). You can use the Application Parameters property to transfer additional BI URL parameters.

BEx Web Application or Query as a Document or Link in KM You can include a BEx Web Application or query that is displayed on the Web as a precalculated document or link in Knowledge Management in the form of an iView on a Portal page. The precalculated documents with historic data are stored in Knowledge Management (not in the BI system). The links in BEx Web Applications or queries access the BI system indirectly through the Repository Manager for BI metadata and then display the current data. A BEx Web Application or query can be generated as a document with the BEx Broadcaster and as a link using the BEx Web Application Designer or the BEx Query Designer. The documents and links are only located in Knowledge Management (not in the BI system). You can use

BI Object	Value
Web Template	template=<TEMPLATE>
Query	query=<QUERY>
Query View	initial_state=VIEW&initial_state-view=<VIEW>
InfoProvider	initial_state=INFOPROVIDER&initial_state-infoprovider=<INFOPROVIDER>
Report	report=<REPORT>

TABLE 16-4 BEx Web Application Query String Properties for the Portal

the Portal Content Studio to create iViews with documents and links. The iViews are of type KM Document iView and have the code link com.sap.km.cm.docs. The most important property is the path to the document. Here are some points to keep in mind:

- With a precalculated BEx Web Application or query as a document, the path is independent of the selected folder in Knowledge Management. You specify the folder in the BEx Broadcaster in the Target in the Portal tabbed page.

- With a BEx Web Application or query as a link, the path to the document is independent of the selected prefix for the BI Metadata Repository Manager and the template ID of the BEx Web Application. You have to enter the following value as the path to the document (the designations in brackets are placeholders for technical names):

  /<BI_REPOSITORY_MANAGER_PREFIX>/activeVersion/WebTemplate/ <TEMPLATE_ID>/launch

You can use the KM-Content iView from the Content Administration Portal role to determine the path for the document.

BEx Web Applications or Queries as iViews in Different Portals   BEx Web Applications and queries that are displayed on the Web can be displayed as iViews in different portals. SAP NetWeaver 2004S Portal is required for displaying BEx Web Applications or queries using the BEx Web runtime functionality in SAP NetWeaver 2004S. This portal can be used either for BI content only (as a BI Portal) or on a company-wide basis (as an Enterprise Portal). If this portal is to be used only for displaying BI content, you may need to integrate the BI content concerned into another (company-wide) portal. This portal may be one of the following:

- SAP NetWeaver 2004S Portal
- SAP Enterprise Portal 6.0
- Third-party provider portal

The following types of integration are available:

- Integration Using a URL iView
- Export/Import
- Global Portal (Federated Portal)

The decision of which one of these possibilities are going to be used is critical and can have significant effects on the portal landscape. Analysis needs to be done for the appropriate decision of which process should be followed for the current web based reporting and the future portal approach for an entire company.

In addition, Single Sign-On (SSO) is also supported, in most cases, for this type of integration. The portal to which the user logs on and in which the content of another portal is displayed is called the *producer portal*. The other portal is called the *consumer portal*. The terms *producer iView* and *consumer iView* are used in the same way. If you want to integrate a BEx Web Application (SAP NetWeaver 2004S) into an SAP Enterprise Portal, version 6.0, the web browser must fulfill the prerequisites for SAP NetWeaver 2004S.

The prerequisites depend on the selected integration:

- **Integration Using a URL iView**   Various settings are required for setting up Single Sign-On when integrating using a URL, in which case a trustworthy connection between two portals is established.

  Carry out the following steps to use Single Sign-On:

  1. Export the portal certificate in the producer portal.
  2. Import the (producer) portal certificate in the consumer portal.

     A third-party provider portal does not normally support SAP logon tickets. However, most non-SAP portals allow the use of X.509 client certificates.

- **Export/Import**   You need to create a BI system in the portal for export/import integration. This BI system in the consumer portal must have the same system alias as in the producer portal.

  The following general steps are required for Single Sign-On:

  1. Export a BI certificate in the BI system.
  2. Import a BI certificate to the portal.

There are additional ways of displaying a BEx Web Application or query in a different portal:

- **Integration Using a URL**   This type of integration uses a URL iView (as a producer iView). You use a URL iView to help call up an SAP NetWeaver 2004S iView (as a consumer iView) in SAP EP 6.0. It is also possible to make a reverse call: An SAP EP 6.0 iView (as a consumer iView) can be called up in the SAP NetWeaver 2004S Portal.

  The difference between BEx Web Applications and queries is indicated only by their differing URL parameters. When you are directly calling the iView or calling the iView via the application integrator, these URL parameters are defined for the consumer iView, so no differentiation is required in the URL iView (producer iView). All required information is defined in the consumer iView. A source portal provided by a third party can use all three options for integrating a consumer iView as long as it supports the display of external content using a URL.

- **Export/Import**   You can export BI iViews in the producer portal as portal content and import them into the consumer portal. The producer portal can be an SAP NetWeaver 2004S Portal or an SAP EP 6.0. This is also the case for the consumer portal.

  The following steps are required for the export and import of portal objects:

  1. Create a transport package using the Portal Content Studio in the producer portal.
  2. Add portal objects.
  3. Export the transport package.
  4. Import the transport package in the consumer portal.

The system alias of the BI iView is retained during the export and import procedures. You must define a system with an identical system alias in the consumer portal.

- **Global Portal (Federated Portal)**   The concept of a global portal allows content from multiple portals to be virtually grouped together and published in one portal. You can use a global portal to integrate BI content from your BI Portal into an Enterprise Portal.

BEx Analyzer Workbook as an iView in the Portal   BEx workbooks are Microsoft Excel workbooks with one or more embedded BEx queries. You can display workbooks in the Portal as iViews. This would allow you the option to have a one-stop solution for a frontend for all of your users reporting needs. In the Portal the workbooks are displayed in a separate Microsoft Excel window. BEx Analyzer workbooks need the BEx Analyzer, which requires a local installation of the SAP GUI for Windows with the BI front end. A possible recommendation would be that you use BEx Web Applications in the Portal that run completely in the web browser. You could use the function Export as Excel 2000 File from the BEx Web Application context menu as an alternative to a local installation of the BI front end if you need to access the functions of Excel. If this is not possible an iView with a workbook can be generated using the Portal Content Studio or Role Upload. The iViews are of type SAP Transaction iView and have the code link com.sap.portal.appintegrator.sap and the next screen - Transaction. The important properties are System, Transaction Code (TCODE), and ApplicationParameter:

- The System property includes the alias on the BI system.
- The Transaction Code for every workbook is RRMXP.
- The value WBID=<WORKBOOK_ID> is in the ApplicationParameter property.

You can determine the workbook ID with the BEx Analyzer by opening the desired workbook. In the design toolbar for the BEx Analyzer, choose Workbook Settings. The Workbook Settings dialog box includes the workbook ID in the upper field Name of Workbook. Note that with BEx Analyzer Workbooks as an iView, the AutoStart property contains the value True (also turn on the process first screen), the GuiType property contains the value WinGui and finally make sure that the property Technique has the value SAP Shortcut File turned on.

BEx Analyzer Workbook as a Precalculated Document in KM   BEx workbooks are Microsoft Excel workbooks with one or more embedded BEx queries. You can include a workbook that was stored as a precalculated document in Knowledge Management on a Portal page in the form of an iView. BEx Analyzer Workbooks as Precalculated Documents can be generated using the BEx Broadcaster. The precalculated documents with historic data are stored in Knowledge Management (not in the BI system). You can use the Portal Content Studio to create iViews with precalculated workbooks. The iViews are of type KM Document iView and have the code link com.sap.km.cm.docs. The most important property is the path to the document. You can use the KM-Content iView from the Content Administration Portal role to determine the path for the document.

BI Documents in Knowledge Management as an iView   The Repository Manager for BI documents and BI metadata allows the display of documents and metadata created in the BI system (especially the documentation for the metadata as well) using Knowledge Management (KM). The Repository Manager for BI Documents enables access to documents created in the BI system. The documents are broken down into three document classes: Metadata, Master Data, and InfoProvider Data (very much like our discussion around the document process in Chapter 7). The Metadata document class contains manually created documents on metadata. These documents are not the automatically generated documents from the Metadata Repository. In the Master Data document class are documents on characteristic values, such as images for personnel numbers, descriptions, and technical specifications for materials. The InfoProvider Data document class contains documents on a combination of characteristic values, such as comments on key figures. You can use the Data Warehousing Workbench to create the documents or you can create them in Web Applications. The Repository Manager for BI Metadata enables access to automatically generated HTML-based documents for metadata. The documents correspond to the information in the Metadata Repository in the Data Warehousing Workbench. You can also store BEx Web Applications or queries as documents or links in Knowledge Management using the BEx Broadcaster. In both cases, documents or links are created in Knowledge Management that represent BI content and that can be used to display and use the functions of Knowledge Management. The ability to support the data in the reports with unstructured information from documents has become more and more important as the key decision makers use information from outside of their core company data to make critical decisions.

Keep the following points in mind:

- **Displaying individual documents as iViews**   The documents can be displayed individually as iViews. For this display, an iView of type KM Document iView is required with the code link com.sap.km.cm.docs. You have to specify the most important property, the Path to Document or Link in KM. Using the KM Content iView from the Content Administration Portal role, you are able to determine the appropriate path to documents from the Repository Managers for BI documents and BI metadata and to precalculated documents or links from the BEx Broadcaster. The appropriate prefixes <BI_DOCUMENT_PREFIX> and <BI_META_DATA_PREFIX> have to be included in the path to documents from the Repository Managers for BI documents and BI metadata.

- **Displaying multiple documents in KM folders**   Multiple documents can be displayed in a KM folder. To do this, you create internal links to the corresponding BI documents in the KM folder of your choice. For example, you may want to add BI documents or the appropriate documentation on BI metadata to a KM folder in which you have stored precalculated documents and links from BEx Web Applications using the BEx Broadcaster.

A KM folder is displayed using a KM Navigation iView with the code link com.sap .km.cm.navigation. The KM folders can be displayed in different layouts. The Layout Settings property determines which layout is displayed.

Web Interface (from BW-BPS) as an iView in the Portal   A Web interface (from BW-BPS) is a web-capable planning application of BW-BPS in the form of a Business Server Page Application (BSP application) that is created using the Web Interface Builder. This allows not only the

BI-IP screens but the BW-BPS planning screens to be viewed from the Portal. Web interfaces can be displayed as iViews in the Portal. A Web interface as an iView can, together with other iViews, be part of a Portal page or can contain the complete content area. A direct call of the Web interface takes place in the BI system with which the current data is displayed. You are not able to use the portal cache. You are able to manually create an iView with a Web interface using the Portal Content Studio. The iViews are of the type SAP BSP iView (for Business Server Pages) and have the code link com.sap.portal.appintegrator.sap.BSP.

The most important properties can be determined by looking at a URL for a Web interface:

<web_protocol>://<hostname>:<port>/<customer namespace>(<session_id>)/bc/bsp/<application namespace>/<application>/<start page>.htm

- The System property includes the alias on the BI system. The values in the URL for <web_protocol>, <hostname>, and <port> can be automatically replaced by the alias.

- The Customer Namespace property corresponds to <customer namespace> and is sap by default.

- The Application Namespace property contains the <application namespace> and is sap by default.

- The Business Server Page (BSP) Application property corresponds to <application> and thus the name of the Web interface.

- The Start Page property is the start page for the Business Server Page (BSP), and it corresponds to <start page> in the URL. The start page has the name of the Web interface in the format <Web-Interface-Name = application>.htm.

- The Application Parameter property is optional and enables transfer of additional URL parameters to the Web interface.

NOTE *When Web interfaces (from BW-BPS) are integrated into the Portal, you have to activate the current web design in the Web interfaces (see SAP Note 629775). If you do not do this, the Web interfaces (from BW-BPS) will not be displayed in the current Portal theme. Also, note that during the configuration of your BW-BPS WIB you will need to make sure that the field 'FIRSTPAGE' in the parameters for the WIB Header page is filled in with the URL location for the BSP. Usually it's a standard short URL which can be obtained from the metadata repository for the BSP.*

BI Components in Portal The integration of BI content into the Portal ideally takes place using BEx Web Applications and queries that run in the web browser. You can also integrate other BI components, such as the Data Warehousing Workbench, BEx Query Designer, BEx Web Application Designer, or BEx Analyzer into the Portal (transaction iViews).

- **Data Warehousing Workbench** The Data Warehousing Workbench is a comprehensive SAP transaction that functions only in connection with a locally installed SAP GUI for Windows. With SAP GUI for Windows 6.20 or higher, you do not have to log on again if you want to display SAP GUI for Windows transactions in a web browser window (Single Sign-On is supported).

You can generate the Data Warehousing Workbench in the Portal Content Studio as an SAP Transaction iView. The most important properties are System, Transaction (TCODE), and GuiType:

- The System property includes the alias on the BI system.
- The Transaction code for the Data Warehousing Workbench is RSA1.
- The GuiType property has to contain the value WinGui.

- **BEx Analyzer**   The Business Explorer Analyzer (BEx Analyzer) is an Excel add-in with extensive OLAP functionality in connection with a BI system. In order to use the BEx Analyzer, you have to have the SAP GUI for Windows with the BI front end installed locally. For technical reasons, the BEx Analyzer opens in a separate window. You do not have to log on again because Single Sign-On is supported. A SAP GUI for Windows appears in the portal window in the work area. You can generate the BEx Analyzer in the Portal Content Studio as an SAP Transaction iView.

  The most important properties are System, Transaction (TCODE), and GuiType:

  - The System property includes the alias on the BI system.
  - The Transaction code for the BEx Analyzer is RRMX.
  - The GuiType property has to contain the value WinGui.

- **BEx Web Application Designer**   The Portal is an application that runs on a web browser. The BEx Web Application Designer is a Windows application. It is technically possible to start Windows applications in a web browser, but this is not recommended for security reasons. Instead, you call the Windows application BEx Web Application Designer from the Windows Start menu. You can generate the BEx Web Application Designer in the Portal Content Studio as a URL iView. The most important property is the URL that contains the value file://C:/Program%20Files/SAP/FrontEnd/Bw/wdbpwpub.exe.

NOTE *The path is dependent on the local installation directory. Single Sign-On is not supported.*

- **BEx Query Designer**   The Portal is an application that runs on a web browser. The BEx Query Designer is a Windows application. It is technically possible to start Windows applications in a web browser, but this is not recommended for security reasons. Instead, you call the Windows application BEx Query Designer from the Windows Start menu.

  You can generate the BEx Query Designer in the Portal Content Studio as a URL iView. The most important property is the URL that contains the value file://C:/Program%20Files/SAP/FrontEnd/Bw/wdbrlog.exe.

These options are not specific to the reporting process but are of interest if the BI Portal is going to be your central access to the BI system. This section of the chapter has provided you with additional information on the basic technical side of each of the methods used to link BW objects to the Enterprise Portal.

You can distribute the BI content using the BEx Broadcaster and the BEx Broadcasting Wizard to the Portal. You can also integrate BI content into the Portal using SAP Role

Tool / Display Type	BEx Broadcasting Wizard	BEx Broadcaster	Portal Content Studio	KM Content	SAP Role Upload
BEx Web Application as an iView			X		X
BEx Web Application as a Document in Knowledge Management	X	X			
BEx Web Application as an Online Link in Knowledge Management	X	X		X	
BEx Analyzer Workbook as an iView			X		X
BEx Analyzer Workbook as a Document in Knowledge Management	X	X			
BEx Query as an iView			X		X
BEx Query as an Online Link in the Knowledge Management	X	X		X	
BEx Query as a Document in Knowledge Management	X	X			
Single BI Document in Knowledge Management as an iView			X		
Multiple BI Documents in Knowledge Management as an iView			X		
Web Interface (from BW BPS) as an iView			X		
BI Component			X		

TABLE 16-5 Overview of the Integration Tools and Display Types of BI Objects

Upload, KM Content, and the Portal Content Studio. Table 16-5 provides an overview of which tool you use to create which objects. A combination marked with an X in the table means that this display type of BI content is possible with the designated tool.

Also, a wide spectrum of users has the option of publishing BI content to the Portal based on their authorizations. The tools are customized for various groups of users. Table 16-6 provides a list of user groups and the possible tools they would use.

User Groups	Tools
Information Consumers	Broadcasting Wizard
Knowledge Worker, Authors, and Analysts	BEx Broadcaster
Administrators	Portal Content Studio KM Content SAP Role Upload

TABLE 16-6   Overview of User Groups and Tools

As mentioned, the Portal Content Studio is the central component of the Enterprise Portal that portal developers will use for consolidating all the reporting needs of business users. The following illustration shows the initial screen of the Portal Content Studio. Notice that the administrator has the ability to create a number of different objects to help with the organization of the reports and workbooks. We will focus on creating the basic structures to generate the results we need for the display of our reports. The folder hierarchy you see is called the Portal Content Directory, and this is where all folders, pages, roles, and iViews are stored in the Portal. Depending on the option chosen from the context menu of the folder or other object, the Portal Content Studio work area will reflect the options available, as you will see throughout our example. This is one example of an approach that can be taken while setting up your user frontend.

Copyright by SAP AG

Developing Pages in the Enterprise Portal   Once you have published the iViews to the Portal Content Directory folders, you need to create the Portal pages. Portal pages are used to present the iViews to the user and can appear in a variety of layouts, such as one- or two-column widths. Each page is stored in a folder in the Portal Content Directory and can be completely different from others in the hierarchy. Once you have created a page and chosen a layout option for the page, you can then add the iViews to it. The iViews can be developed from BI content or other external services such as SAP ECC Transactions, URLs, and other BI objects such as the BW Workbench. For each page, the properties determine how it behaves.

NOTE   *You will notice that as we go through each of these option that some functionality can be accomplished within the WAD versus in the BI Portal. For example, in this case, the use of the Page can also be reflected if you were to use a Container object in the WAD with two ANALYSIS GRIDS included, then publishing the CONTAINER to the Portal.*

Also, each iView added to the page provides the ability to have unique properties. The following illustration shows the properties of a page.

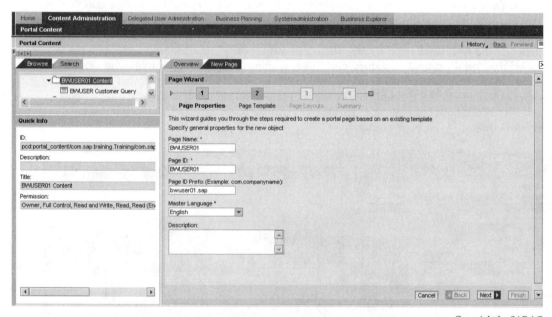

Creating a Portal page requires four steps, but for our purposes all we really need to do is make sure we have the page consistent for the iView. In step 1, the technical name and a description are required. The first of the following illustrations shows step 2. We will be using the Default Page Template option. In step 3 we identify the type of page layout required to comfortably display the reports we will be using. There are a number of options for the layout, but we will be working with a basic two-column view. The second illustration shows this information.

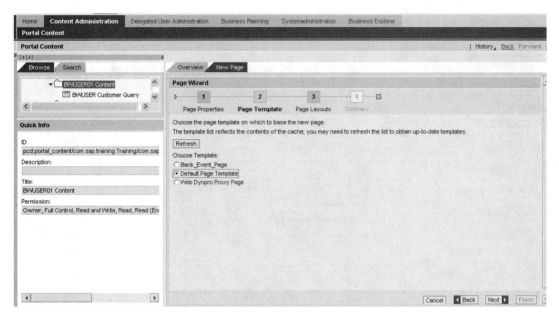

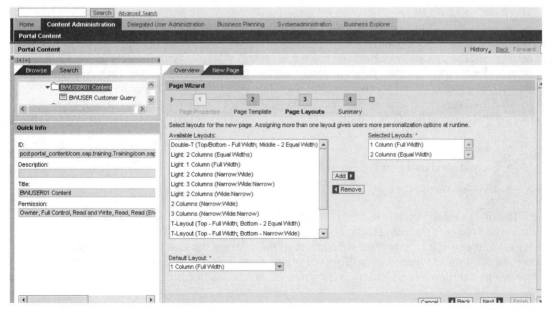

Finally, step 4 involves a review and summary of the properties chosen, as shown here.

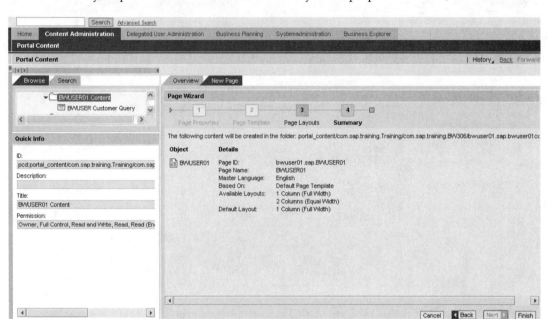

Developing Folders in the Enterprise Portal Once the iViews have been organized on the Portal pages, the process of organizing the pages onto Portal roles with the help of the Portal folder structure begins. Pages are assigned to a role using a hierarchical structure of folders. It is important that you understand the relationship between the folders and the layout of the Portal interface. There are three key layers for navigation in the Portal folders (assume that the role itself is the root of the hierarchy and is not involved in the display):

- First level of top navigation
- Second level of top navigation
- Detailed navigation

The first two layers relate to the horizontal menus at the top of the Portal screen. The third layer relates to the navigational panel at the right of the screen. When the folders are defined in the role, it is important to be aware of these layers because their hierarchical position determines where they will appear on the final screen. The final setup of the role with a series of hierarchical folders is shown next.

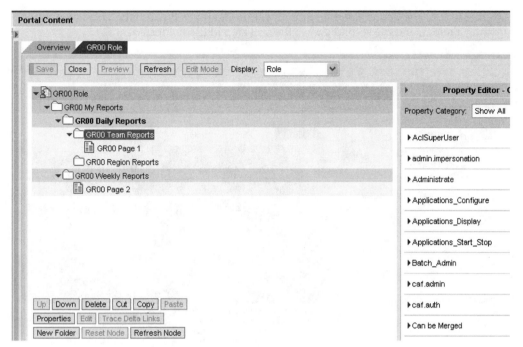

Based on this illustration, the final view of this information shows that the **My Reports** level is at the top of the page, followed by the **Daily Reports** and **Weekly Reports** levels (shown across the top of the Portal page as sub-tabs or in the second level of folders). Finally, the **Team Reports** and **Region Reports** levels, followed by **Page 1** (assigned to the Daily Reports folder) and the **Page 2** (assigned to the Weekly Reports folder) are found in the navigational portion of the screen. The creation of a folder involves the assignment of a technical number, description, and ID prefix. You can also include additional comments about the use of the folder, if necessary. Once all this is complete, click Finish to close and save the folder. The first of the following illustrations shows the initial context menu for creating a folder, and the second shows the first step in the Folder Wizard.

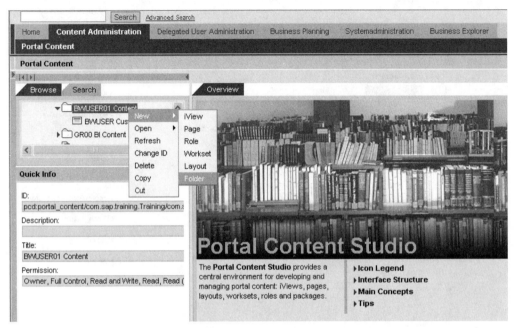

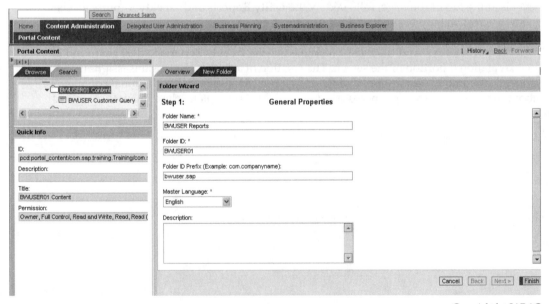

Additionally, the folder saves its file location within the Portal.

Developing Roles in the Enterprise Portal So far, the hierarchy of the Portal has been developed from the bottom up. We worked through the configuration of the iViews from the objects in the BI environment (lowest-level object) and then moved to the pages needed to assign the iViews to the structure (second-tier object). Then we worked through the folders to which the pages are assigned (third-tier object). Finally, we configured the root of the Portal hierarchy (the role). The role is an object that organizes folders into a hierarchical format, and we worked through this organizational process in the previous section. Now the only task left is to confirm the configuration of the role. The following illustration shows the initial step in the Roles Wizard.

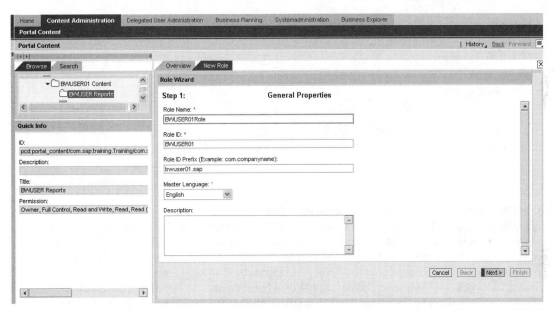

To access this, right-click the content folder and select New _ Role. Enter the technical name and description of the role and click Finish to save it. The final step in configuring the role is shown here.

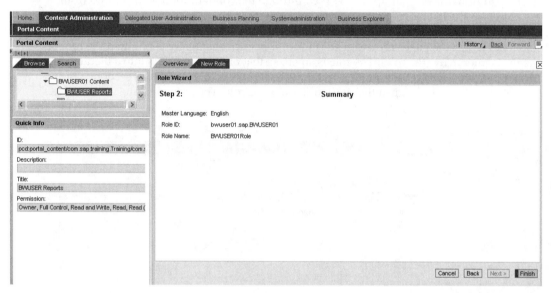

Configuring the BI Content in the Enterprise Portal

Now that we have completed the configuration of the Enterprise Portal structures and have identified the location within the Portal Content architecture where the Portal will be stored, we can begin the process of taking all the pieces and combining them. We have already set up and assigned the BI objects to the Enterprise Portal by linking the object—whether it is a query, BEx Web Analyzer query, WAD query, or whatever—to the Portal. We also created the iView for that object. Now, we need to go through the process of assigning all this to the appropriate levels and objects.

Assigning BI and Portal Objects   Even though we have worked through the configuration of the actual object from the bottom up, the assignment process will be from the top down. Therefore, we start with the role we just set up. The following illustration shows the role we just created and the use of the context menu to create a new folder. This folder will be assigned to the role being used to organize the hierarchy of objects.

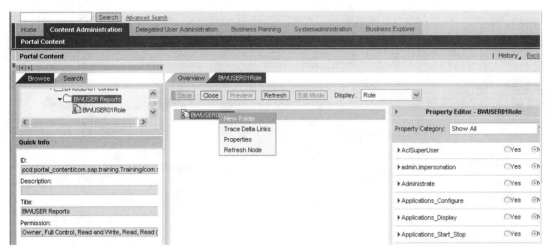

The creation of the folder is explained earlier in this chapter. Once the configuration is complete, the folder BWUSER Quarterly Reports is found at a lower level under the role. This process is very straightforward, and the results are shown here.

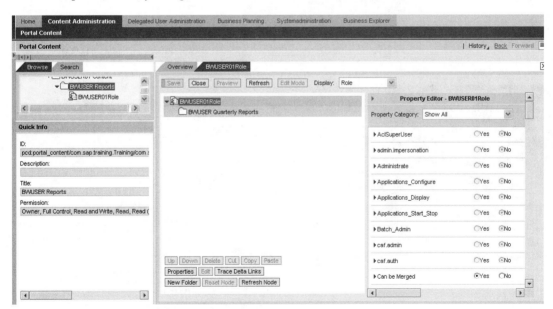

Our next step is to take the page we developed before and assign it to the folder. Remember that during the creation of the page, we would have assigned the iViews. Therefore, once the page is assigned to the folder, the basic architecture of the Portal view is complete. The first of the following illustrations shows that the folder parameter Entry

Point has been set to Yes. This means that when the role is accessed, this folder will be visible immediately and not hidden. Ensure that the appropriate level is highlighted (in this case, the folder BWUSER Quarterly Reports). Find the page that was created and use the context menu option Add Page to Role _ Delta Link, as shown in the second illustration.

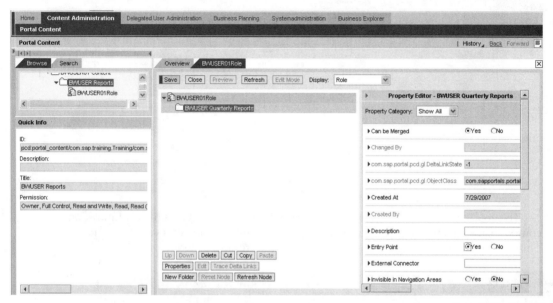

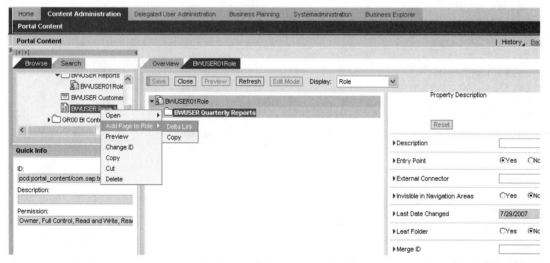

Finally, the end result is that the page is assigned to the folder, and this is the hierarchy view of the information from the Portal. Once this is accomplished, we just need to assign the role to the business user, as shown here.

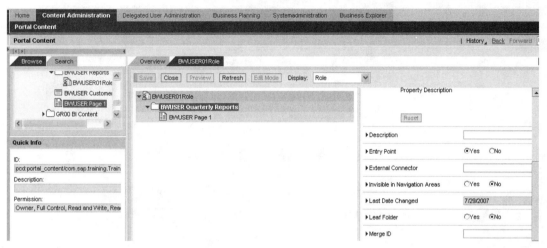

Assigning Roles to Business Users The process of assigning roles to the business users takes us out of the current tab (Content Administration) and moves us to the Delegated User Administration tab, where the assignment will take place. The following shows the initial screen.

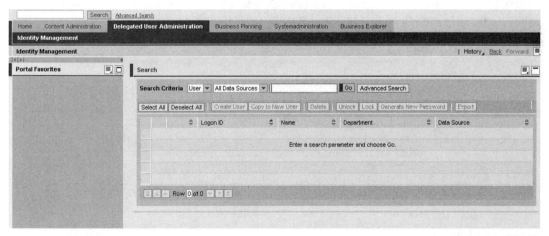

To enter our user into the field, we perform a search to locate the user and have it default into the catalog below. Once the user is located, as shown here, choose the box to the far left of the line to highlight the user. Then, at the bottom portion of the screen, select the tab labeled Assigned Roles, which is where we will make the assignment.

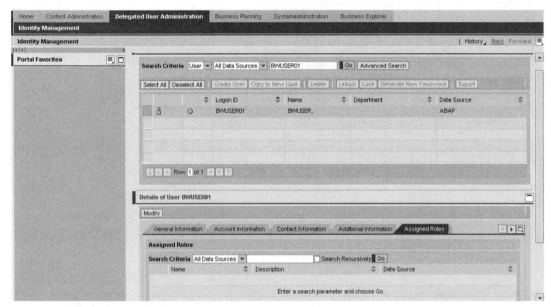

Click the Modify button so that the option for assigning can be completed. A search for the BWUSER01 role causes it to appear in the lines below. Choose the role to be assigned and click the Add button to add the role to the user, as shown next.

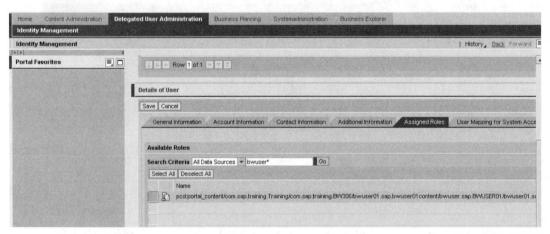

The following shows that the role has been added to the user.

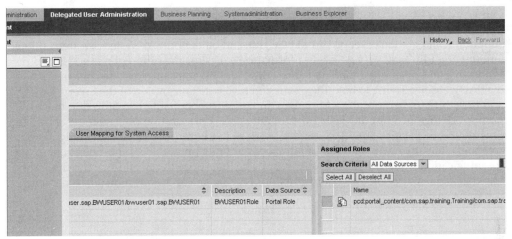

Make sure that you save before leaving this screen. Finally, by executing a refresh of the screen (found on the context menu of the Options button on far right side of the screen), the tab BWUSER Quarterly Reports appears, as shown here.

This is a basic example of setting up the necessary links between the EP and BW to enable the reports, queries, workbooks, and documents to use the functionality of the Enterprise Portal for displaying strategic information for the business users.

Summary

This is just the tip of the iceberg when it comes to the Enterprise Portal—and only the portion that deals with the BI content. In addition to integration with BI, the Enterprise Portal can support the integration of reports from ECC, R3, and other non-SAP systems. A tremendous amount of additional, very detailed information exists for the different methods used in connecting and integrating the Enterprise Portal and BI. You can access this information in the SAP websites. Trying to hold the discussion to just the integration of the Enterprise Portal and BI is difficult because the KM system and other functionality is required to make all parts work together, but the basic functionality and configuration offer you the ability to execute these specific steps to make BW work in the Enterprise Portal. In many cases, companies already have some sort of intranet or Internet process for communication, so a set communication strategy likely already exists. The Enterprise Portal and BW can fit nicely into that architecture, and the Enterprise Portal can be one of the additional tabs on your corporate website.

Other Options with the Analyzer—Integrated Planning (BI-IP) and Visual Composer (VC)

After all the information we've reviewed, the new concepts still keep coming. This chapter focuses on the functionality behind the Integrated Planning (IP) component of BI 7.0 and the Visual Composer. In both cases, we will be reviewing just the specifics of the integration between these two components and the BW environment. These two components are highlighted in this chapter because they are extensions of the basic BW query process. There are a number of other options when it comes to extending the functionality of BW, such as the use of Crystal Reporting, but these two components have really taken off and are being used quite extensively in many customer implementations. They are very different in terms of results and uses, and we will discuss the basic functionality and outcome of each in more detail in this chapter. It is important to understand that the Visual Composer (VC) is an additional component within the NetWeaver platform and is not delivered with BW. On the other hand, Integrated Planning is a part of the BW environment and is delivered with BW.

The Visual Composer is a component of the xApps Analytics, and it allows you to compose model-based and analytical based applications in a flexible way, without manual coding. With VC, you create pattern-based or freestyle user interfaces using simple drag-and-drop services and then define the data flow between them. Because VC is model driven, you can compose an application without having to write a single line of code. This is the best part of this component. It allows people like you and me to create incredible front-end functionality without doing any coding at all. When a model is deployed, SAP NetWeaver VC translates the model into the required code for the application. SAP Visual Composer provides a development environment for rapidly creating and adapting model-based transactional and analytical applications. It has been designed to enable business analysts to create enterprise applications using standardized components that meet SAP standards and quality criteria. Visual Composer has been designed according to the following essential considerations:

- **Simplicity**　Visual Composer enables fast development of model-based business applications, without requiring manual coding skills. The Visual Composer graphical interface is very user friendly and it implements drag-and-drop capabilities, direct layout visualization and a range of other tools for facilitating model building and adaptation. It is also browser-based, eliminating the need for client-side installation and maintenance.

- **SAP NetWeaver 2004 integration**　Visual Composer is tightly integrated into the SAP NetWeaver 2004 suite of applications.

- **Connectivity to SAP and third-party systems**　Visual Composer operates on top of the SAP NetWeaver Portal, utilizing its connector-framework interfaces to enable access to a range of data services, including SAP and third-party enterprise systems. In addition to accessing mySAP ERP systems, users can access SAP Business Warehouse and any open/JDBC stored procedures.

- **Support for different runtime environments**　Visual Composer is a robust tool whose models can be deployed to run in a number of different environments, including Web Dynpro and Adobe Flex.

- **Reusable components**　The building blocks implemented in the models ensure consistency in functionality and UI design from application to application. Using them ensures significant savings in time and effort by eliminating the need to re-invent similar functionality from model to model.

- **Trial and error**　Visual Composer is ideal for trying out a model, quickly simulating it in runtime—or even deploying it—and then going back to the "Storyboard" for correction and tweaking.

In summary, Visual Composer enables business analysts to apply their inherent understanding of their organizations' requirements to create and adapt applications to their specific business needs. These applications can then be subsequently customized and continuously changed in Visual Composer as the organization's business objectives evolve. In terms of the use of VC by the business analyst, there needs to be a comment added. It is important that the business analyst is comfortable with the overall functionality and process to create a VC storyboard. This type of toolset can be a bit intimidating to the higher level business analyst but to anyone that is interested in working with a proactive and interactive frontend set of tools the VC is for them.

Integrated Planning is the new planning component available in the 7.0 BI system and is fully integrated into the BW environment. This means it will use all the BW architecture to help with the planning process. This is in contrast to the component of BW called BW-BPS (Business Planning and Simulation). One question that could be asked at this point is, Why are we going through the IP functionality and not the BPS functionality? Simply put, the Business Planning and Simulation component doesn't have as integrated of an environment as does the Integrated Planning component. For example, the use of the standard BW queries, BW variables, and other areas of BW can be directly used in IP. Whereas in BPS, the creation of BPS-specific objects, such as the Planning Layouts and BPS variables, are needed to handle the planning process, and these BPS-specific objects can't be used in any BW process or activity. This point is the main reason that the IP functionality is being reviewed in this book and chapter—much of what we have seen in the BEx Query Designer, BEx Analyzer, Web Analyzer, and the WAD are consistent and very integrated with IP.

Not to say that there aren't times when you would rather use BPS instead of IP. However, the implementation and reusability of the objects are more apparent in the IP area. You need to remember that in terms of maturity of the product, BPS has been around for over six years, whereas the IP product had its initial version in the 7.0 BW platform and is therefore working through some issues based on the maturity of the product. With all the SBC and additional enhanced functionality being embedded into IP with each support package, it is very important to think carefully of the "why not" in terms of using IP for any new implementation. Although you will see some references to BPS during our discussion of IP, the focus of our discussion is IP. We will not cover all the options in the IP area because to do that would take another book. This component's material is very important to the idea of "BI versus BW" for the system, and to do the entire IP area justice would take an entire book. In this chapter, the discussion will primarily focus on the use of the front-end tools for reporting purposes. This means that the discussion around the back-end configuration for the IP planning functions and other components will be for the purposes of getting to the BEx Query Designer, BEx Analyzer, and WAD functionality and not drilling down into all the activities in these areas. These items could take a full book to go through and discuss in detail. If you are looking for a detailed discussion of the IP items—such as the Planning Sequence, the Status and Tracking area of IP, and other IP-specific planning activities—this is not the place to find that information. If, on the other hand, your IP question is about the use of the WAD functionality or the setup of a query to enable planning and posting, then you've come to the right place.

Some of the background information in this area was covered way back in Chapter 2, "Storing the Data—SAP BW InfoProviders." I will refer you to that chapter for information in the areas of Real-time InfoCubes and the aggregation levels used specifically for IP. This chapter strives to cover all the loose ends when it comes to IP and the use of some of the functionality in the Web Application Designer and BEx Analyzer. There will be times when the concepts require a discussion of the backend configuration or how certain items work in the BW Data Warehousing Workbench, but for the most part our conversation will revolve around the front-end functionality.

Introduction to the Visual Composer

The Visual Composer is a part of the overall concept of Analytical Applications. Analytical Applications (or *Analytics*) provide the users with the ability to execute processes for both tactical and strategic information in a single application. Analytical Applications are also known as Composite Applications. The process involves combining the functions from a transactional system together with the relevant reporting information from a data warehouse environment on the same screen. This could be done by just toggling back and forth from one system to another, but that would drive the most patient person nuts. Thus, Analytical Applications help the different groups of information analysts actually execute their responsibilities—analyze information (rather than driving them nuts trying to remember what system or activity they are working on at any one time). In many cases, the analysis being processed doesn't require the same level of complex tools, so offering the business user the correct toolset is as important as the data itself. If you are reviewing a basic list of expenses posted to a department, not all the functionality of a BW system is needed, but rather a basic set of tools to generate the appropriate view of the data. If we take this a step further, suppose we are not only interested in reviewing the costs by department, but are also looking to do some analysis by department and then forecast the planned costs. These different activities require the use of a number of data analysis functions. Therefore, an Analytical Application is required. This can be a combination of any of the different source systems integrated into the Enterprise Portal.

SAP Visual Composer is a web-based visual modeling tool that enables the business analyst to quickly create and adapt sophisticated application content, without coding. Visual Composer minimizes the effort and time required to create an application, resulting in faster "go live" decision-making, and is a part of an Analytical Application. As the target users for Visual Composer, business analysts are defined as the key users in customer organizations, possessing in-depth knowledge and understanding of the business unit's operations and core processes. Using their understanding of the business requirements and knowledge of their company software to accomplish the various business tasks, the business analysts use Visual Composer as an easily learned tool to "map out" the logical flow of the required applications. Visual Composer has been designed as an application-modeling tool that augments other existing SAP tools, such as SAP NetWeaver Developer Studio and BI Web Application Designer. A leading feature of Visual Composer is that it can accept datasources from a range of different back-end systems (the SAP system, SAP BI systems, JDBC-connected systems, and others) into the same model. It can also compile the models into different UI technologies, such as Web Dynpro and Adobe Flex. A good example of this can be seen in Figure 17-1, which shows a completed Visual Composer web screen. As you can see, the information is broken down into different levels (based on the toolbar items): Country, Sales Organization, and Customer. The user can toggle from one

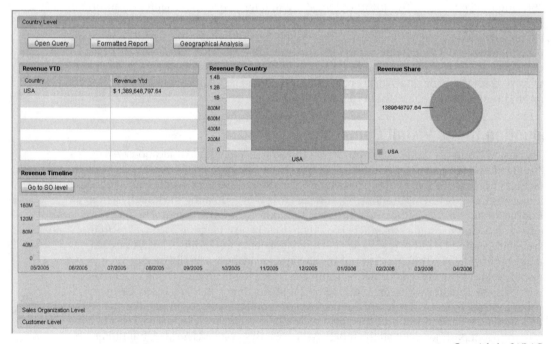

Copyright by SAP AG

FIGURE 17-1   Visual Composer web-based report

level to another. This information can come from different sources—for example, BI from the Country level, CRM from the Sales Organization level, and ECC from the Customer level—but all are available in one integrated screen.

Using the Geographical Analysis button, we can drill down to a different view of the data, as shown here. In this view of the information, additional drilldowns can be done based on the buttons on this screen: Monthly Comparison, Customers, World, and Broadcast. This geographical analysis is enabled by the use of the GIS process (for details, see Chapter 13 on Advanced BEx Processes).

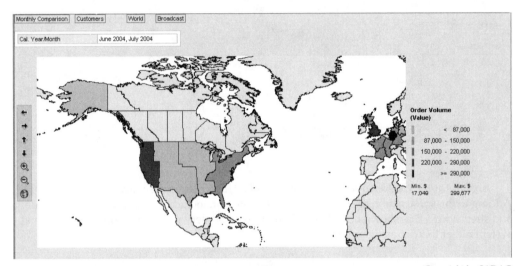

Copyright by SAP AG

The following illustration shows the results of a drilldown from the main report to the report at the Sales Organization level. Additional details by sales organization are available here, and with just a click on any of the sales organizations, the data will immediately change and display the details at that level.

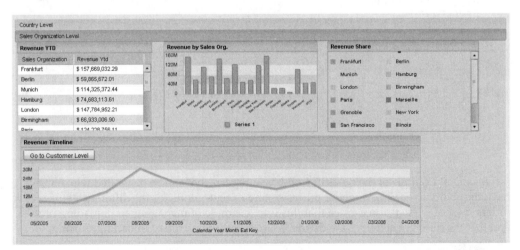

Copyright by SAP AG

The following illustration shows the results of a drilldown to the Munich sales organization and the immediate access to its detailed information.

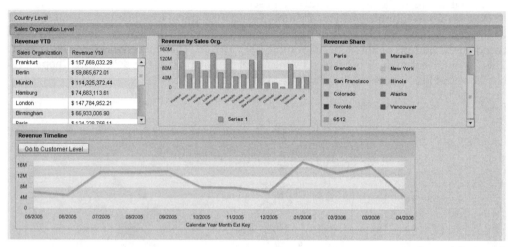

Analysis at the Customer level, with the use of a tachometer-type analysis, is also available. Adding to this information are the details of the customer, including country, city, postal code, and street address, as shown next. This information could very well come from an operational system rather than a data warehouse.

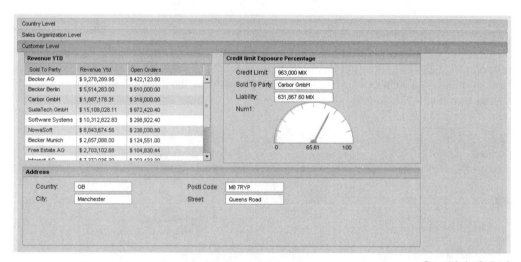

As a final example of the types of web-based reports that can be generated with VC, we have the ability to analyze ongoing processes and execute alerts for the different statuses of orders, as shown next. You can see that this is an example of managing an unloading process and that the different activities are divided into the following tabs: Unloading, Sorting,

Loading, Distance. The status of each activity is displayed, and the expected arrival time, actual arrival time, and so on are available for the different users to perform their tasks and responsibilities.

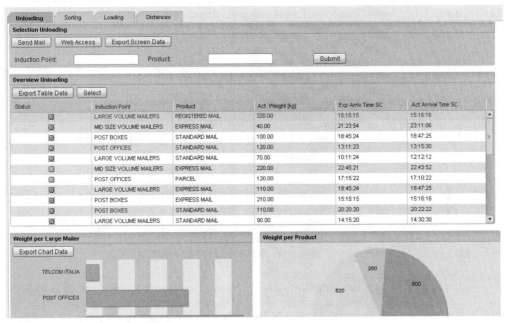

Components of Visual Composer

A prime concept in application modeling for SAP systems involves enabling business analysts to quickly and efficiently design and implement a modeled application that meets specific business requirements. Access to the analytic and transactional data must be direct and intuitive, resulting in a fast response from the structured data. The modeling tools must be powerful and intuitive, operating in a user interface that is user-centric and highly efficient. The model elements and components must be familiar in their graphical look and feel and in their functioning. For example, an input form is displayed and manipulated as an identifiable and familiar view in a portal iView, with all the fields and controls displayed and configured in a logical manner. Deployment should be fast and should give access to the runtime version of the model. Also, the user should be able to easily return to the "drawing board" in order to make subsequent modifications. The following are terms in the process of implementing VC that you will encounter and components that will be used during the configuration process in the Visual Composer documentation set:

- **Design time and runtime** Visual Composer is a design-time software tool in which you can develop an application and then deploy it. After deployment, you can run the actual application in the Enterprise Portal to check its functionality and results. During model creation and configuration, you define all the runtime attributes of the model components, such as the frame of a table, the size and types of toolbar buttons, the type of graphic, and the format of an output form. You can also define a range of properties of the actual Visual Composer design-time tools, such as the use of a background grid, the placement of the various toolboxes used with each board, or the style of the initial graphic display. Design time is mainly driven by the Visual Composer Storyboard (see Figure 17-2). This is the working area of the Visual Composer and is executed in a web browser.

- **Runtime environments** Models designed in Visual Composer can be deployed to run in one or more technologies, including Web Dynpro and Flex. The same model can be deployed to more than one environment, although not all components and controls are fully supported in each. Models deployed to Flex can run on a range of browsers, including Microsoft Internet Explorer, Netscape, and Firefox. Visual Composer implements a proprietary XML-based Visual Composer language as its source code for creating the models. Only during deployment is the model actually compiled into the executable code required by the selected UI technology. The result is a model that can be created once and used anywhere.

NOTE *A Web Dynpro is the development and runtime environment used to create professional user interfaces for business applications powered by SAP NetWeaver. It provides a declarative meta model for developing Web Applications, without requiring much programming code to be written. From this abstract definition, Web Dynpro generates code to create a ready-to-run Web Application for different runtime platforms and front-end technologies.*

- **Creating and adapting applications** In Visual Composer, you can create modeled applications from scratch, or adapt an existing application to your specific needs. For Analytic Applications with standard features, it is much faster to customize an existing application by replacing data services with the required queries, for example, and making other minor adjustments. No matter what, when planning to

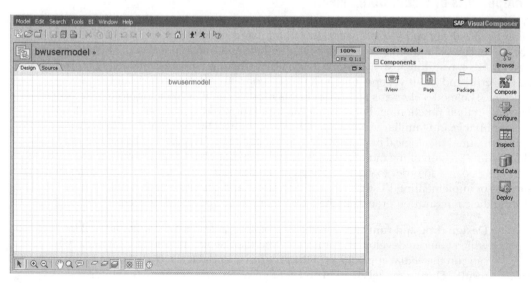

FIGURE 17-2 Storyboard for the Visual Composer

create or adapt an application, you should define the actionable information, detail the target functionality, and locate or prepare all required datasources ahead of time.

- **Data services**   At the heart of any modeled application is the source of the analytic and transactional data: This can be standard SAP RFCs (remote function calls) and BAPIs (Business APIs), Business Warehouse InfoCubes, BI queries, JDBC-compliant stored procedures, Web services, and others. A main strength of Visual Composer is that models can be built around any number of disparate data services and then finely tuned to display only the exact subset of data needed for the specific transaction or function. In our discussions we will stick to the data service of BW objects.

- **Storyboard**   You use Visual Composer to create and adapt applications through a graphical user interface called the Storyboard. This is your "work area" on which you organize and configure components of the application into a logical flow, or model. You build the application model by defining the data services and model components, assembling and connecting them into a task flow that answers the needs of the application. You place the model elements in a screen layout that reflects the actual look and feel of the application in runtime. The Storyboard contains a number of different boards, on which you can compose the model, lay out its components, and view its source code. The Storyboard uses the Microsoft XML Parser, Adobe SVG, and the Adobe Flash client as additional software units. The Adobe SVG plug-in is used to manipulate, scale, and manage graphics in the Visual Composer Storyboard and the XML Parser is used to manage the models in the tool correctly. All models are entirely described in XML as an open markup language.

- **Workflow**   As you build your model in the Storyboard, you drill down from upper-level model entities down to the lowest-level elements. Usually, experts very familiar with their actual business needs will perform the initial modeling of the task flow and screen layout. Subsequent modification and configuration can be performed by other modeling experts and developers.

- **Events**   In Visual Composer, an "event" is used to signal that an action has occurred in the workflow. At that point, the system then performs the actions assigned to the event. Certain model elements—such as data flow lines—are modeled to respond to these events. For example, Visual Composer assigns names such as *evt1, submit (used with input form buttons) and *next (for layers) to data mapping lines or transition lines, indicating the action that invokes the event. These names can be changed, and they can be used for defining controls that invoke the action. A standard event, such as submit or close, occurs when the specific control connected to the line is activated to invoke the event. For example, in the model shown in Figure 17-3, two submit lines have been defined. Also, the use of the asterisk (*) before the event name indicates that if any event of the same name (without the asterisk) is raised, all events of the name *with* the asterisk will respond. In this case, if the button in Input Form 2 is clicked (raising the event), both events (actions defined for both forms) will respond. If the button in Input Form 1 is clicked, only that event will respond.

NOTE   *Notice we have moved directly into the Visual Composer Storyboard component. Access to VC involves a number of steps, but again we are only working toward BI integration.*

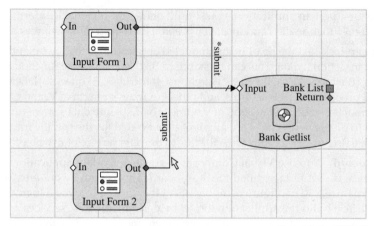

Copyright by SAP AG

FIGURE 17-3   Input events in the Visual Composer

In transitions between layers, if the transition line is given the same name as the event lines within the layer and is prefixed with an asterisk, raising the event in either form within the layer will activate the transition to the next layer. For example, a layer may contain two forms in which the user enters information. If the user inputs data in Input Form 1 and clicks Submit, the transition to Layer 2 will occur. If the user inputs data into Input Form 2 and clicks Submit, the transition will occur as well. This result is shown in Figure 17-4.

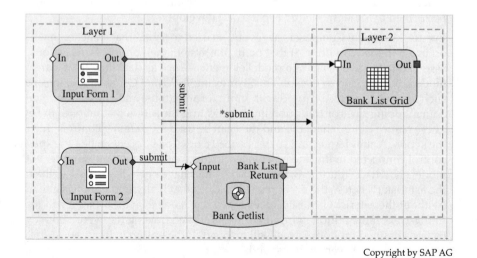

Copyright by SAP AG

FIGURE 17-4   Input events in the Visual Composer for two layers

Configuration of BI/Visual Composer Integration

Integrating BI with the Visual Composer involves a series of steps, including the actual system setup through to the use of the Enterprise Portal to execute the final VC web-based reports.

System Setup for VC

The Visual Composer server is installed on the development server, running on the SAP J2EE Engine, which runs the connected portal. The Storyboard is accessed from the client machine through a standard browser. At runtime, the user accesses the deployed model by calling up the portal using the browser. At the server side, SAP NetWeaver VC is executed in the runtime environment of the SAP NetWeaver application server based on the Java Stack. The Visual Composer server is therefore the central component. When a model is created, the result is stored in the J2EE database and at the file level as an XML description. The content developer can then decide which process will be used at runtime. The model remains without changes, but the iView will be created for Flash or for Web Dynpro for Java as a runtime. In the runtime, transactional content can run through Web Dynpro and Flex, while analytic content may run through Flex. The models deployed by Visual Composer to the portal include runtime metadata, which is stored with the model in the PCD (Portal Content Directory) and exported in the business package for delivery to customers. After the model is deployed, the iView will be transported to the SAP NetWeaver Portal where it will be a component of the EP, just like any of the other objects located there. Figure 17-5 shows this information. Additional details around the actual set up of the VC environment would be handled by the VC and EP Basis team.

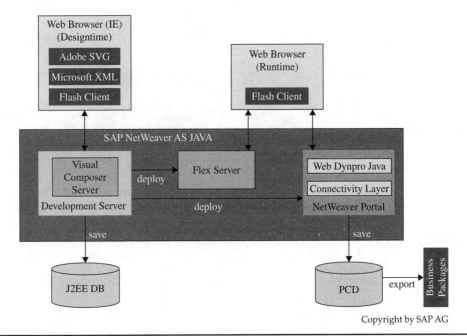

Copyright by SAP AG

FIGURE 17-5   Visual Composer Architecture

Uses of the BI Kit

One of the components of the integration between Visual Composer and BI is the BI Kit or BI Extension Kit for the Visual Composer. The BI Kit is a plug-in that provides users access to a variety of datasources. The core VC allows only the use of remote function calls and Web Services. With the BI Kit, additional types of datasources can be included, such as JDBC sources, ODBO, XMLA, and SAP BI. The addition of the SAP BI is the one in which we are most interested. To help with this process, the BI Kit comes with a wizard that helps with the process of integration. The following illustration shows the starting point to gain access to the BI Integration Wizard. Once you have drilled down to the iView level (you will see this during the configuration portion), you can then use the BI integration Wizard function.

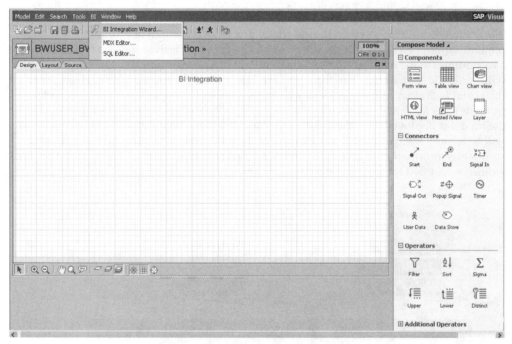

The following illustration shows the initial screen of BI Integration Wizard. Once you identify a specific system, the prompts change depending on the type. For example, if you choose a BW system, the wizard will be looking for an InfoProvider or query. This is the integration point between the Visual Composer and Business Warehouse.

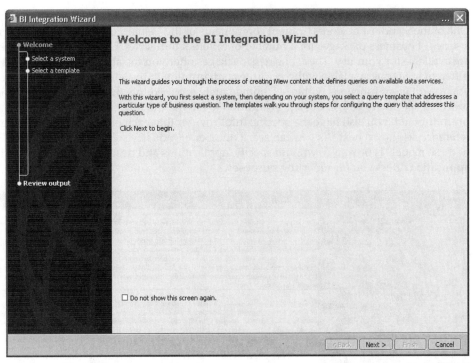

Table 17-1 lists the connector and the access they provide.

Connector	Technology Based On	Provides Access To
Relational (OLTP)		
BI JDBC	Sun's JDBC, the standard API for RDBMS	Over 200 JDBC drivers (examples include DB2, Microsoft SQL Server, Oracle, and Microsoft Access)
BI SAP Query	SAP Query	SAP operational applications (InfoSets from transaction SQ02)
Multidimensional (OLAP)		
BI ODBO	Microsoft's OLE DB for OLAP, industry-standard OLAP API for Windows	OLE DB for OLAP-compliant datasources (examples include MS Analysis Services, MS PivotTable Services, and SAP BW – indicator on the BEx Query Designer)
BI XMLA	MS XMLA, Web Services–based access to OLAP providers	Platform-independent access to OLAP datasources (examples include SAP BW 3.x, MS Analysis Services, Hyperion, MicroStrategy)
BI Web API	SAP RFC and SAP BW WebAPI	SAP BW queries, query views, and InfoObjects

TABLE 17-1   Connectors Provided in the BI Kit

Use of Business Packages for BI

One of the Standard Business Content components of the Visual Composer is the delivery of a series of business packages for a number of different industries. Over 25 business packages are available for your use. These business packages offer you the ability to immediately have different scenarios available with very little configuration in the VC component. These offer you the different functions within VC immediately grouped together based on best business practices specific to your industry. In addition to having the functionality of the VC preconfigured, you also have the specific InfoProvider that each of the business packages reference, as shown next. As you can see, a number of industry solutions are covered. Each of these models is broken down into specific applications and descriptions of what each application offers you for reporting purposes.

Business Package	Application	Application Description
CRM	Order and Lead Analysis of Channel Manager	This Analytic Composite provides channel managers with a quick overview of the orders-to-stock from their channel partners. Channel managers can view the sales performance by product categories and also get further information on the best-selling products within a selected product category. In addition, the Analytic Composite provides channel managers with information on the lead performance of their channel partners.
	Web Analysis	This Analytic Composite provides Web Shop owners with a quick overview of the Web Shop performance. Web shop owners can view the sales revenue over time, best selling products by product categories as well as their top customers by product category. In addition, the Analytic Composite allows Web Shop owners to compare event-based data such as conversion rates (ratio of logons to orders as well as view to order) and the number of viewed/added/ordered items.
	Connection and Open ticket Analysis	This Analytic Composite provides a detailed analysis of open service tickets by priority, average call information by queue, average handling time by category and connection volume per time interval and weekday. This overview of the help desk enables managers to monitor call-related service levels and drill-down into problem areas and fine-tune as needed which enables organizations to identify and fix small problems before they become large ones.
	Marketing Project Performance Analysis	This Analytic Composite provides an analysis of marketing projects. From an easy-to-use analysis based on contribution margins to a listing of all campaigns that have commenced within a specified time period, this Analytic Composite presents the user with an analysis of planned versus actual costs, revenues, margins, responses, activities and campaign details. Additionally, marketers are able to stop campaigns that are not performing well.
	Order and Lead Analysis for a Channel Partner	This Analytic Composite provides channel managers with a quick overview of the orders-to-stock from their channel partners. Channel managers can view the sales performance by product categories and also get further information on the best-selling products within a selected product category. In addition, the Analytic Composite provides channel managers with information on the lead performance of their channel partners.
	Sales Pipeline Analysis	This Analytic Composite provides an overview of the sales opportunities by phase and by month of expected closing date. At a glance, sales professionals can see which opportunities they need to get to the next phase in the sales cycle to stay on track. They can quickly focus on the most promising opportunities. With a single click, they are able to get a full briefing on the opportunity/customer and they can take appropriate action on the opportunity to speed its closure.
	Competitive Win/Loss Analysis	This analytic composite allows the user to analyze won and lost opportunities over time. Sales executives have all the critical data they need to improve their positioning and win against competitors. They can analyze in which phases competitors have strengths and weaknesses and leverage this in upcoming sales cycles

The following illustration shows the business package, the level required for the system configuration, the technical name of the application, and the specific InfoProviders that support these functions. These business packages can be downloaded via the SAP website under Downloads and Installations and Upgrades.

Business Package	System & Release	Technical Name of Application	InfoProvider
CRM	CRM 4.0 SP08	CRM_CHANNEL_MGR	0CSAL_C03; 0MKTG_C01
	CRM 4.0 SP08, Tealeaf Data	CRM_ESALES_WEB_EVENTS	0CSAL_C03; 0WEB_C04
	CRM 4.0 SP08, CTI Data	CRM_HELPDESK_IC	0CRM_CTI1; 0CRM_CTI2; 0CSRV_C01
	CRM 4.0 SP08	CRM_MARKETING	0CRM_MC06
	CRM 4.0 SP08	CRM_PARTNER_MGR	0MKTG_C01; 0OCSAL_C03
	CRM 4.0 SP08	CRM_SALES_PIPELINE	0CRM_OPPH
	CRM 4.0 SP08	CRM_SALES_WIN_LOSS	0CRM_C04
	CRM 4.0 SP08	CRM_SERVICE_TEAMS	0CRM_PRI; 0CSRV_C01; 0CSAL_C09; 0CRM_CODT
Manufacturing	R/3 >= 4.0B	ERP_AVAILABILITY_OEE	0PP_C03
	R/3 >= 4.0B	ERP_CAPACITY_UTILIZATION	0PP_C13
	R/3 >= 4.0B	ERP_EXECUTION_TME_ANAL	0PP_C13
	R/3 >= 4.0B	ERP_INVENTORY_OVERVIEW	0IC_C03
	R/3 >= 4.0B	ERP_MANU_ORDER_ANALYSIS	0PP_C01
	R/3 >= 4.0B	ERP_MATERIAL_CONSUMPTION	0PP_C05
	R/3 >= 4.0B	ERP_MATERIAL_UTILIZATION	0PP_C05
	R/3 >= 4.0B	ERP_OEE	0PP_C03
	R/3 >= 4.0B	ERP_PERFORMANCE	0PP_C03
	R/3 >= 4.0B	ERP_PLAN_REALIZATION	0PP_C01
	R/3 >= 4.0B	ERP_PROD_FLEX	0PP_C01
	R/3 >= 4.0B	ERP_QUALITY_PROB_ANALYSIS	0QM_C09
	R/3 >= 4.0B	ERP_SCRAP_ANALYSIS	0PP_C03
	R/3 >= 4.0B	ERP_SCAP_QTY_ANALYSIS	0PP_C02
	R/3 >= 4.0B	ERP_TAKE_FROM_STOCK_OR_BUY	
	R/3 >= 4.0B	ERP_YIELD_OEE	0PP_C03
	Automotive - BW Info Area: Supply Chain Managment -> Inventory Collaboration Hub -> ICH Alert InfoCube for		

Integration Point for VC and BI

Once the VC system has been configured and the business packages are installed, we can move into the actual configuration of a model to be used by our business user. As we go through this process, keep in mind that this should be a toolkit that some of your power users and business users can comfortably configure and compile to create their own reports and analysis on the fly. We start by logging on to the Visual Composer website. Once the Visual Composer loads up to the Web, we can immediately create a model by using the menu path Model_Create Model. This generates a field where you enter a technical name for the model. Once this is complete, you will have entered into the Storyboard screen. The next step is to create an iView. From the Storyboard, either drag and drop the iView component onto the Storyboard or double-click it. For the example, the iView is labeled BWUSER_BW_CHART, as shown next.

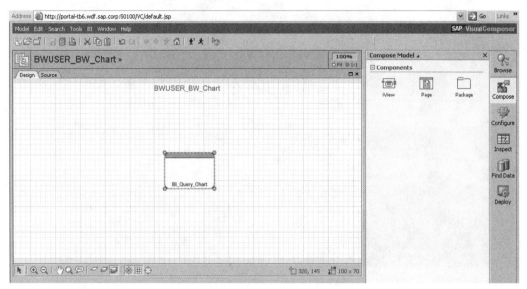

We will be using the data from a specific query to develop this basic chart from the Visual Composer side. Now, using the context menu from the iView object, choose Drill Down and move down to the iView level for additional configuration, as shown here.

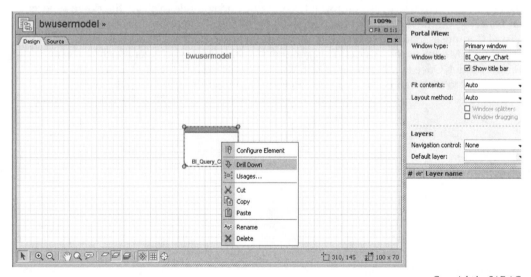

The following illustration shows the drilldown state for additional configuration. Also, on the right side of the screen, notice that the system we have chosen is SAP_BW and the Look For option uses a BW query. In addition to the BI Integration Wizard, this is another approach to linking the Visual Composer to BI.

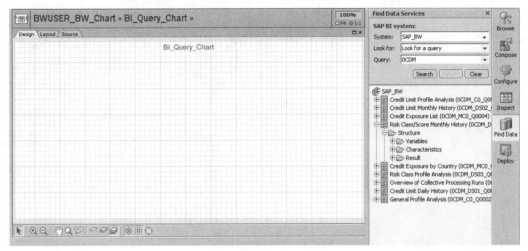

We are looking for a query with the initial technical name of 0CDM. We can do a wildcard search to find this, as shown next. Also shown is the list of options under the Look For field. The use of all these options is very important. With this tool the business user can start from scratch using the InfoCube, query, view, and other options to find the specific BW object required. This means that the business user can directly access the tables rather than needing a query.

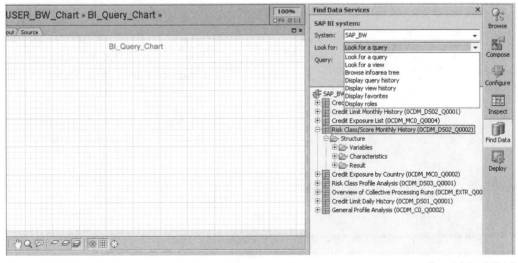

Having found the specific query to be used (0CDM_DS02_Q0002), we can now either drag and drop the query onto the Storyboard or double-click the object. Either way results in the object appearing in the Storyboard screen, as shown next. Notice that additional functions are available immediately upon accessing this query. You have options for using an input screen, variables (BW variables), different output types, information, and messages.

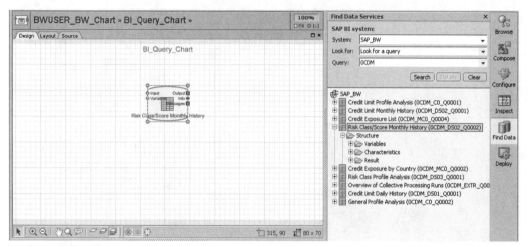

We will be using the Add Input Form option to allow the ability to input values for analysis. This is accessible via the context menu on the object Input Form, which is shown here.

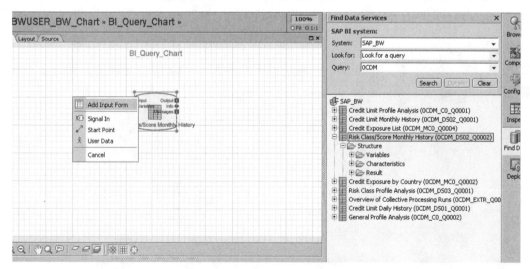

In addition, some minor configuration of the elements in the input form is required, as shown next. In this situation, the title has been changed and the Business Partner and

SUBMIT fields have been checked along the right side. Therefore, Business Partner is going to be used as the master data input, and a SUBMIT button will appear after the value has been entered into the input field.

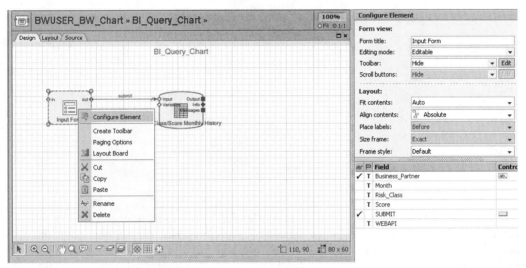

Dragging the option to have this as the "start point" is shown next.

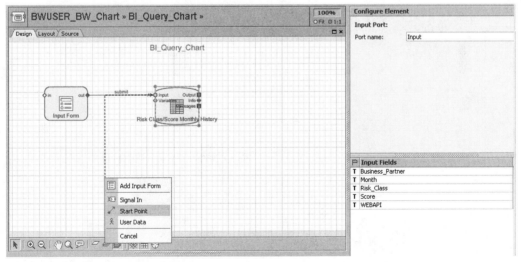

The dialog box for selecting the start point is shown here. In this case, Business Partner will be chosen for master data entry.

The initial data entry is now completely configured. Again, as mentioned earlier, this is just the tip of the iceberg in terms of configuring Visual Composer. We will now direct our attention to the output side of the equation. As the name conveys (output side of the VC, add a chart view), we will be creating a chart for this report. Therefore, drag and drop the output option and choose Add Chart View. The following illustration shows the results of this activity.

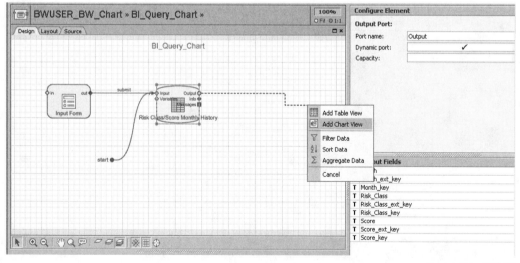

Now working on the chart object from the Configure Element area, we change the label of the axis to Score and add a formula to the calculation, as shown here.

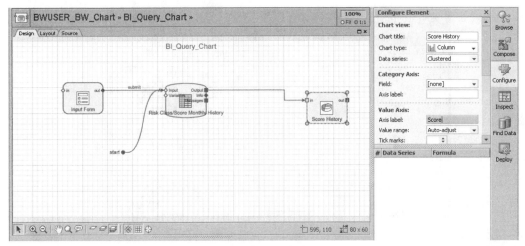

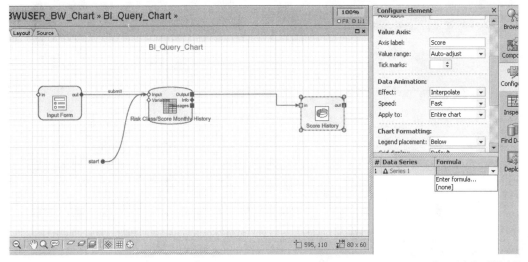

Double-clicking on the formula field causes the following dialog box to appear. Here, we are going to get the net value of the key figure—Score Key—and graph that value.

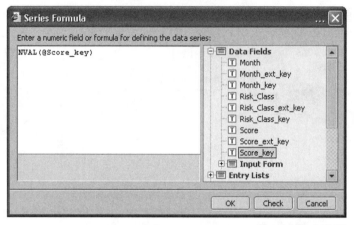

The final result of this configuration is shown next.

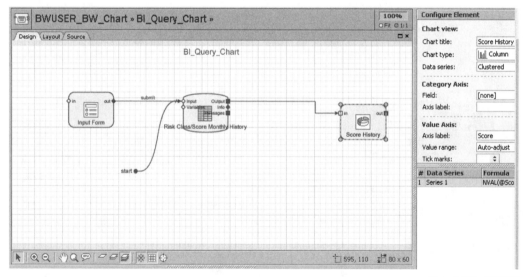

We are now ready to compile the model. Using the Compile option on the right side of the screen, the model is configured and positioned to be deployed. After the compile process, the source code is available and we can preview the model. The final result of the compiled model is shown here.

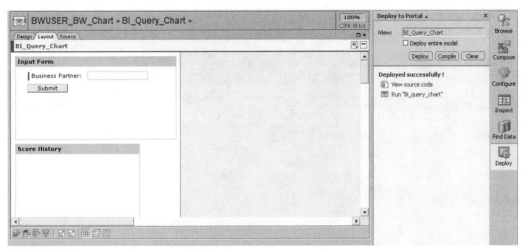

A preview of the results is shown next. Notice the input form with the Business Partner description and the Submit button below. Also, the chart is available below the input screen. We will move that chart to the right of the input screen for additional space.

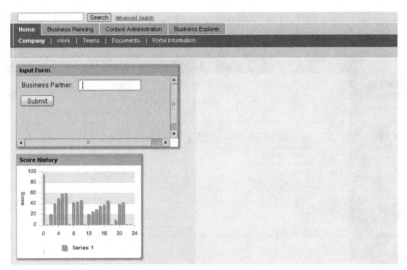

After a review, the business user decides they need additional help with the master data entry into the input field. Going back to the Visual Composer Storyboard screen, we can use the assignment of the Add Value Help option. The following illustration shows the initial step in this process.

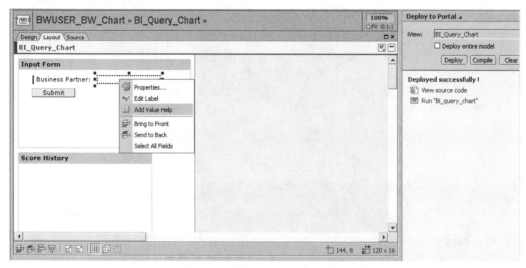

The Value Help Configuration Wizard now appears, as shown next, and helps makes the configuration of the value help quite painless.

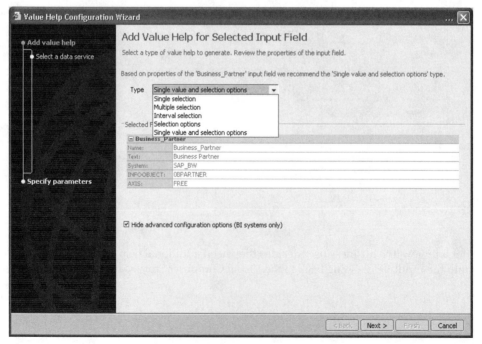

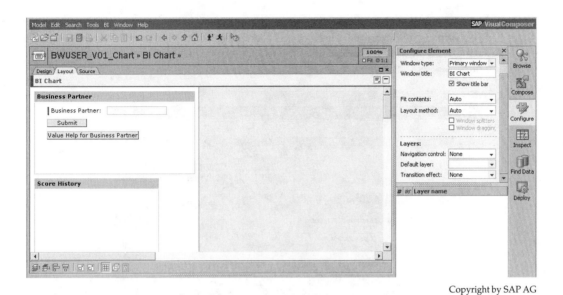

FIGURE 17-6   Visual Composer–based analysis

We will go with the single selection and business partner as the value help. The final result is that the web-based screen can now offer help with master data entry. Figure 17-6 shows the results of this configuration. Notice the Value Help for Business Partner button below the Submit button.

When this option is used, a list of possible values to enter appears so that the business user has an easier time of picking the appropriate value rather than guessing about the value. The result is shown here.

Business_Partner

value or selection options:

| Single Value Selection ▼ | Search |

Text
Jan Fortmann
Deutsche Bank
Citibank
Enterprise
Andrew Sands
John Taylor
Teltel GmbH
Orgatel Inc.
Alu United Corp.
Crocodile Enterprise
Live Computer Sytsems

Finally, by accessing this report from the Enterprise Portal, we can see that some additional changes have been made. For example, the chart has been moved to the left and the input is on the right. Clicking the Value Help button causes the list of possible business partners to appear for selection purposes, as shown next.

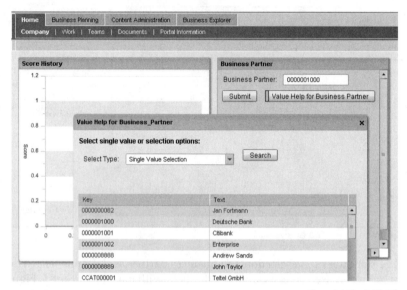

Copyright by SAP AG

Once the information is assigned to the input field, the business user can click the Submit button, and the data is retrieved from the query via the InfoProvider and displayed, as shown here.

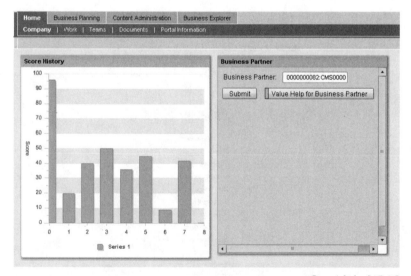

Copyright by SAP AG

This small example of the functionality of the Visual Composer is only the beginning of the configuration options for the business user. As you can see, the use of the business packages with all the preconfigured BAPIs and models is definitely the initial approach to take for power users. Once they are comfortable with the VC environment, tons of additional enhancements to the report can be made.

Introduction to Integrated Planning

Before we begin our discussion of Integrated Planning (IP) and the Integrated Planning process, we'll review some background information about the planning process first. Reporting and planning are definitely linked at many different levels in terms of the data, process, and importance, but there's a definite distinction between setting up an environment for reporting and one for planning. In the process of reporting, we have some interaction with the information in the form of slicing and dicing it, but in the planning process not only do we have this ability but we also have the actual planning activity—that is, posting the data directly into the InfoProvider. From the reporting side of the fence, the data being displayed has already been posted, and we are doing the analysis of the end result. Whether that analysis is a year-to-year comparison, a plan data–to–actual data comparison, or month-to-month comparison, we are still in the mindset of analyzing data and what we can do with this information to further the future business activities of the corporation.

In planning, we have much of the same approach to information, but the difference is that as planners we are on the other end of the data. Rather than having results to analyze, planners have to develop the information and understand the objectives of the corporation and the overall business environment to make sure the business plan developed is achievable and will move the company toward a successful result. In some ways, planning is more important than just plain reporting because it is the driver for the business for both short-term and long-term goals. Planning is an integral part of the management cycle. We plan at so many different levels, and even if we don't plan consciously, we still do so inherently. In the corporate environment, there are many different levels to the planning process—operational versus strategic, public sector versus private, and so on. In fact, there are far too many to discuss all the different planning scenarios that could come up. The analysis of these different planning processes would take another book.

Companies as a whole plan differently based on their requirements, such as whether they are interested in long-term profitability or short term profitability. Are there political issues to be reviewed? And what about the employees of the corporation? Will this plan help them and the corporation? Will the reduction of costs be a priority, thus causing the planning in the cost control area to be more detailed than in the sales revenue area? Will a repurchase of stock be a priority for cash assets, or will the building of a new plant or location be the priority in this current year's plan? These and many more questions will define the planning process a corporation will use.

Figure 17-7 shows the typical cycle of management, and as you can see, planning is a primary driver for all other activities. Initially the corporation has a company mission statement of some sort and uses this as a foundation of the long-term planning process. With the information gleaned from the company mission statement and the addition of external issues taken into account—another company entering the market, currency fluctuation, and so on—we start the process of defining the operational and strategic planning process. This process can take the majority of the year, and it is not uncommon for a corporation to plan

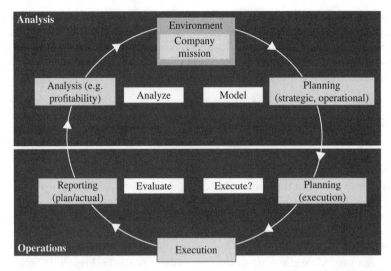

Copyright by SAP AG

FIGURE 17-7   Management cycle

and budget year round. Depending on the level of the operational and strategic planning process—for example, planning at the cost center level or the GL account level or at a higher level such as the divisional level—data is gathered together that will define the goals and milestones for the corporation over the next number of periods or years. Another level of planning and budgeting that needs to be identified is the cycle of planning. Will the planning take on a rolling process, meaning that each time phase the plan is reviewed and adjusted base on the current/actual information? Is the corporate strategy for planning based on a quarterly analysis with review of the variance between the planned and actual numbers? Once the data for each time period is gathered, the reporting and analysis of that information is done. As you can see, this cycle has no ending activity. This is an ongoing process, and once the actual information is reviewed, a corporation will then take that data and refine its plan and budget and also refine its planning and budgeting process.

Figure 17-8 is a very good diagram of the overall planning levels. The two levels of planning that keep the corporation running on a daily basis are the Execution Planning and Operational Planning processes. The Strategic Planning process is the one that reviews and analyzes the long-term planning objectives and takes into account the larger view of planning for the company vision and mission statement. Operational Planning and Execution Planning normally take into account information available via day-to-day activities, such as the activities of the production line, inventory analysis, analysis of sales by customer, and those components of planning that involve more available types of information. Once the two planning cycles are executed, there needs to be a reconciliation of the two plans in order for the Strategic and Operational views of the corporate goals to be consistent. Therefore, the planning process can be very iterative in nature and painstaking at times. Reconciling the view of the corporation at a mission statement level and the needs of the corporation at the operational level is very challenging and, if achieved, can be very rewarding to both the corporation and all the stakeholders.

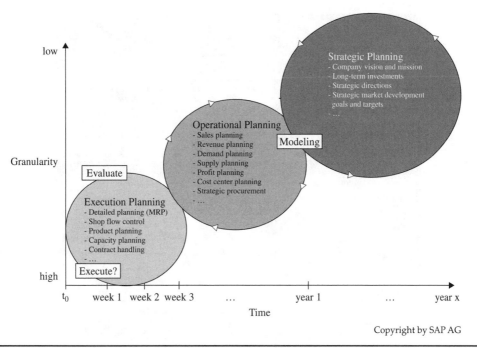

Copyright by SAP AG

FIGURE 17-8 Strategic, Operational, and Execution Planning processes

With all these challenges to a planning process, the software to help with this activity needs to be robust enough to accommodate and enhance the planning process. BI-IP (Integrated Planning) can be very helpful in this process and can offer the functionality that many companies need and seek for doing planning. Because IP is fully integrated with BI, there are numerous areas in BW where IP can reuse the objects and structures built for reporting purposes. This helps with the configuration and implementation process of IP. If the corporation has been planning and has a basic idea of its planning or budgeting cycle and the steps involved based on the specific corporate needs, then the implementation time of IP is reasonable. Figure 17-9 shows the positioning of IP in the overall architecture of BI. Actually, IP is one of the significant changes that has moved the BW concept into the BI environment. This, along with other tools in BI (such as Data Mining), has caused BW to change from a report and database workhorse to a Business Intelligence platform where the business user can review information about the actual results of a specific period as well as post data into the BW InfoProviders and be able to plan at any level of sophistication needed. As you can see, IP can take advantage of all the tools within the BI environment, including all of the front end of BW—Bex Analyzer, BEx Web Analyzer, Web Application Designer, Report Designer, and Information Broadcaster.

In our discussions, we will not be getting into detail about the planning-specific services such as locking, validation options, data slicing, and characteristic relationships. We will also not be investigating one of the options for front ends of IP—the Status and Tracking System. Because this is used as a monitoring process and doesn't give the reporting and planning portions additional functionality but rather uses all the objects and setup developed in IP, any additional detailed discussion would move us into a totally different topic. Express Planning

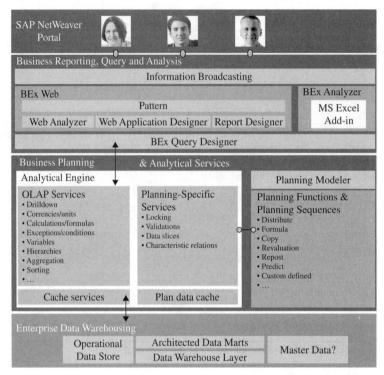

Copyright by SAP AG

FIGURE 17-9   Position of Business Planning in the BI architecture

is also available, but this again is only a monitoring process, and all functionality would need to be designed to be used in the Express Planning screens. If this book were looking at all the details of IP, they would definitely be in the chapter on the available user interfaces. Figure 17-10 steps down into a bit more detail of the sections of IP that could be reviewed. In this diagram, we have the four sections of IP: Modeling, Automatic Planning, Manual Planning, and Process Control. We will be focusing on the Manual Planning portion of this chart, and thus "designing a query." But to get to this level there needs to be some initial setup and configuration of IP. In these areas, the coverage will be at a high level, and just enough to get us to the next level. Even though all these different components are critical to the building of a consistent planning process, we will not delve into characteristic relationships, the use of hierarchies, enhanced designs for modeling, user authorizations; only the basic planning functions, and, as mentioned, none of the process control areas.

As a final comment around the use of Integrated Planning we can definitely see the use of this technology for the what-if analysis and the forecast, planning and budgeting issues but we can also use this type of process for simply reporting needs. For example, lets say that you are try to execute a report that needs to have calculations executed that will require information from different months and days or that need information that is not available but needs to be calculated on the fly using other information. With the use of IP you can easily create the necessary calculation functions to do the trick.

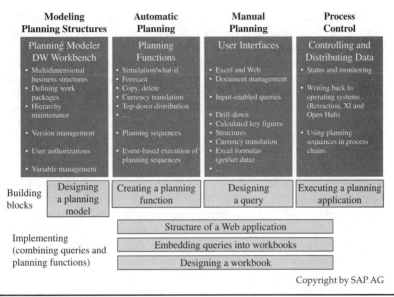

Modeling Planning Structures	Automatic Planning	Manual Planning	Process Control

**Planning Modeler
DW Workbench**
• Multidimensional
  business structures
• Defining work
  packages
• Hierarchy
  maintenance
 	
• Version management
 	
• User authorizations
 	
• Variable management
	**Planning
	Functions**
	• Simulation/what-if
	• Forecast
	• Copy, delete
	• Currency translation
	• Top-down distribution
	• ...
	
	• Planning sequences
	
	• Event-based execution of
	  planning sequences
		User Interfaces
		• Excel and Web
		• Document management
		
		• Input-enabled queries
		
		• Drill-down
		• Calculated key figures
		• Structures
		• Currency translation
		• Excel formulas
		  (get/set data)
		• ...
			**Controlling and
			Distributing Data**
			• Status and monitoring
			
			• Writing back to
			  operating systems
			  (Retraction, XI and
			  Open Hub)
			
			• Using planning
			  sequences in process
			  chains

Building blocks	Designing a planning model	Creating a planning function	Designing a query	Executing a planning application

Implementing (combining queries and planning functions)	Structure of a Web application
	Embedding queries into workbooks
	Designing a workbook

Copyright by SAP AG

FIGURE 17-10   Components of BI Integrated Planning

Results of Integrated Planning

Before going into all the details surrounding IP, let's discuss what to expect and what we are driving toward with Integrated Planning. Because this is new functionality in Business Warehouse, a couple examples of the possible outcomes are warranted. If you have been working with Business Planning and Simulation in the BW environment, you will not find these examples overly surprising. However, subtle differences can be seen between the IP and BPS screens. There are also definite differences and useful functionalities in the workbook examples because in BPS we had to work with the Planning Folders for the Excel approach, and the amount of flexibility in that area was a bit limiting. We will be following a full IP process from start to finish during our discussions, using both the Web Application Designer and the BEx Workbook points of view so that you can see the differences between some of the functionality and the look and feel.

The main goal of either the WAD or workbook options is to have a reasonable user interface for the process of planning. This takes into account a number of aspects in the process, including the type of planning, the methods used in planning, and the system configuration itself, not even to mention the users themselves and what they expect concerning the flexibility and easy of use from a user interface. So while we review these different approaches, I know you will be thinking about the functionality and configuration, but also keep in mind the overall look and feel of the different interfaces.

Web Application Designer Example

As we have discussed, there's a growing trend to move to the Web for reporting and planning needs. Therefore, starting with the final result of a WAD configuration for IP is a reasonable decision. The front end of a WAD-supported IP report can have a variety of look-and-feel options, and this is only one. We will reduce the different bells and whistle that can be added to these screens (such as pictures, dropdown boxes, variables, and so on) to focus on just the use of the IP functionality. Figure 17-11 shows an example of a finished Web Application Designer IP screen, ready for the business users to execute a planning process. Again, not including the possible addition of corporate logos, more background colors, and such, this is a well-thought-out planning process. From the ability to copy information from some other source (such as an actual or estimate) to the plan using the Copy button, to the ability to perform "what-if" scenarios with the planned data using the Aggressive Version tab, this planning process looks at a detailed plan of information from the bottom up, all the way through to the overall sales plan, and then takes that information and uses it as a basis for the what-if analysis.

Notice on this screen the icons that indicate documents are attached to certain cells with master data or key figures. You can assign documents to any of the cells shown in these screens.

Also, notice the blue and white coloring of the columns. This identifies the cells that are not postable (blue background) and those that are postable (white). An additional explanation is available in the field above the tab strip. Within the tab, three different planning functions are available to execute and change the data—Copy, Revaluate, and Planning Sequence. This screen can be used for manual data entry and also can show the results of the execution of each of these planning functions.

NOTE *The terms* planning function *and* planning sequence *will be defined a bit later in this chapter. For now, though, a planning function is a method of executing a calculation or change to the current data within the InfoProvider and a planning sequence is a group of planning functions executed in a specific sequence. The query can show the results of these changes, or the changes can occur behind the scenes (for example, a calculation of different currency values).*

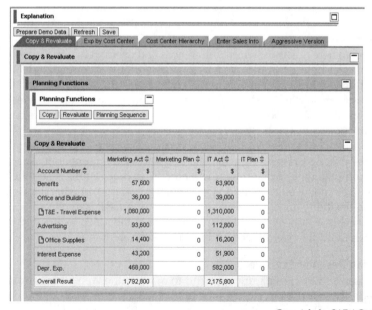

FIGURE 17-11   IP Screens for planning—from Cost Planning to Sales Planning

If we execute the Copy planning function, the actual values are copied over to the planned cells and the planning process is underway. Figure 17-12 shows the results of the process. This is a very basic planning function, but it shows the concept behind the configuration of the different planning functions and what they can do.

Upon executing the Revaluate planning function, we see that behind the scenes a variable was used and that this variable appears in a pop-up before the calculation occurs. This particular variable is a numeric variable for the assignment of a revaluation value. In this case, it's a 10% adjustment to the current planning data, as shown in Figure 17-13.

Finally, the calculation is executed and the values for just the planned data are adjusted up 10%. Figure 17-14 shows the results of this process.

Numerous scenarios exist for planning, and the one you use depends on your company's specific approach to planning, which will control the look and feel and functionality of the planning process. One final view of another tab in this same planning process to show additional planning functionality for currency translation is warranted. In Figure 17-15, you can see that we have the ability to plan in multiple currencies at the same time and can toggle back and forth between currencies while continuing the planning process. Therefore, for a company planning a portion of its business in Euros and another portion in U.S. dollars, this functionality would be invaluable. In this case, we are planning in both U.S. and Canadian dollars at the same time.

We could continue on with various examples for quite some time, but what we've covered so far offers you a good view of the possible user interfaces and the results of using IP as a methodology.

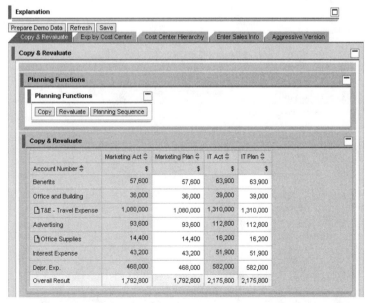

Copyright by SAP AG

FIGURE 17-12   Result of using the Copy planning function

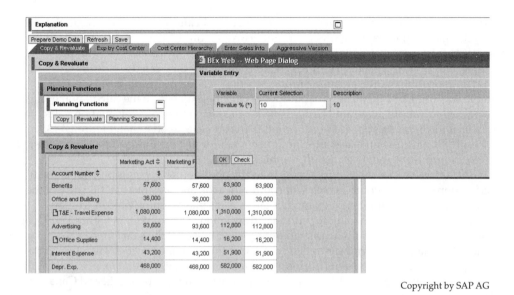

Copyright by SAP AG

FIGURE 17-13   Use of the Revaluate planning function and the data entry of a variable

BEx Workbook Example

The functionality discussed in the previous section is a tough act to follow, but the functionality of the BEx workbook using the IP process is not shabby. Although the BEx workbook was used before, it was not really assimilated as aggressively into the reporting strategy as other

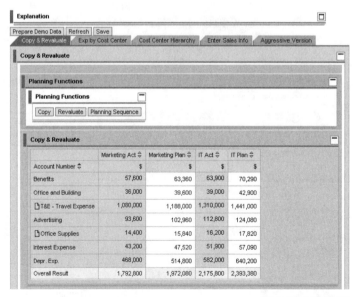

Copyright by SAP AG

FIGURE 17-14   Results of the revaluation of the planned data

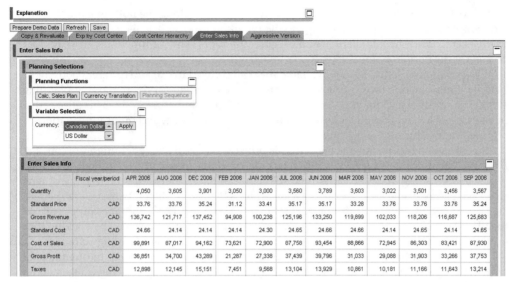

Copyright by SAP AG

FIGURE 17-15   Planning process in both U.S. and Canadian dollars

components in the BEx reporting process. However, with the additional of Excel-based functionality, the BEx Workbook is definitely worth taking a second look at. Figure 17-16 shows the initial screen of a BEx Analyzer workbook. Some bells and whistles have been

Copyright by SAP AG

FIGURE 17-16   Initial planning screen for BEx workbook IP planning

added to demonstrate additional functionality. Notice that along the bottom a number of worksheets have been added to complete the planning process. The user can move from worksheet to worksheet to display and execute different planning functions. Also, notice the buttons at the bottom of the screen.

Other planning functions are available that can be used to execute different activities. The planning function for variables is used to set the variables for the remaining planning steps. The result of clicking the Variables button is shown in Figure 17-17. This allows the business user to decide on the period, year, FYV, company code, and other information required to use during the planning process.

Accessing one of the other screens in this process, we see that even though the concept is the same, the user interface is very different in terms of the look and feel. In Figure 17-18, the user sees something that is more familiar to them—an Excel screen. In this case, the different Excel screens available are controlled by the buttons Plan A/R, Plan Inventory, and Plan A/P, and there are additional buttons for calculating the inventory, DSO, and operating cash. As the planner goes through the process, they can just move to another screen by clicking the buttons along the top or they can move to each worksheet for other planning activities.

We will see additional examples of the available screens and go through the configuration of both the BEx workbook and WAD for IP. As you can see, these options have a tremendous amount of functionality. I have seen companies use IP for adjusting entries for inventory, adjusting entries for managing master data, and updating information via the Excel or web screens, rather than having to work through the traditional approach of posting data into InfoCubes. Be very careful with this functionality, however. We will not be getting into the performance and maintenance of these objects, but questions in these areas need answers before any of the IP and/or BPS functionality is used.

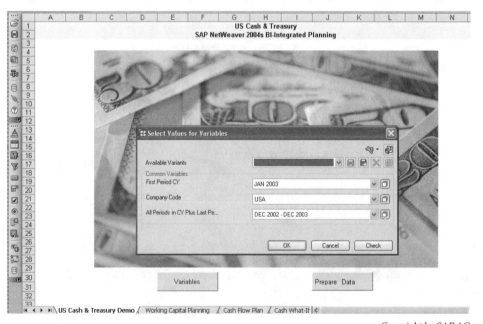

FIGURE 17-17 Execution of the Variable button for IP planning

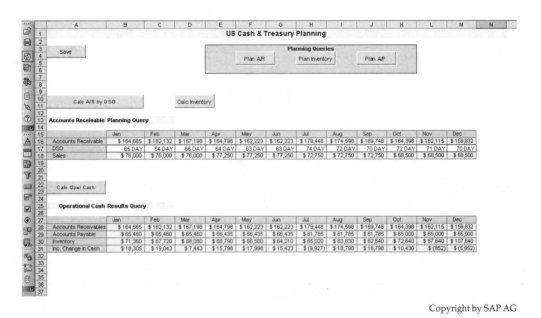

FIGURE 17-18   The initial screen for U.S. Cash and Treasury Planning

Architecture of BW for IP

This shouldn't come as a surprise, but there are a number of different versions of the IP architecture. We will focus on just one to make sure you are comfortable with what is going on behind the scenes before heading into the BEx query build. You already know that the data that is posted into the web screen and/or the Excel user interface makes it into the InfoCube and is saved. The question is, how does this happen? You also know from a previous chapter that we use the Real-time InfoCubes and aggregation levels for IP. We just need to group them together and look at an example of the architecture. Figure 17-19 shows one example of that architecture. In this case, the Real-time InfoCube—the Plan InfoCube—is used for storing the planned data. Notice that the aggregation level is positioned as the structure that connects the InfoCube and the IP activities, such as manual planning and the planning functions. You already know that the aggregation level can be used for reporting.

This scenario works well with our example because we need to get the actual data into the Real-time InfoCube for the initial step of planning, and in this case the Data Transfer Process (DTP) is used to accomplish this task. We are using a normal upload from a standard InfoCube to the Real-time InfoCube to bring the actuals into play. Once this is finished, we can start our planning process. The uploading of actuals can also be done on an ongoing basis if the company's approach to planning is some sort of rolling forecast. Another approach might be that both actual and planned data are stored in one InfoCube, with that InfoCube acting as both a standard and Real-time InfoCube, depending on the task at the time. The ability to switch a Real-time InfoCube to a standard InfoCube, and back again, makes this option possible. Figure 17-20 shows this option. In this case, the upload of actual data would occur directly in the InfoCube, and all the reporting and planning would be done directly on one InfoCube. Other scenarios involve the use of MultiProviders instead of the individual InfoCubes.

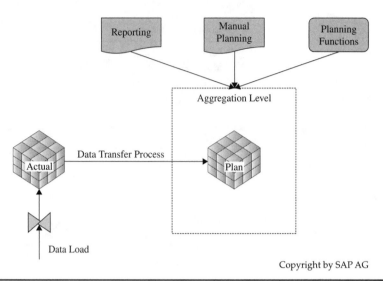

Copyright by SAP AG

FIGURE 17-19 Configuring the IP architecture using two InfoCubes

NOTE *Remember that during this process, we are switching the functionality of an InfoCube from being available for uploading to being available for planning and yet not changing the type of the InfoCube.*

InfoProvider

Based on these different scenarios, we can see that there needs to be a Real-time InfoCube and an aggregation level involved in the architecture somewhere. In terms of these two objects, we went over the basics in Chapter 2. However, one additional item needs to be

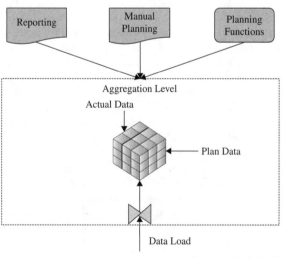

Copyright by SAP AG

FIGURE 17-20 Configuring the IP architecture using one InfoCube

brought to your attention, at the minimum, concerning the functionality of the Real-time InfoCube. Once there are postings from the user interfaces into the InfoCube, the data is saved in request IDs. These request IDs are a bit different from those generated when the data is uploaded into the InfoCube via the normal structure and process. The data is posted into the InfoCube (fact table) and the request ID is "yellow" (not green) at this point. This is not a problem or an issue, unlike what you would be going through if this were to have happened with a normal upload. The request ID stays yellow until there are a total of 50,000 records in that one request. Once that number of records is hit, the InfoCube will automatically generate another request ID and that one will be yellow, as shown in here.

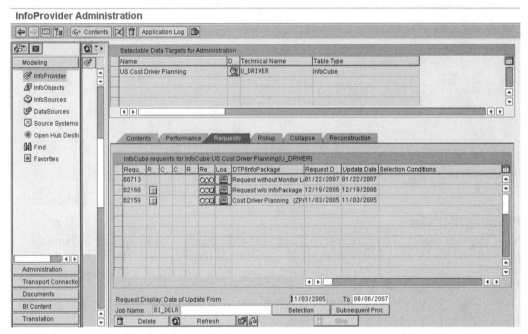

Suppose you are posting data and the total record count in the current request ID is 49,950. You post 100 records. All 100 records will be posted to that request ID and then another one will be generated. I bring this up for the following reason: If you are reporting on this InfoCube and there are yellow requests, the data within that request ID will not be available for reporting because the reporting flag can't be displayed for a yellow request.

Therefore, you will need to include a specific standard-delivered variable in your query configuration to make sure you show *all* the data within your InfoCube, including the data in the yellow request ID, as shown here. This variable can be inserted into the Filter section of the BEx Query Designer, and this will allow the query to read the "yellow" request ID data. Specifically, variables 0S_RQMRC (Most Current Data) and 0S_RQTRA (Most Current Data – Transactional InfoCube) are the ones available.

> **NOTE** *You can also change the read mode of the query in transaction RSRT to allow the display of all the data in the InfoCube, whether the request ID is open or closed. This is more of a technical solution, but is available nonetheless.*

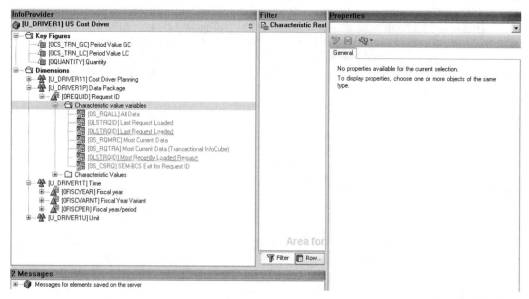

Copyright by SAP AG

Planning Modeler

Now we move into the basic components of the IP architecture. This involves the Planning Modeler and the location where all the objects specific to IP are created. The aggregation level, filter, planning functions, and planning sequences are created in the Planning Modeler. A basic diagram of the connections between each of these objects is shown in Figure 17-21. As you can see, the Real-time InfoCube is used as the basis for the aggregation

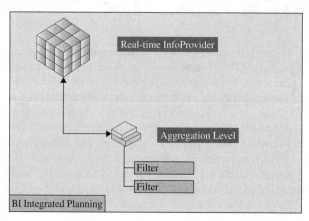

Copyright by SAP AG

FIGURE 17-21   Object architecture of IP

level, and from this level the filter is built. We then use the filter as a basis for the planning functions. The planning sequences are groupings of planning functions. We will work through a high-level discussion of these objects because they will be configured by the IP group or other business users involved with the planning process, so it is important that you have an understanding of these objects when interacting with them.

An example of the Planning Modeler is shown in Figure 17-22. This figure shows the initial execution of the transaction code RSPLAN to access the Planning Modeler. As you can see, there are two options to start the planning process: Start Modeler and Start Wizard. The wizard steps you through setting up the IP process, and the Modeler offers all the same options but you drive the process. We will look at the Modeler in this case.

Once you click Start Modeler, you enter a web-based configuration screen. The Modeler offers a full web-based configuration process. The following illustration shows the results of this activity. As you can see, the request for an InfoProvider field is available. We will review the InfoCube U_AMER_1A, which is the underlying InfoCube for the example we reviewed previously for the cost and sales planning. Notice that all the activities are available from this view. Once you have identified the InfoCube to use, the process moves to the Aggregation

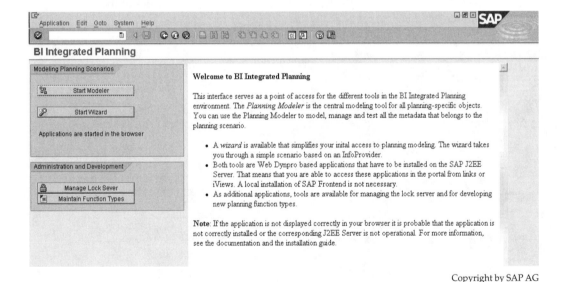

Copyright by SAP AG

Figure 17-22   The initial screen of the Planning Modeler

Levels tab, then to the Filter tab. This is followed by the creation of the planning functions, and then the planning sequences. These activities are specific to IP, and we will briefly cover what is occurring.

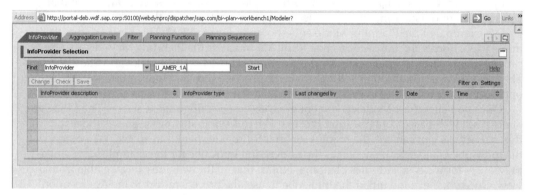

Copyright by SAP AG

When you click the Start button, the fields are filled by the characteristics of the InfoCube, as shown here.

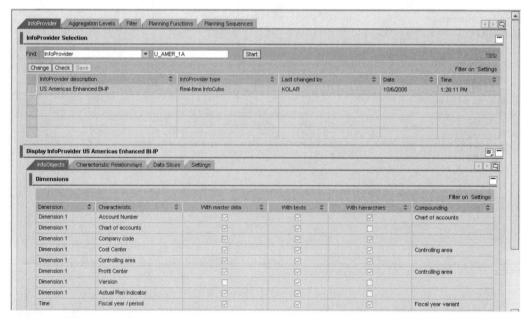

Copyright by SAP AG

Aggregation Level

In the Aggregation Level tabbed page, you can see that two aggregation levels are built on this InfoCube. Cost Center Functions is probably the one where we can see the planning function for Copy, which we observed in the previous section. The following illustration shows this information.

Copyright by SAP AG

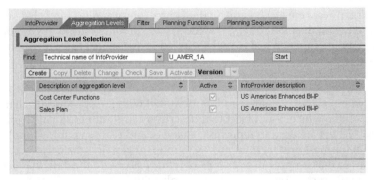

An aggregation level is a virtual InfoProvider that has been especially designed to plan data manually or change it using planning functions. An aggregation level represents a selection of characteristics and key figures for the underlying InfoProvider and determines as such the granularity of the planning. You can create several aggregation levels for an InfoProvider and, therefore, model various levels of planning and hierarchical structures. Note, however, that aggregation levels cannot be nested.

Choosing the Cost Center aggregation level, we see the different characteristics that have been identified as the necessary items for this portion of the planning process. Remember that that the aggregation level is what we need to create the query that will be used as the basis of our planning process. Therefore, identifying the correct characteristic is very important. Make sure that only those that are required are chosen, and don't just choose all the objects. This will cause problems in the long run with the data being posted. The following illustration shows this information.

Copyright by SAP AG

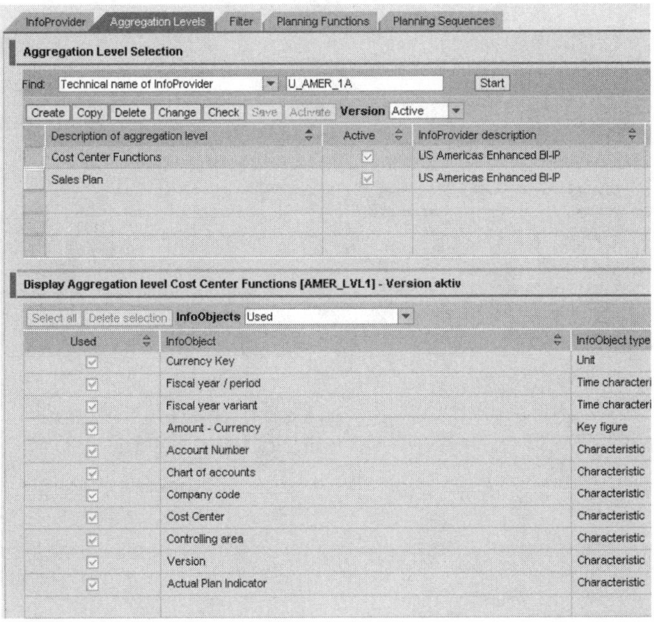

At this point, if we were just creating a data entry query and nothing else, we could stop here and start creating the input query. However, we will follow through with one example of creating a planning function just to make sure you have some basic knowledge of the IP process.

Filter

Once the aggregation level is created and or identified with the appropriate characteristics, we move to the filter, which is an object that describes a multidimensional segment of data from a data set. Filters are used in reporting, analysis, and planning, for example, to restrict data to a certain business area, certain product group, or certain time period. You segment data in this way so that users or user groups only have access to the data that is relevant to them or so that only certain data areas are available within an application scenario. Within BI Integrated Planning, filters determine the selection of data upon which a planning function is executed. In the Filter screen, we identify the actual master data that will be needed or attach variables for those that will be accessed by the planners at runtime. In terms of IP versus BPS this component can be related to the Planning Package. In this case, all the characteristics have been assigned certain values, not variables. These results are shown here.

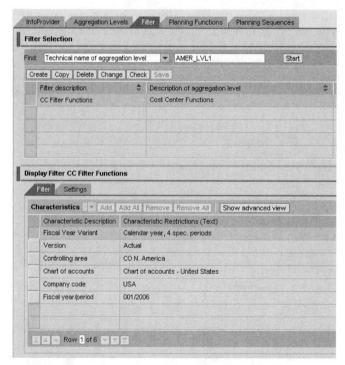

Copyright by SAP AG

Planning Functions

Now we can move into the creation of the planning functions. Planning functions are used within BI Integrated Planning for system-supported editing and generation of data. A planning function specifies the ways in which the transaction data for an aggregation level can be changed. The following are determined for this purpose:

- The name of the aggregation level
- The type of planning function
- How characteristics are used
- The parameter values

The planning function type determines the way in which data is changed by a planning function. The standard planning function types are Unit Conversion, Generate Combinations, Formula, Copy, Delete, Delete Invalid Combinations, Forecasting, Repost, Repost by Characteristic Relationships, Revaluation, Distribute by Reference Data, Distribute by Key, and Currency Translation. You can also implement customer-specific planning function types. We will focus on just one planning function to show the integration between IP and the BEx components. The following illustration shows the initial screen of the planning functions tab. Notice the planning functions AMER_FNC1 – Copy Act to Plan and AMER_FNC2 – Revalue Plan.

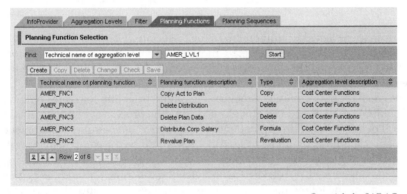

Copyright by SAP AG

These are the two planning functions we executed in the examples. If we choose one of them—AMER_FNC1, for example—and investigate its details, we see that the conditions are fairly wide open. All the data is in actuals. Therefore, everything that is assigned to the version Actual will be copied to the version Plan. The details of this condition are shown here.

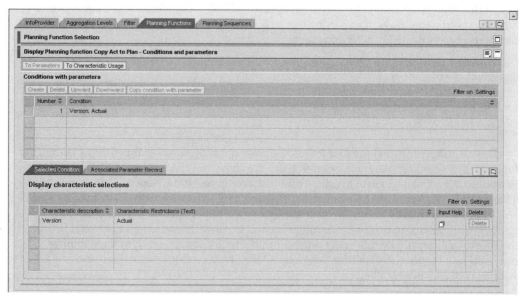

Moving from the Selected Condition tab to the Associated Parameter Record tab, we see that the From and To fields show that we are moving Actual versions to Plan versions. This is demonstrated in the example where everything from the Actual version moved to the Plan version with the execution of this planning function.

The final screen for the Planning Sequences tab offers the ability to create combinations of these different planning functions. Therefore, during the process of planning, the need to execute several planning functions in sequence is required—for example, executing currency translation, depreciation calculations, and so on, This would be the component to use. It also offers the option to test the planning functions. Once this process is complete, we can review the results by looking at the BW Workbench and viewing the InfoCube and the aggregation level we just created. The following illustration shows the results. Notice that the two aggregation levels are available and linked directly to the InfoCube.

These are the basic objects we need to demonstrate the use of IP and BEx tools. Although this review was at a very high level and many different activities have been overlooked for our discussion of user interfaces, these activities are critical to IP in terms of setting up a useable and consistent planning process. Therefore, be sure you review the details of IP on the SAP website or from some other source.

Setting Up the Front Ends for IP

Now we can turn to BEx's involvement in this process. The only way to have the business users and planners view the data is via the BEx components. The setup of the final results you saw in the previous examples covers many of the different toolset we have discussed. Therefore, in a number of areas we will move directly to the required components because, by this time, gaining access to them has been discussed. Setting up these interfaces takes the BEx Query Designer, BEx Analyzer (Workbook) and/or the Web Application Designer. Remember, to enable the planning process for manual data entry, the BEx Query must be created based on the aggregation level and not the InfoCube.

BEx Query Designer

In this section, we will work our way through the setup of the BEx query type Input Ready Query, which will allow data entry. An Input Ready Query is defined for an InfoProvider of type Aggregation Level. It is "input ready" and can be used for manual planning. Whether a particular cell is input ready depends on the drilldown—specifically, if you use the additional IP functionality of characteristic relationships and data slices are permitted for the cell. Once you have defined a query on an InfoProvider (Aggregation Level), you see the Planning tabbed page under the Properties of structural components (for example, in key figures or restricted key figures). The options provided there allow you to determine which structural components of an Input Ready Query are to be input ready at runtime and which are not. With structural components that are *not* input ready, you can also determine whether they are viewed as reference data or are just protected against manual entry. Table 17-2 shows the following options for the structural components.

Option	Description
Data cannot be changed	If the structural components are being used as reference data, they are *not* protected by data locks to ensure exclusive access for one user because this data serves as a reference for many users. This is the default setting.
Data can be changed using planning functions	If you want to protect structural components against manual entries but allow changes by planning functions, you can use locks to protect this data for one particular user. In this way, you can ensure that the planning function works with the displayed data only and not with data that has been changed by other users.
Data can be changed using user entry or planning functions	Data can be effected by manual data entry or planning function processes.

TABLE 17-2   Input Readiness of the Structural Components of a Query

You can also determine whether an Input Ready Query is to be started in **Change mode** or in **Display mode**. You find this property in the **Properties** area of the **Planning** tabbed page (see the following illustration). If there is at least one Input Ready Query component, the query is started in Display mode (as long as it has not been set otherwise).

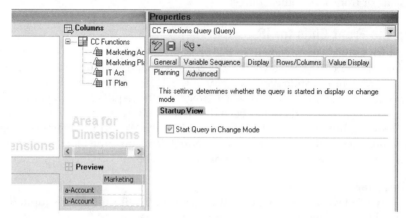

This takes us back into the BEx Query Designer and the setup of a query. Because we have created so many queries at this point, we can get right into the BEx Query Designer and direct our attention to the specific indicator that will allow us to perform this planning activity (see the following illustration). We will simply use the query from our cost center screen example.

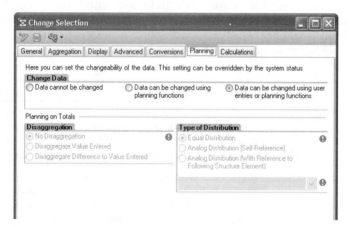

It is important to test the Input Ready Query before finishing in the BEx Query Designer. Therefore, you can execute it to confirm that the query is in fact available for data entry. The following illustration shows the results of the execution of the query. Notice that the cells that are available for data entry are white and the others are grayed out. Remember that the query you just created is the basic setup for manual data entry and can't be used on its own for data entry. You need to combine this query definition with either the WAD or the BEx Analyzer (workbook) for data entry to be available.

CC Functions Query				Last Data Update: 08/05/2007 19:53:17

New Analysis | Open | Save As... | **Display As** Table ▼ | Information | Send | Print Version | Export to Excel | Comments | Filter Settings

▼ Columns
  • CC Functions
▼ Rows
  • Account Number
▼ Free characteristics
  • Currency

	Marketing Act ⇕	Marketing Plan ⇕	IT Act ⇕	IT Plan ⇕
Account Number ⇕	$	$	$	$
Salaries	100,000	0	100,000	0
Benefits	57,600	63,360	63,900	70,290
Office and Building	36,000	39,600	39,000	42,900
T&E - Travel Expense	1,080,000	1,188,000	1,310,000	1,441,000
Advertising	93,600	102,960	112,800	124,080
Office Supplies	14,400	15,840	16,200	17,820
Interest Expense	43,200	47,520	51,900	57,090
Depr. Exp.	468,000	514,800	582,000	640,200
Corp Allocations	996,000	0	373,500	0
Overall Result	2,888,800	1,972,080	2,649,300	2,393,380

Copyright by SAP AG

Another important item to check is the display of the characteristics being used in the Planning Input Query. If you are going to require that additional lines be available during the planning process—for example, the requirement is that additional GL accounts can be added to the planning screen during the planning process—then make sure the display of the characteristics has a key assigned. The setting can be Key and Text, or Text and Key, but in any case the key must be available; otherwise, the final interface will not allow additional characteristic values to be used, but rather only those that are available with the original query.

As a final note in regard to whether the cells of a query view are input ready, keep the following rules in mind:

- In a query that is used for manual planning, a cell is only input ready if each characteristic value of all the characteristics included in the aggregation level is unique. For this reason, none of the aggregated values on the aggregation level are input ready; totals, subtotals, and inner hierarchy nodes are not input ready.

- If a query that is used for manual planning includes a navigation attribute that is restricted using a fixed or dynamic filter or a restricted key figure, the system treats the navigation attribute as a normal characteristic. The preceding rule applies here. The system only responds as if the navigation attribute is *not* part of the query if the navigation attribute is *not* restricted.

NOTE *In terms of allowing the user to select the attribute, this is consistent. In terms of posting data to the navigational attribute in the InfoCube, because the characteristic is not in the InfoCube, posting to the navigational attributes is not possible. Therefore, if you need to have data posted to the navigational attribute make sure that the attribute is also a characteristic in your infoprovider.*

- If you want to use a query in manual planning that is defined on a MultiProvider or a complex aggregation level, the cells are not input ready if the InfoProvider they refer to is not a Real-time InfoCube or is a Real-time InfoCube that has been switched to load mode.

- If an Input Ready Query is executed in Change mode but the requested data is locked by another user, the query starts in Display mode.

BEx Analyzer—Workbook

Once the BEx Query Designer work is complete, we can then use this basic query definition in the BEx Analyzer to finish our manual planning interface. A basic overview of the steps involved with this process are offered in Figure 17-23.

Generally speaking, the process involves taking the query definition and using it as a basis for the BEx Analyzer workbook. Again, numerous options are available to use in these activities, and depending on the planners' needs, you will use additional functionality. Here, our purpose is to show another use of the BEx Analyzer and the workbook. We've worked with the BEx Analyzer for quite some time now, so we can move directly into the workbook and review the required settings that will help with this process. Accessing the BEx Design toolbar, shown next, we can look at the process involved.

NOTE *Quite a few checkboxes and settings aren't covered here. Use the F1 function key to get additional details for some good comments and documentation.*

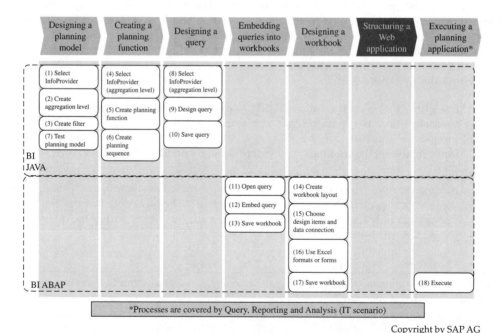

Copyright by SAP AG

FIGURE 17-23   Overview of the steps in the BEx Analyzer for creating an IP Manual Planning workbook

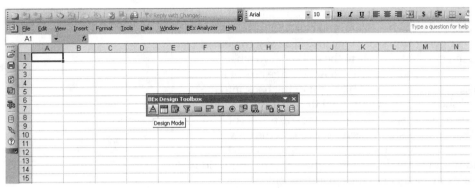

Copyright by SAP AG

We will start by assigning a query to the workbook. There's very little extra introduced at this point. Much of what you will see was discussed earlier on. The result of assigning the Insert Analysis Grid icon to the worksheet is shown here.

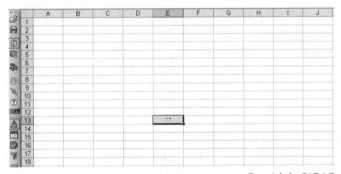

Copyright by SAP AG

Once this is complete, click the Grid icon to open the following dialog box. This is where the query is assigned to the grid.

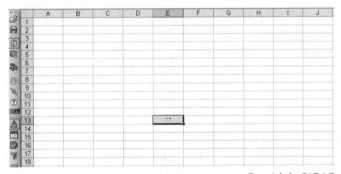

Copyright by SAP AG

When you click the Create icon, a dialog box opens to access the queries. Here, you can find the Cost Center query to assign to the grid. The assignment of the query U_AMER_Q2 to the grid is shown here.

For this example, we will not change any of the basic parameters, so from here, moving back into the worksheet and switching from the Analysis Design mode to the Display mode, we see the results of the assignment, as shown next. Notice that the only difference between what we did in a previous chapter and what we are doing here is that the Analysis Grid is now available to have data manually entered into it and then saved back into the InfoCube.

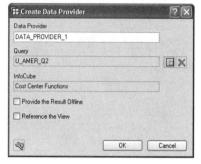

Account Number	Marketing Act	Marketing Plan	IT Act	IT Plan
Salaries	$ 100,000		$ 100,000	
Benefits	$ 57,600	$ 63,360	$ 63,900	$ 70,290
Office and Building	$ 36,000	$ 39,600	$ 39,000	$ 42,900
T&E - Travel Expense	$ 1,080,000	$ 1,188,000	$ 1,310,000	$ 1,441,000
Advertising	$ 93,600	$ 102,960	$ 112,800	$ 124,080
Office Supplies	$ 14,400	$ 15,840	$ 16,200	$ 17,820
Interest Expense	$ 43,200	$ 47,520	$ 51,900	$ 57,090
Depr. Exp.	$ 468,000	$ 514,800	$ 582,000	$ 640,200
Corp Allocations	$ 996,000		$ 373,500	
Overall Result	**$ 2,888,800**	**$ 1,972,080**	**$ 2,649,300**	**$ 2,393,380**

As one final item to check to confirm that the workbook is ready for data input, go to the Query Properties and look at the Display Options tab to make sure the option Allow Input of Plan Values is checked, as shown here. If this is not checked, the screen will not allow data entry. Once the workbook is saved, it is ready to be used for data entry. Several additional objects need to be added, such as a button for saving the data, but these activities were discussed in a previous chapter.

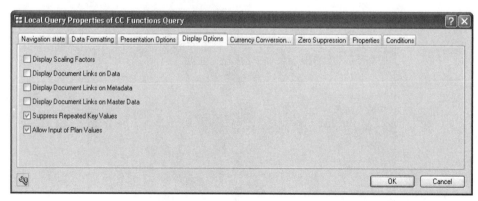

Our next task is to complete the discussion of the use of the Insert button option in Design mode. Again, other than working with this option within the context of IP, nothing different is used in this example versus what we did in the previous chapter on BEx Analyzer functions. The following illustration show a button assigned to the screen in the Design mode.

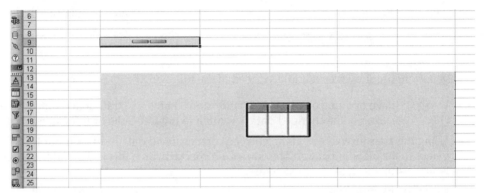

Clicking the button accesses the dialog box for the different functions, as shown next. The function we are interested in is Planning Specific Command.

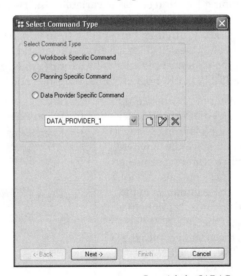

This option has a series of commands available. Table 17-3 details the different options available.

Wizard Option	Static Parameters: Name	Static Parameters: Value
Save	CMD	SAVE_AREA
Transfer Values	CMD	VALUE_CHECK
Execute Planning Function	CMD	EXECUTE_PLANNING_FUNCTION
Execute Planning Sequence	CMD	EXEC_PLANNING_SEQUENCE

TABLE 17-3   Planning Specific Command

These options are shown next and described in the following list:

- Using the Save option, you can persistently store changes to transaction data. If the check is successful, the changed data is written to the InfoCube or InfoCubes.

- Using the Transfer Values option, you can copy changed data from an Input Ready Query to the planning buffer. The entries are checked when this is done. If the check is successful, the data is copied across.

- Using the Execute Planning Function option, you can trigger the execution of a planning function. The dialog box that appears in the subsequent step allows you to select the planning function and data provider. You can either select the planning function or branch to the Planning Modeler, where you can create or edit a planning function. If the planning function contains variables, the system displays these variables in the lower area of the dialog box. Input help is available for selecting the values. By selecting a data provider, you specify from which data provider (with type filter or query view) the selection for all characteristics is to be made. When you choose Finish, the system copies the values for PLANNING_FUNCTION_ NAME and DATA_PROVIDER_FILTER to the button properties.

- Using the Execute Planning Sequence option, you can trigger the execution of a planning sequence. A dialog box for selecting the planning sequence then appears. You can either select the planning sequence or branch to the Planning Modeler, where you can create or edit a planning sequence. If the planning sequence contains variables, the system displays these variables in the lower area of the dialog box. Input help is available for selecting the values. When you choose Finish, the system copies the values for PLANNING_SEQUENZ_ NAME to the button properties.

Using the Planning Function option, we access a dialog box where we can assign the specific planning function to the button. In this case, we will assign the planning function for COPY – AMER_FNC1 – Copy Actual to Plan. The following illustration shows this result.

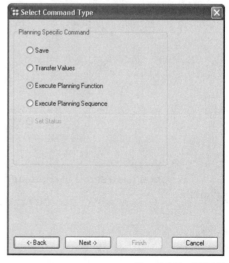

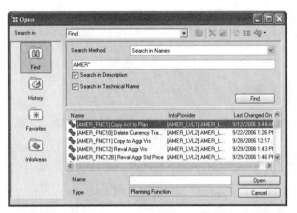

The next illustration shows the final result of the configuration of the button. After adding a label to the button, we then look to test this option.

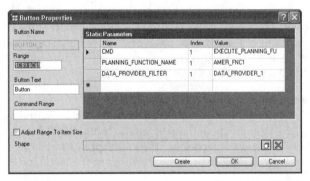

The display results of the button are shown here—that is, the actuals are copied over to the plan columns.

Account Number	Marketing Act	Marketing Plan	IT Act	IT Plan
Salaries	$ 100,000		$ 100,000	
Benefits	$ 57,600	$ 63,360	$ 63,900	$ 70,290
Office and Building	$ 36,000	$ 39,600	$ 39,000	$ 42,900
T&E - Travel Expense	$ 1,080,000	$ 1,188,000	$ 1,310,000	$ 1,441,000
Advertising	$ 93,600	$ 102,960	$ 112,800	$ 124,080
Office Supplies	$ 14,400	$ 15,840	$ 16,200	$ 17,820
Interest Expense	$ 43,200	$ 47,520	$ 51,900	$ 57,090
Depr. Exp.	$ 468,000	$ 514,800	$ 582,000	$ 640,200
Corp Allocations	$ 996,000		$ 373,500	
Overall Result	**$ 2,888,800**	**$ 1,972,080**	**$ 2,649,300**	**$ 2,393,380**

Notice that the other values (Salaries for Marketing and IT Plan) have been replaced with the values from the Actuals column, as shown next.

	Account Number	Marketing Act	Marketing Plan	IT Act	IT Plan
14	Salaries	$ 100,000	$ 100,000	$ 100,000	$ 100,000
15	Benefits	$ 57,600	$ 57,600	$ 63,900	$ 63,900
16	Office and Building	$ 36,000	$ 36,000	$ 39,000	$ 39,000
17	T&E - Travel Expense	$ 1,080,000	$ 1,080,000	$ 1,310,000	$ 1,310,000
18	Advertising	$ 93,600	$ 93,600	$ 112,800	$ 112,800
19	Office Supplies	$ 14,400	$ 14,400	$ 16,200	$ 16,200
20	Interest Expense	$ 43,200	$ 43,200	$ 51,900	$ 51,900
21	Depr. Exp.	$ 468,000	$ 468,000	$ 582,000	$ 582,000
22	Corp Allocations	$ 996,000	$ 996,000	$ 373,500	$ 373,500
23	**Overall Result**	**$ 2,888,800**	**$ 2,888,800**	**$ 2,649,300**	**$ 2,649,300**

Copy Actual to Plan

These are the basics of setting up the IP process with the help of the BEx Query Designer and the BEx Analyzer. You could spend hours working on these screens to make sure that they function correctly and look exactly how the planners' requirements describe but we will leave that additional formatting to your imagination.

Web Application Designer

In this process, we will use the same exact command—COPY—and the same exact query—U_AMER_Q2—to re-create the same scenario in the WAD for the IP process. We just completed the WAD discussion, so accessing the Web Application Designer should be second nature to you now. The basic process of setting up the WAD for IP processing is shown in Figure 17-24.

So, we start with the WAD template for the IP screens from the previous example and will look initially at the Analysis web item, as shown next. This WAD example is complex, and a number of web items are used in this process. Therefore, we need to search for the correct Analysis item. We find our query assigned to the ANALYSIS_ITEM_1 object. Notice the technical name on the General tab for ANALYSIS_ITEM_1.

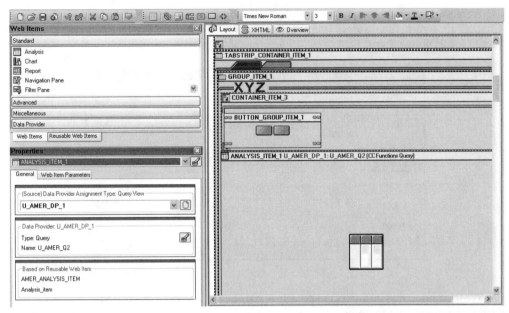

Copyright by SAP AG

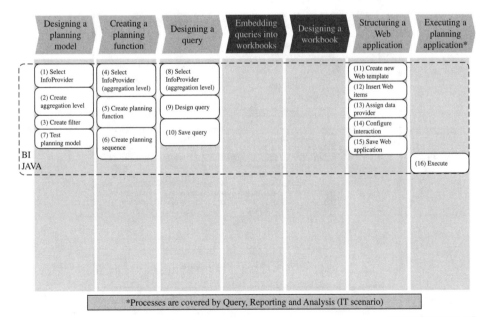

*Processes are covered by Query, Reporting and Analysis (IT scenario)

Copyright by SAP AG

FIGURE 17-24 Steps for Configuring the WAD for IP

Access this by using the Change icon. We then see the same view we saw before in Chapter 15. Again, the result of this process, due to the nature of the query, is an input screen for IP, shown here.

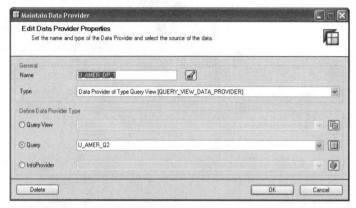

We then open this option up to see the actual list of queries available and search for the data input query, as shown here. We will review the results of this after we finish with the Button group.

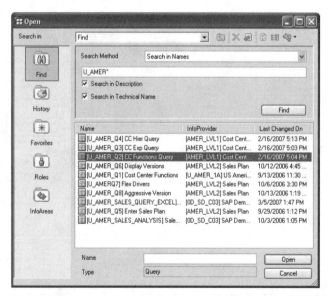

Our final process in this example is to look at the configuration of the Button group. In this case, we are going to focus on the available planning options, which are very similar to those available in the BEx Analyzer. Under the commands for planning applications, you can find a summary of all the commands you can use to create planning applications. The following illustration shows these commands in the system.

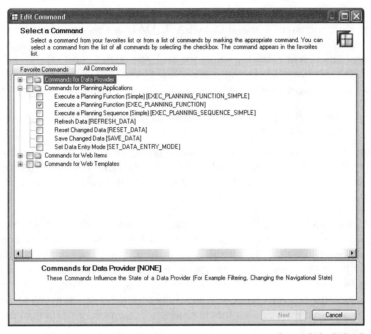

The following commands are available:

- Refresh Data [REFRESH_DATA]
- Save Changed Data [SAVE_DATA]
- Reset Changed Data [RESET_DATA]
- Set Data Entry Mode [SET_DATA_ENTRY_MODE]
- Execute a Planning Function (Simple) [EXEC_PLANNING_FUNCTION_SIMPLE]
- Execute a Planning Function [EXEC_PLANNING_FUNCTION]
- Execute a Planning Sequence (Simple) [EXEC_PLANNING_SEQUENCE_SIMPLE]

Using the Refresh Data command (REFRESH_DATA), you can copy changed data from an Input Ready Query to the planning buffer. The entries are checked when this is done. If the check is successful, the data is copied across. This command is particularly useful if you see the data entered manually into an Input Ready Query and want to know what impact these changes have on other parts of your Web Application.

Using the Save Changed Data command (SAVE_DATA), you can save your data changes within a Web Application persistently. If the check is successful, the changed data is written to the InfoProvider. This command is particularly useful, for example, if you have changed data manually using an Input Ready Query or automatically using a planning function, and you want to save these changes. Using this command, you save all data within the entire Web Application.

Using the Reset Changed Data command (RESET_DATA), you can undo your data changes within a Web Application. This reverses unsaved data changes made manually or by planning functions or planning sequences. You cannot undo changes that you have saved persistently by choosing Save Changed Data (SAVE_DATA). This command is very useful, for example, if you have changed data manually using an Input Ready Query or automatically using a planning function or planning sequence, and you want to undo these changes.

Using the Set Data Entry Mode command (SET_DATA_ENTRY_MODE), for an Input Ready Query, you can switch between Display and Change mode for a data provider.

- **Display mode**   If a query is started in Display mode, the data requested by the query is not locked for the current user.

- **Change mode**   As soon as Change mode is chosen, the system attempts to lock the data for the aggregation level for the current user. This lock attempt is rejected if the data is already locked by another user, and the data provider remains in Display mode.

Using the Execute a Planning Function (Simple) command (EXEC_PLANNING_FUNCTION_SIMPLE), you can trigger the execution of a planning function. All characteristic selections are determined by specifying one single data provider. The type for the data provider can be Filter or Query View. If the data provider is of type Query View, only the fixed filter of the query is used to restrict the selection. Additional restrictions, such as restricted key figures, are not used. When you use this command, you should note which restrictions were defined in the filter for the query so that the planning function does not change more data than required or this may result in performance concerns.

Table 17-4 lists the information for the command parameters in the same sequence that they appear in the Command Wizard when you insert the command.

Using the **Execute a Planning Function** command (EXEC_PLANNING_FUNCTION), you can trigger the execution of a planning function. You can specify for each characteristic how the selection is to be determined. Table 17-5 lists the command parameters in the same sequence that they appear in the command wizard when you insert the command:

Parameter	Description
Variable Screen	You use this parameter to specify whether a variable screen is to be displayed. If you do not select this option, the variable screen is displayed only if mandatory variables are not filled.
Data Binding: Reference to Data Provider of Type Filter	You use this parameter to specify the data on which the planning function is to be executed.
Data Binding: Variant	If the planning function uses variables, you can use this parameter to specify how they are to be filled. Using a variable variant, you therefore specify the parameterization of the planning function.
Data Binding: Variables	You use this parameter to specify the values for individual variables of the planning function. If a variant is also selected, a value assigned using this parameter is given precedence.
Planning Function (PLANNING_FUNCTION)	Technical name of the planning function. You use this parameter to specify which planning function is to be executed.

TABLE 17-4   Information for the Command Parameters for Planning Function (Simple)

Parameter	Description
Display Variable Screen	You use this parameter to specify whether a variable screen is to be displayed. If you do not select this option, the variable screen is displayed only if mandatory variables are not filled.
Data Binding: Selection Bindings	You use this parameter to specify the data on which the planning function is to be executed.
Data Binding: Variant	If the planning function uses variables, you can use this parameter to specify how they are to be filled. Using a variable variant, you specify the parameterization of the planning function.
Data Binding: Variables	You use this parameter to specify the values for individual variables of the planning function. If a variant is also selected, a value assigned using this parameter is given precedence.
Planning Function (PLANNING_FUNCTION)	Technical name of the planning function. You use this parameter to specify which planning function is to be executed.

TABLE 17-5   Command Parameters for Execute a Planning Function

This command is particularly useful if you want to change data using a planning function, and the Execute a Planning Function (Simple) command is not sufficient.

Using the Execute a Planning Sequence (Simple) command (EXEC_PLANNING_ SEQUENCE_SIMPLE), you can trigger the execution of a planning sequence. Table 17-6 shows the information and outlines the command parameters in the same sequence that they appear in the Command Wizard when you insert the command:

This command is particularly useful if you want to change data using various planning functions summarized as processing steps in a planning sequence.

Parameter	Description
Variables Screen	You use this parameter to specify whether a variable screen is to be displayed. If you do not select this option, the variable screen is displayed only if mandatory variables are not filled.
Data Binding: Variant	If the planning function uses variables, you can use this parameter to specify how they are to be filled. Using a variable variant, you specify the parameterization of the planning function.
Data Binding: Variables	You use this parameter to specify the values for individual variables of the planning function. If a variant is also selected, a value assigned using this parameter is given precedence.
Planning Sequence (PLANNING_SEQUENCE)	Technical name of the planning sequence. You use this parameter to specify which planning sequence is to be executed.

TABLE 17-6   Command Parameters for Planning Sequence (Simple)

In our example, we find the Copy command in Button Group Item 1, along with the commands for Revaluate and Planning Sequence. The following illustration shows this information.

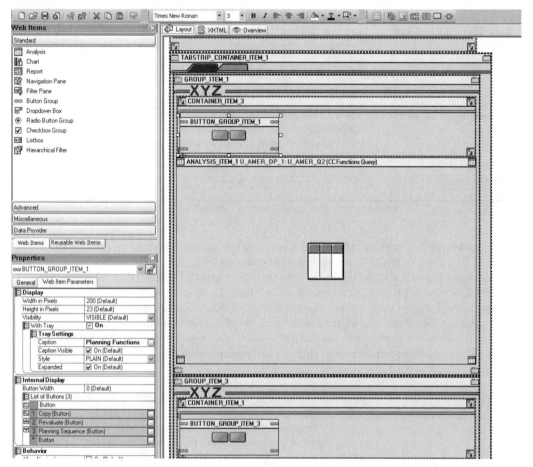

By accessing the option for the Copy button from the group (click the small box to the right of the Copy button line in the Web Item Parameters screen), you can see that a command is required. You can also alter the caption, adjust the execution of the command, and change the design of the actual button, as shown here.

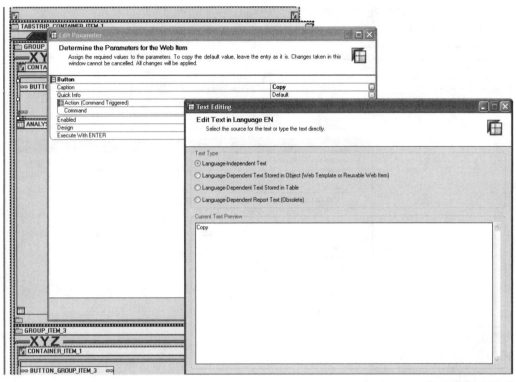

Choose EXEC_PLANNING_FUNC (the small box to the right of the line) to open the dialog box for assigning the planning function, shown here. In this screen, the options allow the use variants, a variable, additional binding options, and the planning functions (at the very bottom).

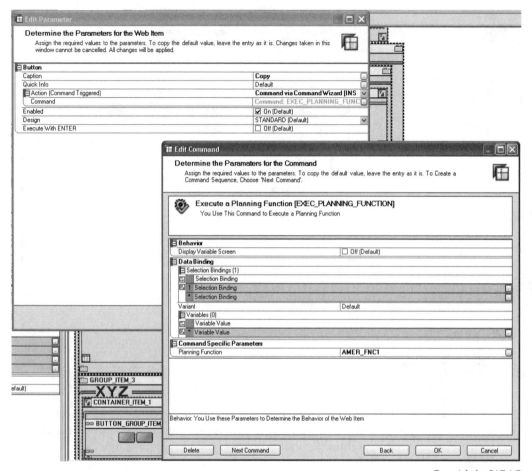

Choosing the box to the right of the planning function causes a dialog box to appear that allows you to identify the actual planning functions. This is shown in the following illustration.

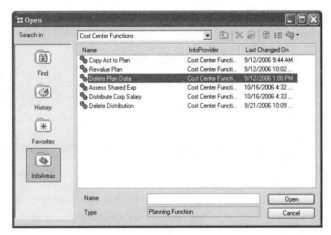

After identifying the correct planning function and saving the parameters, you are now ready to execute the IP WAD template and execute the planning process. This brings us full circle back to the WAD screens we reviewed initially. If we look at another tab in this Web template, we can see that we can use all the functionality of the BW reporting tools. In this case, we can use a hierarchy to display the information in the same manner as a business user might report the data. Notice that the result totals are grayed out so that no postings can occur on these lines, as shown here.

Cost Center	Benefits $	Rent $	T & E $	Advertising $	Office Supplies $	Interest Exp $	Depreciation $
▼America's Cost Ctr	299,196	186,060	5,721,800	495,156	495,156	75,024	2,493,780
▼Shared Services	207,900	129,000	4,010,000	346,800	346,800	52,200	1,752,000
• Procurement	64,000	40,000	1,200,000	104,000	104,000	16,000	520,000
• Corporate Services	80,000	50,000	1,500,000	130,000	130,000	20,000	650,000
• IT Service	63,900	39,000	1,310,000	112,800	112,800	16,200	582,000
▼Product Development	91,296	57,060	1,711,800	148,356	148,356	22,824	741,780
• Marketing	57,600	36,000	1,080,000	93,600	93,600	14,400	468,000
• Research & Develop.	33,696	21,060	631,800	54,756	54,756	8,424	273,780

In the following illustration, we can see that additional functionality has been added to the screen. In this situation, the planner is able to display the results of the calculations as they are executed. Also, one query is available for Strategy Business Driver analysis, and the bottom query is available for a review by month of the effects of these company-specific drivers.

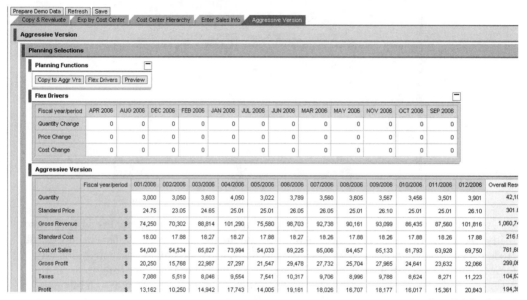

A series of different options are available in both the BEx Analyzer and the Web Application Designer for manually entering data. These options cover a number of situations specific to setting up an IP screen, such as how to manage data entry if initially there is no data available for the screens to access since if this situation exists (no initial data) the screens for IP would show a comment such as 'no data available' and the input screen may not be available. In this case, you have a number of options—from using the settings on the BEx Query Designer to access all master data, to using the settings on the WAD and BEx Analyzer to access the Excel spreadsheet without data. This situation and others are specific to IP. For additional information on to how to handle them, you'll need some training with SAP or you can access the SAP website.

Summary

I'm not sure if you've noticed, but we just turned the corner from a Business Warehouse to a Business Intelligence system. With the additional functionality that the Visual Composer and the Integrated Planning processes offer, anyone working with BW can experience the next step in the overall process of using information to their company's advantage. With these components added to your strategy, the MIS department has now become your best friend in working through the drivers for your company, understanding the overall impact of the different aspects of the economy that impact your business, forecasting the future use of information other than just gathering information within your company to help with this process, and working to take advantage of the market changes rather than thinking you're one or two steps behind when it comes to driving your business. This changes the company's view from reactive to proactive, and rather than relying on lagging indicators for your business, you can now work with leading indicators to move quickly and more aggressively into different markets and avoid problems before they impact your company's future.

Index

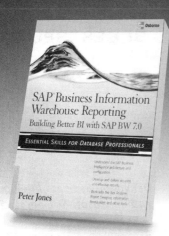
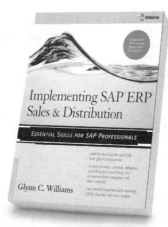

FROM THE NUMBER-ONE BUSINESS INTELLIGENCE PUBLISHER